ArtfromArt

ArtfromArt

A Collection of
Short Stories
Inspired by Art

Selected and Edited by **Stephen Soucy**

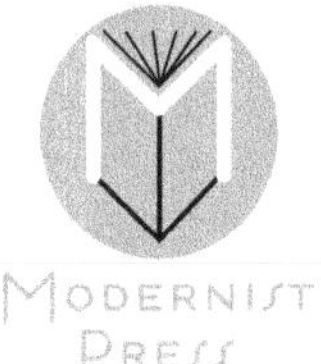

MODERNIST PRESS

LOS ANGELES + NEW YORK

Art from Art © 2011 Modernist Press

Publisher's Cataloging-in-Publication data

Soucy, Stephen, H.
    Art from art : a collection of short stories inspired by art / selected and edited by
Stephen Soucy
    p. cm.
    ISBN 978-0-9832210-1-2 (Paperback)
    ISBN 978-0-9832210-0-5 (Hardcover color edition)
1. Art--Fiction. 2. Sculpture--Fiction. 3. Painting--Fiction. 4. Music--Fiction.
5. Photographs--Fiction. 6. Graffiti--Fiction. 7. Short stories. I. Title.

PS3600.A1 A79 2011
[Fic]   2011902274

Book design by DesignForBooks.com

Visit Modernist Press at: www.modernistpress.com

Contents

Introduction

Stories inspired by works of art.

This simple idea for an anthology began my two-year commitment of compiling these excellent stories, and working with the graphic design firm, Marcolina Design Inc., to create each work's accompanying visual.

Every story featured in *Art From Art* was written with a work of art in mind at the start. What constitutes a work of art? Here's what the authors came up with:

Paintings proved fruitful starting points for several authors. Richard Zimler's *Stealing Memories* was inspired by a painting by Legér; Marshall Moore's *Flesh Blood and Some of the Parts (Le sang du monde)* owes its existence to Magritte. John Morgan Wilson's *The Pull of the Current* was inspired in part by John Singer Sargent's "Tommies Bathing," and Billy O'Callaghan's, *The Things We Lose, The Things We Leave Behind* has a connection to the Irish artist, Jack Butler Yeats.

Vincent Van Gogh's "Starry Night" proved powerful imagery in Martin's Rose's futuristic story, *Scanner Days, Starry Nights*. Anne Whitehouse's *A Visit to the Stock Exchange*, features a main character loosely based on an artist she once knew and a vivid painting this woman had created.

Steve Rasnic Tem was moved to write *La Mariée* based on the painting of the same name by Chagall. Ron Savage was inspired by the Impressionist collection at the Museée d'Orsay and wrote *Retrospective*.

Pedro Ponce was taken with the haunting imagery of Giorgio de Chirico and wrote *The Piazza De Chirico*. Similarly, David Gullen was moved by some disturbing imagery and an idea of horror in his *Installation 72*.

Various street artists at Seattle's Pike Place Market inspired David C. Pinnt to write his *One Penny for Art*. Gustave Caillebotte's "Paris Street, Rainy Day," was in part the starting point for Elizabeth Graver's *Flatiron*.

Nude sketches by Duncan Grant and an interest in Aleister Crowley set Jameson Currier on the road to write *The Bloomsbury Nudes*. Sketches she had made in a sketchbook years before were instrumental for Lauren Alwan's *Self Portrait: Untitled*.

A fictional painting—an image firmly set in his mind—was one of the starting points for Sean Padraic McCarthy's *The Man Who Walks Beside the Sea*. Black squiggly lines, drawn during a writing workshop proved enough of an inspiration for Deb Taber to discover the Aal in her story, *Black Silk*.

An interest in the art of graffiti set Robert Guffey writing his work of the same name. A course she took in Renaissance Painting, and her memories of a woman she met in the class was enough for Lois Barr's *Gesso*.

A work of fiction—a short story by Luis Borges—prompted Michael Mendolia's *Transparent Tigers and Towers of Blood*. Shakespeare's "Merchant of Venice" inspired Keyan Bowles to set her story in space with *The Intra-Galactic Shakespeare Festival*. Even my own story, *Skating*, owes its existence and borrows from the structure of Charles Dickens' *A Christmas Carol*, coupled with a touch of one of my favorite films, *Last Year at Marienbad*.

A work of literature—a Richard Burgin story, a song by Jason Mraz, and The Alamo—was a trinity of inspiration for Sylvia Martinez Banks and her _____ *John* story.

Music was a starting point for two other authors in the book. Stravinsky's "The Rite of Spring" for Tracy Debrincat in her, *Call it a Hat,* and two Nine Inch Nails songs played on a continuous loop, gave Reni Kieffer the sound and the vision she needed to compose, *Right Where it Belongs*.

A New York Times Sunday magazine article coupled with the story of Anne of Green Gables, set Grace Talusan on the path of *The Book of Life and Death*.

Two different Richard Serra sculptures inspired two of the authors in the book. Benjamin Robinson wrote *The Bridge House*, based on Serra's "Torqued Torus Inversion" and Terri Griffith's *Corporate Art* was based on Serra's "Tilted Arc."

The Jean Luc Goddard film—*Deux ou Trois Choses Que Je Sais d'Elle* (Two Or Three Things I know About Her) served as the starting point for Andrew Hook's *Ennui*.

A visit to a tin-mining museum in Cornwall, UK started V. Gebbie on writing *The Return of the Baker, Edwin Tregear*. The Metropolitan Museum of Art in New York City, inspired Kevin W. Reardon to write *Three Shades*—which was set at the Met and features several works of art.

Nathaniel Hawthorne's style (and a voice heard upon waking from a dream) inspired Felice Picano to write his *Absolute Ebony*.

Nineteenth Century photographs inspired Fred McGavran to write *A Photograph From the Permanent Collection*. A photograph of Lawrence Argent's sculpture "I See What You Mean" set author Steve Himmer to create his story of the same name. And Robert McGowan in his, *An Ephemeral Exertion,* was influenced by a set of digital photographs he had taken of sunlight washing over the walls of his home.

In Fred Skolnik's *Creativity,* the work of art in question became the unfinished story and an exploration of why he did not wish to write the piece.

Lisa Annelouise Rentz wrote the first draft of *Glove* in 2000 and built it on twenty-five-year-old memories, and was inspired by a page ripped out of a magazine that she kept above her desk for years.

Alex MacLennan was intrigued by Sam Taylor Woods "Still Life"—the celebrated film of an impossibly beautiful bowl of fruit decaying at an accelerated pace—and wrote is flash fiction story, *Four Minutes Time.*

Richard K. Weems set his *Artistic Endeavor,* in the world of professional wrestling, and presents intriguing characters drawn to self-destruction, abuse, and artistic expression.

The authors spent some time writing about the details of the art behind their story. You can find these at the end of the book, just beneath their bios.

The visuals featured in this book were inspired and created after the stories had been accepted for publication. I owe a debt of gratitude to Dan Marcolina and his staff at Marcolina Design, Inc. for creating and/or finding such arresting images—one for every story in the book.

Additional thanks goes out to Teri Johnson for her assistance in editing the book, and Frank Bruno for his strong (and correct) opinions on the cover art for the book.

I am proud and honored to be publishing each of these stories. After having invited several authors, I went to two well-respected call-for-submission websites and received a flood of stories inspired by art. It took several months to go through each and every one, but it was easy to discern the best of the bunch.

Each of the writers in Art From Art stuck it out with me, and my recently formed Modernist Press, to see their amazing words in print. Writers of various genres, writers with various levels of publishing experience, writers that had a vision to bring these different worlds to the page. And finally—writers from across the globe. Our line-up of authors live in places as varied as Hong Kong, Paris, England, Ireland, Israel, Portugal. Others reside in cities across the United States: Los Angeles, West Hollywood, Long Beach, San Francisco, Boston, New York, Washington, Memphis, and a few others living in more rural locations in between. Each was a delight to work with, and each should be proud of their exquisite work, collected here in Art From Art.

STEPHEN SOUCY

1

I See What You Mean

after a sculpture by Lawrence Argent

STEVE HIMMER

Me and Freddy were refacing a fireplace at one of the houses in Caribou Court, that gated development going up where Delmore Bros sawmill was torn down last year. My father worked there for years, and Freddy's did, too. I've never seen a caribou around here, but the one on the billboard by the entrance is pretty impressive. Bigger than the runty deer in my yard. The fireplace was big, too, big and brand new and we were covering its bricks with smooth, round stones before the owners moved in.

We were almost done for the day. Beyond the big windows, still glazed with the factory's cling film, the mountains had that afternoon glow folks move here for and travel guides call our "golden hour." As I climbed down the ladder to fetch what would be the last stone at the top of the hearth, my skinny legs shook and my head spun so I stopped on the middle rungs to catch up with myself. Climbing all day without eating had wiped me right out.

Through the window, I saw a bear moving among the thin pines on the ridge above town. Nothing strange about that: there are so many bears around here that the rangers have to dope some and truck them away a few times every summer, since we can't shoot them now even when they come too close to town. But it seemed early in the season for this one to be out of his den, and he didn't look scrawny and starved like he'd been hibernating at all. Plus he was blue, which I'd never seen before on a bear, so I thought maybe it was only the afternoon light. I scratched at my xylophone ribs beneath a flannel shirt that seemed to have grown since the last time I'd worn it, and watched the bear rub his blue rump against the bark of a tree.

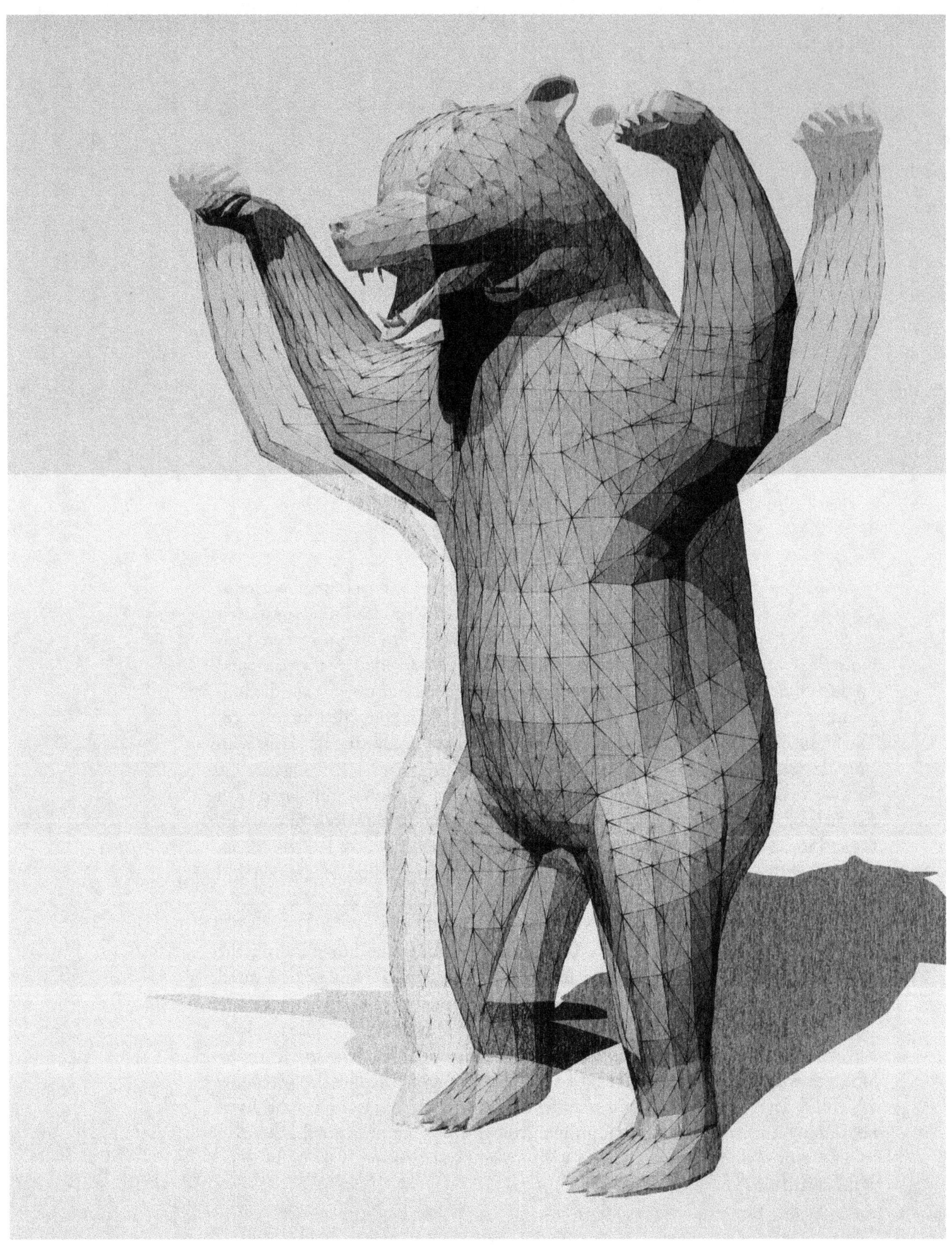

"You see that?" I asked Freddy, pointing at the window with my trowel, a big glob of mud hanging off like an avalanche waiting to happen. I didn't say what "that" was.

"Uh huh," Freddy answered without looking up from the cigarette he was trying to light off the gas heater for drying the plaster and keeping us warm in those houses where heat isn't on until the owners arrive. His belly hung to both sides and his back humped with fat so when he leaned over the heater it looked like he'd curled in a ball. It was easy to imagine Freddy living off himself right through the winter. The light through the windows threw my shadow across his gray sweatshirt like a racing stripe.

I waited for him to look out the window, but he didn't so I let it go. I've gotten good at pretending not to notice what no one else does. I've had to, even things I'd like to tell someone about and things they might even believe. But my probation officer and the counselor he sent me to both say I need to learn what to keep to myself, and how what I say sounds to other people.

"You'll burn the house down," I said, "or do your eyebrows like I did." But the cigarette caught, no problem, and Freddy puffed away in front of the heater instead of getting back to the fireplace so we could go home. With my breath more or less back, I climbed down the rest of the ladder and on the floor my legs felt like they'd come back from sea. My body hurt more than it should've from just a day's work. But I finished the bare patches in Freddy's part of the hearth without saying so, like he probably knew that I would. Like I owed him, which I did.

In the morning I'd been clever and slung a bag full of stones on my shoulder so I could hang a whole bunch before climbing down, because the chimney was two stories high. But the contractor who's paying Freddy came by around lunchtime and bitched me out.

"You crack any stones in that bag, you'll pay for 'em," he hollered from the foot of my ladder. "That's imported river rock you're slinging around, not local shit."

I turned to see who was yelling, and shook a shower of white dust onto the shoulder of his clean denim jacket. He cursed me and brushed at his clothes with a handkerchief like they'd been hit by a bird, then he stormed away and didn't come back. But for the rest of the day I hauled only one rock at a time, just in case. It's hard enough getting hired around here, and I only got that job because Freddy did me a favor. Work doesn't come the way of a guy with my reputation, not anymore. The same stories that used to get me hired and kept me from paying for drinks have me on a blacklist these days. Last time I tried to get on a real crew, health insurance and vacation days and payment by check and the works, the foreman said there was no room on his team for a guy who'd waste a whole afternoon racing belt sanders on a new hardwood floor.

"We all used to do things like that," I said.

He told me, "We don't do it like that anymore."

I said he was just pissed off he'd lost a week's wages and broken his sander in the same race, but he still didn't give me a job.

Even Freddy's got a big, shiny truck with his name on the side, and carries a calculator in his toolbox. He picked it up when I was in jail. I got out and he was talking about profit and loss, and I told him something was lost, all right, but he didn't say anything back. He throws me work when he can, mostly when a contractor needs something done in a hurry and hires as many guys as turn up. Usually it's on developments for folks moving in from the coast, decking out big houses in foreign woods I couldn't afford sawdust from. Freddy goes on about Italian marble like everyone else but he still says it "eye-talian." There's more money piled up in Caribou Court on its own than there used to be in the whole town, and I guess it's spilling out through the gates into pockets like his, but none of it's coming my way. My cabin's too far out of town to catch the runoff.

The finished fireplace looked nice enough. Like one I saw in a ski lodge a long time ago. I don't know if it looked any better than the bricks we'd covered up or better than rocks pulled from the river through town would have looked, but no one asked me what I thought.

Up on the ridge, the bear was further back in the trees but not hidden by them because his coat was so bright. He really was blue after all, but I didn't risk telling Freddy to look. I couldn't tell how tall he was exactly—it's tough to measure something far off against trees, because they look bigger or smaller depending on where you're standing, and whether you're cutting them down or climbing up—but he was much taller than average bear size and taller than most of the trees when he stood. His front paws were cupped over his eyes like he was shading them against the low sun to look in my direction. I doubt he saw much through the windows, maybe the glow of the heater, but I felt like I was being watched. Like those wide windows were a screen with me on it.

"You done yet?" Freddy asked, halfway out the door with his tools already packed. "I'm thirsty."

By the time his truck passed between the brick pillars where the gate to the development will hang, past the billboard with the caribou on it, the hillside and trees had slipped into shadow and the bear was either gone or his blue was too dark to be seen.

Freddy pulled over at the split where he goes east and I go west to get home. I climbed out, and lifted my bike from the bed of his truck. The cab had been warmed by Freddy's body, so when the wind that always hangs over that long, straight stretch whistled through I shivered as the chain rattled on my bike.

"How long now?" he asked.

"Few months," I said. "I'll be driving again end of summer, when riding a bike might be nice. Not too hot, not too cold."

He dropped his empty beer can out the window and it bounced toward the side of the road where I stood. "Sure you won't come to the Rat? I'm only staying for a couple."

"Not tonight." Another can popped inside the cab. "Gotta get home."

"Pick you up Monday?"

"Tuesday," I told him. "I've got something downtown Monday morning. I'll be along after that."

Freddy was already rolling away when he waved the back of his hand without looking. I climbed onto the bike—Frankensteined together from parts picked up all over—and I pedaled into the maze of new houses between the old edge of town and my cabin. When I bought the place it was pretty much by itself, my nearest neighbor around the other side of the peak and out of sight. The last quarter mile of road wasn't even paved until those houses went up with so many side streets between them. It was cheap when I bought it, especially with two of us making the payments, but I couldn't touch it these days and I figure it's only a matter of time before eminent domain flattens my shack for more houses.

Construction was finished on most of the homes in the new neighborhood, and the landscaping looked nearly done. Lots of them were still empty, but lights were on in enough windows and enough cars were parked in driveways to make the streets feel alive. There were kids wheeling bikes into garages at the end of the day, and games of street hockey just breaking up. A couple of mothers stood on the curb with crossed arms and scowls as they watched me ride past. I still wish I'd picked up some of the work on those houses so close to my place that I could've gone home for lunch. I asked around when the project got going, but somebody remembered the time with the Bobcat and how it set the whole crew back a week.

All of a sudden I'd ridden down some cul-de-sac with a bunch of windows staring like eyes in the forest and I couldn't tell which way to go. It was too bright to spot my usual landmark, the cut between Mounts Lewis and Clark I've always aimed at on my way home. With those houses sprung up, all those porch lights and streetlights, you can't make out the mountains after sunset these days until you get well out of town. A guy can circle for hours in the same neighborhood trying to find his way out. Even when he hasn't been drinking. All I found was a perfect green park with paved walking paths and signs keeping dogs out and me off the grass, and a playground with cute plastic sculptures of buffalo and wolves for kids to climb on. In one of the houses, somebody was practicing their violin and it was about the saddest thing I've ever heard.

I rolled past a boulder that looked familiar from when I shot birds in the hills where those houses were built. I bagged a big turkey one Saturday and was having a sandwich at the foot of the rock, when a long yellow cougar slid around one side and there we were, face to face. Me with my peanut butter and jelly and him with his teeth and his claws. We stared at each other for the longest moment of my whole life until the first night in jail, then he walked away into the trees that aren't there anymore. It looked like the same boulder to me, left alone through all that construction, but maybe it was a new one hauled in from wherever those river rocks started.

All those mothers in all those houses were cooking dinner at the same time, and the neighborhood smelled like a restaurant kitchen. My stomach growled and swore at me with each drifting scent, each of them better than whatever cheese crackers or cereal I might scavenge to eat later on. Those streets and those smells got me all turned around and I ended up headed toward town. The damn ring roads and spokes take you that way whether you like it or not. So I took it as a sign to stop at the Rat Cellar before trying again to get home. It was the Rathskellar once, I've been told, but no one could say the name right so the owner gave in and painted himself a new sign.

Freddy was already there, like a mushroom on top of his stool. "Thought you weren't coming," he said.

"I wasn't."

He ordered me a beer before I'd sat down and he said, "You always do."

A few hours later, I wobbled home on my bike because it seemed safer than the ride Freddy offered. I tried to count houses as I passed them, to know how many new neighbors I had, and when I spotted the blue bear standing behind one of them I almost crashed into a mailbox. His claws hung over its roof like Kilroy—he was taller than he'd looked far away on the ridge. I think he turned his head as I passed and followed me with his eyes, but I didn't look up to find out in case he wasn't actually there. My probation officer says it's about self-control for guys like me, even when no one is watching. So I stared straight ahead and pedaled steady—steadyish, best I could—and rode home without stopping and without getting lost. I ride a bit clearer when I've been drinking. I get so lost in my thoughts that I follow the map in my memory instead of the one on the ground, with all its new houses and roads. It's instinct, I guess.

Outside my cabin I leaned the bike against my rusty old truck with its four flat tires and missing tailgate. If I looked west I could still see the mountains, a purple line across the blue night, but the eastern sky was bright all the way into town and even the stars were swallowed. My front door was unlocked like it always is, because I don't need my car keys but if I carried just one key I'd lose it. I'm no good at hanging on to things. I was always leaving my keys at the Rat or at Freddy's or somewhere and had to wake my wife up to get into the house, so now that there's no one to let me in I don't bother with locks. And with all those new houses, who'd come out here to go robbing, where even the fire department won't come? Only the bears, and there's no food in the house to lure them.

I spent most of the weekend on the couch, thinking about the bear and wondering if I was the only person in town who could see him, and how that could be. Maybe the bear wasn't real, or I was the only one looking.

Monday morning while the grass was still frozen I was pedaling toward town to see my probation officer. I don't suppose things get much clearer than a bright Monday morning when the world is as real as it gets, and there the bear was on the corner of Euclid and Twain, lying on top of the parking garage that went up a few years ago but so far as I know hasn't ever been filled. I've heard it doesn't make enough money to pay an attendant and the city takes a loss every year because, says the mayor, we're a city on the rise and we need to plan for it. The bear's blue head hung over the top level four stories up, brown eyes big as planets staring down at the street. I saw his shadow first as it spread across the building's own and kept coming. It got my attention because I swear his shadow was blue.

If I'd been with anyone I might have said, "Hey, look at that giant blue bear," but I was alone. The folks in the street, men in ties swinging briefcases cut from exotic hides and women in shoes sharp as skinning knives, all of them stepped through his shadow without looking up. If they could ignore a giant blue bear on a building they sure wouldn't take any notice if I tried to tell them about it. I'd only wind up in jail for the day drunk or not, and why miss my appointment for that? I'd be risking more time, the way things are around here. Freddy's cousin shotgunned a stop sign last month and they sent him to the state prison. Used to be if the cops caught you peppering signs they'd bet you a beer and take a turn with the gun, but now they arrest you no matter how well you shoot. Or if you don't even shoot but offer them a beer, bet or no bet, by the side of the road. Guys I've known for years, cops I've driven home from the Rat when they couldn't drive their own cruisers, have cuffed me and thrown me into the backseat then told me all the way to the station how much town has changed as if I couldn't already tell.

Fighting the urge to look up, I jumped out of the bear's shadow and into the street where I was almost run over by an open-topped sightseeing jeep taking some tourists up to the ridge to spot birds or cougars or maybe the caribou I've never seen. The driver was wearing a safari jacket and hat with the brim pinned up on side, and he scowled at me from behind his microphone. Some of the passengers snapped my picture as I tripped back onto the sidewalk, but none of their cameras aimed upwards at the blue bear.

After that close call my nerves were shot and I had to stop in the Gold Dust for breakfast, where I knew I could get whiskey poured in my coffee. It's one of the last places you can around here. The counter was filled up with folks wearing plastic nametags on strings round their necks like those ugly bolo ties in the souvenir shops. They were talking about all the animals they'd spotted from their bus the evening before—I guess everyone's out seeing something. I was worried they'd talk all morning before I got a seat, but they ate fast like they had places to be. I was a few minutes late but I made my appointment.

I couldn't swear to it, but I might've seen a blue shadow pass behind a few buildings while I made my way from the Gold Dust to the square where the courthouse stands across from the new natural history museum with the dinosaur statue out front, and the convention center beside it. After calming my nerves with breakfast, I felt more relaxed about seeing the bear and about being the only person who could. I thought I'd seen all I'd see in my life, and I thought I knew all this town's secrets, so the surprise had thrown me but now I thought hey, if there are giant blue bears in the mountains I never knew of after living here my whole life, maybe there are other things, too.

––––––––––

When I left the courthouse a while later, he was across the street and big as daylight with his face pressed against the glass wall of the convention center and paws around his eyes like blinders. I don't know what was going on inside the building because the acronym on the marquee didn't spell anything, but the bear had disrupted it with his head in the window and a whole crowd of folks wearing those nametags I'd seen at breakfast were hurrying out the front doors.

At least everyone else could see him now, too. At least I wasn't crazy for spotting giant blue bears. I thought it would be like an old monster movie, the bear stomping all over the city, and I thought that would be something to see—not because I wanted anyone to get hurt, it just seemed like it would shake things up around here. It might remind us of how things used to be. And if the city got flattened, someone would have to rebuild it. Folks were pointing and screaming and aiming their phones, those ones with cameras built in. Police pushed everyone back from the bear and stopped traffic, and a crowd gathered on the square. He looked heavy, that bear, and I don't know what kept him from pushing right through that glass, hard as he seemed to be leaning.

With all that racket around him, the bear didn't move. He stood with his eyes to the wall even after everyone inside had come out. He didn't smash the building or stuff people into his mouth or even growl. He didn't act much like a monster, or even that much like a bear. And the longer he stood doing nothing the more people made their way downtown and pushed up against the barricades the police had set up. The mayor gave a speech on the courthouse steps and said he would ask for the National Guard to get rid of the bear, but some lady from the tourism board whispered in his ear and the mayor said never mind.

Freddy showed up along with most of the city, and I found him standing on top of his cooler because he was pretty far back in the crowd. He was drinking a beer, and so were a couple of teenagers beside him. He stepped off the cooler so I could get a drink and the white plastic lid popped like a cap on a bottle.

"Bear's not doing much," Freddy said.

"He doesn't have to," I said. "He's a giant blue bear. Seems like that's something already."

No one seemed to be leaving and more folks arrived all the time, and the crowd nudged the barriers right up to the edge of the road. Still the bear didn't move. People started posing for pictures that made it look like they were up near his feet—forced perspective, somebody called it.

Then the cops started posing right next to the bear, and I saw the one who pulled me in the last time and cost me my license. Must've been the whole force with their guns out and aimed at him like they were protecting the city or something. The mayor was lifted onto the blue toes and wagged his finger in the bear's face while cameras flashed and the whole city cheered. And the bear kept his eyes to the window. Finally the police took the barriers down altogether and kids climbed on the bear, and their parents posed as if they were afraid, and the convention got back to business.

By dinnertime, vendors were selling pizza and hot dogs and T-shirts of the blue bear they'd printed up quick. Within a few days, word of the bear had gotten out pretty far and folks started to come from all over. The city put his picture on everything from brochures to shot glasses for sale in all the bars that changed their names to something about a blue bear. Even the Piney View campground out past my cabin started calling itself The Bear View, which wasn't so bad since there had always been lots of bears around the campsites and warnings hung up on the trees about how to keep safe. But after a few weeks folks stopped camping there because the bears in the woods weren't blue, and they stayed downtown in hotels instead. Which is alright with me, since someone has to renovate those hotel rooms with their new blue bear styles instead of the wagon wheels, saddles, and saloon doors they've had all my life. With all that work on short notice, often enough to keep the bills paid that someone is me, and I might be able to buy a new truck by the time I'm able to drive it.

And if I manage to save enough money and sell my cabin, I might build a smaller one farther from the edges of town and stock it with plenty of food so I won't have to leave it so often. Where the lights aren't so bright and the houses so close, there's a better chance of my spotting some other blue bears and seeing what I haven't seen yet. I won't put a lock on it, or even a door, and if bears walk right in then so what.

2

Transparent Tigers and Towers of Blood

MICHAEL MENDOLIA

Albert Rey is gone. I had been strolling next to him, chattering about a collection of South American fiction that was my latest preoccupation, when I was distracted by a blue button on the ground near my right foot. A victim of incurable curiosity, I picked it up, massaged its cool, smooth surface with my fingertips, and then turned to Albert to comment on this peculiar find. Oddly, he was not there at my side, though no more than ten seconds could have elapsed. I looked around me, baffled yet not concerned. After all, people do not routinely dematerialize. I assumed that, waylaid by his own fit of inquisitiveness, he had ducked down an alley or into one of the dilapidated shops we had passed. I moved to the side of the road, prepared to wait patiently for his return.

I am still waiting.

It is as though he were plucked from this universe with surgical precision by some otherworldly force. Despite the absence of clues, I remain encouraged, notwithstanding occasional dejected premonitions of a bruised and misshapen corpse. The whole matter is strangely diaphanous. I have the abiding sense that anything might happen: one of these days Albert could stride forth from the rainforests of Borneo, garbed in the attire of the indigenous natives, or he might ascend, smirking, from the bowels of the Manhattan subway system. Anything is possible; nothing is forbidden.

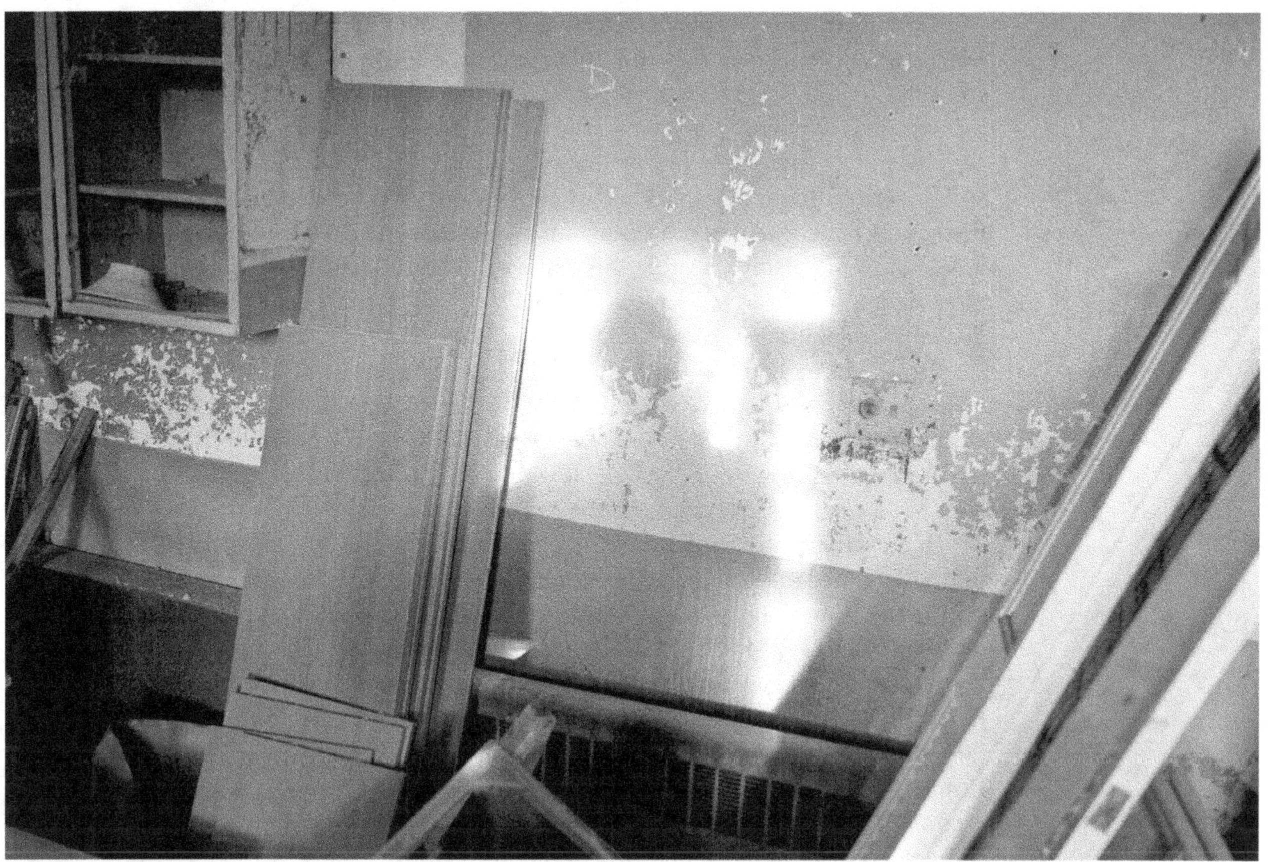

My thoughts inevitably spiral back to the travel essay which is perhaps the fountainhead of this mystery. When I first stumbled upon Margaret Mirto's article "Tranquil Mystics in Maui" about a community of vegans on a Hawaiian island, I had no reason to doubt its veracity. I read with fascination how the Ukbari acolytes bathed at sunrise while their masters intoned sacred verses; how ritual meals were served on platters carved from volcanic ash, described as the most sublime of substances; how the advanced yoga sessions extended six hours or more without interruption. I learned that nearly two dozen individuals had renounced their worldly, carnivorous pasts and been inducted into this island society. Though typically skeptical of any type of congregation, I was intrigued. In fact, more than that—I was captivated with the idea of discarding my empty urban life and joining this idyllic group.

Despite my initial curiosity, several months passed and I gave the Mirto article no further thought until the evening of October 19th, when my friend Albert Rey invited me over.

One of my dearest friends, Albert is a consummate host, his dinner invitations a welcome medley of scrumptious meats, vintage wines, and intoxicating conversation. He is a stocky man, whose soft-spoken manner seems at odds with his imposing stature. While not a writer of any consequence himself, he is a true connoisseur of literature, and we have spent many hours discussing the novel and of what it might be capable. That evening our conversation had a decidedly theoretical bent. For nearly an hour we talked over the device of a particularly unreliable first person narrator who omits or distorts key facts, so that only the most discerning reader could wade through the swamps of contradictions and divine the final truth of the story.

"It would be constructed as a puzzle," Albert proposed. "But the average reader would take it at face value and not discern its obscured, elaborate framework. In this way, it would be possible to create a work which would signify different meanings to different readers. It would be as if you had created two novels with but a single text. It would be marvelous."

The concept intrigued me, as my own novel, a work-in-progress for five years, had mired itself. Its banal linear plot had become tiresome even to me, and during this dinner discussion, I decided to abandon it in favor of a more inventive work which would crush through the very boundaries of fiction.

Albert's ideas are not always in sync with my own predilections. Though he breathes freely in the stratosphere of literature at its most sublime, he maintains an unapologetic fascination for the mundane genre of horror. Sometimes I capitulate and follow him down his sanguinary path of menace and gore. That evening he invited me to create a novel in which multiple murders occurred simultaneously, in a skyscraper which the press would later refer to as a "Tower of Blood." The motivations for the individual murders could be revealed gradually over the course of the novel.

"There might be a supernatural element involved, of course," Albert contended.

For example, it might emerge that the killers shared a sense that they were being hounded by transparent tigers. Albert elaborated on the horror of being pursued by relentless, invisible predators, and I agreed that this premise would offer ample potential for narrative tension. The murders themselves might be accidental, occurring in the heat of the chase as it were, as the unintentional assassins, drunk with their visions, struggled to evade the tigers.

Not to be accused of promoting gore for its own sake, Albert conjectured that such a work might tackle the elusive nature of guilt. Could the tigers be considered the perpetrators of the tragedy, or should the human participants be held responsible? When I tried to dismiss this digression of our conversation as meritless, Albert pressed me to consider it further. Would the answer hinge on the reality of the tigers?

"Yes," I responded. "If the tigers did not truly exist, how could they be held accountable for something which actually happened in the real world?"

Albert licked his lips, and I knew that he was going to try to ensnare me with his infernal webs of argument.

"If more than one individual perceived the tigers, doesn't this mean that they were real, at least in some sense? The alternative—simultaneous group delusion—would be equally far-fetched. And how, after all, can the existence of a thing be measured, if not by human perception of it?"

"Are you saying," I countered, "that if enough people believe something to be true, to be real, then that in of itself makes it so?"

Unable to answer me, Albert changed the subject.

"If the human killers in this story truly lacked the intent to murder, then how could it be right to hold them culpable?"

"Why does anyone need to be held culpable, if the deaths were accidental?"

"Multiple violent deaths in a single building, and no one to blame? Just a series of odd coincidences? No one could accept that," Albert said. "In the end, nothing is ever accidental."

"So what does that leave?" I asked irritably, after a pause. "Evil? Evil as an external force, beyond human comprehension or subjugation?"

Albert beamed at me, as if I were a particularly precocious student. He quickly added that the novel must of course not present any definitive answers to these queries, but instead force the readers to work out their own conclusions.

As though fearful of our conversation losing steam, Albert immediately began suggesting a number of other possible novelistic approaches. I rejected many of them out of hand, since they had already been accomplished or at least attempted by other authors, such as a circular work in which the novel begins mid-sentence and concludes with the preceding fragment, as Delaney did in his science fiction novel *Dhalgren*. We spent some time elaborating on a labyrinthine structure in which the plot involves a man writing a novel about a man writing a novel, and excerpts from these interlocking works could be provided in consecutive chapters without fanfare, so that the unsuspecting reader would only gradually become aware of the conceit. Albert then suggested a trilogy of novels to be entitled *Uno, Two,* and *Trois,* which would take place in America, France, and Italy, respectively, but whose plots would all concern a mysterious disappearance in Argentina.

I complained that such an overweening external structure could stifle the creative spark, but Albert reminded me of his favorite film director Lars Von Trier.

"Consider the documentary The Five Obstructions, in which Von Trier challenges his friend Jurgen Leth to create experimental films with a series of increasingly restrictive requirements—such as remaking a film in Cuba with no shot more than twelve frames. The results were unvaryingly inventive. The restrictions led to a flowering of creativity, not a diminution of it."

"It's a thought. Though not all of the segments in that film were equally successful, in my opinion."

I did not elaborate further, since I had learned that Albert tolerates no criticism of Von Trier. I find it laughable that the director restricts his filming to Denmark and its immediate environs because of his acknowledged terror of flying. This led me to change the subject, as Albert opened a second bottle of Cote du Rhone.

"Have you ever visited Cuba?"

"Never, unfortunately. Though I hear it have wondrous beaches. I have been craving a getaway to some warm, exotic place. In fact, only today I was looking into booking a trip to Hawaii."

My eyes widened, not only because of Albert's uncharacteristic grammatical blunder. I was immediately reminded of the essay.

"I've been interested in going to Maui myself. I would even consider a spiritual retreat there, as odd as that may seem."

Though it had been some time since I had read Mirto's article, I recalled several of the key elements to a degree sufficient to entrance Albert. The prospect of adventure brought further color to his swarthy cheeks. In the end, we decided to visit Hawaii together over the winter, and Albert offered to look into the logistics of spending a week with the Ukbari.

Three days later, Albert called me, troubled that he could find no mention of this community in any of the guidebooks on Hawaii. A phone call to the Hawaiian tourism board had similarly met with defeat. We concluded that quirky communities of this sort were likely to disband and scatter within months, and regretted that we might have missed the opportunity to experience the yogic marathons of the Ukbaris.

Nonetheless, that evening, as I tossed in my bed, discouraged and mentally agitated, I had the startling thought that the essay I had read might not have been factual after all. I was embarrassed that this possibility had not occurred to me earlier, especially after all our discussions of metafiction. I recalled a story by Jorge Luis Borges which recounted, among other odd happenings, how a group of intellectuals created a detailed fictional country called Uqbar which they wrote about as though it truly existed, even to the extent of forging entries in encyclopedias. It occurred to me that Mirto's community of Ukbari could be similarly constructed, its very name a wry nod to the master Borges.

I discussed this possibility with Albert Rey on Friday, October 24th. We spent Saturday afternoon at the public library on the Parkway, searching for the Mirto essay whose source—maddeningly—I could not recall. Good fortune eventually beamed down on us and we were able to locate the brief article in a 2004 issue of the now-defunct journal Exotic Destinations. Rereading "Tranquil Mystics in Maui," this time with a critical eye, was a decidedly strange experience. How could I have missed all of the author's clues and insinuations? She described conversations with several of the acolytes, whose surnames were withheld: Helen K., Joseph Z, and Jorge Luis B. That last name was like a slap on the face. How did I not notice it the first time? Mirto's description of one of the meals was even more blatant: "the concoction of grains and vegetables, spiced up with local Tlonnic herbs, was surprisingly delightful."

Albert and I relished the writer's mischievous homage to Borges, and we scoured the library for other works by the devilish author Margaret Mirto. We even enlisted the aid of the reference librarian, a well-coiffed septuagenarian whose professional efforts ultimately disappointed. As we walked out of the library, I felt strangely exhilarated. I slapped Albert on the back and proposed that we visit Maui together anyway, in a tribute of sorts to Mirto.

On that expedition, which transpired in December, Albert Rey disappeared without a trace, and I found myself embroiled in—

———

I really dig puzzles, all kinds of puzzles. Crosswords, Sodoku, brainteasers, you name it. So when I found those pages that you left on the kitchen table, I was sucked in right away. I had to figure out what it all meant.

Ever since I started renting a room from you, I've been intrigued. You seemed normal enough at first, but it's always different when you live in someone's space and find out what they're really like. You're nice to me, polite, considerate even, but something is a bit off. My first day here, you said that I should make myself at home, eat whatever I want out of the refrigerator, feel free to watch the TV in the living room and all that, but you did have a few ground rules that you expected me to follow. Basically that I was never, repeat never, to go into the room you called your office. And that you were not to be disturbed between the hours of 8 AM and noon.

"Nikolai, that's the most crucial thing," you told me. "That's when I work on my novel."

You insist on calling me Nikolai, even though I've told you a bunch of times that I prefer "Nick." When you met me, my nametag said "Nikolai" and I guess it stuck.

I'm rarely up before noon, so there's little chance that I'm going to horn in on your morning writing sessions. I'm a night hunter, that's what my buddy Alex always says. I have a couple of bartending gigs, one night a week at this swank French hotel bar, and pretty much every other night at the Urban Jungle. I like the Urban Jungle. It's loud and rank and generally crazy. I met you at the swank place, of course. You used to be a regular there, though you stopped coming after I moved in.

You like your gin. That's how this all started. I could tell you wanted to talk to me. Nothing weird about that, lots of customers do. People don't want to just drink, they want someone to yak to. It makes them feel like they've got friends. You were like that. I could feel your eyes on me the whole time. The gabbers are usually good tippers, so I stood in front of you and wiped down some martini glasses and waited.

"This is a decent gin gimlet," you said. Decent. I liked that. Flattering but not really. I nodded my head.

You ended up telling me how you were writing this novel. In fact, that's pretty much all you wanted to talk about. You were fixated on it. It was your life's project, you said, and it should have been done years ago. You were all worked up about it. You even quit your job, manager of something at a big chemical corporation, so that you'd have more time to write. But then something happened, something that you didn't want to talk about, and there were unexpected expenses and now money was starting to be an issue. You worked afternoons at one of your friend's shops downtown, selling candles and greeting cards and crap like that, but it wasn't a huge source of income. So that's when you said that you were thinking about renting out a room, and did I know anybody who might be interested.

I was living with Alex at the time, but knew I had to get out. I was getting wrapped up in too much of his shit. So having a room at your place seemed like a great idea.

I don't know what I thought would happen. I wasn't expecting that you'd make dinner for me, or that we'd do the grocery shopping together or anything, but I guess I was surprised that you were so aloof. I eventually realized that you go out of your way to avoid me. Whole weeks go by and I never see you.

Alex tells me I should just go into your office and start rooting around until I find your secret. Probably dig up a severed ear or something, Alex says. But I pride myself on my character and I'm not going to stoop to Alex's level. Though if I think about it too much, the whole situation does creep me out.

The house itself isn't saying anything. There are no photos of your family, no souvenirs or postcards from vacations or anything. There are never even magazines or junk mail left lying about. Certainly no personal correspondence. The whole place is cold and sterile, and that makes me figure that you must be hiding something.

When I found those pages on the dining room table, I knew they were meant for me. You would never be so careless. "He wants me to see what he's writing"—that's what I thought right away. But by the time I finished the last paragraph, the hairs on the back of my neck were bristling.

I scrambled into my bedroom. On the little shelf on the wall, I have a bunch of books stashed, most of them science fiction. I used to love reading, though I don't have much time for it anymore. I looked up at those books, my heart racing. Two of them are—you guessed it—The Collected Fiction of Jorge Luis Borges, and Samuel Delaney's Dhalgren. I pulled the Borges down. I keep a bookmark in the story "The Garden of Forking Paths" because it's my favorite. I love how it's a detective story and you don't know what's going on until the end. But the bookmark had been moved to another story: "Tlon, Uqbar, Orbis Tertius." The one that you wrote about. I paged through it, and saw a phrase that immediately caught my eye. Transparent tigers and towers of blood. Right from the Borges story.

That was pretty freaky itself, but then I had this vision of you hovering over my bed, reading the titles of my books. I had thought about rummaging about your office, but it never occurred to me that you'd be going through my stuff. You didn't look the type. What else have you been doing in here?

I looked around my room, feeling shaky, feeling violated. First I checked my wallet, though I knew that was stupid. You aren't after my money. My clothes are strewn on the floor, and it would be hard to say whether they had been pawed through or not. I know that some guys like smelling other dudes' underwear and stuff, but I don't really want to think too much about that.

I went back to those pages you wrote, looking for more clues. I have no idea who your friends are, or even if you have any friends, so I don't know if the part about Albert Rey is legit or not. So I did a Google search.

Nothing about Albert Rey, but this is really bizarro: there's an entry about a guy named Alberto Rey, a muscular Latino pornographic actor who starred in the 1999 film, *Pink Prison*. A movie that happened to be produced by the Oscar-nominated director Lars Von Trier. A Wikipedia entry even comments on this guy's poor grasp of the English language, particularly his problem distinguishing between singular and plural nouns, as in "Look at that tits!" That part cracked me up. But it all makes sense, doesn't it? How you tied all that shit together?

I doubt that you'd be buddy-buddy with a porn star, especially a straight one, but the references to Lars Von Trier and to bad grammar seem more than coincidence. It's so weird. How would you know that I'd look up this stuff on the internet? It's like you are playing a game of cat and mouse with me.

And the bit about Albert's disappearance. What's up with that? Is it a threat?

I have to get the hell out of here.

So here's the money I owe you for this month. You can keep the change.

———

As I undertake this writing, I will keep in mind the words of Marcus Aurelius—"Be neither dilatory in your actions, nor disorganized in your conversation, nor rambling in your thoughts." Of these seemingly simple directives from his *Meditations*, the first is in practice the easiest to follow, and in fact, I intend to send this letter to the police tomorrow morning, since, though tonight my mind is flooded with confusion, nearly benumbed with anxiety, I speculate that I might be able to provide some illumination to the investigators. I had considered making an appointment to discuss what I know and what I fear, but after a day of indecision, I have concluded that only a written statement would be appropriate considering the circumstances.

Appropriate, of course, because some of the most important, most intriguing, information—I hesitate to use the word "evidence" at this juncture—that I have to share is itself in the written form. The documents which came into my possession are a curious hodgepodge of contradictions, filled with ominous undertones. The first was apparently written by my good friend George Altieri, and the second a handwritten letter probably meant for him.

Reading of one's own disappearance is an unsettling, almost surreal experience, but my concerns extend beyond the potential threats to my own personal safety. First of all, let me clarify what little I can. Indisputably, my name is Albert Rey; I have never been called Alberto or any other variation. Though of Hispanic heritage, I was born and raised in Chicago. English is therefore my native tongue, though I consider myself fluent in three other languages as well—Spanish, Italian, and French—and I even know a smattering of various Eastern European phrases. I am not prone to sudden grammatical lapses, even under the influence of a fine bottle of Cote du Rhone. Needless to say, I have never been associated with pornographic films, and while it is true that I hold Lars Von Trier in esteem, I was not even aware that he had directed such films in addition to his more traditional oeuvre.

I have never been to Hawaii, and never even discussed such a trip with George. We have never travelled anywhere of significance together, and I certainly did not disappear in Hawaii. In fact, it is my friend George Altieri who has mysteriously vanished.

I met George many years ago, during a difficult time. My life had been nearly demolished by two blows of destiny's hammer. First, Lucinda, my wife of nearly thirty years, abruptly decided to divorce me and moved out with little explanation, leaving me spinning in distress. Then, not two weeks later, before I had even begun to accustom myself to her absence, her loss became more decidedly permanent: while crossing a street not far from the penthouse condominium where we had lived together so blithely all those years, she was struck by a car on a rainy Sunday afternoon, and died immediately on the impact. At the time, I was flooded with a stream of conflicting emotions, including sorrow and rage, compounded by an irrepressible vengeful satisfaction. After years of tempering my volatile nature and adopting the somber cloak of maturity suitable to my years, I had been suddenly reduced to a child in pain, heedlessly craving the destruction of everything related to his misery. I could not speak to anyone without wailing. Weak in spirit, inconsolable, I spent an eternity of weeks at a coffeeshop, where I sat unnoticed and unbothered and pretended to read the newspaper.

Eventually my fog of self-absorption began to lift and I became aware of those around me: the rotating trio of surly barristas who took my order each day with carefully calibrated indifference, the businessmen huddled anxiously over laptops, the students bantering among themselves with caffeinated brio. I could see these same people day after day for decades without ever feeling the slightest inclination to engage any of them. In contrast, I was instinctively drawn to George Altieri. Unlike the restless creatures all about us, he was like a marble sculpture, grave and inanimate, except for the moments when he drew a coffee mug to his lips with a trembling hand. His skin was the color of stone and his eyes had that unfocused quality common in those prone to abstraction. He was like me, baffled, broken.

As I suspected, he too had been a victim of adversity. His mother had finally succumbed, after years of battle with pancreatic cancer, and he found himself at a crossroads without compass. He did not need to tell me the formidable energy required to raise one's head and join once again the rollicking merry-go-round.

"So this is what grief feels like," he told me once. "Most people think it is synonymous with sadness, but it's not. I'm not particularly unhappy. Just tired. Numb actually. It's almost as if I'm the one who died."

We had such conversations sporadically, a few minutes here and there, talking first about our preferred coffee flavors or the wretchedness of tabloid newspapers, and then drifting seamlessly into a discussion of our most personal concerns. Immersed in grief ourselves, we had been freed from society's stricture against the open acknowledgment of death, and we communicated unselfconsciously, as though we were sharing observations about the weather.

As the weeks passed and our rapport grew, we eventually began sitting together at the same table, always choosing a table for four, perhaps so that the two empty chairs could symbolize our own specific losses. George was a laconic man, and there were days in which we shared hours of comfortable silence, but there was one subject on which he would speak tirelessly. With the idealism of an adolescent, he told me he wanted to write a novel of such beauty, such significance, that it would cast into shadow all that been written previously. One day he brought a few typewritten pages to the coffee shop for my perusal, and I feigned astonishment. In truth, his writing was lackluster at best, but I have not the cruelty to wrest from a shattered man his last remaining dream.

Eventually George disclosed to me the most intimate news, guarded more closely than the details of a mother's death or a life's passionate ambition: the issue of personal finances. A confluence of healthcare expenses and poor financial management had left George's fiscal outlook bleak. He had retired a few years back, envisioning a future of frugal comforts, but this was now increasingly questionable. Nonetheless, he remained committed to his fiction, and wanted only a mundane job which would not overly occupy him. I have a number of lucrative business ventures in the city and was able to offer him a job, and for over a year, he spent his afternoons working at my shop Delightful Things.

As an employee, he was ideal: conscientious, trustworthy, punctual. Not as affable as the elderly Mrs. Quinn, but thankfully less prone to hold unwary customers hostage to monologues on genealogy, one of her favored subjects. For this reason, I was filled with worry when I received a call from Mrs. Quinn a week ago, indicating her displeasure that George, already an hour late, had not yet even called the store to explain his absence. I tried reaching George myself by phone, unsuccessfully, and I was forced to relieve Mrs. Quinn myself that day. Odd though it was for George to be so thoughtlessly irresponsible, I held peevishness at bay, and told myself that he must have found himself embroiled in some important matter, or debilitated by a flu, that would be clarified in due course. When he did not come to the store on the second day, I went directly to his house to sort the matter out.

He was not at home. Possibly with subconscious forethought, I had brought with me the spare key which George had given me months ago, in case of "contingency." To be entrusted with the key to another's home is the greatest indicator of trust and friendship. And yet is it not tragic that on a planet so cramped with quivering flesh, there are so few with direct access to our personal quarters? For surely George had given his key to no one else.

The house greeted me with a sinister stillness, and my banal exclamations— "George? Are you in here?"—echoed as if in a cavern. I saw nothing amiss at first: as usual, tidiness reigned supreme. George's bed was made and there were no dirty dishes in the sink, nothing to indicate a sudden departure or an unseemly encounter.

On further investigation, there were elements which did intrigue. One of the guest bedrooms was oddly devoid of all but the most basic furnishings. The shelves above the bed were unoccupied, the dresser's surface barren. It was as though the room had been vacated. Reluctantly, I pulled open some of the dresser drawers and found only a pair of woolen socks and some scattered change. The closet was similarly forsaken.

On the dining room table, I found the two documents I have referred to earlier, along with a stack of crumpled fifty-dollar bills. The handwritten letter and the money seem to explain the mystery of the empty bedroom, but it troubles me that I was unaware that George was renting out a room in his home. As I noted earlier, we were rather close, and this is not the sort of matter that one would hide from a friend.

On the other hand, he might have been shielding himself from my disapproval. I had never met Nikolai personally, but George spoke of this Bulgarian youth frequently, with an uncommon intensity. Though my inclinations take me down other shadowy roads, I can certainly understand George's fascination for a rough young man, and I am sure that drug-dealing only increased the allure. My concern was that George might have crossed over the threshold between idle fantasy and outright obsession.

"Nikolai has such piercing green eyes," George told me once. "Like a cat. In fact, he's feline in many ways, how he slinks about with his long, lean body, how he can be affectionate one moment and then relentlessly indifferent."

I cautioned George once, vaguely, discreetly, that such a young man, involved in criminal activities, might be no stranger to violence, but George brushed my concerns aside.

"Now his friend Alex, that's a different story. That one would mug an old lady with a walker without a pang of conscience. Nikolai's not like that. He's just wrapped up in the excitement of that world. It's a thrill for him. But he somehow retains the innocence of a child."

George would know that I would not support such a living arrangement, though I can imagine the electricity generated from having the object of desire sleeping under the same roof, just a room away. I would have expected that such a situation would not end nicely, but apparently, Nikolai simply absconded when the situation became suspect. There is no intimation that he had been planning any harm to George.

And yet George's letter ends abruptly, mid-sentence. What are we meant to gather from that?

Of course, the second document could have been written by George himself. In fact, it seems quite far-fetched and melodramatic for a young bartender to write such a letter of explanation. Why wouldn't he just pack up and leave? Would such a person truly feel obliged to leave money behind for unpaid rent? Furthermore, it would be rather surprising, after all, for this thug to be familiar with the works of Jorge Luis Borges, which are difficult to comprehend even for many graduate students of literature.

Instead, George may have written both texts as an elaborate exercise in metafiction. The first account refers explicitly to Borges, that undisputed master of the genre, and it would be consistent for such a work to incorporate real individuals (such as myself, in this case) into an otherwise fictional account. Though George and I never had the specific dinner discussion described in his account, we have on several occasions discussed the books of Paul Auster, Dennis Cooper, and W.G. Sebald, those addictive and intoxicating mazes masquerading as novels. I had assumed that George would follow a more traditional, linear narrative in his own work but I would hesitate to assert that my conjectures are always grounded in reality.

Of course, the writers of metafiction often aspire to goals loftier than merely tantalizing puzzles. The Borges story "Tlon, Uqbar, Orbis Tertius," for example, has been considered a diatribe against totalitarianism. It has been proposed that Borges is suggesting that ideas themselves can be spell-binding and dangerous, such as those leading to anti-Semitism or Nazism. George Altieri's work, if read as a metafictional text, may similarly possess another level of meaning beneath its benign prose. Perhaps George is encouraging the reader to ponder the woeful insularity of human existence: his characters, though sometimes interacting and sharing the same physical space, remain disconnected and isolated, somehow trapped within invisible walls limiting comprehension and even perception. The characters occupy vastly different worlds, and all connections to others are fleeting and fraught with misunderstanding.

It is equally probable that George might be commenting on the innate suggestibility of the human nature, on the precariousness of belief systems in general. How easily the reader is misled! How quickly we accept that what we are told is valid without any supporting evidence whatsoever. In this way, the work might be a veiled critique of religion: compare how zealots cling to beliefs which are equally unfounded and unsupportable. Or perhaps this is all my own conjecture, an attempt to force my own atheistic spin onto an unsuspecting author?

Nonetheless, other, more pressing and less abstract alternatives demand consideration. Clearly, there is the matter of George's vanishing, compounded by the seemingly simultaneous disappearance of his boarder Nikolai. Has George abducted Nikolai, and created these documents as a convenient explanation for Nikolai's mysterious absence? Or do I have it wrong? Could it be that Nikolai, driven to rage by unwanted sexual advances, murdered George and wrote the letter to thwart the investigators?

So much might have happened. There seems to be an infinity of possibilities, all equally likely and equally problematic, like an unsolvable mathematical conundrum. Clues abound but there are no facts. Every seemingly firm surface melts away at the slightest touch.

This afternoon, I called the bar at the Crillon hotel. I was told that they have never employed someone named Nikolai, or Nick for that matter. I meant to inquire further whether any of their employees had recently quit, or gone missing, but I was taken for a crank and was promptly hung up upon.

Now even Nikolai's very existence is called into question. A whole new set of potentialities opens itself before me, a gaping rift in the terra firma: perhaps George was simply tormenting me, or entertaining me, by feigning an unnatural infatuation? It might be more likely that the obsession was full-blown and George was simply clever enough to call the boy by a fictitious name—but why would he do this unless he were planning some sort of mischief? And if the latter were the case, then George himself was certainly the author of the handwritten letter. Going one step further into this ever-expanding spiral of inquiry, can we be sure that someone did in fact rent a room from George? Just who, if anyone, has vanished?

The implications extend to the philosophical. The Anglican bishop George Berkeley famously questioned whether a tree falling unobserved in a forest makes a sound; he resolved that question to his own satisfaction by concluding that there is a sound because God is always there to hear it. The writer Borges was similarly engaged with this concept, but unshackled by the strictures of religion. In his story, perception shapes reality, rather than the other way around. By seeing the empty guestroom and reading the documents I have described, am I personally accountable for making Nikolai's disappearance real?

I am essentially a self-interested man so I will brush aside these obscure conjectures and get back on point. What is my own role in all of this? Should I consider myself threatened? After all, my own disappearance has been described in detail, and there are even references to my "bruised and misshapen corpse." I may be well advised to go into hiding myself, to evade these sinister forces apparently all around me.

There is a final matter which may be somehow related, which I feel somehow obliged to reveal now: I wrote a short story which I had once shared with George. It was provisionally entitled, "The Tower of Blood." The plot involved a man who kills his disloyal wife by hiring a young Eastern European drug dealer to stage a hit-and-run accident. The matter is deemed an accident, and the narrator is free of suspicion, but strange things begin happening: one morning, when he turns on the bathroom faucet, blood rather than water is released. The next day, there is blood from the showerhead. Then the toilet flushes with blood. Convinced that these peculiar developments are linked to his own guilt, he finds himself paralyzed with anxiety. The story closes with the narrator sitting in his living room, motionless, exhausted, the body of the strangled young Bulgarian splayed at his feet, as blood cascades down the windows of his penthouse condominium.

I am not sure if this short synopsis, or indeed any of my idle musings, is relevant to the disappearance. If you have further questions, you need only locate me, though by the time you read this letter, I might be anywhere, perhaps in Hawaii or Manhattan or Borneo, just to list a few of the places on this enormous, godforsaken planet of ours.

The principle of Occam's razor demands that we choose the simplest explanation. In my opinion, it should be concluded that all of these documents, not just the first two but this one that you are reading right now as well, are part of a fictional exercise and that George Altieri and Nikolai and even myself, Albert Rey, are merely imaginary characters. If you insist on disregarding my advice, adamant in your frantic pursuit of darkness, then I would suggest reluctantly that you investigate for yourself and go to George Altieri's residence on Poplar Street and look for a splatter of blood in the abandoned guest bedroom, just in front of the bedside table.

3

Creativity

FRED SKOLNIK

Point A is connected to Point B, Point B is connected to Point C. When you run out of letters you go back to the beginning, using subscripts. In this way you can record an infinite number of connections, or "links" as they are called nowadays, though there are in fact only a few trillion. Well, maybe many trillion, but in any case not an infinite number. However, since you are starting a new series every time you reach the letter Z, there is no necessary connection between parallel terms, that is, A is not necessarily connected to A_1 and A_1 is not necessarily connected to A_2. On the other hand, as each point may have numerous connections, A may very well be connected to B_1 and/or C_2, and so on and so forth. These connections are being created every second of every minute of every hour of the day. No one can actually follow them. We can only run off labels and look around for something to stick them on. Furthermore, at a given moment, any of these trillions of connections may present themselves to us, that is, become conscious. For example, all the words in our language are connected and therefore you may say "I think" or "I feel" as the case may be. But not only words are connected, the thoughts and feelings themselves are connected, objects are connected, people are connected. Thus the heat of a summer day evokes the distant shouts of children, ships standing out at sea, women with sun-browned bodies lying in the sand, viz., a cluster of connected points gathered around a central point or nexus like the hub of a wheel

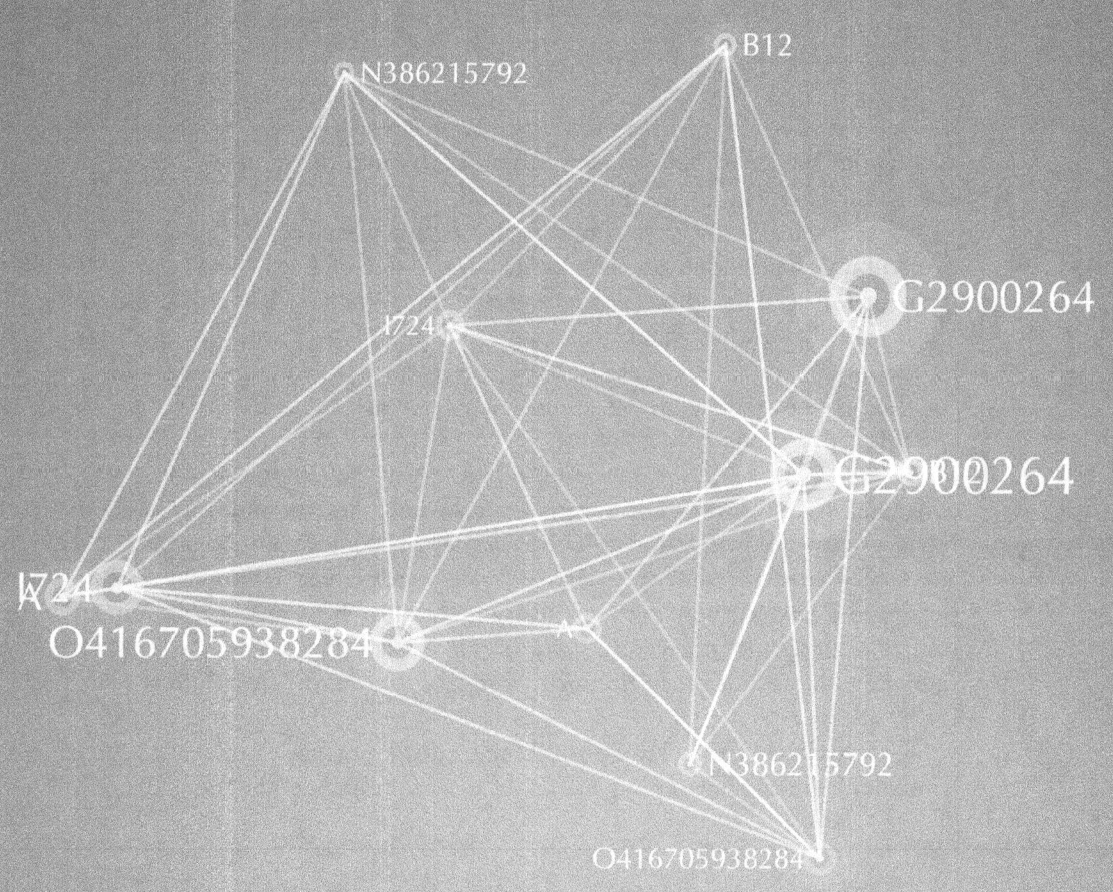

B12
N386215792
G2900264
I724
G2900264
I724
A3
O416705938284
N386215792
O416705938284

(say, A) that subsumes the others, much like Proust's *petite madeleine*. All this may be represented as follows:

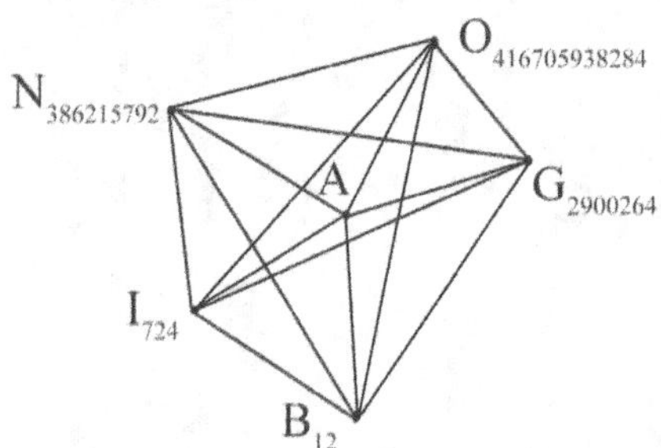

roughly speaking. In this manner I may come under the spell of a chain of associations sparked or ignited by a particular stimulus that touches a center of thought or feeling in my unconscious mind.

I wait patiently for these connections to reveal themselves. Though I may focus all my attention on a certain point I am essentially passive in the process. I cannot reach my hand into a barrel and pull up whatever I like. You cannot know beforehand what your next thought is going to be. I wait for something to occur to me. In the meanwhile I make a cup of coffee and my mind wanders. Random connections come up, unrelated to the task at hand. I look out the window. I daydream. I walk around in circles. Then I come back to the pages on the table. I read: "She was wearing a dark, expensive-looking coat with a fur collar and had a little dog at the end of a leash and a fleshy, handsome face and he knew she would be fleshy under her clothes and found the thought exciting and looked down furtively at her legs and they were perfect." This is the starting point and I can't say why the sentence came into my head at a given moment though I can see the context and frame of reference easily enough. The sentence resonates. I know it is the beginning of a story. I can feel the connections wanting to surface.

Unfortunately I can think of nothing at this point but to introduce some commonplace dialogue to bring the characters to life and get them together:

> *"Hi," he said.*
> *She said hi too and smiled engagingly. "You live here, don't you?"*
> *"Yes, we went to high school together. Remember?"*
> *"I remember."*
> *"Where you off to?"*
> *"Just walking my doggie. I live at the other end of the block."*
> *"I know. I've seen you on the street. But I never saw you like this before."*

"Like what?"
"All dressed up on a Sunday morning. You look great."
"Thank you."
"May I accompany you?"

I don't precisely invent these words. They are offered to me out of, I suppose, various models stored in my mind. Whether I accept them or reject them depends on still other models stored in my mind. I of course feel that I am "writing" dialogue. This is a moot point, as the lawyers say, and also a pretty big philosophical question. Who am "I"? What am I? Am I only a passive observer borne along by the tides and currents of a sometimes stormy, sometimes placid sea? This troubles me. I have a certain difficulty locating myself on the ontological plane though I know I'm right there. If the sea were conscious, I think, it would see itself as we see it, but with the difference that it would know it belongs to itself. Is this the key?

From here I try to pick up the thread again:

She laughed at this, at his fancy way of talking, knowing it was a joke, and said, "Why certainly," in the spirit of the thing, and they crossed the street to the park opposite the row of houses where they lived and walked beside the low retaining wall under the overhanging trees where autumn leaves covered the sidewalk. They were a couple now, a young man and a young woman with a dog on a leash. A car came by and then a boy on a bicycle. Daniel half turned toward her but she was looking straight ahead, almost smiling, as if waiting to see how he would begin.

"Nice day," he said.

"A little chilly," she replied. That was why she was wearing the coat. But the weather was perfect, it was football weather, and after the game hot drinks. He was wearing a sweatshirt and a suede jacket and his black chino pants and his scuffed suede shoes, on his way to the candy store to get the Sunday paper, and now she was here, like a gift. He noticed how clear her skin was. She is blooming now, he thought.

They were alone on the street. The dog stopped at every tree and went through the motions of peeing and she tugged a little at the leash to get him moving again. The steep, grassy incline running down to the retaining wall from the pedestrian walk that traversed the park was also full of trees. He had played there once but had not been there in many years. The park belonged to his childhood. Nothing had really changed, not the neighborhood and not his life. Behind his house there was a little yard, also grassy, but somewhat neglected now, and facing the street there was a garage with an automatic door where his father parked his Dodge and kept his gardening tools, mostly for the hedge out front and the tiny flower bed. All the houses on the block were identical and he imagined that Marjorie's bedroom upstairs looked out on the street where she might have seen him passing by some night.

This is Teller Avenue in the Bronx, opposite Claremont Park. I lived on College Avenue, on the other side of the block. From my bedroom window on the sixth floor, looking across to Teller Avenue, I saw a few elm trees in a fenced-off area next to a big parking lot and also a few of the little yards behind the houses there and the rear of the six-story building on the corner of Teller and 170th Street, whose windows we occasionally broke when we played stickball in the parking lot, and the steep, grassy incline of Claremont Park. I am now, figuratively speaking, at $G_{2900264}$.

In fact, the girl and the picture of Teller Avenue are evoked simultaneously. The moment she appears in my mind I see her on this street, and I also know at the same time that this will be a story about beginnings and possibilities feeding off my own emotions and history but not directly connected to them, a work of fiction then in every sense. The dark coat with the fur collar is what such a girl might have been wearing on a chilly Sunday morning fifty years ago and creates a picture that I find appealing. The dog or doggie, on the other hand, is a prop. An internal editor, created out of many and diverse elements, great complexes of connections touching everything I have ever read, thought, felt, tells me what is needed to complete a sentence. Any object can serve as a prop, a fire truck that a character leans against, a bag of potato chips, a cigarette. The internal editor scans the entire stock of props piled up in the storeroom of the mind and picks one out, saying, "This will do." Sometimes, of course, another voice says, "Not quite," and then the search begins again. In all this I am like a head of state waiting for his ministers to sort out a tricky problem. The dog or doggie is not really my idea. I am reluctant to take credit for it. It is given to me, along with everything else.

I didn't know anyone who lived on Teller Avenue. It was a very quiet street, lined with trees, and the park right across from it. I rarely had occasion to be there, except when I took the shortcut through the parking lot and crossed the street to enter the park by boosting myself up on the retaining wall and then making my way up the grassy incline. The center of my life was College Avenue, the parking lot, the Taft High School schoolyard and 170th Street, the commercial axis of the neighborhood running up to the Grand Concourse and beyond. Later our horizons expanded in ever-widening circles. We discovered Fordham Road, the Paradise and RKO movie theaters, Van Courtland Park. We discovered Manhattan too. Ultimately, we felt at home everywhere. We were New Yorkers. Nothing surprised us.

Teller Avenue thus remained an out of the way street, the urban equivalent of a country road, and I suppose that was part of its charm, or more likely all of its charm. Claremont Park itself was quite large, running from 170th Street to Mount Eden Parkway, about five city blocks, and then down to Clay Avenue. It had big playgrounds, ballfields and basketball courts and endless green fields where we played rough games of football. Thus, when the girl walks up Teller

Avenue on a Sunday morning, an entire physical world is evoked. This is simple memory, without its underside, without its texture. It does not lead me back to its source. It does not proceed from such a source. It is a chain of tangential associations. I am dissatisfied. There is something stronger, deeper here. I want to go back to my original impulse, the image of the girl and the street on that Sunday morning. Instead, working against myself, I am constrained to push the story forward and write some more lifeless dialogue so that before I know it Daniel invites Marjorie to spend the day with him and takes his father's car and they drive up to Van Courtland Park and go horseback riding and then they have pizza in a little restaurant where Dean Martin sings "Mambo Italiano" on the jukebox and they get back when it's almost dark and he asks her to go out with him next Saturday night and she says she'd love to and it's as simple as that.

Here I lose the story. I know that I don't want to write *Goodbye, Columbus* or *Love Story*, but that seems to be where I'm heading. I write a few more pages without much enthusiasm. Daniel thinks about Marjorie all week. He goes to his French class and his science class and his sociology class and daydreams most of the time. The sociology teacher is a Southerner and quite contemptuous of everything, calling scholars who hold certain views "mow-rons" in his Southern accent, and Daniel finds himself thinking that this was not the place for him, the sociology teacher that is, and he would be better off back home in the South teaching in some backward university, and the French teacher is a German who speaks French with a German accent which no one would have noticed, least of all the other French teachers, who were probably all Americans, and they go out a few times, that is Daniel and Marjorie, and he kisses her and they sit on the stoop in front of her house till late at night and she confesses that she always had a crush on him and it is clear that she considers him her boyfriend now and he feels that way too. They are like a small-town couple on their little tree-lined street with the park across the way and when it starts to get cold they go inside and usually her parents are already asleep so they sit on the sofa in the dark and kiss and pet and she resists him a little but always gives in though he would not go too far.

I no longer have any sense of the characters. They have lost their reality. Marjorie's father is a shoe salesman and her mother teaches elementary school and she, that is Marjorie, has a younger brother who Daniel rarely sees. Daniel has a younger brother too and his father sells insurance and does pretty well so his mother has never had to work. Here I gratuitously introduce an aunt who dies of cancer of the cervix, taking her off the shelf so to speak. She is a big, handsome woman who "goes to business," as Daniel's mother puts it, meaning she is a secretary, and always wore sweat-stained see-through blouses and expensive tailored suits and nylon stockings and high-heeled shoes. This was my next door neighbor in the Bronx, a single woman in her late thirties who lived with her elderly mother, and her death made a profound impression on me and I have kept her in mind all these years. I suppose I will have to use her someplace else, as she doesn't really belong here. In any case it is clear that marriage is on the horizon and Daniel and Marjorie talk soberly about sleeping together and decide not to, or rather Marjorie decides not to with a great many rationalizations to win Daniel over to her view, and they continue to pet very heavily on her living room sofa when everyone is asleep but at other times they have long, serious talks, baring their souls as the saying goes, and Daniel begins to idealize the life they might have together and is convinced he loves her and tells her so and she says she loves him too and everything is settled.

As I say, this is not the story I wish to write. It has swept me along in spite of myself. I have no interest in Daniel's married life. I am interested in the few moments that contain the essence of a life. These make up the lexicon of memory and desire, so to speak, these contain the images, symbols, motifs from which all things flow. I contemplate the material at hand. I see that first day taking shape. It will have been a perfect day, of the kind that lingers in memory for a lifetime. But beneath it, again, there is something more. It is this that I am looking for. It is buried in this vision of the girl in the dark coat coming up the street. Otherwise, I am afraid, instead of *Love Story* I will be writing *Before Sunrise*, whose charm I doubt if I can equal.

I make another cup of coffee. I scratch myself. I check my mailbox. All these impulses and inclinations present themselves to me sometimes in a trickle, sometimes in a flood, and are filtered, sorted and displayed by a system of checks and balances whose workings are hidden from me. I am being ridden by these impulses, in a manner of speaking, like a pogo stick, or steered around the house like a vacuum cleaner, if you will. Later I "decide" to have hamburgers for supper and take the chop meat out of the freezer. The thought of having hamburgers for supper gives me a little lift. This is an emotion, produced in that same hidden place and perceived like all the data of consciousness as belonging to me. Clearly, however, it is the thoughts and objects that produce the emotions after being mediated subliminally. Now I perceive an object, now I have a thought, now I have a feeling, now I act. Everyone has a lot to say about feelings but I suppose they can best be viewed as an evolutionary device, varieties of pain and pleasure to warn or encourage us and thereby help us preserve ourselves. The flesh feels pleasure and pain but the "self" feels joy and sorrow and all the other refinements of feeling because its survival and integrity are driven by the same biological imperative as the survival of the body. At any rate, these feelings are not generated consciously. They simply "come up" like so much flotsam and jetsam. Then we act, not like automatons to be sure, though many of us lean in that direction, but with a clear sense of "choosing" a course of action. This is the crux of the matter. A thought, feeling, perception or impression, more or less complex, more or less strong, impels us toward an action—to eat an orange or rob a bank—and if there are no dissenting inner voices we act without further ado. If, on the other hand, objections are raised, a debate ensues and one voice or the other prevails, depending on its force or volume. Not surprisingly, as consciousness is conscious of a choice being made, it perceives it as its own. But consciousness is only a kind of seismograph that recognizes itself as the ground of its own being. Volition must necessarily be generated outside it, asserting itself as from behind a veil. We are in essence unknown to ourselves, we cannot see the process, only the result. To enter this process and discover ourselves is thus to embark on one of the great journeys of life.

She was wearing a dark, expensive-looking coat with a fur collar and had a little dog at the end of a leash and a fleshy, handsome face and he knew she would be fleshy under her clothes and found the thought exciting and looked down furtively at her legs and they were perfect.

I have come back to the beginning. I have gone back to the top of the page. Again I feel the powerful resonance of these words, or rather of the image or vision they evoke. Again I find myself waiting for what will come next, for now the process begins again and again I am a bystander. The day stretches on. I have absorbed thousands of impressions and thought thousands of thoughts. These are duly recorded; they will find their place in the general scheme of things in their own good time. I await further developments. There is little I can do to speed up the process. Whatever expedient is suggested to me pops up in my mind like a jack-in-the-box. I am directed to look here or look there. Sometimes I find something, sometimes I don't. This is of course frustrating and again calls into question my autonomy. I am not the author of myself. I am whatever comes into my head. My only certainty is that all these connections flooding the unconscious mind are uniquely my own. I inhabit myself like the occupant of an empty room hearing voices behind the walls.

The girl in the dark coat comes down the street on a perfect autumn day and evokes or is evoked by a certain sense of a distant time and place that I bear within me. I skirt its edge and feel its reverberations. From the street and the park and then the parking lot and the view from my window high above the street I move now into an inner circle of associations attached to a single image. They have always been there, linked, resonating, giving color to everything I see and think. Now, suddenly, I have arrived at the center of my life.

Point A is connected to Point B and Point B is connected to Point C. Around these centers of feeling gather great constellations like points of light yielding the essence of a life. You may label them like isotopes, if you like, and trace their paths down all your days.

B_{12} then are the shadows moving like bars across my bedroom wall when the cars turned into the parking lot from Teller Avenue and threw their lights against the slatted blinds of my bedroom window. And as I lay in my little bed watching the shadows moving on the wall and listening to the sound of distant traffic I had a vision of the night that was like a call to another life.

I$_{724}$ is the rain beating down on the sidewalk in the dim, yellow light of the streetlamp on the corner of our street. And I would watch the rain for hours from my kitchen window, dreaming of that other world without knowing what it was.

N$_{386215792}$ are the long, narrow streets like canyons steeped in shadow where I walked alone one quiet Sunday afternoon when the day was winding down and the air was hot and still, and I could almost touch what I was looking for.

G$_{2900264}$ are the young mothers with infants in carriages and their milk so sweet, their breasts so full and white. I remember the young mothers and the sloping lawns and the mornings in the park. It must have been during the War. And I must have looked out at the world from beneath a woolen cap with hunger in my eyes. In that time and that place women wore long skirts or dresses and high heels and nylon stockings and the sky was always blue. And you saw a squirrel run up a tree and heard the shouts of children playing in the vast green fields. And there were beds of flowers and little ants and dogs on leashes and bikes and roller skates and bouncing balls, so much noise and movement and color and light and the sun so bright and a pale quarter-moon still in the sky and you wanted it all and you said, "Me! Me!" and she looked too, or maybe she didn't hear you.

O$_{416705938284}$ is a young woman sitting on a fire escape in the hot summer night with the smoke from her cigarette curling into the air.

And A? And A? A must be the lazy, distant drone of a plane high overhead in the cloudless summer sky. I could hear the excited voices of children all around me and such a hum and buzz and then it came so far away and I looked up and saw it and heard the distant sound and it made everything seem so right and filled me with such wonder and such peace, and fixed forever on that perfect day my sense of the world and the promise it contained.

I know that I do not wish to write this story. I wish to leave the image that lies behind it unresolved. I do not wish to go beyond the moment that contains all the possibilities of my life. So great is the tension within this moment that it could fuel the birth of an entire universe. As long as this tension resides in me all things remain possible. The girl in the dark coat embodies this possibility. I shall forever see her coming up the street. Nearer and nearer she will come and I shall wait for her.

4

The Return of the Baker, Edwin Tregear

V. GEBBIE

Unlike so many, I came home in July. Some of the lads got off the train at Exeter, some at Plymouth. I must have gone to sleep. I woke at Penzance, my stop, when someone shouted, *End of the line, mate.*

Mr. Olds was outside the station in the trap; that was a godsend. It was a long walk to St Just.

"Edwin Tregear. Well I never," he said. Indeed, that's all he said for the first five minutes of our journey. "Edwin Tregear the baker. Well I never."

There was bunting outside the cottages. Kiddies with flags. "'Spect you're glad to see that then?" Mr. Olds said, waving at the kiddies. I didn't wave, just held my bag on my knee.

Mr. Olds asked questions. "'Spect you'll be baking again?"

I looked at my hands and tried to imagine them twisting dough into pretty plaits for the mine owner's wife. I couldn't. Still saw them trying to hold a rifle steady.

"Maybe not, Mr. Olds. Maybe I need to do something else."

"They are recruiting up Levant," he said.

It would not be long before we saw the first mine chimneys, the first engine houses.

I shut my eyes. "I dare say," I said.

Later, there was the sound of voices, excited, and Mr. Olds tapped me on the shoulder. "You awake, lad?" We were passing through Newbridge. More kiddies, more flags.

We passed a small stone house on the road outside Newbridge. No bunting here. Front door closed. Curtains drawn. Mr. Olds didn't take his eyes off the pony's hindquarters, just flicked the reins. "Young Matty Harris, shot for desertion. 'Spect you know."

It was cold, suddenly. I shut my eyes again. The trap lurched, bumping me and Mr. Olds together like dice in a shaker. Then I had to stop. And before he could rein in the pony, I half fell into the mud, knelt and retched.

When it was over, I leaned against the wheel of the trap, shaking, wiping my mouth on my sleeve, just breathing.

But then there was no trap, no Mr. Olds, no pony. My wrists were raw, tied to another wheel with a strap, my arms stretched wide, pulled almost out of their sockets. A young lad's body being dragged away, his head not quite covered, mouth open like he was trying to say something. His boots gouging small furrows through a different mud.

"You alright, lad?" Mr. Olds said.

I think I nodded.

What a homecoming it was—even if home was just a room above a bakery.

What do I remember? The village kiddies grown so much, lifting paper chains up round my neck. The hottest, sweetest tea served in the best Royal Albert cups. A great cake decorated with flags and *Welcome Home Edwin* piped no doubt by Baker Jebb.

Baker Jebb himself—so old, his hands trembling. Mrs. Baker Jebb, unchanged, red-faced, hair white as good flour.

"We kept your room exactly . . ."

I remember how the bakery door flew open, neighbors pushing to slap me on the back, shake my hand.

"Welcome, welcome back." Pots of jam, bottles of home brewed beer. I remember some lads rapping on the window, sticks over their shoulders, grinning: "What's it like killing Germans?" and Mrs. Baker Jebb shooing them away.

I remember the brass band playing a bit ragged in the square. Less three cornets, the tuba and the bandmaster.

The publican from The Tinners' carried round a gallon jug. "A soldier needs more than tea now, Mrs. Jebb."

Later, after the homecoming, I went up to my old room. I could not sleep. The bedstead creaked with every movement, it seemed. But I must have slept in the end, as it was late when I woke to the smell of flour and yeast heavy in the air.

I lay there, stretched my arms up towards the roof, flexing my fingers like I used to, get them ready for kneading. I did not go downstairs for a while. Then, when I did go down, I stood in the doorway, watching Baker Jebb setting the early loaves to rise. It was so, so familiar.

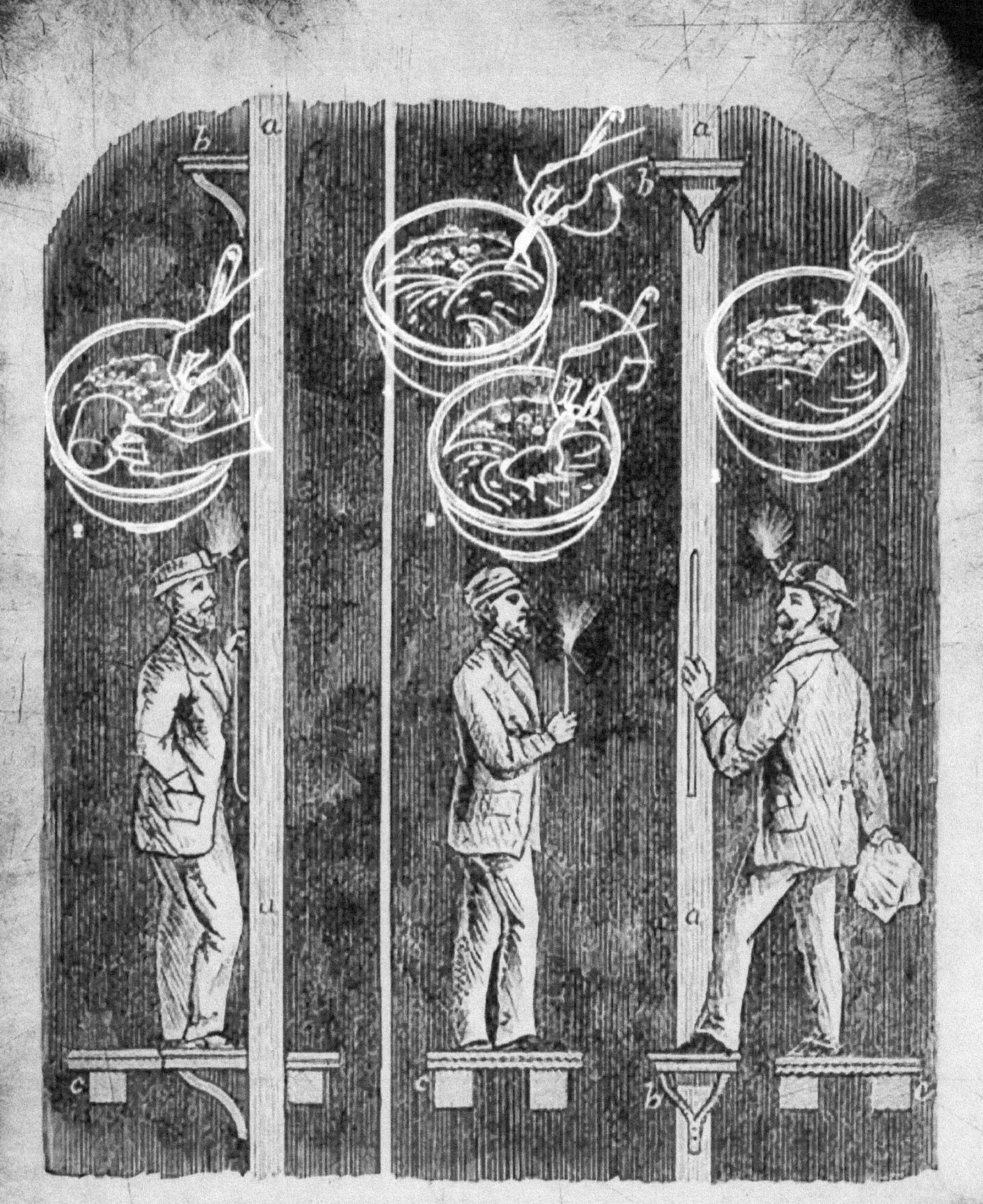

Baker Jebb looked up eventually, wiping his hands on his apron.

"Edwin—been waiting on this day. 'Bout time you took the place over, then? "

"I'm sorry, Mr. Jebb," I said. "I don't think I can do that, not now."

It was not easy, that conversation. Baker Jebb came over and held his hands up for me to see. Old, twisted. "Painful, they are," he said. "Been waiting on you, Edwin."

I didn't reply.

"Best baker in Cornwall, you were," he said "Never seen a lad take to baking like you done. I can't be doing much more."

True enough, I loved baking, before. I loved the feel of the dough. The smells, rich and round, the sweetness of sugar, the sharpness of orange and lemon peel. The depth of saffron for the saffron bread. Its color.

But not with these hands. Not now.

"I'm sorry, Mr. Jebb," I said. "I'm going down Levant, if they'll have me."

The mine manager's office was not that different from the recruiting office in St Ives. One thing was different though. In the corner of the mine office there was a great boulder on display, lines of tin and copper ore running through.

A sign:

A time to cast away stones
a time to gather stones together

Mr. Nicholas sat behind his desk and looked at me over his glasses.

"Recently back from the War, isn't that right?"

I nodded.

A hooter sounded somewhere in the mine. It echoed like the whine of shells and the howls of half-men.

"Ah," he said. "Well, you look fit enough to me. Monday next, five thirty."

He gave me some papers, told me that I'd have linen trews and tunic supplied by the mine, one set every six months. One strong hat and candles. I was to bring my own boots, food and match tins.

Then he said, "The first week you'll have a helping hand with Fritz."

I half laughed. "Fritz?"

"Ah. The man-engine. The mechanical lift down the mine. Boche contraption. Been here for years."

"They get everywhere," I said.

I must have looked like a daisy the next Monday, my work clothes so painfully new. The older miners' clothes—stained red from the clay—were stiff from a night over the hot pipes in the dry. That dry stank. Sweat.

There was a man sitting at a table taking down who was at work. The Marker, he was called.

"Make your mark," he said. I signed my name. He looked up.

I had trouble with my strong hat when I loaded the brim with clay and candle. The whole thing felt as though it would fall off any second, and I must have been holding my head at an angle until a small man with a broken nose said to stand up straight while I could.

"Jarvis," he said. "No Miners' Federation here . . . I run something like it, unofficially. See you afterwards for your dues." Then I dropped my food and match tins in the passageway. I held up the line of men waiting for their turn on Fritz, until Jarvis grinned and showed me the knack of holding both tins in one hand, leaving the other free to grasp the handles of the man-engine.

Extraordinary contraption. Beam engine in the engine house up top. Then a great wooden rod that rose and fell over and over again in the shaft, little ledges fixed to the rod, made to take a miner's boots.

The noise was deafening. Thudding and hissing, shouts. My ears rang with it all. I watched as the man in front grasped a handle on the rod, stepped forward, then disappeared, standing, down into the darkness.

I stood on the wooden platform, feeling it give slightly under my weight. I reached for the metal handle as it rose back up, my boot found a ledge on the rod, the rod plunged, and my breakfast nearly reappeared. Twelve feet. Then the rod slowed and Jarvis shouted from above to step off . . . "Backwards!"

I stepped back and my foot met a platform on the side of the shaft. I forgot to let go. My arm was jerked upwards as the rod rose . . .

"Let go, man!" Jarvis shouted. I did, and just stood there, shaking. I peered between the boards; could just see another platform below mine. The candle on the strong hat of the man below.

Half an hour, this journey would take. Half an hour to the bottom, hundred and fifty men at once, they said.

Then other sounds. First the hiss and thud of that beam engine up at ground level, getting fainter the deeper we sank. The scrape of hobnails on wood, as the column of men slid on and off their perches. Coughs.

Then singing, the men's voices rising up the shaft for all the world as though angels had fallen into the dark. Slow pieces, chapel hymns, the words all lost as the music bounced round the walls and echoed down the adits.

Someone was singing loudly, out of tune.

"He's a voice that'd crack granite . . ." shouted a voice from the below. And another replied: "Perfect! Bring him along here . . . let the man sing . . . do my work for me nice."

Working at Levant was tough. Plunged into darkness, just you, despite what they said about teamwork. Backbreaking, the only light the flicker of candles on wet red walls.

At the end of each shift we brought a little of that somberness up with us, with the painfully slow ride in silence up into the fresh air. Then the long walk back to St Just, unless Mr. Olds passed by on his trap.

Then one day the shift end silence seemed greater than normal. The passageway at the top of the man-engine leading to the dry seemed full of a heavy quiet. Where were the sounds? Where were those half hearted bursts of singing, when someone usually called out to shut up? Where was the talk of payday, and arguments about the strength of the beer being better in St Buran than Pendeen?

I came up the steps pulling the work shirt over my head. There was a knot of men waiting, silent. Looking at each other. Then a voice, "So how's the hero Edwin Tregear, then?"

I stood there, shirt in hand.

"He's fine, thank you . . ." I said.

The men said nothing. Just looked at me.

There was a laugh, and Jarvis, the Miner's Federation type, pushed his way forward.

"So tell us, Edwin Tregear . . ." he leaned against the wall, folded his arms. "Tell us . . . what exactly did you do to be a hero?"

I shook my head.

I said nothing. Just stood there, naked but for my work trews, bootlaces undone, sweat running into my eyes.

I could hear a sound like the biggest shell flying straight for me. The biggest bloody shell the Hun ever managed to put together. I waited for the impact.

"Aaah. Go on . . . hero," said Jarvis. "Go on . . .you can tell us. We're your mates." He turned to the men. "Aren't we, lads?"

There was no answer. Not one word from them, or me.

Then he spoke again, and his voice rang against the granite steps.

"Our hero Edwin Tregear shot young Matty Harris."

The silence that followed came deep. Then a few men, still red with clay, broke forward.

"You bastard, Tregear . . ." A fist swung, I ducked.

Jarvis laughed,

"Not yet, lads."

The men gathered closer. What had been silence swelled into a hum and the hum into a growl. Then Jarvis' words came again.

"Had it from my cousin up Plymouth. He's no hero, isn't Edwin Tregear, he's a murderer. A fuckin' murderer. Cowardice is one thing, can't abide that, can we lads . . . but murder?"

All I could do was shake my head.

There was a long pause.

Then I said, quiet, "Yes. I shot Matty Harris. And no he wasn't a coward."

Hard to say exactly what happened then. A fist caught me on the jaw. I fell. A boot in the stomach . . .

But then it stopped. Someone was standing between me and them. The Marker, turned up for the next shift, to take down the names.

"What's going on here?" he said.

I lay there, shaking.

"Tregear," said Jarvis. "Just explaining how he shot Matty Harris from New-bridge."

"You want to hear?" I said. Then louder. "You want to hear?"

The Marker stayed put.

"I'd say if he's explaining, you let him finish," he said. Didn't help me up. But I stood.

Jarvis said nothing. Held up a hand, and they went quieter.

Then I told them.

I told them how Matty Harris shook in his boots. How he slapped his hands over his ears at the sound of gunfire. How he buried his head in my chest and cried when he saw a man's head blown apart right next to him. How he shouted to be let home, that he lied, he wasn't of an age. He wasn't of an age.

"I took him with me," I said. "Kept him by me, as much as anyone can. I had him by my side. Looked after him, but you can't properly, not out there. No truck with cowards, that's what they called them—him and others—and Matty was no coward, just frightened out of his wits. But they couldn't have that either."

Silence, then. No one moved.

"I told him," I said. "I tried to tell him to buck up. I did . . . tell him . . . just before Vimy Ridge it was, but Matty Harris just wanted to go home, that's all. Kept talking about Newbridge.

So he went. Ran away. But he was no coward, I say."

Then Jarvis laughed. That was too much.

I reached for the bugger, grabbed him by the shirt.

"You got no idea, have you?" I said. "You wanted to hear? Well damn well hear."

The men surged forward, but the Marker shouted to wait.

Then I told them the rest.

"Three of them there were. Three kids. Matty and two others. Some quick court martial that took five minutes, and a little ceremony to keep us troops in line . . ."

Jarvis had a sort of grin on his face. I pulled him round to face the men.

"They do that," I said. "Didn't you know? Get men from the same troop to form the firing squads? Only no one wants to do it. So they pick."

I jabbed a finger at a tall man in the front.

"You."

And at the man next to him, "You."

And at the Marker, "You," and he flinched, shook his head. I ignored him.

Then I pointed straight at Jarvis, whose grin wavered. "They have to shoot *you*," I said. "Their mate."

I turned back to the men.

"They chose me. Matty's mate."

The men said nothing. But they were listening.

"No choice. Or you get shot yourself. Insubordination. Refusing an order. Then, they give you rifles already loaded. And they tell you that one has been loaded with a blank. So. Go on. What would you do? Eh?"

At first no one spoke. Then it started.

"I'd not shoot straight, tell you that for nothing."

"Nor would I . . . give the blighter a chance, eh?"

"I'd go for his legs. Maybe . . ."

Jarvis was saying nothing. I turned to him. Lowered my voice. "What would you do, if you were them?"

Jarvis, red-faced now, "Nothing. I'd bloody do nothing."

That struck me as funny. I almost laughed. "So you'd like them to blast you open and leave you screaming until some bastard officer finished you off?"

That shut him up. And the rest of them.

"What to do?" I said. "I tell you what was to do. I could put a bullet straight into Matty's heart, that's what. No sodding about. Finish it. I still hear him at night, standing there while they were about to cover his eyes, not understanding anything, shouting . . . *Edwin? Let me go home?*"

And I held up my hands, still red with clay, and shaking, now. "With these. Used to make bread, then they killed people. Hundreds."

I waited a bit. Collected myself.

"And, yes. They shot Matty Harris. I didn't wait for the command. Aimed for his heart, reckon I got it. Went down before they covered his head, never knew what hit him. I got shackled to a gun carriage for my pains, but at least, I did him well."

Don't mind admitting, I couldn't see, then. I must have shrugged on my clothes and just walked out. But I do know I shouted it again, and my words echoed round the dry like it was a chapel.

"I did him well."

The next day, the village lads still played at soldiers. But this time they tied the smallest to the tree in the square, formed a firing squad, and one broke ranks and shot first with a stick. And Mr Olds still said "Morning, Edwin," as he passed. But his eyes said something different.

At Levant, the morning shifts were long now, silent. There was no singing on Fritz on the way down. Only the great thudding of the engine. Down at the bottom, the air was thick with things unsaid. When someone spoke, their words seemed to flail against the tunnel walls and fade out into the dark.

The days seemed full of echoes.

Then, a few weeks later, at shift end the first man to shaft bottom rang the bell. One ring. *Ready to come up.* And painfully slow as always, Fritz began to move, picking up speed, until he was ploughing up and down, taking the usual four men a minute on their journey to the light, to dry clean clothes, the walk back home, and tea.

I was one of the last on. Over a hundred and twenty men above me on the rod, all getting on and off at the same time. The weight of a hundred men . . .

I caught the handle when it was my turn, and stepped on. On, off, on off. The dance up the shaft started. By now, my boots did the dance themselves, finding the rhythm of the rod and moving with it. On, off. On, off.

Suddenly, it paused, breaking the rhythm. It paused at the top of the up-stroke, as though it was taking a breath. It began the downward stroke, I dropped my tins on the platform. By the time I picked them up, the rod was on the upward . . . I reached for the next handle but it didn't come. I felt a thud. That's all.

There was a kind of silence. Then it fell. And everything and everyone fell with it.

A great crashing, a rumbling; chaotic sounds, shouts, a single high scream, then that scream became two, then a hundred. Dreadful, it was. Howls. I crouched on my platform, tried to hold onto the shaft wall. Wet, rough. Complete darkness, no candle-ends left.

Into that shaft poured the things the earth wanted back. Whole sections of rod. Wood, splintered planks torn from the platforms. Stones, larger and larger, beaten from the sides of the shaft. Metal from the bindings. Water, from some broken piping.

And men. Shaken from their perches, flung down the shaft, pennies into a well. Thudding off the rock walls like dough slapped onto a tabletop.

Beaten as they fell by the great rods of the engine, broken at the top, as they strained at the metal collars linking the sections, fracturing them, shaking free from their fetters, lunging downwards in a rush, tearing into everything, everyone, taking everything with them into howling chaos.

Then something hit into me. I fell into the shaft.

The shell hole was not empty. There were men there, groaning so softly it sounded like a choir.

Thing is, I was lying across some blokes, and there was a leg, no body with it, just a boot. Wet red meat. Couldn't see it properly. Couldn't see it at all. But the smell was iron. If I moved my fingers, I felt sharp bone.

Not easy to breathe. But at least the barrage had lifted. They were shelling the lines now, soon be time to carry on. Wait for the all clear and go. When this blighter moved off me, at least . . . off my legs, off my back. Heavy bloke.

Someone was asking for water. But water was dripping—I could feel it, cold, hear it splashing.

Men must be moving out there. Stupid. Dislodging stones, rattling little stones, bouncing down into the hole. Better be bloody careful . . . idiots, wandering around out there . . . you never know . . . even when you think they've cleared off, even when you think the barrage has done for them in the trenches . . . Bloody Hun pops up all over.

Dropped the rifle when I fell. Couldn't find the bloody thing now. Wait until sunup, maybe before . . . when the sky lightens. Men groaning, only so much air down here. Stink of earth, metal, sweat, piss. A man's shit.

Extraordinary, these places. Then the men moved. Falling. Vertigo probably. The barrage did that, got the eardrums something chronic. But god, this fellow was so heavy. Tried to shift him, he made a terrible noise.

Tried to push myself up, hand on the ground . . . just bodies, soft, damp, no earth, lying on hardness. Tried to push the chap off, he was wedged, poor blighter. Something hard on top, pinning him down. "You OK there, mate?" I said. No answer.

"You OK there mate" I said and it echoed over and over, "OK there mate, 'K there mate, there mate."

Then someone said too loudly, "Water over here."

Someone said, "This one's alive."

Someone said, "Need lifting gear."

I remember that. How loud they were. I hissed, "Be quiet, lads. Not here. Not out here. No. Lifting gear's too big, too much, you'll get us all fucking shot."

Someone said, "OK mate, we'll get you out now, hold tight."

Someone said, "What's your name?"

"Edwin. My name's Edwin Tregear. Have to get back to the trench. Have to change, walk home, after a nice drink of water. Who is asking for water?"

Someone said, "Bloke on top's alive, just . . ."

Someone said, "You're lucky mate. The beam'd have got you if it wasn't for that blighter. Saved your skin, he did, poor bugger. Poor bugger."

Lucky.

Two days it took for them to get to me. They brought me up in an ore bucket. I was cut about, bruised, thirsty, otherwise OK.

The ambulance was on its way back from Camborne, and there were two nurses working in the dry. They were very kind.

One nurse was no more than a girl, black shadows under her eyes. She tended men on the concrete floor. I saw four bodies, unmoving. Thirty in all, gone, she said. She looked up at me, shook her head.

She said Mr Olds' trap would be coming back soon, and it would take me back to St Just.

"No," I said. "A drink of fresh water, some bread, and I'll be fine."

I walked up to the road and turned towards home. Here, at least, nothing had changed. Out at sea, cloud-shadows still chased each other towards the horizon. I could almost hear them laughing.

I did not look over my shoulder. I knew there was a knot of men walking just behind me, in silence.

At St Just, I went straight to the bakery and through to the back. I shouted to see if Baker Jebb and Mrs. Jebb were in the parlor. But they were not. I washed under the tap. Drank some more.

I fetched a tin measure, filled it from the sack and covered the slate in flour. I filled the white jug with milk to the third mark, just like I used to. I broke a piece of yeast, opened a twist of saffron. Sniffed them both. Found sugar. I heated the milk for the yeast, dropped in the sugar and the saffron, watched the milk turn golden. I took salt. Set a bowl of currants on one side. Then slowly, I worked at it. I worked the milk into the flour, my fingers stiff, sore, working it, working it, loosening my fingers . . . until I was surrounded by scent, warmth, swelling in my head. I watched my hands warming in the dough and working, working, bending and pulling, bending again, knuckles pressing into the dough as though my fingers were kneeling.

Mrs. Jebb came back at some point. I saw her in the doorway, one hand on her breast, watching me gathering the dough together.

I slept while the dough was rising.

When it had risen and risen again, I made two loaves and set them to bake. And when they were done, I put them out to cool on the windowsill.

Later, I took one loaf of saffron bread through to the shop, and wrapped the other in muslin. I walked out of town towards Newbridge and I stopped outside the small stone house where the curtains were still drawn.

I went to the door and knocked. I waited, listening for a moment. Then I put the loaf on the doorstep, turned away and walked back to St Just.

5

Stealing Memories

RICHARD ZIMLER

In September of 1931, the French painter Fernand Léger visited the United States for the first time. He was fifty years old and already famous for his darkly outlined, colorful figures. In early October, while in New York, one of his lower molars became infected. At the time, my father did all the dental work for Marcel Berenger, the Madison Avenue gallery owner. One evening, Berenger called our home. Could his close friend and compatriot Léger come by that night?

Near midnight, Léger arrived wearing a tweed coat and cap. My father told me years later, "He had panicked eyes, and I knew he was going to be a difficult patient. " In fact, he sat frozen in the dental chair and mumbled in French when my father didn't have his hands in his mouth. Was he cursing? Praying? My father spoke little French and couldn't say for sure.

"I remember that he sweated a lot and that he smelled of some peculiar floral soap," Dad told me.

The problematic molar was easily cleaned and filled. Léger shook my father's hands exuberantly and thanked him with great praise for his dental skills. In his awkward English, he confessed that the toothache had made him forgetful, and that he only had two American one-dollar bills in his wallet—just enough for cab fare back to his hotel. Of course, he had no checking account in America. If my father were willing to wait until the next day, he would mail a check drawn on Monsieur Berenger's account. My father said not to bother, that it was his

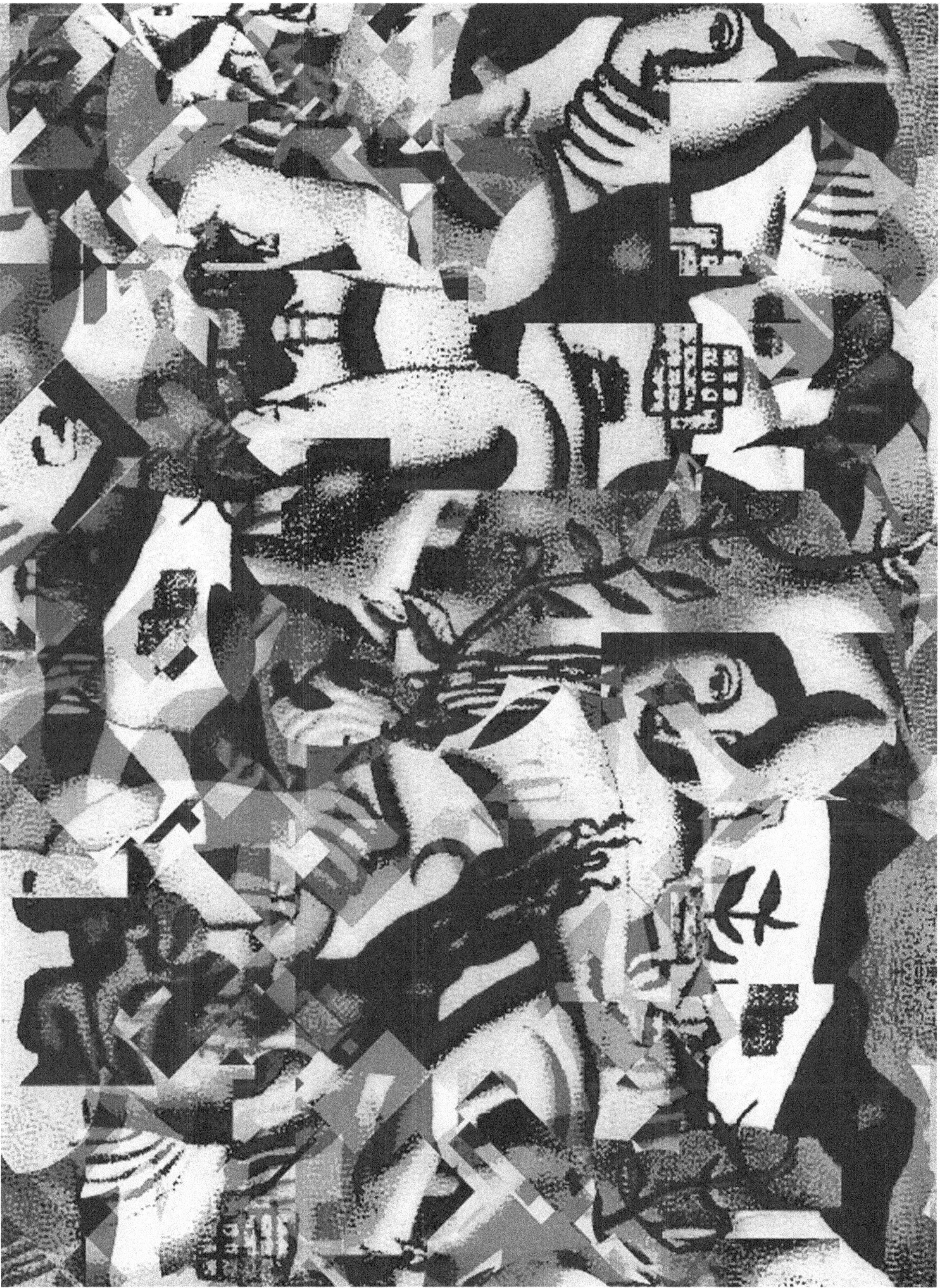

pleasure to work on the molar of so talented an artist. Léger reluctantly agreed and parted a happy man.

Exactly three days later, however, a small flat package arrived by messenger. It was twelve inches square, wrapped with brown paper and tied with red and white bakery string. "I thought your Aunt Rutya had sent us some of her strange Rumanian pastry," my father told me with a laugh. Inside the package, however, was a small painting Léger had apparently just completed and a signed, two-word note written in French: *Avec gratitude.*

As children, my brother, two sisters and I called the painting "The Woman with Stone Hair."

It's a portrait of a young woman seated on the ground with long black tresses done in such a way as to make them look solid—like polished obsidian. She has the soft pink skin and dreamy face typical of Léger's female portraits at the time.

The painting was my introduction to modern art. It used to hang in my parents' room, above their bed. Years later, I realized that it must have been a study for Léger's famous work, "The Bather," completed in 1932.

Both my parents adored the painting, and after my mother's death, it seemed to take on the importance of an icon for my father. Sometimes, I'd find him sitting on the green armchair where he usually piled his dirty clothing, holding the canvas, daydreaming. Once, late at night, I found him asleep with the Léger on his lap. At the time, I had no idea why. Children sometimes don't understand the simplest things.

My mother died on June 6, 1954, of breast cancer. By the time the lump was detected by our family doctor, the disease had spread to her lymph nodes. I was thirteen at the time. I didn't understand why her hair was falling out. My dad explained that Mom was really sick but that I shouldn't worry about her; she was getting the best possible care.

Before I realized that she was dying, she was already dead.

My mother and I had been very close. During her illness, we played endless games of gin rummy after school. Sometimes she liked to draw portraits of me. I'd sit in her bedroom by the windows facing Gramercy Park where the light was strong. She'd sit on her bed with her box of colored pencils. She wore a bright blue beanie to keep her bald head warm. Her eyes were large and brown. She smiled a lot, as if to encourage me. As she sketched, she nibbled bits of Hershey's chocolate bars; it was the only food she could keep down.

Sometimes, she and I would clear off the dining room table and paint together with the sets of Japanese ink that my father found for us at a tiny art supply store on Hudson Street. Mostly she'd paint finches nesting in pine trees. I have two of these studies hanging in my office at Barnard College. Visitors always say, "Oh, so you've been to Japan . . ."

One strange little painting that she did hangs in my bedroom, however, over my bed. It's a finch, but it has human eyes—my eyes.

My mother was buried at Mt. Sinai Cemetery in Roslyn, out on Long Island. I refused to go to the ceremony and spent the afternoon alone, eating the rest of her chocolate bars in front of the television until I got sick and threw up all over an old Persian rug we had at the time.

After she died, I felt as if I'd been left behind on a cold and deserted planet. It was my father who rescued me. He let me come into his bed at night for a couple months after her death, never uttered even a single complaint for my disturbing his sleep. Nor did he listen to my older siblings' warnings that a 51-year-old man shouldn't share the same bed as his adolescent son. "Forget what they say," he used to tell me. "They don't understand." To get me to stop shivering and fall asleep, he'd rub my hair gently and tell me stories of his youth back in Poland. He spoke of demons from Gehenna, shtetls turned magically upside down, chickens with angels in their eggs. He took great pains to make all the endings happy.

On my insistence, he wrote down two of these stories and tried sending them to children's publishers, but all we got back were mimeographed rejection letters. Editors didn't regard dybbuks and Cossacks as fitting for American children. I still have the manuscripts at the bottom of my linen closet; maybe Jewish lore will come into fashion one day.

My brother and sisters were off on their own by the time my mother died; they were all in their twenties and married. So for the next six years, till I went off to college, my father and I lived alone in our apartment at the corner of Irving Place and East 20th Street. He was a good man, heartbreakingly lonely and prone to distant silences, but attentive when I needed him. After my mother's death, the pride which she'd taken in my smallest accomplishments was magically transferred to him, just like in one of his crazy stories. When I won my high school English award, he sat in the front row of the parent assembly with the tears of an immigrant father streaming down his cheeks.

When my father turned sixty-five, he sold his dental practice and moved permanently into a cottage in Hampton Bays out on Long Island. He gardened, watched New York Mets baseball games, and scratched out Bach suites on his violin. I spent every other weekend with him.

In later years, when New York winters forced him indoors for weeks at a time, he spent all of January and February with me at my apartment on 91st Street and West End Avenue. He'd read his magic realist novels in the bed that I set up in my living room, snooze, water my plants, browse in the local bookstores. When I'd get home from classes, he'd make me verbena tea. I used to make him jambalaya, his favorite dish, every Saturday.

In February of 1984, he suffered a minor stroke. In the hospital, he developed bacterial pneumonia. Then, something seemed to snap inside him and he grew delirious. One specialist said Alzheimer's disease. A couple others suggested various pathogens that could cause brain lesions. Tests were ordered, but none proved conclusive. It was agreed by default that Alzheimer's had set in, that he'd managed to keep it hidden until illness weakened him. He was 81 years old. I was the only child still living in New York. That spring, I took a leave of absence from my post in the Art History Department at Barnard and spent long afternoons in his cottage, keeping things clean, preparing meals, reading to him on occasion, and watching him snooze. He grew progressively weaker and would sleep most of the time, in the most cockeyed positions, legs and arms dangling over the side of his bed, his head twisted to the side and mouth open. One day, I dared to straighten him out and discovered that he was pliable, like a rag doll. I gingerly moved his legs together and placed his head straight back into the valley of his down pillow. He looked as if he were prepared for burial. So I took his right arm and laid it over the side of the bed and twisted his head. He looked much better that way.

Anyway, the important thing is that after I arranged my father in his bed, I noticed out his window that the crabapple tree in the backyard had become a cloud of soft pink. And that a male cardinal had alighted there. Red feathers and pink petals—life doesn't get much better than that.

Now, a decade later, I still associate the cardinal and the crabapple with my father's illness. When he wasn't sleeping, he'd sometimes kick and scream, froth at the mouth, rant about being held hostage. Toward the end, during the few moments of lucidity that gave both of us a bit of peace, he'd reach for me. "Paulie, you're still here," he'd say. "When will it end?"

His grip was that of an eagle; talons biting into flesh.

Then he would begin to shout again. "I want out! Out! You can't keep me here against my will. I want to see the manager! Where's the manager?"

Pieces of the verbal puzzle I put together made it clear that he often thought he was being held captive in a hotel in San Francisco. At other times, he was convinced he was being dunked underwater by a Cossack marauder—and that his entire village of Jews was being butchered.

I found out that an eighty-one-year-old fights like a teenaged boxer to keep from drowning. His doctor recommended low dosages of tranquilizers. Half a five-milligram Valium usually did the trick.

Once, during a calm moment, I found him sitting on his bed facing the Léger, just like in the old days. We held hands without talking, and then he struggled to his feet to make us verbena tea as a treat.

All of us who loved my father knew he had been constructed of more fragile materials than most people—a man of balsa wood with a rubber-band engine flying off to foreign lands inside his head. So dementia was not totally unexpected. In fact, my two sisters and brother all told me—independently of one another—that they were only surprised he'd stayed sane for so long. They said it easily, as if they were discussing a family pet who'd been gently weakened by an invisible cancer.

My own interpretation of the visions my father had that spring is that there was always a kind of fairy-tale landscape inside him that engulfed him completely in the end. It was a world of shtetls hidden deep inside the forests of Poland—a land of Talmud scholars and kabbalistic magic, but also one of Cossacks and pogroms.

For many years, he escaped such a world successfully, but then, when he weakened physically, it claimed him back.

As we reach the end of our lives, do we all return to our ancestral landscape? Will I, too, return to the threatening forests of Poland even though I've never set foot inside that country?

After he died, when I was sitting alone by his side, listening to the room exhale with relief, I began to tremble. There was no one there to make me verbena tea or rub my hair. No cardinal perched in the crabapple tree.

For about a week, I didn't feel anything but the gaping absence left by his death. My brother and sisters flew in for the funeral. They were willing to help by then because there was no one to nurse. They brought me barbecue chicken from the deli in Hampton Bays and cookies to nibble on in bed. Sometimes I'd go to Westhampton Beach, where I could walk down the strand and think about the past.

I didn't go to the funeral itself; that morning, my body seemed to give out, and I woke up shivering with a high fever and stomach cramps. I wasn't sorry; I was dreading having to share my grief with people who didn't help me take care of him.

Like my mom, the only thing I could keep down was chocolate. Real food tasted thick and stale.

Two weeks after my father died, I was alone in his house, beginning to inventory the Florida seashells, ceramic figurines, glass paperweights, and other *tchochkes* that he and my mother had accumulated over the years. It was then that I discovered that the painting by Léger was missing. "The Woman with Stone Hair" had been in his bedroom, of course, right above his nest of pillows. I'd seen it there every day for three months while nursing him. All that was left of it was a tawny square where the sun hadn't been able to bleach the wall.

I didn't panic. I called up my brother and two sisters to see if they'd seen it; they were the only people who'd spent any more than a few minutes at my father's house since his death.

I called each of them in turn, and they all denied knowing anything about the painting's disappearance.

I don't believe that my describing the personalities of my siblings will help anyone understand why they lied to me. What is important to know is that they hated my father for things that had happened many years before I came along, during their childhoods. After his death, they each made a point of telling me that he was a very different person when they were growing up: strict, unfeeling, vindictive. He didn't listen to them or our mother. They said he liked to humiliate the kids by slapping them in the face when they misbehaved.

They all mentioned these things to explain why they weren't visibly upset at his death. They spoke forcefully and slowly, as if they were prosecutors presenting the evidence against him.

Although it's hard for me to believe, I suppose that their portrait of my father may be accurate; after all, children grow up in different families according to their age. Also, parents often grow more tolerant as their youthful self-righteousness fades, and very possibly my father had changed his whole attitude toward childrearing by the time I came along. Another possibility is that his relationship with my mother improved over the years; when I knew them, my parents were affectionate and playful with each other. Apparently, that was not always the case.

When I told my older brother Mark about the painting, he raised his eyebrows in a theatrical way. "I didn't even know Dad still had it," he said matter-of-factly.

Hard to believe he could forget a painting worth a few hundred thousand dollars, but I didn't say anything.

When I called Sarah, next in line in our hierarchy, she shouted: "You lost it? You lost the Léger?"

I replied, "It was right there all the time. And then it was gone. Someone stole it."

"How could they steal it?" she moaned. "You were living in the house."

"I wasn't watching every minute. Someone could have walked in, just picked it off the wall and carried it off. If you'll remember, I was pretty depressed at the time and wasn't thinking about such things."

"Well you should have been thinking about them, because now you've really screwed things up. You should have put it in a vault, goddammit."

Then I called Florence, number three in our line of descent. When I was a kid, I was close to her. She played baseball with me, took me to foreign films, taught me how to roller skate in Gramercy Park. She had been bright and daring, had had thick dark hair, a quick smile, and long, elegant hands. After my mother died, however, she hardly ever came to visit me and my father. Now, she considered herself the only intelligent member of our family—the scholar. She taught Anthropology at Oberlin College and spent her summers digging up Hittite tablets in Turkey. She had neither a lover nor partner—no children, no friends. Her conversations with me had grown more and more bitter over the years. She was like a never ending winter whose days grow darker and colder with each coming year. Her particular brand of contempt for our father had mostly to do with him supposedly belittling her for pursuing an academic career. She hated me because I didn't hate him.

"That's just great," she told me when I informed her about the missing Léger. "Do you know how much money I make a year?"

"More than me, probably."

"Clever," she said. I could see her sneering. "I need that money," she continued. "We could've auctioned it and made a fortune. I was counting on it."

"So what do you want me to say?"

"You could start with you're sorry."

I let an angry silence spread between us to let her know that she'd reached the limits of my patience. She understood, and she spoke more gently. "Did they leave any clues?" she asked.

"None that I could find."

"So who could it be?"

"The only people who ever entered Dad's bedroom were me, you, Sarah and Mark."

She suddenly shouted, "If you're making this up . . . if you've hidden it so you can sell it later, I'll kill you!"

"Florence, what the hell are you . . ."

She was screeching at the top of her lungs: "I swear I'll kill you, I'll cut out your heart, and I won't give it another thought."

That was the first time I thought that something might be seriously wrong with her.

The police came twice to my father's cottage to dust for fingerprints and interview me. Florence even insisted on hiring a private detective. We each chipped in seven hundred and fifty dollars. But the painting didn't turn up. Until three weeks ago.

Meanwhile, within months of the painting disappearing, we all stopped talking to each other. At first, Florence suspected me, Sarah suspected Mark, and Mark suspected Florence. It was like a bad imitation of Shakespearean comedy. Then things got really wild; Florence convinced the others that the villain could only have been me. After all, I was the only one who'd been at my father's cottage all the time. So I had far more opportunity to take the painting and find a buyer. As for my motive, that was harder for her to concoct, since I'd never been known to care that much about any inheritance. But she managed to come up with one. According to Florence, I needed the money to pay secret debts. Her diabolical reasoning went as follows:

I'd been promiscuous during the 1970s and had therefore caught AIDS. I'd stolen the painting because I didn't want to admit that I had the disease and desperately needed to make hospital payments. Of course, I could have used my Barnard medical coverage, but I didn't want to confess my illness to university administrators for fear of being ostracized, even fired. This was 1984, and that sort of cramped reasoning made some sense back then. Anyway, Florence claimed that she'd actually searched through my garbage and found bills for thousands of dollars that had been stamped overdue by Roosevelt Hospital. Naturally, she said, I couldn't admit that I'd stolen the painting or had such hospital bills because to admit either would be to virtually confess that I was tainted with plague.

I found all this out from Sarah's eldest daughter, Rachel, the only person in the family with the courage to call me up and ask if I was really ill.

Thanks to Florence's creative storytelling, my three siblings have never talked to me again.

It has always been hard for me to believe that reasonably intelligent and sensitive adults could behave like this, especially if they really thought that I had AIDS. But, as I found out, such things happen all the time. Since the end of 1984, I've never even received so much as a Christmas card or birthday call from any of them. And until three weeks ago, I really did believe that they accepted Florence's story. I figured that they must have regarded it as an absolute miracle that I managed to live more than a few years.

During kind moments, I used to say to myself that when Florence started these rumors everybody was in a panic about the new plague striking America. And my father had just died. None of us was behaving rationally.

Occasionally, however, I speculated that Florence had stolen the painting and had accused me to cover herself. But mostly, I didn't care. Dad was dead. I had a tenured teaching job that kept me fulfilled, good health and close friends. At a time when people really were starting to die in the long, drawn-out viral war that was just then beginning, these were the important things. As for the painting, I hoped that it had been sold to a museum where people could appreciate the nobility of the peasant girl with the obsidian hair. If I gave in to anger at times, it was only because I thought that the loss of the painting had somehow ripped out the very last page of my father's life story.

Then, one June day in 2001, I flew off to Porto, Portugal to attend a series of lectures on French 20th-Century Figurative Painting at the Serralves Foundation, expecting not much more than seeing a few old friends. Martin Roland was there, the painter and professor of Art History at McGill University. The title of his talk was "Léger, the Female Nude and Solitude." I didn't know what this meant exactly, but I liked the way it sounded. During his lecture, he showed slides to illustrate his theory that Léger's women were fundamentally more isolated than his men—that they inhabited what he called espaces fermées—closed spaces. Additionally, Roland suggested that such an attitude was fundamentally new; the Classic and Romantic attitude being that women were far more in touch with the world—connected to the cycles of birth and death—than men. One of the slides illustrating Roland's thesis was of my father's painting.

When I saw it, I gasped; it was as if a loved one had risen from the grave. *So is she still here?* I thought; I realized at that moment that I'd imagined for many years that the young woman in the painting had died at the same moment as my father. Strange what the mind comes up with.

More importantly, I also realized that the young woman in the painting looked like my mother. How I could have missed that is beyond me. Maybe it was the trauma of losing her. Or maybe I needed to be older to see the subtle correspondence in their attitude rather than their physical form. There was no denying, however, that they had the same serene but knowing look in their eyes, the same inner elegance. Was this a coincidence? Or had Léger met my mother that night when he came to have his molar filled? Maybe he, too, recognized the similarity and offered the painting in tribute.

When Martin's lecture ended, I ran to him to ask about "The Woman with Stone Hair."

"I got the slide from the Fondation Maeght," he replied. "I suppose the painting must be there, but I've never actually seen it in person."

From my hotel I called up the Fondation Maeght in Nice and spoke to a helpful young woman who told me that the painting in question was owned by a private collector in Princeton, New Jersey. She was a miracle worker and called me back later the same day with his phone number and name—Carlo Ricci.

When I spoke to Mr. Ricci from Portugal, he was friendly. Yes, he had the painting. It was hanging in his living room, over his couch. He remembered very well the circumstances under which he'd bought it. He voice was deep, his accent slightly British.

"At the time, I was collecting Léger, everything I could find," he told me. "I was in love with his scope, his size. A dealer in Boston called me one day. Jensen . . . Richard Lloyd Jensen. Do you know him?"

"I'm afraid not."

"Well, he called me up one day, out of the blue, and he said he had a lovely portrait in the style of 'The Bather,' and that the people who owned it wanted to get rid of it quickly—that I could get it for a bargain price. "

"Did he say who it was who was selling it?"

"Not that I recall."

"You wouldn't have Mr. Jensen's number, by any chance?"

"I have his gallery number. If you'll wait just a moment . . . ."

But Ricci couldn't turn up the number; he'd stopped buying paintings years before and had moved on to antique cars.

When I got home a few days later, I managed to find Mr. Jensen through a series of phone calls to gallery owners in the Boston area. A man named Levine told me that Jensen was now retired, but still occasionally dealt in paintings. "His house is a treasure trove," he said.

When I got Jensen on the phone, I said, "Let me tell you a crazy story," and I proceeded to tell him about Léger's toothache and the history of the painting.

"I remember it very well," he said when I'd finished. "Personally, I didn't like it. But I knew Ricci, and I knew I could sell it."

"Do you remember who offered it to you?"

"I'm afraid not," he replied. "Fifteen years is a long time. But I still have my files. If you'll hold on . . ." I waited twenty minutes on the line. Twice he came back to tell me, "Don't hang up, I'm coming closer," then, the third time, he said, "Got it . . . Mark Kumin and Sarah Halper."

"Both? You're sure?"

"It's right here—they both signed the forms."

"And no one else?" I was thinking of my youngest sister Florence.

"No one."

"Do you have the date of their contract with you?"

"June 17, 1987."

So they'd hidden away the painting for three years before putting it on the market.

"Do you mind telling me the price?" I asked.

"Oh, it was a bargain. Two hundred and seventy-five thousand. Minus my commission, of course."

After I hung up, I sat for a long time with my head buzzing. For maybe a hundred thousand dollars each, Mark and Sarah had stolen our father's painting; had been willing to let lies about me go unchallenged; and had never spoken with me again. It didn't make much sense. And Florence? Had she been involved behind the scenes? I suspected so. She was clever enough to have developed the plan and found a way around actually signing anything.

I couldn't sleep that night. The sheets were icy, the bed too small. I watched TV and thought about the past as if I were searching for clues to a murder. At nine the next morning, I called Mr. Ricci back and asked if I could see the painting. He explained that he was an old man, seventy-seven, and was no longer in the habit of receiving guests.

"I'll come whenever you want and I'll only stay a moment," I said. He simply sighed, so I added, "I'll pay you five hundred dollars just to stand in front of it for a minute."

"Oh dear, that won't be necessary," he answered in an apologetic tone. "How about tomorrow, say early afternoon?"

His granddaughter got on the phone to give me directions to his house. That night, I fished out my father's old medicines from the bottom of my linen closet and took a Valium in order to sleep. In the morning, I rented a car and drove to Princeton. I'd never been there before. Ricci lived in a wealthy neighborhood with towering oaks and perfect lawns about a mile west of the University. His house was English Tudor. When I rang the bell, a young woman answered. She introduced herself as the granddaughter I'd spoken to. She was tiny, with short brown hair. She wore jeans and a baggy woolen sweater. When I thanked her for giving me such good directions, she smiled warmly. "My grandfather is waiting for you with the painting," she said.

I'm usually quite observant, but I have no idea even today what the foyer looked like or how exactly we got to the living room. I suddenly couldn't seem to get my breath, and I was worried that I was going to faint. All I remember is my feet pounding on a wooden floor for the longest time. Then, I saw Ricci seated in a wheel chair at the center of a large, brightly lit room, with all the walls painted white. He was bald and shrunken. A blue blanket was draped over his shoulders. He was holding my father's Léger in his skeletal hands. He smiled, and I remember his teeth were too large.

"Is this the painting, Professor Kumin?" he asked.

I nodded.

Objects must soak up memory and become aligned to certain events; looking at the Léger, I was overwhelmed with the feeling of being with my mother. It was as if we were about to play a game of gin rummy on her bed.

It was then that I understood why the painting meant so very much to my father, and why I'd discovered him once sleeping with it on his lap.

"Professor Kumin, would you like to take a closer look?" Ricci asked.

When he held it out to me, a hollow ache opened in my gut. I wanted to run my finger over her hair, but I was sure I'd burst into tears if I did.

"No, thank you," I whispered. "I think I should get going."

I turned and rushed past Ricci's granddaughter out of the living room. While running to my car, she called my name once, but I didn't turn around. I cursed myself for having visited.

At home I went through old photographs of my parents. I kept looking at my mother as if there were a mark I needed to find—later, I figured I was looking for the first sign of her cancer. Then I had this overwhelming urge to see her grave. I felt like a character in some feverish detective novel. So I drove out to Roslyn and found the Mt. Sinai cemetery. It was past closing time. The sun was setting, and the gates were locked. But the brick wall around the cemetery was only four feet high. On hoisting myself over, I found scruffy lawns, pink azalea bushes, and neat rows of white marble headstones. I rushed around like a trespasser till I found my parents' graves. It took less time than I thought, maybe a half-hour. By then, dusk had veiled everything a solemn gray.

Isadore Kumin, January 12, 1903—June 18,1984

Gnendl Rosencrantz Kumin, December 4,1906—June 6,1954

I gathered pebbles and put them on their headstones and kept putting them there till there was no space left for anything. Then I put some more stones in my coat pockets till they felt heavy enough for me to leave.

When I got home, I typed one-line notes to each of my three siblings: "I know now for sure that you stole Dad's painting."

It seemed important to let them know that I had found out about their treachery, but not to say anything more.

Florence was the only one to write me back. She sent a typed, single-spaced, seventeen page letter. She wrote about all the bad things my father and I had ever done to her. Eleven times she told me that I was a "queer without balls" and that if I'd had any courage I would have admitted years ago that I'd done everything I could to ruin her life. I had the feeling that she typed the letter with a hammer in each hand. A lot of incidents she referred to were totally invented: *Don't you remember how you and Dad abandoned me after Mom's death. And then when you made fun of me for having an abortion when you knew I had no way of raising a baby . . . It was too much to ever forgive.*

The madness shrieking from her pages frightened me, but I couldn't stop reading. On page twelve, I learned more about why she, Mark and Sarah had stolen the Léger. She said that when she was in high school, they'd pleaded with our mother to leave our father and divorce him: *Mom was so good and kind, but you weren't old enough to know. And Dad was evil, a secret man of silent plans whose very presence was toxic . . . .*

When their effort failed, and when our mother died, Florence realized that she couldn't bear to see our father keep "The Woman with Stone Hair": *We had to get the portrait of Mom away from him. He had her in life, but would never keep her in death. I had to make sure of that. And we knew you wouldn't agree, so we never told you.*

————

When I was growing up, I always thought that as an adult I'd be friends with my siblings, particularly Florence. I also thought that as we age we must each inevitably grow more accepting of our parents and their failings.

Over the last three nights, I've gotten calls at two in the morning, but when I answer, no one is there. The last time it happened, I had enough of my wits to say, "Florence, if this is you, then please don't call again."

Sometimes, in my dreams, I see her trapped in one of Léger's *espaces fermées*—closed spaces. She kicks and screams, but she can't get out. Even so, I'm not taking any chances. I changed my phone number today and workmen are coming over in the morning to install a security system.

6

The Bridge House

BENJAMIN ROBINSON

In the bejewelled, electro-festive streets old habits bit deep. A squad of synapses lined up in his head: don't panic, stay calm, success is on the way.

Gavin had only one habit left, the bones of an itch he'd been trying to scratch ever since he walked through *Torqued Torus Inversion*. New York, nineteen eighty-five, made him feel alive, standing in that metal hoof, riveted something in his brain.

Three years later, he enrolled in Art College to study sculpture. Set in acres of atrophied concrete, the foundation year occupied the top floor of a run-down Secondary School. A late bloomer beating a hasty retreat from life's evergreen grind, he thought he'd found his vocation. Two years in, he'd dropped out, moved back to Dublin and was renting a studio above a second-hand bookshop. To hell with the system, he was ploughing his furrow.

Four years of trying to get his work exhibited, weaving in and out of part-time jobs, he was still dropping. These were the days when people still took him aside. He still had that look about him: half-cocked and headstrong with a hesitant gait, like he was heading for the edge of somewhere and didn't quite trust himself to stay well back when he got there. He'd yet to discover what constituted a wasted life, what sealed the deal. He'd a vague idea it involved beating your head against something, but he was still waiting for the definitive crunch, the smack down that would see him depart the field of play for good.

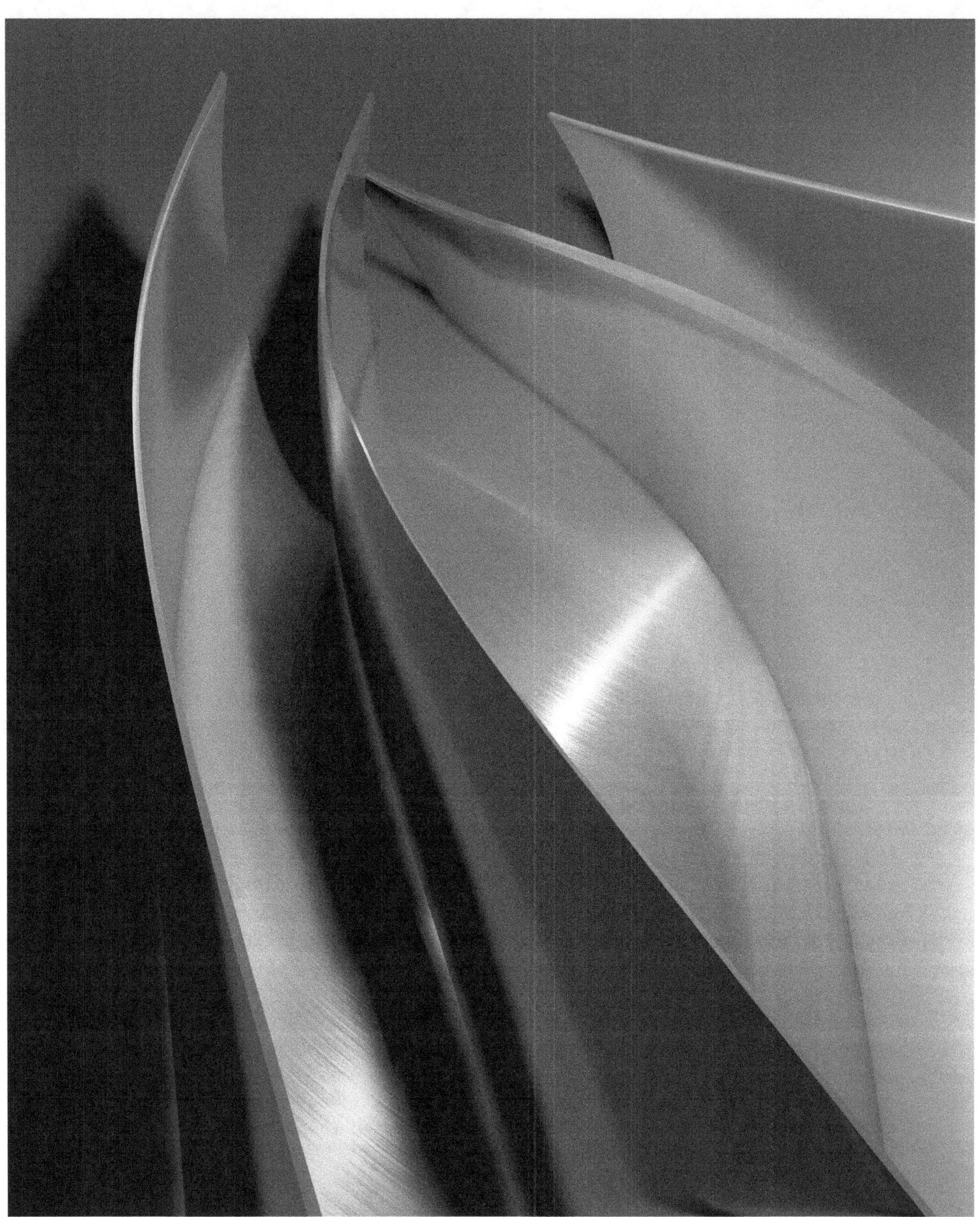

Three years later, he was living in a bedsit over a butcher's, a three bar relic on full tilt and the meat freezers wheezing beneath him. He slept with sheets of newspaper between the blankets to keep warm. If he wasn't in the pub, he was in the library's dog-eared armpit, reading up on stress fractures and metal fatigue.

He got a phone call from an old college friend. He'd met Brendan on and off over the years, discussions about art with a capital A usually leading to the two of them grappling outside on the pavement.

"Doing any art these days?" Gavin asked him.

"I'm in The Bridge House." No time for chitchat.

"I'll be there in about half an hour."

Gavin walked into town, no point in wasting money on the bus and it was crisp as a new bank note out there.

He started humming a yuletide carol. God rest ye merry something. People were scurrying round with parcels and presents. The lack of cynicism was outrageous. He'd considered having a quick can before leaving. Quick in the sense of not sitting down and savoring it in one of the many beer glasses he kept polished to impenetrable ping. His father said you could judge a man by whether or not he used a glass to drink beer. Real men, he said, don't use beer glasses. Real men don't go to Art College; they toughen up and knuckle down.

He walked along the riverbank. Wind was ripping over the wall. He pulled his hood up over his head and stared at the frost tapering into oblivion. The bridge's crossbeams loomed. As he watched the frost expand and contract, he pictured his latest creations on plinths in the Royal Hibernian Academy. He saw himself wandering down a brightly lit corridor, a glass of wine in his hand. He came to a room full of his sculptures. People were turned in on themselves, muttering and whispering.

The Bridge House was dim, pleasantly so, and verging on empty. Brendan was up at the bar, nursing a pint.

"How's it going, horse," he said, downing the dregs. "You couldn't lend us twenty quid, could you?"

Gavin eyed him up. Still thin as a *Giacometti*. "I'll get these," he said with a wave of his hand.

Brendan glanced round and acknowledged the act of charity. "Cheers, man," he said.

Gavin nodded. "So what are you up to these days?" A degree of flattery was expected, Gavin having agreed to sponsor the night's drinking, and restraint to a point of drunkenness beyond which open season would bring the inevitable questions about Gavin's flagging career in inverted commas. Destined for anything but art, Brendan was the plain speaker in College, the hard drinker who'd said Gavin would give up sculpture because he didn't have it in him to sell his soul.

"Been doing some writing. A novel."

Gavin felt something sharp in his back. He wanted to say, yeah, who isn't, but it was Christmas so he said, "A novel, really? That's great."

"Finished it a year ago."

Pints of stout arrived like undertakers.

"Nice timing," said Gavin paying the barman. "So what's it about?"

"The North. Heavy stuff." He raised his glass. "Cheers, man."

Watching other people drink made Gavin feel slightly sick. "Heavy," he laughed, "what is it, a doorstop?"

Brendan lowered his pint and wiped the cream from his top lip. "Bon appé-tit," he said, belching.

Gavin pushed through the foam and drank deep. What's a bogtrotter like him doing using a phrase like bon appétit?

"Get it down you, boy," Brendan said.

Gavin nudged the base of his glass, boy stuck in his craw.

They continued to exchange pleasantries, Brendan pulling his punches till the pints tamped down, Gavin simmering like a kid stacking shelves in a heat wave.

They drank the pints quickly and Gavin reordered. He ordered shorts as well, doubles—it was Christmas—and the drinking slowed to a canter. "This novel of yours," he said, relaxed enough to broach the subject. "The North. Bit passé, isn't it?"

Brendan frowned amiably. "I was up there talking to some ex-paramilitar-ies. Hard men. Most of them active in the community now. Social justice initia-tives. Everyone's eager to bed down the process."

"It's still a divided society, whichever way you slice it. The contingencies inherent in the . . . ." He struggled for the right word. It was his father taught him to read, beating it into him, night after night. He took a long draft of stout and mumbled, "the transition to peace."

"Some of them studied art in prison. There's an education programme here too, you should look into it, man, you might swing something."

"I don't want to swing anything."

"Check out the website, it's called Escape."

Gavin laughed. He found the idea of escape preposterous.

"The European Site for Creative Arts in Prison Education."

"And what do your ex-paramilitaries bring to the table?"

"A back catalogue of atrocities."

Gavin had half a Diploma and beginner's First Aid. "I'll stick to sculpture," he said. "Do you want a sandwich?"

"Yeah. And the same again, cheers." Brendan raised his glass. "So. Any exhi-bitions coming up?"

Gavin tried to get the barman's attention. "Just trying to get a body of work together," he said straightened out the corners of the note.

Brendan raised his arm and the barman came over. "I see Sweeney got another bursary," he said swiveling round on his stool. Sweeney, an Art College classmate, was the fallback when the conversation flagged. "For one of his video thingamajigs." He faced front again. "Ten thousand quid and he was in Berlin last summer on a travel grant."

Through the *Brandenburg Gate* with a swagger.

Gavin ordered pints and sandwiches. "Thought he was still teaching." He pulled his shoulders back. "They're called video installations, by the way."

"Gave that up when he won ev+a. Been a bit of a bore ever since. Met him a few months ago, after a couple of pints he was on the 7up. Going out with this French intellectual now." French said for Gavin's benefit like it was the quintessence of sophistication; and intellectual like it was a debilitating disease. He picked up a sandwich. "Fucking stunner, the jammy bastard," he said taking a bite.

Gavin made a series of little slash marks in the condensation on his glass. "I haven't seen Sweeney," he said, "in oh it must be four five years." Six years, three months, but he preferred to keep it vague. Something buried in him burrowed to the surface. "He's an asshole, a glorified interior designer."

The pub was throbbing with voices.

"Must have something to be such a high flyer."

"He's not weighed down by talent."

"What?"

"Weighed down by talent," Gavin shouted.

"Right," Brendan nodded. "So are you still working on that small scale? The last time I saw your stuff it had a restricted feel to it. Maybe you need to try and—"

Gavin bristled. "Try and what?" He lifted his pint and put it down again.

Brendan's hands rose in a slow-motion explosion. "Blow them up or something. It's like those little sculptures you made in second year—"

"They're called maquettes."

"Yeah, what was it your tutor called them?"

"I don't remember."

"It was part of the reason you left, wasn't it?"

Gavin looked down at the cigarette burns on the floorboards, scorched eclipses with tarry brown halos. He wanted to laugh, but felt more like crying. "Balls of trepidation."

Brendan clenched his fist. "Little balls of trepidation, that was it."

"They were just models."

"I admired what you did, man, you stuck to your guns, you blew them off."

"The finished pieces would've been bigger."

Brendan nodded in a show of solidarity. "You'll pull an IRA spectacular one of these days," he said grinning.

In the last year, Gavin's work had stalled in a series of semi-readymades—a black leather wallet filled with shards of photographs, the exterior cut and fashioned into a rose; a matchbox covered in gold leaf filled with toenail clippings; and Yield Point, a half-finished installation project based on the linear *stress-strain* relationships of composite steel superstructures.

He looked down the bar. People were maneuvering through streams of meaningless chatter. "That's your department now, turning butchery into bedside reading."

Brendan tapped his fingers on the counter. "So are you thinking of jacking it in?"

"It doesn't give me the buzz it used to." He flinched at his use of buzz, a word he associated with winos with flagons of cider. He pointed to Brendan's empty glass. "I suppose you want another?"

"Cheers, man. You could always try writing."

"About the Troubles?"

"About anything. And it's post-Troubles now. Your old man's from Belfast, isn't he? Ex Harland and Wolff."

"Was, died last summer. Have you sent it to any publishers?"

"What?"

"Your novel. Have you sent it to any publishers because you'll need to get an agent first. Publishers aren't interested in reading unsolicited manuscripts."

Brendan stared into space. "I have, man," he muttered. "I mean I did. Faber picked it up."

Something in Gavin, a realisation that had lain dormant, recoiled like a stricken animal. He raised the back of his hand to his mouth, clipping the edge of his pint as he did so.

A lake of beer spread out between them.

"Take it easy, man," Brendan said righting the empty.

A frothy stream trickled over the counter. "You take it easy. I'm sick of carrying the likes of you." The legs of the barstool screeched as he pushed back. "And stop calling me man." He hated that *man*, hated hippies, arty types sitting round smoking dope all day taking about how Warhol was a god, how Hirst's a fucking genius. *Tracey fucking Emin and her fucking unmade bed.*

Brendan got off his stool and pushed through the crowd.

The barman arrived with a rag. "Do you want a replacement?"

"A what?"

People were pressed up against the bar, trying to order. "Another pint," he said, mopping the slops.

"A bottle. Thanks. And no glass."

The barman returned with the stout. Gavin was turned to the man standing next to him. "Koons's wife sued him," he said with a smirk, "his porn star ex-wife sued him."

The barman put the bottle down on the counter. "Who's wife sued him?"

Gavin gripped it and twisted the top in his palm. "Jeff Koons. Balloon Flower magenta?"

"Balloon Flower what?"

The room started spinning, like the motorbikes on the wall of death his father took him to when he was fifteen, hurtling round the steel hoof, the world turned on its side. He threw his head back and drank himself clear. "It's a big stainless steel sculpture in the shape of a balloon twisted into a flower. Like the ones made by clowns. It sold for twenty-five million."

"Jeff Combes?" the man said, "is he local?"

The barman held a tumbler of ice up to the spirit dispenser. He pressed the rim to the lever. "And he's a clown, you say?"

"Something like that," Gavin said as the measure dispensed.

Outside, Christmas lights danced on the river and the streetlights were chiseled with snow.

Brendan was halfway across the bridge when Gavin caught up with him. Gavin called out for him to stop, but Brendan kept walking.

The bottle shattered on impact, leaving a jagged stub in Gavin's fist. And when Brendan dropped to the ground, Gavin tore into his face like it was a piece of Carrara marble.

7

An Ephemeral Exertion

R O B E R T   M C G O W A N

Collectors collect for many reasons and they're typically complicated, intertwined like snakes in a bucket.

Paul Weycliff's reasons were however purer than most: he genuinely loved beautiful (but of course meaningful as well, as goes without saying) things. He liked having them around, works in a wide range of mediums—paintings both vast and tiny, sculptures figural to minimalist, prints, pottery, glass, fiber, works ancient and works of the present uncertain moment—all manner of marvels everywhere in sight. It's possible that motives other than personal aesthetic response were from time to time at play somewhere in him, perfect purity being a somewhat uncommon trait in the human animal, but such motives would have served him in but the merest subordinate roles. Paul, a learned, broadly sophisticated man, truly and simply did pursue his acquisitive passions with a guilelessness of near-childlike quality, his advanced years notwithstanding. A refreshing phenomenon within the not altogether undefiled sanctum of art-world carryings on. He bought out of delight.

Never for investment. Or for glory, for the prestige of having been the first to see the importance of some lately anointed art-world luminary. Not as the byproduct of a penchant for slumming in the lowly haunts of struggling artists (all of that romantic bullshit about the impoverished but free-spirited life of the creatively driven). Not in consequence of a compulsion to manifest his own taste through the accumulation of the work of others. Or in order to build

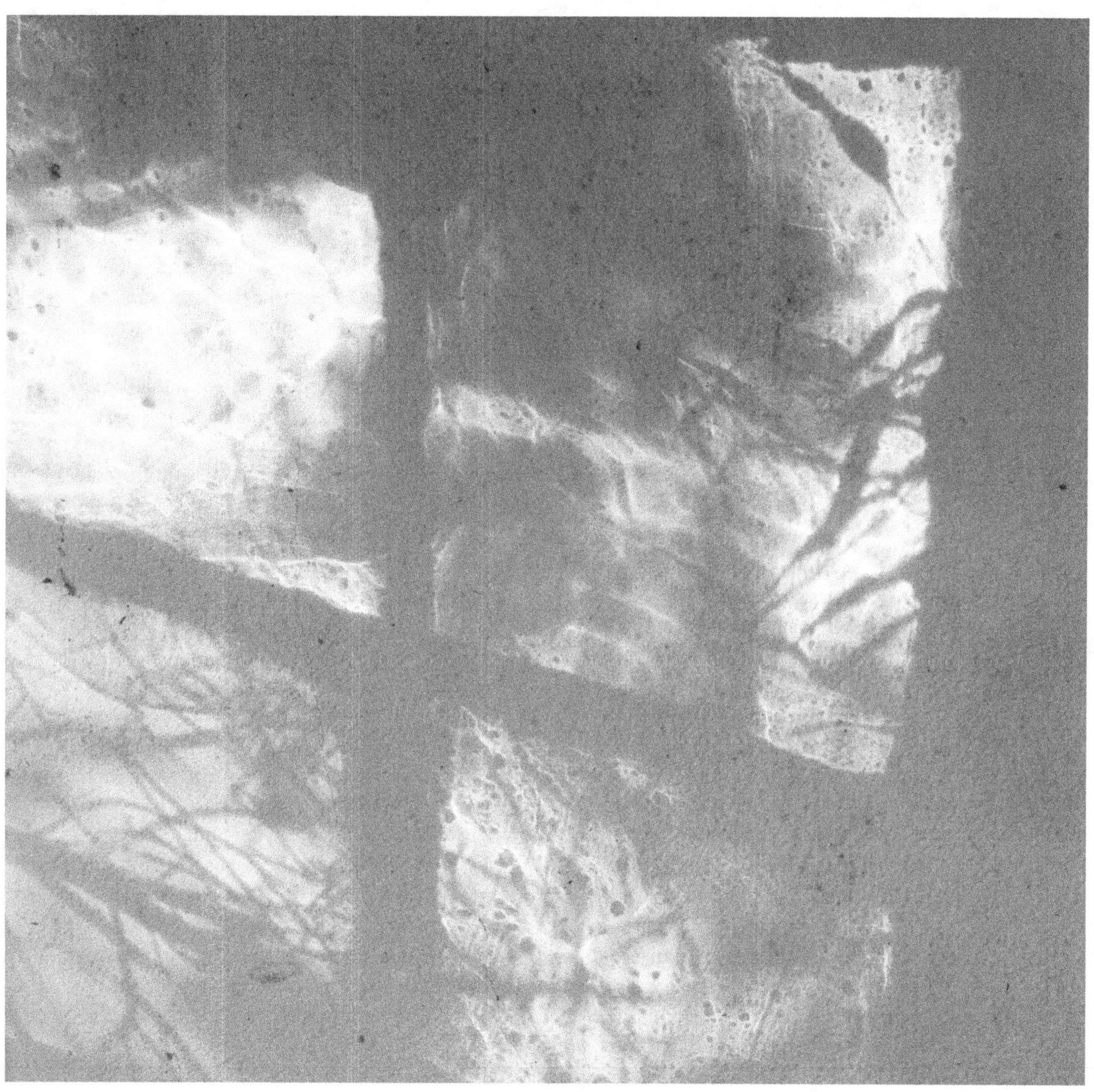

and then eventually donate to The Major Big Deal Museum of Art a worthy collection destined to immortalize, by the selfless grace of the collector, the artists whose works are included in the collection . . . thereby immortalizing as well—unavoidably alas, can't be helped—the collector himself. Not because he was in love with some artist or another, or, over time, with a series of them. And in truth not because of an altruistic wish to support the arts. But because of the pleasure certain objects engendered in him and because he therefore desired, sometimes with the intensity of carnal lust, to make them his own.

The money Paul spent to satisfy his object-lust was from a family fortune accumulated over three or four generations by pursuits not altogether legal. By, that is to say, criminal enterprise. Paul had never himself been directly involved with these activities, their having moderated and then ceased altogether during the years of his childhood, but the fortune survived entire and was now his alone. Paul did remain yet in the acquaintance of a few of his father's and grandfather's old associates, men who retained the shady skills and shady connections by which the Weycliff family wealth had been amassed, but of course Paul had no hand in whatever mischief, if any, these old fellows might still have been up to. He now and again had contact with them socially, as one might with relatives, but he thought of them, understandably with some affection, as nothing more than colorful ties to his family's unsavory distant past.

It might be well to note that by whatever motives or methods art is collected, whether they're saintly or selfish, and with whatever money it's bought, whether that wealth was acquired by means honorable or corrupt, a very great deal of compelling work that would have disappeared, or that would have been at best left to languish in obscurity, has been instead preserved and even celebrated, which in the long run is what matters more than the ephemeral exertions by which its salvation occurred.

Concerning the artists whose work the collector collects: Although the very rare ignominious exception now and then comes to light, it's nonetheless an overriding axiom in the art world that any artist, any authentic one, any honorable one, would view as anathema an expectation, however subtle, whether by gallery or collector, that he alter a work, or contrive one afresh, with a view toward satisfying a collector's particular wishes or taste. How about blue here instead of green? Could you do one of these a little smaller so it'll fit on my dining room wall? Such requests might have been altogether acceptable a couple of centuries ago when artists were still craftsman, but not nowadays. When it does happen that an artist assents to such a request, or is at least rumored to have done so, such an instance exists only as a shameful blotch on the integrity of artist and collector alike. Almost always in this modern era artists labor without compromise, without *conscious* compromise anyway, to manifest their own visions, whatever the consequences. Money and fame are iffy; self-satisfaction in the work itself is the only thing the artist has at least some measure of control in achieving.

Paul Weycliff would never have behaved badly as a collector, and Aubry Allen, the artist for whose work Paul felt an exceptional affinity, and which he bought frequently over a period of nearly forty years, would never have compromised his expressive imperatives even for a collector as loyal and as important as Paul.

They'd over the years become friends. Artists and their major collectors do often become friends, the bonds between them forming, at least initially, around the collector's interest in the artist and the artist's interest in the collector's interest in him.

They respected each other's integrity, Aubry as artist, Paul as collector. Once when a museum—the institution's identity need not be revealed—was showing a group of works from Paul's collection—*Twenty Years: Selections from the Weycliff Collection*—the museum's exhibition designer/installer placed a series of Aubry's sculptural reliefs, not one beside the other along the wall, all at eye-level, as would have been proper, but stacked one atop the other, three high, so that the lowest and highest of the works could not be seen without dipping and straining and without therefore a degree of distortion caused by the consequent skewing of perspective. It took them three separate trips, but Paul and Aubry together, in full view of stunned-speechless museum staff, and without comment to them, simply removed from the wall and carried out of the museum all three of the sculptures, afterward sending to the museum's director, over both of their signatures, an overnight letter decrying the museum's lack of professionalism. In response to which they received separate letters of abject apology. The incident was remembered by both of them as one of their proudest moments. A lesser artist and a lesser collector would have endured without protest the museum's insultingly careless treatment of Aubry's work.

For an extended period very late in his life, after he'd achieved a major prominence as sculptor and painter, and as though weary of producing the more imposing, generally large-scale work for which he'd become known and which were by then physically exhausting for him to construct, Aubry began turning out an endless stream of relatively diminutive drawings on rag paper. Rarely larger than about twenty-two by thirty inches, sometimes half those dimensions or even smaller, lyrical nonobjective images of sunlight that, having entered through his windows, through curtains and blinds, landed in staccato spikes or edgeless pools and swaths on wall and ceiling. He did the drawings in his apartment, on his dinner table. Color pencil, pastel dust, blown on and rubbed, other materials at hand, and the very finest archival fixative.

They were ethereal. Vast sensual expanses of space. Color so exquisitely delicate in gradation as to appear to have been applied by breath, as indeed in a sense it had been, indistinct light-formed shapes as ephemeral-looking as the light they were born of. Utterly celestial. As though truly immaterial.

Aubry worked at them devotedly for more than three years before his unforeseen death, for which the drawings seemed to those who knew him to have been uncannily preparatory. They were as though the expressions of a sensibility no longer world-bound.

And there were hundreds of them.

All but the very last few having been handed over bunch by bunch in those last years to Paul. "I'm tired of galleries and shows," Aubry had told him. "I don't want to be bothered by any of that anymore. I just want to keep drawing. They're yours, Paul, all of them."

Which was in violation of Aubry's exclusive and ruthlessly constrictive contract with his dealer, the imperious Markus Korbin, into whose entrepreneurial care alone all works leaving Aubry's possession were to be relinquished, and who upon discovering the existence of these drawings and that they'd been given to Paul, brought suit demanding they be delivered to him. Forthwith, as certain attorneys so much enjoy saying.

Which is what happened: Markus Korbin got them all.

The Korbin Gallery was one of the most important, one of the most influential, but Korbin was beneath all else a profiteer. A huckster is how he was commonly characterized by those familiar enough with his operation to know. He could move art and he could make people famous, but his every move in those directions was motivated first by self-interest, by prospects of personal material gain. He might almost as well have been selling furniture, or cars. Aubry wouldn't have become involved with him had he been less naive about career matters; all he'd ever really wanted was to do his work and be left alone. Korbin made a lot of money on Aubry for a lot of years. Aubry did in Markus Korbin's care make a good living on his work, and because of the prominence that came to him by way of Korbin's machinations on his behalf he would always occupy a place of at least some small—or greater; who can say?—measure in art history. But these last works, these drawings . . . Korbin thought them frivolous, he thought them the last feeble emissions of a waning creative energy, he thought them insignificant. But valuable, monetarily, because of Aubry's stature otherwise.

He set about selling them as quickly and for as much as he could wrangle while the suddenly deceased Aubry Allen still generated a marketable art-world aura, celebrity being after all fleeting, lasting fame uncertain. Despite his foolishly unfavorable assessment of the drawings' artistic merit, Korbin might nonetheless have taken a more careful approach to them were he not bitter about Aubry's having disregarded their contract by giving them away to Paul, and were he not angry at Paul for accepting them—underhandedly, Korbin thought, although it had never occurred to Paul that accepting Aubry's own work from his own hands was legally or even ethically problematic. It's certain that Aubry himself had thought nothing of it either, especially in his very last years, given his innately lackadaisical attention to such pesky instruments as contracts, which he once naively remarked, "have nothing to do with anything that really matters."

Korbin never even mounted an exhibition of the drawings. He merely sold them out of the back room. And with little concern about who bought them . . . about whether the drawings were going into responsible hands or not . . . whether into important private collections or alas to those from whose possession the drawings might well in time disappear, be lost . . . whether into medi-ocre corporate collections where they would reside in unflattering company, perhaps to be damaged by inept handling, careless framing, display or storage in detrimental conditions . . . And Korbin certainly made no effort whatsoever to place even a few of the drawings into museum collections. He treated them like pricey disposable curios.

It's true that paying a hefty price for a work of art will go far to enhance its chances of survival into the future. For the simple, if hardly exalted, reason that what an object costs in money is commonly taken, though very often errone-ously, as a measure of its value otherwise as well. But high prices can't alone reliably secure an object's immortality. If a work of art isn't safe-guarded by those who value it *beyond* mere monetary considerations, its survival will remain always in jeopardy.

Some time after Korbin triumphed in his legal contest concerning the Allen drawings, the gallery suffered a burglary. A scattering of artworks by various art-ists were taken, including all several hundred of the Aubry Allen drawings not yet sold, probably ninety-five percent of the total turned over to Korbin by the court.

A decade later, Paul Weycliff, grown elderly now, made to the celebrated New Museum of Contemporary Art a gift of all the Aubry Allens he'd assembled during his long and faithful association with the artist, including as well a number of important pieces he'd acquired after Aubry's death. An incomparable collection of Allen works representing every stage of the artist's productive life: paintings, sculptures, prints, even a group of sketchbooks providing poignant insight into Allen's most personal tentative explorations. A uniquely comprehensive survey of Aubry Allen's development and a collection of stunningly marvelous works of art.

Included among the vast number of Allen works presented by Paul Weycliff to the Museum were seven large archival storage boxes, locked and sealed, donated with the ironclad stipulation they remain unopened in the Museum's climate-controlled vault for a period of forty years, by which time Paul Weycliff himself, as well as Aubry's soulless dealer Markus Korbin, would surely be long dead, Korbin's gallery long closed and forgotten.

8

Glove

LISA ANNELOUISE RENTZ

I wanted the installation to be uncomfortable inside, close and used like an airplane seat, displeasing enough to make exiting a relief. The installation first, then, had to be alluring—*what could be in here?*—so from its polished shell inward, cleanliness welcomed like green gingham fabric still on the bolt.

Inside, the little cabin-on-wheels did not reek of former occupants or hidden mildew or simple staleness. Fresh air pressed the viewer, down from the ceiling a light bulb's length away, in from the three-quarter-scale cabinets that formed a hips-wide aisle leading to a bed and bunk that were wedged in the tail-lights-end of the 1963 Bellwood camper travel trailer, which I had found advertised, For Sale/Best Offer, in the Monck's Corner Trader. *You Don't Pay Till It Sells.*

The same day I received my final copy of the contract to exhibit at Block Gallery, I decided to not renew the lease on my apartment. When I held the contract—just a laser-printed doc about liabilities—I decided to move. I wanted to exhibit, out of habit. I wanted to move away again, out of having wheels. Packing boxes and disconnecting cable and transplanting pigments and scissors and mylar into the crannies of the Bellwood was less work than exhibiting. My work *was* often enjoyed (". . . constructed of toy animal pelts, her 'Hugs' was cuddly and lasting," stated one review, "a respite from the daggers and grenades of the rest of the group show") but it was less-often purchased. Exhibiting or moving, I had a bad habit of thought, of expecting people to read my mind, like wonder-

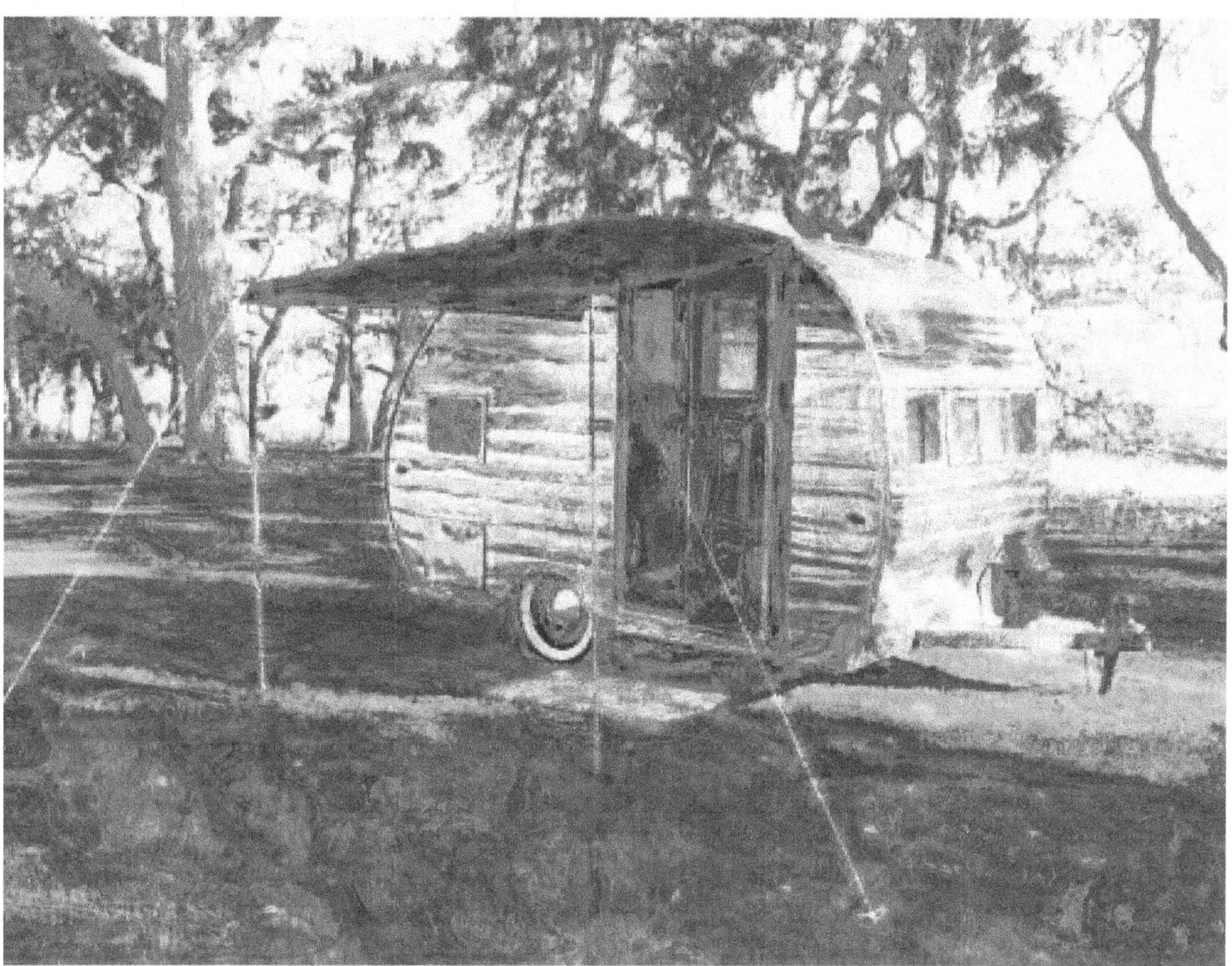

ing to myself, *where are some strong men?* while out on the sidewalk surrounded by boxes, and actually waiting, with the certainty of a spider, for one or two to walk by. (We were all done in ten minutes that particular day.) This habit, this undue expectation of other people, was encouraged by my job—creating visuals that often did successfully convey what I was thinking, without having to verbalize a thing. Though sometimes, when I was done painting and gluing and clamping, my meaning had changed without me. My decisions were separate from me, like an indistinguishable wineglass set down carelessly at a party.

The exterior of the camper was glinting, polished aluminum with three bevels running around the midriff like the belt on a terrycloth robe. The windows were wide robot eyebrows, crank-to-close. I cocked them open. The outer camper was wind-smooth, designed to tow behind your car. My car had a tow hitch.

The exterior and the smoothness were the second thing I addressed: something needed to be applied. To keep with its lines, I encrusted the aluminum with nail polish: Underbelly Pink, Nuegrass Green, and Lilting Lilac. And a little Bone Blue for shadowing. I brushed on the lacquer, after buying out five dollar stores ("there are better way to refinish your trailer, ma'am," one clerk responded, after I asked about more in the back) in an un-ruffled feather pattern, multi-colored like a lorikeet, glinting like a shield. The feathers, the biggest as big as my forearm, laid tight and overlapping, like the cabin was designed to dive underwater too.

From a distance, the tones I chose barely interfered with the original finish. I applied at the most two coats to any feather, to keep things nice and translucent. The colors overcame the form of the trailer only when you were nearing the door, and even then the colors, trapped in lacquer, floated over the aluminum. The metal was a gaze away, sealed in, not stained. The lacquer could be chipped or dissolved, but it fit like pantyhose.

I painted the feathers for four relaxing days. That was the launch of my project, the decision sealed in too. I enjoyed standing, or at times lolling on the ground, with the smoothing paintbrushes, watching the lush but wimpy colors dry and get in formation, picking out bugs that got stuck, wondering about disclosing to exhibit-goers that some animals had been harmed in the making of this installation.

When I work, there's a rectangular-shaped space that I have to work around. It's about my height, it's about claustrophobia, it's about breathing, it's about arm strength. This unblinking rectangle comes between me and my artwork, and then it stays between my artwork and everyone else. It's an involuntary distance. My work has a meaning to me that is of no use to anyone else, just like an interpretation ("A nisus of Americana, oil-based economies, and self-indulgent beauty products . . .") has no impact on that meaning of mine.

The cabin's message to me, at that point, was *lust.* A desire to make off with a particular man, like a trailer hitched to a car, a Conestoga hitched to an ox, a chariot towing the sunrise, pulling and going and never stopping: how would he look walking under the roots of a redwood, how would I look eating at the counter of a truckstop. By exhibiting this trailer, I institutionalized my desire for Mark Hohlram, and wanted him to get the 1,300 pound hint so that I would not have to summon the breath over the next two or three years it would otherwise take me to squeak it out.

Mark and I were intermittent friends. He was a successful painter. When I faced Mark, sitting or standing, he felt to me like he was holding open his wedge-shaped runner's thighs, forming a ramp. He talked about Beauty and Art to everyone (thereby selling much of his work himself) and when I first moved to town (he was one of the first people I met, his black curls and wide brow eclipsing everyone else) I felt that it was his elbow around which I should lace my arm. "Don't ignore the magic in art," he said, thinking he was introducing me to art when he was showing me the city, "don't deconstruct it. Beauty is not something you can get to by picking or symbolizing or interpreting." Mark assumed that everyone was working towards Beauty, and that everyone saw his beauty too. In my case, he was the latter-half right.

The cabin's colors stood out even more in the brick courtyard of Block Gallery. The courtyard floor was a herringbone pattern of long yellow bricks. The perforated brick walls and the leggy rhododendron were a supportive backdrop to my featherings.

Underneath the feathers, amidst the fifteen linear feet of worn upholstery, glitter-dashed formica countertops, rubber-backed curtains and planks of cedar paneling, I placed vases of gerber daisies, maps magneted to the coolerator, a deck of cards neatly stacked out of the box, a hollow limbed Barbie knock-off wearing only short-shorts, and a few old silver plated butter knives. I taped a museum-shop poster of Martin Tink Martin's *Ladder* to the bowed ceiling. He was my long-time GPS; the ladder he had painted telescoped into the clouds. I wanted the trailer to appear lived-in, in the middle of an action, as if the occupants had just run outside to see the big, caught fish.

The butter knives were in practical, in-use spots: one laying on its side next to the sink, a few scattered on the table, one dropped on the floor, all very clean and harmless. I liked the pastel glint of the silver, it picked up the exterior colors. The thick, antique patterns of the handles stood out as especially real and solid in the little playpenmobile. At that point, I had placed all the objects in expected locations, and but for the excess of butter knives and the absence of other eating utensils, the layout was textbook America on the Road.

Once I took in the effect of the desultory knives, I made another scavenging trip to the thrift stores, for more: I was creating this piece to surpass the expected, to exacerbate it. People have high expectations of both the message of contemporary art and of trailers: political and parked on cinderblocks. I didn't want to be interpreted as presenting any commentary on the sardine-encapsulation of poverty, or the materialism of towing houses behind carbon dioxide spewing SUVs, or even just an illustration of one of the many cramped, dead-skin-flakes covered and dust mite-infested places in which people are willing to copulate. The trailer is a vehicle, and motorless and roadless as it was now, it always had and always would take people somewhere. I wanted to go.

Placing the objects was like helping out with Thanksgiving dinner at someone else's house. I let the piece alone for a day. I kept my next step in mind, but pushed it—the undertaking—away so I would work hastily but correctly the next day, a Thursday. This was mainly because the exhibit opening was then Friday; and on that opening day as I continued to work, primping, on the piece in its new setting, Mark would also be there. He would be preparing too, which would consist of hanging his paintings, already framed, each singular on a wall.

The lighting would already be set— not by him—and Mark would have time to meander out to the courtyard to look at the sky, and to walk up the dirt path I had already thrown down on the bricks and stamped flat with my feet, prints in all different directions as if I had many, noisy neighbors in my trailer park.

The dirt path led to two metal steps suspended from the undercarriage of the trailer, and then to the narrow doorway, which I had lined with thick yellow leis like ruffled Elizabethan collars. That Friday I was contentedly working because my plans for Thursday had succeeded. The rest of my chosen tchochkes were in place; to follow up the leis, the first interior object visible was a hip-shaking hula girl figurine out on the counter, head-height as you took the first step up. She was the touchstone of the entire habitation, and quaked with the allure and discomfort of travel.

Opening night afternoon came and Mark stepped into my personal welcome center before anyone else, as I glued the last butter knife to the wall. 224 silver butter knives outlined the message, prying out relief, throwing little linear shadows like Monet's black outline of The Fifer's red, blousy pants. The number of the knives on hand was comforting in their useful bluntness, as if I had plans to suddenly turn the trailer into performance art by making toast for everyone.

Mark was not comfortable in the trailer because of his height. Once he was in, and once I watched his self-protective, slow response—and saw, therefore, the whole installation anew as if he had switched on a blacklight to reveal the dribbles and cracks—the rest of the visitors were unimportant, like bad kissers. Mark the good kisser, even in greeting and even in tipsy, crowded good-byes.

I sat on the bed-couch-bench as he perused my incarnation of *come see the world with me, good kisser man, settle into this comfy, long-lasting spot built for two.* Mark was to the point.

"Ahhh," he said, making the sound and not the word. "A piece you can ennnter." The trailer shook here, because Mark bounded his weight to the ball of one foot, to see if the trailer would shake.

The camper felt like a sanctum. All inner.

"It is quiet out here," Mark agreed as he wedged himself in the booth, sitting sideways with his feet in the aisle, and giving me a look indicating I had gotten too Freudian.

The trailer and courtyard were quiet because inside the gallery was the bustle; worried artists and the curator Mr. Lemonardt, the press and caterers, the people who manage to weasel in early.

"Lemonhead's containing it. I didn't expect it to be cool in here. These vents keep out the sunlight," he noted, betraying a sudden interest in RVs. Our first few minutes together were often stilted by *today's weather, geesh* talk.

I flapped a window gill for him. I had chosen maptone blue for the walls, to establish a misty-picture-taken-at-a-high-altitude background. Gaps in the decor were painted a deep blue-green (indicating, perhaps, unexplored areas), and the table was fringed with jade, silky tassles. The colors integrated the oceans of the maps that were pinned up.

"Like one giant school map. Looks like someone's been living here for years."

People have been, with their pocketknives and fish-scooping nets and Classics Illustrated comic books.

"Want to join me in the gallery for a drink?" Mark said, headed to the relief of the exit, holding out his arm more powerful than a guest list to get in.

Block Gallery was originally textile tycoon Thaddeus O. Block's inletside home, probably used for something obscure like his second daughter's birthday in leap years. A bronze bust of his proud head monitored visitors in the vaulted entrance hall. Exhibits poured through Block, in fact it was to here that Martin Tink Martin was driving, on his own one-man show opening night, when he wrecked and was killed. His exhibit went on. So having Mark scoff at my camper was not the worst thing that had ever happened to an artist at Block Gallery.

By sunset people were pushing themselves through the doorway like arms into incubator gropers, ready to *grasp*. I stood outside and smoked, or wandered through Block and ate smoked salmon from platters. I watched people interact in front of Mark's paintings. His paint was dense and oily, glopped on, but halfway smooth and "deftly formed" (as per the reviews.) In all those dark jewel tones, any earth in his paintings was bloody. Couples responded to the scenes, women in little black dresses with their dates in sports coats looking at supine, naked women laying in the grass under live oaks. After standing a moment to take in the poses, some would touch each other, an arm wanting to be around a waist.

As he walked through, people jumped to Mark, to similarly gather his presence to them. He was polite. I heard him answer journalists' questions, and forcefully recognize strangers who acted like they'd known him since grade school, and repeat lines I'd heard him repeat at other shows: ". . . my art is about looking at women. I look at women a lot. Women are beautiful, and I'm fascinated by their lines. They send me into reverie." I circled the gallery, wondering which woman he was with that night, which was like picking flowers for a certain shapely vase.

Mark had hanging a painting I hadn't seen before, it was called Revolution. The composition had the structure of a wagon wheel. Looking at it with my feet on the floor, the painting and my line of vision and I formed a buttress as I looked at the top of the eight figures' heads. Mark had painted one man and seven women from above, the women in a circle, and the man the axle. The man's arm was held out bent back at the shoulder, his hand leaving a trail of apples in their cheeks, setting their bare breasts ajiggle. The women, who to achieve this angle must have been leaning back on their heels, were mainly in classic three-quarter profile, and though they all had similar It-girl bow lips, their burning red cheeks variously expressed pleasure, surprise, anger, fear, want, sultriness and sorrow. Paint swirled to form the turning man, who looked to be gaining a somewhat orgasmic momentum. I joined Mr. Lemonardt in perusing it. As he would say, "in welcoming it to the gallery."

Mark is totally conscious of his impact here. It relays all his power—what he has to do to be. He likes his impact.

"I disagree," Lemonardt replied. "Mark has elegantly placed the phases of a relationship on one canvas. Like a flipbook." Lemonardt was constantly indignant and guarded Mark jealously; both were locals and guzzled their hometown like mother's milk.

That too, but those women are individuals. In fact, he seems to have captured, with studied political correctness, a rainbow of women. I think the one universality he got right is the man. He's a jerk.

"This is not a man versus woman thing." Lemonardt started, outraged at the thought of such a banal and Steinem-ed commentary in Block Gallery. "I think you should be interested in how people are interpreting your piece," he then directed. "We are."

I haven't slept with him, you know. I ought to, before I leave.

"What do you mean, now?" Lemonardt asked, used to such suddenness in Block Gallery. He was right though, the end of opening night was the point of departure. It could be a part of my exhibit, as a matter of fact. Lemonardt gave me a busy scowl, and left to circulate.

In the night air, in the city-code outdoor lighting, my trailer glowed. I had the taillights and the interior lights on and, of course, a string of electric lanterns scalloping across the roofline. My car was parked in the closest parking space, perhaps the same spot where Block's carriages had awaited him. I went inside the trailer (someone had left the screendoor open, moths were spinning around the light fixture) to find a couple making out on the bunk. They were excused. I put a freshly mixed drink in the coolerator for Mark (which was already stocked with five jars of maraschino cherries, benne crackers, two three-packs of Parmalat and an orange) and sipped mine, sat on the bunk and waited. Sang a little song, neverminded that no other viewers or make-outers came to visit, stared up at the ladder in the clouds, had an imaginary conversation with Martin Tink Martin, first making a pass at me, then I decided it would be better if he just offered me a joint.

Martin Tink Martin has no space between his paintings and me. He's the only dead artist I know; inside my brash piece, inside my manufactured dollop of self expression, the filmy presence of his paintings wrapped directly around me. His crystal clear, crystal blue geometries fitted precisely on his unframed canvases, left no room for words, not even in the nib scratches into the bone of the canvas. I saw Martin Tink Martin's *Glove* when I was about fourteen, at some gallery accessed through an alleyway. My mother and I parked and walked down the alley. It was late and the gallery was crowded, inside I walked around alone as my mother visited with people, their drinks held at elbow level, blocking the bottom half of paintings. *Glove*, though, sat on a low white cube. It was a leather work glove crinkled by hard work, cast in sterling. It looked to be X-large, or more likely engorged since the thumb, laying on its side, the slight angle of the hand causing the fingers to rest on it, was decidedly phallic. As in comin'-to-get-you. Those sterling gleams. The glove at my knees. Martin Tink Martin who I'd eventually followed to Block. Physically followed was as good as I could do. How fine it was to feel Mark shrinking in the argentine light of Martin Tink Martin's paintings that shone through my eyelids.

Finally when Mark did come in, giving me a *let's congratulate each other* kiss on the lips. I quickly excused myself—*just wait one second!*—and locked him in. I backed my car into the courtyard, waved at some smokers, set the hitch pin in place with a flourish, and drove off quickly. I felt like a cavewoman dragging her mate by his pubic hair.

In quotes, I had scripted the title of my piece like the name of a boat on its prow: Actions Speak Louder Than Birds. In the past when I had moved, I'd always found the newness of my environment stimulating and purposeful, as if I was meant to be there in that spot. As if the people who had been there before me had laid down their navigational signals purposefully, as I would. Mark was of course the fish that got away: I stopped for gas and couldn't resist checking on him, four hours later; he was angry and jostled and demanding to be left there at the buggy full-service truck stop.

"What the hell?" he had said, popping out of the narrow door as I opened it, all sweaty and breathing the night air hard, "What are you thinking?" Too exasperated, he stalked off into the hotdog-laced glow of the convenience store. "And get some new shocks for that thing!" he yelled back, almost sympathetically, considering the situation.

My kidnap-performance was duly noted by a few arts journalists as the pranks, the hijinks, the shenanigans, "so" Breton, etc., etc. Soon after arriving, empty-wagonned, in my new hometown, I received a request for my biggest commission ever. Without a word from me in my own defense.

9

Flesh, Blood, and Some of the Parts

(Le sang du monde)

MARSHALL MOORE

After Chaz Mistry's third attempt at killing himself, his parents insisted he return to school right away.

"I didn't bring a note from my doctor to excuse my absence," Chaz told Philip Teo, his guidance counselor. Chaz held up his bandaged forearms and beamed. "When I got here this morning, the receptionist was giving me shit about not having a note. I showed her my stitches and asked, *Will these do?*"

"I heard."

Philip admired the kid's audacity but couldn't let it show.

"And when I walked into homeroom, half the kids clapped," Chaz said.

Philip winced. He wanted to keep a poker face but couldn't. At 36, he hadn't been working with children long enough to be inured to their casual brutality. Kids these days were bioengineered to be almost indestructible, but Philip still worried. He wondered if he had chosen the right line of work. He glanced again at Chaz's bandages: stark white contrasted with the boy's tan skin and plain black T-shirt. No brown scab-smudges could be seen in the weave of the gauze. Philip expected as much. Kids who drive BMWs to school are seldom permitted to leave their gated communities still oozing blood.

"What about the other half?" Philip asked.

"I don't know. They didn't clap, I guess. They didn't have to. The ones that were clapping, they didn't clap long, because Mr. Fujiwara looked like he was

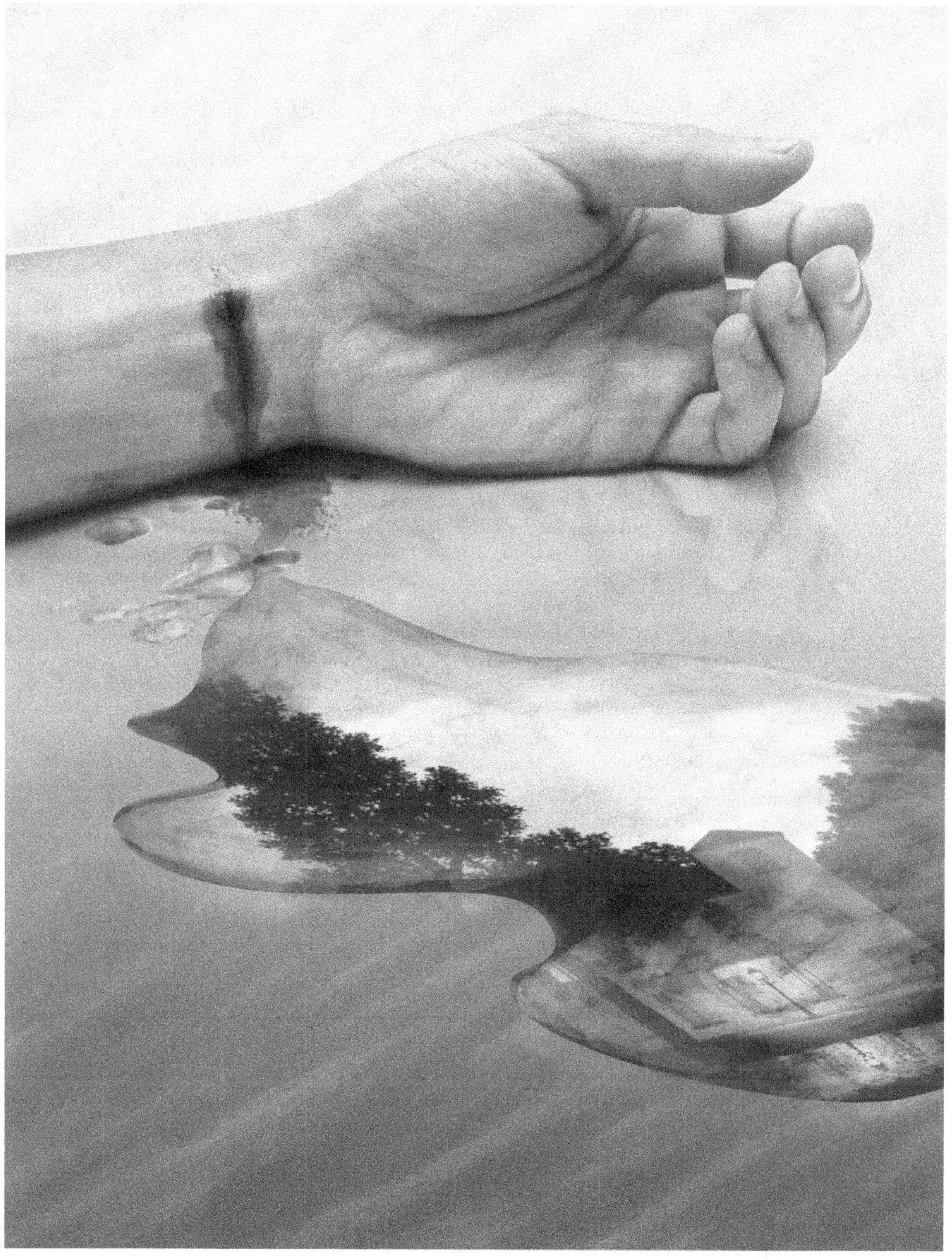

going to start screaming at everyone to shut up. His face turned really red, like he was about to have a stroke, you know?"

"He usually looks like he's about to have a stroke," Philip said. "And when he doesn't, it's because he looks like he's just had one." Time to change the subject. "Would you like some water? Grab a bottle from the refrigerator. I bet you're feeling parched after all the fanfare."

When Chaz turned and opened the miniature fridge, Philip continued: "This wasn't the teenage cliché, was it? You weren't crying out for help? This wasn't a misguided attempt to make your parents pay more attention to you?"

"Is that what you brought me down here to ask?" Now it was Chaz's turn to wince: when he twisted the Evian bottle open, the motion clearly hurt his wrists. "Fuck!"

"I'm surprised you're still hurting," Philip said. "Aren't you taking anything?"

"My father's old-fashioned that way," Chaz said. His face wrinkled with disgust, and Philip caught a glimpse of the adult behind the boy's youthful features. In an exaggeration of his father's Indian accent, he said, "When I was a boy, I drank too many Pepsi Colas, ate too many sweets, and one day the dentist found cavities. Three cavities! Two of them were quite bad. My father wanted to teach me a lesson, so he told the dentist to fill them with no anaesthetic. None at all. The pain was almost unbearable, but I endured it. Do you know why? Because I knew he was teaching me a lesson. It was for my own good. So I am not going to allow the doctors to use accelerated-healing sutures, or glue . . . none of it! You're getting stitches, young man, and if you feel sore afterward, you had better hope Tylenol is strong enough!"

Philip thought back on his own childhood—first in Hong Kong, then Toronto. His parents were too busy jetting from one city to another, managing their business concerns, to let children slow them down. A succession of nannies had raised him. In Hong Kong, they were Filipinas and Indonesians; in Canada, a patient retiree from Argentina. Philip felt like an orphan most of the time, but the nannies taught him several languages he wouldn't otherwise have learned. Plus, he had inherited well. Things even out.

"I remembered how much you like history," Philip said. He returned to his present. "I thought I'd do you a little favor."

"You're rewarding my bad behavior? Pulling me out of my least favorite class to ask why I cut my wrists? I should act out more often. Maybe I could get the rest of the year off."

"You're smiling," Philip said. "If you'd rather be in history, you're welcome to go back to class. I can't force you to stay. But I think you'd rather be here. So answer my question, Chaz. You weren't crying out for help, were you?"

"The psychologists kept asking me the same question, you know. And others. Like, do I use drugs, am I having sex, is it with a girl or a boy or both, are my parents abusing me, am I abusing them, all that bullshit. I thought they were going to take me apart and look at my guts under a microscope if I didn't give them answers they liked."

"Yes, nowadays there's always that risk. What did you tell the psychologists?"

"All of the above. None of the above. I told them I just felt like doing it, you know? It was necessary. Like, I had this overwhelming urge not to be alive. Fuck the bullshit, I'm done, let's get it all over with. Move on to the next incarnation. Maybe next time, I won't be like one of those puzzles where you can only fit the borders together, but you're missing something important at the center." Chaz stared over Philip's shoulder, out the window behind him. "It's all bullshit."

"What's all bullshit?"

"All these questions. Everybody's expectations. Like, I'm supposed to get good grades, go on to the Ivy League, med school, the whole thing, and I'm supposed to have this big traditional Indian wedding even though I'm only half. That's what my father wants. My mom, you know, she's British, she doesn't give a shit what I do. She's always like *Pour me another drink darling, and should we go to Acapulco for the holidays, or Jamaica?* They control everything I do. What can I do? I'm just a collection of spare parts. I barely exist! But . . ."

"But that's not why you did it."

Chaz shook his head. He brushed a tuft of lint off the front of his T-shirt.

Philip thought back to previous meetings. Working for a small private school had its advantages: fewer kids to keep track of, for example. What did he know about Chaz, without sneaking a look at his file? Track team, cross country, and what the hell else does he play? He's smart and athletic, the cuts will heal quickly, but what the hell got broken between the ears? Philip wondered whether Chaz's father had pulled strings, to save face. It wouldn't look good for the head of surgery to have a son upstairs in psych.

"Can you talk about it?"

Chaz shook his head again. Philip quietly took a deep breath and concentrated. He didn't expect this to be easy. Even when teenagers cough up their secrets as freely as TB patients cough up blood, there's still always more to the story. Philip thought back: he'd had what, four sessions with Chaz since the start of the school year? Five?

"I'm Chaz the Spaz," the boy said. "I'm not supposed to talk about it; I'm supposed to act out, remember?"

Philip had never heard the nickname before. He decided not to pursue it: either Chaz would elaborate, or he wouldn't. Being effective as a counselor sometimes means shutting the hell up. People will always tell you what they want you to know. Too many of Philip's colleagues used their jobs as platforms for cramming advice down kids' throats until they choked on it.

"I can't tell whether you're joking," Philip said after taxiing around the subject like a plane on a fogged-in runway. "You're bright enough to know when I'm being subtle, you're avoiding all the hooks when I go fishing, you're not giving me a damn thing, so I'm going to be blunt. If you can't convince me you're not going to try again, I have to take you seriously. Do you know what that means?"

"Enlighten me," Chaz said. "Or should I guess? Another trip back to the asylum? You're going to call my psychiatrist and tell him I need more medication?"

"Or some combination of the above? It's up to your parents, ultimately. Even you don't get the last word, because you're not legal yet. So what's it going to be? Are you going to keep away from sharp objects, tall buildings, and lethal pharmaceuticals? Or do you need to spend more time in the hospital to think things over?"

Chaz sighed and said he didn't want to go on like this. "I'm just tired."

"I need an answer, Chaz. Something more specific than *All of the above* and *None of the above* in the same set of quotation marks. Are you going to harm yourself?"

"Of course not," Chaz said. He heaved a sigh and rolled his eyes as if he hadn't heard a stupider question in months.

Philip kept the cobalt-glass vase on his desk full of fresh flowers: daffodils today, plus a couple of branches he'd snipped off the cherry tree out front. The arrangement provided camouflage for a small travel alarm clock.

"I guess we're out of time, then." Five minutes remained but Philip wanted to collect his thoughts. Certain phrases bothered him. Spare parts? He barely existed? Philip thought, *Let me never be arrogant enough to think I've heard it all before.*

———

Megan Galloway looked around the Samovar Café, eyes wide.

Philip thought, *You'd think she'd never seen red walls before.*

A whiff of perfume drifted Philip's way, sharp and sweet, borne on currents generated by the slow fan churning the air overhead. The people dining at the next table were sharing a pasta dish made with enough garlic to kill every vampire on the West Coast. The strange mélange of smells combined with Megan's overt nervous tension to ignite a minor headache at the base of Philip's skull. The pain glowed small and dull like the tip of a stick of incense.

"You seem uncomfortable," Philip said. He fished in the leather backpack he used instead of a briefcase. Had he taken the last of his Advil? "Don't tell me you're sorry to be missing French. We can go back to school if you like."

Megan shook her head. When Philip looked up from his rummaging, Megan's blond curls caught the light. He wondered whether the color came from a bottle, and abandoned his search for pharmaceutical relief.

"It's just that . . ."

"Yes?"

"Like, everybody in school knows you take students to lunch at nice restaurants sometimes.   Nobody thinks you're up to anything dirty, you know. God, I shouldn't be talking like this."

"Tell me," Philip said in a tone of voice meant to sound as if he didn't care much but wouldn't mind hearing anyway. "I know I'm famous for my unconventional methods."

Megan sighed and slumped back in her chair. She sipped her Diet Coke and looked as if she could breathe again.

"That's it, basically. It's like, what have I done? Am I in trouble? Or are you pumping me for information?"

Philip drank the last of his Perrier and chose his words carefully. "You're not in trouble or even close. I'm pumping you for information about Chaz Mistry. You're a smart girl, Megan. You've got to have guessed that by now."

"I've got to have guessed how smart I am? I thought that's what all those academic achievement tests were for."

"Now you're giving me a hard time." Philip smiled at her. "We won't get anywhere if I beat around the bush. Chaz tried to kill himself two weeks ago. I can't repeat what he said during our sessions, but I do want to talk to the kids who know him. You two were dating for a few months at the beginning of the year, right? And my sources tell me you're still on good terms?"

Megan chewed the tip of her left index finger. Philip noticed the polish on that nail was cracked and grooved, but the rest of her nails gleamed with a carefully applied shade of metallic green, except for the left pinky nail: onyx black. Her silver nose ring sparkled. The sun had come out, then. Philip looked outside just in time to see a blue fissure in the grey sky seal itself up. A strong wind herded rain clouds toward Seattle. Some days, he wondered why he had moved to the Northwest.

"You own this restaurant, don't you? Everybody at school says you own a couple of restaurants, and all this other sh . . . stuff, too."

Philip nodded. "No point pretending otherwise. I'm a partner, that's all. I could take my meals here for free but that's no way to run a business."

Busted, he thought. *What made me think I could get away with bringing a kid here, of all the restaurants in Seattle? I should call the police and file a missing persons report on my own brain.*

Their food came. Philip thanked the waitress, a fair-complected black girl he hadn't met yet, and asked for another bottle of Perrier.

"Do you ever feel like you're all alone in the world?" Megan asked.

The whir of a passing tram prevented an immediate reply. Philip and his business partners had chosen this site for their restaurant because of the view of Lake Union and the proximity to a streetcar line. Philip looked from the sky, now dense with a flock of grey clouds, to the water, silver over slate, and tried to think of an answer. *I was raised by nannies in two different countries. I have never talked to either of my parents for more than an hour all at once. My partner is a writer who has more of a bond with his laptop than with me lately.* Sometimes, the truth needed sentries at its borders.

"Everyone feels that way at times," he said without looking at her.

"I don't know what it is about Chaz," Megan said. "Maybe it's just, you know, the way he's made. Like some of his circuits don't connect. On the surface, he's fine and everything. He's smart, he's cute, he's good in . . ." She broke off and blushed infrared.

Philip smiled and said nothing.

"Sports," Megan said. "Chaz is good at cross country. You know, he's athletic and in really good shape and all, but without being an asshole jock."

Philip nodded. "Stamina."

"Right." Megan wouldn't meet his gaze. "Oh look, here comes our food."

Two courses later, Philip gave up on her. She couldn't tell him anything he didn't already know. Chaz had a few screws loose, everybody knew that, but Megan couldn't explain why he wanted to kill himself. When Philip dropped her off at the school (he called the receptionist from the restaurant and asked her to cancel his afternoon appointments, so he could go home and nurse his headache), she left him with one piece of advice: *Just ask him yourself. I'm sure you already have, several times, but maybe you're not asking him the right way. If you're not getting the answer you're looking for, are you sure you're asking the right questions?*

———

Chaz tried again. According to his mother, he had drunk half a bottle of tequila—*Don't ask me where he got it because neither Danesh nor I can tolerate the stuff. All we have in the house is vodka and single malt scotch*—and snipped the stitches with a pair of cuticle scissors. Next, he sliced through healing flesh to get at the same veins he'd cut two weeks earlier. Crude, but effective. His bathroom looked like a slaughterhouse afterward.

"We barely found him in time. I set the house's central computer to filter the air, and if the level of iron increased, to alert us. That was the most I could do without installing cameras in every room. And at the hospital, the bloody social worker asked me why we didn't lock up all our sharp objects." Angela Mistry's voice hitched. "Chaz is seventeen, Mr Teo. Seventeen! Do you think we didn't think of that? That we didn't try? If he wants something sharp, he's old enough to know where to find it!"

"I'm not the hospital social worker. Have you considered taking his arms away from him until he promises not to cut them up?"

"Yes, but his studies are so important. I know he could get notes from a friend, but it's just so inconvenient! And what would the other kids at school say if he showed up without his arms?"

"It sounds like you'd prefer him dead rather than embarrassed," Philip observed. "Death is inconvenient, too. You might want to think about that."

She was silent so long, Philip thought she'd hung up on him.

After seconds that dragged on like hours, she conceded he had a good point.

"I'll think it over," she said. "And I'll talk about it with Danesh. We only want what's best for him."

"I'm sure you do," Philip said. "If there's any way I can help, please call me again."

"I'll consider what you said," Angela Mistry told him.

Philip thought, *I'm sure you will. For a maximum of fifteen seconds after the end of this conversation.*

———

Time doesn't pass. It crumbles like sandstone, becoming smoother and less distinct. Philip blinked: three days vanished in a blur of meetings with colleagues, sessions with students, and evenings at home with a man in the last stages of writing a novel. Most of the time, Philip expected bustling incompetence from his colleagues and high-spirited disinterest from the kids. Alan, however, disappeared up his own ass in the last few weeks of every book he wrote. He rarely showered and shaved before late evening, when closing in on the end of a novel. They'd been together for four books now, and Philip still felt bereft and abandoned during this part of the process. Those characters (whoever they were; paranoid and superstitious where his work was concerned, Alan refused to discuss his unfinished projects) got more attention than he did. Philip wished he could break off another handful of time and crush it between his fingers, maybe a week's worth, so he could have his boyfriend back.

"How does Corsica sound, after I've finished this?" Alan asked, the third night. He had been quiet during dinner, and his eyes kept glazing over. Philip hoped Alan's characters were all about to die violently. A plane crash, perhaps, or nuclear armageddon. A plague would be nice, or zombies. "When I was a kid, I set a story there. Didn't have the first clue what the place was like, but that didn't stop me. What do you think?"

Philip rinsed the dregs of their pasta down the sink. Phantoms of olive oil, garlic, chicken, and citrus dish soap fought little wars in his nose. He'd used too much red pepper and was going to sneeze. Behind him, Alan scraped the last wilted shreds of a salad into the trash.

"I'm not sure now's the best time. I've got a student who seems determined to kill himself . . ."

"We wouldn't have to leave immediately. Wait until the kid's out of the woods, put in for some time off, and let's go relax. You're juggling too much, and I haven't been present at all. I miss you. I have no idea why you put up with me."

"Because you say things like that. And because we go to places like Corsica and Marrakech when you finish books, among other things." A question crossed

Philip's mind. He considered not asking it, then thought twice. "What would you do in a case like this? I'll be honest, I don't know what to say to this kid. My mind's not on my work lately, even at the best of times. Then this happened. I'm over my head. He cut his wrists a couple of weeks ago, and earlier today his mother called to say he'd done it again. He cut through the stitches and took a knife to the same veins. I suggested she take his arms away from him . . ."

"Harsh," Alan said. He scratched his stubbly jaw and looked surprised, as if he had forgotten he hadn't shaved. Philip, whose shaving needs amounted to a couple of quick swipes across the chin with an electric razor every other day, gave silent thanks for not being white.

"I know it's harsh. But I think they've tried everything else. I don't think I like them, but I feel sorry for them. What would you say? What would you recommend? If his parents are even willing to detach his arms for a while?"

"The same thing, probably. If all else failed."

"But what if he jumps off a building next?"

"You can't save everyone, Philip. No matter how much you may want to, you can't. I'll make a deal with you: I'll stop working on this book for the rest of the night, if you'll promise not to worry about this kid. He'll be all right for now. Let later be later."

"It sounds like you have something in mind."

"Possibly."

"Are you going to tell me?"

"No, but I'll show you if you ask me nicely . . ."

———

"You could strip graffiti off a wall with that scowl," Philip said.

"I want to fold my arms across my chest," Chaz said. "BUT I DON'T HAVE ANY FUCKING ARMS!"

"There's no need to yell," Philip said. He remained calm. He hadn't meditated in years but the basics came back without effort. Breathe in, breathe out. Tune out the rest of the world; turn down the volume. The storm would pass, and the white noise machine purring in the corner would neutralize most of Chaz's thunder and lightning. "I know you're frustrated."

"I can't take notes in class," Chaz said. "This lady from the Special Services Office came in and asked someone to let me have a copy of theirs. *In every class.*"

"Frustrating, I imagine."

"You have no idea," Chaz spat. "You don't have the first clue."

"I've never been separated from my arms, no. In high school, back in Toronto, I broke my wrist once. It was my right one, but I'm left-handed. It was inconvenient, and it hurt of course . . . not the same thing as having no arms at all."

"Wanna know what else I can't do?"

Philip didn't, actually, but he nodded anyway.

"I can't hold my own dick when I need to take a piss. I have to sit down like a girl. How would you like that?"

Philip kept his face blank. He wouldn't like armlessness at all. Among other things, none pleasant, it would ruin his sex life, and he'd never be able to moisturize his chronically dry skin.

Someone else's story crossed his mind. A friend—another Chinese guy—had been circumcised as an adult. The foreskin was too tight, if Philip remembered correctly. There were hygiene issues. Or, more to the point, there were boyfriend issues. The friend endured a rather unpleasant recovery period and found, after a month, that his aim was impaired. *Now I sit down whenever I have to pee, the friend had told him. I can use a urinal if I have to, but it's safer if I don't. I don't regret it, but at best I traded one set of problems for a different set.*

"I wouldn't like it," Philip said. He idly wondered whether Chaz was circumcised.

"I can't jerk off," Chaz continued. "I can't wipe my own ass."

Philip resisted the temptation to ally himself with Chaz, against his parents. To do so would make him a hypocrite. Detaching Chaz's arms had been Philip's idea, after all.

"Those are definite disadvantages," Philip said.

"You're so mild-mannered. *Those are definite disadvantages.* It fucking sucks, man. Do you want to know what I have to do after I take a dump?"

"No," Philip said. "I don't. If you have a way to adapt, then that's all we need to say about your bodily functions."

"Next you're going to say we should discuss what I need to do to get my arms back," Chaz said.

"You're right: I wanted to talk about that next. Unless there's something you consider more important?"

"What are you getting out of this?" Chaz asked. He slumped to one side like a large sack of rice, and shut his eyes. Philip had never seen a more perfect expression of misery. "Why don't we talk about that? Who do you think you're helping? Why are you here? Like, everybody says you're this rich guy who doesn't need to work here. You aren't in it for the money. You drive that old car to work, but everybody knows . . ."

Philip interrupted: "Never mind what everybody thinks they know. Money is not the issue here. Chaz, half the people at this school—including the faculty—drive Benzes or BMWs, yourself included. I have an old Citroën. Big deal." Time to stop this before it got started. "Besides, what I drive has nothing to do with your arms. Neither does my income, my personal history, or anything else you might come up with. Let's leave that for another time, okay?"

Chaz scowled again.

Philip thought of graffiti and warehouses. Rail yards and razor wire. Urban blight was its own language. He thought of Corsica. He wanted to be somewhere else. He and Alan needed to clear some space in their schedules. A couple of weeks in the Mediterranean would do them some good. He could soak up the sun and smile privately at (fair-skinned, tattooed) Alan's attempts to hide from it. They could drink too much, sleep late, and spend time getting reacquainted.

"Dude, you're zoning out," Chaz said.

Philip snapped back to full attention. "Busted," he said. "You got me. It's been a long time since one of the kids I work with had his arms taken away. That's pretty extreme. What are you going to do about it?"

"I can't cross my heart and stick a needle in my eye without my hands," Chaz said. He smirked. "Guess that leaves the part about hoping to die."

"Why am I not surprised to hear you say that?"

"Because you know me so well," Chaz said.

"That must be it. Come back tomorrow when you've had more time to think," Philip said. "Now get back to class."

————

At the beginning of their session the next day, Philip set two items on the desk between himself and Chaz: a roll of toilet paper and a porno magazine.

"Sorry if the porn's not to your taste," Philip said. "You never really know."

"You son of a bitch," Chaz said. "I could get you fired for that."

"I told the principal I was going to do it. She thought it was a good idea. As a matter of fact, she told me which one to buy." Philip picked up the magazine and flipped through the pages. "Not bad if you like that kind of thing." He showed Chaz a picture. "Do you think these are real, or are they silicone?" He made as if to hand the thing to Chaz, stopped himself, and set it on the desk again. "Besides, the school's private, and my partner's on the board. We donate a lot of money each year. Good luck firing me. How are things working out in the bathroom, Philip? Or are you trying to hold it until your parents give you your arms back? I can call the school nurse if you want. She'll give you an enema if you explain the situation. She told me she did that for a couple of other students. She even cleaned them up with baby wipes afterward. Don't tell anyone but I think she kind of gets off on it."

"Motherfucker," Chaz spat.

"Just making a point," Philip said, in his most mild-mannered voice.

————

Philip got home to find his partner sprawled out on the sofa, looking dazed. Next to him, the neck of a champagne bottle poked up from a bucket of ice. On the coffee table, two flutes sat beside a bouquet of white tulips. Philip wondered what white tulips signified in the vernacular of flowers. Probably something like *I'm sorry your baby was stillborn*. It wasn't the sort of thing either of them would know.

"I finished it," Alan said. He sounded husky. Had he smoked a victory joint on the back porch? Philip tried to remember whether they still had any weed in the house, and if so, how long it had been there. "I want to cook a huge disgusting gluttonous dinner for us. I've had a tuna steak the size of Gibraltar marinating all day, and I'm going to saute spinach with garlic . . ."

Philip carefully placed his leather backpack on the floor. They exchanged a look, Alan stood up, and they both jumped up and down, whooping in celebration. Alan danced around the room like Snoopy after three cans of Red Bull, chanting *I'm done I'm done I'm done* until he ran out of steam and collapsed on the couch again.

"Now are you going to tell me what it's about?" A tendril of mild irritation penetrated Philip's aura of joy. He sat down and, needing to do something with his hands, pulled the champagne out of its nest of ice. Might as well open the bottle now—no reason to postpone their intoxication. "Or are you going to keep me guessing until after you edit the next draft?"

"It's called *Empire of Sound and Light*. Remember the Magritte exhibition at the KunstForum in Vienna? That's where I got the idea . . ."

Philip and Alan had celebrated their first anniversary in Central Europe. At the Magritte show, Alan could not take his eyes off the two *L'empire des lumieres* paintings: daytime skies over nighttime landscapes. He had seen the paintings before, or others in the series, at a show in San Francisco. Neither the images nor the title would get out of his head. *The empire of lights.*

"The literal English translation doesn't sound very nice . . . it's not what I had in mind. But add the word *sound* and it works better."

Philip's own favorite had been *Le sang du monde*, an organic, reef-like landscape of limb-like ivory curves and cylinders shot through with red and blue veins. From a technical standpoint, it was no match for Magritte's later work, but, like an unattractive date with a great personality, it had its compensations.

He extracted himself from his memories. Vienna had been a happy time for them both. Alan was still talking: something about ghosts, a haunted iPod, and some crazy Southern women. The book. Philip smiled and said *Watch out* as he uncorked the bottle. Alan ducked and kept talking. Champagne flowed over Philip's fingers. He smiled and thought of what else his fingers would be sticky with, later.

"You haven't heard a thing I've said, have you?"

"No," Philip admitted. "You got me thinking about Vienna."

"What you're really thinking about is that kid, right?"

Philip shook his head. "No, honest. I was thinking back. Vienna was like . . .

I don't have your way with words. It was like staying inside a large jewel box. It doesn't call much attention to itself because it wants you to look at the treasures it holds."

"I'm going to use that," Alan said. "And don't say you don't have a way with words. Nobody who speaks as many languages as you do has a right to say they don't have a way with words. Would you roll up your trousers so I can kiss your kneecaps?"

"Don't you have spinach to saute?"

When the phone rang, Alan answered it before Philip could tell him not to.

"It's for you."

Philip accepted the phone with a tremor of dread.

"Is this Mr Teo?" asked an Indian-accented voice. "This is Danesh Mistry. I'm sorry to call you at home, but I thought you would want to hear it from us first. Our son Chaz has run in front of a speeding car. He's at Swedish Hospital."

Philip went numb as Dr. Mistry recounted the details. *Pour me a drink*, he mouthed at Alan. Philip grabbed a flute with his free hand and wiggled it in his partner's direction. *Now.* Whatever elation he'd felt upon hearing Alan had finished the new book was cancelled out by the news about Chaz. So much for celebration. Storm clouds formed over the parade and commenced to piss horizontal rain.

"We've decided to detach his legs."

Philip estimated that Angela Mistry had not slept in several days. Without makeup, all the signs of insomnia were plain on her face: puffy eyes, blotchy skin, chapped lips. She sat in the same chair her son had occupied several days earlier and looked equally miserable. She kept crossing and re-crossing her legs, as if she needed to use the ladies' room, and she couldn't keep her hands still.

Philip stared through her for a second, trying to picture Chaz without limbs. Who would carry out the amputations? His father? Or was Chaz engineered for easy partition? Pulling off his legs might be as easy as unplugging electrical appliances, or picking tomatoes off the vine. Philip had attended a couple of workshops during staff development days at school, but couldn't bring himself to rip the limbs off the terrified test subjects. Time had passed. He had too much on his plate, and the details of his Modular Children refresher courses faded away.

"Just for a while," she continued. "Until he snaps out of it, this phase he's going through. Just for a while."

Phase? Philip thought of Picasso's Blue Period, or Gerhard Richter's photorealism. Mondrian, while he was still trying to be Picasso or Braque, before the right angles and primary colors. Maybe Chaz would benefit from paint, if he could be convinced not to drink it, and some canvas? If his parents wouldn't consent to give him his arms back, he could hold the brush with his teeth.

"Is he all right? Where is he now? Still in the hospital? Or have you been able to take him home?"

Angela shut her eyes. "No, he's not all right. His injuries were very minor, which was a miracle. But he's not all right. No seventeen-year-old who is this determined to commit suicide is all right. Yes, he's in the hospital. Danesh will supervise the procedure. I'm sure you had guessed that much already."

Philip recalled Chaz's imitation of his father—the trip to the dentist, cavities, no anaesthetic. Yes, of course Danesh Mistry would supervise the removal of his son's legs.

I need a shower, Philip thought. *A long hot one. And then I need to take a long drive through the country. Alan's finished with the book; he can come with me. I need to get away from this woman. I need to get out of this office.*

"How will you know when he has snapped out of it, to use your words? Did you and your husband discuss that before you decided on this course of action?"

She looked up, and brushed her bangs away from her eyes.

"I . . ." The shocked look on her face told Philip everything. She quickly plastered a veneer of self-control over it. "We're his parents, Mr. Teo. We'll know."

Philip nodded. "I'm sure you will," he lied. "Please let me know if there's anything I can do."

The second the door swung shut behind her, Philip called the principal, pleaded a headache, and took the rest of the afternoon off.

———

We should buy a cabin in the woods somewhere, Philip thought. *Or in Provence.* Preoccupied, he called Alan from the car and told him not to cook dinner; they should eat out.

"You're off early," Alan said.

"Mental health day. Tell me you haven't started editing the book," Philip said.

"I haven't. I've been generally useless today. Postpartum depression, maybe. I feel sort of hollow. Where do you want to eat?"

"Someplace Thai. Preferably in walking distance of our house, and with a good wine list. I want to drink until I look sunburned."

"That won't take much," Alan said.

"Don't remind me."

"It's the kid, isn't it?"

"It's the kid," Philip said.

———

Visiting Chaz in the hospital had not been Philip's idea. In fact, he voted against it. Alan brought it up at dinner, and Philip almost swallowed a chopstick. *You've got to be kidding. That's the last thing I need to do,* Philip had protested. Alan countered with, *No, he's gotten under your skin. If you don't see it through, you won't be happy with yourself when this is all over. No matter how it ends.* Requests from both parents, as well as an e-mail from Chaz himself—dictated, using voice-recognition software—tipped the scale.

The first thing Chaz said when Philip entered the room was, "They took my dick and balls too. They're in that jar. I'd point but I don't have hands. How's that for fucked up?"

"Which part?" Philip asked.

The shape under the blankets was all wrong: flatness where legs ought to be. Someone had pulled the covers up to Chaz's neck after propping him upright, against several pillows. Philip couldn't see any bruises on the boy's face, but he was several shades paler today. Tubes and cables snaked under the blankets: a catheter, for sure, and an IV. Monitors for his vital signs.

When Chaz grinned, it looked like his first one in weeks. Perhaps it was.

"You don't really want me to look at your dick, do you?" Philip asked.

Chaz shrugged. Philip had never seen a limbless torso shrug before. When the blankets covering (what was left of) Chaz's body shifted, Philip felt a tight burst of panic: what if Chaz's hollowed-out shoulders looked like bloody sockets with the eyes torn out, but bigger? On second thought, Philip decided he'd seen too many horror movies.

"Why should I care? It's not like I'm really attached to it," Chaz said.

Philip looked. The genitals in the jar looked just like genitals in a jar. There were no other words to describe them. He remembered something and squinted to see better. Yes, Chaz was circumcised.

"Thank you for not laughing," Chaz said.

"What's there to laugh at?" Philip genuinely didn't know. He wanted to cup his hands over his crotch and squat down in self-protective sympathy. "Why didn't they let you keep your gonads?"

"Before they did it, I asked the sperm donor what I was supposed to do if my balls itched. You know how you can sort of cross your legs and squeeze, if you want to be discreet about it? Now I can't even do that."

Philip nodded. "The sperm donor?" What he really wanted to know was whether the severed genitalia still itched like phantom limbs. Or did Chaz get an urge to reach toward the jar containing his cock, with hands that weren't there?

"My father. Mom's the egg donor. Don't tell me you haven't heard that one before."

"I haven't."

"How does it feel, being so deprived?"

"Don't worry about me. I can be vulgar in half a dozen languages," Philip said. "And I'm going to change the subject now. Don't make that face. Chaz, I want you to listen to me. Your parents have taken your arms away." *And please let them not tell you it was my idea.* "And your legs. And your private parts too. You have to reconsider this suicide thing. Do you want to spend the rest of your life like this?"

"While I'm like this, I don't get to decide," Chaz said. "I could decide to kill myself tomorrow, but it wouldn't matter. Physically, I can't do it. The decision is invalid. That's the whole point, isn't it? They're turning me into a null set."

"No, they're trying to keep you from turning yourself into one. It's not the same thing. Haven't they set some conditions? Like, a timetable for restoring your arms and legs?"

"And the hogleg," Chaz said.

Philip stole another glance at the jar. Hogleg? Sure, why not? This would be the wrong occasion to say, *I've seen bigger.*

"What do you have to do, then?"

"Convince them I'm not going to kill myself." Boredom again.

"And?"

Chaz looked at the ceiling. Philip followed his gaze: nothing but white acoustic tiles up there, a fluorescent light, and motes of dust waltzing in midair. For a second the world went quiet. Philip tuned out the bleeps of machines and the dull buzz of distant conversations. He thought about his priorities. When had going to Corsica surpassed steering Chaz through this crisis?

I'm in the wrong line of work. Philip admitted it to himself for the first time. *I should be more involved with the restaurant, if it's going to succeed. I should give myself more time to manage our investments. I should try to make Alan open up about his work, and let me in. I don't like being a silent partner.*

"You have to mean it," he told Chaz. "That's what I'm not hearing. Otherwise, your parents won't put Humpty Dumpty back together again."

"Because they love me *so much*," Chaz said.

"Whatever's wrong, Chaz, you're going to have to open up and talk about it. You have to get through this. Killing yourself won't solve anything."

"Not all problems need solutions," Chaz said. "Some of them just need erasers. What am I supposed to tell my parents? That I want to be a real boy? Or do I tell them how much I hate them? If my father wanted a son who'd grow up to be a perfect replica of himself, why didn't he have himself cloned? If he wanted gratitude so badly, why didn't he go to India and buy a kid on the black market? And how about my mother? *I'm rich, drunk, and glamorous, darling, so fuck you.* Under the surface, she's an empty human being. I don't even like being in the same room with her."

Philip thought, *Neither do I, actually.*

"Has your social worker talked about family therapy?" he asked. Another memory of Magritte's *Le sang du monde* surfaced. If the ceiling tiles were to warp and bulge, and to sprout a red and blue network of capillaries . . . Philip reeled his attention back in. He needed to remain in the moment. Zoning out like this was never a good sign. He thought, *I need to get the hell out before he asks me to pick him up and throw him out the window.* "If this is how you feel, then your parents need to hear it. They need to listen to it, and they need to deal with it."

"Family therapy is for people who still love each other," Chaz said.

"Ending relationships can also be an option, if they are ruined past repair. You're really not in a trap, Chaz. No matter how much you want to believe that you are, you're not. Now I have another appointment," Philip said. "Is there anything you want me to tell the nurses on my way out?"

He expected a caustic request—Pull a plastic bag over my head and tie it tight around my neck, for example—but Chaz just shrugged. He was listing to one side, but Philip didn't stick around to see whether he'd topple over. The nurses could handle it, if he did.

––––––––––

Philip almost choked on his halibut when Chaz and Megan strolled through the front door of the Samovar Café.

Two weeks had passed since the hospital visit. Chaz had not returned to school. According to his mother, he had been reassembled, on the condition that he transfer to a school for disturbed children as soon as a space became available. He needed full-time supervision.

"What?" Alan asked. He turned to look. "Oh. Is that the kid?"

"Yes," Philip said.

"They're coming this way."

"I noticed."

"May we join you?" Chaz asked, after introductions were made.

"I'm not sure that's the best idea, Chaz," Philip said. "Shouldn't you be at home with your family?"

Chaz pulled out a chair and sat down, then gestured for Megan (who looked mortified) to do the same thing.

"They're sending me off to that school tomorrow. It's up in Bellingham. I talked them into letting me out for a few hours. Why not spend them having a good dinner?"

Alan was frowning, and Philip could almost read his mind. He was thinking the same thing he saw on Alan's face: *You're teenagers. Shouldn't you be at a horror movie, or out getting drunk and having sex?*

"So you came here," Philip said. He thought it over. "I'm not crazy about the idea of inviting you to stay for dinner. We're half done, anyway. But you're already here. If you want to order a coffee, that's fine, but we have to leave after that."

Chaz nodded. Then he excused himself to go to the restroom. "Be right back," he said, and Philip nodded acknowledgment. Megan looked frightened for a split-second, as if unsure what to say or do in the company of these two adults—the school guidance counselor (Philip wanted to reassure her that he'd be an ex-counselor as soon as the school year was up) and his author boyfriend.

On his way to the bathroom, Chaz stopped and spoke to the young man dining at a nearby table. They exchanged a couple of words. The young guy laughed and shook his head.

"Man, that's just weird," Philip heard him say.

Chaz spoke to two women at another table. One listened for a moment and the other seemed to be tuning him out. The first woman's smile froze on her face. Philip strained to hear what Philip was saying. Perhaps Chaz knew her from somewhere. A friend of his parents, maybe. She stopped chewing, then swallowed her food like a mouthful of tacks. Chaz said something else, and a whole spectrum of ugly expressions passed across her face. The one ignoring him changed her approach and said "Leave us alone" loud enough for Philip to hear. The dining room went silent for a moment as people turned their attention to Chaz and the two women.

"What are you looking at?" Alan asked. He turned to follow Philip's gaze, and saw Chaz walking away. "What did he say to her?"

"My bionic ear is at the shop," Philip said. "Is yours working? I should apologize to them." He thought about it. "No, better wait and find out what he said, first."

"That was weird," Megan said. "But you never know what he's going to do next."

"I wonder if we should be worried," Philip said.

"That woman said to leave them alone, right?" Alan said. "What the hell did he say?"

"Are you asking me? I don't know. I shouldn't have brought him here. I'm sorry—I thought it would be a good idea to say goodbye, Mr. Teo," Megan said. "He said that's all he wanted to do. But now that he's got his arms and legs back, I'm not so sure. He tells lies, sometimes."

"Why did you bring him here, then?"

"He's going to that new school and he wanted to tell you goodbye?" she said. "Honest. That's what he said. I wonder what kind of goodbye he meant."

She looked across the dining room at the two women Chaz (who had gone on to the restroom, and could no longer be seen) had spoken to. They had stopped eating and seemed to be arguing in hushed tones. One wanted to stay and the other wanted to leave, if Philip read their expressions correctly. The room was too dim for him to be sure.

In the kitchen, someone shouted. Philip couldn't recognize the words. Pots and pans clattered. Glass broke. More shouts, this time in both Cantonese and English. The blood drained out of Philip's head, but before he could stand up and rush into the kitchen, Lawrence, the chef, stalked over to their table. His face burned infrared, but Philip thought he looked at least as embarrassed as outraged.

"There's a naked boy in my office," Lawrence said. "With butcher's diagrams drawn all over his skin. He was at your table. What the fuck is going on, Philip? We're too busy to deal with bullshit from psychotic kids . . ."

"I'll talk to him. This shouldn't have happened, Lawrence. We had no clue. Please believe that."

"You wouldn't have arranged something like this on purpose, Philip. Not in your own restaurant. The kid may be a psycho, but you're not. Just come and do something with him, okay? We're busy, and it's creepy, you know? The kid needs help."

"You have a gift for understatement," Alan said. He tossed back the last of the wine in his glass and poured himself a refill from the bottle they were sharing.

Philip whined in his head half a second (*Why me?*), got over it, and followed Chef to the office. Someone had given Chaz an apron, but it didn't conceal all of the lines on his body.

"I asked the other diners which parts of me they'd like to eat," Chaz said. "I even offered to take off my clothes and show them."

"Chaz, people don't go to restaurants because they want to eat teenagers," Philip said. "People in restaurants want to be left alone with their companions and their food. Why the hell are you doing this?"

Chaz shrugged. "I thought maybe the chef would cook me if I asked nicely? I've read about him a few times. The food critics say he pushes the envelope with Asian cuisine, so, you know . . . I wanted to give him a bigger envelope to work with."

"That's bullshit, Chaz. Why are you doing this? And why are you doing it in *my goddamn restaurant?*"

Chaz shrugged again, and for a dirty second Philip wished Lawrence *had* butchered him. Detachable limbs meant less muss and fuss. They probably wouldn't have to hose blood, gore, and bone chips out of the kitchen afterward. What did the health codes say about bio-engineered pull-apart children? Were there even laws yet? And what did they taste like, anyway? Chicken, or something gamier? Venison?

Corsica, Philip thought. *I need to be in Corsica. We're buying tickets tonight.* He visualized flying into Nice or Marseilles and taking a ferry, one of those long slow ones that take an entire day. They'd have a cabin to themselves. They'd have no floor space, because of all the suitcases. Nothing but peace, quiet, their bed, and the Mediterranean all around them . . .

"Wouldn't you rather be eaten in a good restaurant than a bad one?" Chaz asked.

"I'd rather not be eaten," Philip said.

"I found these in the men's room," Lawrence said from the doorway. He handed Philip an armful of clothes—Chaz's. "Now if you'll excuse me, I have a kitchen to rescue."

"You're not going to give me an answer, are you?" Philip asked. His exasperation rose like the mercury in a thermometer. He told himself to relax—you can't blame people for their pathologies—but it didn't work. What he really wanted was to call Lawrence back into the office for a quick consultation. They could take little bites out of one of Chaz's biceps. Maybe he'd taste good in a simple curry, maybe? Or was it too much of an Indian cliché?

"No, he's not," said a woman's voice from the doorway.

Philip recognized Angela Mistry's accent before he turned to look, and when Chaz slumped over unconscious, it came as no surprise. She stood in the doorway, with Lawrence behind her glowering. *There are too many people in my kitchen,* said the look on his face.

"What's that?" Philip gestured toward the gizmo Chaz's mother held in her right hand.

"The remote control. We had him modified while he was in hospital," she said. "We were hoping it wouldn't be necessary."

"I guess Chaz is going to have to get used to life as a head in a jar, then?" Philip asked.

She looked grim, then sad, then grim again. Philip almost felt sad, himelf, when Angela Mistry directed two men in paramedic uniforms into the office. They loaded Chaz onto a gurney and took him out the back door.

"I can't apologize enough for this," Angela said.

"It's not your fault. Don't apologize. Just . . . I don't even know what to say. Take care of him?"

She nodded again, curtly, and left.

In the dining room, Philip found only Alan sitting at the table. He had taken a book out of the backpack he brought everywhere and was reading, and sipping coffee.

"I hope that's decaf," Philip said.

Alan looked up, and nodded.

"Still want to go to Corsica?" he asked.

"Yes, and I want to buy the plane tickets tonight."

"I meant to tell you, I was surfing the web today. There's going to be a Magritte retrospective in Nice, in about two months. Want to time it around that? *L'empire des lumieres?*"

"*Le sang du monde,*" Philip replied. "Sure, why not?"

10

Artistic Endeavor

RICHARD K. WEEMS

We are cuddled together on his living room couch when Mike takes my hand. It is like watching a Venus fly trap devour a chigger—my fingertip can barely cover one of his weightlifting calluses. He somehow manages the edge of his pipe-thick thumb between the bones leading to my middle and ring fingers.

"It's a ch'i spot," Mike says as he pushes down. His thumb presses apart my knuckles. "This is going to hurt something awful."

It isn't long before I feel the urge to pull away, but Mike's hands are strong and he has me tight. He presses harder. To shut out the image of compound fractures and reconstructive surgery, I stare into the scars on his hand, the pink tracks from barbed wire and the puncture dots that look like burst pimples.

"Just make like there's no pain," he says. "This is nothing. Try not noticing a fence staple while it's getting plucked out of your hand."

Mike is a performance artist, a professional wrestler to the uninformed. To pay the bills he trains well-off slugs with sedentary lifestyles, but once a month he and his mortal enemy, his former tag-team partner gone bad (or vice versa), fight with cheese graters, with baseball bats wrapped in barbed wire. They fight with flaming fold-up chairs, with fence staplers. They dress the same and dye their hair the same color so no one can tell them apart. There is no hero, no villain—no one to root for. The crowd cheers solely for the violence itself.

9 IRON
FLAMING CHAIR
SPIKED BASEBALL BAT
WIRE CUTTERS
THE
Art
OF
ENTERTAINMENT

Videotapes of his matches sell big on the Internet and in Japan, but Mike won't let me watch one. We've only been seeing each other two weeks, and he wants me to experience one of his shows first-hand.

He wiggles his thumb as though attempting some kind of massage.

"He does this to his own girlfriend," Mike says, meaning his opponent. "He says it keeps down her urges." Mike abstains for three days before a show. He says the build-up heightens the performance.

"A broken hand would definitely cool my jets," I say through my teeth.

He presses even harder a moment to show me he's been holding back. "You're a fragile one," he says. "I could've popped your arm out already if I were so inclined." He gives my hand a slight jerk. "Clunk," he says, and he smiles.

Mike has a good smile—warm and sexy. His gray eyes gleam when he is showing off his strength. Odd to think I'm on the verge of jumping the bones of a man about to break my hand into two distinct halves, but the idea is there just the same.

"Maybe I'll go back to my place," I say.

"Weren't you there just yesterday?" Mike pulls in his lips, ready to make this a fight. He leans in over me as though ready to block my escape.

"I can scream," I say.

"I'll silence you," he says. "I'll break you into submission and keep you under wraps until I'm ready for you."

I laugh, but I'm only getting hotter.

"Uncle," I say.

"You're damn right, uncle." Mike considers my hand, from there looks over every inch of me, then lets me leave. The back of my hand has a wide, red spot already tingling of bruise. In the elevator going down, I avoid eye contact with a scruffy man in a dirty pullover and an older woman who doesn't look like she gets out much. I feel guilty of some crime.

Martha must know how I sound when I'm trying to sneak past her floor on the way to my own. That, or she's been poking her head in and out of her apartment half the night.

"Are you all right?" she says as she marches up to me. She puts out her hand, as though she expects me to need assistance.

"Sleepy, but fine," I say. I continue up the stairs, but she comes along beside me, visually inspecting me for the battering she's convinced Mike is going to give me one day. I keep the end of my sleeve over my hand the rest of the way up the stairs, but I drop my guard when I unlock my apartment door. My bruise, now full-fledged, probably glints like opal to her critical eye.

"I told you, Karen," Martha says. She stomps right into my one-room apartment and has a seat by my bed. She crosses her arms and puts on her Let's Talk About It face, but I just want to sleep.

"He gave me a deep muscle massage is all," I say. "People pay a hundred bucks for thirty minutes of the same treatment." I close the door, then take off my shirt. I hide my hand behind my back as I undo my bra.

Martha keeps her game face at full force. "Deep muscle massage," she says. "The kind the secret police use just before they resort to hot pokers." Martha's known me since we were cashiers in a bagel shop—me a scared art student new to the City, smuggling poppy seed and everything in my waistband come quitting time, Martha toting a fresh Masters from NYU and out to convince someone she'd make a good editor. She claims she can smell bullshit as easily as a pot of fresh Ethiopian.

Before I take off my glasses, I look at myself, down to my panties, in the mirror on the closet door.

"He's a fine-tuned machine," I say. "And I'm all soft and puffy. He would have barely noticed the same amount of pressure." I get into bed and wiggle all the way under the covers. When I look up, I can see a glow of light coming through the sheet. When I look down, it is as though I am not there.

Out there, beyond the walls of my cocoon, Martha says, "That man has invaded you like a Hun, and you've already given him access to the Citadel. He knows you're a sculptor, and he gets all stigmata on your hand. Tell me at least you're still working on your boxes."

I hesitate, trying to find a positive way to say, "Not for a couple of weeks," but Martha's chair is creaking before I can think of something. I make shoebox-sized wood sculptures. Each one its own universe: couples foxtrotting under mauve palm trees with a bowl of Wheaties as a backdrop, that kind of thing. I have a whopping five of them currently on display in some back room gallery I haven't even seen yet.

"He's in my next one," I say, finally. "I'm just doing research."

Martha was with me when I first met Mike. We were checking out a gym and its clientele. Mike and his partner were tossing a seventy-pound dumbbell back and forth with practiced rhythm. Martha thought they could have been twins, but I knew which one I wanted. He was the one who looked at his partner with a slight alpha-male smirk each time he caught the weight. There was also something I liked instantly about the way he wiped at his sweat as though angry with it. When his partner went for a heavier dumbbell, I introduced myself. He seemed more annoyed than anything to meet me, but I kept pressing even when Martha was trying to pull me away. When I told him I was a wood sculptor, he said, "That's a lot of sitting around, isn't it?"

"Jesus, Martha," I say. "This is just my hand. Imagine how it feels to dive backwards through a table from ten feet up." The darkness under the blankets keeps my hand from hurting too much.

Martha responds so quickly I know she's been waiting for the right opportunity to say this: "Karen, you should have maced him in the face the second he started busting up your hand. Being safe is ninety-nine percent prevention, picking up on the warning signs and acting on them before they get worse. If you find yourself in a bad situation, you've already failed—the trick then becomes to get yourself out before you become a trophy on the wall." Martha has all these principles because she's been through a couple of bad situations herself. Every Tuesday night, she and other renounced victims kick dummies and scream dissent from the diaphragm. Some Tuesdays they get to kick a volunteer in padding that makes him look like sumo. She brought me in for Bring a Sister night, but the guy in the suit was a laugh. As if he had much concern for the kind of damage a girl could do to him.

"I need my beauty sleep," I tell Martha. I throw the covers down to show her I'm serious. Martha holds her ground for a bit, then finally stands and makes sure I see that her feelings are hurt before she starts for the door.

I let her get her hand on the knob before I say, "I know how to take care of myself. Let's drink too many margaritas soon, on me."

Martha turns back. "Tell me precisely when."

"Not tomorrow," I say. "You can guess why." I bury myself under the covers again before she can give me one of those disappointed stares.

In the morning, my hand is plenty stiff. A spot in the middle of my palm hurts when I bend my fingers. The bruise is like looking into a storm cloud from above—an inky black mass with streaks and spots of purple. It is 8 A.M., and I know Mike is in his kitchen, separating the yolks out of three extra-large eggs. He eats eight times a day, every bite scheduled to his metabolism. He weighs his food. I picture his arms making curling motions as he coaxes the whites into the blender. Watching him mix his 9:45 A.M. yogurt with grapes, granola and 4 oz. of banana is like watching a ballerina warm up. I put a mug of yesterday's coffee in the microwave and run cold water over my hand.

Martha says you can learn a lot about me from my hands—precision, a natural talent for fine arts, that kind of crap. She says ancient Mediterranean cultures would have had festivals to celebrate my latest works, but I find that about as likely as someone yelping like a run over dog at a gallery show and going home to tell his friends of this kick-ass wood sculpture they just GOT to see for themselves. When Mike first saw one of my pieces, his reaction was as blank as white paint. It was the one I have mounted over my sink: a pyramid of green army men assembled before a river of braided Halloween garlands, black bats and witches abroom poking up like crests and waves. Fiery wisp-like creatures I made by chopping the hair off a dozen Troll dolls ride the currents.

I can think of the steps I took in making this monstrosity, how the snipers looked like a good foundation to build up from and how the pyramid created the need for an audience and how good it felt to cut the blue and orange hair from those stupid, stupid dolls—but what good was any of this effort but to make art intellectuals like Martha give thoughtful nods and engage in critical analysis in a way loud enough to let others appreciate their smarts?

When I know Mike is finished drinking his protein shake, I call.

"How's the hand?" he says.

"Bruised."

"Is that it?"

"It hurts some when I move my fingers."

"A deep bruise, at least."

"Satisfied?"

"I should have kept you around while I did my nighttime calisthenics. You could've slapped my abs while I did crunches."

His exquisite musculature is all part of his performance—the horror of an electrified barbed wire match juxtaposed with two tanned, firm specimens of male perfection. With this kind of intensity in the world, what chance does a piece of shit box sculpture have? I hear Mike cut apart an apple, put it on the scale a moment, then spread soy butter on the slices. My coffee tastes like there's Saran Wrap keeping me from its full flavor. Mike tells me I can't come over tonight because he has to meditate on the beating he's going to be taking.

"The sensation you call pain," he says, "is surprise, the nerve endings suddenly deluged with a torrent of impulses. So I anticipate the worst. I prepare to have my ear ripped off by a strip of barbed wire, so when all I get is a harsh yank with a nutcracker, I barely notice it happened."

"I guess I'll have to spend the evening with Martha," I say. Mike is quiet a moment, clearly trying to remember who Martha is.

Then, out of the blue he says, "So how's the sculpting?"

I take a moment to find the words that will say what I mean. "I used to like it," I say, "like doing it, I mean. But I'm starting to wonder the point of it." It's easy to say these kinds of things to Mike because he lets me finish my thoughts. Martha is always trying to find a response to what I say, especially if it's something negative, as though she has an allergy to self-deprecating comments and can't let them go unrefuted.

"It's been a struggle lately to get any work done," I say. "It's like walking with fat thighs, fatter than I have now."

"Then you need to skinny down," he says, of course while his mouth is full.

"So what do I do?" I say. "Shut myself away and forget to eat until I die of starvation?" I bang my mug audibly on the counter. Does that bastard think I'm drinking coffee for breakfast?

"That," Mike says, "or do a sun dance. Tearing off a nipple should inspire something. You'll see what I mean. I'm on tomorrow night, and you're on the guest list."

"He'll plead artistic endeavor," Martha says. She's waving a long, thin spoon at me menacingly. "He'll pound you into to a bag of bargain meat, then defend himself on the evening news with words like 'inspiration' and 'freedom of expression.' He'll make John Wayne Bobbit the next Laurie Anderson. While you

shake and blubber at a survivor's group, the son of a bitch will get an NEA."
We've started our evening at an ice cream shop. Martha treats me to a chocolate
double-malted just to make sure I know what's unhealthy. After this, she wants
to go back to her apartment to watch Friday night prime time. She's considered
showing me *Sleeping With the Enemy* so I know there is always hope in moving
on to another relationship, but who's to believe that skinny-ass Julia Roberts
ever had a finger lifted against her? About as much empowerment as a fat-free
Twinkie.

"He'll surely be responsible for selling out the premiere of *Beating Lorena*."
Martha hacks at the brownie at the bottom of her bowl to let the Death by
Chocolate seep into it thoroughly. "Funny he should advise you to slim down
your thighs. Legs are the strongest part of the female body. I was going to suggest you take up kickboxing. Testicles hurt worse when you kick up rather than
straight ahead."

I decide not to tell her that I'm going to Mike's next show. She would worry
about me ending up like Talia Shire, embracing Rocky's battered shell after the
match, promising my undying love.

"Eat up," she says, "and we'll get a movie."

"What about too many margaritas?"

"Too many margaritas it is then."

At the bar, Martha makes eyes with a couple of coffeehouse-types and entices
them over. Martha tells them I'm into artists, says it like I'm free and on the
make, but these boys with their stylish shirts and literary references don't look
like they could write their way out of a polite yawn. I've drunk a little much, but
I make a valid point anyway.

"Hot coffee in the face," I say to the one who knows how to pronounce
Vladimir Nabokov's name correctly. This boy laughs as though he has the foggi-
est notion what I'm talking about. I turn in my stool and face him straight on.
Martha gives me a look.

"Hot coffee," I reiterate. "Coffee on the plateau of boiling, multi-million-
dollar-lawsuit kind of hot. And I put the whole mug; no, say the whole fucking
pot in your face." I say this with a gesture and ample volume to beat out the
jukebox. "Tell me what kind of reaction that'd get out of you."

"Sounds painful," the boy says.

"You'd scream like a bitch," I say. "I'd like to see your poetry do something
that painful."

In the cab home, Martha says, "You're losing your context, kid." Two definite signs she's in lecture mode: she's calling me kid, and she's not even trying to
meet my eyes. "It's like you've been reborn a pack animal, only able to relate in
a competitive mode."

"I've just lost patience with pretension," I say. I say Nabokov's name a few
times and make flighty hand gestures.

Martha opens the ashtray, then snaps it shut as though it's just disagreed with her. "At least they looked safe. At least they wouldn't require Navy Seal training for you to make it through a first date."

"Children," I say, countering Martha's lack of eye contact by looking out the window on my side. "Sucking on latte-flavored binkies."

"You still haven't gone to your own exhibit, have you?" Martha turns and looks at me for this one, since she knows I won't bother answering.

"Maybe someone will buy one for a bookend," I say. "Put it to some good goddamn use."

"I think your work is improving," Martha says. "Art comes from the soul, and you just need to spend some time on yours." Martha is just a copy editor who now and then writes poetry so full of Greek corpses it's indecipherable, but it's enough to let her consider herself an expert on art. The gist of what she says next is this:

Martha worries that I'm sacrificing my own identity to please Mike. She says I would be happier with someone who wants a woman who is herself, but to me that sounds like complacency, like getting stale. I say something back, something about liking the challenge of finding something new about myself. It's my summation that worries her the most.

"Even if someone has to beat it out of me," I say.

The cab pulls up in front of our building, and together we pay the fare and walk up the stairs to Martha's floor. I look at Martha, and she winces as though she's expecting me to say something unkind. Her intentions may be in a good place, so I just nod farewell. I rush up the rest of the stairs and call Mike.

"I'm busy," he says. "I'm about to dive over the rope with my head caught between the rungs of an aluminum ladder. So leave me the hell alone and I'll see you tomorrow night."

I'm about to doze off when the dial tone kicks in, and I hang up.

The performance is at a Catholic youth center in New Jersey. It takes me three trains and a bus to get there. I am wearing black jeans, a dark blue turtleneck, and my army surplus trench coat. The preliminaries are already underway, so I take a seat in the pullout bleachers at first, away from the small crowd standing around the ring. But the bleachers hum with the stench of stale beer and old chewing gum, and who knows what I could be sitting on, so I move in amid the fans, who are mostly men of course. Though they are holding hubcaps and street signs and copper pipes, they seem quite benign. Some biker-types and guys wearing leather and spikes, even a gang of skinheads ringside, but nothing that sets off any kind of fight/flight response. To tell the truth, they all look like shoppers who have been at a flea market too long. But they do make me feel conservative—I must be the only woman not wearing a concert tee or flannel tied up against the ribs.

I make my way to a spot where I have little trouble seeing the ring. Inside, two guys in neon tights are jumping around and on top of each other. Their efforts look rehearsed and dispassionately choreographed, like a grade school dance recital. Even a backhand chop to the chest, though audible, seems to have little more impact than a movie slap. Next to me is a scrawny kid too tall for his age, his hair a mess and his goatee little more than an uneven scrape of charcoal. When he turns to me, I pretend to be interested in the dance, but he keeps staring at me, and after a while I figure it's better to let him say his piece and be done with him.

"I hate the prelims," he says, his smile full of false confidence. "A bunch of pansies trying to be Kerri Strug. I come to see the real men get it on." He nods to a box he has on the floor between his feet.

I consider blurting out to the kid that I'm banging one of his real men, but all I do is nod and hint at a smile.

The kid continues to make side comments to me now and then during the rest of the match and the one after it, which is also unremarkable for its clumsy acrobatics. His every comment questions the sexual orientations of the performers: "They should call that move 'The Cornholer,' or He might as well kiss the guy first."

The crowd thickens a little by the time the next preliminary ends, but still I manage to get a couple side steps away from the kid, who remains protective over his box and doesn't come after me.

The lights go down, and the crowd starts vibrating a little, moving in steady tremors. People around me who haven't already been brandishing weaponry start pulling things from concealed places. Tire irons, bicycle chains. A guy in full beard and kerchief pulls out a portable drill. Objects are passed over me and into the ring. The kid with the box reaches down and pulls out a battery-powered blender, which he turns on puree and waves over his head horror-movie style before passing it up.

Then without warning, out of the entranceway come Mike and his opponent. They have each other by the hair, and they are punching each other tempestuously. I have to weave like a sparring partner to see around the bodies hopping up and down in front of me. Mike and his opponent both have on jeans and sleeveless black Harley tees and I can't tell them apart at first. Both even have blood spread across their foreheads already. After a few roundhouse exchanges, they pull each other down the ramp towards the ring. It takes me a minute or so before I recognize the slight waddle Mike has when he walks, but by then he's through the ropes, and he and his opponent go for the weapons that have been offered up.

They start with some of the more tame items—trashcan lids, a folding chair, No Parking signs. For a while, they do nothing more than take turns whacking each other over the head. This is obviously a preamble, and I tingle tip to toe with the anticipation of something much much worse happening.

Then it's worse. The opponent shatters a fluorescent light rod over Mike's head, and Mike makes it clear to everyone that he's mad now. As the cloud of gas around him settles, he reaches for a Formica tabletop, and all hell breaks loose.

A woman up on someone's shoulders shows her fallen tits for a round of approval. The skinheads up front lock their arms together so they can move as a single mass. When Mike swings the tabletop so hard that it splits in two over his opponent's head, the mass bounces in place and chants, "Ho-ly shit! Ho-ly shit!" Their movements cause ripples, and I am suddenly being pushed from all directions. I pull my arms up against my sides and I realize how safe I've been all my life. I've felt nervous in dark alleys, dreaded the immediate prospects of my future when approached by Dahmer-looking weirdoes at bars, but being in the middle of this near-riot (at best, a mosh pit) makes my lungs feel as though they're being force fed burning marsh gas.

I instinctively look for the exit signs, but they're too far away, and I feel like a neon pink couch in a room painted black. I'm conspicuous, a target. I'm dressed all wrong. I wear glasses. Even worse, I am completely unable to get into the spirit of things. When Mike has his hand shoved into the electric blender, the kid who brought it beams as though he's just had a personal visit from Ed McMahon and the prize committee, but I'm involved. It matters to me when I see Mike get a pizza cutter rolled over his forehead because I'm the one who's going to have to look at him the next day, but I also can't seem to shake my innate need for justice. When Mike takes the portable drill and runs it a moment behind his opponent's ear, I feel he is only right—after all, he just had his nose pulled with a bolt cutter. When the opponent pours out a sack full of thumbtacks into the ring and slams Mike onto them, the guys around me groan with sympathy pain and delight, but I have a lump like putrid hardboiled egg in my colon.

In the end, there is no finality, no sense of completion. Neither man pins the other, nor attempts to do so. Mike and his opponent roll from the ring and fight their way out of sight. The people stir and chant and stomp feet for a couple minutes (I'm surprised no one holds up a Zippo), but when the house lights come up, they obediently turn and leave. The blender kid and I meet eyes, and I expect him to come onto me again, but he's had the fight taken out of him. He smiles at me in a congratulatory way, welcoming me to the club, and moves on. My arms feel as though they've been holding back boulders, and only now do I realize I've been clenching my teeth through the entire show.

When the gymnasium is almost empty, I go back to the locker rooms. I hover in the hallway between the Men's and Women's, not sure which Mike is going to come from. Guys periodically emerge from both, looking showered, their eyes to the floor. One looks at me hopefully, as though he wants me to bug him for an autograph.

Finally, Mike comes from the Men's lockers, a square of gauze taped to his forehead and a white t-back shirt despite February. There's a deep blush of red on his right shoulder, where he landed on the thumbtacks. Otherwise, he looks fresh from the gym.

"I thought you'd come out looking like a bowl of borscht with legs," I say.

Mike smiles, though with effort. "I clean up well," he says. "They keep a cut doctor on hand." He grimaces as he slings his gear bag over his good shoulder.

The locker room door opens again, and out comes Mike's opponent and his own girlfriend.

"You've met Carl," Mike says. I nod to Carl, but his nod back has a real fuck-off attitude to it. I figure it would be a bad idea to tell him it was a good show. He's wearing a neon blue tee that's a size or two too small. It makes his upper body look like a steroid detonation.

The girlfriend is standing a pace behind Carl. She is tall, even without her heels and stiff, bleached hair. She's pretty too, somewhere underneath all that makeup, and she's bright as hell—her spandex is neon, and her top could control air traffic. I'm surprised she's not snapping gum.

"That's Katrina," Mike says. I put up my hand, and Katrina turns on a smile just long enough to wave back.

"Pleasure," I say, but that's not the word I would use to describe my assessment of her. On one hand, I am glad that we don't resemble each other. I would hate to think that Mike has been trying to score a replica of her for himself. But coming out of tonight's testosterone fest, it would have been nice to meet a woman who looked like she could discuss something more than the best cream rinse out on the market.

Besides, I get the distinct impression that Katrina would rather be the only female along with these two guys, and it rears up my antagonism better than cattle prod.

Carl looks right past me. "We're thinking of getting a bite," he says to Mike. "Something greasy no doubt. You in?"

Martha would have some biting reminder that she's not chopped liver, but she's never stood between these guys. Carl's biceps alone wash all want of equality right out of me. I look at Katrina, and she gives me this blank look as though she's waiting for me to do something interesting, like go away.

Mike puts his hand on my shoulder. "We're going to head back," he says. "Those thumbtacks put the hurt on me something awful."

"All part of the game, bud." Carl rubs his forehead up by his own gauze, which is closer to the hairline. "Thumbtacks hurt."

"Next time it's you," Mike says. "And it's going to be something on fire, I can assure you."

Carl smiles and laughs once like he's gotten a joke he doesn't think is all that funny. "We'll see," he says.

I don't know how I ever thought Carl and Mike looked so much alike. Carl looks like a comic book cover. Exaggerated and empty of substance. A perfect model for one of my boxes.

"Last chance to talk me into buying you a meal full of lard," Carl says. I notice he is trying to keep his weight on his right leg.

"I think Karen here wants to get home," Mike says. He leans forward, and I can feel his breath on the top of my head. "It's her first, so I'm sure she'd rather spend the rest of the night doing something a little more low-impact." He gives me a slight pat on the ass as a signal for me to comply.

"Great," I say. "Blame it on me."

Carl waits, as if the last word on this can only come from Mike. He shifts his weight momentarily, then back when his left knee buckles a bit. Finally he says, "Fine. Fuck off, and I'll see you Tuesday."

As Carl walks around Mike and me, Katrina following, Mike says, "You're getting soft if you want three days to rest up."

"Soft, soft," Carl says. He reaches back, takes Katrina's hand, and brings her alongside him. "You'll see who's soft, pal."

Off they go, towards the exit at the end of the hall, Katrina double-timing her heel-retarded steps to keep up with Carl's tired and injured lope. He lets go of her and works his hand up and down her back.

"I'm out the near door," Mike says, pushing lightly on my shoulder. "Carl thinks parking too close to the dressing rooms makes for a bad show."

We get to Mike's Honda, and he has me drive. As he clambers into the passenger seat, he favors the right side of his back.

"Katrina sure didn't want me along," I say as we pull out.

"She's a good egg." Mike is turned toward me, but it's because of his back rather than any concern for my being odd-peg-out. "She's real good for Carl. His last girlfriend never came to shows, found the whole business horrid. Katrina knows it's a big deal for him."

"Probably helps that she carries his gear bag," I say. I look into the rearview to pretend I'm not noticing Mike's glare.

"That's not all he wants," he says.

"Don't be so sure," I say. "Most guys go for a personal lackey. I didn't even know girlfriends were allowed in the locker room." My temples are tight, my hands pinching the wheel. If Mike's expecting another high-haired porter who for all I know scrubs Carl's back in the shower, I'm going to make his hurting ass walk home, even if it is his two-door I'll be kicking him from.

"Ah, shit," Mike says. "They were in a huff because Carl thought we sucked tonight." He stretches painfully and closes his eyes. "There's an artist about Katrina, believe it or not." He mumbles something, maybe, "Like you," but when I look to him to confirm this, he looks asleep.

Back at his apartment, Mike falls face-first onto the couch.

"I can feel every goddamn hole that's been put into me," he says.

I go into the kitchen and fetch an ice pack. "I never heard a crowd gag like that," I say. On my way back to the living room, I grab peroxide and a wad of cotton.

"That was disappointment," Mike says into the cushion. "Last time they saw us both fall onto razor wire, but that shit cut me up so bad I couldn't shower for a week."

I sit on the edge next to him and rub the ice pack gently over the red bumps in his shoulder. I know it's bullshit, but I keep telling myself this is not what Katrina will be doing for Carl. I have a lighter touch, since I have such sensitive hands. After chilling the thumbtack wounds, I put the ice on the back of Mike's neck and grab the peroxide, just like Mike says to do.

The thumbtack wounds look ready to infect, despite the peroxide. After a rubdown all over his back, Mike sits up. He has me get behind him, then leans back until I must be lost from view. He is pressed so hard against me I can feel his groans in my breasts.

"Tell me what the hell I do this for again," he says as I rub his shoulders.

"You like the pay," I say.

Mike turns his head part of the way toward me. "I get paid?"

"And you get to meet exciting new people and count their teeth on one hand."

Mike laughs, then warns me not to make him laugh. "You should talk," he says. "You come to a wrestling match dressed like a math professor."

I give his shoulders a hard squeeze, though I'm sure he barely feels it. "Don't cross me," I say. "I got my own bag of thumbtacks."

"That'll have to wait for tomorrow night," he says. He closes his eyes and puts his head back. He has ridges on his forehead from the scars piled upon scars piled upon scars. He dozes a while, but when I start feeling claustrophobic I wake him. Then we clean the cut on his forehead, and he checks his back in the bathroom mirror.

"I'm going to look like Quasi fucking Moto," he says.

I show him how some rouge on his left shoulder evens out the thumbtack marks and gives his back a ruddy, healthy glow. He submits to this willingly with no hint of sarcasm, no sense that he's humoring me. He already knows how to apply some base to his forehead so his ridges are noticeable only from close-up. From five feet away, his body is smooth and healthy. He has me stand back to make sure of this.

Soon after that, we go to bed. As he's nodding off, Mike tells me three times that he needs to be touching me every moment while he's asleep. It sounds so important to him that I feel dishonest and undependable the one time I do slide out to call my apartment and check my messages.

The next night, it's like this:

We're naked, and Mike breaks out body paint, the heavy duty Ultimate Warrior stuff that goes on thick and rubs off only with a hard sweat. We paint targets on each other's bodies. He paints KICK ME in cartoonist letters over my ass. When he turns off everything but the black light in his bedroom, we glow like aliens.

Then we go to the interview.

"Tonight," I say, "you have a big match with Pussy Galore" (the glint in his eyes, fury at the very mention of my wrestling name—his nemesis, his new greatest opponent). "What are your thoughts concerning your upcoming bout, this First Blood match, with this most fearsome adversary?"

"Pussy Galore," he screams, his beautiful naked body painted and glowing in the black light, an arrow and THE BUCK STOPS HERE hovering over his manly penis, which swells subtly as he goes into his act. "The things I'm going to do to that Pussy, so bad its own mother won't recognize it!" And here it's about breaking bones and bending bodies in unnatural ways, all of which he pantomimes with trained clarity.

No surprise that my messages last night were all from Martha. "Just checking up on you," she started with each time. By the third message her speech was groggy and slurred, her voice barely audible over the television.

"It'll help me rest," she finally admitted in the last one, "if I know you're home safe, so give a ring whatever time you get in." She paused as though making sure there was only silence on the other end. Then, "I've got a dog story for you." Code—call me when he's not around, especially when he's not around.

I realize now, while Mike glows and struts and gesticulates violently before me, that I pity Martha for wanting to live in a sealed bubble of safety, and for me pity is the same as anger. I erased her messages and went back to bed. By the time Mike found me in the dark and pulled me up against him, I had decided that letting Martha worry about me for a day or two might teach her that there will always be things beyond her control.

I sidle backwards on the bed, lowering and lowering my guard to Mike, opening my painted body. I could taunt him, fuel him on some more, but there is a line you don't cross. Mike and I, our play puts our bodies so close to that line we can kiss it.

11

Scanner Days, Starry Nights

MARTIN ROSE

Vincent's mother died in the gutter.

He remembers the year 2010 like a pulsing, bloody ruby, fractured in red: her upturned face in the rain, her pressing hand in his as she died with her mouth open in the gutter water. They had spent a year previous living in basements of whatever landlords would take them, and wherever they went, that damn picture followed.

He was a boy when she died, but it seems the picture obscures even the memory. When he recalls the blowfly making a modest one-room home out of his mother's left nostril, the lines seem to blur, and his dead mother runs like a watercolor across the page, morphing into . . . that terrible picture. Starry Night.

He never had a father, so when Maynard Dartmouth became his employer it was clear to Vincent, from the moment he shook hands, the kindly old gentleman considered it his duty to be Vincent's surrogate father. It leaves a bad taste in his mouth like an after-school special—the wayward child and his hopeful, yearning parent figure who leads him on the right path.

During the interview he wears a white button-down shirt, carefully ironed and tucked into his tastefully chosen black pants. He looks impeccable and he knows it; underneath the white fabric of his shirt, and under this, his undershirt, winds a snarl of lines and tattoos that travel across his skin in a never-ending, self-generating spiral.

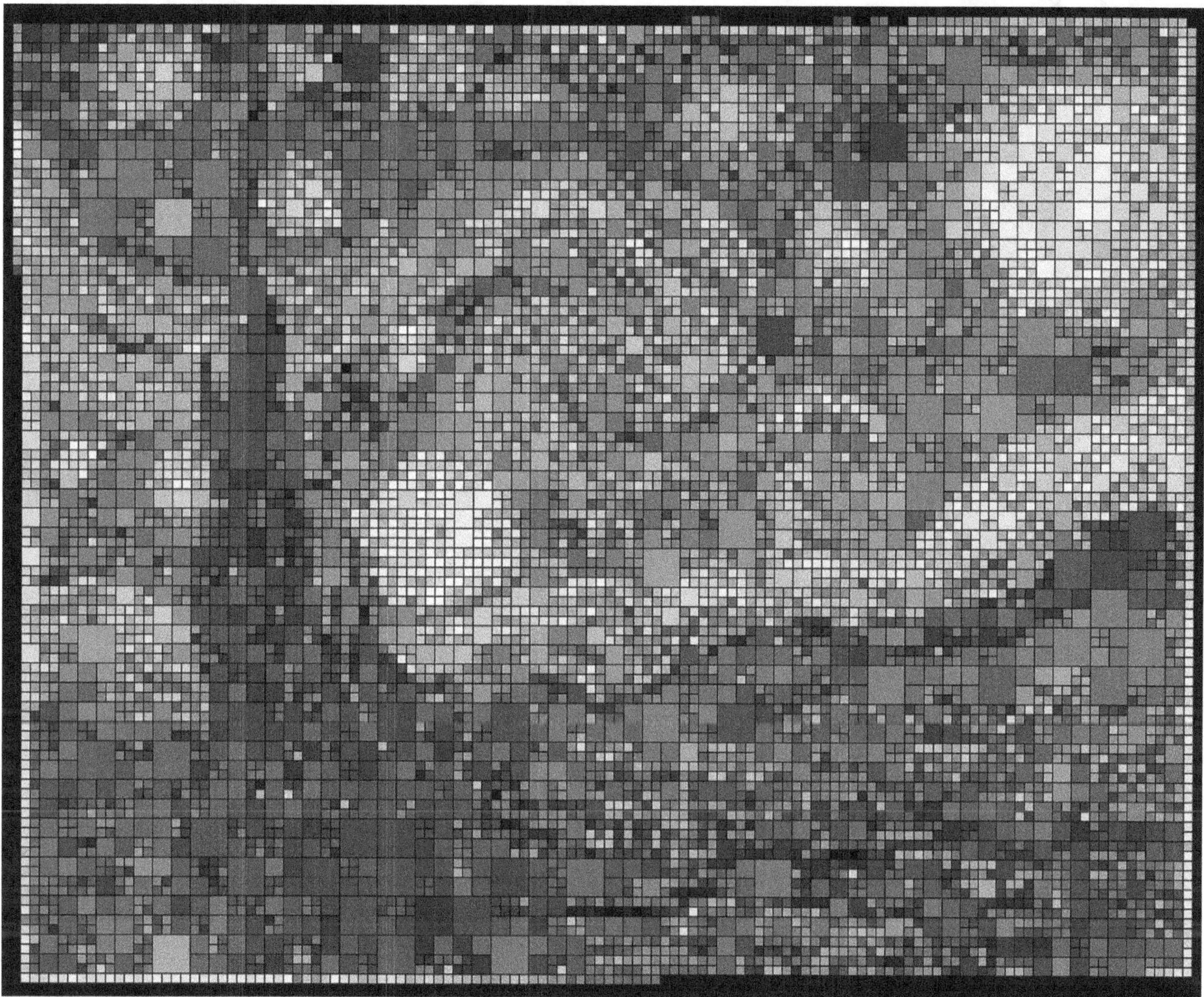

After years spent homeless, without his mother alive to take care of him, and his eventual journey to the edges of the affluent (which would never deign to accept him into their ranks anyway), he keeps his marks and scars carefully hidden. All the tattoos were acquired after her death.

Maynard Dartmouth is the curate of the new First American Digital Museum and he needs someone to maintain the virtual load, the servers, the web pages that will house the tired and obsolete paintings of yesteryear. This project is brokered and funded by a very prominent Chinese bank, who snapped up some of the world's most renowned art. The problem with owning so much art is that ancient paintings generally require maintenance and care, security and storage.

Why not, the Chinese and American bankers mused, cut costs by scanning the originals, and post the digital version on the web in the First American Digital Museum (charging web surfers per view, of course)?

"What happens to the originals?" Vincent asks.

"Ah," Maynard says, and rubs his chin uncomfortably. "That's where I need someone with your special talents."

Vincent doubts that he is qualified for the work, but since the great Housing Bust of the early century, people had been scraping by, and fifteen years later, jobs were still hard to find. Vincent had struggled to volunteer at a local library and care for their monthly art displays. He wasn't sure if he would go so far as to call dusting off a glass case every month a "special talent."

"What you're asking me for has more to do with my social standing," Vincent flatly points out.

Maynard laughs, a long, slow chuckle with pale blue eyes beneath his white hair. "It's the sort of thing that someone of principles might have trouble with."

Vincent purses his lips to ask what they were really discussing here, but his mind makes the leap. "You're destroying the art after you scan it for the Digital Museum, aren't you?"

"No, my boy. You will be."

He accepts the job on site.

He always shows up in his cleverly ironed, button-down shirt, buttoned all the way up to the neck to hide the ravenous snarls of ink over his back and chest, which bear a single, iconic image that people used to have imprinted on credit cards, back in the days of yore when credit was easy to obtain: Starry Night.

He pulls the Caravaggio up from the machine, where the lights reflect off ancient oils and capture the image forever in an unnamed database. Pixels inside pixels. The painting itself is huge, bigger than he thought it would be.

"Burn them," Maynard instructed, the wrinkles at his eyes crinkling in deep thought as they narrowed. "Burn them or bleach them, but whatever you do, nothing can remain."

They do not even spare the frames, which he tosses into an incinerator for the very purpose, closing the black grille over the consuming flames. He tears the canvas off, but in the case of older art it often comes away in a puff of centuries-old dust, all too happy to fall apart at the slightest urging. Van Eyck follows Caravaggio, then comes a lovely Vermeer. There are many works he does not recognize, and familiar ones his mother once adored, before she died. In some cases, he had seen them in the museums himself, when she was still alive and would take him there as a boy, unmarked and unchanged.

Degas, Renoir, Whistler, Wyeth, Kahlo, Dali. Art school staples and the arbitrary gods of the academic world. What raised one artist above another, Vincent is not entirely sure. He has many artists for friends, and cannot say he particularly likes them or their art.

Then he comes upon the sunflowers, waiting in the newest load of paintings arrived from the delivery truck in the alley. The packages are all waiting for him to open them like a fresh, Christmas Day, tear away their coverings and lift them, large or small, onto the huge scanner that will flash searing, unforgiving light upon every brushstroke, oil and line upon the canvas. Centuries-old art reduced to a surgical instant of light, he operates on each in their turn.

Until the sunflowers. He rips away the paper and holds the gilt frame in his hands. There it is, brighter than day, big, bobbing sunflower heads in a vase in an unknown room. He stares at it for a long moment and briefly, his mother dead in the gutter surfaces. A lump in his throat.

Then he swallows it down and consigns it to the flames.

He should have known the sunflowers were only the beginning. Where there is one Van Gogh, there will surely follow another. Without further preamble, that December afternoon with light pouring through the window over his computer and work table, Starry Night lays exposed before him like a wanton woman, giving itself away.

His hands tremble, and he finds he cannot bring himself to touch the canvas. He can safely grip the frame, but he holds it like it is on fire, every moment burning his fingers to touch it. He lets it fall to the worktable.

Reflections on Maynard, the ever helpful surrogate parent, who enjoys reaching out and patting him on the back, likes to congratulate him on a job well done, as he is busy destroying some of the most essential and life-changing artistic creations the world has ever known. He wonders just what Maynard really thinks of him, that this is the task he feels a perfect fit for Vincent's skill.

This reflection spawns still another, and he recalls, the way one might accidentally bite into a rotted tooth, dragging his mother up the length of the flooded gutter by one, dead hand. Touching the frame of the canvas is very much like that. Dragging it through the gutter, killing it a little more every step of the way.

He snatches the painting from the table, hastily wraps it in the butcher paper, and tucking it under his arm, leaves the office where the First American Digital Museum is busy being born.

They miss it immediately, of course.

To his satisfaction, it takes them three days to find him.

Who knows the streets better than he does? The trouble was hiding a rather large masterpiece by Vincent Van Gogh. He went the first place he could think of, the local public library, where he slipped it into the display case for local collections and art works.

Nobody recognized it, but then, when was the last time anyone had ever seen it? Probably not since the Chinese had bought it in the early century. In buying the painting itself, they renewed the copyright, forbidding duplication of any kind, digital or otherwise. With the Americans acting as lap dogs to Chinese interest, they found no trouble with enforcement. Piracy was rampant, but you would be hard pressed to find a picture of any classic painting that the Chinese had acquired.

Vincent, however, found a way around that.

When he had turned eighteen, he had it tattooed upon his body, spent hours and hours in the chair with the needle buzzing over his flesh; he paid for it by working for free at the tattoo parlor. Whenever he unbuttoned his corporate uniform, out unfurled the stars, the moonlit sky, the driving wind over a midnight hamlet. Out spilled his mother's beloved Van Gogh. Of course, that was a crime, but ink is much more difficult to trace than internet images. Anyone can hack into a computer—no one could hack his skin.

Until now.

They burst upon him in the attic. He knows they are there, the game done and over with before it even commences. He finishes the top button of his shirt when they burst through the door and the police officers take him downtown. They print him and throw him in a cell where he waits. He expects to be there awhile, for without living relatives there is no one he can call upon to bail him out.

Sometime in the morning, as he lays on the bench half dozing, a figure walks before him as the bars pull away. He opens his eyes and sees Maynard Dartmouth standing there, in his gray suit and blue tie, his pale eyes like paper.

"My boy, whatever were you thinking?" he says softly.

Maynard had put up the bail, and without a word, Vincent follows him out of the jail cell and to the car. He never asks where they are heading, though he has a terrible idea of just what awaits him.

"I didn't think I would be able to come back to work," he says finally, when the car stops in front of the office building, home to the world's First American Digital Museum.

"I need you," Maynard says quietly. "No one else will do it."

Vincent does not respond, but follows him out of the car, into the mirrored building with glass upon glass. Up the elevator, to the endless hall with the rows of anonymous white doors, until there stands open the one he must walk through.

When he enters after Maynard, he sees everything as he has left it, incinerator door open, the flames licking inside, the light streaming through the mirrored windows. On the table, as if it had never left: Starry Night.

They both regard it, side by side.

"You want me to scan it, destroy it?" Vincent says softly as he comes abreast of the painting, staring at it once more.

"No," Maynard sighs. "It's nothing that I want."

"We don't have to."

"We do. They'll take everything from me. My grandchildren will be on the streets tomorrow if I refuse."

Vincent's face twists briefly, recalling when the street had been his permanent home, and then it smoothes out, carefully concealed behind his chosen, corporate mask.

"You're going to make sure I finish it?"

Maynard nods, but the set of his shoulders is helpless, distraught.

Vincent approaches the worktable, and lifts the knife to slash canvas. It reflects Starry Night back into his eyes, but what he sees there, he isn't entirely sure. The blue of the paint is like the blue of his mother's dead, cobalt eyes.

"Then I'd best do it quick," Vincent says solemnly.

It is quick; he reaches out until he can feel the whisper of Maynard's white, brittle hairs on the soft, inner skin of his palm, and slams his head onto the open glass of the scanner.

Maynard screams, a blood smear stretches across the glass as the scanner bulb flicks on, searing heat rushing in with the light.

"When we have our adequate copy of you, Mr. Dartmouth," Vincent says through gritted teeth, "than we will no longer need the original."

And with this, his screams rise to match the high-pitched whine of the scanner, and Vincent patiently waits to capture the final image.

12

The Book
of Life and Death

GRACE TALUSAN

Ever since I left the Philippines to try my luck overseas, I've been lugging around a series of mismatched plastic-covered photo albums and scrapbooks I call the Book of Life and Death. When I start a new album, I tape a ribbon to the center page, splitting the photo book into two chapters: life and death. I fill the pages of each album with snapshots of those who have just taken their first breath and those who have taken their last.

Without my mother's help, my collection would be incomplete. Whenever someone is born or dies back home, my mother grabs the elbow of the person with the camera and begs, "Don't forget reprints for Marybelle." Then she wraps the photos in plastic and sends them to wherever I've been working—Lebanon or Saudi or Hong Kong.

At first she didn't understand my albums. But many years ago, when I brought Volume Two home during my annual visit, my mother plopped down onto the milk crate by the kitchen window and studied each page. After a while, I blurted, "Say something, Ma. Don't just sit there and cry." She flipped between a page in Death, then turned back to Life, back again to Death. She grimaced a smile, "It's too beautiful."

For the life chapter, I accept entries of baby's first photo only. These photos are always the same: a blue or pink knit cap, eyes puffed into slits, head slightly pointed at the top. I've instructed my family not to bother me with photographs of baptisms or first Christmases or the endless parade of children's birthdays.

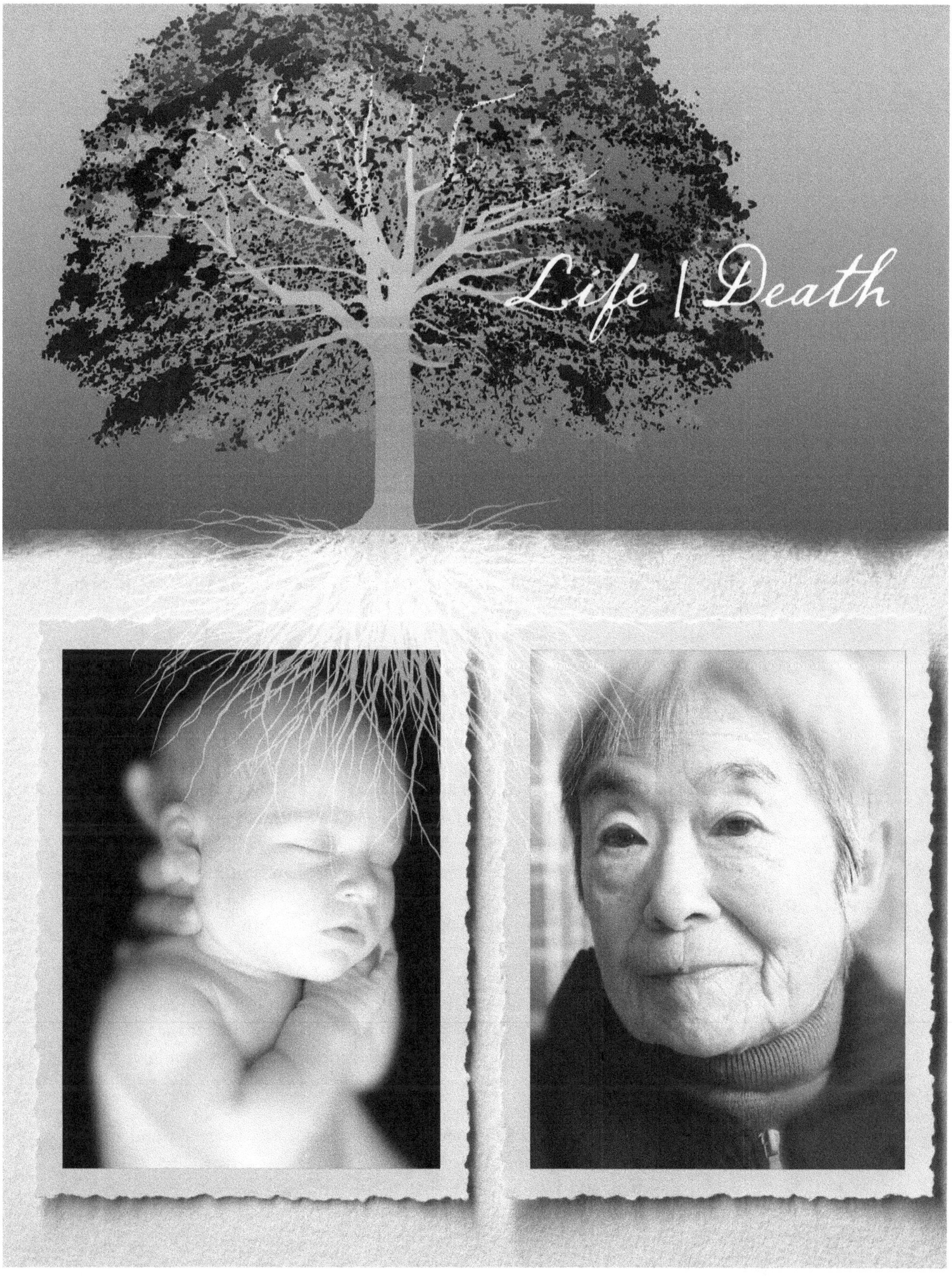

Life | Death

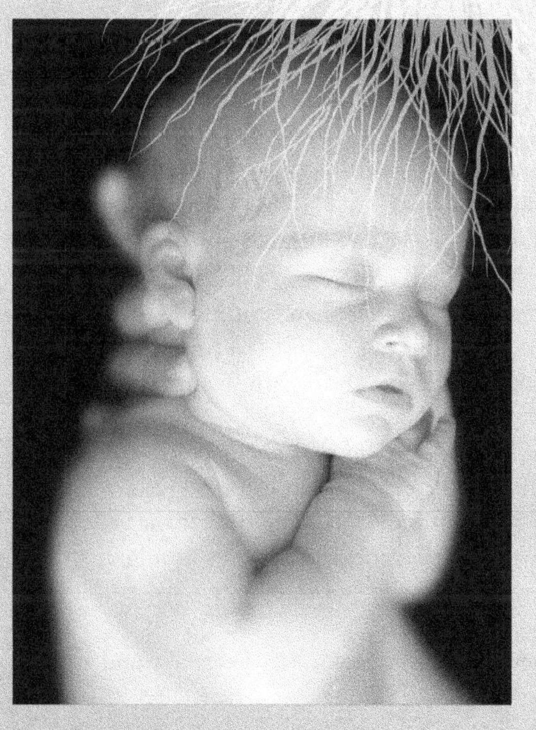

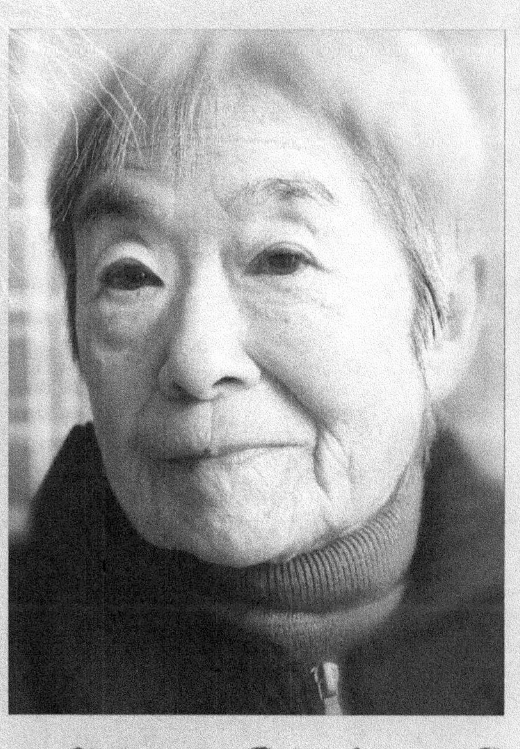

My own daughter, Anne, appears in Volume Five. These are the pictures of lives waiting to happen.

For the death chapter, there are variations on a theme. Sad, smiling children and widows pose next to caskets. Displayed behind the family on wooden easels are birds-of-paradise and sampaguita, its white bells ringing fragrant jasmine. Silk banners, the kind that beauty pageant contestants wear, cross the bereavement wreaths, but instead of Miss Massachusetts or Miss Guam, the painted letters read, Beloved Father. Devoted Husband. Loyal Brother.

Over the years, some patterns emerge. The baby photos are split equally between male and female, but I've noticed more men fill my death pages. It was all their bad habits: the cigarillo breaks every half hour and—without the pressure to maintain their figure—the breakfasts of fried rice, eggs, and spicy longaniza sausages with cubes of pork fat in each bite.

Some deaths were sensational and noteworthy enough to be written up in the Times or Bulletin, and I saved the corresponding newspaper clippings inside the plastic photo sleeves. A handful of family members appear in both sections of the Book of Life and Death. In the 11 months of the year I was working abroad, my sister's daughter Uta lived and died before I even met her. My uncle's ninth child, Francis, was crushed under a crowded jeepney during the Manila rush hour.

After making these books for 20 years, I know that despite the best and worst, life goes on. Widows remarry. The mourning laugh again. We try so hard to be happy despite life's most depressing news of all: one by one, we will lose those we love until that inevitable day when we lose our own life.

After a long day of anticipating the needs of others, I relax by reading from either the Book of Life and Death or my special-edition box set of Anne of Green Gables. I always read my Anne books in order, starting when orphaned Anne arrives at Matthew and Marilla's farm on Prince Edward Island, then continue through her school years, her friendships, and romances. When I've finished the last page of Rilla of Ingleside, when Anne is older than I am now, I return the book to its space in the box. I press my palms flat against the container, my left hand against the first book and my right against the eighth, feeling the span of Anne's life between my hands.

For the past decade, I've worked for the Chows, first in Hong Kong and now in the States, where three years ago, Professor Lincoln Chow was offered a teaching position. Now we live on the first floor of a triple-decker that has been renovated from its former life housing three generations of an immigrant Italian family, and thankfully, my room is down the hall from where my employers sleep.

When Jing Chow first interviewed me, she said, "The Professor and I plan on having too many children for me to handle alone." Ten years later, there are still no children, and I know better than to ask why.

Working for an economist has inspired me to think about the world in numbers. If I wait my turn with American immigration and petition for my daughter Anne once I get citizenship, she will be 43 before she can legally join me. However, if I work three hours every weekday, sneaking out while Jing takes her nap, I am able to earn extra money while the American women have their careers. These dollars will pay the government officials who have the power to move Anne ahead in line. And while college is in session, I earn even more, as the fraternity boys hire me on weekend mornings to clean their basements of crushed red cups and spilled beer.

More numbers: Both Jing and I turn 40 this year. My female relatives live an average of 74 years. Tipping the balance in my favor: daily bowls of oat bran cereal and regular physical activity in the way of housekeeping. I've calculated my lifespan at 80 years. As my age clicks over this year, I estimate that I'm halfway between my days.

It's midnight and my bedroom door creaks open. I squint beyond the yellow glow of my bedside lamp. The whites of Jing's eyes shine at me. "Marybelle, the Professor is snoring again. Can't you hear it?" Jing doesn't wait, but steps into the room. She's wearing her nightgown printed with the blue flowers, a newer version of the one I'm wearing now. Jing and I share the same tube of drugstore Midnight Black to rinse through our gray. We paint our faces with the same makeup, mine from the free samples that Jing receives like a prize every time she makes a purchase over 20 dollars at the department store.

Jing swipes the Tiger Balm from my nightstand, and sighs, "I was looking for that." She walks to the other side of the bed and crawls in beside me. She unscrews the hexagonal container and presents it to me, the ointment's odor of camphor, menthol, and spices familiar and pungent. I raise my eyebrows at Jing, blink down at my reading material, and stare back at her. Jing takes it for granted that I will minister to her every need. On TV, the sitcom mothers say, "Do it yourself. What am I, your maid?" But I can never say that.

Jing ignores my annoyance and slides her feet underneath my calves. "Warm like oven bread," Jing says. "Oh, Marybelle, your album of death. Any new pages this month?" Jing always forgets the life part of the book, but I don't correct her.

"Hay, naku," I say. "Your feet are ice."

Jing shrugs her nightgown from her right shoulder, then takes my hand and places it against her back. "Marybelle, it hurts."

I dip two fingers in the Tiger Balm and sear the ointment into Jing's skin, feeling her back muscles, as hard as bone. Jing sighs, "There's no one like you."

My irritation melts and I ask Jing, "Remember my cousin's missing husband, Boyet?"

"So, did he run off with another woman?"

"They found him pulled over on the side of the road. He was stretched out in the back seat. The windows were rolled up, and the air-con used up all the fuel. He was two weeks in that back seat. By that time, the car was covered in vines and banana leaves and palm fronds. Imagine the odor."

"Imagine!" Jing grins. "No other woman after all."

"Heart attack. He was just lying there with his hands behind his head as if he expected to wake up twenty minutes later."

Jing repeats something she's said before, "You Filipinos, with your passion and Spanish blood. Always so much drama and emotion. Not like us Chinese." Jing always forgets that my father was part Chinese.

When my mother was 15, sewing soles into designer shoes, she was impregnated by the factory owner's son. He was 19, the rebellious college dropout of a wealthy Filipino Chinese family. He didn't believe that I was his. When he was still alive, my mother would mail me newspaper clippings about him from the society pages of the Manila Times. The last items my mother sent were his obituary and the accompanying article, "Shoe Baron Drops Dead in Manila Hotel." The article described how his young mistress had lain beneath him for an hour as she waited for paramedics to remove his body. Under the headline, my mother had scribbled, "Finally, the other shoe drops!"

I pass Jing the album and point out the grainy newspaper photo of Boyet's car, which is a casket of sorts. "I think those are his feet," I say.

Jing asks, "Is everything ready for the party tomorrow? All those economists make me nervous."

"It'll be fine," I tell her. I soften the wings of muscle in Jing's back with the heel of my palm. "I've even created a special appetizer for the occasion. Imagine a pink pork peony. It's an assortment of deli meats arranged into the shape of a giant flower. Professor's guests will love it. A piece of resistance."

I peer over Jing's shoulder and stare at the snapshot of my cousin. She is posing in the funeraria next to Boyet's closed casket. My cousin's eyes are mapped in red lines and her face is splotchy pink. But a camera points at my cousin, and she, nine months pregnant with her husband's first and last child, can't help herself: she smiles.

I've thought of changing my situation many times, but one year turned into five, and suddenly, seven. And when Lincoln offered to arrange my visa to the States, how could I refuse?

Lincoln said, "Change your luck, Marybelle. Give your daughter opportunities, the American ones."

I didn't answer right away because I couldn't believe my fortune. America. The States. Growing up in my parents' squatter hut, I understood that I needed to make my own luck. I sold bottles and scrap metal to earn my trike fare to school; I won a scholarship to a small Catholic women's college. But no teaching job paid as well as overseas domestic work. Now, college grads stay home and work for call centers, but those jobs are only for the elite. At last, here was my chance.

"Alright, alright," Lincoln said. "I know it's far from home, but look, I'll raise your salary twenty percent. I need you to come with us. Jing needs you."

By that time, I'd already given up any notion that I could ever find work in the Philippines. I'd already hired a domestic to raise my daughter. "Of course," I told Lincoln. But now that I'm here, I often fantasize about making my escape.

During Jing's dark days, when she doesn't get out of bed and barely eats, I want to leave even more. Once, I was reading a magazine and came across one of those quizzes, Do you suffer from depression? I realized that Jing would've gotten an A+ on that exam. Professor brings her to the psychiatrist appointment, but sometimes I notice Jing dropping her tiny pill into the sink. I don't say anything. Who am I to criticize Jing for keeping secrets?

Every month, I visit Western Union to remit my salary to home. I know Lincoln would cringe to learn how much of my pay goes to wire transfer fees. He would faint if he knew that my life's earnings are wrapped in plastic, stacked in the old refrigerator in my parents' kitchen, earning no interest. But I've seen what's happened, how over a weekend, the peso will devalue and a person will find himself significantly poorer on Monday morning.

The money from my side job is tucked under the sofa cushions, hidden behind books on my bookshelf, and stashed under my mattress. I dream of leaving every day. But if I left, what would become of me? I would become TNT, tagot na tagot, and literally "hide and hide" from immigration the rest of my life.

Americans show up to parties right on time, some even early. In the Philippines, you wouldn't expect anyone to arrive until at least an hour or even five hours past the invitation time. And when they do show, smiling sheepishly with eight or ten of their relatives and neighbors in tow, you wave them all in.

I'm ready when the first guest, Kevin, arrives at our dinner party at 12 minutes to six. He seems nervous as he storms past the shoe rack and bin of guest slippers by the door.

"Sir," I start. "Your shoes."

But Jing pinches my waist. I bite the inside of my cheek so as not to imagine the grains of salt and sand, remnants from the winter's snow, shedding from the man's shoes and being ground into the floorboards.

I offer Kevin red wine. He drinks it in three gulps and smiles at me with Merlot-stained teeth, "Where's Lincoln?"

With my lips, I point to the backyard, where Lincoln grills steaks. Kevin exits through the sliding glass door.

By half past, most of the guests have arrived. A knot of graduate students huddle around the grill with Lincoln and punctuate their points with amber beer bottles. Two faculty members, Ben, a statistician, and Linda, an ecological economist, sit back against the sofa, their heads turned to each other. They whisper softly to one another, while their spouses, who are both in advertising, lean forward, discussing the merits of the midseason network lineup.

I know the guests' professions because what they do for a living is the second thing Americans say about themselves, after their name. In the Philippines, kin counts. Upon introduction, we want to know which province your family is from, who you belong to.

No one accepts my offer of pork petals. I've sorely miscalculated the popularity of my creation and each rejection makes my head bend lower. When I present the platter to Linda, I barely shrug the platter at her. Linda takes a slice. As she dangles the piece of ham in her mouth as if she were a baby bird, I realize my mistake. "The bread," I say. I dash into the kitchen and return with the bag of rolls and cocktail napkins.

After making a finger sandwich, Linda clasps my wrist. She is the first person to look directly at me. Her hair is gray, cut neatly against her neck, but her face is smooth and flushed with wine.

"I'm Linda. And who are you? You have gorgeous eyes."

I'm embarrassed by the compliment. "Linda," I say. "Pretty."

"Excuse me?" Linda slurs.

"In Spanish, linda means pretty."

"No," she says. "I spell it with a y. So I guess I'm not pretty."

Suddenly, I smell Jing. No matter how hard she tries to mask it, Jing always smells of Tiger Balm. "Marybelle is our domestic," Jing offers.

Lynda stares at my eyes and nose. "Hawaiian? No, don't tell me. Thai. No, Filipina!"

Jing slinks away as Lynda fires questions at me. "What dialect do you speak? Which island do you come from?" She asks how I came to work in the States, how I got a visa, whether there was fierce competition in Hong Kong for employment, whether I had gone to college.

I dutifully answer.

"Jesus," Lynda says. "You're an English teacher? How did you end up doing this? Serving ham and wine to a bunch of boring academics?"

"No jobs back home," I stutter. "And I have a daughter."

The other guests in the room are shifting in their seats and finding pieces of lint to pick off their shirts. Ben whistles quietly.

"I'm sorry to be so nosy, but I just read an article recently about this very subject," Lynda says. "Anyone catch it? The Sunday Times on overseas Filipino workers?"

"I read it. *A Good Provider Is One Who Leaves*," bursts Kevin. I hadn't noticed his return from the grill.

One who leaves. Kevin and Lynda summarize the article to their audience in the living room. It's an odd experience. I've become invisible again, listening to them tell a story that is and isn't about me.

Lynda continues, "So the parents leave the country to make money and they feel so guilty about leaving their children that they buy them a bunch of crap.

Video games, cell phones, things like that."

"Depreciable assets. Material goods," Kevin says.

"It makes you wonder if it's all worth it," Lynda says.

"It's ironic," Kevin says. "First-world mothers hire third-world domestics who in turn hire native domestics to care for their children. Ah, capitalism."

The guests don't notice how my feet sink inches into the floor; how my head buzzes with flies. I'm furious; I want to tell them that they don't understand. Sure, I'm not physically raising my daughter, and yes, I'm guilty of buying her designer fashions and even jewelry for her cell phone, but my absence also buys Anne's future, a little bit of land and a private school education. What I started overseas will change my family's luck.

To my relief, Lincoln appears in the living room, tongs in one hand and a heavy platter of meat in the other. "Dinner is served."

During those empty days in Hong Kong when Lincoln was working for tenure at the University of Hong Kong and Jing couldn't get out of bed, I'd read aloud to Jing from Anne of Green Gables. When Anne is in the depths of despair, she asks Marilla if she's ever felt this pain. Marilla answers, "No. To despair is to turn your back on God." No matter how many times I read this scene, Jing clucks her tongue as if hearing it for the first time. Like me, Anne was a servant. Like me, Anne went to college to study education. Except Anne became a teacher and I stayed a servant. Later in the first book, when Anne meets her best friend, Diana Barry, her kindred spirit, I always imagine that Jing and I are kindred spirits, too.

Jing wasn't surprised that I'd named my daughter after Anne of Green Gables. For years, my parents mailed me cassette tapes with Anne's voice. Anne would parrot my parents. "Ma," she would repeat. "See," my mother would say on the tape. "Anne knows who you are. She knows her mother." But I couldn't see how Anne knew me, so I bought my parents a camcorder. Then they sent me video-cassettes of my Anne, but it didn't solve the problem. As I played and replayed moments from her life, Anne was forever growing up without me.

The wine glasses are filled and the guests are stuffing themselves full of steak and salad in the dining room. In the kitchen, I dump the platter with my pink peony into the trash. The flower slides from the plate, clumping together. It hasn't fooled anyone into believing it is anything but what it always was: super-market deli meat.

I wash dishes as quietly as I can. Lynda sets a wine glass on the counter.

"Sorry about all the questions," she says. "I really put you on the spot. I apologize."

"Ma'am, you don't have anything to be sorry about."

"I used to be like you," she says quietly. While she was in high school and college, Lynda tells me, she worked summers cleaning toilets and washing windows with a maid service. "The managers would drop us off at clients' homes in pink cars, and we wore pink uniforms. I don't know why they bothered—no one was ever home to see us."

I nod.

"I couldn't wait to peel off those pink clothes. Talk about motivation to get an education. Not that you didn't get an education—you're a teacher, after all." She places both of her hands on my shoulders as if we were new adolescents at their first dance. Her breath smells like a fraternity basement and her eyes are full of tears. "It's just the luck of the draw. I had the luck to be born here, and you . . ."

I finish the sentence in my head. I slide my shoulders from Lynda's grasp and blot small puddles from the counter.

"What I'm trying to say is—"

I notice Jing in the doorway. Jing has heard it all. "Lynda," she sings. "My dear husband wants your expert opinion on sustainable growth."

By the time I've finished cleaning after the party, Lincoln is snoring. Jing's slippers flap toward my door, but pause, then pad downstairs. The water runs for tea and then the microwave beeps. I hope she'll drink her chamomile tea and return to Lincoln's bed.

I am under the covers, flipping through Volume Five of the Book of Life and Death. I find Anne's Polaroid snapped 10 minutes after her first breath. Then, my eyes drift to my bedside table and the framed photo of Anne in graduation cap and gown. It used to annoy me when the old folks would grab my wrist, lean close to my face, and say, "Life goes by before you know it. Be sure to enjoy it while you can."

But now, I understand. When I look at newborn Anne's face, still puffy from the journey through my body, I enter that moment like an attic room and I'm back there, full of hope and overwhelmed with love. The pain was so raw, my body was a stranger. But I had done something big.

I'm yearning for Anne and soon I'm crying. Then I hear the tap of one finger against my door. Jing. She taps my door open. Her eyes are wide and bright.

"What." Jing acts as if my face were always red and tear-stained.

"Marybelle, our luck is turning." Jing holds something behind her back. "You won't believe it. This is a sign."

"Oh?" A quick shock of electricity pulses through me; my scalp sweats.

"Why aren't you excited?" Jing asks.

"I'm just tired from the party."

"This will perk you up. Look," Jing unhooks her arm from behind her back and thrusts a rectangular packet at me.

"What is it?" I stare hard at the packet so Jing can't see my eyes quiver.

"Money. Cash. Dollars."

"Gosh, there must be hundreds," I say flatly. It's four days' worth of house-cleaning clients and three Sunday mornings on fraternity row. Exchanged for

Philippine pesos, those dollars alone would pay two years' tuition, room, and board for Anne at the University of the Philippines.

At least Jing hasn't found all of it. It's not a fortune in American terms, but enough to start a new life. Enough for my own place.

Jing is giddy. "Thousands." She spreads six other packets onto the bedspread. "I found them behind the pots and pans in the back of the pantry cupboard."

"What were you looking for?" I've lived with these people for years; I know their habits better than they do. Jing was never one to stick her hand deep in a dark cupboard.

"My red kettle, who cares?"

"Maybe it belongs to the Professor?"

"No, no, no. He invests," Jing says. She slaps one packet against her palm. "I think someone in the Italian family was saving up, secretly. Maybe the teen-age daughter was pregnant and planning to run away. Or the husband had a mistress. Perhaps it was one of the grandparents—those people from the Depression never trust banks. I bet the person died without ever revealing his secret."

"Are you going to find whose money it is?"

"Was," Jing answers. "Finders keepers. I could buy a leather couch or a widescreen HDTV or several pairs of designer shoes before my bunions get too big."

"Sure," I say weakly. I calculate in my head how many hours it will take, straightening other people's magazines and wiping their toilet seats, for me to make up my loss.

Jing gathers the envelopes and stacks them. They are as thick as a paperback book. Despite my exposure, I'm impressed with my ability to turn hard work into dollars, which turn into opportunities for my daughter. "Marybelle," Jing says to me. "Our luck is turning. This money is a sign. A good luck omen."

Jing's eyes are serious as she takes my hand and presses it between hers. "Stiletto heels? A couch made from a cow? Foolishness." Her lips are dry. "Mary-belle, this money—and any more that we find around the house—I want you to have it. It belongs to you."

"I can't take it," I say. "You should wear Jimmy Choos. If that's something you want to experience." I really mean it. I want Jing to feel stylish and beautiful for once in her life. And it's in that moment, imagining her hobbling through the hallways in Jimmy Choos, that I understand that I love her.

Jing snorts. "This is for your future. And I'll ask Lincoln to invest it so your money grows."

"If you insist. Thank you." Jing's gesture makes her feel good. And by accept-ing her gift, I allow her to feel large and good. Isn't that how life works best—when we trust give-and-take, when we're not afraid of generosity?

I hold Jing's gaze as I take the money from her. I touch my finger to the corner of my eye and feel Jing's Tiger Balm, always on my fingers, stinging.

Sometimes it feels as though Jing and I have spent a lifetime waiting for Lincoln to return from work. Afternoons, Jing lies on the couch, and I sit in a chair behind her head. As I pluck stray hairs from her chin or scratch itchy spots on her head with my thumbnail, Jing shares a thought or an observation; or sometimes she reminds me that I need to pick up tea or milk. When Jing's not depressed, she narrates the stories of her life. We're bonded in our losses, our buried hopes: for Jing, her brood of children who never materialized; for me, my Anne who knows me as well as she knows Santa Claus. We spend our days together like an old married couple.

One afternoon a few months ago, while I was kneading her feet, Jing broke the silence and said, "Marybelle, promise you won't ever leave. I don't have a child like Anne who will take care of me when I'm old."

"You and I are exactly the same age."

"I already know that I'll go before you. And when I do, include me in your book of death."

"*Oo*, yes," I said. I wanted to tell Jing that we can't predict the future, despite Lincoln's calculations, theories, and projections. The future hasn't happened yet, and there's always the possibility we might change it.

"I've seen it all in a dream. Me, slowly dying in the bed upstairs. You, feeding me meals through a straw and wiping my emaciated body down with warm washcloths."

"You make it sound so romantic. And where's your dear husband in all of this?"

"Long dead and gone. Men have shorter life spans."

We laughed nervously about it, but Jing made me promise. I crossed my fingers behind my back as if I were a schoolgirl again and said, "Yes." Later, as Jing napped on the couch, lying stiffly on her back, her hands folded across her belly, I had a guilty thought: this is how she will look.

13

A Photograph from the Permanent Collection

FRED MCGAVRAN

I did not know neurosis was contagious until I attended the photography exhibit at the art museum. It was our first special exhibition; our former director was an introvert who had spent all his time in the archives. Despite substantial bequests, the collection on display never changed. Then the new director arrived and quickly converted two storage rooms into exhibition spaces. "Photographs from the Permanent Collection" was the first.

At the opening reception, the assistant director, pretending youth in a too blue dress with unsupported bodice, poured champagne. Fresh paint tinctured the air. A gray monolith in the doorway proclaimed the title of the exhibit and asked in elegant script: "What is reality when the object has disappeared and only the image remains?" Guards tugged self-consciously on new blazers, and those of us who had pledged $1,000 or more for the renovation smiled happily at one another. Around the walls were daguerreotypes and photographs taken over a period of one hundred sixty years. I declined an audiocassette tour, preferring to explore the exhibit alone.

I began at the first photograph and was immediately disappointed. It was covered with a gray cloth. Had someone defaced it, or had the director found it inappropriate for public display? I had moved on to a brown print of a sailing ship on an iridescent sea, when a young woman in a strapless gown, wearing oversize shoes and audiocassette machine, lifted the cloth. She looked at the first

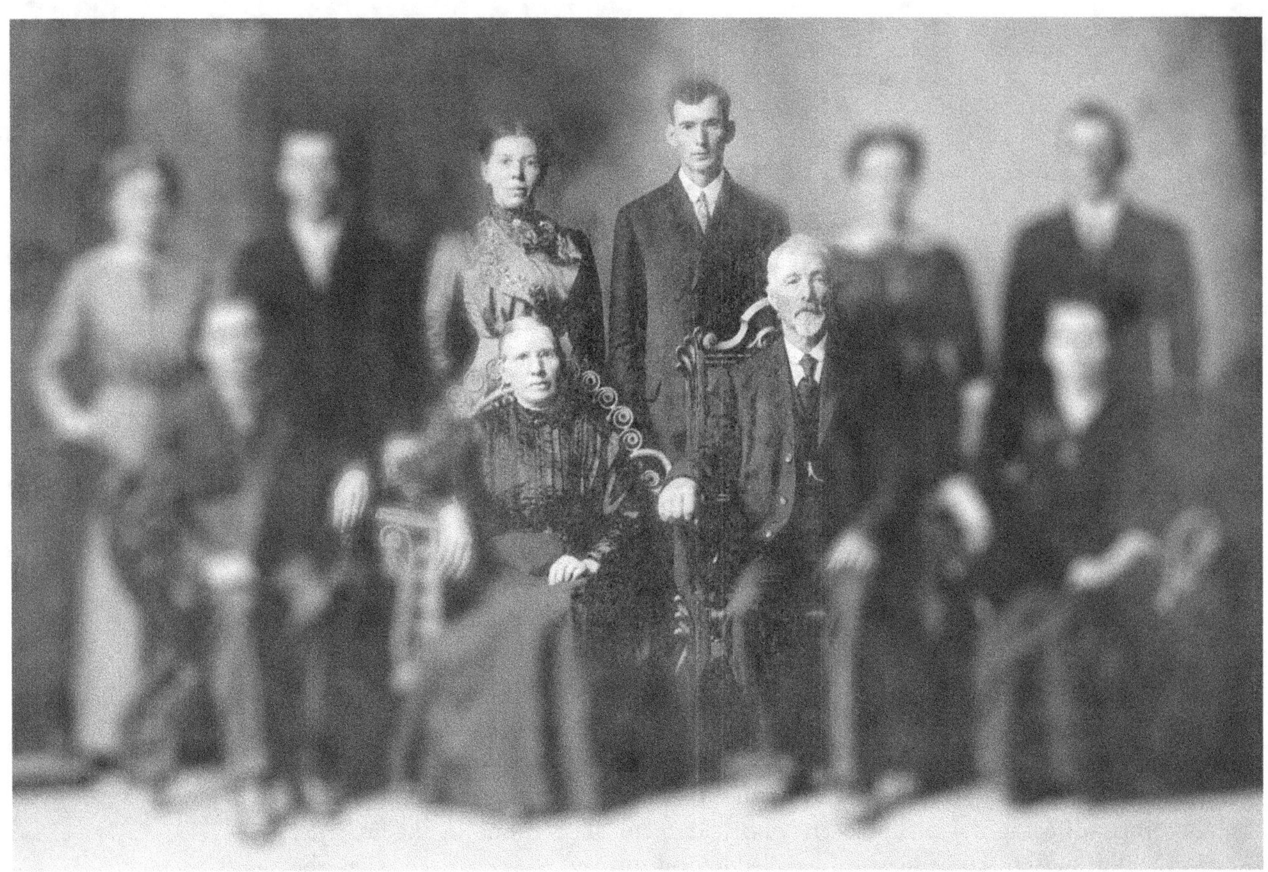

photograph and dropped the cloth to continue her audio tour. The covering was to protect the ancient print from light.

I touched the soft cloth and hesitated. Uncovering the photograph was as intimate as undressing a woman. Was there something here that should not be seen? The young woman had looked and had not been struck dumb. I raised the veil.

A woman in plaid sat next to another woman in a black high-necked dress. Behind them, facing each other, were two slightly older men in black waistcoats. A typical mid-nineteenth century pairing, except the woman in plaid was looking at the man standing behind the woman in black, and the woman in black was staring at her. The photographer had caught a moment of almost unbearable tension and suspended it for one hundred fifty years. I leaned closer. This was not a family portrait; none of the faces were enough alike. These were two couples caught in a moment of longing, discovery and guilt.

Lowering the cloth, I read the note beside the photograph. The curator wondered how the anonymous photographer had persuaded the woman in plaid to hold her head at such an angle throughout the long exposure. He did not say who the people were or why they were photographed together.

I moved on through the exhibition, a collage from before the Civil War to Life Magazine, growing sharper as the years came closer until the blacks and grays burst into vivid colors. Of all the photographs, however, the first was the most intriguing. Why were the men facing each other and why was the woman in plaid looking over her shoulder? No other photographer had caught such mystery and tension.

Clad in the latest Italian fashions and flashing his most superior smile, our new director was receiving plaudits beside the champagne. I congratulated him on his triumph and allowed his assistant to pour me another glass. More confidently I returned to the first photograph and raised the cloth again. The woman in plaid had turned her head and was staring straight at me.

I dropped the cloth so quickly that one of the guards turned her head. Stepping aside, I reread the curator's note. It was as frustrating as looking for a lost object on my desk.

"Is something the matter, Mr. Mattingly?" the guard whispered.

I started, not realizing she had come so near.

"No," I said.

She stepped away. But something was terribly wrong. The description no longer referred to the agony of the woman in plaid holding her pose. Instead the photograph was said to be a typical antebellum portrait, with the subjects' fixed stares ascribed to the long exposure.

"What do you find so fascinating about it?"

Our former director was standing beside me. I had not seen him since the board had delegated me to tell him it was time to retire.

"The subjects seem to change their positions as you look at them," I replied.

He had spent so long in the archives that he had acquired the sheen of those luminous insects one sees in caves and old bookbindings.

"So you see that, too," he said, as if relieved of some great burden, and walked away.

That night I could not sleep. Every time I closed my eyes, I saw the odd foursome. Sometimes the woman in plaid looked over her shoulder; sometimes she stared straight at me. When I opened my eyes, I saw her face floating above me, like a dark spot on the ceiling after looking away from the light. I went to the museum as soon as it opened the next day.

The guard was surprised to see that I had returned so soon.

"I wanted to try the audio tour," I explained.

It took me several moments to learn to operate the cassette. In an almost therapeutic voice, our new director thanked each sponsor by name, then directed me to the first photograph.

"Raise the cloth," he coaxed. "The anonymous photographer has caught two couples stunned between the camera and each other."

What an odd choice of words, I thought, but they had indeed returned to their original pose. Even the description on the wall was the same as when I first saw it. Exhausted, I let the director's soothing voice guide me through the rest of the exhibit. Giddy with relief, I returned home, undressed and went to bed.

I closed my eyes, and there they were again, staring back at me.

"Damn you!" I said, sitting up.

What was the matter with me? The photograph was the same as it had always been; I had just seen it. But something in me refused to believe. How could I convince some dark spot in my unconscious that the subjects of nineteenth century photographs do not change their poses? I got dressed and returned to the museum.

It is strange to sense that people are looking at you, but when you try to catch their eyes, they look away. Well, I can be deceptive, too. This time I went to the far end of the exhibit and slowly made my way back, as if intrigued by a life-size photograph of a New Orleans brothel at the turn of the last century. When I reached the covered photograph, two guards were standing beside it.

"Do you mind?" I said.

"So sorry, Mr. Mattingly," they whispered and stepped aside.

I raised the cloth and caught my breath. They were all staring straight at me, and the man behind the woman in black had his hand on a revolver.

"Mr. Mattingly, can we help?" asked one of the guards.

"No," I replied.

I hate it when they act like everyone over sixty is falling apart. I walked to the entrance like a man in a dream, who finds rooms and windows changing as he wanders through them. The drive home I don't remember. All I remember is lying down, too tired not to sleep. I awakened when the men stationed themselves before and behind me and the women on each side, like watchers around a casket.

"What did I do to you?" I screamed.

If I had not awakened, they would have told me, and I would have died.

Have you ever been so exhausted your eyes ached, and you were afraid to go to sleep? For the next seven hours, I lay sweating through the sheets, waiting for the sun to save me. Was I going mad?

There is an inner voice that can save us from our fears. As clearly as the voice on the audio tour, it told me to go to our former director.

It was a New York style apartment house fifteen stories high that had once guarded the avenue to an exclusive neighborhood. When I asked to call up to the former director on the house phone, the attendant told me had left that morning on an extended vacation.

"Did he say where?" I asked.

She handed me a brochure for Barefoot Cruises. He was going on a sailing ship to the Windward Islands and would be unreachable.

I cannot describe the agony of those next days. If I closed my eyes to sleep, the figures in the photograph would reach for me; if I did not close my eyes, the light would blind me. So I sat alone in a dark room, rocking slowly back and forth to stay awake, wondering how long until I was hopelessly insane. Then they would make me sit in a sunroom with old women in wheel chairs and feed me mashed food on a tray.

I could hear the soothing voices; I could feel the needle prick; I gasped as the pharmaceuticals surged through my veins and even tinged my breath. Like a spider stung by a wasp, I would lie paralyzed yet conscious, waiting for the eggs to hatch and the larvae to devour me.

No escape was possible, unless like Mithridates I could sip the poison slowly before swallowing the full cup. The only psychiatrist I knew was Harold Meiner, M.D., who had been on our board nearly as long as I. Once, when we were discussing the gift of a modern painting, he said something about Jungian imagery that led us not to put it on display. And he had suggested that I be the one to tell the former director to resign.

"It's the psychodynamics of the organization," he had explained.

His nurse was surprised to receive an emergency call. Dr. Meiner was a psychoanalyst.

"Doctor has had a cancellation at four," she said.

"What time is it now?" I asked and made the appointment.

His office was near the university in an old house with a large front porch. There were several back issues of Connoisseur in the magazine rack. Perhaps I was not his only patient from the museum.

Why are symbols so comforting? A tweed coat, a pipe rack, diplomas on the wall and a bald head evoke compassion and confession to a man of my generation. Dr. Meiner had all these attributes, plus a wonderful ability to listen without passing judgment or taking notes. Perhaps I was not his first patient to complain of moving images in nineteenth century photographs.

"Avoidance therapy," he finally said. "You must confront the fearsome object to overcome it."

"Impossible," I said. "Every time I see that damned thing, it gets worse!"

"You must trust me, Garrett," he replied. "We will begin with little steps."

What matter the steps, when you confront a phantasmagoria? He wrote a prescription for a sleeping pill and urged me to return the next afternoon with the catalogue from the exhibition.

"But I'll have to go to the museum for the catalogue," I said.

"Yes, you will. I recently had a patient so afraid to leave his office that his employer fired him. He was cured by travel brochures."

"How can travel brochures cure neurosis?" I wondered.

"What he feared most was sunlight and meeting new people. And do you know where he is today?"

On a cruise to the Windward Islands, I was about to say, when he answered his own question.

"On a cruise!"

It was my first night's sleep in a week, if you can call that sleep. It was as if someone had wrapped my head in black velvet, then tore it away when I awoke. The only thing that had changed was the time. My eyes still burned; my head ached; my mouth was bitter. But I had not seen their dark, unyielding eyes for nine hours. Perhaps I could force myself to return to the museum for the catalogue.

That afternoon at four, I entered Dr. Meiner's office with the catalogue in a brown paper bag, self-conscious as a man leaving a pornography store.

"Very good," he greeted me. "Now open it up and show me the picture."

"Doctor, I can't."

"Of course you can. Come on."

Half closing my eyes, I opened the catalogue. First the preface, then a section on daguerreotypes, and there it was on a page by itself: the woman in plaid looking over her shoulder at the man in the black waistcoat, who was staring at the man behind her. Who had betrayed whom? How could we judge them if we did not know?

"Show it to me, please, Garrett."

I handed him the open book.

"So this is the picture," he exclaimed, glancing at it and smiling. Then he handed it back to me. "Here. Look again. Tell me if anything is different."

I felt the agony of a patient awaiting the results of a biopsy, or a defendant watching the jurors return with the verdict. If they changed their pose this time, I would never leave this dim room sane. He would ask if I felt well enough to drive to the hospital and tell me to bring a change of clothes and pajamas.

But they were the same. The figures, the description—nothing had changed.

"For our next appointment, we'll meet at the museum and go to the exhibit together."

We never had that final appointment, so I suppose my cure is incomplete. Leaving his office, I remembered I had left the catalogue on his desk. I turned and saw him staring at the photograph with a look of such surprise and horror that my chest constricted. Then his eyes, like the eyes in the picture, focused all their anger and hatred on me. I was not mad. He had seen it, too.

"You must confront the fearsome object to overcome it," I said and walked out.

That night I slept without his pills and dreamed intermittently about a sailing ship upon a glassy sea. At our next board meeting, everyone congratulated the new director on the show. Remarkable progress in such a short time, we agreed. Only Dr. Meiner was absent.

I did not visit the exhibition again. Mass hysteria is well known; consider the Nazis or the Khmer Rouge. Mine may be the first case of a neurosis passing seriatim from one person to another. If so, it disproves Freud's thesis that neurosis arises from repression. Instead, neurosis arises from some distortion of reality that is validated by another person accepting it as his own. Thus the first victim is cured and the next infected. I find that strangely comforting. We need each other to go mad.

14

The Pull
of the Current

JOHN MORGAN WILSON

I was sitting in the special exhibition gallery on the second floor of the Met, immersed in John Singer Sargent's *Tommies Bathing*, when I became aware of a young man quietly entering to stand behind me.

I'm not easily distracted from that particular work, even by an attractive man. But I was feeling especially wistful—another way of saying lonely, I suppose—which had drawn me to the museum in the first place. On days like that, I often came here to view Sargent's famous 1918 watercolor depicting two naked soldiers sprawled drowsily on a grassy river bank, intimately close yet not quite touching. If I was lucky, I'd find the viewing bench free and the room empty, or nearly so, and the gallery churchly quiet, as a sacred place should be. Then I'd lose myself in the idyllic scene, dreaming of another time, searching for something Sargent might have hidden or I might have missed.

The stranger stood a few steps back to my left, seemingly as engrossed in the painting as I was. As I glanced back, he reminded me so strikingly of someone I once knew that it gave me a jolt. His eyes shifted briefly to meet mine. They were vividly blue, framed by dark blond lashes and handsome features that were disturbingly familiar. When I faced the canvas again, my heart raced and my mind was in a swirl.

I tried to concentrate on Sargent's work, the skillful use of gouache and graphite on white wove paper, sketchy in nature yet capable of surprising with the odd detail—the shadows of the long blades of grass, for example, caressing

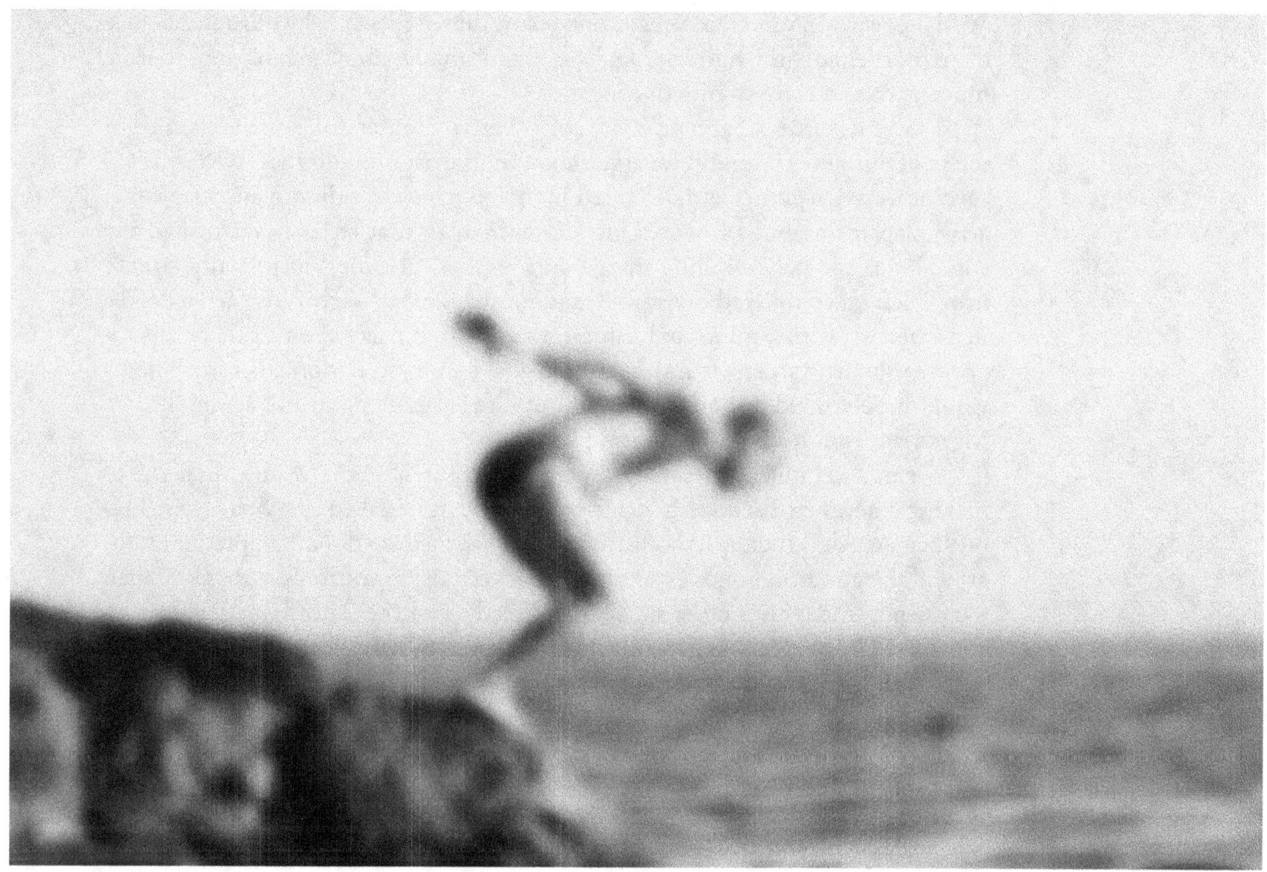

the pale bodies of the two sleeping men. But were they asleep? Or is it possible one gazed longingly at the other through half-closed lids, as my friend Victor had suggested so many decades ago?

At the time, the question had caught me off guard, causing me considerable discomfort. Victor had a way of doing that with me. Looking back, I believe he was testing me, gently prodding, to see how I might respond. Perhaps opening the door a crack, hoping I might step through, but in a way that left the choice to me. He was considerate that way, as decent and sensitive a man as I've ever known.

We were so different, Victor and I. Yet he seemed to truly like me, to tolerate my reserved and fastidious nature without reproach or bullying, to accept me as I was while encouraging me to expand my margins. Before Victor, no male had ever treated me that way. I believe it was the first time in my life that I felt genuinely happy.

———

We'd met early in our third year at university, drawn together by our mutual love of art, particularly the more naturalistic American oils and watercolors of the late nineteenth and early twentieth centuries.

I was a devotee of Sargent, Victor of Winslow Homer, the more acclaimed of the two. But never once did we argue about one artist over another. We respected each other's viewpoints and delighted in introducing the other to an exceptional artist or painting one of us had just discovered. In that respect, Victor had the edge. I was pre-law, fulfilling my parents' wishes, planning to join my father's firm when I'd completed my studies and passed the bar. Victor pursued a degree in art history, with a minor in business, hoping to one day open a gallery to support worthy new artists. It was a personal goal I admired but one that my parents would have scoffed at and forbidden, my life structured for me as rigidly as a Mondrian from his Neo-Plasticism phase.

Victor and I quickly became inseparable, caught up in the heady experience of making a new best friend. My name is Wallace but he called me Wally, which no one had ever done before. As our friendship deepened, so did our appreciation for art and the powerful bond it was forging between us. In truth, we were more than just friends, though we never spoke of it directly. Not then, nearly sixty years ago, constricted by the social rules with which we'd been raised. Victor challenged them, giving me every chance to express how I felt about him, using art as our secret language. But I didn't. I lacked the courage, you see. Victor was the brave one.

"Do you come here often?"

I started upon hearing the young man's voice near my left ear; he'd moved a step closer. His tone was deep but pleasant, reminiscent of Victor's.

Before I could reply, he said, "I don't know how I'd live without the Met. Of course, I would. One has to live, to go on, whatever one's circumstances. But my life would be awfully diminished." He laughed a little, and blushed endearingly. "That probably sounds silly, doesn't it?"

I was so stunned by his remark—Victor had expressed a similar sentiment not long after we met—that I stammered in response.

"It—it doesn't sound silly at all. I—I feel much the same way."

I ventured another glance at him. He had a lovely smile, his lips soft and full, his teeth a bit crooked but gleaming white. I was reminded painfully of Victor's mouth, almost too pretty for his otherwise masculine face, with those inviting lips I'd so often longed to press against my own, but never dared to.

I asked the young man if he had a favorite painter, which allowed me to study him less discreetly. He cocked his blond head, looking thoughtful.

"It's impossible to pick just one, don't you think? I mean, it's not a beauty competition, is it?"

"I suppose not."

I must have sounded stung because he added quickly, "But if I had to, I suppose it would be Homer. I love the boldness and virility, the wildness he captures. Especially the dramatic scenes at sea. There's an unadorned truth to them, don't you think?"

Homer, of course, had also been Victor's favorite. It felt unreal, hearing the young man make the same declaration. My head was spinning again and I was feeling faint.

"But I appreciate Sargent's work nearly as much," he added, turning his eyes back to the painting before us. "A different sensibility, but brilliant nonetheless."

Even his manner—earnest, confident, straightforward—reminded me of Victor. The resemblance was so extreme that I became seriously unsettled. Facing forward, I resolved to ignore him if he attempted to speak to me again. If necessary, I would remind him that the galleries were meant to be hushed spaces where one could commune privately with a work of art, and not be bothered by strangers.

Despite his hovering presence, I was able to slip back into the dreamlike world Sargent had created. *Tommies Bathing* was special, you see, because Victor and I had often sunbathed by the water, just the two of us. We'd take off from school to find a secluded beach, where we'd lay side by side, reading or discussing art. For us, it was usually the ocean; yet Sargent's river setting still spoke to us in a personal way. Although Victor was the more developed and athletic, I was the stronger swimmer, taking laps regularly in the university pool to stay fit; I'd even had some lifeguard training. After some innocent splashing with Victor in the shallows, I'd go for a long swim in deeper water while he stayed behind, exerting himself with pushups and sprints to maintain his fine physique. From a distance, I'd see him dashing along the shore on his muscular legs, like a golden god glistening in the sunlight. Then he'd stand at water's edge, looking out to sea, awaiting my safe return. How joyous I felt seeing him there, so loyal and protective! We'd race back and flop together on our towels, exhausted but exhilarated, basking in the sun's warmth and the security of each other's company.

No pressures, no troubles, no one else to disturb us. Just Victor and me.

He was the first to mention how the figures in *Tommies Bathing* could have been the two of us. My response was typically prim and evasive.

"Except, of course, that they have no swimsuits on," I pointed out, not quite meeting his eyes. "And they're resting by a river, not the ocean."

"But isn't obliqueness one of Sargent's trademarks?" Victor asked. "The opaqueness with which he uses his watercolors, the sketchy style?"

"I'm not sure I follow."

"Nothing's quite distinct, is it? Not the water, not even the faces on the figures. Perhaps that's what Sargent intended, for the viewer to bring something of himself to the painting, to lend his own interpretation to the work."

Victor chucked me playfully on the arm.

"Use your imagination, Wally! Who knows what you might discover?"

From that moment on, despite my timidity, Tommies Bathing became my favorite of all the Sargent watercolors. Victor was right—it might very well have been us lying there together, unknowingly captured by a voyeuristic painter. Victor most resembled the sturdier soldier, the one on the right, stretched out on his side, facing his companion. I was closer in build to the slim figure on the left, lying on my back, eyes upward. Once Victor planted the notion in my mind, it wasn't difficult for me to transpose our souls into those two British Tommy Boys, taking a respite from the horrors of war, or perhaps just the rigors of life. With reluctance, I even acknowledged—only to myself, of course—the obvious sensuality between them. In time, I realized Victor had changed the way I saw the painting, the way I experienced it. He had opened my heart to it, my feelings and sensations. I never again viewed an artwork with quite the same detachment as before.

Still, with Victor, I held back, unable to break free of my self-imposed constraints. Fighting the current, if you will, afraid of where it might sweep me.

One afternoon, toward the end of our third year, we were leafing through an illustrated book on iconic American painters that Victor had discovered in a secondhand shop near campus.

The day was warm, humid. We were both wearing shorts, sitting side by side on the unmade bed in Victor's rented room. The big book was spread like a bridge across our laps. Sunlight dappled and enhanced Victor's golden beauty. As he turned a page, we came upon a reproduction of *Tommies Bathing*. We studied it in silence, mutually absorbed, though I sensed a strange tension in the air, like the moment of stillness before birds take sudden flight from a quiet wood.

Victor shifted on the bed, pressing himself so close that the hairs on our legs mingled damply. Touching him like that was electrifying, but also unbearably frightening.

"What if the two soldiers are spent," Victor asked, studying the watercolor, "not from swimming, but from making love?"

He turned to me with unusual directness, forcing me to meet his eyes.

"Is that what Sargent intended us to see, Wally?"

I sat there petrified. Seconds passed that felt like minutes. Finally, Victor closed the book and set it aside. As he turned back to me, he placed his hand on my bare knee. I jumped at the contact, feeling flushed, prickly with heat. His eyes were on mine again. I looked away, stricken. He leaned close, brushing the nape of my neck with his lips, before whispering in my ear.

"I love you, Wally."

I froze, barely able to breathe. Panic scrambled my feelings. We were alone but there was a window in the room and I was certain that a thousand pairs of eyes were watching us. Judgment crushed me with the weight of centuries. Terrified, I bounded from the bed and fled.

I didn't see or speak to Victor for a week. When I finally worked up the courage to face him, something had changed between us. He was still kind to me, even affectionate. The incident in his room was never mentioned. But I perceived a distance now, as if he'd given me a final test, one last chance, and I'd failed.

"Are you as fond of the other *Tommies Bathing*?"

In the gallery, the young man's voice encroached again. I tried to muster up some irritation, to offer a rebuke, but I couldn't. He sounded so sincere and sociable. Barely more than a boy, I thought, also alone in this cavernous museum, without a girlfriend in tow, or a special male friend. It occurred to me that he might be lonely too, needing someone to talk to. It couldn't hurt, I told myself, to be polite.

I glanced up to find him even closer than before, nearly at my shoulder. His inquisitive eyes darted to the painting on our right, the one some refer to as *Tommies Bathing 2*, a companion piece to the first one and also painted in 1918. Three soldiers in this one, one wading into the water, the other two remaining on the river bank. I studied it a moment, as I had so many times before, however reluctantly.

"I'm afraid the second *Tommies Bathing* has never quite captured my fancy."

"There's something disquieting in it, isn't there?" the young man asked. "The tranquility of the first painting is gone. The third soldier seems like an intruder. He's upset the balance of things."

"That's very astute," I said, and stole another glance. Who was I kidding? He was Victor reincarnate. And his analysis of the second painting—it was beyond uncanny. I didn't know what was happening to me. I was afraid I was losing my mind.

There was another man, you see, a third, who came into the picture during our senior year.

I'd begun dating a girl my mother had introduced me to, going out with her once or twice a week, almost as an obligation. She was pretty, intelligent, and quite nice—definitely marriage material, my father routinely pointed out, more sternly each time. We'd kissed and fooled around a bit, though we hadn't gone all the way, as fornication was referred to in those days. I experienced a kind of relief having her around, but also guilt, feeling like a fraud for using her that way. I never invited her to the beach. I still reserved those special times for Victor and me, even though much of the old magic was gone.

Then, one day, as we lay on our towels studying our textbooks, Christopher appeared. Victor had invited him without asking me. He was a good-looking man, slim and dark-haired, with a hint of the Mediterranean in his olive coloring. He kept his hair rather long for the time, which gave him a pretty look, and wore bathing trunks so skimpy and tight they clearly marked him as a fairy. I was mortified, and thankful the three of us were alone on that stretch of the beach, but Victor seemed unfazed by it. Christopher was an art student, Victor said, as he introduced us, shifting on his towel to make room for our visitor, though there was hardly space on it for two. Not just any art student, Victor added, but one with great promise.

That spring, Christopher became a regular on our outings to the beach. For Victor's sake, I tried to be friendly, but it wasn't easy. As the days passed, and graduation grew near, with so many decisions to be made, I became increasingly confused about what to do, which direction to take, how to live my life. Victor, on the other hand, seemed to grow more relaxed and sure of himself, especially in Christopher's company.

One afternoon, only weeks away from graduation, I went for a swim while Victor and Christopher stayed behind on Victor's towel to study for exams. I intended a long, strenuous workout, out and around the point and back, hoping to expend some of the tension coiled up inside me. But halfway out, I encountered a powerful undertow and realized how dangerous it was, even for a strong swimmer like me. I didn't panic and try to stroke against it. Instead, I began swimming parallel to the shore, as I'd been trained. The riptide was wide and it took several arduous minutes, but I was finally free of it, catching my breath as I made my way back up the sand.

That was when I saw Victor and Christopher kissing.

The sight of it staggered me. I'd never seen two men kiss; it simply wasn't done in those days, not in public. But it wasn't just prudishness that caused me such distress. It was the acute realization of what I'd lost, of what my cowardice had cost me.

They looked up as I approached, abandoning the kiss. But they left their limbs entangled, without the slightest shame. My eyes locked on Victor's but neither of us spoke. He clearly felt he had no reason to explain or apologize. How I envied him and wanted him and despised him at that moment, all at once.

Christopher broke the silence.

"How's the water?"

I shrugged, attempting nonchalance. "Refreshing, as always."

Victor suggested to Christopher that they go for a swim.

"So we can cool off?" Christopher asked, grinning slyly.

They laughed, turning it into a lurid joke. It was like a knife through my heart.

"You go," Christopher said. "I need to finish this chapter. You've wanted to take a dip ever since we got here."

"Just a quick one," Victor said. "Out beyond the waves and back."

He scrambled to his feet and dashed for the water. Christopher picked up his textbook and resumed reading. I watched Victor dive in, right where the undertow was strongest. Most people don't notice an outward current rippling the water, unless they've been taught to look for it. As with so many things, it's what's beneath the surface that's so treacherous.

Victor had no trouble at first. Not until he realized the errant tide was taking him out, faster and farther than he'd intended. A minute passed, then another. I watched his stroke weaken as he fought the ocean's relentless tug. Out he went, becoming smaller and smaller in the rough water, until I saw his head bobbing beyond the most distant waves, then his arms flailing as desperation set in.

"I don't see Victor."

Christopher spoke as he rose from his towel, his book tossed aside. He shaded his eyes with a slender hand, scanning the wide bay.

"I believe he's in trouble," I said, and pointed. "There, just beyond the biggest breakers."

"We have to do something." Christopher turned to me, wide-eyed. "We have to help him."

I felt paralyzed by a chaos of emotions, so unaccustomed to trusting my feelings I wasn't sure what they were anymore, or how to act on them. I was totally lost at that moment, floundering helplessly in my own way as Victor was in his.

Christopher stared at me with alarm, knowing I was the more able swimmer. When I made no move, he turned and raced for the water, screaming Victor's name, pleading with him to hold on. I watched him leap in and thrash about with frantic, awkward strokes, until the ocean took him too. Farther out, Victor disappeared among the whitecaps. I remained where I was, my arms folded across my chest like a shield, feeling a strange calm come over me, but also cold and empty inside.

Hours later, Christopher's body washed up on the shore, a half mile south. Unlike the rescued woman in Homer's *Undertow*, Victor was never found.

―――――――

Sitting in the gallery, it occurred to me that I might ask the young man to join me on the bench, where he might be more comfortable. Perhaps he came here seeking solace, I thought, and we might find some common ground. We could even go for a coffee afterward, if he didn't find my invitation too ridiculous, given the great difference in our ages. If nothing else, I thought, I might make a new friend. But when I turned to speak to him, he was gone. Just like that, without a sound, as if he'd never been there at all.

Probably for the best, I realized. I'd become gravely tired; my sight was fading and my limbs felt tremulously weak. It was late; the gallery would be closing shortly. But I wasn't ready to go, not just yet. I turned my faltering eyes to the first *Tommies Bathing*.

I tried to see it the way Victor might have. What would have happened, I wondered, if one of the drowsing soldiers had reached out, placed his hand on the other's sun-warmed flesh, and left it there? How would the other man have responded? How might their relationship have changed? How might their lives have turned out differently?

My eyelids fluttered as I shifted my attention back to *Tommies Bathing 2*. It seemed more inviting now, less intimidating. A river, an ocean, what did it matter? Wasn't Sargent's painting only vaguely defined, and full of possibilities?

In the quiet of the gallery, I surrendered to his vision, until I was there at the water's edge, among the three companions given eternal youth by the brush-strokes of a gifted artist. Except for the images within the frame, everything around me grew hazy and dim. A great lassitude overcame me, but I wasn't afraid anymore.

Deeper and deeper the painting drew me in, until finally I plunged into the turbulent water and felt the pull of the current, taking me to Victor.

15

The Intra-Galactic
Shakespeare Festival

K E Y A N   B O W E S

The Globe Holo-theater rings with the immemorial words: *"Once more unto the breach, dear friends, once more!"*

King Henry swings his massive tail majestically. With a huge roar, his troops rally to him. The theater is full of battling soldiers as the French defend the wall. Screams, shouts, and squeaks punctuate the clashing of steel. Tentacles are sliced off, tails crushed, heads roll. Purple gore sprays the audience.

"Syndoans," someone in the audience explains to someone else, "They're using Syndoans for all the martial roles. Their limbs regenerate overnight."

Brinna is worried. Her partner, Redmond Rallis of Redmond's Shakespearean Troupe, exudes tension like static as he glares at the ten-foot holo-screen of the Virtual Mermaid Holo-tavern. The screen shows the opening play of the Intragalactic Shakespeare Festival: *Henry V*, from the rival Cranmer Company.

Around him, the timbers of the Virtual Mermaid Holo-tavern resound with the happy shouts of roisterers. Rough wooden tables crowd the room, which is lit only by lanterns, and smells of smoke and ale. Spot-lit over the actual bar hangs a gigantic mermaid with a fish's head and a woman's leather-clad body astride a bicycle. Mistress Mary, dressed in the full skirts and white apron of an Elizabethan taverner, dispenses ale to some of the galaxy's most enthusiastic Shakespeareans.

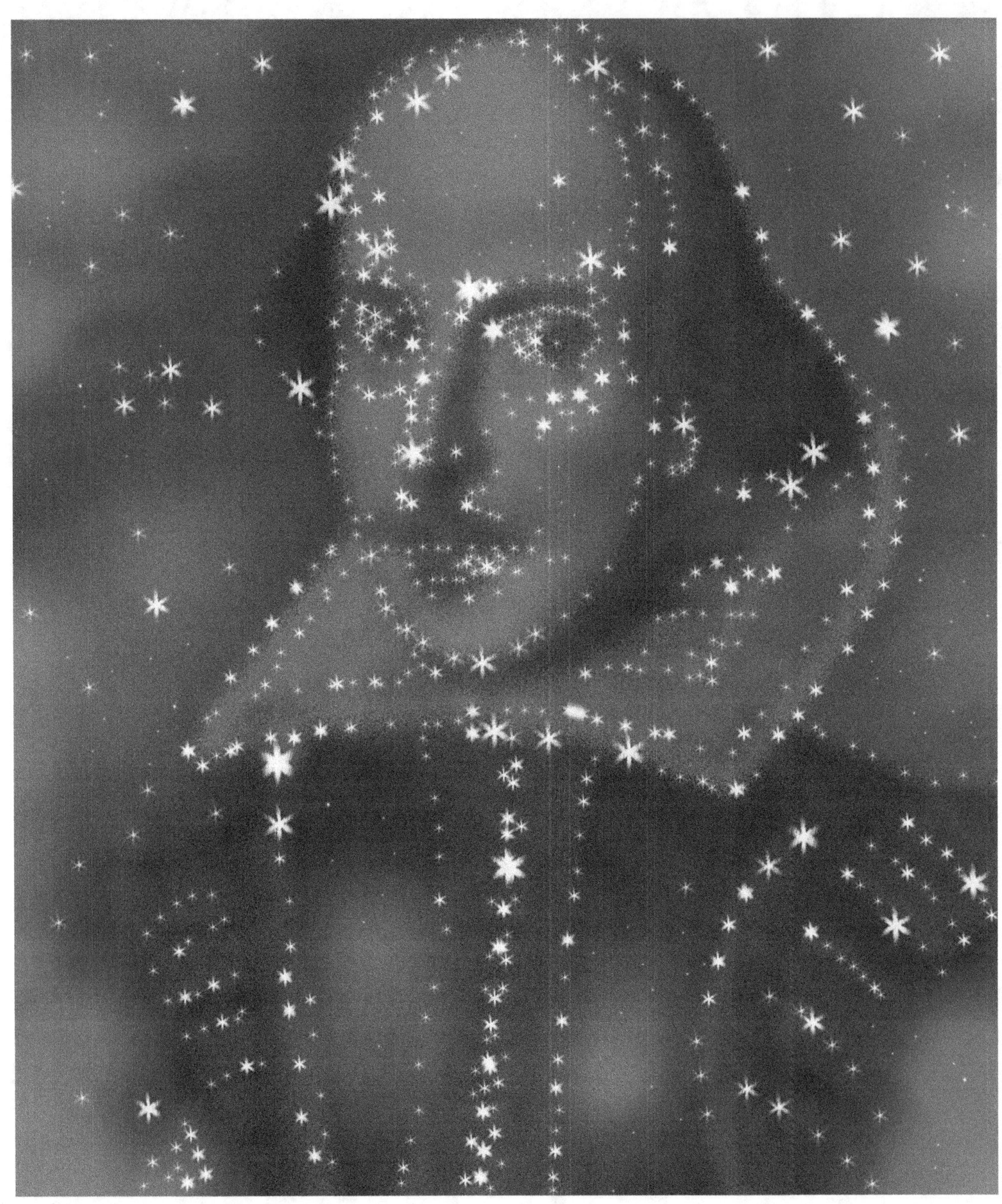

Redmond is oblivious to everything but the holoscreen. "Using Syndoans is not True to the Spirit of the Bard!"

Brinna, manager and auditor of the troupe, runs slender fingers through her long dark hair, beginning to look like a disheveled madonna. "It's a Festival play, Red," she says gently. "They must have cleared the Syndoans. Why risk disqualification?" She takes a sip of ale, sets her tankard on the ring-scarred table.

"Maybe." Redmond's hazel eyes narrow. "How would Cranmer get so many Syndoan actors? Theatre's not a big art on Syndoe. They must have cyberplayers mixed in with the real ones!"

Brinna wishes he wouldn't get so upset. It no longer matters anyway. They're out of the Festival.

"Leave it," she advises, "I doubt they've got cyberplayers. Cranmer orbits too close to the sun sometimes, but even he wouldn't risk cybers in a Festival play."

Redmond draws his vidphone. "I'll call them on it if you won't."

Brinna sighs. "Oh, give here, Red. I know their auditor." Placing the unfolded vidphone on the table where Redmond can see the screen, she dials her counterpart and asks her question.

"Warriors," the Cranmer auditor says, waving his pseudopodia for emphasis, "They're Syndoan warriors, holding their ceremonial tribal battles in the holo-studio. They're under contract to pause for the speech and observe the timing. Each clash is a fresh bout."

"Isn't that a violation of Truth?" demands Redmond. "Tribal warfare instead of a stage battle?"

Edwin Cranmer appears on the vid-screen, pushing his auditor aside. His slick white-blonde hair almost disappears against his white skin. "*Henry V* is exactly about tribal warfare. It's a territorial battle between the English and French." His smile is full of teeth. "Too bad about your Festival attempt, Rallis. You don't have the right to Challenge us, do you? Since you're not in the Festival? Even if it was our Challenge Week, which it's not?" He leers at Brinna. "When you're fed up with that failure, come over to us."

Brinna quickly disconnects. "What a tail-pipe that man is."

"His play's in the Festival's top three," says Redmond bitterly.

Redmond's gone off somewhere, leaving his ale on the table. Onscreen, King Henry courts a rotund, giggly Katharine with clumsy gallantry. Unable to stop watching, Brinna examines the production with an expert's eye.

Katharine bounces away in mock horror as Henry essays a kiss, then rebounds off a throne into him as he declares, *O Kate, nice customs curtsy to great kings.* The production engineers must have manipulated the virtual mass controls. That was about all they could play with in a live performance.

Ever since holo-tech enabled people to interact through personas beamed into a holo-space, "live" became difficult to define. Now the Actor's Guild regulates what's legally a Live performance. Brinna knows the rules down to last subclause and exception. But so what? Her troupe hasn't qualified for the Festival, the cycle of plays held twice every decade, culminating in the William Shakespeare Award (known as the Billy).

Meanwhile, Cranmer, Redmond's old rival in love and theater from their Academy days, is doing brilliantly. Redmond's much more talented, but ill luck's haunted him like some disastrous comet returning every five years. They've just missed their chance, again. The third time.

"Well, Cranmer was right," Redmond says, returning from wherever he'd been. "Perhaps you should have gone with him."

Brinna shudders. "Cranmer!" She drinks her ale as though washing a bad taste from her mouth. Redmond sits down opposite her, putting his mug down too hard.

"We're out of credit, Brin." He takes a gulp of ale. "If you're headed for the Festival, everyone loves you. Credits are as thin as space dust in this economy. We have to disband."

Brinna stares at him in shock.

"The others just talked to me," he says. "They can't take any more delayed wages. Everyone but Sapan's found other gigs."

Brinna's stomach hurts. Their troupe, the troupe they started as young dreamers and kept afloat through the years and bad times, has finally run out of funds and luck.

They stare glumly at the holoscreen as Cranmer's play ends to loud applause.

———

From the dimly-lit bar of the Mermaid a rousing chorus of *Hathaway was a Termagant* announces the arrival of a bunch of the regular patrons. Brinna toys with her drink, not in a boisterous mood.

"Brinna! Redmond!" calls someone. She looks around to see a slim blond figure waving his comm-pad, searching for them in the gloom. Assistant Director Sapan is a recent Academy graduate, as young as Brinna was when she and Redmond started the troupe. He picks his way around the bar-crowd, which is bellowing the chorus, "*Hathaway was a termagant, Old Shakespeare was a nut, he wrote a play 'most every day or she would kick . . .*"

"We're in!" Sapan shouts, his trained voice carrying easily above the noise. "Piffex's *Richard III* was disqualified."

"Piffex?" exclaims Brinna, "But they were the favorite to win!"

"They broke the rules. Their Prince Edward was a simulation and Cranmer's auditor caught it. They're out, we're in! We drew *The Merchant of Venice*."

They're in! So small, so unknown, so late in the season—and yet, here they are, in the IntraGalactic Shakespeare Festival.

"Yes!" Redmond shouts and jumps on the table in an impromptu war-dance. Someone turns the spotlight on him. His lanky figure, hair and beard flying, throws animated shadows on the walls behind. He flings his glass at the view-screen that had, only minutes earlier, displayed Cranmer's *Henry V.* It bounces harmlessly off and drenches patrons with its contents. Sapan and Brinna yell the news to everyone. The crowd from the bar cheers and showers the Redmond Troupe with ale.

As they leave the tavern amid ribald shouts of encouragement, Mistress Mary pulls Brinna aside. "You're headed into an asteroid shoal," she warns. "Don't forget what happened to Piffex."

————

Redmond looks so dejected that Brinna's heartsick. His hair and beard are uncharacteristically neat, the curls tamped down to waves, but his eyes look exhausted. He's been on the vidphone all day, holed up in the private room Mistress Mary kindly provided. "That was the last call on my list," he says. "We're too late. All the sponsors have committed their funds elsewhere. We're done."

Brinna swallows, unable to speak. They've worked so many miracles over the years, but there are no miracles left.

"Someone has got to have money," says Redmond.

"Yeah," says Sapan. "Troupe Cranmer." It has recently augmented its considerable wealth with the whistle-blower bounty for Piffex—half the disgraced troupe's confiscated assets.

Brinna pauses. "Troupe Cranmer!"

"You wouldn't!" Redmond says. "Ed Cranmer's not funding us to stage a competing Festival play. Anyway, he hates us."

"Wait here for me," says Brinna, disappearing into the holobeam. There's a way.

An hour later she's back, waving a credit certificate signed by Cranmer. "Here. Twenty thousand. Enough to start."

Redmond takes it. "Why did Cranmer do it?" he demands fiercely. "What did you promise him? A pound of flesh?"

"A personal bond," Brinna says, stomach knotting. "If we don't repay by the end of the Festival, I'm bonded to his Company for fifteen years."

"Fifteen years!" says Sapan.

"Bonded? You can't do that!" shouts Redmond. "Give it back! We'll withdraw from the Festival."

"Brinna, it's too much risk," says Sapan. "What if something goes wrong?"

"He just did it to humiliate me," says Brinna. "Look, I'm useless to him. They already have an Auditor, and Ed Cranmer micro-manages everything. He probably wants to see us struggle on their handout while they roll in with a golden war chest."

"Oh really?" yells Redmond. "He's always been after you!"

"We'll be fine, Red," says Brinna. "No Festival play ever netted under forty thousand. We can't lose. We just have to stretch the twenty and put on a play. We don't have much time. Let's get on with it."

Under her breath she adds, "Anyway, the thing is already signed."

———

The decrepit rental holo-studio, all they can afford, contrasts starkly with Cranmer's new custom-build. At least the studio has its own staff: a mostly Frl crew, under a Terran Chief. He's an older man, ginger hair and mustache touched with white, and an air of competence. He's run the holo-studio for thirty years, though his experience runs more to low-budget advertising pieces than to a full-on Festival play.

"Thirty years? Can holo-studios even run that long?" Sapan whispers to Brinna.

"Cross your fingers for thirty-one," she says.

———

Redmond would not have chosen the *Merchant of Venice*. Leftovers, he grumbles. Most troupes go for the big, spectacular plays, where they can stage impressive crowd scenes or display magnificent settings.

Those are gone: *Henry V* with its battle-fields to Cranmer, *Midsummer Night's Dream* with its magical woods to Aslow, *Julius Caesar* to Loidll. *The Tempest* with its shipwreck, Hamlet with its castle and ghosts, *Macbeth* with its moving wood and weird sisters, all gone. Others are playing princes and queens, sages and warriors. Troupe Redmond are left with *The Merchant*—and the moneylender.

"Perfect," says Sapan with satisfaction. "We're a small troupe. We'll play it small, intimate, intense."

———

Redmond casts himself as Shylock. Sapan's to play Portia and direct the play. For other roles, they'll need outsiders. The casting call across the galaxy draws dozens of responses.

"But they're all unknowns," laments Redmond. The big names like Minotaur or Qahon or Celia James were all signed months ago.

"We couldn't afford stars anyway," Sapan says.

Now it's up to Brinna to ensure the play remains Authentic, Live, and True to the Spirit as the regulations require. Piffex's terrible fate—and her unspeakable personal risk—settle into permanent tension in the pit of her stomach as she waits in the play-space for the actors' personas to beam in from around the galaxy.

A bell chimes, a blue light flashes. The first arrival wants to read for Antonio. Earth-human, handsome as a cyberplayer, he looks the part. The play needs a sympathetic and noble Antonio for the great courtroom battle. Brinna winces at a memory of a performance she once saw, where the audience shouted for Portia to go away and let Shylock get on with his dinner (of Antonio).

"In sooth!" declaims the actor, "I know not why I am so sad!"

His delivery is a loud rant. Sapan shudders, and calls for the next player.

———

Brinna's extremely wary. Deceitful actors can present simulations instead of their real selves; or use recordings instead of appearing real-time; or use emotion enhancers or mind benders to augment their performances. All these break the "authentic" requirement, and would disqualify the play from the festival. Like Piffex's *Richard III*.

The rules on Live performance are more flexible. Many people who acted together have different biologies: They needed different atmospheres, or different pressure or temperature conditions, or different gravities.

The holo-beam neutralized the differences. From holo-studios on remote planets, actors could beam their personas to a holo-theater across the galaxy, and interact with colleagues from other worlds. Virtual mass allowed them to touch, to leave footprints, or to fall with a convincing thud. The Guild allowed adjustments to virtual mass: that permitted high-grav people to work with actors from low-grav worlds. It allowed the timer switches that compensated for the holo-beam's travel-time. Other than that, the holo-beam had to be pretty much untouched to qualify as "live."

It's Brinna's job to ensure they stay within the bounds.

If all goes well, their own Live performance in this rickety holo-studio will beam into the celebrated Globe Holo-theater, before an eminent holo-present audience, for the renowned Festival. All over the Galaxy, holo-screens would be tuned eagerly to Globe.

———

A beautiful Terran reads for Jessica, Shylock's daughter. Her dark hair shines about her shoulders. Her perfect complexion suggests a climate-controlled colony world. Her voice, low and supple, is perfectly pitched to the audience.

"Yes!" says Sapan.

Yes, such a Jessica would justify Lorenzo's passion and the frenzied reaction of a betrayed father who had huge hopes for his only child. But Brinna pauses. "Uh," she says, "We'll get back to you."

"Soon, I hope," the actress says as she leaves.

"What did you do that for?" asks Sapan plaintively. "She was wonderful!"

"A little too perfect," says Brinna. "Did she use enhancers? Let me scan the recording."

She plays back the holo-cam and runs a quick diagnostic. No abnormalities.

"See? You over-reacted!" says Sapan. "Can I call her?""

"Give me time. This evening, okay?" Mary's warning at the Tavern has made Brinna edgy. She runs more and more sophisticated programs testing for increasingly esoteric violations, each taking longer, and each coming out negative.

"Well?" asks Sapan impatiently as hours pass. "Can we call her back?"

Finally, Brinna writes a customized program. As it runs, she's coming up in goosebumps. "She's not real," Brinna tells her partners, "She's completely cyber, not even based on a human palimpsest. No wonder she looked like a cliché."

"The cyber-bitch!" exclaims Redmond.

"She was perfect," says Sapan sadly. Then he brightens. "Anyway, she'd have upstaged my Portia. Who do you think sent her?"

Brinna can guess. What's missing, what she needs, is evidence.

––––––––

The next candidate for Antonio is a Tral, quadruped, large and heavy by Earth-normal standards. But as he moves deliberately to stage centre, the bulk seems to melt away in the ease and grace of his movements.

"In sooth, I know not why I am so sad

It wearies me, you say it wearies you . . ."

The tone's humorous, self-deprecating, but the underlying seriousness fore-shadows the grave threat he would face. Sapan looks over eagerly at Brinna, who carefully scrutinizes the actor, then nods. But she makes a tape, just in case.

The cachet of the Festival attracts high-caliber players, even if they're not yet stars—and also the fakers. The team casts most of the roles, including Jessica. Brinna sends away three more inauthentic actors using prohibited techniques at their auditions.

––––––––

Bassanio, though, remains elusive. The role of Antonio's protégé and Portia's love is pivotal but tricky. The actor has to play a cad who's borrowing from a loan-shark on a friend's bond with the objective of marrying money—and he has to make the character likeable, even loveable.

Then Greth from Plawan appears in the audition hall, his hooves clicking on the floor. He smiles up at them, confident of his welcome but coming as a supplicant, and addresses himself to Mreyaj the Tral. Antonio.

"Tis not unknown to you, Antonio, how much I have disabled mine estate." Greth looks down with endearing embarrassment as he delivers the next few lines, then raises his elegant head courageously.

"To you, Antonio, I owe the most, in money and in love,
And from your love I have a warranty,
To unburden all my plots and purposes,
How to get clear of all the debts I owe."

"I pray you, good Bassanio, let me know it," says Mreyaj, joining him in the stage-space and wrapping his trunk indulgently round his protégé's withers.

Sapan and Redmond turn as one to Brinna. She nods.

————

One week into rehearsals, Lorenzo quits. He can't evince any emotion for Jessica, and doesn't see why he has to.

"How did that happen?" says Sapan, "I thought I cast them right."

"Jessica's not in season any more," says Brinna. "Lorenzo's no longer attracted to her."

"That Frl calls himself an actor?" says Redmond, "Why can't Texl act attracted?"

"Frl males change color when they're interested. It's obscene for Texl to mimic attraction when he's the wrong color."

Redmond swears. "Why didn't you say anything before?"

"One of the Frl engineers just told me," says Brinna.

The replacement, also Frl, runs through the "Moon shines bright" interchange with Jessica with a convincing display of adoration. Sapan turns to Brinna questioningly.

"Clean. No problems."

"No color change issues?"

"No," says Brinna, with amusement.

"Why no?" asks Sapan.

"She's female. They don't change color."

————

Brinna tunes their holo-screen to the Globe. Several Festival productions are now playing. Cranmer's *Henry V* remains popular, eclipsing Maryknoll's pastoral *As You Like It*, and even Nakasone's dark atmospheric *Hamlet* that stars the great Minotaur. With Piffex's *Richard III* out of the way, *Henry's* the front runner.

Eventually, despite the tight schedule, despite technical problems for the Chief, despite the squabbles between Redmond and Sapan, they progress to dress rehearsals. Sapan keeps the costumes simple; floor-length capes in rich colors. People with nudity taboos wear black bodysuits. Others wear nothing else.

This starts their Challenge Week. Any other troupe can watch their performances, and if they see a broken rule, challenge them. Everyone's curious. Unlike the other plays, Redmond's *Merchant* is an unknown quantity. They all have spare time: Challenge Week for the other plays is long since over. The rival auditors circle around the latecomer.

———

"Maryknoll made five complaints," Brinna reports in the Virtual Mermaid at the end of the day, "and Nakasone made three, all so flimsy that their auditor couldn't raise her crest!"

"Good," says Redmond. "One day done, five to go." Even as he speaks, the vidphone chimes. Brinna opens the connection. It's Loidll's auditor, tentacles folded to indicate a formal Challenge.

"Untrue to the Spirit of the Bard, casting an earth-male as Portia."

"What?" Brinna exclaims, barely suppressing her amusement.

"Violates the traditional gender dichotomy of Earth."

"Males played female roles in Shakespeare's era," said Brinna. "Check your facts."

———

Challenge Week is nearly over. Brinna's relaxed as she heads to the Studio's shabby lounge for a morning coffee. The objections have been getting weaker. The last few were insubstantial as space dust. Suddenly, she stops dead. It's been too easy. Where were the asteroid-shoals? Could be their play's coming in below the radar, but the explanation is probably more sinister.

What would I do, ponders Brinna, if I wanted to kill a troupe? Piffex had cast a simulation unawares, despite all their experience. But none of our actors are sims . . . She'd taped each one and run the detailed diagnos . . .wait a minute!

I'd switch them. I'd suborn an actor in a minor but crucial role. Or plant an actor. Then I'd build a very careful sim, and substitute it—just before Challenge week ended.

———

The previews impress the critics.

"You find yourself inside the scene," writes the reviewer from TheGreenRoom in a posting entitled Merchant/Spoiler, "eavesdropping on a conversation at the next table. Director Sapan has woven an intimate and moving story.

"A brilliant jewel of a play. You've cheered for Henry. You've seen Birnam Wood march. You've seen the ghosts and the witches and the fairies. Now, leave your swords at home and come and meet the Merchant."

———

Whoever chose the Prince of Morocco for the planted simulation was a genius. The actor would definitely get the part—he was dazzling in the role. A Flamer, he moved across the stage emitting flashes of light like a star. He was utterly convincing when he said "Mislike me not for my complexion, the shadowed livery of the burnished sun, to whom I am a neighbor and near bred." It also made substitution very easy; most people could not look at him very closely.

"But why would they?" asks Sapan, when Brinna breaks the news of the sabotage, probably by Cranmer. "They're the frontrunners, we're no threat. We don't have assets for a whistle-blower bounty. And we'd default on the loan."

"Ancient grudge," says Redmond darkly. "He'd love to lay hands on Brinna."

"Maybe the good preview notices needled him," says Brinna, trying not to remember Cranmer's lecherous smile. "But we can't prove he did it."

"The Morocco sim can't stay, can he?" asks Sapan.

"No. And the members of a company are locked in by Challenge Week. You can dismiss, but you can't hire. Can you switch someone over or double up? Morocco's a small role."

Sapan thinks about it. "Arragon could double if he wasn't so visible, with those tentacles and the two heads. Maybe Gratiano . . . no, possibly Nerissa?" But no. No one was right for Morocco. "Brinna, you're in the company," says Sapan, "It'll have to be you."

"Me?" says Brinna, "I last had a toddle-on role as the Indian prince in *Midsummer*."

But they're only days away from Opening. She thanks the stars it's a short role.

The Week finally ends with no more challenges. The saboteur who planted the simulated Flamer must have been shocked when Brinna appeared as Morocco instead. All she has to fear now is stage fright.

That's when random technical glitches start to occur.

"Mislike me not," Brinna begins, moving to stage center. Unexpectedly, Mreyaj is standing right there in her way. A millisecond earlier and she'd have been crushed by the large Tral, who isn't even in that scene.

"Stop!" shouts Redmond. He storms out. "Where are the engineers?"

The Chief storms in. "Who's messing with the timer switches?" he shouts, "I don't want actors tampering with my timer switches! Someone changed the settings on the timer switches!"

Everyone looks baffled. Brinna wonders who, if anyone, is acting. Sapan calms everyone, and the Chief stalks out to reset the switches. Redmond returns. The rehearsal restarts. Brinna brandishes her scimitar, a perfectly balanced prop she can move with the illusion of exquisite control. It whisks by Portia's ear . . . and then suddenly, it's too heavy to hold. Brinna drops it with a crash, denting the auditorium floor.

"Stop," says Redmond. "This can't go on."

"We can't stop now!" says Sapan. "How would we open? We'd get disqualified."

"We'd be finished," says Brinna, visions of servitude to Cranmer looming.

Even as she speaks, there's a crash. A stagehand lies under a large tree he'd been moving. Brinna rushes over, removes the prop. It's unexpectedly heavy. Others gather around and drag it off the injured man. Sapan calls an ambulance.

"He's lucky," says the paramedic. "If that landed on his exo-brain . . . ."

Brinna shudders, imagining a crushed holo-present corpse, imagining the empty husk at the holo-beam's origin. "Sapan. Redmond. We can't risk lives."

Sapan is silent. Then he orders all the actors out.

The Chief calls in his crew for a complete diagnostic. "I want every system checked," he orders. "We'll not be allowing this play to fail."

Brave words, thinks Brinna, but she doesn't say it. She's just back from visiting the injured stagehand, who's not returning. "Not worth the risk," he'd told her. "It wasn't the first time. That thing's a ball of junk."

They'll have to pull out of the Festival. She has a vision of herself as a toy dangling above a Cranmer-faced cat with slicked-back white fur. Redmond seems to read her thoughts and puts a protective arm around her.

"We're not giving up, Brinna," he says. "We'll do this play somehow."

Sapan clasps her shoulder. "Don't worry, Brinna. The Chief will fix this."

She leans back, eyes closed, trying to blank out her mind.

By that evening, the Chief swears the holo-studio is functional again.

"Look, I'll deploy my entire crew," he says. "Even the reserves and back-up. They can work double shifts for a few weeks."

"We have no choice," agrees Redmond grimly. "We can't move to a different Holo-studio. The show must go on."

Sapan restarts the rehearsal. "From the top."

The Tral, Antonio, moves gracefully into place. His friends surround him, crowding round the café table.

"In sooth . . ." he starts.

The table flies into the air, knocking over Gratiano. Then, suddenly heavy, it crashes to the ground.

"Engineers!" bellows Redmond. He charges into the hallway to the control rooms. The cast follows.

They find the crew in a free-for-all. A wildly screaming, hooting, wriggling mass of humanity struggles on the floor, while the Chief stands to one side screaming, "Hold on to him, no don't hit Donast, let go of Janet, grab Bwley. Bwley, I say, Bwley! Nilla! Not Ger, Bwley! Pin him down, don't let him up." A strange odor envelops the scene; Brinna recognizes it as a Frl skunk-defense.

"Shut the doors!" orders the Chief as the cast stream through. Then he disassembles the scrum on the floor. At the very bottom is a sorry-looking Frl, firmly held by a large Tral.

"That's Texl," says Sapan. "What's he doing here? He played Lorenzo before I let him go."

"Texl?" says the Chief. "That's Bwley. Studio Crew. Works below, with the engines."

"Bwley?" says the Frl who currently plays Lorenzo, "I recognize you. When I last saw you, you were Swrt." She turns to Redmond. "This Swrt was banned from the thespian arts. He fixes competitions. He sabotages plays. He boos at actors. This Swrt . . ." She makes the name sound obscene. "Who do you work for?" she demands of the captive.

"Shall I interrogate him?" says the Frl who plays Jessica. She sounds rather eager. Swrt breaks from the Tral's grip and runs for it, pulling out his vidphone as he goes.

Half the group sprint after him. Seeing where he's headed, Brinna runs around by another passageway. Swrt comes pelting up the corridor. She tackles him and they both go down. The vidphone's flung some distance. Swrt scrabbles from under Brinna and grabs for it, but the pursuing pack of actors and crew arrive and catch him again. Another stink-cloud rises from the captured Frl.

Brinna scrolls back to view the most recent call on the vidphone. Cranmer's face appears. "Take a look at this," she says to Redmond, smiling grimly.

Redmond bares his teeth. "Hand this fellow over to the Actors Guild," he says. "He'll talk to them."

"Do you realize," asks Brinna, "if the Guild de-registers Cranmer, we get half their assets?"

"Good," says Sapan. "Let's get on with rehearsals. We open tomorrow."

———

Opening Night. Two heralds come forward, shake their spears, raise trumpets to their lips. Red velvet curtains whisk upward and disappear, leaving—

—a tight group of friends at a sidewalk cafe, the Tral effortlessly the heart of the group. Sapan's used a small stage, so when it's projected into the Globe, the characters appear larger than life and very close. Antonio speaks, humorously, apologetically, "In sooth, I know not why I am so sad . . ."

And the play is on.

A love story, of sorts?

Portia stands before Greth, gazing adoringly at his slender silver muzzle. "You see me, Lord Bassanio, where I stand," she says, and places her ring in the palm of his center hand.

Greth looks down at the ring as though he cannot believe his fortune, and then up at Portia. "Madam," he says, "You have bereft me of all words." His silver horn glints. He almost touches Portia with it, then draws back and stammers, "Only my blood speaks to you in my veins; and there is such confusion in my powers . . ."

Or a story of revenge?

Antonio stands in chains, held for his debt to Shylock, doomed by his contract to die under Shylock's knife. "The duke cannot deny the course of law . . ." The Tral's voice is reasonable, dignified, unflinching. He nears the end of the speech, and raising his trunk says, very softly: "Pray God Bassanio come to see me pay his debt, and then I care not!"

There are tears in the three large, luminous eyes. The Tral turns away, embarrassed at showing this weakness to the audience.

Or a courtroom drama?

Portia, impersonating a lawyer, walks over to Antonio. Her garnet cape swirls about her. "Do you confess the bond?" she asks, as though expecting him to deny it. He doesn't, and she's stymied.

It's written on her face: It had seemed a fine trick when she thought it up in Belmont. Save this unknown man, if she could, and amaze her new husband. But now, the unknown Antonio stands vulnerable before her, and it's not a game any more. "Then must the Jew be merciful," she says.

"On what compulsion must I? Tell me that!" demands Redmond. A small muscle works in his face.

Portia looks shocked. Clearly, no one's ever been so rude to the Lady of Belmont, who is used to giving orders. She launches into a lecture on the quality of mercy, convincing no one, especially not Shylock. Someone in the audience boos. The Duke looks stern and taps the table with his gavel.

All eyes are on Antonio now; the chained Tral with his cloak wrapped about him. Shylock leans over and touches him with the knife, almost as though knighting him. Antonio shudders, but holds his ground.

"Be merciful!" urges Portia, "Take thrice the money . . ." But Shylock argues relentlessly for his bond.

At length, Portia instructs Antonio, quite gently, "Lay bare your bosom." Looking past her at Bassanio standing with bowed head, he pushes his cloak back over his shoulders, baring his chest. His fine brown fur is erect, as though he's cold.

The court seems frozen. The Duke, presiding, says nothing. Portia speaks slowly, mechanically. "The law allows it, and the court awards it." Only Shylock is animated, eager. "Come, prepare!"

Slowly the Tral kneels, bringing himself within easy reach of Shylock and his knife. Shylock rolls up his sleeves, pulls out a large apron, and puts it on. Portia eyes him in puzzlement. What's that about? Then, suddenly, she sees. Blood. Not in the bond. Sharply, she says: "Tarry a little . . . !" Shylock turns to her, impatient.

It's over. The audience allows itself to breathe.

———————

The Virtual Mermaid is overflowing. Mistress Mary can barely get the tankards out fast enough. When Troupe Redmond beams in with cast and crew, the place explodes with noise and congratulations and a new verse of *Hathaway was a Termagant*.

"Next time," Redmond comments, "We'll enter the Festival early. We'll get a different play. *Hamlet* maybe. Something really spectacular."

The rest is not silence, not exactly, but a raucous round of doggerel:

> *When Redmond got the Merchant,*
> *He thought it rather silly*
> *But ent'ring last*
> *With a super cast*
> *They've gone and won the Billy!*

16

Right Where it Belongs

RENI KIEFFER

Watching all the insects march along
Seem to know just right where they belong
Smears of face reflecting in the chrome
Hiding in the crowd I'm all alone

Voices.

More voices.

The door opens and closes again. Same old bitch shoving things into my mouth. Same old bottle getting handed to me. Then she's gone. Door closed and I'm alone again.

The room isn't ugly. It's one of those plain, white walled, simply furnished classic hospital rooms. The bars in front of the windows are a little bit annoying. But that's about it.

It's not fair. He should be here by now. Only he's not and I have to keep watching the world outside through the bars.

Sunshine.

People on the lawn.

I don't want to go outside alone. He said he'd come and then we would go together. Down to the trees at the very end of the grounds and then sit in the sunshine. We do that very often. But it's late. I don't think he'll keep his promise.

The cleaning woman forgot to take my tray with her. There's a fly sitting on top of the untouched food. Even if I was hungry I wouldn't want to eat it any-

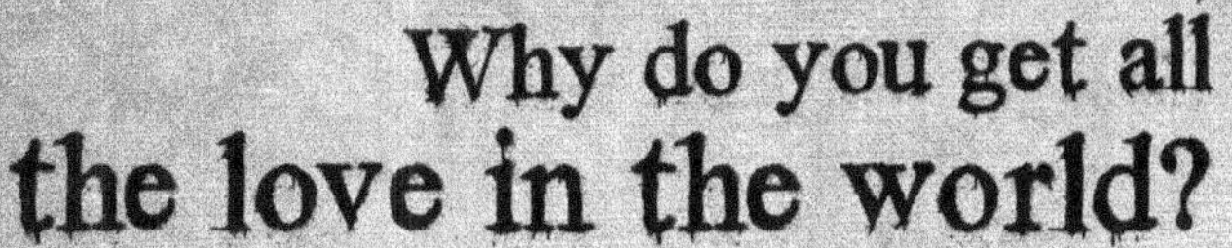

Why do you get all the love in the world?

When I keep silent about his last
statement he sighs quietly
I change the topic

Its a sick kind of self torture
to do that. Asking about them
Still I always do

I tear my eyes away and look down
Misfits. As usual I gave him a similar
I wonder if he still has it

Curling up on the
same spot on the bed I face the
wait hands curled into fists
images everything from on
the bench family from on
stage. An endless stream of memories
and images, feelings and impressions
slowly invading my mind
caused by a simple thing

A kiss

more. Just imagining what this little evil fly might have been sitting on before it landed on my standard sized piece of cutlet makes me want to gag. I can't watch it any longer. I need to keep my meds in.

I swallow.

Once.

Then again. Turn my eyes back outside and that's when I see him. I can see the entrance from my room. I can see the gates and sometimes I just sit here for hours and watch the cars drive by, visitors entering the grounds, walking along the path before they disappear out of sight.

He's dressed in black. As always. I think I can count on my ten fingers how often he was wearing something else but black. He's got a few blue things. A pair of ugly blue trousers. I don't like those. Thankfully he is not wearing them today.

I would have loved them anyway.

The prospect of him being here soon makes my face light up as I grin stupidly through the bars and touch the cold glass with my fingertips. He can't see me yet though he knows where my room is. But he's not looking up to me, he's talking to one of the nurses. They all know him. They all love him. Everyone always loves him. He can get everyone to love him. It's not that complicated and I wish I knew how he does it. Cause if I knew I would make everyone love me as well.

But they all hate me.

Why do you get all the love in the world?

I get up, almost stumble as I push my chair back. My low curse goes under in the loud clatter that follows my hurried jumping up. I look at the grey floor, shake my head at the chair but don't make a move to pick it up again. Instead I crawl on my bed, make myself as small as possible on the neat white covers and wait.

It takes him seven minutes to reach this room. He always takes the stairs, never the elevator. He hates them. I hate them as well. I'm scared of them too. They make weird noises and I fear I'll get stuck. It happened once. I thought I would die.

There are voices again. And for one split second I'm afraid he won't come alone. That he would bring *her*.

That bitch.

But when the door opens, it's just him. His shoes make funny noises on the floor as always, making me smile a bit. He brings in outside air, he brings in the faint scent he's always wearing, fills the plain room with life as soon as he's closed the door behind him.

I sit up too quickly, too overjoyed to see him and then feel stupid for reacting that way. He doesn't seem to notice. He just walks over and settles down on the bed beside me. I reach out for his arm idly but withdraw my hand quickly again.

"Hey."

He's late. And he apologizes for it. He was busy and couldn't manage to come by sooner. I understand that. Of course I understand it. I understand and at the same time there's some nasty images popping up in my head. Images of what might have delayed him. I need to stop this. He made his choice. He's just here out of pity. No love. Never love.

We go outside and I'm cold. It's not really cold but still I shiver as we pass the other patients on our way.

He tells me about the tour and some funny things that they've done. I laugh quietly while just watching as he talks. He's got that sort of soothing tone in his voice. The tone that normally makes me calm down immediately.

Today it's different. Today I'm overcome by an almost unbearable craving for him. I want to wrap my arms around him and never let go again. Of course I don't do this. And he probably doesn't notice. He's not exactly the most attentive person on this planet.

My hands are cold as we sit down, I rub them together gently and force myself to turn my eyes away from him and look over the grounds instead. It's a beautiful day. I hate it. I hate the happiness and the laughter. Hate that there's a family sitting across the lawn, laughing and joking around. You can tell who's the odd one out. The one like me. The one they brought in shattered and broken. He's wearing the same ugly clothes that I'm wearing. He's got the same look in his eyes. Empty staring while everyone else's life goes on. I hate this place.

He asks me what's wrong and I shake my head, touching his arm for a second and even smile a bit. His skin is warm under my fingers and just like before I withdraw my hand just as fast as I reached out.

Too warm. Too much life. Too close.

"I'm just tired." Tired of this waiting. Tired of this place. But then this is where I belong. This is where they're going to help me. Make me "normal" again. Right now I'm not so sure if I want to be normal. I actually never was. And I doubt that I will be when I get out of here. And look at him. He's so far away from being normal. We both are.

He's still smiling and seconds later reaches out and wraps his arms around my neck. He pulls me against his chest and rests his head on my shoulder while squeezing me lightly against him. I can't do anything but sit and breathe. It's something so typical for him. People are sad and he hugs them. That's how he is. It's one of those lovely habits that I learnt to admire so much. Me. Admiring him. Loving him for being able to be lovable. It's a bad habit. Bad obsession. And I need to be careful because it's not where he belongs anymore. Those arms around me are not mine. This breath on my skin doesn't belong to me anymore.

This heart inside his chest is not beating for me anymore. This is not his place. This is my place. And he is just a visitor.

> *No one's heard a single word I've said*
> *They don't sound as good outside my head*
> *It looks as though the past is here to stay*
> *I've become a million miles a . . .*

He asks about therapy and how it's going. I give him the same answer as always.

"Good." I'm lying. It's going far from good. It's going average if anything. Not bad though. Cause if it was going bad I wouldn't be allowed outside with him just like that.

I don't talk. But that doesn't mean I'm not making progress. I make my own personal progress. It doesn't match their expectations, doesn't come up to their "standards" and I'm constantly regarded with worried glances and sighs.

I really couldn't care less. And besides I fear if I told them what's really going on in my head, if I let lose all the bitterness and depression, I would spend even longer here.

I'm not sure if he realizes any of that but he's smiling anyway. Smiling this little soft smile and telling me I'll be fine and that I can leave it all behind soon.

He's wrong there.

I won't ever leave it behind completely. Some things you can't just brush off. You can't erase your past. And just like I'll never forget what we had, I will never erase all the pain and struggle that followed.

The deep fall. The nothingness. The void.

He doesn't know that. He doesn't know what it feels like when you hold on to something. Or maybe he knows and doesn't show. I'm not so sure about that. I always had problems understanding him at times. Still he's moved on. I'm still the same. Two worlds sitting next to each other, holding on to each other. My arms wrap around his middle. Gently, barely touching him. And once upon a time it would've made me smile. Not anymore.

When I keep silent about his last statement, he sighs quietly. I change the topic. I ask about his kids. It's a sick kind of self torture to do that. Asking about them. Still I always do. Not every time I see him. But still. I ask. He loves them to death and maybe I need him to talk about them so I don't totally lose it and drift back into old habits. They're all just bad for me.

He leans back against the bench, lazily sprawling on the wooden planks right next to me. I sit and watch him talk, words washing through me, my mind refusing to grasp their meaning. His eyes light up and there's a smile on his lips again as he talks. I tear my eyes away and look down at his shirt. Misfits. As usual. I gave him a similar one once. I wonder if he still has it.

All the jagged edges disappear
Colors all look brighter when you're near
The stars are all afire in the sky
Sometimes I get so lonely I could . . .

I cut him off mid-sentence with the kiss. I didn't even mean to and I'm more shocked that he doesn't push me away than I would have been if he had reacted otherwise. I don't even know why I'm kissing him. It's not like it'll change anything. He won't save me. But it just happens sometimes. Sometimes I'm so overwhelmed by his presence, his scent and sound of his voice and the way he's still acting so normal when he's around me, like nothing ever happened between us, that I get those urges. They're hard to fight. When trying to keep yourself together already takes up all your energy, you are unable to fight such urges.

Last time he turned away before I got the chance to lean in closer. He got distracted by a noise, just a patient on the corridor yelling some incoherent nonsense and he turned his head in surprise. By the time he looked at me again I was curled up on the bed next to him, staring at the torn edge of his shirt, fingers clutching the covers.

Today it's different. He was just sitting there. Talking. Being wonderful as always. And there was no noise or anything else that could have made him turn his head. In fact he was looking at me the same second I decided to lean forward and find out if it still feels the same to kiss him, if his lips still taste the same, if it still feels the same when I close my eyes, curl my hand around the back of his neck and get lost in this feeling.

I know now.

Then I get up and leave, probably confusing him even more than I already did with this small but rather gentle attack. I don't have much self control right now. And I feel odd after having done this. Embarrassed. People saw me kissing him. And you just can't kick the bench or beat up the nearest tree around here just because you feel stupid and have to get rid of this anger directed towards yourself. No. You go back and curl up and wait until the anger is gone. Then all you have left is the embarrassment.

He doesn't follow me. I picture him still sitting there in the sunshine. He's watching me as I leave and he's probably shaking his head as well. A gesture I've seen so often. He's probably also laughing a bit at me. Not angry. He doesn't show anger anymore since I came here. Nothing but understanding and gentle words. Hugs. Caresses. Sometimes he strokes my hair for a while. Or my shoulder. Sometimes his simple presence is a caress. He doesn't realize that he only makes it worse for me. And I don't tell him because maybe then he won't come back anymore.

He might leave me like he did before.

I guess.

I don't know.

Curling up on the same spot on the bed I face the door and wait, eyes closed, hands balled into fists, images about him in my head. Him on the bench. Him with his family. Him on stage. An endless stream of memories and images, feelings and impressions slowly invading my mind, caused by a simple thing:

A kiss.

Why do you get all the love in the world?
Why do you get all the love in the?
Why do you get all the love in?
Why do you get all the love?
Why do you get all the?
Why do you get all?
Why do you get?
Why do you?
Why do?
Why?

Why?

17

Ennui

ANDREW HOOK

Solange leaves her apartment dressed in a black leather skirt that stops at her thighs. She steadies herself on the side of the doorway as she steps to the pavement. Her hand traces the edges of tiny tiles: pale browns and blues, nondescript. Over her shoulder a green bag is made of feathers and fur. Her blonde hair curves on her neck, drapes over her black cardigan which is patterned at the breast and sleeves with silver swirls.

She nods to the man on the corner, who follows her with his gaze as she walks. Her heels teetering on the pavement. Tiny balances.

From the pavement oak trees break through the concrete and urge skywards. Their roots buckle her way.

In 1878, the photographer Eadweard Muybridge used fifty cameras to prove that all four hooves of a horse are off the ground at one point during a gallop.

Solange turns onto the Rue des Archives.

She reaches into her bag and pulls out a single cigarette. Leaning towards a young man she genuflects and he lights her smoke. She nods her head, and he watches her as she continues to walk.

Overnight, when the UFO approached Paris, the city became tinged in milky blue and orange light as though it were twilight. Solange had looked out of her apartment window and viewed a hazy opaqueness that seemed impenetrable.

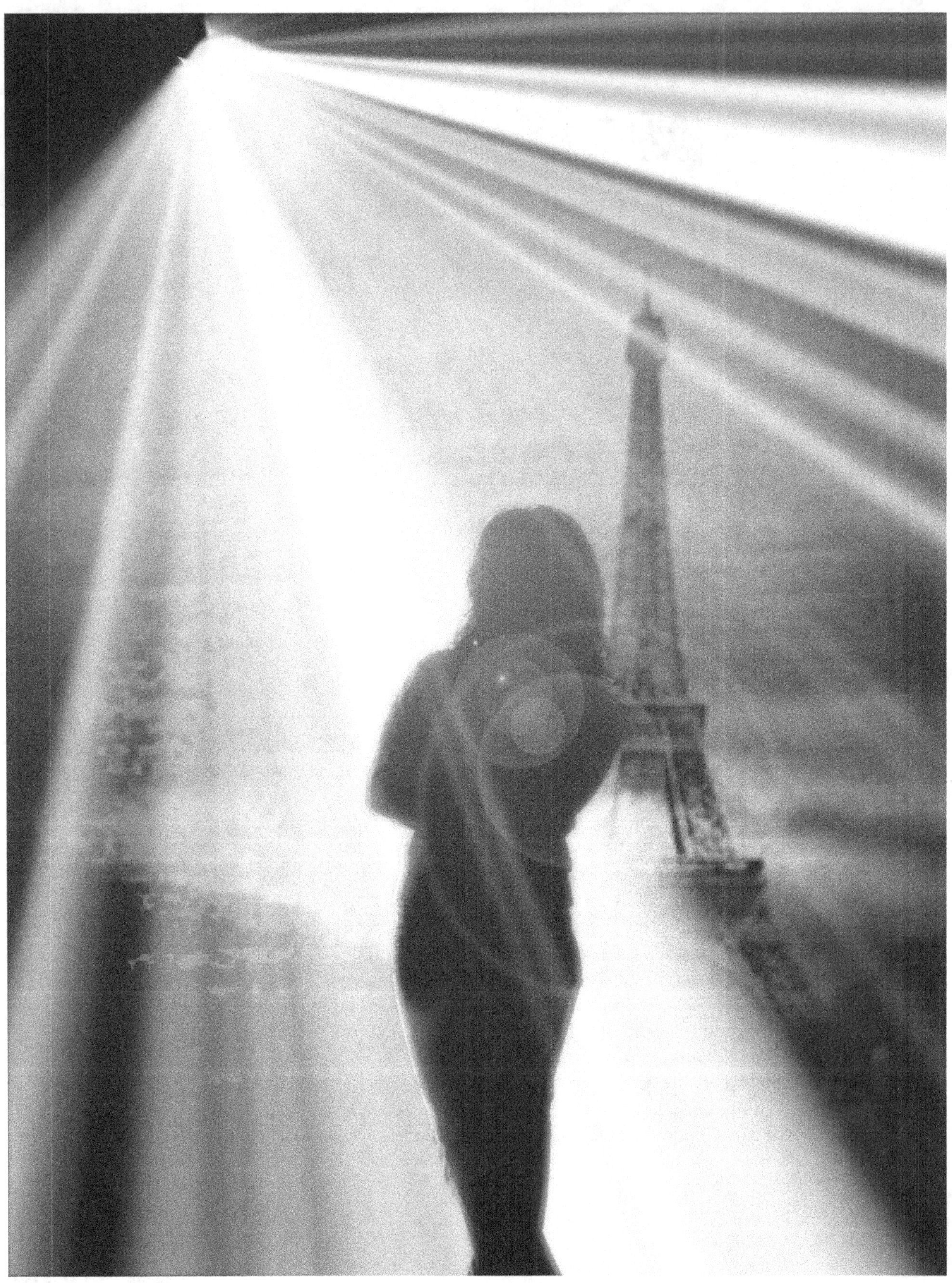

Now, as she regards those who pass her on the street, it is as though the UFO has shrouded Paris in a fog of ennui and numbing complacency, rendering the inhabitants blank and even a little alien-looking themselves.

"Salut!"

The bottom of her skirt rubs against the tops of her stockings.

An arm waves back at her, disappears within traffic. Solange shrugs, turns left onto the Rue de la Verrerie, pulls smoke from the cigarette in her mouth, blows it away so that it heads up.

It dissipates, merging with the air around her face, absorbs.

Her heels click on the pavement like the sound of a determined child using an old-fashioned typewriter. In the sky above her the UFO dominates the city, but whilst a pancake-shaped shadow should cloud Paris the sun illuminates the scene. Light will always find a way.

Solange shakes her head to one side so that her hair reveals her neck in profile. She runs a hand through it, accentuates the skin. Tiny beads of sweat punctuate her. She watches pedestrians pass by, most with their heads to the ground. Those looking upwards wear dark glasses so she cannot see if their eyes are open or closed. She is aware it is all about perception.

Again she turns left, along the Rue des Moussy. Buildings pass by her as though it is they who are moving and not she. Cars crawl. Whereas sometimes the sun makes everything slow liquid today it is different. She rolls up her left sleeve to regard her watch but is confronted with a thin strip of lighter skin.

Briefly, a flicker of a frown creases her forehead. Her lips are lightly paled, her eyebrows etched cleanly. Her blue eyes can't hold a gaze. The muscles in her neck define the sides of her throat. She decides to look up. Can't.

Shortly she turns left onto the Rue Sainte-Croix de la Bretonnerie. She has made a full circle, or rather a shaky rectangle, closer to a rhombus. She approaches her apartment. Leans a hand on the pale tiles again. Pushes the tip of her cigarette into the cracks. Obliterates some grout with ash. Black on white. Entering her apartment she walks through into the living area and stands before the window before the sky before the UFO.

Slowly, she draws the curtains closed.

Francine stands beside a tree in the Jardin du Luxembourg. She sighs and a breeze which until then was inconsequential emulates her. She shudders. She moves away from the tree and stands by a metal lamppost molded with a coat of arms and set into the ground within a circle of cement. She rests against it, then holds it. Her red-painted fingernails follow the curves of the mould, traces patterns which she doesn't think to recognize.

She is dressed for warm autumn weather. A long-sleeved brown woollen dress stops at her thighs. The belt is purely decorative. Boots the same color as the dress rise to a couple of centimeters beneath her knees. A thick pair of lighter-brown tights completes her ensemble.

The previous evening, when the UFO had ascended over the city, she was turning tricks in the park. On her knees, her mouth full, her eyes looking upwards, she saw the shape punctuate the darkness with more darkness. She kept looking, kept the rhythm going. Grass blades patterned her tights when she stood, spitting into a tissue. She stayed there until the next client edged his way through the night's shadow, reaching out for trees to mark his way, to steady him.

Now she leaves the park and finds herself on the Rue de Vaugirard. She turns left, follows the road around the edge of the park. Her long brunette hair flows out behind her as though caught in an updraft.

Unlike Solange, she is not afraid to look overhead. She tries to reconcile her abstract, intellectual knowledge with real, tangible, human understanding.

The UFO is silent.

She passes a couple arguing softly on the corner of the Rue Guynemer. She finds herself wondering what they are saying, walks slower to catch a sentence.

All dialogue is imperfect.

What was it you were trying to tell me?

Why do you love Paul and not me?

I don't love Paul; Madeleine does.

Oh, sure. Why?

I don't want to talk about it. Besides, it's none of your business.

Don't you like going out with boys?

Francine walks beyond earshot. She keeps walking, turns left onto the Rue Auguste Comte. Her arms hang bleakly by her sides. Her dress has no pockets and she has forgotten to carry her bag. The bag contains her credit cards, everything. She is without identity, free. She takes another left, then another, and before she knows it she is back in the park.

She finds a place on the grass that has lost its morning dew. Sits with her legs underneath her, her knees pointing west. Does nothing more. Sits. Stares. Listens.

———

Solange is lying on the couch in her apartment. Outside the traffic has increased. She hears it yet cannot differentiate the noises. Like conversation in a crowded room they become more than individual sounds. The dichotomy between words and sounds blurs. Under her closed eyes everything becomes one. A mass of existence. She lies there and tries to just be.

Something comes to her. She was supposed to be somewhere else.

The presence of life is too heavy for her. She can feel it pushing her into the couch, the fabric leaving indentations on her skin, temporary tattoos, pictures in Braille for the blind.

She thinks of fingers on her body, reading her curves. The curtains over the window fluctuate. A breeze cools her skin. She opens her eyes. Sees nothing. Wants to see nothing.

After a while, she opens her legs.

The telephone rings. Solange listens to its plea.

After a short while the tone, whilst exactly the same, takes on an urgency that it doesn't really have. She knows she is anthropomorphising the object. It isn't really shouting at her, insisting that she leave the sofa, getting wilder and madder with each ring. As she acknowledges this the sound becomes uniform, until eventually it stops altogether.

She sits up. Can't help but feel a part of her has been taken.

When she walks to the window, a few moments later, the curtains are still. She draws them open. Unlatches the window. Opens the glass outwards and into the day. The vacuum inside her becomes filled, and in an involuntary motion her left hand touches her stomach.

The UFO has become another building in the sky. She steps onto her balcony, suspended over the street below. To her left she sees her neighbor, also standing on his balcony, and beyond him, also to her left, is his neighbor. She notes that both of their faces show the same dazed expression tinged with a hint of finality, as if they are floating in a sterile world of hastily-built concrete box buildings and artificiality, waiting for it all to crumble at any moment.

Francine slides her legs straight, shifts onto her back, lies prone in the park with her gaze only skywards, looking into the belly of the UFO.

Just as sunlight finds its way through the structure, so can she perceive the sky beyond. Simultaneously she sees the UFO and sees the sky. She shields her eyes, puzzles the puzzle. Realizes she isn't seeing through it, just that both views exist at the same time.

When she tries to focus, tries to determine what substance the UFO is made of, tries to distinguish patterns and possible doors, she finds herself looking at trees, her head to one side without any discernible trace of movement.

Her eyelids are shadowed in light brown. Her lips are full, slightly parted. She turns again to look at the UFO, but try as she might she can't really see it. Unlike objects which we only notice exist when we turn our attention to them, the UFO becomes less real when it is seen.

Her left hand reaches over her head. She folds a blade of grass between her fingers as she slowly opens her legs. Francine creates a star-shape with her body. A grass angel.

When she closes her eyes the noise of the traffic increases in proportion with the loss of one sense and the heightening of another. The warmth of the sun creates miniscule cracks amongst the foundation on her cheeks. To follow them would be to route an unknown planet. Tracery paths and canals on Mars.

Above the UFO a cloud passes across the sun. Francine shivers, sits up, cross-legged. She places her left hand on her stomach. When she looks around she sees the park is populated. Both males and females are standing or sitting, some leaning against trees. Francine reaches down and unzips her boots, slides her legs out and kicks them off. One boot rests horizontal, the other falls vertical. The cloud passes away from the sun and her toes begin to glow.

She doesn't see any of this.

When she sees this, she doesn't impart meaning to any of it.

When Solange leaves her apartment for the second time her feet aren't touching the floor. Like a horse in motion she is captured in an instant in flight. Somehow, she remains there.

She can't quite remember why she is outside.

On the corner, the man who lit her cigarette is selling newspapers.

She finds that she can't read the headline. Or rather, the words won't allow themselves to be read by her.

It is as though the newspaper and the words upon it exist in different planes. Solange ponders the syntactical difference between an object's meaning and its significance. There is an implicit duality between the two states which lend her the desire to return to the origin of the fracture. A chill suddenly runs through her and she looks up.

The UFO is exactly the same yet totally different.

She turns left at the next junction.

She is unsure whether people are avoiding her gaze or whether she is avoiding theirs.

She can no longer hear her heels clicking along the pavement. On the Rue de la Verrerie she stops for a coffee.

When she sits, the coffee is already there.

She takes a spoon and stirs. Watches the recurring image of an attenuating vortex swirling within the cup of black coffee, sees the allusion to organic genesis in the pattern's coincidental resemblance to spiral galactical formation and nuclear mitosis.

She shakes her head.

What is all this?

Francine stares at the underbelly of the UFO. She makes a decision to no longer prostitute herself. She makes a decision to always be a prostitute. Somewhere in her periphery she understands she will always be prostituted whether she makes a decision or not.

The closer she looks, the clearer she believes she can see a curved M on the surface of the UFO.

"Salut!"

She turns her head to one side.

The greeting wasn't aimed at her but she feels part of it. She realises she has been lying on her back, and rises for a second time whilst understanding that it could be the first. In the park she has been searching for something, she has always been searching for something.

She recognizes one of her clients. He looks different in the daytime with a girl on his arm. Their faces seem pinched, drawn, not haggard but tired. No longer human, she thinks; then realizes she doesn't know what that means.

She stands. Her head feels sore. She must have been sleeping. When she touches her hair a mild electric shock tingles her fingertips.

There is just enough here, she realizes, for humankind to carry itself as normal. Until the time comes that it doesn't need to carry itself at all. Until there is just a state of being, rather than passing moods.

———

That evening, both Francine and Solange look into the sky as the UFO rises vertically, almost imperceptibly, until they can only determine where it was by looking into the place where it no longer is.

Then, a little later, Solange and Francine realize they are only looking at stars.

Under their breath, they make a wish.

Within days, their stomachs are distended.

18

Four
Minutes Time

(after "Still Life" by Sam Taylor-Wood, 2001)

ALEX MACLENNAN

:3:59

Here I am. Arrested in a gallery on the third floor of the Tate Modern, out of place among the high, smooth walls and banks of thirty-foot windows that overlook the slate Thames. In front of me, the painting is pinned to the wall, high above a river as blue as a weathered blue house.

Like me, the still life is framed in a gilded shell (I wear soft leather-tasseled loafers and a crisp jacket that resists the summer heat). Like me, the picture does not fit among the calculated discernment of art students, the flushed pink exhaustion of Americans on holiday, the Chinese that swell and crash past, eager for provocative, pre-approved art. The painting seems odd and abandoned in its ornate, distressed-gilt frame.

:3:46

The classically beautiful still life—gold-brushed fruit on a burnished silver plate—absorbs me and grounds me as the people move by. Vermeer light. Dutch angels.

Claire would have loved it, this warm, spotlit beauty amidst the angular work of creators twice as smart as they truly need to be. Two men enthuse something about *the video,* but I ignore them; I want this for Claire and I.

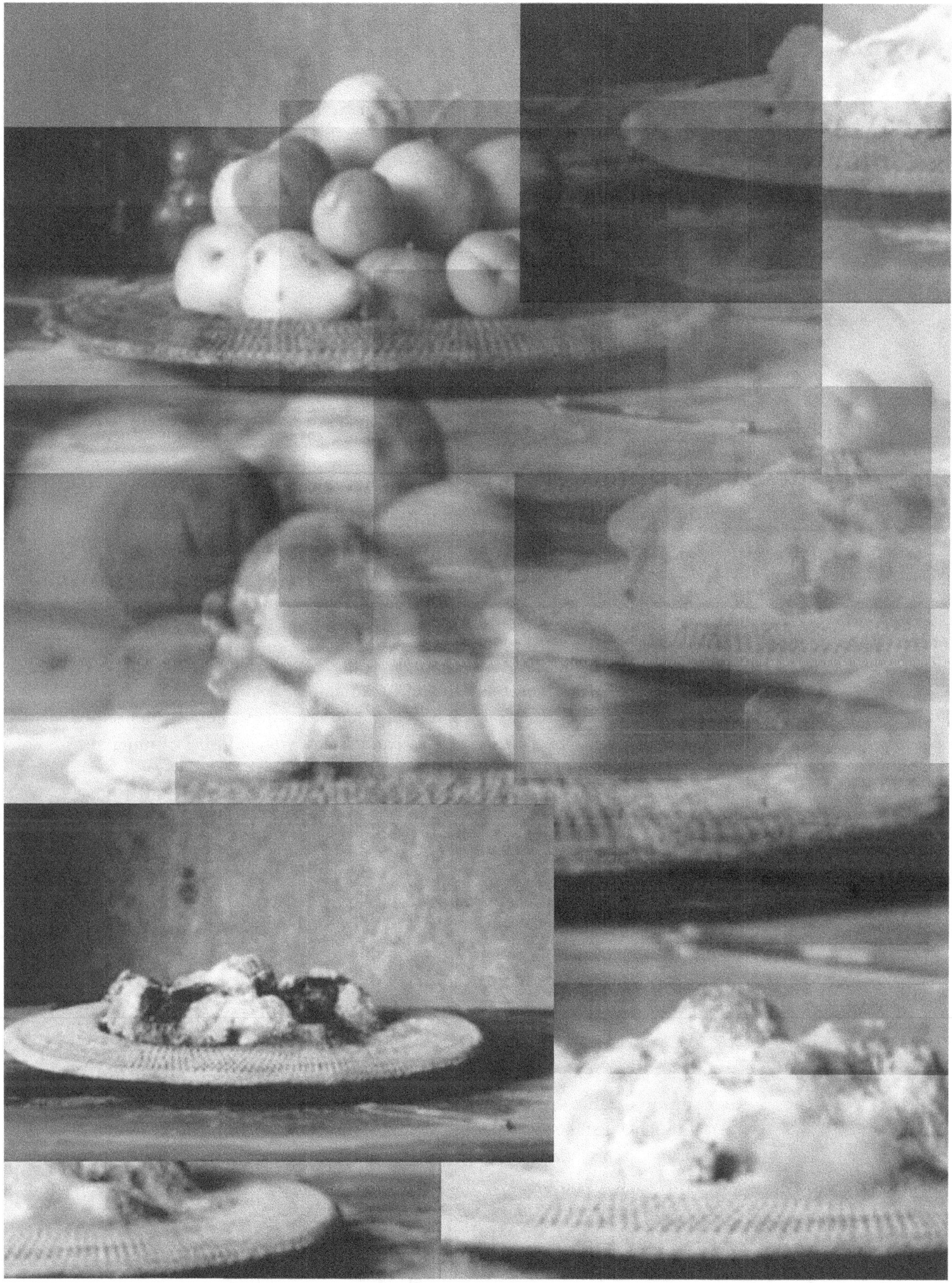

The painting gives off a slow-changing pattern of light over the pears and ruddy apples, the twigs growing from fruit-top, the ornate cloth underneath the plate. A presence at my left—feminine, floral from the smell—flickers. I peer more closely at the still life. The fruit seems to be shrinking in on itself.

:2:59

The fruit is shrinking.

:2:58

And the woman to my right has sighed.

She is noticing that the still life is not, in actuality, still. It is shifting, not in its place on the wall, but within its frame. The fruit is settling in on itself, the light is changing, barely. A dark blush softens the pears' undersides, making me think of a Rubens ass. If it were still, the painting might have been commissioned for a merchant's dining room, paid for with rugs or tapestries or salted meats sent for across the immense distance of a black and chopping sea. I swallow hard and the woman sighs again.

:2:36

There is a slump in the way the apples' soft skins sit on the plate. My eyes flick to the curator's description on the wall and I read *film, plasma, aluminum.*

The woman's pale scent has coalesced; she is a real presence; her blouse is a creamy wedge between dark jacket and dark slacks. We could be standing at a funeral. Claire's, even. A plum begins to implode.

I remember that chapped and unforgiving spring Tuesday and wonder if my arm will brush this other woman's arm, if—as I shift onto my right foot and she cups her elbow in her other hand—I reach back to brush my fingers through my hair . . .

There! The fruit has blossomed with a filigree of gray-green mold—a slow creep around their fleshy bottoms, a lessening of their shape and firmness, a weakening of their essence as fruit. My neighbor shifts, toward me, but I lean toward the painting instead.

:1:59

A hairy gray blanket, like hills of grass or the feel of my tongue after another night of too much wine, covers the fruit. The fruit is losing its shape, like a hill seen through a distance in the rain.

The light is not changing. The fruit is changing. It has utterly, totally changed. My companion mutters something to herself, the soft smacking of lips and teeth, and I imagine her lying in a bedded tangle of white sheets, her black hair unruly, her eyes slow like a child being woken on a dark morning full with snow. Claire had red hair, not black. The rotting fruit makes me want to retch.

The ghost of movement flickers across the picture (at this advanced stage, even I can no longer call it a painting). Insects have found the soupy fruit and are feasting in erratic, sporadic loops and leaps. The insects themselves are invisible. The woman next to me is intangible. Claire has been gone for three months, but her skin remains, in my mind, alabaster and firm.

:59

A dark stain has spread below the fruit, filling the plate's indentation and lapping its edges with the sticky sweet clot of decay. I rock back, immersed in the final, dissolving pool of what was once such a respite. It is like something the first fish crawled out of, in order to colonize the land.

My mouth fills with hot saliva and I want to couple with my neighbor viciously, to take her like a dog. I don't care who she is. I want to be the only two people left on a steaming earth, naked and comforting each other with our skin. I sway away from the painting, afraid of the vertigo but unwilling to give way, and push back against the crowds, the chatter, the museum, the very London air.

The backdrop behind the fruit—a pattern of brushstrokes—is misted as if time or the fruits' effluvia is climbing the wall. I can feel her open her purse, look inside. She has unraveled the painting's mystery, the video-shill, and is becoming bored. She will leave soon. A black puddle spreads across the table's surface, matching the black creep upon the wall.

:03

I should have told Claire,

:02

I loved her more often.

:00

The screen flickers and snaps back to life.

4:00

The still life, illuminated, promises the scent of lemon rind and cauliflower. It takes my breath away every time.

19

Self Portrait: Untitled

LAUREN ALWAN

The pages of my drawing books, the ones from girlhood, are filled with women. Women eating breakfast surrounded by teapots and hat boxes, women in seasonal clothing, in cars and on bicycles. I drew my friends as teenagers, as busy wives and mothers. I drew a girl I hated, rendering her in scrupulous detail, then scratching her out with a pen until the page was torn and spattered with ink. Most often though, I drew my mother. I showed her tanning on the patio, her oily, coconut-scented fingers trailing the sides of the chaise, or standing at the sink in bare feet, warm water trickling down her arms. She was newly divorced, beautiful and young and alone, a kind of movie that I watched, flickering in front of my eyes in recurring scenes: flagging down a car when ours broke down, stirring a Bloody Mary as she turned the pages of a book, or polishing her toes at the edge of the bed, her arms glossy against the sleeveless black knit. I drew these daily portraits, my mother and the objects that surrounded her, and nothing in them seemed labored or difficult. I embraced each challenge of mood and setting, the gleam of her ring against a cracked teacup, her tousled hair against a wrinkled blouse worn on days when she cared little of what the world thought.

My reporting was offset by invention and a preference for the ardent. I dashed over the unfamiliar and avoided the kind of technical drawing I saw in the notebooks of boys at school. Their blueprint-like diagrams showed mechanical things: rocket engines and drag mobiles. These were of little interest, but if needed, I drew them anyway. What I didn't know, I was happy to embellish.

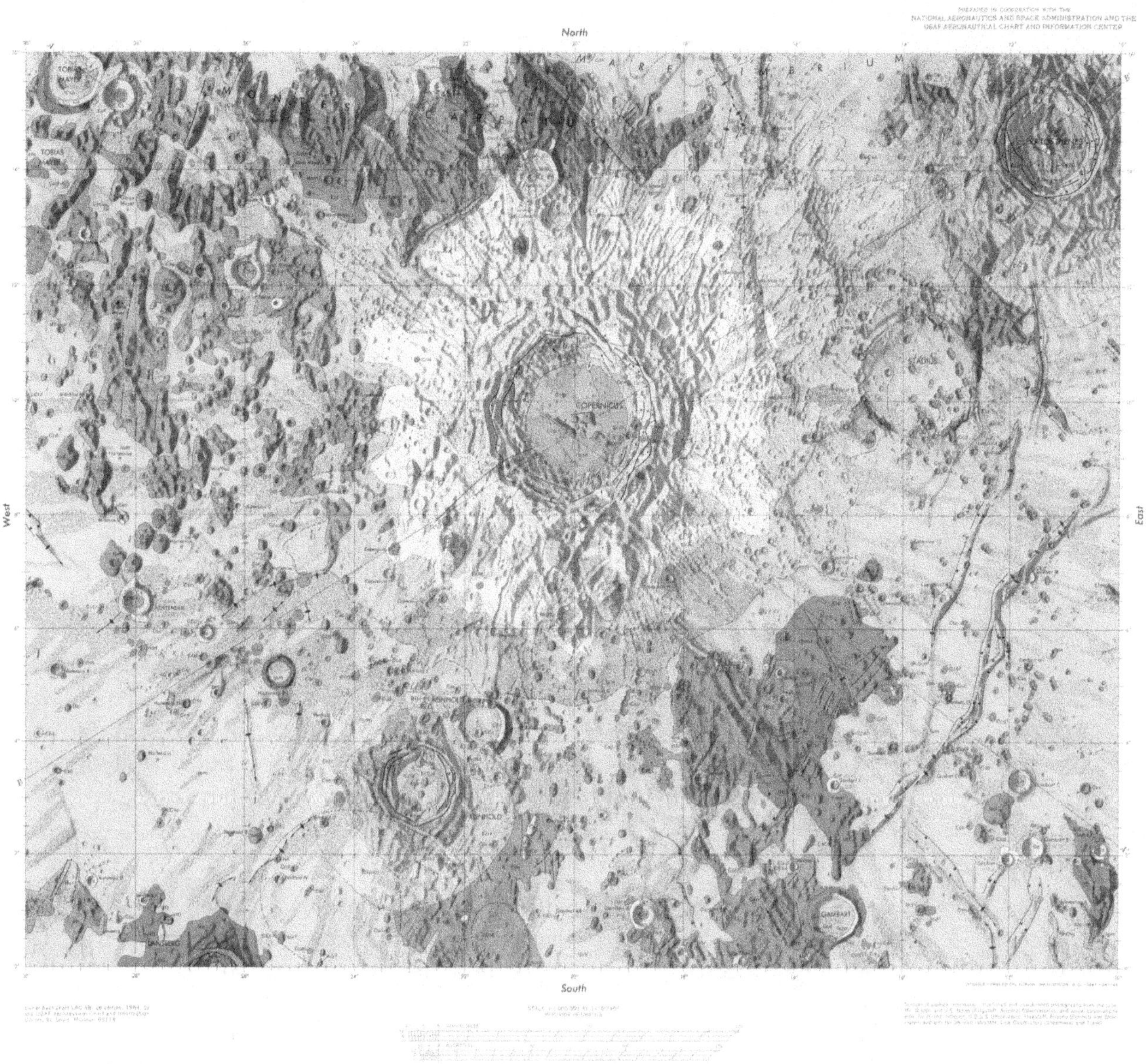

I recall though, the challenge of drawing an embrace, wanting to portray my fingers laced at the back of my mother's neck, the way it felt to brush against her poised arrangement of complexion, eyes and hair. But it proved to be a subject too elusive, the dynamics of anatomy too complex. And so instead I drew an abstract swell of clouds and sky, temporal as an embrace, nebulous as the place where one person ends and another begins.

———

We lived in Los Angeles then, and my mother was seeing a man named William, a man who seemed to steer his life into ours by simply driving up in his car. He would wait for my mother at the curb, languishing in the sunlight. Sometimes, distracted as he waited for her, he would circle his car, front fender to rear, pushing the hair from his face as he checked the finish for scratches.

Cars were important to William. He always owned more than one, and in the ten years he was with my mother he owned thirty-seven overall, including motorcycles. When I needed a ride after school, William would appear in a sport coupe or convertible with my mother beside him. Other parents didn't have cars like that. The girls thought William was handsome. The boys envied his cars, awed by the chrome and horsepower.

William was where he wanted to be, at the forefront, selling the world on new ideas. He worked inside a cluster of windowless buildings, part of a team that would engineer the moon landing. He worked with athletic fervor, considering himself more akin to the astronauts than the support. His job was to cajole the players, the administrators and naysayers who couldn't think outside the lines. The contract, William said, was secured by emphasizing maneuverability. He liked to toy with the government men's straight approach to things, using analogies he knew would escape them, adding off-color references just to make them ill at ease. He wasn't one of those die-cut types, he said. Never would be.

The lunar module unfolded before us in the cast-off bits William scattered across the coffee table. I hoarded them as treasure, spun them like tops, and strung them onto yarn to wear at my throat. Machined into atomic shapes, finely wrought as sculpture, their polished edges glittered in the sun, and arrayed on my bedside table at night, glowed like luminous planets in a distant sky.

———

William became the man my mother wanted to make happy. She knew what William liked to drink, to eat, the people he'd take interest in. She knew what clothes to wear, what topics to discuss at dinner. She orchestrated evenings that put him at the center of things, and I suspect she was successful, though at the time I didn't quite know how. I only recall the times when awakened by voices, I would peer down the hall to see candlelit limbo games or clouds of smoke hovering above glasses and brimming ashtrays.

I preferred the parties that I drew, the kind I imagined other families had—tree trimmings at Christmas, Easter brunch beside a swimming pool. I drew daughters with glossy hair who said endearing things. I drew mothers, attentive and sexy, casual in bare feet and Bermuda shorts. Fathers, the most difficult, came last. My attempts to render them in suits and ties produced unconvincing figures that wouldn't anchor on the page. When I dressed them in something easier, like a golf shirt or a tennis sweater, fathers resembled boys at best, and at worst, girls.

But William is there throughout my sketchbook, rendered with substance and rhythm. I drew him at the office, persuasive with a client on the phone. I drew his reel-to-reel tapes and stacks of car magazines. After a while I set fathers aside altogether and drew William instead. And if I were to draw him now, it would be as a cautious man, one who didn't give anything without making a mental note first; a man who, when he first saw my mother, felt an uneasy pull toward a woman he felt he didn't deserve and a discomfort in such a woman's attainability.

When William came for dinner and spoke in future tense, my mother fixed her eyes upon him, placed her hands in her lap, and listened. If she fell asleep in front of the television, William would carefully tuck a coverlet around her, his hands becoming careful, tender. I speculated whether my mother would marry William, and in my drawing book I began a series of weddings: brides in Denmark, flower girls in England, a ceremony in Japan set against a snowy landscape. I drew the seamstress fitting the bride, the florist with the arrangements. I wanted to draw my mother and William deeply in love. How tightly they might hold each other, how hard it would be to let go.

———

William's lab announced a dinner, a tribute to his project team and the impending conquest of the moon. When the evening arrived, I drew with energy: my mother as she dressed for dinner and dancing, smoothing her hair into a pageboy curl, with spray that fell in a mist of silver beads. She was applying the Miss Dior when William came for her in his tuxedo. As they drove away, I ignored the baby-sitter and her comic books, and drew tables adorned with trophies and martini glasses, my mother in a black dress with a rhinestone buckle at the back. I drew William basking beside her at the head of a U-shaped dais. I added an awning-covered entrance, alabaster doors, valets parking cars, and though well aware they no longer existed, cigarette girls wearing short dresses.

That evening, I fell asleep on my drawing book as I imagined their return—the scent of night air in their jackets and the flush of champagne on their cheeks. When I awoke, my drawings were imprinted onto the pale underside of my arms, and I could hear my mother's voice accompanied by the sounds only adults made, the tear of a match as it is lit, ice shaking in a steel tumbler. I moved to the shadows in the hall, only wanting to see my mother and William, to remember so I could draw them again.

They stood together in the kitchen, ice rattling in their fresh drinks. They used glasses from a set William bought, the kind of glass he liked: one that filled the space in his palm, with a weight at its base and thickness at the rim. He joked about the people they sat with that evening, how attentively a man named Ross had refilled the wine in her glass.

William leaned against the sink and pulled my mother to him. My mother's legs gleamed as she shook off her shoes. He set his hands on her shoulders. He described the way she looked at dinner, the way the rim of her glass warmed where it touched her lips. Outside our house, cars sat in darkened driveways, garbage cans were set out on the sidewalk, and the streetlights turned the lawns pale gray. Lights in other houses had been turned down long ago. William's cufflinks shone gold in the dark, and he lifted the glass and drank.

There are things about my mother and William, about this scene, I couldn't have portrayed, things I didn't know yet: the nights she left me sleeping to go to him or quietly let him in after I'd gone to bed; the late calls from William after he'd been eighty-sixed from a bar and needed a ride home. But I knew other things: my mother's shifting group of friends, a concession to his self-doubt, his need to be unchallenged. I knew without realizing it, how a man comes to a woman, at odds with himself and in great need.

If I could, I would have drawn the drink and what it did, the flush of heat on his brow. I would have drawn the way my mother stood before him, intricate as lace, and the burning tip of his cigarette that hung close to her ear as he steadied himself against her.

William poured another drink while my mother hummed the evening's last song, repeating the chorus, trying to get it right. "How did it go?" she asked. William was no longer paying attention. He was looking into his glass, most likely thinking the things I know now men like William think about: having a better physique, more women who desire them; saying simple, important things to the right people, and knowing without confusion who the right people are.

My mother's humming sounded reedy, off key. William reached toward the window, as if something tugged at him from the streets beyond our block. He wiped away the condensation, revealing our car in the driveway. It was old, its oxidized paint as dull as a plum, dents rusting into cavities. The hood was scattered with my dolls and empty juice cups and half-eaten sandwiches from our lunch that afternoon. William did what he could to keep the car running, was always begging her to at least wash the thing.

"See that?" he said, his words snagging on the gin.

Maybe her humming was just a device until his mood passed. Maybe she didn't hear him. William looked into his drink. They had argued about the car before. She couldn't afford a new one and said more than once she would drive it into the ground. If they were married, she had told him, things would be different.

"Do you see that?" he asked again. She was fiddling with something on her dress, humming the song, trying to get it right.

She looked up, but the glass had already left his hand. It rumbled across the tiled counter, and hit the window. Glass shattered into the sink, bits erupting like sparks. The crash rang beyond the house, beyond the neat hedges and dark flower beds. William reached up and pulled the bead chain, killing the overhead light. He turned on his heel in the center of the kitchen.

He leered into my mother's face. He grabbed her by the chin. "Now do you?" he said, "Now do you see?"

There was a beat of silence in the dark room. She pulled away from him, moved to the sink and set her hands on the rim. She remained there, her back to him. She might have been assessing the broken glass, she might have been remembering what came next with William, steadying herself for that. She picked pieces of glass out of the sink, carefully one at a time, and dropped them into a brown paper bag. At one point she paused to look out across the street, maybe to let him know that she understood their evening was over, the part she loved anyway.

"Is this about the car?" she asked after a moment.

"Right answer," he said, opening the cupboard. He pulled down a new glass and brought it down hard on the counter.

"Well the car is something I can't change."

William smiled as he poured. His eyes narrowed at the ice rising in his glass.

"Don't be like that honey," she said. "You know we don't take anything you do for granted."

He turned, his neck taut, shoving his glass at her. "Corinne," he said, "I don't owe you. Not now, not in the future. Do you see that?"

She looked at him a moment then moved to the table, her hips just resting where our breakfast dishes waited.

"Nice dress," he said not looking up. "Short. Just what Ross likes."

He rolled the name around in his mouth as if he were appraising the texture of the name itself. "Ross," he said, "Great guy." Had they made plans, he asked. He was handsome enough. "Go on ahead," he said and cast a smile into his drink. "You could do worse."

She turned away from him then, and he swatted her backside, told her to be careful, that she was getting fat. The sound of his hand against her, and the way the word fat smacked against the wall stripped the room to outlines. A man, a woman, the blank face of the cabinets, a chain to turn the light off and on. I drew those lines on my leg, my fingernail making right angles in the skin, a line of dots of chain.

The house quieted, settling into the stillness of the rest of the world. William leaned against the wall and closed his eyes. "I'm tired," he said, "Just tell me that you want me."

———

My sketchbook was now nearly full, so I decide to review it. I assigned myself grades, made corrections, and added comments. I gave myself a C+ for a scene of ancient pyramids and an imposing priestess, grading down for unsuccessful execution and poorly drawn facial features. I gave myself a much better grade, an A+, for a drawing of my mother seated in the kitchen, with extra credit for the curls at her temples, her arched eyebrows and strong profile, and for the detail of the book she read, From the Terrace by John O'Hara.

I left one drawing ungraded, thinking it looked incomplete. It was the abstract swell of clouds and sky, my attempt at the embrace. At the center was a small figure, a girl with her arms out-stretched, her eyes and mouth a rapid shorthand of three marks that read as crestfallen, despite the smile. There was no background or foreground, little on which to hang the subject. Only a figure with a quizzical smile on her face and the disparate pieces of a drawing wanting to be whole. At the bottom of the page I wrote Untitled.

———

My mother and William made plans to be married in Las Vegas. They drove away in William's convertible MG. It was a scene that resembled one of my draw-ings—with luggage and road maps, suntan lotion and soda bottles. My mother waved goodbye carelessly in the summer air, her newly manicured fingernails glittering in the morning shine. Her arm came to rest on the back of William's seat, her coral-colored fingertips just touching the back of his tanned neck. And it seemed just then that her hand was a guide—a force that had already been to where they were going and had returned to show them the way. I imagined her hand leading them in an unwavering line from our driveway to Las Vegas and on to every place else they would journey together.

And as the car disappeared at the corner, the place I stood grew bright under my feet. I had a clear sense then of what I wanted and of the things I knew apart from drawing: the way in which a woman might exist beside a man, how to shimmer beside him like a contrasting hue, how to harmonize light and dark until the picture is a self-contained universe of form and color. Inspired and jumpy, I ran to my drawing book, imagining my own stretch on the horizon, irresistible as a blank page, certain as the asphalt beneath me.

———

In the five years between that day and the lunar descent, my gaze turned inward. Using a small hand mirror, I drew myself one oval-shaped piece at a time. I care-fully recorded each flaw, each despondency with draftsman-like precision.

William moved us to a house in the desert, set amid a labyrinth of shining houses and newly paved streets ringed by an eight-foot wall. The ground was a carpet of orange dust marked with Joshua trees, their shaggy silhouettes like unkempt boys loitering outside our door. It was the summer of 1969, and in the clear sky above us, the moon shot was in progress.

On Earth my mother stood in a manicured garden—an engineer's wife in heeled sandals and white linen, discussing landscape design with her guests over cocktails before dinner. At the edge of the garden, I sat on a red boulder, warming my legs on the daylight still there, and watched the sky fade to a lavender wash. Overhead, a jet trail advanced in a thin white line. The air seemed eerily occupied, filled with silver rockets, smoke furls and the deeds of men.

As the guests made their way inside, William had my mother stand beside the pool where he photographed her with waves of reflected light washing across her neck and arms. She did not look into the camera, but up into the mountains, to the filigree of brush and rock intertwining over that sheer drop in the same way that the marriage she had entered was mapping its way across her life.

The guests chatted around the television in the living room, occasionally glancing at the screen where men at control panels adjusted dials and spoke into headsets. I left the party to watch in my room on the television William had bought for me, but the reception was poor, so I turned off picture and listened to the sound. The garbled exchange between Apollo and Houston made me drowsy and I rested my head on a clean white page of the sketchbook.

I can't remember if I dreamed as I lay there, but the dreams I had during those years were filled with the boys I longed for, the same ones who would take me by the hand, up some trail where we would kiss and kiss until the wind turned to a whirling stream around us. Later, those boys became the kind of men people warn you about, but they were the men I understood. I knew what they liked to drink, to eat, the music they'd want to hear. They were the kind of men who are uneasy in their own polished skins, fearing the smallest scratch on their finish, men whose minds are always replaying the last thing they said, or rehearsing the next. I recognize these men before I see them. I know them by the timbre in their voices, I hear them knock before they step up to the door. I can draw their likenesses from memory, seeing the shape of an ear or the curve of an arm as clearly as an afterimage that remains from staring at a thing too long.

That evening in the desert as the Eagle prepared for its fiery descent, I slept on my drawing book until static from the television woke me. I opened my eyes to a sky grown dark. The air was thin and cool, the night sky bitten with small stars that sparkled all around. My heart beat faster at the thought of the night and the emptiness in it that begged to be filled. Outside the screen door, the future pulled at me like elastic. With the grain of drawing paper imprinted on my cheek, I remembered that tomorrow men would be walking on the moon. I raised myself up to draw while waiting for them to land.

20

Absolute Ebony

FELICE PICANO

On a hot and stifling Roman night in the middle of the fifth decade of our century of the Steam Engine, a desultory tête-à-tête between two markedly different Americans was enlivened by a sudden barrage of knocking and shouting several floors below at the level of the Via Ruspoli. The younger seeming of the two men went to the wide ledge of the window and, peering down, reported that two rough contadini were attempting to gain admission to the pensione.

"Leave them, William," his friend replied, with the same torpor and indifference he had displayed during their reunion-dinner—fragments of which now littered the uncovered trestle table in the large, gloomy dining chamber. "The housekeeper, Good Antonia, will see to them."

"Shall I go then?" William asked. "Would you like to rest?"

"All I have is rest in this infernal city during this most dreadful summer. No. Stay. Your talk and natural high spirits bring me much comfort."

Although his companion had reason to doubt the exact veracity of these words, an acquaintance that extended some years back to their childhood across the ocean obliged him to remain.

Even before William had set forth upon his European journey, he had known of his friend's various misfortunes, and the consequent disordered mental condition they had apparently imparted.

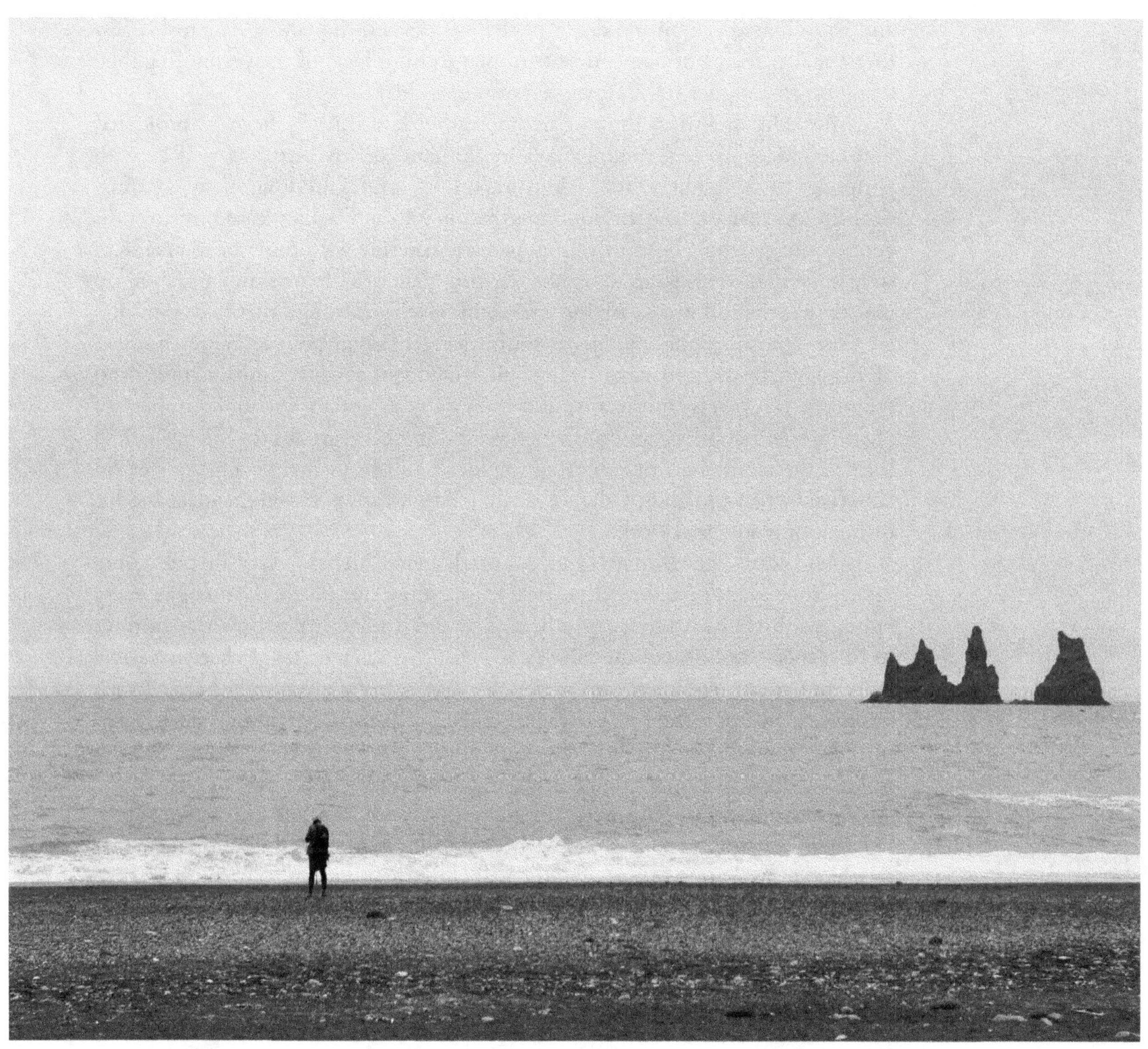

A man in the prime of his life, Michaelis, as he called himself and was so known now, had been an artist of such extraordinary promise that a lifetime of the greatest renown and most elevated rewards had once appeared to be his natural birthright.

As a lad, his talent in draughtsmanship and the application of aquarelles had been so precocious as to attract the notice of the venerable Charles Wilson Peale. Under such tutelage, an inherent genius for the plastic arts was both nourished and coordinated. Upon the death of the old master, the young heir to his aesthetic mantle had but one course left open to him: leaving the young Republic he set off to conquer Italy, art capital of the world.

Michaelis' arrival in Rome a decade earlier had initially been embroidered with accolades no less ringing than in the land of his birth, as well as with patronage of the highest order. He worked long hours, fulfilling many commissions in the spacious fourth floor apartments on the Caelian leased by an indigent Contessa who'd been driven by penury to reside with more prudence than style outside the city gates. Nor was the young artist's life one only of labor, no matter that the toil was satisfying and conducive to earning others' admiration.

The handsome and confident youth was early sought out by representatives of the highest cultural circles the capital could offer—not only painters and sculptors, but poets, musicians, and eventually scientists and philosophers of great lore and subtlety and abstruseness. From these intellects, Michaelis had learned the rarefied art of exploring the ideal; and from their examples, he had conceived a new possibility: that of useful relationships between the ideal and his own, entirely material work.

There were lighter matters to counterbalance such sobriety in the young man's life: teas, salons, dinner parties, balls, riding out on the Campagna every fair day; churches with frescoes to be copied and studied, palazzos with paintings to be inspected. Nor was the fair sex absent or indifferent to Michaelis. Several ladies of varying age, rank, and nationality had secretly given their hearts to the dashing artist upon the first or second meeting. In turn, Michaelis had selected his lady from among the four handsome daughters of the Anglican minister, unofficial director of the English-speaking community in the Italian city.

Because the young woman, although apparently sensible and reciprocal in her regard of the artist, was below the age of consent at the time of their first meeting, more than six years would pass before their engagement could be consummated. When at last they did wed, Michaelis' happiness was unsurpassed. He had recently completed the commission of a large mural for the reception chamber of one of the most powerful prelates of the Roman church. His work was never in such favor, in greater demand. His fame, and that of his colleagues and circle of friends, spanned the Continent. And his Charlotte was the flower of his existence.

Such extreme content was to last but eight months. During a trip to the Campagna, the Signora Michaelis was suddenly taken with a fever. Fragile by constitution, she succumbed within a fortnight.

As was to be expected, Michaelis was utterly distraught. His great disappointment in Charlotte's death caused a melancholia that only deepened long after the natural period of mourning had been protracted. His clerical father-in-law of so short a duration listened with growing anxiety but was able to offer little real balm to the young artist, who set out to lay blame for his romantic misadventure with a liberal trowel, involving not only human but also superhuman personalities. Once the minister had been exposed to Michaelis' more bitter imprecations, he found the artist to be dangerously heretical.

One year passed, then another, and Michaelis found himself still unable to renew his previous connections, nor, more important, to return to that labor which had once been the very mainspring of his life. Previously esteemed for his flights of fancy and unforced humor, he was shunned now by friends for the various perorations of gloom he evinced at the least provocation. Former companions fell away, visited infrequently solely as a duty.

At one time the joy of all who beheld it because of its bright, noble evocation of youth and hopefulness, Michaelis' painting too underwent a transformation consonant with his much altered sensibility. He began to espouse a new theory of art: that color itself was an aberration of the senses, a snare, and an illusion. He declared that all colors ought to be resolved into a more coherent system. Studying earlier theoreticians of chromatics, Michaelis found that half-truths and errors constituted the greater part of their writings. Finally, and by some never adequately explicated chain of reasoning, he declared that only by a subtle, yet complete, mixture of the chromatic scale would color be true both to the mind and to the senses.

When he picked up his brushes and palette again, at last, his tints began to darken, his hues became scarcely distinguishable from each other; reds diminished to deep indigoes, brilliant cobalts became muddied midnight navies. His skills were as evident as before—indeed intensified, more discriminating colleagues attested. But few sitters wanted portraits so dark, so evidently color-saturated that a brace of candelabra were needed to illuminate even the penumbral foreground, and where details of feature and attitude were as transitory to the viewers' eye as a taper's flicker in a dungeon.

Baffled patrons soon began to eschew his studio. Patronage dwindled. Michaelis' once brilliant renown was distorted into that of an eccentric, or worse: a fraud. That his new work was mocked and scorned only confirmed his private belief that he had discovered the long hidden truth of art. He applied himself with renewed vigor to elaborating the darkening of his palette, the complex obscurity of his vision. Bitterness and poverty soon seeped into and throughout his existence. Voluntary seclusion, loneliness, and desolation of any joy in human activity coarsened his courtesy. Mistrust, misanthropy and a growing sense of the growing enmity about him soon silenced him.

Thus had William found his friend, and thus Michaelis remained throughout his visit, despite all efforts to rouse him and elevate his spirits by the recollection of shared youthful joys and follies. Nor was William persuasive in suggesting alternative courses of action to a future even Michaelis himself now could foresee as one of deepening decline. The American pleaded for his friend to return with him to the less somber environs of their mother commonwealth, and to the more wholesome memories and occupations the voyage home would surely entail. But the painter could not entertain the idea of leaving the locale of his greatest happiness—and of his most utter devastation.

Sadly, William acquiesced, again scanning the haggard appearance of his friend which once had bloomed so vigorously, as though he too were an artist and wished to memorize each cruelly imposed new distortion of feature for a future portraiture.

Michaelis' continued silence, and his companion's own resultant silence became suddenly intolerable. William had just stood back from the table to signal his intention to depart, when there was a knocking on the apartment doors, which, while less clattering than that earlier heard, had a more portentous resonance due to the echoing of the high-ceilinged rooms.

His host bade William stay a minute more while he answered the summons. From the outer corridor, William heard the housekeeper's rapid sputter of Italian, followed by his friend's morose accents in that same tongue, soon intertwined with another lighter voice, speaking in a dialect of the language.

Michaelis reentered the room with an astonishing alteration of demeanor. Energetically gesturing, he ushered inside the two grimy contadini William had early seen without. They gazed about them with hesitancy and awe at the apartment's size and elegance, for even in his squalor the artist remained a great man. The artist cleared half the table and asked the men to set their parcel down and open it.

When the moldy cloths had been flaked off and the peasants served flagons of wine, Michaelis touched and fondled a rough stone-like object, the size and shape of a three pound loaf of freshly baked bread.

William was as perplexed by his friend's sudden transformation of mood—hectic, ruddy, enthusiastic—as he was by the object itself.

Taking up a small mallet such as marble-carvers use, the artist inserted an iron wedge into a hairline crack that ran along the top of the stony loaf, and began to gently tap at it, all the while talking excitedly to his compatriot.

"These men, William, are from the countryside near L'Aquila in the Abruzzan Apennines where lie the deepest natural anthracite pits in the entire peninsula in all Europe, it is rumored.

"If they speak truly, then I have at last found the pigment I have been searching for these past three years; the inevitable, yet almost ideal result of my studies and experiments; the base color I shall have ground and then mixed to make a linseed oil to complete my most perfect masterpiece—there, that large shrouded canvas you beheld earlier and questioned me about, and which I would not show you nor any man, and which has lain incomplete awaiting this final color."

"If these men speak truly, William, we have before us what I have dreamed of, what I have required to prove my theory. I will be at last vindicated, within the fortnight, when the new salon of Rome opens and my painting walks off with the greatest acclaim."

Michaelis tapped a final soft blow upon the wedge and the stone gave off a sound soft as a sigh before it fell apart onto the surrounding cloths. Within it, the size of a man's fist—of a man's heart—lay a mass so black so dense that the contadini and William too were forced to gasp and draw back form it.

Michaelis stared, merely emitting a guttural murmur. "Ah, my beauty!"

William was unable to draw his eyes from the dark mineral on the table. Its blackness was so intense it seemed to recede from his vision, drawing his sight deeper within itself.

"What in the Creator's name is it?"

"Only a fine chunk of anthracite now. But when it is made into a pigment, William, then it will be Absolute Ebony!"

William repeated those last two words to himself, with growing uneasiness.

"All colors composed of light in our world mix to pure white," Michaelis explained. "Goethe proved that. But all colors composed of earthly material mix to form black. Therefore I have painted a masterpiece in black so comprehensive as to make Rembrandt's darkest works seem like summer fripperies. We must see how the coal pulverizes. Good as its hue is, it must powder correctly or it will mix poorly and be worthless to me."

So saying, he scraped one side of the wedge against the lump until a fine powder descended. This the artist held up on one finger, inspecting it by candlelight with great care and eventual satisfaction.

"It will do," the artist said, then sat down and sipped more wine, once more becoming pensive.

William believed the arrival of the contadini with the coal represented a turning point in his friend's life. He had never doubted Michaelis' skill or ingenuity, but he sensed disaster impending from this latest event. In applying to an all black painting a pigment blacker still, the artist would surely seal his fate in Rome. His canvas would be completed true, hung at the salon, but surely it would be scoffed at, made the butt of jokes and lampoons. Michaelis would be utterly crushed. Then, William's arguments for a return to his homeland would fall upon more open ears, since that might be the artist's only remaining alternative. Forced to consider his error, like the virtuous and true man William knew Michaelis to be, the artist would undoubtedly return to a more moderately developed philosophy, to a life of light and color.

Yet the coal itself was strangely disturbing, and William was forced to busy himself in order to avoid having his eyes continually drawn to it. He paid the peasant out of his own purse and finding the housekeeper, sent her to fetch Castelgni, the pigment maker, explaining that Signor Michaelis had urgent need of him, and he must be roused of sleep.

The artist did not move from his seat. He sat on, regarding the coal with a concentrated attention, as though he foresaw more than vindication in its depth, as though he could envisage an entirely new universe potential within its dark heart.

So entranced was the artist, William had to at last shake him out of his reverie so he might take his leave.

Passing out the front door of the building, William was greeted by the pigment-maker, nervously, hurriedly ascending the wide, dim stairway to Michaelis' studio.

————————

After the pigment-maker had scraped a chip off the lump of coal, he ground it to a fine point, then swept the powder into an old bronze dish aged with many previous mixings. Water was sprinkled in, the binder added—a concoction Castelgni had learned from his father, his father from his, going back it was said to the days and to the very studio of the great Veronese himself. When he had done, Castelgni called Michaelis who meanwhile had been busying himself uncovering what seemed to the old Roman guildsman to be a large, obscure canvas.

"How does the color look, old man?"

"Nerissimo!" the mixer replied. "Blacker than any black before it."

Indeed, the flat dish, coated with but a quarter inch of the new pigment, seemed to hold more than a pint of it, as though it had suddenly dropped open to the size of a large flagon, as though ordinary laws of depth and foreshortening no longer held true in its presence.

"Chip and mix all of it! But carefully, mind you," Michaelis warned, "I'll need all of it. Bring it as soon as you're done."

He wrapped up the remainder of the coal, carefully sealing it back within its mantle of rock.

"As soon as you're done, you understand? No matter the hour. Leave the dishful. I must test it."

When Castelgni had gone, the artist picked up the dish, looked once more into its depths, and brought it to the palette board that had been set up facing the uncovered painting.

Not even the Roman night was dim enough for the subtleties of darkness he had already committed to the canvas. Two dim candles in wall sconces were foreshadowed by painted black baffles. Within this rare obscurity stood Michaelis' new painting, the summation of his life's work, unlike any work conceived of before.

It was a life-sized painting of Michaelis himself, clad in the masquerade of a Spanish Grandee of a previous era. In the painting, he half turned from the observer, as though he had been walking away and, suddenly called, had turned back to face his caller—a most difficult view to achieve, even were it done with a live model. For it to be a self-portrait was amazing; especially as Michaelis' care and technical skills insured that the portrait would be a compendium of every refinement of proportion and perspective.

But the unusual angle of the subject had another, a more crucial purpose: to provide more than half the entire space of the canvas to one single area— which he would fill in with the new pigment—the area of a full length cape that Michaelis wore. It fell heavily from his broad shoulders, plummeted leadenly, and swung slightly at the tops of his boots to effect a sudden movement, as though by the exorbitant force of gravity.

This area had been long prepared for the new color. For months he had covered it with a base coat of his own perfecting, designed to totally wed pigment to canvas. Once that had dried, the artist had painted over the area with Lamp Black, the darkest hue available to artists. To others, that might appear to be the end of the matter. However, Michaelis had looked upon the Lamp Black with an emotion close to pain, knowing as he did how far from his ideal the Lamp Black proved to be. Yet after it too had dried and he had tediously scraped the entire area of the painted cape, he was pleased to discover how well his base had held. The razor point he wielded was so thin it almost sliced the canvas at moments. The area now to be repainted was so fine that should a person stand behind the canvas he or she might almost be discerned through the area; and yet it was black, front and back, fully primed for the final application.

Michaelis decided upon yet another refinement—a caprice. He would let remain a thin border of the Lamp Black, no more than half an inch, to outline the cape, to bring into relief the new pigment, and then—as a further act of bravura—he'd also paint-in various undulating lines of Lamp Black to suggest the vertically flowing hints of the cape's folds. Though Lamp Black themselves, against the new black they might appear almost silver.

He dipped a brush into the dish of the newly made pigment, careful not to miscalculate his touch because of the curious effect of extra depth. Emerging with the utter dab of darkness on the fine cat-whisker hair of his brush, he lifted it to the canvas.

The pigment almost sprang onto the portrait of its own accord. Only a faint inkish stain remained on the bristles. It was fully, instantly absorbed onto the prepared canvas, standing out against the other blacks like a speck of eternity.

Quickly, greedily, Michaelis dipped his brush and applied more of the pigment, broadening the spot, adding more, then more still, and then all of it, until the dish was merely blemished and once again possessed its natural flatness, and the new pigment, to the size of a man's hand, covered the upper right corner of the outlined cape.

"Nerissimo!" Michaelis whispered, repeating Castelgni's words. "Blacker than any black ever before."

The artist pulled up a bench and sat staring at the canvas, pondering his work, admiring the new color until the hours of night were obliterated. When finally, in answer to his housekeeper's knocking, he at last left the studio chamber, and was astonished to discover that it was some time past sunrise.

At dusk, the pigment-maker arrived, accompanied by an apprentice who helped carry a large covered vat. When Michaelis had the lid pried up, he thrilled seeing the intense depths of the black pigment they had labored to produce. As he'd been promised, it mixed beautifully.

The guildsman apologized for their tardiness. His wife, the old man said, would not allow the block of coal into her house. The superstitious old woman had lighted candles and had muttered litanies all day. Castelgni had been forced to beg work space in the atelier of a fellow craftsman to complete the grinding and mixing.

Upon hearing this, the simple-minded young apprentice, already frightened by the intense blackness of the pigment, whined and pleaded for them to depart.

"But it was a very easy pigment to make," the phlegmatic old man said with a smile, ignoring his younger's pleas, "Almost as though it was eager to become paint for the Signor."

"It is said that the great Frans Hals knew twenty-seven different shades of black, and when to use each of them for perfect effect. Rembrandt himself provided twenty-nine different shades of black for the hats and doublets and backgrounds, to differentiate each of the doctors in his mass portrait, The Anatomy Lesson. The Chinese have an entire school of ink painting where no colors are admitted. Their gradations range from grays so indistinct as to seem the mere smudge of a virgin's finger upon the petal of a white chrysanthemum, to that deepest of blacks, which is used to write but one word in their curious visual language—that signifying the eternal restlessness given to those who seek to usurp the throne of heaven. Their shades of black number thirty.

"Already I have discovered one more shade than they. Intimate to me as to those Mandarins are these various tints and black hues with iron oxide bases and the merest hint of scarlet which seems to me to be the true color of bloodlust in battle and the fever of pestilence. Other tints of black with browns ands green hinted at are luxurious, as though embedded in velvet plush. Some blacks are the colors of certain practices of Roman courtesans whispered in my ears by masked women during lewd street celebrations, while other shades speak of quiet diplomacies, of saddened courtesies, of the final noble words spoken by highborn men and women meeting their ends by treachery and the executioner's block. Other blacks still are almost charming: one with a hint of blue indigo is as tart as a Parisian soubrette. Yet others are somber as widow's weeds, heavy as the unheard curses of decades-old prisoners in airless dungeons. I have acquainted myself with these varieties of despair and in turn invented new hues to reflect those new despondencies I myself have experienced.

"A pure Lamp Black from Liverpool is so black that in bright light it glitters almost silver white. But there! That only proves my point. What I've wanted, what I searched for, was a different kind of pigment, one that would not reflect outwardly, by prismatics, but inwardly, by secret refinements upon nature itself."

Michaelis ceased to speak and fell into a brooding silence. William could do nothing but sigh

"Will you begin tonight?" he at last asked the painter.

"The very minute you leave. And I will work on until it is done."

"Then good-night. Tomorrow morning I ride for Pisa and thence on to Venice. But I will be returned before the exhibit is to open its doors. Promise me that day to return with me to America."

"After the exhibit, sweet friend, I will no longer need to go anywhere," Michaelis said. "I will have arrived."

––––––––––

It was in the earliest hours of morning, the following day, when Michaelis applied the last dregs of the ebony pigment to the final uncovered square inch of canvas. As with every previous brushstroke, the paint seemed to leap off the brush onto the canvas, as though rejoining that portion of itself divided in the act of application.

During the exhausting labor, the artist had scarcely glanced at the canvas before him, or if he had it was only to ensure that the pigment lay evenly alongside the Lamp Black outline he had devised for its entire perimeter.

Now, finished, he stood back to inspect his self-portrait and instantly felt a catch in the back of his throat. It was precisely as he had fore-visioned it: the figure in its usual attitude against its dim background, his face half hidden by the gleaming Lamp Black domino he lifted with one black gloved hand, the shadows, the thirty other individual shades of black he had used for the costume, shading of silver blacks cross-hatched to suggest the sheen of satin, golden blacks delicately embossed for the silken expanses of his doublet and pantaloons, blue blacks and indigo blacks in whorls and minuscule circles to intimate the textures of a throat ruffle, of shirt cuffs bursting from each dark sleeve, browner blacks in careful streaks for details of facial hair and for the highlights of the broad-brimmed hat he wore, all wrought so ingeniously as to offer a palette as rich and complex as the brightest chromatics of David and Delacroix, his esteemed contemporaries.

And even if one were so myopic as to misapprehend these many dark subtleties, dominating the portrait was the new pigment; the immense utter blackness of the cape.

Looking at it, Michaelis felt as though he were seeing through a portal into an entirely new dimension—one intrinsically opposed to any ever seen by man before. Where the Lamp Black edging ended and the new paint began, so sharp a delineation occurred, that it seemed to signal that another reality existed.

The dark cape curved inward by some curious property of the pigment, drawing his vision inward, spiralling counterclockwise deeper and deeper within, until Michaelis felt unable to fix himself to any stable underpinnings of floor or walls or ceiling, nearly weightless. Suddenly afraid that he would fall into the blackness of the cape, he pulled himself away from the canvas and carefully sat down in an armchair at a fair distance from he easel.

That precaution failed little to dispel his initial impression. From a dozen feet further back in the room, his sense that the newly painted area was both more and yet less than a flat surface was much intensified. As though he had assisted in representing the abysses of the heavens themselves, a starless heaven, somehow pulsing alive with the very negation of matter.

A further curious side effect of the new pigment was that the large, gloomy studio itself seemed smaller, almost intimate, especially at that end of the chamber where the canvas was placed. One might infer that light itself could no longer exert its periodic powers or proportions wherever existed that utter lack of light.

It was a bitter triumph, this ultra-black painting, yet it was a triumph Michaelis experienced. So entranced was he with his creation that he sat hours in front of it, before falling asleep on the rough studio cot.

When he awoke from his extended yet un-refreshing sleep, the day outside his window was damp, gray and airless. He was still fatigued, chilled by the sudden wetness that seemed to hold the city in thrall all that day. He passed the afternoon and evening enraptured by his masterpiece, discovering within its maw of absolute black echoes of all the suffering and unhappiness he had so long felt.

That moment he was able to draw himself away from the canvas, particularly from the yawning chasm of the cape, he was filled with a vague sense of unease and restlessness. He picked at his solitary dinner, distractedly began and then put down unread a half dozen volumes of poetry and philosophy he had been wont to turn to previously as balm for even his most melancholy hours. That night, as he began to slip into slumber, he thought he heard the distant approach of floodwaters rising.

The consequent days were spent by Michaelis in an attempt to overcome a sense of exhaustion that strangely persisted. His housekeeper said she hoped he wasn't ill, but as he could find no specific symptoms to complain of, the doctor that was sent for could do nothing for the artist, and went off again baffled, prescribing bed rest.

Michaelis took advantage of this new regimen to actively avoid all contact with others. In fact, he had begun to find the presence of others intolerable to his sensitivities. He asked that his food be set outside his apartment door, where, often enough, Antonia would happen upon it, hours later, scarcely touched. He moved from sleep to waking through far easier transitions than ever before and a great deal more frequently during a single revolution of the hours. Soon it became difficult for him to fully separate these states of consciousness with his prior conviction.

Instead, he began to inhabit an intermediate state, and in this he would find himself gazing out a window for hours, or—more frequently—leaning against the studio doorjamb, his work chamber grown tiny to his eyes, except for the portrait, looming immensely, its awesome depths flickering and breeding odd presentiments.

He began hearing soft sounds which seemed to derive from somewhere behind, and then upon closer inspection, somewhere within the canvas; sounds like those he had first taken to be rising waters; as though some liquid medium of great viscosity had been stirred somehow to life from a vast distance. The movement appeared to be caused in a quiet, yet dark, viscous pond, insistently, tediously lapping against the edge of the canvas.

He began to have inexplicable fantasies, sleeping or awake, of a small, misshapen creature—black as the blackness of the cape—who hid within the pigment, and who softly whimpered its dreadful, unfulfillable need.

Once that was heard, the delicate lapping noises ceased. But the whimpering continued, sometimes for hours, at times barely audible, at other times so loud he could not hear himself think. Nor could he escape it. He found he was unable to step beyond an invisible yet still defined radius around the canvas without experiencing an unspecified although all-encompassing panic, and actually physical pain in the form of a megrim headache. At times, he fancied the whimpering noise so near that it was within his very veins and arteries. He dared not nick himself shaving, or his life's blood would pour out of him not humanly crimson, but absolutely black.

––––––––––

The childlike whimpering was approaching the door of his bedchamber. Although he slept and dreamt and knew he both slept and dreamt, still it slowly advanced through the precisely described dimensions and details of his bedchamber, black and small, almost viscous itself, moving toward the edge of his bed. A fearful thing! He turned away, but could not awaken. It came to the bed's edge and slowly, clambered onto the bed linen, the whimpering subsided now into a soft panting, not so much respiration as the inverse of breathing. Still unable to awaken or move away, he huddled further away from it, within himself, dreading its approach, curling his body like an infant to avoid it. The maddening sound was in his ear now, the creature from within the chasm that was his self portrait stretched itself next to him slowly, with infinitely minute pressure as it leaned its form against his shrinking, dreading back, legs, and neck, as a freezing child might timidly approach a sleeping stranger for warmth. It caused him to tremble then shiver, then shake so violently with its sense of living blackness and nothingness come to life and its sapping of all warmth and life and color from him, that he did at last awaken, with a start. He leapt from the bed and rushed out of the room.

He found in a cupboard a flagon of brandy and drank a cupful, to warm and steady himself. It's half-century of bottled spirits helped a bit dispel the more immediate palpitations from the terrible nightmare, and he wrapped himself in his outdoors cloak and more deliberately sipped another cupful of the old brandy until his hand no longer trembled about the chalice and his breath no longer frosted the cold metal edge. Yet he dared not fall asleep again, but passed the remaining hours before dawn huddled in a dining room chair, peering into the studio doorway left half ajar, and, at times, out the window awaiting the first warming ray of the morning sun.

The nightmare had shaken him out of his previous week of lethargy. He bathed and dressed rapidly and even before Antonia could come to him, he went down to the ground floor for the first time since the pigment had arrived, and asked leave to breakfast at the common table set daily for her family and for several other pensioners.

After so long and so complete an absence, he was congratulated upon his recovery, as evidenced by the new prodigiousness of his appetite.

Cheered, he gathered up a wide-brimmed hat against the hot Roman sun and decided upon a long, morning walk. Antonia was free to clean and air out his apartments, a task she'd long anticipated after weeks of being denied her housekeeping there.

Michaelis returned past noon. Already most of the Roman citizenry had escaped the debilitating heat of the outdoors for cooler afternoon siestas. The artist felt renewed by his walk, his fears of the night dispelled by the benign morning sunlight. He had just settled himself at his table and had begun reading his weekly Corriere, attempting to catch up on news of the town, and was anticipating the coming evening's dinner with William, who was expected back, when Antonia appeared before him, her various implements of trade in hand, and an arch expression upon her kindly face.

"You have worked very hard, Signore. Too much work, it is poor for your health. When you first appeared at our table downstairs, we were persuaded you were some baleful spirit."

Michaelis murmured the appropriate response.

"Never have I met such a persevering artist," she said, shaking one finger as though scolding him for his industry. "Why you even paint in your sleep!"

"How do you mean?"

"Come look!" she said, leading him to the bedchamber. "Ecco! What did I say! Ecco! There! Those spots of black resisted all my efforts to remove them."

At the far side of the bed from where Michaelis usually lay, two spots of the new pigment lay upon the floorboards. The artist wondered if he had been so distracted during the last stage of his work on the canvas that, unawares, he had tracked them into his bedchamber. He dismissed Antonia, assuring her he would ask the pigment-maker for a solvent to remove them.

After she had gone, however, Michaelis returned to the side of the bed to more closely inspect the spots. This near, they took on a more defined appearance: one was a mere half-inch or so of black smudge, the indistinct shape of a semi-circle. But as he looked more closely, it suddenly struck him that the other black mark could be nothing other than the pad and first three toes of a small foot: large and clear, the very impression that would be made by a small child with paint on its feet as it leaned to climb onto the bed.

———

"I was certain the painting would be done by now," William protested. "You look as though you've worked on it without a minute of sleep since I've been away."

"Only one more night of work. Then I am done," the artist replied, not unaware of his friend's vigorous health, almost a censure to his own haggard appearance.

"Do you still mean to display it?" William asked, looking toward the studio where the painting remained covered. "The salon opens tomorrow."

"It will be done."

William was yet to be appeased. "We were to celebrate its completion tonight. And, also my return. We were to dine out. I have already accepted an invitation to a fete for us both, at the *Marchesa* de B___________'s."

"You must go to that alone. Tomorrow night, after the exhibit, we will celebrate, you and I. Have a bit more patience with an old friend, I beg you."

"Tomorrow night for certain, then," William agreed brightly. "You'll have no way out, I assure you. I feel duty bound to see you done with this canvas. Its last stages of labor have taken a terrible toll on you, I fear."

Although exhausted and sad, Michaelis was calm, which William misperceived as the serenity of near completion rather than the resignation it in truth signified.

"Let me only step into this pharmacy," the artist said. "I am promised a draught to sustain me during the last hours of labor."

William left his friend at the herbalist's shop. Michaelis received his prescription and ponderously took his way home.

Arrived, he mixed the potent stimulants the pharmacist had prepared into a flagon of strong hot espresso and sighing, he brought the cup with him into the studio.

Two large canisters sat before the shrouded portrait, delivered by his orders, via the pigment-maker and his apprentice. Michaelis pried up their lids, then drank the potion he'd received, along with the first of a half dozen *espressos* he would continue to consume in the coming hours.

A great initial effort was required for him to dip a paintbrush into the vat before him, and even greater effort to lift the brush to the area of the canvas where the absolute ebony had only just dried. But Michaelis made his nerves iron to his task. Only his heart was a waste of icy emptiness the moment he applied the brush to the canvas and began the destruction of his masterpiece by applying over it the purest, thickest, whitest Zinc White to ever come from Castelgni's workshop.

Perhaps it was because of the precautions he had taken before beginning the task—the dozens of candelabra with the brightest tapers illuminating the chamber as though the grandest party were in progress—perhaps for other, unknown reasons, but he had already emptied one large canister of the bright new pigment onto the canvas and had begun dipping into the second when he began to sense a sort of pulsing from the remaining black pigment that formed the cape.

He worked faster, dipping the brush more rapidly, applying the white in great swaths over larger areas of black.

He became aware of the lapping sound, at first so quiet he merely sensed it at the tips of his hair, on the very surface of his cheeks. It went on, growing ever stronger, louder, until Michaelis could hear no other sound. He worked feverishly now, with greater dispatch to cover the remaining areas of the terrible black. Several times he felt the brush he was using almost twisted out of his hands by some force from within the canvas.

When only a square foot or so of the original pigment remained, he switched to a larger, rougher brush. That's when the whimpering started up. Like the lapping sound before it, it began scarcely audible, but as the artist dipped his brush and raised it with yet more Zinc White to the canvas, it became louder, growing to a crescendo of piteous, fierce moaning so encompassing he was certain everyone in the surrounding dozen streets and houses must be able to hear it.

He filled his ears with wax melting off the many candles around him. Temporarily protected from the terrible sound, he worked on yet more feverishly.

Now only a few inches or so remained of the black. But when he dipped his brush into the canister of white, it came up dry. The pigment was gone, used up. He frantically scraped enough from the sides of the canisters to cover a minuscule section of the canvas, cursing, kicking over empty buckets.

The large canvas began to belly outward, as though attempting to reject the application of the white, as though whatever existed within it was pushing through, to get out—and at him.

Michaelis ignored its buffeting as best he could, shuddering all the while, concentrating to devise how he might cover that last spot of black. His heart beat wildly with the memory of last night's visitor, and of the footprint he had seen, and the whimpering that now pierced through the wax stuffed in his ears, as though the sound derived not from without, but from within his very brain.

Not a thimble full of white remained. It was four o'clock of the morning—impossible to secure more pigment. How could he cover it all?

Michaelis almost went mad then. He sensed a power within that tiny remaining spot of black pigment that had to be obliterated lest it annihilate all else. The canvas continued to shudder from top to bottom, sometimes vertically, other times diagonally, as though to shake off the new paint. It would. It would, he knew, unless he managed to cover every last bit of the infernal hue.

As though by inspriation, he suddenly recalled his own supplies not looked into for the past several years since he had turned to darker colors. Ah, and there in the small cupboard it was, not a great deal, but still clean, clear, unsuillied, an almost full tube of ancient Zinc White he had used for children's dresses and maiden's hands. Deafened by now, near to maddened by the piercing whining form within that still screeched on, he worked to extract the pigment into a dish. Looking up, he saw the canvas blowing in and out as though it were the topmost sail of a Clipper ship under a typhoon's gale.

He managed to get enough white pigment mixed with water and binder, rapidly stirring until he supposed it thick enough to completely coat the last bit of black.

He dipped his thickest brush into the paint, swirled it to soak up every atom of the liquid. But as he lifted the brush from the palette dish to the spot, the billowing canvas went utterly flat. From the remaining portion of absolute ebony the color seemed to emerge so completely as though the black had taken on full life. Before Michaelis' unbelieving eyes, the pigment grew forward, forming itself into the grotesquely black lineaments of a small, unnaturally proportioned, three-fingered hand reaching out for him.

He clenched his teeth to stifle an utterance of terror then dabbed the brush with the Zinc White at those fingers, covering them with lines, blotches and streaks of white. As he did, the hand pulled back and a shriek emerged from the canvas so high-pitched, so fraught with fear and pain as to send him reeling backward.

The scream ended as suddenly. When his head had ceased to ache from the sound, he once more approached the canvas. All was silent: the whimpering gone, the surface still and flat. Quickly and ruthlessly, he painted over that last spot. Calmer, he inspected the canvas, and returned that brush of Zinc White over every possibility of insufficient pigment, no matter how thread-thin any possible crevice, until he was satisfied that not a single iota of the awful black pigment remained.

Exhausted, Michaelis slowly and arduously, dragged himself out of his studio and swooned onto his bed.

———

"Arouse yourself, dear friend. It's past four o'clock in the afternoon."

Michaelis sat up in bed and looked about him as though he had awakened in a strange land.

"Have a cup of this *cafe latte*," William pleaded. "It will help you awaken." He sat in a chair near the bed, holding out an earthenware cup. Late afternoon daylight played over the floorboards through the open curtains of the window.

"The exhibit has been open since midday," William went on. "But now you must rouse yourself and have a bit to eat before we go."

The artist sipped the almost insipid liquid, coming slowly more awake, as though from some long dream.

At once he started. "The portrait! It still must be brought to the salon."

"On that you may rest assured, my friend. It is already accomplished."

"But . . .!"

"Accomplished. Carted to the salon. This morning, when I called on you, I found you sound asleep, fully dressed, wearing the paint-daubed wear you now sport. You had wax in your ears, I supposed so as to not be disturbed by noise during your well-earned rest. I called for Castelgni and his man and they carted it off."

"Did you see it?"

"Alas, no. It was already covered over when the two brought it out, for its own protection, I presume. Meanwhile I tried unsuccessfully to awaken you."

William insisted that food be taken at a local *trattoria* nearby the salon, a place much attended by artists of various nationalities. At one time, during his palmier days, it had been Michaelis' favorite haunt.

Several times during the course of their meal, the artist was recognized by colleagues and acquaintances and though he greeted each, he held no converse with them.

But, as their sweet Zuppa Inglese was served, Riegler, the noted art critic and prestigious historian, came to their table and requested discourse.

"I have seen your self-portrait on exhibit," he said, taking Michaelis' hand in a warm clasp. "Allow me to be the first to congratulate you and to acclaim it a masterpiece."

Seeing Riegler not repulsed by the formerly misanthropic artist, others now approached more closely. All had either already seen the portrait or just heard of it from others. All were filled with congratulations and that unrestrained heartfelt pleasure that true artists feel in a deserving colleague's triumph over their shared and recalcitrant material and even more elusive muse. French Champagne was ordered by Reigler. Toasts were proposed to Michaelis and his work. The dinner became a fete.

Soon the party spilled out into the piazza, and from there, it moved toward the salon with ever increasing festivity.

Michaelis had barely stepped over the threshold of the salon when a man, who for the past three years had mocked him to all who would listen, stepped forward to embrace the artist.

"You have been awarded the *Palma d'Oro*, the highest honor Rome can bestow upon a work of art."

A cheer rose from the crowd. Others in the salon, hearing of Michaelis' arrival, rushed to greet him.

The President of the Society of Arts himself arrived, and pinned the palm tree medal to Michaelis' jacketfront and launched into a speech of flowery laudation and excessive length.

The artist heard and witnessed all this with a scarcely hidden sneer and with no great enthusiasm. What did these fools mean? The painting was a failure. A mere whisper of a possibility of what he had once intended, what he had idealized, what he had achieved if only briefly, and oh so perilously. Could these idiots not understand what he had done? What he had been forced to *undo* by his own hand? Would they never understand the depths of darkness which he had plumbed, first in his imagination, then—when the pigment was actually produced—in his art, in his life? If his undoing was the cause of so much honor, what would they have thought of the painting as he had planned it, as he had first painted it?

The president was at last done speaking. Applause was followed by more congratulations, more toasts and by the drinking of more champagne. Michaelis was asked to speak too, and he demurred. But William—who among all the others the artist truly believed was delighted in his friend's good fortune—persuaded him to attempt it. So the artist spoke quietly and sadly of his travails, of his search for new modes of expression, of his experimentation with new and old forms and themes and techniques, of how the ideal he had envisioned would live on, although the finished work was compromised and would always be a failure, a mere cipher of that ideal.

"Enough modesty. Let us see this marvel!" the President declared. "We have installed it at one end of the great salon, with no others nearby, for all would doubtless suffer by comparison."

"The others are mere exercises by comparison," Michaelis heard his former enemy declare.

Nor was he the only man to utter such sentiments as the crowd, Michaelis in its midst, flowed into the great salon, past one fine painting after another, each one ignored or subjected to abuse and invective from the onlookers.

When they had gathered and opened a space around the painter and his portrait, it was William who read out the inscription: "Self Portrait in Absolute Ebony."

"Amazing, isn't it?" Reigler demanded of his companion.

"Astounding!" several agreed.

"Utter genius!" oner man declared. "Who would have dreamed of outlining the cape in Lamp Black?"

"And the cape itself . . . remarkable!"

"Of course, of course! The cape! The cape!"

The President was speaking into Michaelis' ear during the hubbub.

"When the canvas was first brought in, we feared it had been damaged during the carting. Two tiny spots of white in the lower center of the cape seemed to mar the edge of the cape. Fortunately, within seconds, they were gone. They vanished as we looked on."

Michaelis did not appear to hear the words. Instead he seemed entranced, his eyes completely filled by what he beheld: the portrait, exactly as he had finisihed it a week and a half before, with the cape painted in absolutely ebony.

"Why, I feel as though I could put my hand right into the pigment, there at the cape," Riegler reached toward it.

"No!" Michaelis shouted. "Don't touch it!"

"He meant it no harm," Williams said.

"Don't touch the canvas," Michaelis repeated more softly, but with as much anxiety in his voice. "Don't go too near it. Not ever! Not if you care for your sanity."

"As though it were a window cut into some other dimension," he could hear another man saying. "One of utter blackness, naturally."

"Why, even the room appears smaller at this end," yet another viewer observed. "As though it were made smaller by the portrait."

"There's never been a painting like it," several agreed.

Michaelis turned away, grasping Williams' arm.

"We must go," he whispered.

"Go? Where?"

"To Boston. Tonight. Immediately. The first packet that sails."

"But surely you're jesting. after a triumph like . . . "Then, seeing his friend's face, he changed his words to say, "The packet doesn't leave until tomorrow afternoon."

"I must gather a few necessities tonight. Now. You will help me," the artist said quietly, drawing William away from the others still gathered in wonder about the portrait.

"I'm delighted, of course, to help you leave," William said, "Since that was the purpose of my mission to you here in Rome. But why such haste? We were to celebrate tonight, surely? And to leave Rome now, at the height of your success?"

William had to repeat his question, then repeat it again.

Although Michaelis stared at him from only inches away, he could not hear his countryman's words. All he could hear was a soft, lapping sound, then the awful familiarity of a barely audible whimpering that spoke of an unfillable abyss that would reach out slowly, inexorably, and draw him in, deep into the maw of absolute ebony.

21

The Things We Lose, The Things We Leave Behind

BILLY O'CALLAGHAN

A mile or so outside the village, I stop, just for a minute, to watch four boys kick an orange plastic football around a field. Through a heckle of laughter and calls to attention, young legs battle the tangle of long grass, the ball looping from one to another to another without hardly a pause, their play dictated by some pattern or set of rules that is far beyond my comprehension but which seems to make perfect sense to them. They look happy, and I try to recall how it had been for me at that age, when I too had been full of running and careless as to my direction, but my old world and this one now seem like vastly different species of the same beast.

Our pasts pool around our ankles, dragging at every forward step we take, but it doesn't do to dwell too deeply on what has gone before, even if we sometimes use those past events to explain or excuse the things we've done. So much has happened to me here, enough to chase me away, enough to call me back.

I watch until the boys become aware of my presence, then I raise a hand in salute. "Grand day, lads."

The boy who has killed the game moves a few paces closer, then stops, hands on hips, ball pinned beneath one foot. He studies me while chewing the innards of his lower lip, his head inclined ever so slightly to the left and his eyes pinched nearly shut in resistance against the washed-out glare of an April sun. He is all worn edges and scuffed knees, and his yellow hair has the same shorn, stubbled look as the fields after the hay has been taken in. Short and a shade too thin,

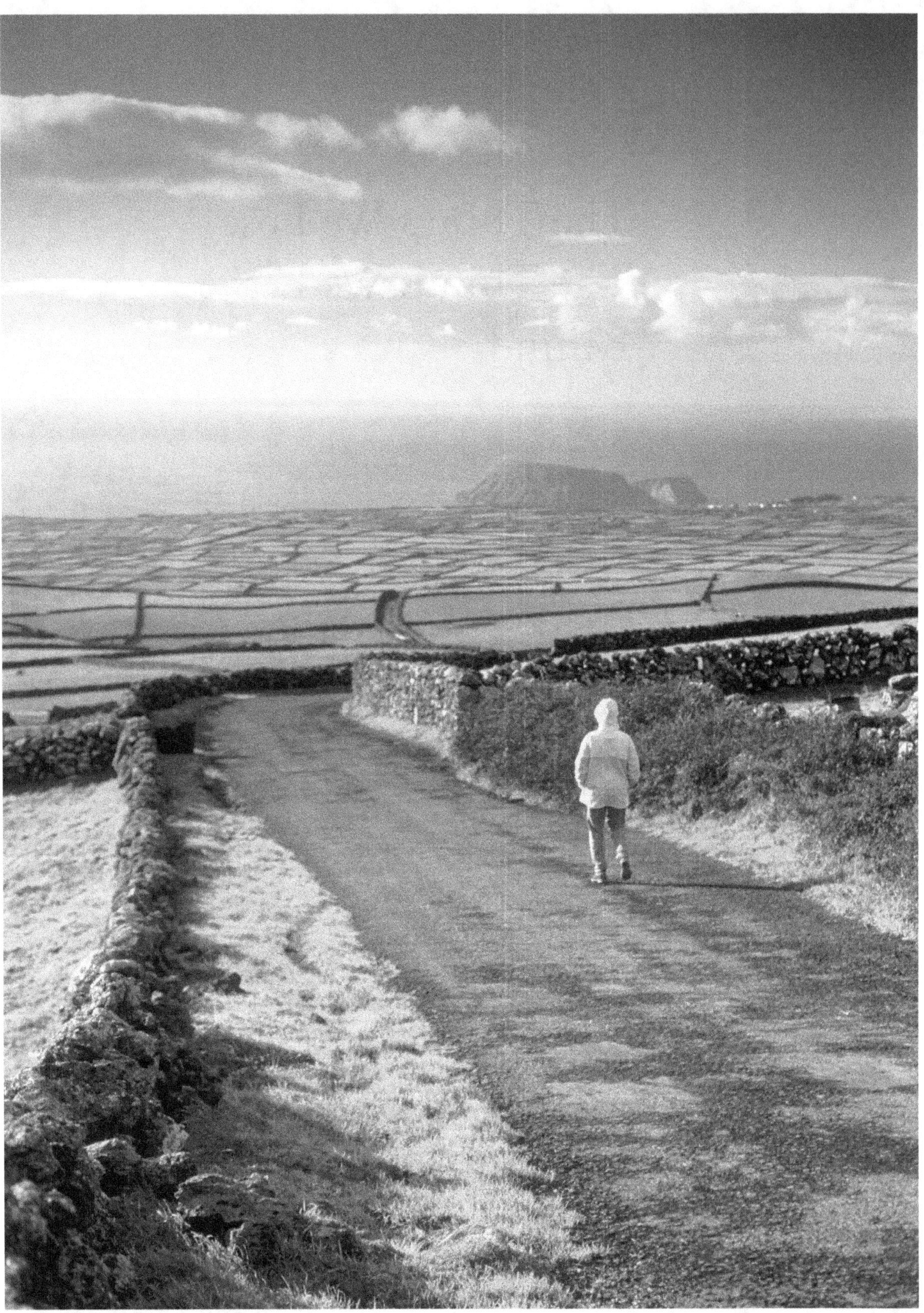

perhaps, but still just right for a child of his age—seven going on for eight, if the signs match the facts. Short because it is not yet his time to stand tall, thin from so much running.

"You lost, mister?" he asks, after a minute or so has passed. It is only the middle of the day and there is no need to hurry.

The others mutter their amusement at his question and I, for my part, feel obliged to break open a smile, but suddenly I have a lump in my throat that makes it difficult to swallow. I shake my head.

"No, boy. I'm not lost. No one can get lost on an island of this size. Out here you can see every direction coming. For real lost, you'd want to try a city. Dublin isn't bad, London is better still. Best of all is New York."

"You've been to New York?" asks one of the other boys, in a small husk of a voice that pokes up out of a crowd and that knows all there is to know about the ocean, even at such a tender age. Boys grow up hard on islands, those that manage to survive.

"I have," I say, "and believe me, it's not all that it's cracked up to be."

The lead boy rolls his foot off the ball, drawing it up into the air. He shows me his tricks, which work like a slow but stately magic, even in the long grass. Needing, for some reason, to impress me. His control isn't perfect but his put-on swagger of confidence more than makes up for that fact, and when the ball slips loose of its invisible leash he shapes his face so as to pass the mistake off as intentional. It spins away but he doesn't chase it, not even with his eyes.

"You need directions to somewhere?"

Age is such a conceptual thing. Eight-year-old mouths can shape ancient expressions just as easily as they can chew gum. Boys long to be men, to say and do the things that men can say and do. Men, meanwhile, waste years of life on dreams of childish things.

I shake my head again, and wonder if he knows who I am, if he has at all sensed even a suggestion of the bond that once bound us so fast together. No matter. I recognize him even if he fails to recognize me. I suddenly long to use his name, to feel it from my own mouth. Jack. Spoken as a brazen sigh, put out here for the whole island to hear and contemplate. A word for the wind, and an acknowledgement of sorts. Or an admission. Jack. But I can't. When a man walks away from his infant son, he gives up all rights in that direction.

"That's all right, lad," I say, forcing my tone to steadiness. "I guess I know the way well enough. Why don't you boys get back to your game."

There is a murmur of breeze, a teasing glimpse of first summer carrying the smell of the ocean on its breath. Hands in pockets, I keep a casual pace, drifting on up the road but less than eager, really, to get where I need to be. Being back here is hard to take, almost as hard as knowing that I will soon be gone again. I walk, slowly, because that is the sort of pace this place demands, and I know that if I was to turn, I'd find the boys still grouped together in the field, still watching me. They know who belongs here on this island and they know how to recognize tourists. Fitting neither category quite right, I have triggered confusion.

The only difference in six years is the fresh coat of whitewash. Six years. Christ. Standing here now, it feels impossible that so much time has passed. Time should change things, really change them, not merely tug at the seams. Since the day I left I've held a picture of this place in my mind, a matted image that hardly varies from any of the hundred such scenic postcards that they peddle to the tourists in every seaside town and village up and down the country. A small farmhouse cottage set back a little from the twist of dirt road, its thatched roof touched up with season after season of newly cut reeds and always keeping to just the right side of the sunken abyss. And five or so acres back beyond the cottage, the land finally rolls away, collapsing down into the jagged spokes of shale that rake the sea. A huge cloak of sky completes the picture, a sky always working, from minute to minute moiling to churn out yet another new trick of the light, now the glare of a tilted looking-glass, now the deception of smoke. The sea today is calm, another April lie in a place that has practiced that skill to perfection.

Tommy is in the kitchen, sitting hunched over in a hard chair with his elbows resting on his knees and his hands laced together in a prayerful grip. He looks up when I come to the back door but his eyes have the watery resonance of a dream and it takes him a moment to register my presence as something real. Then he rises slowly but not quite fully, courtesy of the hard-won lumbar kink that keeps him off-balance and constantly at odds, and by way of greeting he offers a hand that is nothing but rags and sticks. I come inside and sit at the table and he finds a bottle in the cupboard by the range.

I have known Tommy all my life, and I have known him as a father-in-law since the age of nineteen. We have plenty to talk about, but for a while it is easier just to sit and drink. The whiskey is a brand name type, nothing special, the stuff they make in big factories and sell in every licensed premises in Ireland, but here in this kitchen it takes on new properties. I can taste the flavors of the island filtering up through the heat, and stones grate inside my throat. Not molten lava, but certainly blazing dust. The old transistor radio in the corner is skipping out a fiddled reel that seems without beginning or end but the station is slipping in and out of tune in a way that brings a wonderful and priceless sense of distortion to the piece. A happy accident, like so many of the best things in the world.

"So," he says, at last. "Where'd you end up, then?"

I'm not sure why I have to think about the answer, but I do. "America," I say, when I can.

"New York first, then some other places. But one is much the same as the next until you give up on the cities." My voice sounds unfamiliar to me, and feels worse. The tone has dropped a notch, a semitone at least, and feels airy. It takes the better part of a minute for me to recognise the fact that we are conversing in Irish. Old words and older ways, ways that I have long since put aside.

He nods at what I have told him, sucks down the whiskey in his glass and dashes off a refill. I hold my hand across the mouth of my glass to indicate that I'm fine for the moment, that I want to take things slowly, but he waits with the bottle until I give up and then he pours anyway. I try not to stare but can't help myself. And I see that I was wrong in my earlier assumptions of time and its effects. Six years might not have touched the rocks and the dirt of this island, but people are not rocks and dirt. The weather has all but torn Tommy asunder. His face is a ruin of years hard spent. Ashamed of the part I have played in making those marks, I want nothing more at this moment than to turn away, to lower my eyes, hide myself among the kitchen's thickening shadows, maybe to run again and this time never look back. But I owe him more than that.

"You got my letter?"

"I did. A week back. I had just about given up expecting you."

"It's been a while, all right. I never meant to stay away so long."

He recognizes the lie and looks away.

The kitchen looks the same now as it did when I first sat here. Same furniture, same worn paper on the walls, same curtains on the window. But such sameness only serves to emphasize all that has been lost. Without discussing the matter, we decide to give the whiskey a bit of a beating. I have a bad stomach and hardly touch the stuff anymore, except when the occasion demands. But I'm not at all sure that I can bear to sit in this house without the sustenance of something strong. I suppose Tommy feels the same way, at least today.

"I was sorry to hear about Bess."

He smiles at that, a nice, heartbroken ache of a smile that widens his eyes. "I know, boy."

"She was a good woman."

"The best," he says, then pulls again at the whiskey in his glass. "And she was always fond of you. But it was an ease to her, in the end. The other thing had her eaten away so that you'd have been hard pushed to even recognise her from the way she once was. It's a terrible waste, you know, having to watch something like that happen to someone who was always so strong."

"How long has it been, now?"

"It'll be two years come June." He empties his glass and looks at me, and I am shocked to see the surface for what it truly is, a cracked and crumbling façade. "I'll tell you, Bill. If it wasn't for the boy, I don't know how I'd have coped."

Big subjects lie between us like jagged shards of glass. Neither of us wants an argument, so we thread lightly. The words prove difficult to come by, and when spoken don't seem nearly enough to cover all that needs saying. I look around again. The picture of the Sacred Heart hangs crooked on the wall beside the window. That picture was crooked when I first set foot in this house, the better part of ten years ago now, to ask Elisabeth if she might like to come out for a walk along the shore with me. And it was crooked, too, on the day I left, the day

I turned my back on all the sorrows and all the joys and just walked out, with England in my sights but America very much on my mind. Elisabeth was already gone by then, gone in the toughest way imaginable and buried over on the stony hillside. A name chiseled into rock, but more than that too. Everywhere I turned I could see her, every voice I heard shifted with her own musical timbre. America lay a full huge ocean away, and I wanted to believe that that would be more than far enough. But it was not. Home can be like a disease. It gets in your blood and poisons everything; it's with you for every heartbeat, hammering away until finally you have to give in, you have to come home. And this land, I know, has a way of paralyzing time, because out here all you really see is rock and ocean and sky, elements that keep a count in aeons rather than years. What was real back then seems just as real now, and your have to dig deep beneath the ancient veneer before that illusion comes apart.

I clear my throat but my voice, when it comes, feels as if it belongs to someone else, a paper thin croak driven by my rush of breath.

"How *is* he?"

"Jack? He's grand. He's good as gold."

Tommy licks his mouth, bunches his chin in a way that squeezes up his face, the pasty flesh rippling and then holding its folds. He is thinking of something that won't be shared, and a smile breaks, setting his eyes to glistening. Outside, the sky is doing something new to the light. The sun has slipped behind the fringe of western clouds. The colors feel too raw to be natural but the salt-flecked window frames a scene that is undeniably immaculate to a painterly eye.

The boy enters the house at a run, draws up with an audible gasp when he sees me. By now, the kitchen is swathed in twilight, and I recall such moments as these from the springtime days of my own childhood, the few minutes when night feels close but not yet quite here and it is still too soon yet to think of sparking awake the lantern. Of course, these days it will be the electric light because lanterns belong to a generation gone, but the sense remains the same. A groggy dusk but a most comfortable pocket in the day, time enough to take a breath, maybe to whisper a prayer for those still wandering out beyond the walls and beyond the waves, the lost ones.

"Hello again," I say. This time I mean the smile I wear, but its edges still feel anxious.

Jack glances around, then studies me carefully. "Hello," he says, after a long moment. "Again."

I'm not sure what to say because I'm not sure how much he knows about the way things are. I find myself wishing for Tommy to act as our buffer, but he is outside, drawing water from the pump. "Good day for a game of football," I say. "Did you win?"

"There's no winning or losing," Jack says, and shrugs his shoulders. "It wasn't that sort of game. We didn't have enough players for a proper match." He considers sitting, decides against it. I feel like I can read the careworn jumble of his thoughts. "You know my granddad?"

"I ought to, since I'm sitting here drinking his whiskey." I widen my smile, trying to keep things light between us. But he still looks uncertain.

"Why didn't you say something earlier? About where you were going, I mean? I could have walked up with you."

"You had your game, and a sunny day. You wouldn't have had much business being cooped up with us, listening while we rattled our teeth about things from long ago. You'd have been bored stupid."

He should be nothing like I remember. At his age, six years is as good as a lifetime. Details sharpen and wane, hair changes color with the sun, and running picks away every ounce of fat even as eating piles it on. The fact that, back in the field, I could have picked him out from the scuffed pack of others, doesn't seem quite right, somehow. He should have been just anybody, another stranger who happened across my path, but he wasn't. And now, standing just feet apart, I can't help noticing that the way he squares his jaw was the way Elisabeth squared hers whenever she was trying to be strong in the face of something troubling, or that he has her eyes, her shade of green that is nearly grey, a peculiarly coastal shade of eye, mirroring the sea but only at a certain dying moment of the day, when the light has been mostly sucked out of the sky and the surface turns reflective, hiding its greater depths. I see the details of Elisabeth in him, and I know that if I just consider the nose or the little crooked corner of that mouth, I will see details of myself there too. But I know when to look away. It is the pretence that keeps this house of cards upright, and denial becomes easier with practice. Anyone who has ever run more than two steps worth of escape knows that.

In many ways, I can't quite believe that he is standing here before me. I have thought of him often, of course, wallowing in my guilt until it lost the worst edge of its sting, picturing him as he once was, an arm's worth of flesh all sleeping smiles and wise, familiar eyes, and then imagining how he might have been with every passing year. But time's wicked trick was to make him seem less real to me, somehow, more a thing of fantasy than flesh and blood.

"I'm starving," he says, at last, and twisting away into the shadows he finds a large knife in the cutlery drawer and proceeds to cut himself a doorstop slice of soda bread. Not the baby that I had rocked to sleep or tickled to hear him squeal with laughter, but already halfway towards being a man. He uses the same knife to cut a wedge of butter.

"We don't get many visitors," he says, over his shoulder. He takes a bite. "Actually, we don't get any. I'd say you're the first. Ever."

A pot of stew has been simmering away on the range. Another feature of my younger days, part of the smell of this cottage, the scent of onions and thyme and the thick chunks of mutton filtering into the aura of the place. About an hour after my arrival, Tommy had dropped some potatoes into the pot.

"You'll destroy your appetite," I say, just for something to take the edge out of Jack's comment. "We'll be eating dinner soon."

He looks at me again, for longer than he should, really, even with the dusk thickening walls between us. I get the sense that he is studying me too, matching details as I had done. Then he takes another bite of soda bread, chews it with a daring that will probably stoke a heap of trouble for him in years to come but which clearly makes up a big part of who he is. I'm responsible for that chip on his shoulder.

The night passes in snatches, the essences of sleep and wakefulness so diluting one another that in short order they become two sides of the same tarnished and constantly spinning coin. After the sickly gloaming of those half-nights in the cities, the darkness feels absolute. Riptides of memory claw at my mind, and I toss and turn in this old bed and try to ignore the ghosts that whisper reminders of late-hour embraces and last broken breaths. The dreams, when they come, are time trips that deepen and dissolve, and then I am back again into the waking pit, gasping at the turgid air. I tell myself that it's the whiskey, but it's not.

A little after five, I hear movement, the creak of a floorboard, outside the bedroom door. Five minutes later I am dressed and sitting at the kitchen table. The electric light now feels like an almighty gift, as would anything that can so completely dispel the predawn shadows. Tommy boils a kettle of water for tea, lays a few strips of bacon in a pan. I sit there and watch his shuffled moves as he tends to his business, and decide that this sort of hour does no one any favours. He wears yesterday's clothes, the same as I do, but everything seems ill-fitting on him. Braces hold up his trousers, his heavy grey shirt is only partially buttoned. Worse, his salt and pepper hair spools wildly from the back of his head, giving him the wizened look of the truly infirm.

"Can I do anything?" I ask, but he doesn't answer, maybe doesn't hear, and I leave it at that. Lard spatters and crackles in the pan, and the heat of the range chases away whatever little chill the early morning might carry.

We eat mostly in silence. The food won't be mistaken for gourmet, but the bacon tastes the way it should and the eggs run when cut apart. I'm not that hungry but that doesn't matter. Here on the island, food takes on the qualities of a ritual, one of the many duties to be fulfilled. Tommy wipes his plate clean with a piece of buttered bread, chews it thoughtfully and then sits back in his chair.

"So," he says, barely loud enough for me to hear. "Is this about something?"

For a moment, I am lost.

"Your visit, I mean."

I shake my head, no. "It's like I said in the letter. I just had an urge to come home. Elisabeth's anniversary seemed like as good an excuse as any. And I suppose I wanted to see the boy." The heat of the tea in my mouth should feel better than it does. Confession never sat well with me.

"And that's all?"

I meet Tommy's glare, then bow in surrender. "That's all."

"Because he wouldn't want to go, you know. Even if that was what you had in mind. He doesn't even know you. And I'd nail him to the floor before I'd let you take him out of here. So help me Christ, I would. This is where he belongs."

Outside the window, the darkness is splitting. Dawn isn't far off but it is more of a feeling than anything else, and there's little proof to the eyes.

"I didn't come to take him, Tommy. That's not what this is about. He'd like America for about ten minutes. Believe me when I say that it's not like here. Besides, I know he's not mine to take, not anymore. It's just that, well, after all this time I had lost the picture of him in my mind. I wanted to see him, that's all. And I needed to come home, just to see that there is still such a place."

Tommy stares at me, reading the rest of my story in silence. Then he looks away. It's been probably three or four days since he last bothered to shave, his small concession to God as he took up his place in the back pew of early Mass or to the people of the village as he tended to some errand deemed too complicated for the boy to run, and the blue-white dusting of stubble gives him a look of wild horses and wind-battered sails. Tourists would pay pretty pennies for a picture of that face so full of weathered character. He smiles at something and I know that a memory has broken across his bow. I wait for him to share the thought, but he doesn't, and it's not my place to push.

Minutes pass. We drink more tea and watch the window fill with sullen grey.

"He's all questions, you know. I can see them, piled up high in his head. They wrinkle his brow and age him fifty years. But he doesn't ask, not when it comes to serious business. In a few days he might mention something in passing but he's never outright with it. He's bright as a buttercup, that boy. Takes his time on things, figures them out. Does it properly. He understands, I suppose, that if I want him to know something, I'll tell him."

"Does he know about Elisabeth? How she died, I mean?"

"Some. Not the details, though. It was Bessie who told him bits and pieces, over the years. Made a story out of it and filled in most of the blanks, softened it up. Going on about a mother's love, and all that."

We sit until the silence becomes too much, and we are stuck in the same direction. Then Tommy stands with a groan and gathers up the plates, leaving the cups. It is early, and we'll drink a lot more tea yet before it is time for me to catch the ferry. He scrapes what little waste there is, the bacon rinds and a few crusts of bread, into a small bin, then lowers the plates into a large yellow plastic basin so that they can soak for a couple of hours. Watching his back, I slip an envelope from inside my shirt. Whenever I had money, they had money too; when I was on my heels they learned to do without. Lately, I've been doing okay. I have learned the hard way that money only tunes the material world, but it does hold a few keys and I do what I can to help. Making a small difference is still making a difference. I set the envelope in the middle of the table and stand, try to stretch out the knot between my shoulders that has become so familiar of late. It shifts a little but not far.

"Sun's coming up," I say, in a thoughtful tone that doesn't encourage an answer, but it's my excuse to step outside, just for a minute or so, to gaze out at the ocean still black against the last of night and to feel the dawn breaking at my shoulder. The darkness feels tempered, and crumbles by degrees even in those few moments.

Back in the kitchen, Tommy is sitting again and the envelope is nowhere in sight. We drink tea until I am sick of the taste of it, and then we keep drinking to fill up the time. There is no more, really, to be said. I have a question that I want to ask, whether or not Tommy has any idea why Elisabeth did what she did, but that question is always in my mind, always, and I know better than to cut it loose. Instead I ask him to tell me how Jack is doing at school, and how he is in general, and I lean forward with my elbows on the table and make sure that I absorb every word of reply. Tommy talks with ease, now that I am no longer a threat to the world that he has carved.

"Do you think he knows who I am?" I ask, when I have heard everything else. He is becoming more real to me now, the boy, my son, the added colors making all the difference.

Tommy shrugs. "Difficult to know. As I've said, he's a bright boy, but deep. He chews on things. I give him all the room he needs."

"Does he ever ask about me? I mean, you know, who his father was, that sort of thing."

"Sometimes, we'll be doing something. Mending nets, say, or getting the boat ready for the season. He knows his father was a fisherman, and that he was good with his hands. Damn good, in fact. Did you see him watching you, last night? Did you happen to notice him checking out your hands? He'll never say so, but he knows. He knows enough, Bill."

I nod, understanding I can't hope for any more than that.

By eight o'clock, I've had enough. The ferry doesn't sail until eleven but I make the excuse that there are a few things I'd like to do before I leave. Call to the old graveyard, pay my respects. Maybe look in on a few of the neighboring families. And I want to walk, alone, just for a little while. Visit some old ghosts.

I shake Jack's hand, because a hug would be too awkward, even though we both probably want it. "So long, boy," I say, hoping in my heart that it's not goodbye. He clenches his mouth and nods, then goes to sit in the corner. Tommy looks at him for a moment, then follows me outside.

We walk out onto the road. "It's been good seeing you, Bill," he says. "Take care of yourself, you hear?"

My throat aches in that dull way when tears are near but trying not to fall. Down in the harbour a boat has come in after two or three days at sea. The men, bone-tired, will be gutting and crating their catch for the mainland markets. A breeze is blowing from the east and it carries the impatient screams of the gulls as they circle and perch in anticipation of the scraps.

"I'll write," I say, the best that I can manage, and I slip my hands into my pockets and stroll away, counting the steps so that I won't look back.

Installation 72

DAVID GULLEN

I'm left looking at the installation after everyone else has gone to collect their white wine and canapés.

It consists of a galvanized steel tray a meter long by half a meter wide, with ten centimeters walls. Round tubes, like wide, metal drain-pipes, are fixed to the floor at each corner, and slightly inward leaning. They give a superficial appearance of an inverted table. The legs at one end are roughly sixty centimeters high, taper towards the ground and are lined with padded suede.

The other pair of tubes are wider and shorter, with a vertical hinge allowing the rear of the tube to be opened. There is a cutaway at the base of each hinged section. One tube is open, the other closed, held shut by a small, brass padlock. The whole installation is spotlessly clean.

Footsteps echo across the birch wood floor of the white-walled gallery room. "What do you think?"

Standing beside me is the beautiful, slim girl from the video. It takes me a moment to recognize her: she's cut her blonde hair shorter and it makes her look quite different. She studies me patiently while I stare at her, feeling disoriented, struggling for words.

"Very powerful. Intimidating."

Her light laugh tells me she thinks my answer predictable. In some way I have confirmed her expectations. Tucking a strand of hair behind her ear she holds out her hand. "Chloe Adams."

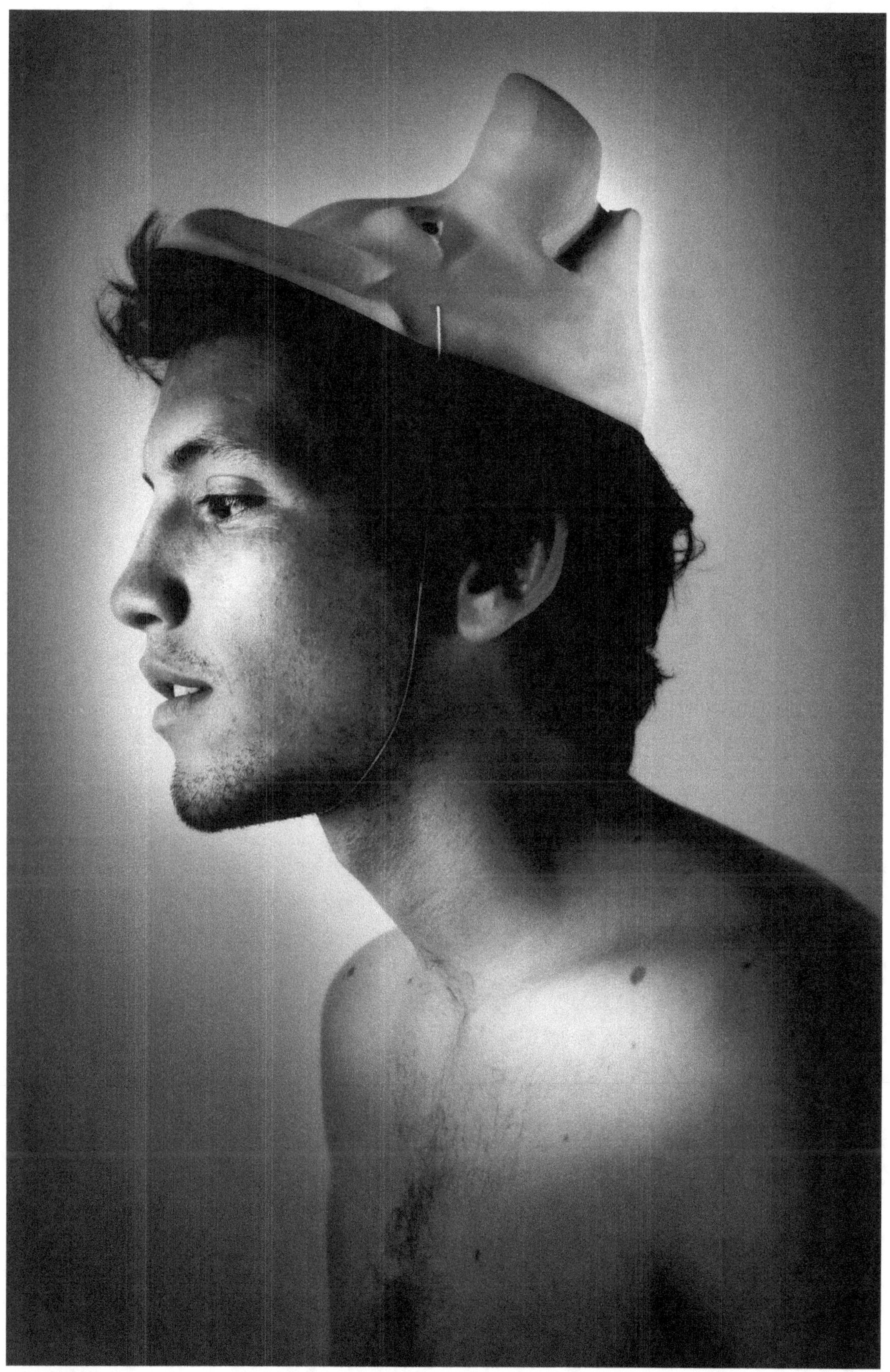

I take her hand. The grip of her cool slender unpainted fingers is firm. "David . . ."

"I know who you are, everyone does. The video—did you actually like it?"

The sound of voices from the next room swells as people begin to move away from the buffet through the gallery rooms. Holding the hand of this attractive young woman in her revealing black dress and bare feet, I feel as if I'm about to begin an unexpected journey.

"Did it turn you on?"

"No, not really. Sorry."

She laughs again, pulling her hand free of mine. "You take things so literally. Not many critics take things at face value."

"I write what I see, say what I feel."

"There's more to art, more to me, than surfaces. Probe deeper, you never know what you might find." Chloe moves closer, pressing her stomach against my belt and whispers. "It was real."

My laugh is less confident than hers. "Of course it wasn't. That's why you're still here."

"It wasn't me. I have a twin sister, Veronica. We tossed a coin."

"Where is she tonight?"

"Where do you think? Somewhere—different." She licks her forefinger. Slides it between her lips, squeezing it between her teeth. "It got me so hot. My own sister, it was like watching myself. I get wet thinking about it." Chloe looks at me, her pale eyes widen as she presses her palm between her legs. "We could find somewhere."

I feel my cheeks redden. Despite her casual eroticism, her loveliness makes me feel awkward. "Who . . . who was the other girl? The young one."

"Some trash Marlowe found."

"I'd like to meet her."

She looks disappointed. "I didn't think you were into that. It's okay though."

"Is she here?"

Again, that superior laugh. "Not likely."

"Where?"

She wrinkles her nose and grins. "Where do you think? Ask my sister. See you around, Romeo."

"Wait." But she is gone, slipping through the returning crowd, moving deeper into the gallery, sleek hips swaying, raised arm waving across the room, shaven armpit pale as white silk.

"David. Hi." Petra, camera swinging from its shoulder strap, kisses my cheek. Her scarlet lips leave a faint, and enticing musk. "The girl in the video, you were talking to her."

"Her sister, Chloe."

"Are you all right?"

"I'm fine. The installation . . ."

"Strong, yes. What else should we expect from Marlowe? I'm not surprised you're feeling a bit disoriented. I haven't decided if he's gone mad or just taking the piss. What do you think?""

"It looked very real."

"In a way it was. What is the difference between fantasy and reality if they look the same, if they make us feel the same things? Reality, like truth, is subjective. Everything's processed in our minds, it's an individual decision."

"Chloe told me it was real."

"A decadently exciting idea, but that's Chloe Adams for you. And when she refers to her sister she's talking about her muse, what she calls her Aspect of Art. It's how she isolates her performances in Marlowe's installations from her own internal psychic spaces."

"She told you that?"

Petra's dark eyes hold me. "Use it in your review, David. I expect you to." She strokes my arm affectionately. "I'm going to find her, get some photographs for my magazine. And don't worry, Chloe's sister doesn't exist. I'm sure she's an only child."

I move through a gallery filled with the usual first-night invitation mix of young artists wearing black, their eccentric friends, colorful, aging groupies, journalists, collectors, critics, the rich, the pretentious, and the intermittently notorious. Drifting from room to room I try to focus on the other exhibits but can't connect with their message. Tonight everything, every conversation, is about one thing, Marlowe's installation:

". . . typical transformation of the crass and mundane."

"Imagine kneeling there. I don't know what to think."

"A classic study of depersonalisation."

"Being able to touch the installation afterwards was so empowering . . ."

". . . that girl, so lucky."

"Tragically original. She's here tonight."

"Impossible. Where?"

"I despise myself for loving it."

"I love myself for despising it!"

"You've always been in love with yourself."

"No, darling, just the idea of self . . ."

I owe it to the other artists exhibiting tonight, and the readers of the magazine I write for, to spend some time viewing the other work. There is a white stone bench in a short passage between two of the rooms. I sit there and try to clear my mind, mentally touring the gallery, trying to recall my impressions of the other photographs, constructs, paintings, sculptures, and installations.

I'm broken from my reverie by the sound of spontaneous applause. Marlowe, dressed in a black polo neck and dark slacks, breaks free of the gathered crowd, bowing, hands pressed together like a Chinese emperor. I can tell he's seen me. He says something to his appreciative audience and there's more applause and a few cheers. It is quite remarkable. Turning away, Marlowe comes towards me followed by Chloe, the woman who looks so similar to, but I fear is not, the person in his video.

Marlowe holds out his hand. "David, are you ok? You look lost."

I take his hand and stand up. "My head is full of your compelling art; I'm trying to empty it."

"What would you replace it with?" Marlowe looks up at me. He's quite short, shorter than the blonde woman beside him in her high-collared, backless black dress.

"Concepts, sensations, phantom echoes from the soul," I say.

"I wish I could visualise my drives so easily. Sometimes I find it hard enough to simply recognize them."

"My writing is going through an impressionist phase. It means I can make some of it up."

"I'm sure in your case it would be a product of morphic resonance, emergent truths from a subconscious pond. You've met Chloe Adams?"

"Yes. She was telling me about her sister."

Marlowe frowns. "Veronica?"

"In the installation."

He burst out laughing. "Chloe's sister lives in Paraguay. They haven't seen each other for . . ."

"Seventeen years," Chloe yawns.

Marlowe takes my elbow, draws me down. His other hand rests lightly on my hip before artlessly slipping across my buttock.

"Don't bother," Chloe says, "he's more interested in your jail-bait."

"We're all a little afraid of you, David," Marlowe whispers. "Everyone will read your column first."

"Tonight I'm a little freaked out."

"I take it you liked it then?"

"That's not the right word. When I shut my eyes I can still see your work. You've made tonight your own, listen to the crowd. This evening everyone is talking about you, tomorrow everyone will be reading about you."

Marlowe opens his arms in acceptance. "To what else can an artist aspire?"

"You're not worried about a counter-reaction?"

"Of the media? From ordinary people? Artists have to exist outside of nations and societies. How else can we observe? If I show them something about themselves they don't like, they shouldn't blame me."

"Can I quote you?"

"New art forms new impressions. Installation 72 opens deep inside you, lodging there forever to make you a part of the work itself. Tonight should be conceptualized as a mental seed, nourished by a communal, consensual, psychic vibe." Marlowe's eyes glint under his close-cropped dark hair. "This is the first piece of a new movement, a new school of art thought. Come to my winter show and you will understand more."

"I don't doubt you. I look forward to it in trepidation."

Marlowe looks at me thoughtfully, his eyes twinkle and I can almost hear the mocking laughter inside his head. "Petra Foelke said something similar when she was photographing us. I understand your concern with Chloe's imaginary sister. Think, David. How could I do such a thing if the authorities weren't satisfied?" He leans closer, confidentially. "I don't like talking about methods, but I see it's necessary. I used CGI, computer graphics. Very clever, honestly."

"I see. Yes, how else."

"Quite. Chloe, show David your scar."

Chloe's eyes slide back into focus. "What?"

Turning to me Marlowe explains: "Chloe got a little cut on her tummy while we were filming."

"Gorgeous, love it. Blood's the best colour to wear against skin." Chloe looked around the room. "There's Pedro Agenbite. I love what he does with fabrics."

"Show David your scar, darling."

Chloe looks down at her dress. "What, here? There's nothing under this you know."

"So?"

"It doesn't matter." I say.

Chloe ducks down and grips the hem of her dress. "Don't you want to look at my cunt?"

"No, darling, he doesn't." Marlowe pries open her fingers. "Sorry, David, we did a lot of stuff last night, excited about the show. Chloe's come down a bit hard."

"Don't worry."

"After tonight my installation will be destroyed. From then on it will only exist in people's heads, only survive on reputation and, perhaps, your review."

"A good test of your theory of lodgment."

"Very perceptive. Look, we're going to run it again. Coming?"

"No, Once is . . ."

Chloe wiggles her hips and takes my hand. "Come along. You can see your little girlfriend again."

———

The white-painted room is empty apart from Installation 72. The viewpoint doesn't change for a long while. I can hear the whirr of a projector, and wonder if Marlowe really used film, or if the sound is part of the installation. Then the view swings round to the door, which is already opening. Young, slender and fair, dressed in a dark skirt and white blouse, a woman enters. As she begins to undress I know that Chloe's body would look exactly the same. The woman looks at the camera as she unfastens her bra and smiles, then bends down and steps out of her plain black knickers.

Perhaps it is Chloe's sister who ties back her long, fair hair. The camera smoothly zooms to her profile as she lifts her arms over her head, then pans down across her bare flank and back to the installation.

She swings open the wider pair of tubes and kneels down inside them. Reaching behind her, a beautiful, arching, graceful movement, she closes the tubes, her lower legs protruding from the cut-outs, and locks them shut. She kneels upright for a moment, her fingers on the rim of the metal, high up against her bare thighs. Then she tips forward, seizing the other pair of tubes and slides her arms into them. Her arms disappear almost to her shoulders, the metal tubes straightening her elbows.

It is obvious that having placed herself in this position it would be extremely difficult, if not impossible, for her to get out without help. Naked, she is kneeling on her hands and knees across the metal tray. I wonder if she is comfortable. The metal tubes encase her arms and her thighs. Her legs are apart and her breasts hang down. The bright lights warm her bare back.

A naked man wearing a pig's-head mask enters the room. He is pale, hairy and slightly paunchy, and is carrying a large, white card. He stands to the rear of the installation, holds up the card then places it against the leg-tubes. Picking up the discarded clothes, he takes them out of the room.

The card reads: "Installation 72".

The sound of the projector slowly grows louder, then fades away. Finally the woman lowers her head and closes her eyes. The scene is static for several minutes. The prolonged tableau, her immobility, the encasement of her limbs within the installation's metal, minimize her, blend her into the object. The projector noise is gradually replaced by a sizzling, like the sound of frying.

The pig-masked man comes back into the room and squats in front to her. He says something, but the mask muffles his voice. There is a beating pulse in the woman's neck. She looks up at him and nods her head. All sound stops.

The man quickly walks round behind the installation, scoops something up from behind the tray and straddles her. He transfers the object to his other hand and we see it is a knife. He reaches under her, between her breasts, drags back hard, pulling the blade into her body. He opens her quickly all the way down into her hips, twisting the knife free of her pubic bone. A split-second later her entrails slop and spill into the tray in one great slithering mass.

There is still no sound. In utter silence the woman grits her teeth and blows out her cheeks. Her breathing is short and quick, ribs flaring under her skin. Blood sheets down from the wound in a red curtain.

The man climbs off her and squats in front of her again. Inside the metal tubes her arms and legs are shaking violently.

The woman looks up at him. Already her face is greying, her lips blue from loss of blood. Her mouth sags open and her eyes are losing focus. All she can do is shake her head.

Going behind her again the man begins to bugger her. The woman moans and rolls her head as he spasms and grips her hips. He pulls free and she collapses, her body held up only by the tubes encasing her limbs.

Still erect, blood smearing his thighs, the man in the pig mask leaves the room. He instantly returns, now wearing evening dress, leading a coltish young girl wearing blue jeans, trainers, and a pink t-shirt with a sequined heart on the chest. The girl kneels beside the woman, goes down on her hands and knees and peers under the body. Lifting the thick edges of the wound with her thumb and forefinger, she studies the entrails cooling in the tray. Then she squats in front of the corpse, lifts its head with both her hands and wedges an apple between its black lips. Finally she picks up the sign and stands to one side of the installation.

She turns the sign over. Now it reads: "Woman split like a pig."

After the viewing I go to the toilet. I try to reach the basins but vomit onto the floor, the stink and wet sounds blending with the increasingly noisy applause coming from the gallery.

My hands are trembling as I rinse my mouth and wipe my shoes. Outside there are shouts, excited screams, the sound of breaking glass as Marlowe's art depersonalizes its audience into a single object. I hear a sound more akin to barking than laughter and realise with bleak relief that I am outside the expanding event horizon of his installation. As I put my hand on the restroom door a low chanting begins.

When I go outside they're showing the video again.

Retrospective

RON SAVAGE

*He seemed not to care for the thing itself, the bowl of fruit, the pond beneath
the bridge, the girl on the roof, none of that mattered. He was concerned
with the way the light and the shadow played on the thing. This was first,
always first, this was what infatuated my father. He had to know how the
light and the shadow brought these things into the world.*
—LAURA GAUS-DAULTON
A biography for the Thomas Gaus retrospective

That morning Margaret had arranged her husband's first show at a Chelsea gallery on West 27th Street. That night she slept with their three year old on the fold-out sofa in the living room and didn't talk to Thomas until the evening of the second day and only to ask him to pass the oregano during dinner. What have I done? Thomas wanted to know. Then he said, You shouldn't be carting Laura off and disturbing her sleep.

She is an old woman standing at his door. The old woman was once his wife and still is his wife, legally, technically, and she wants to see the daughter she hasn't seen in God knows how long. That thick rust colored hair nobody could comb has gone white on the sides and frames her face. She is also half a foot taller than him, mostly angles and pale long arms, and her eyes go to this and that, taking in the details. He hasn't seen her in, it must be, twenty years.

She says, What do you think, Thomas?

He thinks, Uh-oh. Then he says, Look at you. I thought you'd be dead.

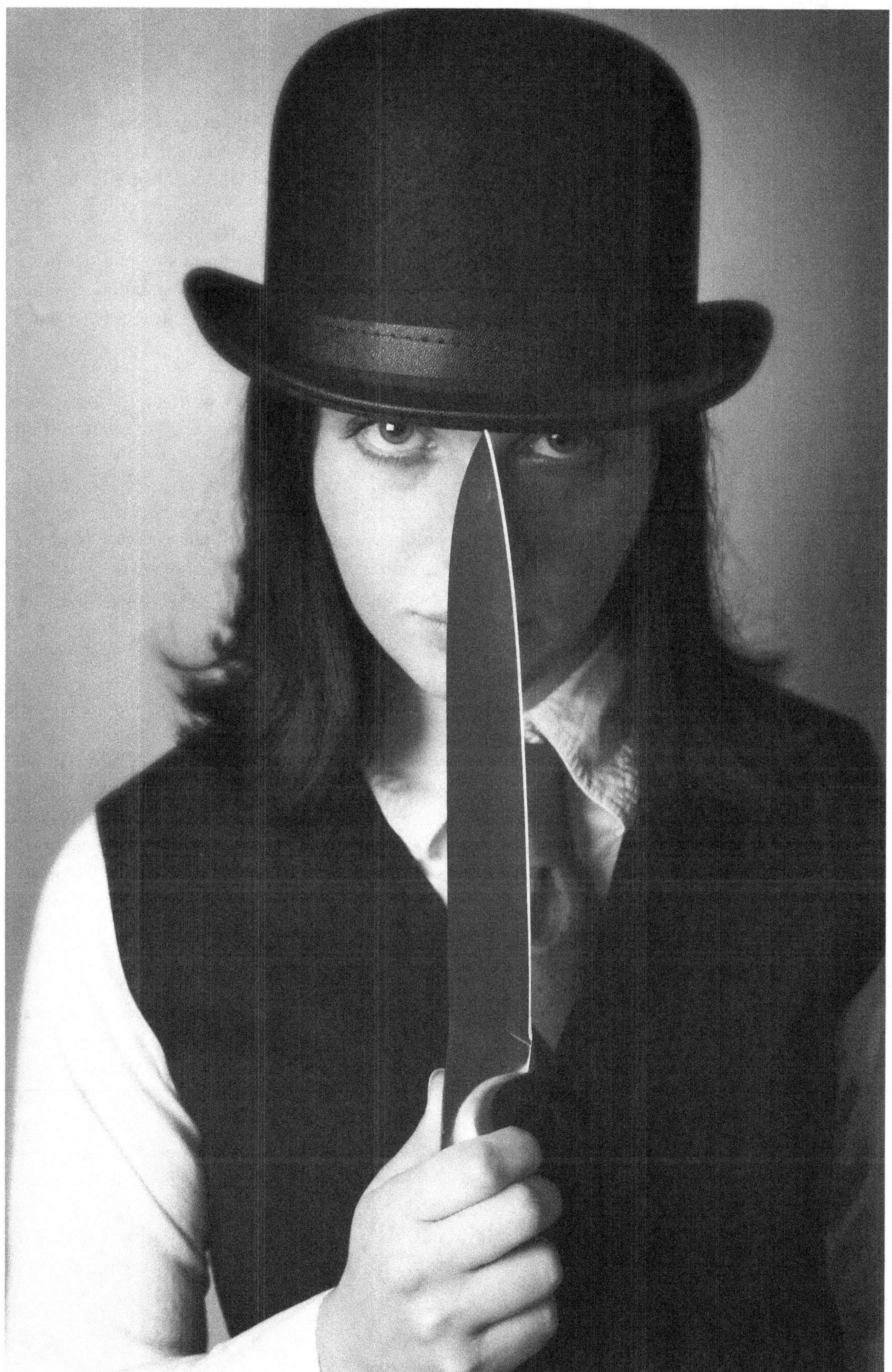

Thought or wished? She says and gives him a quick anxious smile.

Both, he supposed.

His wife tells him she has had a few wishes herself. She tells him she isn't well but death is playing hard to get. Too much smoke or drink or both, she isn't sure. Her liver doesn't work right, and her heart has problems of its own.

What can I say? she says. I was always a disaster, and now I'm an older disaster. But I'd like my Laura's address or maybe her phone number, either one. She steps inside his apartment before he invites her. Then she says, You got any wine? White's fine but I'd like a nice red, something dry.

I remember, he says.

I want to talk with my daughter, she says again. I want to apologize and listen to her tell me what a hideous mother I was. His wife glances around his living room for clues.

Thomas is already nervous. He doesn't want to undo his solitary life, the years he took getting to this reasonable and safe place. But she isn't here for him, or so she says. She isn't here to apologize and listen to him tell her what a hideous wife she was. His wife has come to find her daughter and not to see her husband, or so she says. Thomas thinks he is more afraid of what he may want than what she may offer.

The painter was hospitalized in 1963 for mania and depression. He liked to use alcohol to even out his moods. Red wine was his favorite but the wine only helped until the depression got bad. Then Thomas Gaus would sometimes cut on himself, a razor, a knife, broken glass, whatever he had available. That was how it happened in '63, when he turned thirty. His friend Fat Willy found Thomas naked on the roof of his mother's Bay Ridge townhouse in Brooklyn. The air felt warm and damp and the sky was filled with charcoal clouds. Thomas sat cross-legged on the tar roof. He had a skinny, delicate look in those days. His hair was curled and dark and to his shoulders; his eyes were dark, too. That day he smelled of vinegary sweat and cigarettes. When Fat Willy found him, Thomas was holding his cut left wrist above the canvas and painting his blood into the picture with a steady right hand.

Thomas met his wife during a Friday-night social at the hospital on First Avenue. The room was the size of a school gym and had a blond wood floor and fluorescent lights that were either too intense or burnt out or blinking on and off and buzzing. Patients had collected in the shadowed corners and covered the dance floor. Some of them smoked and talked in small groups. Some danced slow and they hugged each other. They hugged each other while the Beatles sang *Yesterday.* They didn't care about the song and the tempo. Others danced at arm's length so they could look down and watch their feet. Cigarette smoke rose to the ceiling in bright layers.

I feel like Olivia de Havilland, the young woman said. Margaret McFerrin was a year older than Thomas and taller than him, but not much taller, and just as skinny. She had rust colored hair that fanned out and gave her a shocked look. Her eyes were large emerald eyes. Thomas thought she was beautiful. Her eyes quivered when she talked. Margaret leaned down to whisper. She said, Mama and me love *The Snake Pit.* It's our favorite movie. We like to sit on the sofa with popcorn and a box of tissues and have ourselves a good cry.

Margaret also cried when she wasn't watching movies. That's what happened the evening her mother took her to the hospital. I'd been crying off and on for three days and didn't know why, Margaret said to Thomas. She sometimes heard a woman's voice, too. The woman liked telling Margaret what an ugly, disgusting person she was and that her talents were mediocre but Margaret ought not to worry because these talents would soon vanish entirely. She thought the woman had her mother's voice. Margaret kept that part to herself.

I'm an illustrator for an advertising firm in midtown, Margaret told Thomas. She supported her mother and knew people Thomas had only read about in magazines. Then she had said, You want to sneak out and drink some wine?

We can't leave the hospital, Thomas said.

Who's leaving the hospital? Margaret said. She said it the way people talk to the less educated. I got wine in the garden, she said. You like red? I got a good Cabernet, nice and dry.

Thomas Gaus was not above having heroes. He loved Monet and Pierre Renoir and Pissarro and Sisley. My father believed the Impressionists understood our limits and gave us our freedom. He used to say, How can we know the exact look of a thing? Only God knows the absolutes. All we have is what we see and the light and the shadow. My father was unyielding about this. Nothing stirred his rage more than anxious critics who missed the comfort of nineteenth century realism. Thomas Gaus believed the world came to life through personal and shared experiences of it. How we make sense of our senses, that was what he used to tell me.

Four years into their marriage, toward the end of the summer, Margaret got her husband into an uptown gallery on East 77th. By midweek Thomas had sold sixty-eight of seventy-two paintings and had received praise by both the *Times* and the *Voice.* Margaret withdrew again and wouldn't talk to Thomas. She also started sleeping on the roof of their apartment building with the baby. The baby had Margaret's rust colored hair and her father's dark brown eyes. Six days passed before Margaret would talk to Thomas and sleep in their bed.

The afternoon the Guggenheim called to ask Thomas to show some of his work, Margaret took a serrated kitchen knife to ten of her own paintings. She had cut straight down on each painting three times then straight across three times. The paintings were a project she had labored over for the last six months.

Thomas and Margaret stand in front of the wine shelves at the Korean grocery on West 4th Street. Margaret sneaks a look at Thomas, and Thomas guesses his wife doesn't think he is telling her the truth about his drinking. She doesn't believe he has quit. Her big emerald eyes have started to vibrate. His wife is talking about wanting to see Laura again. I was too busy with myself, she says. I couldn't live with you and be satisfied with my own painting, my own work. I always felt bad. But you can't be a mother and constantly focus on yourself. This is when Margaret saw Thomas keeping his distance from the wine shelves.

It won't bite, his wife says.

I'm sorry, what? He hears her and for a moment she is a stranger.

The wine, she says. It's awful but it won't bite.

Thomas was remembering their lives together. All the drinking, yes, but he also didn't know where he ended and his wife began. His moods swings had subsided after a month or two of marriage. He had quit his medication and the depression never got bad enough for him to cut on himself. Margaret was healing him by her presence alone. Still, their troubles could get dark and out of control. They were too tangled in one another. If they drank too much they could become petulant and cruel and they drank too much most of the time. Then there was baby Laura who cried for things and got them angry but kept them in this world and responsible. Laura was a mother long before she knew they had given her the job.

Now his wife is telling him, I want you to have a drink with me, Thomas. We haven't seen each other in twenty years. One drink. Why would you deny me? What's the harm in it?

Mr. Kim sells both jugs and boxes of red wine. The jugs have a finger loop near the mouth and the boxes show pictures of vines and wet red grapes. The two wine shelves are between the rice, pasta, and macaroni and cheese products to the right and the rye and white breads and English muffins to the left. Mr. Kim is sitting on a stool behind the cash register. Mr. Kim is in his early eighties and likes calling Thomas 'young man.' As in, Young man, you buy that or not? Mr. Kim's eyes and his tan bald head are just above the cash register.

Margaret is seventy-five and there isn't a line on her face. Maybe three or four lines but nothing like an elderly face should be. Crazy people don't age the way normal people age. Thomas knows that from his days at the First Avenue hospital. He sees it in his own face. Crazy people have the faces of old children.

When I quit I quit, Thomas says.

You mean you don't drink period? Margaret says and sounds bewildered.

I stopped drinking a while ago, Thomas says.

He feels scared telling her he stopped drinking. During their time together he didn't think about telling her no. Disagreeing with her wasn't what his mind considered. These were the years Thomas thought and felt only what Margaret thought and felt. He didn't know he had a 'no' in him. What she wanted was okay with Thomas. He did not need to upset her and lose his comfort.

Thomas wants to tell Margaret that he had to stop drinking or the social worker and the judge would have taken their daughter, his daughter. But he doesn't say that.

The social worker and the judge are a fear, not a fact. He gets too nervous around his wife. Thomas doesn't want to backslide and get all twisted up in her again. The way she saved his life was far too expensive.

What's a while ago? Margaret says. She wants to know the starting date of his sobriety. She says, Two months, a year, what? Margaret has the suspicious tone of someone who doesn't trust a quitter. She closes one eye and looks at him with the other.

I don't know, Thomas says. Thomas does know and feels irritated with himself. Why does he lie? What can she do? This is an old woman. He touches one of the boxes of red wine with his fingertips. His forefinger and middle finger are stained yellow from cigarettes. Thomas says, I quit six or seven months after you left us. That's when I quit, six or seven months after. His tone is too forceful, lying isn't his strong point. He quit drinking the night Margaret left him but telling her this would upset her. Six or seven months of drinking lets a person know he struggled over the loss.

Margaret smiles a sly smile then she brushes aside a strand of white hair on her cheek. She isn't as beautiful as Thomas remembers but she is beautiful enough. That's okay, Thomas, she says and rubs his thin shoulders the way she did when they first knew each other back in the day. This was when he relied on her to keep him alive and sane, to keep his moods from consuming him. She rubs his shoulders there in the aisle beside the glass jugs and the boxes of wine, the breads and the macaroni and cheese. She rubs his shoulders while old Mr. Kim looks at them over the cash register. Margaret is humming a tune Thomas used to love but now can't recall. Her hands are delicate bones; her nails, long and red. That's okay Thomas, she says. He hates how her touch can still calm him.

Thomas and Margaret had not left the Friday-night social to go outside and drink.

Margaret brought the Cabernet to his room and they drank the wine there and talked and Thomas showed her the drawings in his black leather sketchbook. The room had a bed and a lamp on a gray metal nightstand. There was a wooden chair with a crimson vinyl seat and a bureau that looked expensive but was probably particle board. The lamplight put shadows in the corners and across the ceiling and the polished concrete floor. His room smelled of disinfectant and spice aftershave.

Margaret was balancing his sketchbook on her lap. She would turn the page and say, God, look at that. God, look. This was when Margaret told Thomas that she drew, too. But nothing like this, Margaret said. Not anything like this, believe me. She was an illustrator for a midtown firm and drew men in expensive suits and women driving their children to ballet. I'm not an artist, she told him. Thomas thought his sketches had hurt her feelings or left her sad or maybe both. Her compliments came with an undefined struggle. Each praise was delivered the way a doctor might tell a patient the bad news. She could have been saying,

You have cancer. These sketches are incredible. I'm sorry, you're H.I.V. positive. One drawing is better than the next. I think it's a fatal blood disease but we should do a few more tests. I love what you do with your light and shadow, the way it brings out the object. Thomas didn't understand her reluctance. He wanted to look inside her and get the truth. He lighted a cigarette, instead. After Margaret and Thomas drank more wine they said they had never been good with people but they felt good with each other.

Why do what the camera can do? I remember my father being emphatic about that. The first photograph was taken in 1826 with a wooden box camera invented by two Parisians named Chevalier. The Impressionists came along some years after that. My father said the Chevaliers changed what artists ask themselves. The camera forced the artist to rethink everything, he said. Our bowl of fruit, our pond beneath the bridge, the girl on the roof, the camera clipped each thing from the world. All we needed to do was paste these things into scrapbooks. The artist had to look for another path, ask a different question. What do I see and how do I feel about the thing I see? That became important, that was my father's argument for the Impressionists. What do I see and how do I feel about what I see? These became the eternal questions of Thomas Gaus. He would ask me, Isn't that paramount? Isn't that more intriguing than what the camera can do?

Margaret had crept into her husband's studio the night before the movers were scheduled to transport seventy-five of Thomas's paintings to the Guggenheim. This was close to one-fifteen in the morning. She used a serrated kitchen knife on each painting. She cut them three times straight down and three times straight across, the way she had cut her own paintings two weeks before. Then she scooped Laura up from the bed and put a finger to the four year old's lips and told her not to fuss and to do what mommy said to do. Laura wanted to know if they were going to sleep on the roof again. Margaret told her, No, hon, not this time, and the child nodded and laid her head on her mother's shoulder.

They did go to the roof. The night was warm and clear and there were traffic noises far below them and the air smelled of frying foods from the nearby restaurants and the exhaust fumes from the traffic. Yesterday Margaret had laid two boards across a six foot space between their apartment building and the building next door. The drop itself ended in an undefined blackness. She began crossing the walkway with Laura pressed to her chest. The baby was thin with thick rust colored hair like Margaret and dark brown eyes like her father. Laura started to cry and wriggle, trying to escape her mother's arms. Margaret told her to stop that now, please. Laura said she was very tired and wanted to go home and sleep in her bed. This is when Margaret got angry and left the baby on the roof next door to their building and never came back.

Margaret has decided on a small glass jug of the red. We'll have one teeny drink, like we used to, she is saying to him. She says, Do you remember those days, Thomas? God, we were nothing but crazy. Margaret's big emerald eyes start to vibrate. Her hair is thick and unkempt but more white than rust colored now. Her voice has a thready, frantic edge. You remember the fun? she says. How good everything felt when we were together?

Music plays in Mr. Kim's grocery store. The music is far away, the sort Thomas hears in elevators. He has to concentrate to recognize a tune. These are songs of the sixties but done with violins: Kyu Sakamoto's *Sukiyaki*. Mr. Kim's store smells of fresh bread and pickle brine and floor wax.

Thomas doesn't get why his words don't matter to Margaret, why she is ignoring him. She tells Thomas that she is sick. It's the second time she has told him. She says death keeps playing her like a coy young girl who is all flirt and no action. Too much smoke or drink or both, she isn't sure. Margaret's liver doesn't work right, and her heart has problems of its own.

Promise me you'll have a drink, Margaret says.

Let me pay for that, Thomas says and lifts the wine jug from her hands before she can agree or protest. He is walking toward the cash register and Mr. Kim.

We can talk about our Laura and drink this awful wine, Margaret says. She smiles at Thomas again but her heart isn't in it. She says, Maybe you can give me her phone number.

Then Thomas does something he has never done with Margaret. He sets the wine jug on Mr. Kim's gray wood counter and grips Margaret's shoulders with both his hands and looks into those big vibrating eyes.

I don't drink, he says. Thomas doesn't yell this at her. He says it as a fact. I haven't had a drink since I don't know when, Thomas says. And I'm not going to start drinking now by having a drink with you, he says. Not now, not ever. I'm not giving you Laura's address, either. I'm not giving you her phone number. And Thomas tells Margaret what he knows will hurt her. Thomas says, There are things we do to people that can never be forgiven.

Tears rise along the bottom rim of Margaret's vibrating eyes. She shakes loose of Thomas and runs from the store.

Mr. Kim frowns and nods at the jug of wine. Young man, you buy that or not? He says.

Thomas had awakened that night with thoughts about his new paintings and the Guggenheim. He followed his wife and the baby to the roof but got there too late to see Margaret leave. Thomas got there when his baby was balanced on the two boards and crawling to their building from the building next door.

Daddy's here, baby, Thomas had said that as he walked to her. Thomas didn't rush it, didn't panic her. Thomas took his sweet time. Like everything was okay. Like you could kiss it all and make it better. Meantime he was making deals with the Lord. He would go back on his medication, no problem. What's a few pills, anyway? If a man can't take a pill, he doesn't know his priorities. Let me get my kid and you can do what you want to with me, he was thinking, and I'll be sober when you do it. I'll be sober every minute I'm with her, he was thinking, and all the minutes I am waiting to be with her. Then Laura was up into his arms, hanging on, her arms hooked about his neck. Thomas gripped her tight to him and she said, Daddy, I can't breathe, and Thomas said he was sorry.

Thomas Gaus seemed not to care for the thing itself, the bowl of fruit, the pond beneath the bridge, the girl on the roof, none of that mattered. He seemed concerned with the way the light and the shadow played on the thing. What do I see and how do I feel about the thing I see? That became paramount for him; that was my father's mantra to the Impressionists. This was the constant focus of Thomas Gaus. What my father saw and how my father felt about what he saw became everything, became his life. And for that, for his steadfast vigilance, for his love that never wavered, for all things too sweet and fragile to reveal, the girl on the roof was, and is, eternally grateful.

Three Shades

KEVIN W. REARDON

In a far corner of the American Wing, Bryan paused before a horizontal world painted by Thomas Eakins: a Philadelphia riverscape, autumn gold leaves mirrored in polished slate water, a sky which defied the confines of its canvas. This idyllic scene existed only to frame "The Champion Single Sculls," Max Schmitt, the artist's buddy, in an idle moment, glancing back at the viewer, his boat adrift, oars at each side. The artist painted himself into this eternity, in a separate scull, lagging twenty feet behind his friend, forever isolated. Then, Bryan registered physical excitement when he noticed that each man was reflected in the water, specters made of paint and will, but less defined than actual persons, free to leave their constrictions and find community in some other instance.

Bryan's reverie was interrupted when he stepped back, bumping against a petite woman who was standing while she sketched a bronze cast of a boxer. Bryan apologized, but her polite smile turned to a snarl as he peered over the top of her sketchbook to see if she was any good.

From a labyrinth, Russell arrived at the top of the stairs and was pleased by the two-story gallery, bathed in natural light. In a corner, the concrete was cut away and he looked out through a vertical window at the urgent Sunday in Central Park: joggers, cyclists, families with strollers and a place to be. Sealed outside the Met, their silent rush was an absurd amusement.

Before he could flatter the petite artist, Bryan was distracted by a gaggle of noisy French tourists. One of the boys stood out: bedhead, a down coat that was

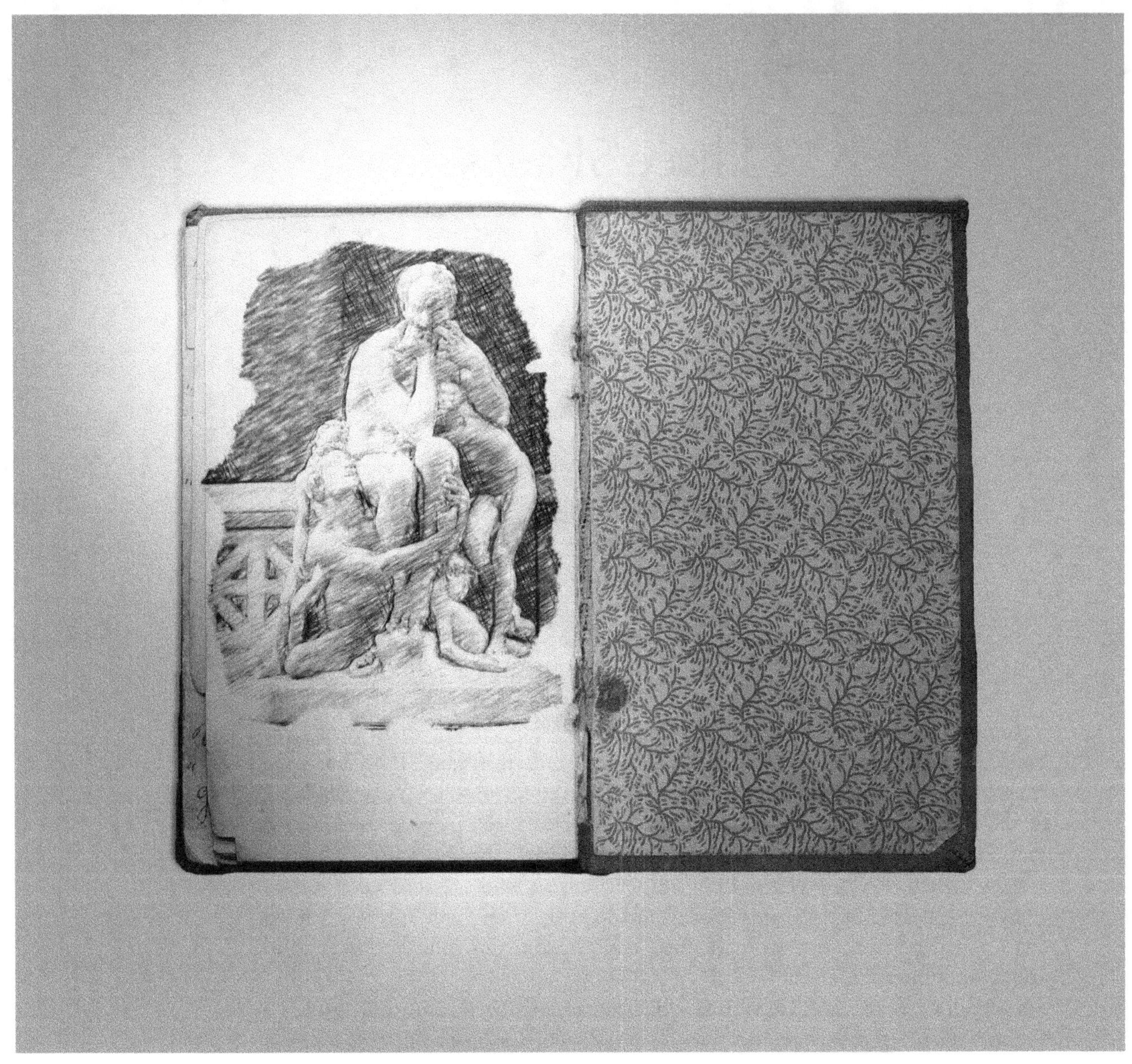

too heavy for the season, tight trousers stretched over an obvious anatomical feature. He didn't talk to the rest. Yes, this one would do quite nicely, Bryan thought, as he crossed his arms and pretended he was still looking at the painting.

Russell wished the French guys would stop babbling so loudly. He came to the Met to be alone with his thoughts, which is possible on weekdays, but a challenge on Sunday, unless you're interested in the pre-Columbian, Oceanic,

Islamic or some other, unpopular classification. One of the French guys stood out mostly because of his tight jeans, though the boy needed to comb his hair. That was the pain of the Met, Russell thought, you open up some aesthetic sensibility which enables you to appreciate all this art, but then you're vulnerable to longing. If he'd seen the French guys on the street, he'd have passed them thinking only, hey, there go some hot foreign tourists, but here, he saw each in his own beauty.

Bryan posed with his hands in his jeans' pockets, hip slightly cocked, projecting a come-hither attitude for which he possessed a particular gift. Pheromones or brain waves may also have been involved, but Bryan was no scientist. He just knew what he wanted and how to get it. He was so convinced of his own appeal that he sustained his pose after the French guys, who might have been heterosexual, moved along to the next gallery.

Russell was relieved when the French bevy disappeared and he was left with nothing but the Thomas Eakins paintings and some little woman sketching. But then, at first he thought the Frenchmen had left one behind. Ouch, the way those jeans fit his ass was so fine. He was standing like that on purpose, with one hip out, just to the side. Russell hadn't seen anything quite that provocative since leaving his old job. Bryan, a hopeless flirt, had worked under him for three years. Russell hated that job; in fact he hated being a copy editor. But he was here to forget. Renewing his dedication to the art, Russell decided to work his way down the wall, beginning with a portrait by Eakins of his father: aged hands, withered face, compassion and sorrow.

An assemblage of green and flesh caught Bryan's eye and he crossed the room to look. Eakins had painted three nude boys, two playing Pan pipes, languishing at a verdant country estate. The brush strokes were less exact than in most of his work, which conveyed the frivolity of the scene, or perhaps the painting was unfinished.

Russell stole a glance over his shoulder. At first he assumed it was his wishful imagination, but then he realized that the guy with the perfect ass was the very same Bryan who had worked two desks away for more than three years. Five months had passed since Russell had left that job. Russell could speak to him. Bryan had no right to be angry. And he wanted to. But just now, Russell was not capable of conversation with anybody. So he returned up the stairs and through the labyrinth, departing the American Wing, annoyed that his intended course had been altered.

Oblivious, Bryan closed his eyes and tried to imagine more exact details of an adolescent boy who romped naked a hundred years ago in Thomas Eakins' Arcadia.

Though Russell had been a communications major, he'd taken a survey class which covered 600 years of western art in sixteen weeks. It all blurred together then, as it did now: past a Saint Gaudens Diana; into a darkened room filled with lutes, brass horns and harpsichords; around suits of armor. He just wanted to get far enough that he wouldn't have to talk to Bryan. A tour group congregated in front of Rembrandt's Aristotle petting a bust of Homer. Russell fell into their ranks to give himself time to think.

Mary Cassatt is such a snooze, Bryan thought as he whisked past her pastel maternities. In each painting, a woman performed an intimate kindness for her child. "She painted mother's day cards," he muttered to himself.

In front of a Winslow Homer seascape, Bryan saw something he liked: the boy was twenty, twenty-two tops (Buzz cut, stud in his ear, flare-legged jeans which had worn away where the fabric dragged on the ground. The jeans rode low on his hips. A trucker's chain connected the front belt loop with a wallet in his back pocket). Waves crashed on Homer's New England rocks and Bryan could feel the mist on his face, until this chick (with a backpack cut into the belly of a teddy bear and a coat decorated by ostrich feathers) came over and took the hand of his young man.

It occurred to Russell that he could leave, perhaps see a movie. But he'd paid the full suggested admission. He would not be deterred. He simply would not think about Bryan. Lingering amidst the Dutch Masters, he eavesdropped on conversations, and pretended he too was a tourist, innocent to the splendor of New York.

Despite himself, Russell's mind wandered to Bryan's hair. When it was cut short, as it was now, Bryan was an oaken brunette. In their first year working together, partly because Bryan was always broke, he refused to get his hair cut. It grew out into corkscrew curls and Russell thought the blonde highlights were natural until Bryan confessed they were the result of lemon juice and sunbathing. Russell never sunbathed. His own bald spot, which had grown rapidly in the past year, was all the more reason Russell resented Bryan's thick and wavy crown.

American painting is good for only so much entertainment, Bryan thought, as he passed through a greenhouse sculpture garden, eager to indulge in a guilty pleasure. Though he was raised as a Jehovah's Witness, Bryan had scorned that faith as absolutely as it had rejected him. As a result, he took perverse delight in the Byzantine icons, medieval reliquaries, imperious Madonnas, and vulgar, worldly representations of Christ. The blasphemous gilt and ostentation would have driven his mother to despair, yet the biblical narratives resonated with him.

Russell decided a cup of coffee was the only way to redirect this expedition. He asked a guard for directions and made his way through European Sculpture and Decorative Arts. It should not have been a surprise to find Bryan at the Met. Talking together about art was one of the few pleasures Russell took in his last years crammed into that office, bound by economic necessity to desks of proofs, late into the night at least one week a month when they were putting the magazine to bed.

When Bryan was still "the new guy," he walked by Russell's desk and chatted. Russell was planning a trip to Italy, a lifelong desire, and was reading a Thames and Hudson book on the High Renaissance. Bryan always had time to chat, which was probably why he was a less-than-productive proofreader.

Bryan said that he had been an art history major. He was pretty, and if Bryan knew what he was talking about, he would disprove Russell's fondly held belief that all pretty men are dim. He decided to test Bryan.

Russell said, "Maybe you can help me. I'm really loving this book, but they keep talking about contrapposto. What the hell is that?"

"It's a fancy term, about sculpture, for the distribution of weight around a central axis."

"Un-huh."

"Look, think of the David. He's posed like this," and Bryan raised his left hand to his shoulder, let his right arm drape to his side, and drew back one foot just slightly, offering his body as an example, knowing the full effect of his agile, solid form.

Russell was seized by awe, envy and delight. Perhaps Bryan's flirtation was to be taken seriously. Russell was only a few years older, a few pounds heavier, just slightly more financially secure.

"It's the way Michelangelo made David's stance look natural while achieving classical balance."

"Yeah, uh, I think I get it."

Bryan relaxed his pose.

Russell found himself standing in front of a marble Bernini Bacchanal, a faun teased by imps. He stepped out of the way to allow the passage of a swift adolescent, only to back into a wide midwestern couple.

The jovial nudity of the Bacchus made Russell uncomfortable; the product of a Catholic family, he approved of Bernini mostly for his depiction of overwrought saints. Russell was active with Dignity, an apologist group of gay would-be Catholics. Dignity promised that Russell would not be permanently isolated from the belief system with which he was raised. His gratitude to Dignity, coupled with ingrained modesty, compelled him to look away from the Baroque revelry.

Willing his eyes to the floor, Russell walked briskly through the 18th Century rooms. The stale air smelled of reproduced fabric. He found himself in another of the Met's greenhouse spaces, looking out at the park, on the far side of a cluster of cafe tables.

In the darkened caverns of medieval art, Bryan contemplated the flagellation of Christ. The gaggle of French boys announced themselves with their chatter. The bedheaded one, who now carried his down coat at his side, deliberately caught Bryan's gaze.

Bryan moved along to a walnut, gilded, aquiline lectern. He leaned close to see the grain of the wood and a discrete chime immediately summoned the guard.

"Please step back, sir."

Bryan apologized, but insistently stood at the lectern. Wood mites were eating the eagle from inside out. The thick holes grew darker with each passing decade. Bryan touched skin about his lips and at the corners of his eyes. For a moment, he was sad that none of this would last.

The guard, a tall Black man, would not look away. Bryan wondered if he was interested. But then Bryan noticed his wedding ring and, deciding it wouldn't be worth the effort, he moved on.

Stopped by a riot of life realized in marble, Bryan was delighted to find good ole, over-the-top Bernini treating a mythological subject. Three plump cherubs teased Bacchus, forever in a moment of surprise and delight, forever to inspire such moments among those fortunate enough to happen upon this wild tribute to temporal existence. Bryan lingered and savored.

When he finally moved on, Bryan was still giddy on his discovery. He made his way into the sky-lit, glass-walled cafe. The overcast afternoon was bright in contrast with the depths of the Met. Bryan adjusted his eyes and decided that, since he was there and he had just paid homage to Bacchus, he should have a glass of wine.

As he waited on line, he noticed a familiar figure, slumped in a far chair, holding a cup of a cappuccino. Sallow eyes atop full cheeks, the man was, unmistakably, Russell Schuur. Bryan remembered how much he liked chatting about art with Russell. Bryan knew, when he talked about art, he sounded more intelligent than he actually was. Once he had paid for his wine, Bryan walked over to say hello.

"Oh wow, it's you. How are you?" Russell asked, avoiding looking directly at Bryan.

"Fine. You're looking well."

"You too."

"How's the new job?"

"It's great." Russell lied, and wondered if he should ask Bryan to sit down.

"What are you doing at the new place?"

"I'm still a copy editor."

"Still?"

"Yeah." Russell locked Bryan's varnished brown gaze. "How are things at the magazine?"

"The same. The woman who took your place is a real bitch, though."

Russell was silent, seized with guilt and shame, thinking that Bryan must know.

Bryan took the silence as an opportunity to backtrack. "Oh, God, I shouldn't have said anything. I'm so indiscreet. I'm such an idiot."

"No, no, not at all. I won't say anything."

Bryan noticed that Russell was closer to bald now, and he may have put on weight. His own indiscretion, talking ill of the new boss, had made Bryan uncomfortable.

Russell was about to ask Bryan to sit down, when Bryan said, "Well, it was good to see you."

"How's Ellen?" Russell asked, picking a co-worker's name at random just to continue the conversation.

"She's fine." He is so into me, Bryan thought. "I'll tell her you said hello."

"Yeah, cool." Russell stood up, holding his mostly empty cappuccino cup.

"I'll see ya."

"Yeah, bye."

Bryan took his wine to a table, shadowed by a mammoth black Rodin bronze of The Three Shades. Bryan remembered how he filled in for Russell while he was in Italy for two weeks. He resented that this idiot, who had no appreciation of art, got to go to Italy, and he, who struggled to put himself through school, had never been. As a thank you gift, Russell bought Bryan a lavish Caravaggio picture book. Bryan accepted, even though he knew why the gift was so extravagant.

Russell, wandering aimlessly amidst Mayan relics, remembered their boss at the magazine. Mr. Snyder was a petty man who relied on Russell's judgment. He took it as a personal affront when Russell gave two weeks' notice. Behind closed doors, Mr. Snyder berated Russell's future employer, but ultimately accepted his inevitable departure.

Alone in the atrium, Bryan assumed a cross-legged pose and sipped his wine. He would have preferred to forget his thirtieth birthday, but Russell had arranged a surprise party in a bar after work. When mostly everyone had left, Russell presented Bryan with another lavish gift, a coffee table book of paintings by Guido Reni. This time Bryan insisted Russell take it back. Russell refused, claiming that it had been a bargain at The Strand. Bryan didn't believe him. Russell had been on the verge of tears.

"I don't understand," Russell said. "You liked the Caravaggio book so much. I thought this would be just the thing."

Bryan was insulted to think that someone like Russell thought he stood a chance with someone like him. It was a relief when Russell quit the magazine, even though that bitch took the job that should have been his. Mr. Snyder was an asshole.

Putting that thought out of his head, Bryan noticed that the wine was of a better quality than he had expected. He contemplated The Three Shades. Twilight had fallen outside the museum, but spotlights cast these muscular male figures in high relief. They dangled their heads and reached out their hands toward a central point. But they lamented at too high a pitch to be affecting for Bryan. He thought to himself that, if his body was as developed as theirs, even if he was stuck in

Hades, he could make the best of it. And he smiled to himself, then realized that he had almost missed the bedheaded French guy, who was now leaning against the glass wall, casting inviting glances in Bryan's direction.

Somewhere in Arts of Africa, Oceania and the Americas, Russell stood in front of a glass case filled with treasures of ancient Mexico.

That last day, in his office, Mr. Snyder asked Russell, "So that other guy, Bryan, can he handle your job?"

"How do you mean?"

"Should I promote the bastard?"

Russell thought for a moment. Bryan teased but offered only rejection. Russell saw no reason he should do any favors.

"Well, Mr. Snyder, he's not a great copy editor," which was absolutely true.

And within a week, Mr. Snyder had hired this new woman, and Russell had done his part to train her.

Russell took a bench across from an intricately carved South American canoe. He wanted to think about anything else.

The French guy introduced himself and sat down across from Bryan. Laurent's shirt was open at the collar. Perspiration condensed on his skin.

Bryan asked, "So how long will you be in New York?"

"Three days more," Laurent said with a thick, charming accent.

"And what have you done, while you've been here?" This was not the first time Bryan had made a friend from another country.

"Oh, many things, I sink. zee Statue of Liberty, zee Empire State, uh, und zere iz a bar near my 'otel, zee name of zee bar iz Chase."

It was a gay bar and, from his grin, apparently Laurent thought he was very clever to mention it in this way.

"Oh, yes, I know that bar," Bryan confirmed.

Laurent smiled like a Watteau courtesan.

"So what happened to all your friends?"

"Friends?"

"I saw you before with a lot of French people." Bryan suppressed an urge to mimic Laurent's accent.

"Oh, zay went to zee rest-au-rant."

"And you didn't go?" Did you stay here for me, Bryan was asking.

"Non, I wanted to zee more of zee Met."

"Well, zee Met is about to close, I zink," Bryan couldn't help himself. Laurent probably had one of those concave Eurotrash chests, but he couldn't have been more than twenty-five, and younger was always reassuring.

"Zo eat iz," Laurent said.

"We could go to dinner."

"Yez, if you like."

"Do you need to go back to your hotel to change?"

"Change?"

Bryan was beguiled by Laurent's perplexed look. "Change your clothes. . . Before dinner."

Laurent looked down at what he was wearing, looked over at Bryan, got the idea, and said, "Yez, we go first to my 'otel, zo I can change clothes. Zank you."

"No, Laurent, zank you."

They got up and made their way toward the exit. The awkwardness, as they figured out how to walk together, was familiar to Bryan. He knew how to defuse it. He playfully bumped against Laurent. Laurent bumped back.

Russell re-entered the cafe just after Laurent and Bryan had left. The restaurant was closed and busboys in white jackets wiped down the empty tables. The Met, on weekends, was always a bad idea. Russell resolved that, one day in the coming weeks, he would call in sick. He'd come back to the art when he could have it to himself.

Patrons flowed toward the main exit, but Russell delayed departure to consider one of his favorite sculptures. The marble group depicted Ugolino and his sons: nude, tense, muscular. Dante recorded their fate in the Inferno. They were sealed in a Pisan wall for crimes against the state. They starved to death. Ugolino's face bore all the world's fear and shame. His boys looked to him for food and an explanation.

For Russell, this horror recalled a gorgeous Tuscan afternoon. He had completed the requisite tourist visits at the Campo Dei Miracoli, the leaning tower, the baptistry, the duomo. Then he wandered through Pisa, charmed by the gray stone, golden light, arcaded streets and exquisite strangers. He happened upon a plaque that marked the building where Ugolino and his family had died. When he saw the name, Russell remembered the statue in the Met. He couldn't wait to get back to the office to tell Bryan what he had found.

25

A Visit to the Stock Exchange

ANNE WHITEHOUSE

In the early eighties, in the beginning of the bull market, I visited the New York Stock Exchange. But it was not any interest in stocks, bonds, futures, or money markets which took me there. An artist brought me to see her painting.

The idea of going to the Temple of Mammon in search of art appealed to me, not least because in my experience the making of art has little to do with the making of money. Naturally, this is not true of the world-at-large. But that world was only incidentally my world. I had never benefited from it or been its victim. I made my living, such as it was, by getting children in the New York public schools to write poetry, either an innocuous or a dangerous occupation, depending on how you look at it. But the fall I met Elizabeth I was temporarily on leave, having been granted a residency in an artist colony in New England.

Elizabeth was fifteen years older than I, and she seemed more from my mother's generation than my own, a divorced woman with grown children. She had been an art student when she met her future husband, also an art student, some twenty-five years ago; and after they married (a quick civil service at City Hall), she had stopped painting to be her husband's helpmate and, quite soon, a mother. I learned from Elizabeth that there had never been any question but that her husband was the one who was the "real" artist. He was the one, after all, who won the grants which took them to Italy where the second of their two children was born. Not until years later, when they were living in western Massa-

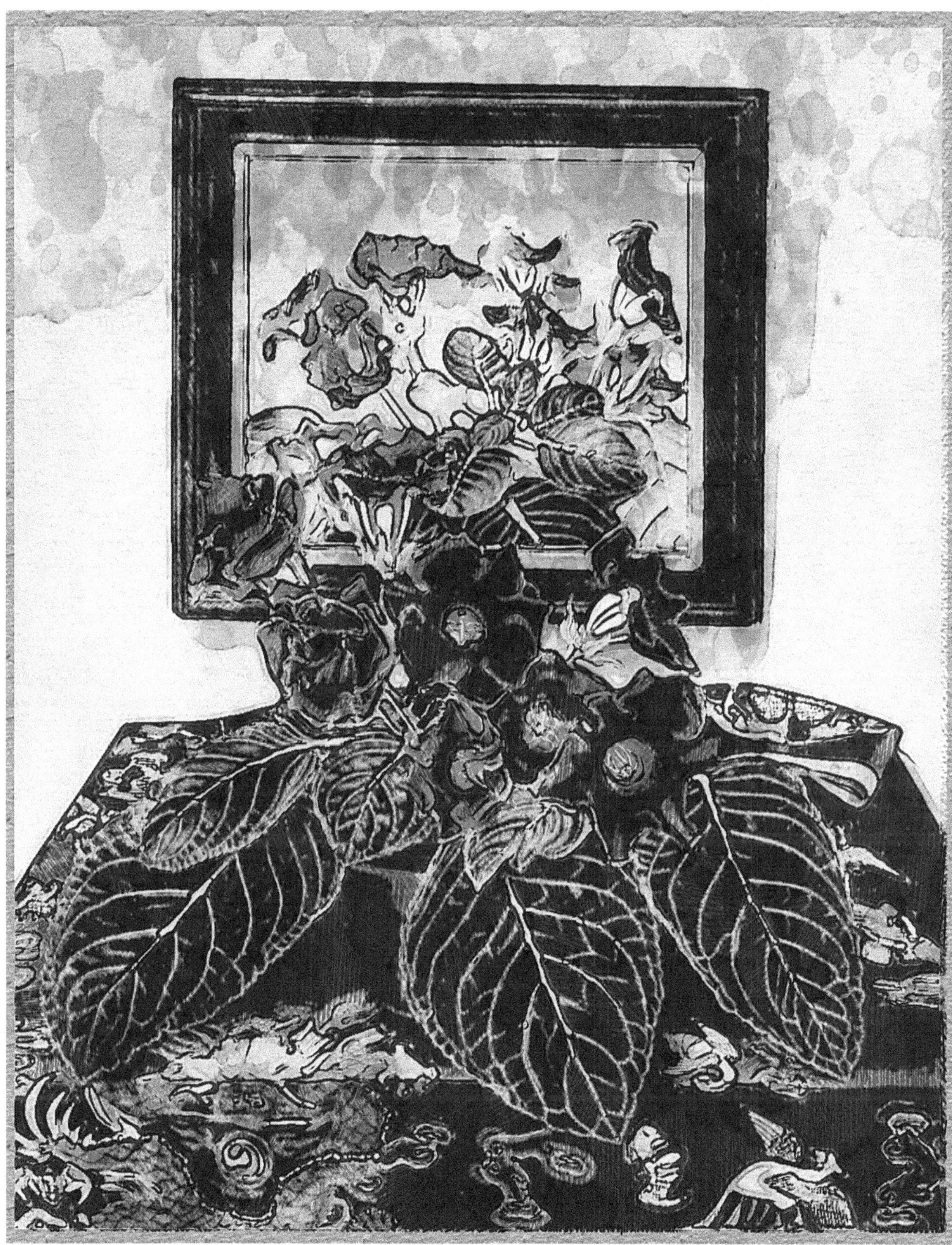

chusetts and her children were adolescents and her marriage had broken up, did Elizabeth go back to painting. "I'm a late bloomer," she said. In some ways she was like hippies I had known in my own adolescence, interested in "alternative lifestyles," yoga, and health food. She fit right into the artist colony with its communal fellowship and long periods of solitude for working, and, indeed, she had enjoyed its advantages a number of times. When she talked about her life—she liked to tell her story—she was both deprecating and defensive about the years she'd devoted to wifehood and motherhood. Was it facetious of me, hearing her, to think of my mother's comment about her long-ago cigarette habit, "We didn't know it was bad for you then"? In any case, I was not terribly interested in her struggles to "find herself" and "assert her personality." But I was interested in her painting.

Elizabeth arrived after I had been at the colony for two weeks. From the moment I met her, I knew she would be an extraordinary painter because she has such an extraordinary face. And if this seems somewhat simpleminded on my part, I have always set great store by what I see in people's faces. Although she was forty-three years old, her skin was entirely smooth, the color of light toast, spattered with freckles so close in shade they made her complexion appear darker. Her head was large, supported by a short, almost childish neck; and her body, too, seemed young—small-breasted, sturdy and athletic. But it was her eyes which were so extraordinary. Enormous and round, fringed by dark lashes, they were the closest I've ever seen to an owl's eyes in a human face. Hers was not a penetrating glance; she looked constantly astounded.

Elizabeth had a number of friends at the colony from previous visits, and they often teased her affectionately about her eyes. She blushed to hear them; their attention excited her. My impression was that she was a favorite, for she was generally held in high regard. She struck me as awkward, both in manner and speech. She seemed anxious to please and unsure how to, and at the same time rather dogmatic. The first pronouncements I heard her make were about health food. But while she eschewed coffee, she had a consuming fondness for sweets, whereas I made café au lait daily on the hot plate in my studio, yet could never finish the brownie sundaes the colony's cook treated us with, which Elizabeth spooned up with great enjoyment. Only her hair revealed her true age, dark and streaked with gray, cut short in an easy-to-care-for style I've always associated with mothers.

One evening soon after her arrival, I found her sitting alone on the sofa in the lounge before dinner, enjoying the fire burning in the massive stone fireplace, and I joined her. "What are your paintings like?" I asked, wondering, and wanting to get to know her better.

"I've been painting flowers mostly."

"You mean like Georgia O'Keeffe?"

"No, I hate Georgia O'Keeffe."

"Why?"

"I think her paintings are sensational, and I don't like her colors either."

Her assertiveness amused me. I like people to have opinions. It doesn't matter whether or not they agree with me. "I love her sensational paintings. I suppose yours aren't sensational."

She didn't crack a smile. "I'm a realist painter. There were a group of us interested in realist painting in the late fifties when everyone else was an abstract expressionist. Conrad, too." Conrad was her husband.

"I guess your time has come now," I said.

"Do you think so?" She considered, "I like painting flowers, but I'd like to paint portraits, too. It's just that it takes me at least a year to finish a painting, and it's hard to get people to sit that long. I painted a portrait of my daughter once. It took two years. By the time I finished she'd grown breasts, and she was so self-conscious she didn't want to pose with her shirt off anymore."

"I thought you said you didn't paint when your children were growing up."

"Not when they were little. This was one of my first paintings, after I'd gone back to it. Alyssa likes it now, but I'd never do it again." Elizabeth sighed. She'd already told me she had problems with her children, as well as with her ex-husband.

It turned out Elizabeth didn't like the Impressionists, or Picasso. She liked Matisse with reservations. But she loved Ingres and all the Italian painters and the artists of the Northern Renaissance. When I mentioned that I wanted to see her paintings, she invited me to her studio. "I have two, one I just started and one that's over halfway done."

"Do you mind my seeing something unfinished?"

"No. I have a card of my best painting. I can show it to you."

On the next day in the late afternoon I paid a visit to Elizabeth's studio. I walked through a beautiful woods. The air was still and the sunlight warm and yellow on the turned and the fallen leaves. I'd been writing, and my mind felt expanded and cleansed. I felt I'd earned this leisure, and I looked forward to our meeting as an interesting diversion.

Elizabeth had the largest painter's studio; with an attached apartment, it was considered very desirable. When I knocked, she called for me to come in, and I found her in the kitchen, mixing up some cold zucchini soup in the blender. The kitchen was a mess, dishes and silverware strewn over the counters and dirty pots in the sink. Vegetable parings had fallen on the floor. Elizabeth seemed agitated and nervous. As I came to know her better, I realized she was often this way.

"Do you want some soup?" she asked me; and before I could answer, she started telling me what was in it and how nutritious it was.

"No, thank you. But you go ahead."

She poured some in a bowl, spilling a glop of it on the counter. It dripped over the edge as she watched helplessly.

I tore off a paper towel from the roll that was lying on the counter and wiped it up.

"Are you sure you don't want some?"

I shook my head. "Do you mind if I look at your paintings?"

Elizabeth was spooning up her soup so rapidly she left a moustache above her lips. I repressed a smile. "Please, take your time. Just tell me where they are."

It occurred to me then that I wasn't so much asking permission as taking charge. It was a way of being with Elizabeth that seemed easier at first, and only later became hard.

"They're over there," she said, gesturing to one end of the big studio outside the kitchen. "One's on the easel and the other's leaning against the wall."

I was glad to meet Elizabeth's paintings without her watching me, thinking her nervousness would distract me. From across the room I approached the painting on the easel. It was large, about four feet high and nearly as wide. In the center of the white canvas, a huge bunch of purple flowers with curving leaves under them had been meticulously painted in. As I came closer, I saw that the rest of the canvas was not really blank; a grid had been blocked out in pencil, and the composition had been sketched in. The flowers were in a pot sitting on a woven tapestry that had been laid over a wooden dresser. Attached to the dresser by two posts was a bevelled mirror in a frame. I saw it first drawn in the painting, and then I saw the actual still life assembled nearby. My eye went from one to the other, comparing the painted flowers to the real ones.

She had painted them exactly, and still a transformation had taken place. The leaves appeared huger than in reality, bristling with life, more animal than vegetable. They seemed metallic, almost treacherous, below the velvety purple blooms. The leaves looked hard, and the flowers so soft.

From the next room, I could feel Elizabeth waiting for me to speak. "I'm impressed."

"Are you really?" I heard her high-pitched voice, the clatter of the bowl being set down. She came up next to me; she'd wiped her mouth. I glanced at her, then back at the painting. "I've never seen leaves like this before, ever. I would have never thought to see them as you have. I'm in awe. I mean that."

She didn't speak, and I felt a little shy. I noticed, leaning against a table, a large wooden frame that had been strung across and up and down with wires. "So that's your grid."

"Yes, I had it made for me in Italy." And she described to me how she plotted her compositions, sighting them through the grid.

"It must be hard for you to be so painstaking and methodical," I said.

"I guess you can tell I'm not naturally that way. Only with painting." She sighed. "I stand in front of them so long I've gotten varicose veins. The flowers die, and it's hard to find new ones just like the old ones. That's why I usually paint them in first."

"What are these called?"

"Gloxinias."

"I wonder how you've gotten their textures. It seems I can touch them with my eyes. And this is your other one." The smaller canvas leaning against the wall had only been plotted. I could see the penciled outlines of a single, large lily-like flower. I looked around the room for its original, but I missed it in the clutter of boxes, scattered clothes, tubes of paint, jars of brushes, and at least two palettes. Elizabeth was rummaging through a pile of papers. "I want to show you the postcard," she said. "The one of my best painting. Oh, damn, where did I put it?" Papers slid off the table onto the floor. "Here it is."

Eagerly and awkwardly she rushed towards me. I thought she might slip and fall, but she delivered the card into my hand.

I looked at it for a long time without saying anything. Even reproduced on the card, it was clear that this was a striking painting. It was so full—exuberant and at the same time intensely still. In the exact center was a large Chinese vase with a scene of a man kneeling before an emperor. Five large white chrysanthemums leaned out of the vase on long stalks. The vase sat on a dresser—the same dresser before me now—covered in an Oriental cloth. Both the vase and the cloth were blue and white against a deep red ground. The mirror was tilted down at an angle, reflecting the cloth, the Chinese vase, and the flowers. Where the cloth fell over the edge of the dresser, it was embroidered in blue zigzagging stripes suggesting the sea, with toothed, rearing whitecaps. Above, lying on the dresser, were three circles embroidered with blue dragons and peonies. The vase was placed exactly on the center circle.

The symmetry was explosive, the clarity intense. Not a brush stroke was visible. I turned the card over and read the inscription on the back: "Elizabeth Schultz Howell, *Alyssa's Vase*, oil on wood, 60" by 60", 1980. Courtesy of Babette Berné Gallery, N.Y."

"I think it must be an incredible painting, Elizabeth. And you're an incredible painter." As I gazed into those staring, waiting eyes, I realized that before I had been humoring her, and I was embarrassed. I hadn't anticipated this startling mania for perfection, this art at once so cool, vivid, and impenetrable. I thought of how there was this mysterious depth to Eliazabeth, that she was another person besides the one who was awkward and blurted out private things to me without the slightest hesitation, who complained constantly and bored me with her praises of health food and her conflicts about women's liberation.

I think in that moment I loved Elizabeth, or at least loved the being in her who made this art that I had not imagined anyone could make. I gazed at her sturdy body in a rumpled turtleneck sweater and the same black knit pants she had worn almost everyday, and the trivial thought crossed my mind that she was careless about her clothes. I could see that she believed in me, and that she was pleased. "Let me see your hands," I said, putting the card back down on the pile of papers and reaching to take them in mine. "Let me see the painter's hands."

As I held them, it seemed to me that something in us met that was deeper, that could not be touched so easily, but because I was never again to feel it so precisely, it is hard for me to say what it was. I felt it in Elizabeth's silence, in her absorption. For once she did not chatter or attempt to explain herself. I had seen her awkward, nervous, earnest and still willing to be teased, but I had never before seen her graceful, as now she was. I wondered if this was the self in her that painted, that I had not known and that she could not explain to me. I felt intimate and unembarrassed with her as I would never feel again. Why? I still don't know. Perhaps it is because in that moment we waited and were surprised by each other, and later we could not meet each other's expectations.

"You have hands like a child's hands. They're soft and chubby and so opaque you can't see any veins or bones in them."

She let go of me to examine them. "My daughter wrote something about my hands. It made me cry. I told her I didn't know anything about writing, but I wanted to show it to my friend, Naomi, who's a writer, to see if she thought it was good. You're a writer. Maybe you would know how to talk to her about it."

What Elizabeth said made me sad. I had been thinking of the artist, but now I saw the mother and felt pain for the daughter. "Elizabeth, if your daughter wrote something about you and gave it to you, she wasn't asking you for criticism, she was trying to communicate. Why didn't you just tell her that you loved it so much it moved you to tears?"

"I thought she hated me."

"I'm sure she loves you, or she wouldn't have written it. She's trying to reach you. She needs you to reach back."

"I think if she worked harder and found a good teacher, she could be a writer. She needs to apply herself, to find some kind of art to sustain her. But she's so shy. You should see her. You wouldn't believe she was my daughter—her breasts are so large. She has a voluptuous figure but she always hides it under shapeless shirts. I tell her if I had what she does, I'd flaunt it."

I shook my head. "How old did you say she was? Eighteen or nineteen? Why do you push her so much? Why don't you let her grow up? And besides, Elizabeth, not everybody is an artist. She's probably better off if she's not. I think you should only be an artist if you're too miserable not being one. Aren't you always telling me what a hard time you have of it?"

"But if you have a talent, it's your duty to develop it."

"Is that what you believe? That life is one course after another of self improvement? Is that how you've lived?"

Elizabeth looked angry. She said fiercely, "My father committed suicide when I was eight years old. For a long time I didn't know what happened to him. He was often away. I just knew he had died. And my mother was a Communist and there were always all these people talking about politics, and in the summer I got sent to the Communist camp. It was nice to be in the country and I made friends, but I never liked Communism. I always believed in the individual. We were poor and my mother didn't know anything about art, but she had a picture in her bedroom; I think it was cut out from a magazine. It was the reproduction of a painting of a landscape. I used to sit on her bed and stare at it for hours. It seemed like I could go inside it. I thought, if I could make something like that, I would be happy."

"Elizabeth, I don't want to fight you. So you had an unhappy childhood and became an artist to escape from it. No one will take that away from you. But Alyssa is not you. She probably just wants a mother, and you're trying to turn her into a woman too fast and make her be an artist."

I felt I'd said enough and changed the subject. "The vase in the painting. Is that your daughter's vase?"

Elizabeth took a breath and seemed calmer. "No, Alyssa is my friend that my daughter Alyssa is named after. It's her vase. It's a wonderful vase. It's been in her family a long time. I'd never read Keats until a few years ago, but when I read his ode, it made me think of this vase. I know he wrote it about a Greek vase, but I like to think it was about a Chinese vase."

I felt better now that we had strayed from the dangerous ground of parents and children. "Where's the painting now?"

"Babette sold it last year. There was a chance that the M.F.A. in Boston would buy it, but she let this rich man at the New York Stock Exchange have it. He could pay more, and, what's more important to her, she wanted to cultivate him as a buyer. But I'd rather have taken less and have it in a museum where people can see it. And besides, because there were two dealers, Babette and the dealer for the Stock Exchange, they each took a cut, so my share was less anyway."

"How much did it sell for?"

"Twenty thousand dollars. I got ten, and I had to pay income tax on that."

"I guess it doesn't seem like so much when you think of what you put into it to make it."

"You know, I'd like to see it again," Elizabeth said.

"Can you?"

"It's written into the sales contract that it can be lent to a show every other year, and I can arrange for permission to go see it. But I've never yet done it. Would you like to go see it with me?"

"I'd love to."

From time to time during the rest of my stay, Elizabeth and I discussed this expedition. I was to leave the colony the week before Thanksgiving. Elizabeth would remain for two weeks longer. Sometime during the winter, after she was back in Massachusetts, she would make the necessary arrangements with the Stock Exchange. Her schedule was flexible. She didn't have a job, but lived off alimony from her ex-husband. Money was a sore subject. From what Elizabeth said, Conrad made a good deal of it. His paintings were in the collections of major museums all over the country. She held it against him that the children went to him for money, so that their closeness to him was reinforced by the financial tie. It made me uncomfortable to hear her talk about whether the children were on her or Conrad's side. When she discussed the situation of her friend Alyssa—mother of five children, also divorced—she praised the fact that Alyssa's children had unanimously sided with their mother.

"I think it's terrible to make them choose sides at all," I said.

These were unpleasant moments with Elizabeth, when I felt bound to object to her. But she could also entertain me with stories. She made Conrad sound so bizarre. She told me that during their years in Italy he became obsessed with the ochre walls of the buildings in Rome. He spent days searching out walls through the city. The luster of their color, their peeling, uneven surfaces appeared in his paintings, meticulously and lovingly described.

Conrad's obsession struck me as such a strange way to see a place and to remember it by. It appealed to me and it repelled me; it was so narrow a focus. One part of me argued, perhaps it is worthwhile to want to know one thing so entirely in all its variations. If you cherish it and reveal it to other people as you see it, isn't it justifiable, even humanistic? And yet Conrad's obsession also seemed barren to me because, in focusing only on walls, you miss so much else.

Elizabeth related this story with evident pride. My reservations did not occur to her. This was because in many ways she shared his compulsions. But all her commentary on Conrad was tempered by her sense of hurt, of wounded pride, and, not less importantly, of exasperation. If he was successful now, it wasn't because he was careful about money. She told me that in Rome, when he used to receive his grant money, he would leave the bills lying in piles around his studio and forget about them, and sometimes the mice would eat through them. When the cleaning lady hired by the foundation discovered this damage, she was horrified and refused to come back. She was a hardworking, frugal Roman housewife, and to her to treat money like this was a desecration.

"But didn't you notice it?" I asked, my own bourgeois sensibilities also shocked.

"Well, there were so many notes anyway," Elizabeth defended herself. "You know how Italian money comes in these huge denominations that turn out to add up to almost nothing."

"So you didn't lose so much."

"Maybe about a hundred dollars. But we didn't really lose it. We brought it to the bank and got them to take it back."

"Oh God, that must have been interesting."

"Well, in some of the bills the faces were completely eaten out. We had to do a lot of convincing."

Elizabeth told this with a straight face and her staring eyes, and made me laugh. Hers seemed a fantastic life to me, but one that I would never want to be part of. I am too careful; I need an orderly existence, and I am afraid of mess and chaos. The more I got to know Elizabeth the more it surprised me that her art was so controlled, and she was so uncontrolled in her life. She was a puzzle to me. She believed that to be an artist is a virtue, and she felt allied in solidarity with other artists against the world; and yet when it came to naming artists, particularly contemporaries, one by one, she disparaged them. Her tastes were narrowly defined; she said she only liked realist painting. In all of this I sensed the shadows of her Communist upbringing, but for once I chose not to mention it to her. However, I did take issue with her on the subject of realism.

"I wouldn't call you a realist painter," I told her the day before I was to leave the colony. She had asked me to her studio again to see her progress on the Gloxinias. "And I think that's a good thing, because I'm not so crazy as you are about realism. In your paintings you don't slavishly copy what you see, it gets transformed. The way the planes flatten out or come forward, the reflections in the mirrors—no one could see so much at once in real life. It's more than life, it's heightened life."

Elizabeth listened avidly to what I said. "Whatever I paint, it always comes out differently from what I see. Even though I grid it. I don't know why."

"I think that's what makes your paintings good. That change that somehow takes place without your willing it."

Since I had last seen the Gloxinias, Elizabeth had begun to paint in the tapestry. It was of a hunting scene; it looked old and European. Speaking rapidly, Elizabeth began to talk about how she had borrowed it from an antique dealer in New York and had to return it. That was why she was painting it now, she said. She seemed nervous, describing how she'd had to leave the dealer a thousand dollars as collateral, and then launching into the story of how she'd gotten a friend to bring the dresser up to the colony in his truck. I listened without paying much attention, thinking how this painting was a rectangle instead of a square like "Alyssa's Vase," and the mirror was tilted at a different angle—Elizabeth was painting variations on a theme. It was filling in, coming together, growing richer, and I admired it, praising the leaves particularly, but when she tried to involve me by asking what color I thought she should make the background, I tried to advise her, but couldn't come to a decision. I felt unequal to the task.

Back in New York, I quickly slipped into my old life. I had three residencies in different elementary schools, and, starting in January, I would also be teaching an evening course at a college. I was also trying not to let my writing lapse entirely. Although I was very busy, I was looking forward to hearing from Elizabeth.

She called in December. I asked her about her last two weeks at the colony, and we chatted for awhile, and then she told me she would probably come to

New York in January, but it was mid-February before she was able to arrange it. She telephoned on a Sunday.

"I'll be driving to New York tomorrow. I'll return the tapestry to the dealer then and get my money. I have an appointment at the Stock Exchange on Tuesday afternoon. I have to call them Tuesday morning to confirm it. Is that all right with you?"

"I have to teach on Tuesday in Bay Ridge, in Brooklyn. But I can get through by the early afternoon. Where will you be?"

"At my mother's in Brooklyn Heights."

"I can meet you there, and we can go to Wall Street together."

Tuesday was a day of cold, drenching rain. When I emerged from the subway at Fourth Avenue and 69th Street, I looked for the Verrazzano Bridge as I always did. Today it was almost hidden in mist.

I called Elizabeth at her mother's from the school's office. At first I thought I had the wrong number, because I heard a black man's voice answer the phone. But he said, "I'll get her," when I asked for Elizabeth.

"Who was that?" I asked Elizabeth when she came to the phone.

"He works for my mother," she said.

"Is it all set for this afternoon?"

"Yes. We're supposed to be there at three thirty."

"Great. Do you want to have lunch? I've finished my teaching, and I can leave."

"Where do you want to go?"

"We'll decide when I get there. There're a lot of places."

"Well, hurry, because I'm dying to get out."

"Okay."

Twenty-five minutes later I was ringing the buzzer in the brick apartment building where Elizabeth's mother lived. There was a tiny creaky elevator that smelled, and it took me all the way up to the third floor. The corridor was in need of cleaning. I didn't see a bell, so I knocked.

A huge black man opened the door. Taking up the whole frame, he eyed me up and down. Automatically I felt afraid. "Elizabeth, Elizabeth."

"I'm coming." I caught a glimpse of movement in the space between the man's gigantic arm and his torso.

"Hey, baby, what's your name?" he leered at me.

I stepped back. I saw Elizabeth was behind him. "Let her out," I said. I felt about to cry, but he stepped aside. "Hurry up," I said to Elizabeth. "Is your mother coming?"

"No. She wants to go with us to the Stock Exchange, though. I told her we'll come back to get her."

"Can she meet us at the restaurant instead?"

"But which one?"

"Tell her we'll call her when we get there.

"Is that all you're wearing?" I asked Elizabeth when she finally came out into the hall. The man still stood there with the door open, not impeding us, but watching us. "It's pouring down rain. Don't you have an umbrella or a raincoat?"

"No. I can look for something."

"No, you can use my umbrella."

"I thought we would never get out of there," I said when we went down the stairs, for I refused to wait for that elevator. "Who is that man, and what is he doing with your mother?"

"Isn't he awful? Five minutes after I walked in, he asked me to go to bed with him. I went into the kitchen and he followed me and started putting his hands all over me."

"Why didn't you leave?"

"I didn't want to leave my mother."

"What's he doing, keeping her prisoner?"

"I told you, he works for her. She hired him to go shopping for her and do errands and carry her bags. He's an ex-con and he couldn't get a job. You know she's a Communist and believes in helping the less-fortunate."

"Isn't she afraid he'll attack her? How old is your mother?"

"In her seventies."

"I think she's crazy. Is he going to be there all day?"

"No, he leaves in a half an hour."

"Thank God. You aren't staying with your mother?"

"No, she doesn't have room. It's a tiny apartment. I'm staying with my friend Alyssa, in the Village."

We stood in the doorway of the building. The rain was lashing the pavements and the street. "Here," I gave her my umbrella. "I have a raincoat and a hat. I'll be okay."

We went to a Chinese restaurant and didn't discover until after we ordered that it didn't have a phone. Elizabeth went to call her mother from the street. It took a long time, and our food arrived before she returned. I took a few bites and then waited and watched it grow cold. Finally Elizabeth returned.

"She's coming, but I forgot the name of the restaurant. I told her where it is. I hope she can find it. Maybe I better wait for her out front."

"What about your lunch?" I was growing exasperated, starting to worry that we'd never make it to the Stock Exchange, and wishing I had never committed myself to this expedition, but I wasn't yet willing to give it up. "Why don't you eat something? If you told her the address, I'm sure she'll find it."

"You don't know my mother."

After about ten minutes, Elizabeth went back outside. "Patience," I warned myself. "Just be patient."

And, despite my fears, Elizabeth returned not too much later with her mother in tow. Mrs. Schultz was a tiny, thin woman. Only the shape of her large head was like Elizabeth's. She was wearing a too-tight sweater and skimpy pants under her coat. She, too, did not seem to possess an umbrella. Mrs. Schultz refused offers of our lunch. It turned out that she was a fanatic about health food, whereas Elizabeth was only a convert. Elizabeth asked me if I wanted to drive to Wall Street.

"God, no," I said. "You'll never park. It's five minutes by subway, or, if your mother wants, we can take a cab."

"My mother never takes cabs."

Mrs. Schultz had only spoken to us to tell us all the bad things we were doing to our body by eating this lunch. I noticed her clothes were dirty. I didn't feel like talking to her. I kept remembering that man in the dark doorway of the apartment, and I was repelled.

"We better hurry. It's after three now." I was annoyed that Elizabeth and her mother were so impractical—that was the word I used to myself. They made me feel vulnerable, and at the same time I felt I had to take responsibility for them and guide them through the city. Now there was only one umbrella between us, and the rain was still coming down.

"You take it," I said to Elizabeth's mother.

"No, no, Elizabeth should have it. I'll be all right."

I thought I was going to scream, but Elizabeth persuaded her mother to take the umbrella. We made our way to the Borough Hall station. At the line for the token booth, Elizabeth bought only two tokens for her and her mother. They would have to wait in another line to go back, but I wouldn't be with them then. Finally we stood peering up at the imposing gold doors of the Stock Exchange. They were a bedraggled pair, and I wondered if I resembled them. "What are we waiting for?" I said, as they hesitated. "Let's go in."

Elizabeth had the name of the owner of her painting on a slip of paper, and she showed it to the guard. We were directed to a bank of elevators. We went up to a checkpoint and then were sent to another bank of elevators. "He doesn't want to meet me," Elizabeth explained, as we were in transit, "I can only come when he's out of town. Now I have to see," she squinted at the paper, "Ms. Norbert. That's his secretary."

Ms. Norbert was a tall, haughty woman in a swirling skirt. "Can you tell me how long you'll be?" she demanded.

Elizabeth didn't answer, and I saw she was turning red. Mrs. Schultz mumbled to herself, pacing aimlessly on the carpet in front of Ms. Norbert. "We're not sure," I replied.

Ms. Norbert gave me a withering look. "I'll unlock the door for you. Call me when you want to leave." Our steps were soundless on the carpet as we followed her down the hall. She unlocked a door, and her hand slipped in to turn on the light.

"All right," she said, "don't touch anything."

"Does she think we're thieves?" Elizabeth muttered to me once she'd left. We'd been let into a pleasant, spacious office. It, too, was thickly carpeted and furnished with antiques—a massive desk, a wardrobe, two chairs and an end table, a small sofa and lamps. The walls were painted a pale green, and floor-to-ceiling green curtains were drawn over the three windows. I didn't see Elizabeth's painting at once. I had to come farther into the room to see it. It was on the wall opposite the desk, close to the sofa.

It was magnificent, and yet somehow not quite what I was expecting. I stood in front of it, trying to sort out my impressions. Perhaps because it was so large it didn't seem as jewel-like as the reproduction. It was impassive and riveting. I stared at the curling petals of the white chysanthemums, the perceptible shadow of the mirror against the wall, the extravagant, even joyous, curve of the vase. There's so much to see, I thought. It would take a long time to grow tired of it. It dominated the wall on which it hung, but it didn't take over the room. It fit into it.

I filled my eyes, and then walked around the large office, studying it, too. I stood behind the desk and thought of how the man who occupied it had hung the painting so that he could always see it when he sat here, and yet he was adamant in his wish not to meet the artist. He was a collector. On the wall behind his desk was an arrangement of framed, signed autographs of famous Americans—Thomas Jefferson was one, and Alexander Hamilton was another. There was another painting, too, near the door, an abstraction with flowing tongues of color. I had to admit that it didn't hold up to Elizabeth's painting, but I didn't put this, as Elizabeth probably would have, to the superiority of her genre over the other. It was just that Elizabeth's was by far the better painting.

I was curious to see how Elizabeth and her mother were taking it all in. Mrs. Schultz wasn't looking at her daughter's painting, but walking slowly around the room, with a tentative, wondrous step. She stared down at the floor and chanted over and over, in a litany, "See how thick the carpet is, see how heavy the curtains are." My skin crawled to see her; she was like a ghost. Elizabeth stood absolutely still before her painting, with her back to us, oblivious to us. I approached her, wanting to share what she was seeing.

I wasn't prepared for what it was. Elizabeth turned to me with tears in her eyes, wetting her cheeks, and a voice choked with emotion. "He's ruined it, look what he's done," she cried.

"What do you mean?"

"I paid a lot of money for the right frame. I had a heavier, more ornate one, and now he's gone and put it in this modern frame. It's all wrong, it's horrible. And the color of these walls. This sick green changes the whole cast of the background color in the painting. It makes it look nauseous, too. I hate it."

Elizabeth spoke with such vehemence, and then, to my profound shock, she began to sob. "I wish I could buy it back right now. If I had twenty thousand dollars, I'd buy it back. I tried so hard. I'll never paint another painting like this, I never will. And now it's here, and it's all wrong, and no one will ever see it."

Perhaps I ought to have embraced her right then, kissed her and stroked her hair to soothe her, but I didn't. Still, it seemed I was closer to her than her mother, who looked up at us as though across a calm, meditative distance, and said in a voice that sounded almost pleased, "That's how it always is. The rich do what they want. They don't care about us." She nodded with satisfaction.

I was embarrassed. I hated her. I felt it acutely. I worried that Ms. Norbert would swoop down on us and throw us out. My reaction kept me from holding Elizabeth and comforting her, but not from feeling her pain or believing that she was right. But I wasn't adequate to it. I didn't know what to say to make her feel better. I stood next to her, silently, absorbing her awful unhappiness.

I saw how Elizabeth would always feel an alien in this room and the other rooms like it in the world. And she was right; her art was welcome here, but she was not. Part of me wanted her to be different, to be less disheveled, better behaved, more equanimous, to be able to ignore the snubs and come away feeling proud. But she couldn't. She cared too much.

It was everything to her—how much she cared, her sacrifice and her love. Nothing else could equal it. It was ridiculous, and at the same time, it was what made her great. It was distressing and ennobling that she couldn't fit in, that she didn't know how to.

"I'm sorry." I was apologizing for myself as much as expressing sympathy, that I couldn't give her what she needed.

"You'll have to go now," said Ms. Norbert, appearing in the doorway. "You've been here long enough. I can't let you stay any longer."

Elizabeth looked back at her, her cheeks still tearstreaked, without speaking. Her mother didn't even raise her head. "We'll be out in a minute. Don't rush us." To myself, I sounded angry and fierce, though I hadn't known I would.

"Arrogant artists," I heard Ms. Norbert muttering to herself as she flounced out. She was nowhere in sight when we walked to the elevator bank. We went down the way we had come, in one elevator and then another, and left the Stock Exchange and "Alyssa's Vase" in the room of its owner.

26

La Mariée

STEVE RASNIC TEM

Jan couldn't remember exactly when he'd acquired the print. Sometime early in his college years, certainly, not long after he'd first discovered Chagall. Then he'd seen it hanging on the dusty back wall of some bookstore, priced at more than he could afford—he couldn't afford anything in those days. But he'd wanted a Chagall on the wall, even though he didn't understand much of what he saw in Chagall's paintings. He just admired the way they made him feel, and it didn't really matter which Chagall, so he'd bought the first one he saw.

Despite his affection he didn't look at it very much in those days—he didn't really know how to look at art. The pieces he really liked always filled him with an indefinable sense of longing. And although "longing" was an emotion he did not want to feel, or even to think about, he fully understood its importance.

The painting appeared to portray a world much better than the world he had lived in. Not necessarily safer, or more luxurious, but certainly more interesting than his world, and furnished with the things he'd cared most about. It was all too much, in the end. Jan could not think about these things and still have a normal day. So although he did not consciously intend to, he hung the picture too low on the wall, and very quickly there were pieces of furniture in front of it. He always remembered it was there, and now and then would catch a glimpse of the beautiful bride's face when he moved things around in the room, or he would see the fish with arms holding the candle on some shadowed part of his wall where it could not possibly be.

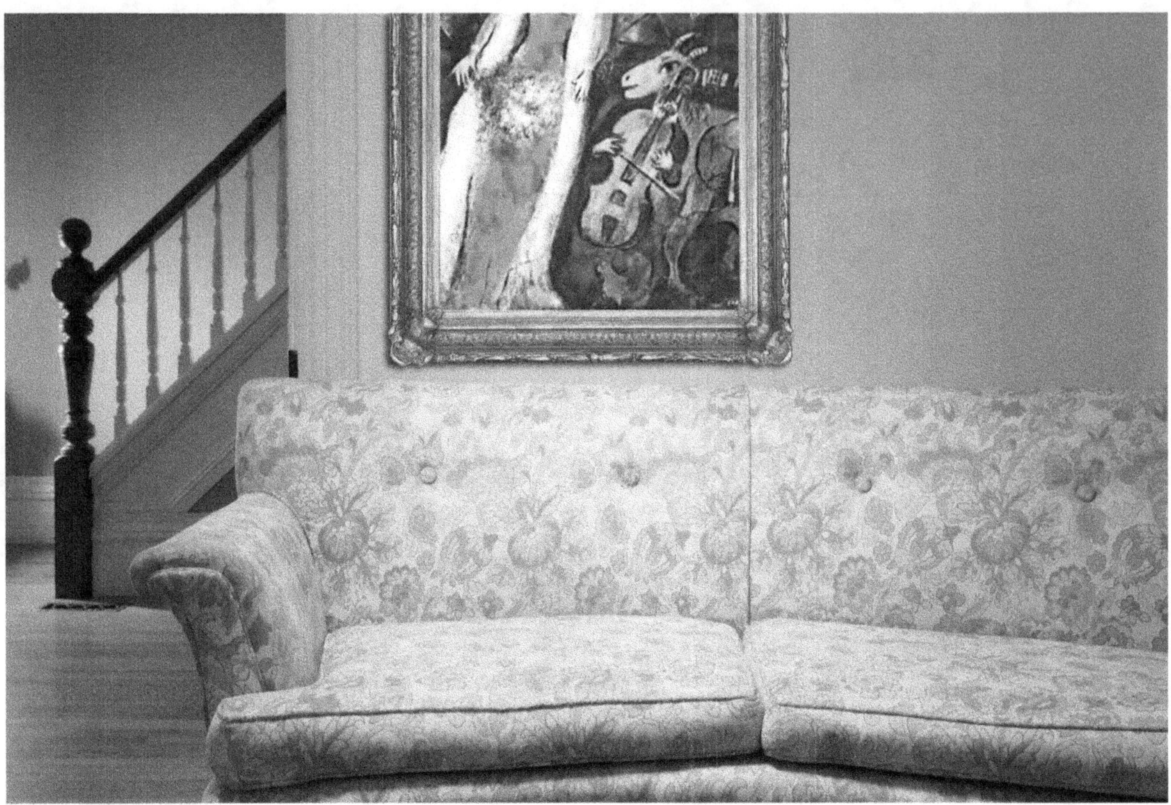

The young bride in the painting wears a red dress. She stares forward, doll-like. Her eyes are wide and her mouth is so small perhaps her lips are pursed in amusement or for a kiss. Perhaps she simply has an extremely small mouth, and that, coupled with her incredibly long neck, more horse's neck than woman's, makes him think she is no ordinary bride but someone magical—if you married her your life could never be ordinary again.

The way she stares, the stillness of her, might lead you to think she's not a real woman but a mannequin the dressmaker has outfitted for a wedding shop window. See, there he is fussing around her head, positioning the bridal veil so it looks perfect on her.

But then you look at her hands, and they are so expressive, the fingers of the right spread in order to delicately hold the bouquet of white flowers, the left slightly open to hold the fold of the long veil back so that she can see more of the dress, so you know that she is a living, breathing bride, staring at herself in the mirror, and she is still because she is overcome with emotion—never in her life had she imagined she could look this good.

But Jan kept her in the shadows behind the furniture in his crowded little apartment, his little secret. Over the years he brought many women to this apartment, some he thought he loved and some he knew he did not, and he never told any of them about the painting. And if they noticed a dusty edge of the frame and wondered what the rest of it looked like they said nothing about it to him.

Perhaps he never mentioned La Mariée because he knew none of these women loved him. Or because he suspected that once he exposed this young bride in the red dress she would never mean the same to him again.

When Jan was in his fifties a woman moved into the apartment next door. He supposed she wasn't a very attractive woman, and the fact that he should care to think such a thing filled him with shame, particularly since he avoided looking at his own body. He had two mirrors in the apartment, one above the bathroom sink and one mounted on the wall between his bathroom and his bed, tall enough that he could use it to judge his outfit before going out for the day. He used the one in the bathroom for shaving, for cleaning his face, a broad pale face which seemed to have little to do with him. He barely recognized its rounded square shape, the wrinkles around the eyes, the hesitant mouth and weak chin. When he took a shower he moved swiftly through his bedroom to his dresser, the blur in the mirror nothing more than a wraith, an approximation, a pale memory of who he used to be.

He'd never married, not by choice but because he'd never been able to make the proper connection. He supposed some people had a talent for making such connections, although he couldn't be sure, because he had no knowledge of how such a talent might work. He'd lost touch with the basics of dating—it had become a foreign land he no longer had a visa for.

He'd listened to the woman as she'd moved in, two men in blue coveralls hoisting the large items up the stairs—the dry steps popped and cracked so loudly under their weight he almost expected some catastrophic collapse. She handled the rest of it herself, puffing and groaning and cursing under her breath as she struggled up the stairs. Unlike in a Chagall painting, objects did not float around until they had found their perfect placement. He knew he should have gone out and helped her, but he didn't know exactly how to begin such a transaction.

In his agitation he got up out of his chair and started to rearrange his own furniture. He wasn't exactly sure why he had decided to do such a thing, except if he were asked later (and who would ask?) why he hadn't helped her move he might say he'd been so busy moving his own belongings he hadn't been aware of her struggle. To make this anticipated lie more plausible, he moved rapidly around the small apartment with his arms full of his displaced possessions to make as much noise as possible. He pushed and pulled chairs and tables and bookcases and cabinets around the room, leaving them at barely-considered locations, going completely on instincts he knew he did not have. And in the process brought La Mariée out of the shadows for the first time in years.

He stopped then, exhausted and a little dizzy. Sweat trickled down his body in discrete tracks, like tears. It was a ridiculous thought, the body crying, not out of sadness and not out of joy, but out of the relief of purposeful movement.

Jan stared at the print mounted in the same spot for all these years, the painting he'd loved but had never felt comfortable looking at and had never been able to stop thinking about.

She was younger than he remembered her, her face less defined, but still as beautiful as ever. The man floating above her—whether a dressmaker or impending husband—seemed overjoyed just to be able to look at her.

The flowers she carried had not wilted, and the goat-headed man beside her still played a lively cello, but much of the original blue background was laden with dust.

Jan found a rag and began to gently wipe the dark away, the dust smearing where it mixed with his sweat. He tried to touch the surface as softly as possible, afraid that age and rough handling might deform her. He still felt slightly light-headed, which resulted in small, barely discernible movements, or transformations, in the figures. An enraptured fish appeared suddenly out of the darkness holding a candle aloft, slowly blinked his eyes, moving his tail fin ever so slightly in order to remain in the same position. It felt almost as if he'd been resting deep in some other place until Jan rediscovered him. And was that red-topped table behind the fish just beginning to dance?

As the dark night began to seep out of the painting, and the deep Chagall blue—the color of oceans, or the color of dreams—began to appear, the houses of the painter's lost village became visible, and the figure of a man Jan had not remembered began to play the flute, his energized limbs seeming to fade in and out of abstraction. This flute player didn't even look at the beautiful bride. He was so intent with his performance it was obvious he was in love with something else.

Jan understood the painting no more than he had decades before. Apparently the years had taught him little that would illuminate the mysteries of La Mariée. But still he understood there was something vital about these two-dimensional images which generated longings he could not quite understand.

Some time that afternoon music began to drift out of the woman's apartment. He was not well-versed in classical music, could not have provided the names for more than three composers, the names of any of their compositions, certainly couldn't have matched a composer to a specific song, but he was able to distinguish the separate voices of their instruments, sometimes even when they were part of a swelling wall of sound. Out through the woman's door, down the short hall and into his rooms floated violins and cellos, flutes and oboes, and drums soft as distant cannon.

He took off his shoes and walked to his door in his stocking feet, turned the knob slowly and pulled the door open an inch or so. His new neighbor was just coming up the stairs: a vintage floral scarf over her head made her look old-fashioned with her wide face, reddened cheeks and nose. As she trudged higher up the staircase he saw that she carried a bag of groceries in one arm, and a bouquet of white flowers in the other hand. She was old enough to be someone's grandparent, but then again so was he.

She turned her head and their eyes met. There was no way he could pretend—she knew he was watching her. He closed the door softly, quickly. No doubt she thought him some sort of pervert, or at least someone closeted and eccentric, someone who did not know how to behave normally in the presence of other people. He walked away, putting some distance between himself and the door as if that would protect him.

A few minutes later there was a knock. Of course it had to be her seeking some sort of accounting. He could simply not answer, but she certainly knew he was there. And if he didn't answer now, what was he supposed to do in the future, hide in his apartment as long as she lived next door?

He eased the door open. She stood there, the music sweeping out behind her from her open apartment door. She smiled (she *did* have a wide face), and examined him up and down. She still wore the floral scarf over her head, and she still carried the bouquet of white flowers.

"May I help you?" he asked hesitantly.

"We're neighbors now, did you see?"

What did she mean by that? "I heard the movers earlier."

"Correct. An arm and a leg, I tell you. I decided to handle a lot of it myself." Was she about to accuse him? "But it's done. Do you have a vase I can borrow, for these?" She shook the bouquet.

"I've—I think I have a jar."

"That's great, I'll give you some." She walked past him before he could catch his breath.

He practically ran to get the jar from the kitchen. When he got back with it half filled with water she was close to La Mariée, examining her. "Beautiful print," she murmured. "I just love Chagall. I take it you do as well?"

"I like the picture." He thought about it. "I don't understand it very well."

"Let me take that before you spill it." She eased the jar out of his trembling hands. "Why don't we sit down? I'll take care of this." She put the flowers in the water and placed the arrangement in the center of the coffee table. She glanced around. "Oh, did you just move in as well?"

Embarrassed by the mess, he wondered why he had allowed her to—guide him like this. Then he replied, "just rearranging things."

"*Feng shui!* Absolutely." She sat down near him on the couch, looking not at him but at La Mariée. Her forwardness intimidated him, but there was an awkward quality about her that reminded him of himself and put him at ease. "You have a lot of Chagall's standard imagery here. The goat-headed man, the musicians, so much music, the language of love, you know?" Amazingly, she winked at him.

He again became aware of the music pouring out of her open door. Should he remind her it was still open, anybody could walk in? He didn't think it was his place.

"His main subject was love. The musicians play at births, deaths, weddings? Every time you're at a crossroads, but these are also important events in your love calendar." Love calendar? Was she talking astrology here? "There are tons of fish in his paintings—his father worked in a fish factory. All the houses are from Vitebsk, his home town. He must have missed it terribly. They signify memory, and dream, as does all the blue."

"I *thought* the blue might be dream," Jan said, surprising himself.

"There you go! See, you may understand this painting better than you know. His use of space, the arrangement of the objects, I think he's suggesting that memory, dream, the past and the present, they all exist at the same time for us because of love."

"What about the bride?"

"Well, it is called La Mariée. Maybe she thinks it's the most important day of her life. Everything's floating around her, including that happy gentleman fixing her veil. They thought that way about marriage back then. I wouldn't know, never having been married myself."

So they sat there, both of them propped awkwardly on the couch, staring at this painting, neither of them young, or good-looking in any conventional way. She talked some more about the picture, but he had stopped listening. He was listening only to the music from the other room. He gazed at the way the man adjusted the bride's veil, and totally unexpectedly, reached over to touch this woman's scarf where it lay against her head, and immediately felt he might float away.

27

Call it a Hat

TRACY DEBRINCAT

Dmitri Shostakovich—Concerto in C minor for Piano, Trumpet, and Strings, Op. 35. Orchestration: solo piano, solo trumpet, and strings. Igor Stravinsky—The Rite of Spring. Orchestration: piccolo, 3 flutes, alto flute, 4 oboes, English horn, 3 clarinets, E-flat clarinet, bass clarinet, 4 bassoons . . .

Lydia tried to concentrate on the program notes, but couldn't keep from glancing at her wristwatch. Three minutes past eight. The orchestra was seated, the instruments tuned, the conductor had yet to appear. Ushers continued seating latecomers. Lydia's heart pounded wildly, and the nape of her neck dampened behind the collar of her creamy satin special-occasion blouse. She fought the urge to recross her legs, and forced herself to remain still. Just a bit longer and second-row center was hers for the night.

In the Concerto for Piano, Trumpet, and Strings, Shostakovich combines humor and introspection side by side. Sudden shifts from one temperament to another juxtapose the naïve with the complex, and humor with sorrow.

"Excuse me," a gentleman tapped her knee. "I believe you're in my seat."

"I am?" she drawled softly, feigning surprise. It was acceptable practice at the symphony for cheap-seaters to migrate forward to fill vacant seats after Intermission, by which time it was assumed the rightful ticket holders wouldn't arrive. But Lydia loved to be up close to the music and hated to wait. She had become expert at occupying the empties at the beginning of the performance and had never been questioned before. "Are you sure?" She looked up slowly and smiled, hoping the diversion would grant her some time.

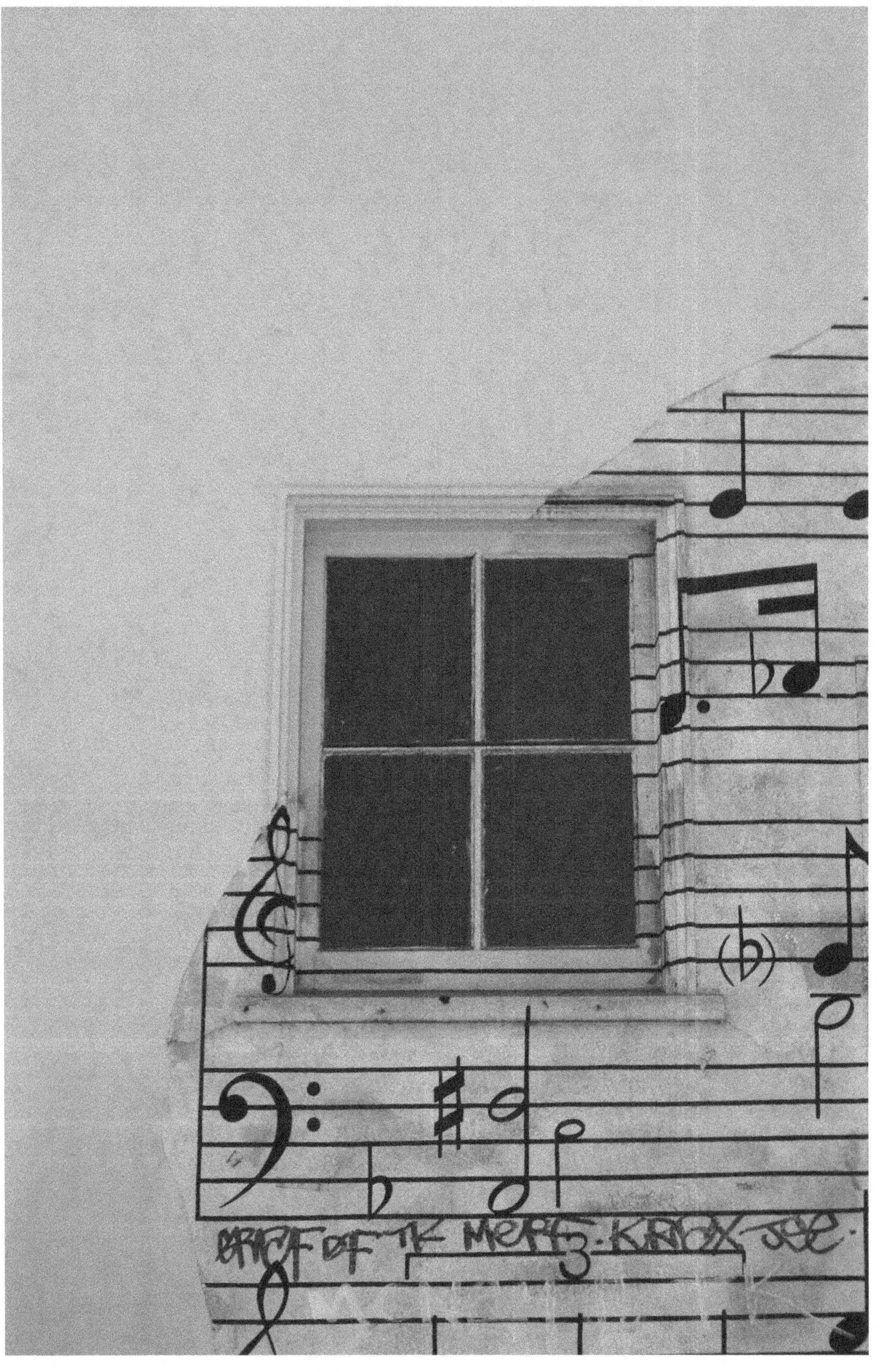

"No harm." His eyes were deep espresso brown, shot through with shards of amber. They smiled back in a way that made Lydia think he knew her secret. He had a high forehead, sandy hair, full lips, and slightly protruding ears. A little like Stravinsky, Lydia thought, and bit her lip to keep from smiling. Just beyond him, on the paneled walls, the crystals that dripped from the wall sconce shot prisms of light around his head. "I'll just sit here." He settled into the adjacent vacant seat. "It's about to begin."

Lydia smiled, and quickly returned to her program. She felt a flush deepening in her cheeks, and dried her moist palms on the velour seat cushion.

The gentleman set his elbow (forest-green herringbone, suede patch) on the armrest, unleashing the scent of apples and bedsheets, and there it remained when Lydia innocently raised her hand to turn the page and flicked her finger against his hand. He didn't start, didn't look, didn't even acknowledge the contact. She wondered whether to retreat, thereby surrendering the armrest for the duration of the performance, or whether to hold her ground and battle out the boundary during the first movement, when a second masculine voice interrupted.

"Excuse me," this one said, standing just beyond Lydia's neighbor and addressing them both. "But you're in our seats."

"Are we?" Lydia's neighbor asked.

"We've had the same ones for twenty years!" the man snapped, emphatically waving two tickets.

"Looks like we're busted," Lydia's neighbor said. He helped her to her feet, took her arm, and by the time they crab-walked out from the center of the row and stood at the aisle to scout for two vacant seats, the lights had dimmed, and an usher appeared to firmly escort them from the auditorium.

Stricken, Lydia followed the gentleman into the deserted lounge, where she found herself inexplicably holding his hand. "Exiled from Shostakovich," he sighed. "May I buy you a drink? Champagne?" Lydia nodded mutely, watching their reflections in the large plate glass windows, through which she could see the plaza, with its trees wrapped in sparkly lights, and towers of water shooting up from a fountain. He returned and raised his flute. "Maybe we can sneak back in after intermission. Those front rows are fine, aren't they?"

"I know everyone's footwear by heart," Lydia smiled.

"To the *Concerto in C minor*," he said.

She clicked her glass to his. "To *The Rite of Spring*." Lydia drank, then cocked her head to listen to the muffled music from behind the paneled walls.

"Hmmm." He nodded and closed his eyes, listening, too.

When the piano's leisurely movement ended, she finally spoke. "My name is Lydia."

"Franklin."

They gravitated toward the bar for a second round, neither of them having much else to say. When the bartender, in an effort to kickstart their conversation, confessed he was an undertaker during the day and had once built a custom casket to house both a motorcycle enthusiast and his Harley, Lydia and Franklin laughed and quickly moved on to childhoods, books, and a surprisingly lovely session in bed.

One year later, Lydia and Franklin had successfully merged their lives to include one address, a wall of books, a tasteful CD collection, and Johann, a goldfish Franklin had bought Lydia "just because." By fortuitous coincidence, the philharmonic was performing the same program he and Lydia had missed the night they first met. To celebrate the anniversary of their meeting, Franklin purchased second-row balcony tickets and supper at a tony downtown grill that specialized in tiny, exquisite portions for the pre-concert crowd.

He was quite garrulous over dinner, engaging the wine steward in conversation in a mixture of Italian and French, planning idyllic vineyard vacations that hinted suspiciously of honeymoons, asking whether Lydia preferred summer to spring, if she had ever crashed a symphony hall in Vienna, proclaiming her collarbones luscious, then gazing at her meaningfully with his espresso eyes over forkfuls of chicken Marsala.

Behind the collar of a new taupe satin blouse, Lydia's nape grew feverish. Was Franklin going to ask her to marry him? Was this the moment? Was this "It"? They shared a chocolate crème brûlée for dessert, during which a staticky recording of a tin-pan piano and a jazzy blues singer begging "do me like you do" purred from the speakers. The queer song suddenly reminded Lydia of Lester. He was the one before Franklin, the one who made Lydia feel invisible by day and uninhibited at night. Lester held no promise for the future, nor did he ever pretend to. Even after eight months, he wouldn't let Lydia call him her boyfriend, wouldn't even show her his apartment.

When Lydia called Lester shortly after meeting Franklin to tell him their nighttime flings were history, he asked her to go out with him one last time. She impetuously agreed, then phoned Franklin to tell him she couldn't attend his mother's birthday party that night due to a migraine. As soon as she hung up, she ran out the door to meet Lester, without even stopping to brush her teeth or splash between her legs.

Once at the Prestige Inn, Lydia and Lester fell into bed without preamble. She was twelve, she was twenty; she was bad, she was good; she was shy, she was nasty; she was sweet, she was mean. It didn't matter how she was—Lester fucked her, with no distracting murmurs of love or charm. She left exhausted the next morning and threw herself into bed to soak up the last bit of fucking Lester before she had to dress to go to the movies with Franklin that night, who had left a message enquiring about her migraine before assuming she could keep their date.

Lydia had not heard from or even thought of Lester again, until now. But because of that song, all she could think of was the way Lester rubbed his face red between her legs until she cried. She didn't miss Lester. Of course she didn't. Not when falling in love with Franklin was so easy. Easy and pleasant. Franklin was kind, dependable, spoke bits of French and Italian, included Lydia in all aspects of his life, found her collarbones luscious, and, like Lydia, enjoyed the occasional breech in the social contract.

"Nice song," Franklin said, and insisted on buying the CD on the way out to play in the car on the way to the philharmonic, which was now housed in a sumptuous new space, with stainless steel curves that made the building seem like a galleon prepared to set sail. By the time they were riding the escalator up to the lobby from the bowels of the parking structure, "do me like you do" was seared onto Lydia's brain, and her mood had progressed from a loathsome nostalgia for Lester to annoyed loathing for Franklin. What if he did propose? Could she say "yes" to a lifetime of pleasant, easy, and "do me like you do?"

They reached the lounge on the terrace, where Franklin went to buy cordials. Lydia looked out across the steel and glass atrium and shivered. She turned to see if Franklin had remembered to bring his gloves, and thought she saw him smiling at someone across the room, but when she looked to see whom, she saw only a woman in a red dress. The sort of woman Franklin wouldn't look at twice—wearing makeup that tried too hard—in a style of dress Franklin wouldn't care for: ill-fitting, flashing with rhinestones.

"Who's that?" Lydia asked when he returned.

"Who, darling?" he said, placing his hand on her nape. "Mmm, you're turning me on," he whispered close to her ear.

"No one." Lydia felt sad for the woman in the red dress, who chewed gum with her mouth open, swung her pocketbook on her hand a bit too wildly, and placed her hand over her mouth to stifle a belch that offended no one. A year ago, it had been Lydia standing alone before the performance, trying to savor the Kir Royale she desperately wanted to slug down; attempting to appear at ease in her solitary excursion. Lester would never have accompanied her, nor would she have wished him to.

The last bells chimed. Franklin took Lydia's plastic cup and tossed it into the trash. They walked to a side door marked "Orchestra," where a red-jacketed usher held up a gloved hand. "Tickets, please."

"Oh, we just want to go in for a look," Franklin said smoothly, waving his tickets in the absent-minded professorish way Lydia found so beguiling.

"Sorry, sir. You can look all you want," the usher said, staring him down behind thick-lensed spectacles. "After the show." She appropriated his tickets and brought them close to, then far away from her eyes. "You're up at the top, sir. In the back. Let me escort you to your seats. They're just about to begin, and there's no late seating."

The usher led them up three flights of winding stairs covered in garish, floral wall-to-wall, then down a crooked hallway lined with glass. When they emerged from an ill-lit, oddly-angled passage and found themselves eye-level with the wooden ribcage of the auditorium's light scaffolding, Lydia felt like she had entered Alice's rabbit hole. She leaned over the rail to peer down onto the orchestra far below, nearly swooned, and fell back on her heels.

"We're in the belly of the whale," she said, and laughed to disguise the stars that swam in her eyes.

"It's all this Douglas fir. Makes you feel like you're inside a cello," Franklin said. "Will you look there?" He pointed down to the second row on the main floor, at two empty seats toward the center. "Waiting for us." He touched Lydia's hip to guide her down the steep stairwell. "We'll try again at Intermission," he whispered, then directed her to their row.

Focus, Lydia told herself, and found a point in the near distance, letting it become a beacon to help her maintain balance, a lighthouse to prevent her from toppling absurdly over the thin, burnished aluminum side rail into the open-lidded grand piano. Lydia imagined a swan-like, headfirst dive, her meadow-colored skirt fluttering at her ankles until she hit the strings with a cacophonic screech, and the skirt flopped over her shoulders, revealing to the audience that on the first anniversary of the most successful relationship she had ever been party to in her life, she had defiantly donned the most pathetic piece of under-wear in the drawer—frayed and saggy, with shredded elastic. Lydia worried the panties signaled an underground act of rebellion. Did she unconsciously wish to undo her future with Franklin? And even so, hadn't the hints he dropped at dinner blasted that desire for the uprising into general disarray?

"Almost there," Franklin announced. "Seats thirty-nine and forty-one."

Lydia maintained course, grateful for the serene beacon that distracted her from the whirl of color, babble of conversations, honk-and-blurt of instruments, and intersecting planes of the walls around her that conjoined to create a preco-cious visual and aural screech. So determined was Lydia to stave off vertigo, it wasn't until she stood in front of her seat that she realized her lighthouse was not just a lighthouse: it was the toupee of the man in front of her.

And not just any toupee. This toupee seemed to have been fashioned from matted, bloodless roadkill. It was a dreadlock skullcap, a welcome mat of frizz. A hideous, frightful concoction that perched on its owner's head as though it owned him, not bothering to cover his hairless pate past the tops of his catch-er's mitt ears, and leaving the eggshell skin on the back of his head naked and exposed as a baby bird.

The toupee's owner turned and looked up at Lydia. She abruptly cut her eyes away to a place just above it. To safer, higher ground. *Make no mistake,* this new spot promised. *Lydia is not looking at your head. Or your hair. What-ever you call it. Your hat. Lydia is looking at me, this spot just above it. In fact, Lydia is so very much* not *noticing you or your hair, she's going to look you straight in the eye.*

When she did, she saw eyes that sparkled like lasers in the shadowy lamps of the hall. Eyes that burned, flickered, and smoked. Blue lights in velvet darkness, illuminating the way for stealth jets of insight. Eyes with a manic stillness that saw too much. Of everything. Pain. Wasted paper. The extravagance of ideas that went nowhere. Slings and jeers, imagined or real; it made no difference, they were seen, and felt.

Lydia hovered halfway between standing and sitting, grimacing a smile. I acknowledge you, the smile relayed, *but not your extravagant hairpiece. I may sit just behind you, but our worlds orbit furiously in opposite directions. Our ticket numbers are identical save for one letter, but we have nothing in common, nothing.*

Franklin was already seated. "Comfortable?" he asked, opening his program to find the length of the pieces, calculating his intermission hustle to the men's room and bar.

"Perfect," Lydia said. She sat and pulled her embroidered blazer about her shoulders. As she bent to stow her matching bag beneath her seat, she quietly breathed in her neighbor. He had no smell. None at all. He was neutral, as though he had no effect whatsoever on his surroundings, made no ripple in the pond.

Good, Lydia thought. I won't have to worry about sneezing. She settled back into her seat. The lights dimmed and the Shostakovich *Concerto in C minor for Piano, Trumpet, and Strings, Op. 35* began. Lydia closed her eyes and slipped away on the opening flourish for trumpet and piano, then down into the broader, darker themes underscored by the strings and the solo trumpet's solemn, sustained notes.

His name was probably something like Alistair. He would speak softly. With a lisp. Perhaps an accent. Definitely orthodontic scaffolding hooked into pink gums, guarding soft palate, guiding crooked teeth into place. There was a general disregard for hygiene, which Lydia fact-checked in the smattering of dandruff across the shiny shoulders of last decade's gabardine. If she were to nudge his shoulder with her pump, he would turn around and apologize, and when they engaged in that full-on eye contact, she knew she would be locked into his gaze. If Alistair spoke, she would have no choice but to listen, for beneath the unfortunate skullcap no doubt was a razor-sharp intellect. She would be kind, witty; she would be free to flirt. He would be thankful for her attention; she would be beholden to his gratitude. Beneath his rayon and worn cotton vest beat a generous, true heart; a soul milled with passion and flair. The knowledge that she was one of the few who knew this would embolden her to laugh and (somehow, in her fantasy) place her hand on his thigh, which would be surprisingly hard from all the miles of walking he did, miles alone, and there would be a sharp intake of breath on both sides. A meaningful, long-lasting relationship was certain, for she would never be able to tear her gaze from his eyes, whose manic calm she now saw more clearly as the sparkling of a child or the knowing, impenetrable bead of a crow, and she was no longer ashamed of his mangled toupee. She would just call it a hat. Yes, a hat, and it was merely another part of him that she loved and indulged, like his penchant for radishes and glen-plaid vests, or his habits of rising to pee in the middle of the night and forgetting to buy new socks.

Lydia was wondering if Alistair wore his toupee during sex, when the first movement abruptly ended. She coughed discreetly along with the rest of the audience, who had been saving up throaty ejaculations since its beginning. Franklin offered Lydia a tissue and a lozenge, but she waved them away. When she realized she might have seemed annoyed, she grabbed Franklin's hand and pressed his knuckles to her lips, inserting the tip of her tongue between two fingers. He smiled mischievously at her and winked as the elegant moderato began its brief, rich interlude.

Its simple eloquence made Lydia feel violently modern; she peeked to see if Alistair had noticed their wanton public display. Franklin was her treasure, Lydia knew this in her heart. Yet, as the violins swelled anew, tears sprang to her eyes, and her chest tightened with a suppressed sob. For how did she repay Franklin for his kindness and devotion?

First, she removed Alistair's clothes. He would want her to pair his mismatched socks and hang up the pants that didn't suit his jacket before she climbed onto him. She would refuse. Maybe even reprimand him for making such a request. Alistair's hands were soft, like a woman's, and she tied them to the bedposts with the long, silky scarves she reserved for chamber orchestra events. Alistair seemed frightened. And why not? What woman had ever captured him the way Lydia had? She reassured him with her eyes that he was in no danger, but no words issued from her mouth as she brought her lips to the velvety skin of his hard, muscular thighs.

Alistair moaned and writhed in response, his head twisting from side to side beneath the resolutely stationary toupee. Why won't he take it off when we make love? Lydia wondered. Didn't he know she would love him without it? What if she were to become obsessed with what was under there, or where it came from, and why? When she gently prodded him for information, Alistair would tease her at first.

"Who wants to know?" He'd smile over the rim of a chipped teacup and offer a basket of scones.

So she would stop asking, because she loved him, she loved scones, and if everything else was right in their world, there was no need to delve. But someday, maybe it would be after an argument, or the morning after a night of bad sleep, or maybe it would be a repercussion from an unfortunate dream of broken teeth, someday, the question would come up again. And after a while, Alistair would stop offering scones and become close-lipped and tight about his toupee, until one day Lydia would realize he's back in his own universe, he's let go of her gaze, he's shaken her off. And she wouldn't even care anymore, because she could no longer see the gleam of his eyes in the shadow of his snaggletooth and the smell of the radish breath, and it was all she could do not to suggest Head & Shoulders, and they would sadly shake hands and say goodbye. There'd be no fighting or bickering or name-calling or therapy, and Lydia would be sad but enlightened as she walked away and wondered why she couldn't just be happy the way she knew how to be back when she was able just to call it a hat.

Franklin's program crackled. Lydia watched him turn the page ever so slowly, in order to make the least possible noise, a practice which Lydia felt actually compounded the annoyance factor, a theory she and Franklin had once debated so hotly that Lydia accidentally closed the car door on her hand and dissolved into tears in the parking structure, and Franklin put her fingers in his mouth to make them feel better.

The moderato drove into the final movement, fraught with madcap chases, a brilliant Spanish-sounding trumpet, and delicate pizzicato strings that buzzed under Lydia's skin like bees in a hive. He was still turning the goddamn page.

Lydia snatched his program, snapped the page shut, and slapped the book in Franklin's lap. Franklin gasped, and the row of heads immediately before them jerked and shushed in disapproval.

As soon as the clapping ended, Franklin rushed away to the men's room. Lydia followed leisurely. She would go to the ladies' room and then meet him at their prearranged spot. She flushed the toilet and wondered how couples managed to stay together for years and years; not only how but why? As she was washing her hands, Lydia noticed the sparkling red dress in the mirror over the basin next to her.

The woman caught Lydia's eye and smiled. Her top teeth protruded over her bottom lip in a way that was half beautiful and half beaver. Lydia smiled back, and watched from the corner of her eye as the woman applied bright red lipstick over those big, soft lips, which pressed together, then opened in a smile, revealing the terrible, amazing teeth.

"I saw you before with Franklin," Lydia imagined the too-red lips forming the words. "Does he still swing? Does he still take those crazy photographs?" The prospect was so thrilling and confusing, that Lydia found herself attempting to rinse soap from her hands three inches above the spigot. When she finally located the water, the ladies'-room door had shuddered and closed behind the woman. Lydia remained at the basin, where she applied frosted peach lipstick with dripping hands, threw away the tube of lipstick, and wiped her hands on her dress.

Lydia approached the bench in the courtyard next to the fountain that looked like a gigantic rubber-band ball, where Franklin chatted with the woman in red. Their shoulders touched as they laughed, and an air of intimacy pervaded, as obvious and overwhelming as the syrupy scent of night-flowering jasmine. "You were right, darling," he said when Lydia joined them, as he handed her champagne, in a real glass flute this time. "I was smiling at this woman earlier. I didn't realize that I recognized her, but I did. We're old friends. Janice, meet Lydia. Lydia, Janice."

"Old, old friends." Janice smiled her awful smile. "Franklin was just telling me how you met."

"Yes," said Lydia, stupidly.

"It sounds thrilling," said the too-red lips.

"We've waited a whole year for *The Rite of Spring*. And if we're going to get into those orchestra seats this time, we should be going." Franklin grinned and slid his hand down the length of his silk tie, flipping up the end with a flourish.

"The idea of The Rite of Spring *came to me while I was still composing Firebird," Igor Stravinsky recalled, 45 years after the ballet's first performance in 1913. "I had dreamed of a scene of pagan ritual in which a chosen sacrificial virgin danced herself to death."* Franklin had secured the second-row seats, as promised. While he chatted up the usher about the use of material on the grantors' wall, Lydia slipped by, then pretended to need assistance removing her wrap. Now, head down, studying her program, heart percussing wildly in her chest, throat, and ears, Lydia found herself reading the same sentences over and over. All she could think of were the words she had put in that woman's—Janice? Janet?—mouth: "Does Franklin still swing?" "Does he still take those crazy photographs?" *The evocative opening, with the bassoon playing in its highest register, immediately transports the listener to some vague, primeval past as Stravinsky conjures what he described as "a sort of pagan cry."*

The music crashed and thundered with jarring percussion and offbeat rhythms. Lydia's mind leapt to one possible future. Some Saturday afternoon, with her husband Franklin out returning videos and Lydia home in her pajamas, holding a fan of glossy Polaroids of anonymous body parts, red, shiny, engorged; opened and spread by manicured fingers, wrists with gold watches. Quick! What kind of watch did Franklin wear? A brown leather band. Was it cracked? Crocodile? A gold face. She really had no idea and was more ashamed for not knowing the kind of watch her husband wore than she was for going through the photos in the manila envelope that she'd imagined she'd found in the drawer behind his shorts.

Franklin had a right to his sex life before he met her, of course he did. They were adults! But these! She studied each photo carefully, dreading the next for fear that he'd be there, her Franklin, naked but for a pointy party hat and those dumb sport socks he favored, surrounded by a harem of housewives, nuzzling his neck or energetically bouncing their heads above his cock. Lydia might understand if they were beautiful women, models or porn stars or strippers or whores, who represented fantasies that Lydia herself could never achieve. Would never even *want* to achieve! But to think that Franklin partied with—was that the proper term?—"swung" with regular people like themselves, was unfathomable to Lydia. She imagined a PTA meeting of parents and teachers, then removed all their clothes, put gin and reefer into their hands, and watched as they screeched and howled and paired off in groups of twos and threes to grunt and moan and spill drinks and burn holes in bad orange carpeting. For some reason, they always wore hats and shoes; she could never make them all the way naked.

She held her breath as she flipped to the next photograph, and because it was her fantasy, her worst nightmare came true. Here were Franklin and Janice/Janet, not just together, not just naked, not just wearing hats and shoes and drinking cocktails from Dixie cups, wearing cracked, brown leather watches and too-red lipstick, not just ignoring receding hairlines and long teeth, saggy, lopsided breasts and stretch marks, heat rashes from thigh rubbing and carpet burns, but holding hands, dammit!, and smiling.

The music was wild and stark. She peeked at Franklin and was surprised when she found him watching her and smiling. She laid her head on his shoulder and, through her lashes, searched for Alistair's toupee, her beacon, in the row far above the orchestra where they had sat during the first half. She imagined a young woman in a wooded glade, encircled by bears and other beasts; dancing, dancing, dancing, until she dropped.

28

The Piazza De Chirico

PEDRO PONCE

Arcade

One does not enter so much as encounter the Piazza de Chirico. We are roused by a strange conjunction of statuary and architecture: the head of a horse emerging from an archway, a supine nymph fanned by the spray of a fountain, the face of a clock emerging like a querulous moon from behind the leaves of an artichoke. We avoid the Arcade if we have somewhere pressing to be. One moment, traffic harangues us as we hazard a crowded crosswalk; the next, we turn onto a vacancy of cobbles, lined by archways receding far into the distance. If we follow our instincts—which, in the interests of propriety, we mostly ignore—we pocket digital porters, ignore the ringtones of concerned friends or fretful dates, and set off in the direction of diminishing columns. We are never alone in our fecklessness. Scattered like tribute at the base of pedestals are abandoned briefcases, purses, grocery bags, and bulging totes which, never claimed, are discarded or collect dust on the shelves of the Lost & Found.

Kiosk

The Piazza is not our most popular attraction. We are better known for our Rustic Quarter, which preserves the picturesque simplicity of another age, down to the elaborate glass fixtures that crown streetlamps. The Menagerie District is considered more family friendly; the Natural History Museum more educa-

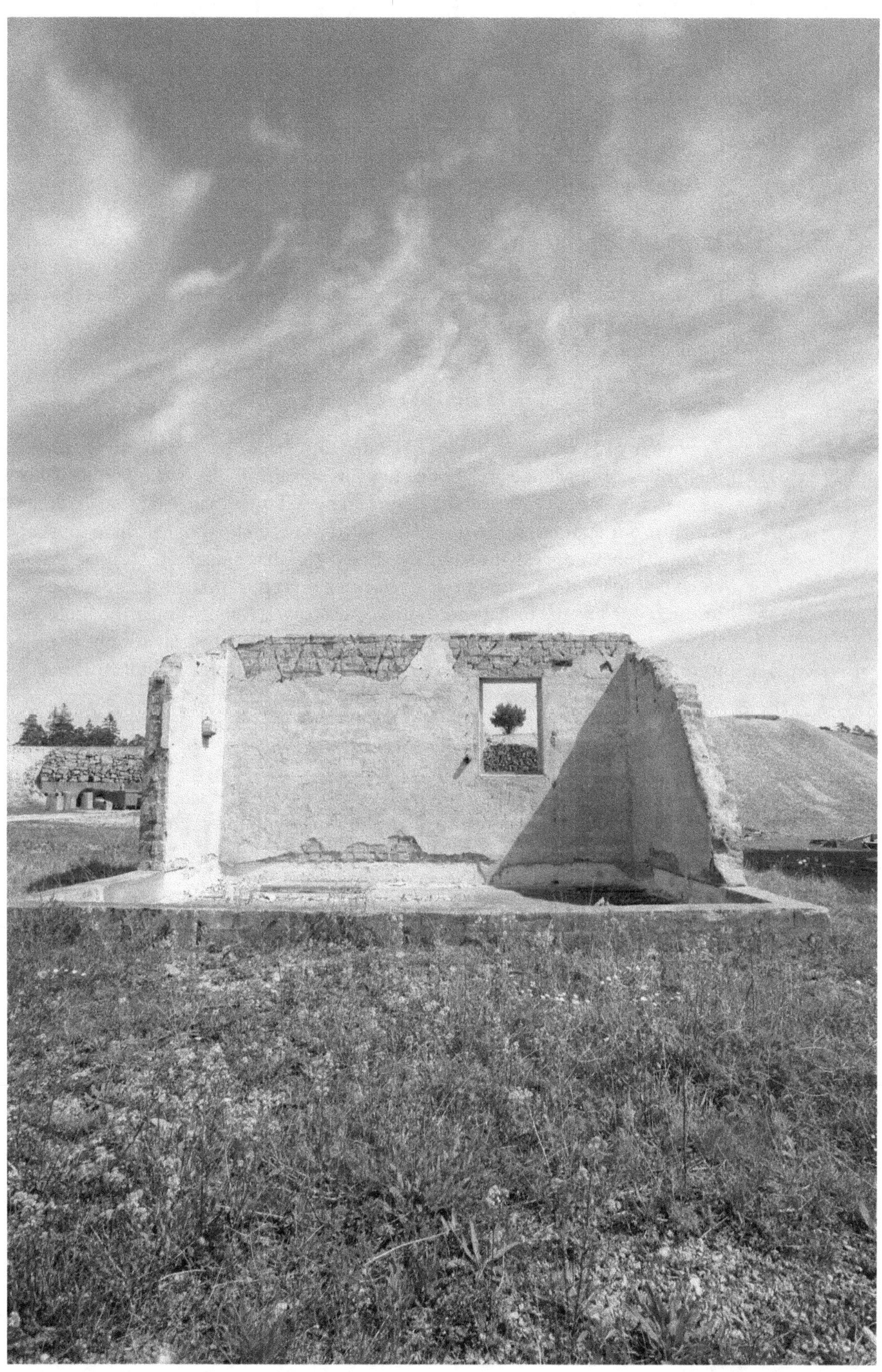

tional; the Botanical Preserve more picturesque; the Empyrean Falls more sublime. The Piazza's proximity to the train station was intended to attract visitors with its convenient location. Despite the efforts of our Chamber of Commerce, attendance remains low. Brochures are careful to describe the park's distinct atmosphere as contemplative rather than desolate, its disorienting vistas a trick of design. Complaints nevertheless accumulate at the feedback kiosk, so many that Piazza volunteers have been overwhelmed and replaced by boxes that, by the end of a given week, are packed with scrawled survey forms, their corners waving from crammed slots like flags raised in surrender.

Enigma

Regardless of how many times we wander the Piazza, new vistas always reveal themselves. The Mannequin Grove lures us inward, limbs beckoning as if for partners in a dance. We traverse a series of deserted squares joined at corners that widen at our approach. The squares seem to rise acutely in our path, an optical illusion. Still, we are exhausted by the time we reach the furthest colonnade. The clock that marked our entrance is unreadable from this distance where we pause to catch our breath. In haste to retrace our steps, we almost miss the limbs of mannequins emerging from a nearby niche. They are posed identically as they were where we began. Beyond the nearer brush, the familiar chuff of delivery trucks, the cloying of chapel bells. We follow the noise to our point of origin, the same pavement traced by windblown refuse, the same awnings limp with rain.

Ariadne

Critics of the Piazza are an infrequent but vocal minority. Our election cycles invariably begin with weekly editorials calling for its redesign or demolition. Campaign buttons feature the iconic figure of Ariadne, who occupies the Piazza's central square, her bare breasts obscured by a censor's bend sinister. Her profile is framed by slogans admonishing us to reclaim the moral fiber of our community. Despite this, no prevailing candidate has ever attempted to legislate the Piazza's closure.

Ferry

Those who defend the Piazza extol its cunning design: kaleidoscopic perspectives are created by the deft placement of stationary structures, without the mechanical gimmickry employed by major amusement franchises. Rumors persist, however, of hidden machinery, if not present from inception then recently annexed in a desperate bid to swell flagging attendance. Silhouettes appear and vanish from windows and colonnades; shadows gather and extend with little conformity to the natural paths of sunlight; sails swell incongruously against the sides of tenements. We are dared to trace the trick to its source and end the mystery once and for all. We nod in determined complicity before discreetly changing the subject, unsure of what perturbs us more, the revelation of gears and levers, or a waiting ferry poised on the shores of a nameless sea.

Voyage

We are a landlocked city. What we lack in venturesome terrain and romantic vistas, however, is offset by the values distilled from our native topography: integrity, moderation, forthrightness. We are consistently voted "Most Navigable" by the major travel magazines. Our streets map themselves in seamless grids on the memories of newcomers. Those seeking more variety may enjoy the man-made marvels of the Canal District or the natural wonders simulated twice daily at the Museum of Virtual Knowledge. We emerge to pristine food courts, our sleeves damp from rainforest dew or whitewater falls, the pavement at our feet rendered jagged by the scrim of stereo lenses. Eyes readjust to the unmediated taupe of bus shelters and city squares streaked in neon. We stutter homeward, blinking in the glare.

Tower

Brochures advertising the Piazza make note of the eight towers that form an enchanting skyline within a skyline. This is an exaggeration, if not an outright fiction. There are at most two towers in the Piazza de Chirico, the Great Tower in the northwest corner and the Red Tower that bisects the southern wall. The others are merely versions of these two, seen from different angles further distinguished by the Piazza's uncanny geometry. Some go even further, claiming that the two towers are one and the same merely observed at different times of day. A growing faction agitates from the opposite view, claiming that there are indeed eight or perhaps more towers in the Piazza, and that praise for the imaginative design is a mere ruse to placate the taxpaying public.

Moon

In spring, the Piazza extends its hours, opening to visitors after dark. Beneath the gloss of a full moon, sculpted fruit sprouts from the cobblestones with particular succulence. Even the passageways through desolate colonnades are not without their charm, threaded by silver moths and blossoming vines. Between a screening at the local art house and a late meal taken al fresco, couples often stroll the Piazza's length, noting mutual reactions with dissembled interest. If nothing more, the moonlit vistas are fodder for conversation. The fortuitously paired will recognize a shared amusement at the strangeness of the Piazza, indulging its wonders with the mild gasps and knowing laughter reserved for haunted houses or wax museums. A tree branch creaks overhead; footsteps echo from distant corners. We welcome the sudden clutch these provoke in our companions, the closeness afforded in traversing the unknown. We regain the well-lit avenues arm in arm. Yet occasionally, the Piazza lingers beyond its role in our designs. We make small talk, consider menus, weave fingers emboldened by wine. Across the table, we sense an absence behind nods of understanding, a distraction focused just beyond.

Map

Despite repeated attempts by the Bureau of Public Works, no accurate map exists of the Piazza de Chirico. Every updated version is followed by weeks of indignant calls from parents led to dead ends on their way to birthday parties; breathless octogenarians lost to walking groups; weeping dog walkers who looked away for mere seconds; aspiring fiancés foiled at the crucial moment by the apparent disappearance of the Palm Grove. Indeed, the Piazza is not one square, but many. Its spaces proliferate with every visitor. From the height of the Great Tower, we could be looking at our kitchen tables, fruit ripening on a nearby sill, juice cooled in a fluted pitcher. From the ground, the pitcher acquires limbs and a torso, speckled rind the enormity of monumental sculpture. The overhanging loggia resembles a giant's backrest. Later, we will ignore amused whispers and irritated stares to finger transit tokens and cigarette lighters, toll slips and canned sardines, ruins newly excavated.

Shadow

There are days we resent the Piazza. Its stark vacancies strike us as bland, its poetic appositions precious and crude. We forsake its shadowy cloisters for the aisles of the All-Mart. We relish the store's tidy geometry, shelves piled with all manner of tangible distractions: bowling balls, fishing rods, tires, plastic lawn fixtures, oven cleaners, stock pots, dish cubbies, door stops, espadrilles, hiking cleats, aromatic candles, concealers, revealers, duvets, bathing salts, cosmetic masks, analgesics. We fill baskets, carts, and canvas bags. We sign for the total, names etched in duplicate. Traffic swells at our return; we signal by horn and gesture the urgency that impels us. Amid construction cones and terraces of blinking letters, the Piazza's turnstiles sway feebly in the rusting light.

Clock

Visitors are surrounded by clocks, mounted on pediments overhead and reputedly accurate. There is thus no excuse for malingering. Nevertheless, we find ourselves giving the same excuse to skeptical faces: We lost track of time. How to explain the experience of the Piazza, where time is marked not by what is but what is about to happen? The houselights dim. A curtain rises. We wait, silenced before the bare stage.

Still Life

The story is told of a voluble matron—never a native of these parts—who accompanied her more saturnine husband to the Piazza for an afternoon. Her amazed exclamations funneled bluntly from between faraway columns, coaxing birds from the eaves of porticos. She resolved to record every monument and trick of perspective for the benefit of her book club back home, eagerly notifying each recipient using the phone function on her camera. So distracted was she by her growing collection—the Great Tower a mere trinket pinched between fingers, a display of mock terror at the giant fish on stilts—that she was soon separated from her husband. She ignored his absence until sudden hunger reminded her that she had skipped lunch in an effort to stay on itinerary. She searched with growing concern for her husband, spotting him at last in a narrow corridor formed by the back legs of a rearing horse in bronze. She would later recall how she recognized him in minute detail, despite the intervening distance—his scalp, burnished to a dull rose by an excess of sun cream, his shirt collar dog-eared to one side despite her patient smoothing on the shuttle downtown. He faced away, in the direction of an empty expanse walled in by segments of brick and freestanding columns; she could discern him raising his camera—as always, reluctantly, for he could never be bothered to document the most picturesque parts of their trips. She forgot her annoyance, relieved at the prospect of departing for an early supper. She was only vaguely aware in her eagerness of how the scene eluded any apparent progress, how the surrounding buildings seemed to rank ever tightly at either side of a diminishing aspect. Conscious of the time, she quickened her steps. The blow came directly to the face, her just-lowered wristwatch eliminating any chance of dulling the impact. She never lost consciousness—an important factor forestalling litigation. At her feet, an easel creaked to rest. The sky of her vision, tufted with clouds, the brick and stone baked to gold in the afternoon sun, bore the dimple of her forehead. A corner of the toppled canvas drew her eyes toward a darkening plinth.

Fountain

On a typical visit, we pause before one of the Piazza's fountains, stark quadrangular basins centered on a single narrow spout. We dig in our pockets for spare change, indulging the traveler's custom of tossing coins to the trickling waters to earn a speedy return. We find our tokens but hesitate over the burbling stone, wondering what's the use. We know we will return, whether from nearby stoops and office vestibules, or from distant chambers steeped in the rarest dust.

Melancholy

Those who favor the Piazza's closure see it as more than a drain on public resources. Anecdotal evidence—given greater credence by the occasional exposé on the evening news—suggests that visitors experience a range of symptoms associated with their wanderings, mostly short-term melancholy, but also occasional anxiety, intermittent panic, and suicidal thoughts. We are discouraged from returning by concerned community leaders, who encourage more salutary distractions in newspaper editorials and posted bills. For a time, we resume long abandoned hobbies, tackle living quarters with sprays and dusters, browse catalogs of interior design. At odd moments, we muse on the disarray of our industry, skeins of wool and spilled flour, chicken wire and wallpaper, motor oil and calisthenic balls, compost and muffin tins—tableaux familiar from dreams, purged of alchemy.

Glove

The Piazza subsists on donations, the occasional hosting fee for large events, and sales of merchandise. Postcards sell briskly, as do bookends pairing miniatures of the Piazza's best-known landmarks: the Red Tower, the Endless Arcade, the marble bust of Apollo. Less popular are the pastries and biscuits modeled on the outsize specimens festooning monoliths scattered throughout the grounds—stale and chalky, these often melt to unappetizing mush at the base of our morning coffee. For a time, a version of the enormous hand pointing the way to Lover's Grove was a popular souvenir. It remains a striking fixture of the odd costume party, sporting event, or price slashing storefront.

Train

We have a train to catch. There is always a train to catch, but this train, the train we await on this platform, cannot be missed. We have arrived even earlier than usual to ensure catching it with time to spare. The newspapers customarily perused as we wait remain folded beneath our coat sleeves. Perhaps the corner of a page ripples to distract us, but we ignore it, fixing sights firmly on the vacant track. We check our watches; the dials are blurred by mist. We wipe fastidiously at the slick glass. In the distance, a keening engine approaches. We move quickly to join the growing rank bordering the platform's edge. Legs bar our progress, splayed rigidly over briefcases and blood-colored loafers. The louder the engine's approach, the deeper the thicket of legs, arched ever higher in colonnades stabbing the horizon. We see smoke funnel sluggishly into the pale sky, a line of cars opaque as beetle backs, the cuff of the ticket taker, our palms spread empty before the jaws of his punch. We start to sprint, our progress arrested by carpet plush, furrowed pillows, and the questioning faces of cats.

Interior

We never wander the Piazza aimlessly. We always have a destination, however veiled by the derangement that pauses our steps. We seek the interior, the origin of the Piazza's divergent footpaths. If attained, some believe, the significance of its design will be apprehended in full, revealing the secret architecture of all space. Others dismiss this as, at best, amusing folklore for tourists, at worst, yet another symptom of our compulsion for symmetries.

Corridor

We sink into repose under shady archways, lulled by the chime of fountains. But we startle just at the point of giving over, our fingers pale fists at our sides. We shake off stupor and rise to the exits. We conduct the day's remaining business with particular diligence and expediency. A satisfying exhaustion loosens our necks and shoulders as we make our ways home. In the after hours din, we gossip over pints and tumblers, cheering another day's end. At some point, caught between conversations, we opt for neither to search the street outside. Dusk traces the dim outlines of lowered grates, mute hydrants, the bobbing heads of sleeping men casting for dreams.

Curtain

To those who avoid the Piazza and those who habitually wander its paths, one may add a third group. At one time, they too were habitual wanderers, by far the most frequent. Once acquainted with the Piazza's expanse, they would spend entire days there, convinced of eventually mastering its secret. Their search would lead them to obscure corners rarely frequented by the public—an archway's vacancy, the curtained void between ornamental statues. Having determined the source, they vacillated before the hieroglyph of monument and minutiae. They watched the curtain ripple over stone seams, revealing a wedge of shadow. Walls made firm by trick of light opened out into thresholds scattered with sand. Hesitancy overcome, they turned aside, in the direction from where they started, never to return.

29

One Penny For Art

DAVID PINNT

SATURDAY 3:15 P.M.

"One Penny for art, folks!" he cried and Darryl stopped, looking for the voice's source as Sara pulled away from him. The crowd at the Market, tourists mainly, pushed around him, some muttering beneath their breath, others elbowing him in the back. Sara's bobbing golden ponytail disappeared into the throng.

"Just one copper coin to support an artist!" The voice cut through the din and Darryl fixed its origin. There, next to the railing at the near edge of Victor Steinbrueck Park, the Artist had set his pieces along the green metal railing. He jangled a coffee can in one hand. He was thin and short, but his words boomed out over the street musicians and the fish-hawkers. "A single penny's all I'm asking. You've all got a penny, don't you?" He shook the can, rattling coins. Dreadlocks stuck out in all angles from his head. His blue-hooded sweatshirt, splattered with paint, was unzipped to reveal his bony chest. Faded army fatigue pants that had worn through at the knees, unlaced high-top tennis shoes, no socks. His wide eyes followed the passersby, but there was no pleading in his gaze, instead Darryl saw confidence, joy. "Just one—"

He turned his head and coughed, covering his mouth with the back of his hand. Darryl couldn't hear the Artist coughing, but he could see the violent way his thin shoulders shook. He could see the man's emaciated chest buck and heave. After a moment, the Artist wiped his lips and returned to his cry.

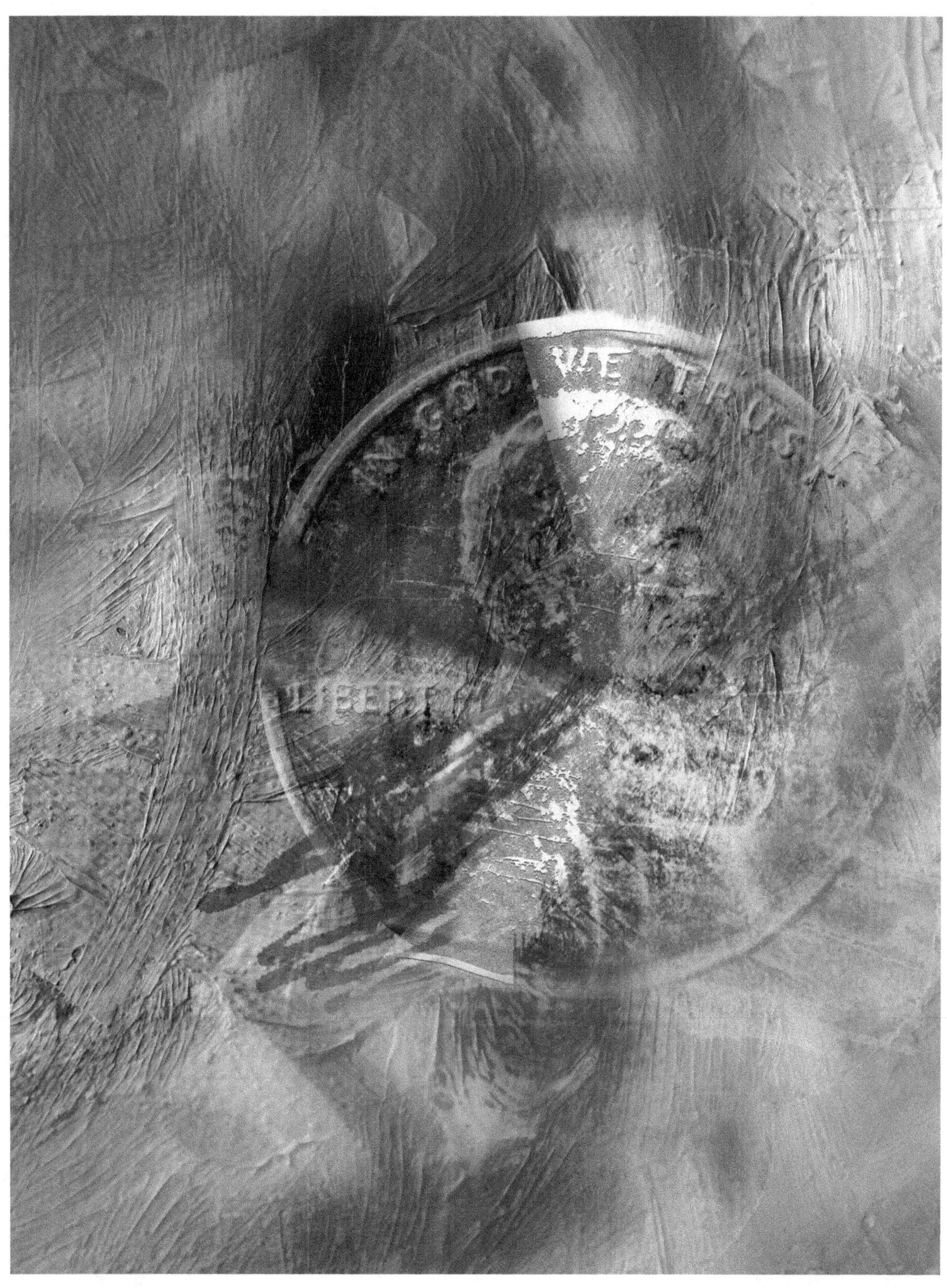

IN GOD WE TRUST
LIBERTY

Darryl frowned and stepped off the curb, meaning to cross the street to the railing. The half-dozen paintings behind the Artist were all odd sizes, one at least six feet wide and four feet high—another barely a foot square. Explosions of color and random patterns, they seemed to be painted on something other than canvas, but from the distance Darryl couldn't tell for certain. One of the paintings looked . . . warped, the top right corner curling down and the bottom left curling up. Mixed in with the starburst of blues and yellows were overlapping white rings, some malformed as they followed the curve of the painting.

The Artist shook the coffee can again and Darryl was certain he could hear coins rattling against tin. But not many. He extended one foot and pulled it back as a black Mercedes slipped by, its driver oblivious, chattering into her cellphone.

"Darryl," Sara hissed in his ear. One hand, all bones and sinew, clamped his elbow as she drug him back onto the sidewalk. "What the hell's wrong with you? I'm walking down the sidewalk, talking to myself like an idiot, thinking you're there, and I look back and there you are about to step into the middle of traffic."

Darryl wanted to ask her how far she'd wandered down the street before she'd noticed he wasn't there, but the double wrinkle between her eyebrows and the set of her mouth warned him against it. "Look at the paintings," he said, instead, indicating the Artist with a jerk of his head. The man rattled the coffee can, but didn't approach the pedestrians too closely. His plea carried out over the crowd, but he made sure to not obstruct the view of his paintings

Sara's nose wrinkled in a way Darryl remembered finding endearing. "Eww, Jackson Pollack on acid. He should show a little . . . I don't know . . .dignity— just get one of those 'Will Work for Food/God Bless' signs. It all amounts to the same thing." Her skeletal hand dug further into his arm and her other hand pressed into the small of his back, gently but firmly turning him back onto the sidewalk. "Now listen—this is important."

She pulled a little closer to him, but didn't relinquish the hold on his arm, as if afraid he was going to bolt back across the street and empty his pockets into the Artist's coffee can. While Sara talked, she didn't look at his face, but navigated through the crowd, anticipating the choked clots of tourists as they stopped to watch a salmon flung from the ice-packed cooler at the front of a fish counter, arcing ten feet back to the scales, where it was deftly caught in a swath of butcher's paper. A scattering of applause rose from the crowd. Sara guided them between two parked cars, past the crowd, and then pulled him back into the flow.

She twisted her hand just enough to look at her watch. "Steve and Lee are showing up in five hours. What I'm thinking is . . .Fusion of some sort, like shark with cilantro and lime, but maybe we can chunk it up, put it in spinach tortillas with Jasmine rice—like a wrap, with, like, a mango chutney or something, but that means Chablis. And God! Fish and rice. That'll get Lee to start in on the Paella they had in Spain, and how absolutely 'orgasmic' it was, and how 'You just can't get cuisine like that here,' well, no shit, Lee. We aren't in Spain, are we? Maybe we should do something Italian, but I get such a headache from red wine."

Darryl glanced back over his shoulder at the Artist. The man's deep brown eyes seemed to be looking straight back at his own. One paint-splattered hand tugged at the open front of his sweatshirt. As Darryl bent his ear to listen to the merits of veal versus risotto, he could feel a clump of change jangling in his pocket.

SUNDAY 12:45 A.M.

"Could you believe her?"

Darryl cupped his wineglass in one hand, peering at the distorted pads of his fingers through the crystal. The whorls and curves were splayed out, mashed against the glass. His hands appeared stubby, Troglodytish. For just an instant he flashed back to fifth grade, trying to find the right keys on his saxophone as Mrs. Rhodes leaned over his shoulder, stale denture breath on his ear. Your fingers are just too fat, Darryl—they mash down three keys at a time. Musicians, artists, they all need thin fingers, supple fingers. Art is expressed through the hands, painting, writing, music, all through the hands. Darryl drained the last bit of wine from the glass.

Merlot, Chilean.

Because she wasn't sure about the vintage's lineage, Sara had insisted upon putting it in a decanter before Steve and Lee had arrived.

She stepped into the bedroom, one towel wrapped around her body, the knot tucked between her breasts, another, turban-like on her head. Her forehead was high, rounded, scrubbed red and shining. She'd removed her makeup and her eyes looked so much tinier, pale green pupils that almost blended into the whites of her eyeballs. "I mean, could you?" She sat on the edge of the bed next to him.

"Could I what?" Darryl frowned into his wine glass. He didn't want to look at her eyes again. He had the disconcerting feeling that she would suddenly peel back that high, shiny forehead to reveal some mottled alien beneath it, some slavering, B-movie, rubber monster.

"Believe, her—Lee." She unwrapped the towel from her head and briskly rubbed down the ends of her hair. "All that crap about how many hours Josh and Seth are putting in. She doesn't fool me—she's not fooling anyone. God, I can't stand her sometimes." She put one leg on the bed and ran her hand along the calf, squeezing the muscle. Her skin was tan, beaded with water still. "We should go to the gym tomorrow. I'm feeling . . . squishy."

Darryl finished the Merlot. "If you can't stand her why did you invite her?"

Sara's eyebrows arched, "She'll be a full partner in six months. The board likes her. The board likes her a lot. So I need to like her too, or at least she needs to think I do." She pursed her lips. "Don't look at me like that. You don't have to play these games at your job. You don't understand. Don't go judging me."

Darryl lay back on the bed and closed his eyes. Explosions of colors behind his lids—the wine, he thought, but they seemed to be starbursts and warped, concentric circles. He felt Sara lay down next to him. One hand, warm against his skin, lightly trailing along his chest, up along his clavicle.

"Penny for your thoughts," she whispered in his ear.

"The Farouz watercolor," he kept his eyes closed, thinking of the painting in the living room, a Monetish wildflower field, "I know it goes with the couch, but do you really like it?"

"Art's the farthest thing from my mind, right now," Her breath was hot in his ear and he felt her tug the towel loose from between her breasts, press herself against him, a combination of cool water droplets, warm skin, softness and firmness. Darryl tangled his hand in her wet hair and pressed his lips to hers, riding things out. For Sara, a sudden shift in mood was the norm, not the exception.

Afterward, as she lay pressing his arm into the mattress, breathing deep, hard asleep, he found himself watching the rain hit the open window sill, knowing he should get up and close it, but not feeling energetic enough. "Things are good," he whispered to himself, "things are just fine." He closed his eyes and didn't think about the change in the top drawer of his dresser.

MONDAY 11:45 A.M.

Darryl chewed on a dry bagel as he made his way through the marketplace crowd. The latte he'd grabbed on the way out from the office was still too hot to drink. When he'd first moved to Seattle, he'd laughed out loud at the thought of paying three dollars for a cup of coffee, but now it seemed a daily habit—yet another way to thin out his wallet. He took a small sip, swirling it through his teeth, and swallowed a chunk of the bagel.

What am I doing here? At work he'd told the temp receptionist he didn't know if he was coming back that afternoon. He didn't want to think about the mountainous piles of paper he was leaving behind. His job seemed just that, right now—a job, not a career, not some real part of himself, just a job. Certainly not a calling.

The marketplace wasn't as congested as it had been on the weekend, but there were still quite a few passersby. During the week the locals living in the high-six-figure condos on the waterfront shopped here, paid twice as much for vegetables from the open-air stalls. Sara always liked to point out to their guests that the "raddichio came from the Hmong stall, fourth from the north entrance" Darryl supposed it sounded better than that they'd picked it up at Safeway.

He dropped the last of his bagel in the trash and headed for the north end of the market. *What am I doing here?* He mumbled the words beneath his breath. Was he losing his mind? He wasn't sure. He only knew there were seven contracts laying on desk, seven procurement managers to be called, seven butts to kiss, and he wasn't at work.

The Artist had moved about twenty feet farther from the Market, still against the railing, but as close as he could get to the little green sward above the marketplace, a municipal "park" the size of a decent subdivision lot. It seemed as if all the same pictures from Saturday were still lined up against the railing. In the same pattern, the warped plywood six feet long, the squares no more than twelve inches to a side.

Several pieces of frayed nylon rope hung over the railing and Darryl had a sudden image of the Artist winding his way down to the market from the Denny Regrade or the U-District in the wet, early morning hours, the warped paintings concavely stacked within each other and tied together, resting on his thin shoulders, bowing them forward.

"Like what you see, man?"

Darryl twitched at the Artist's low voice. He had crossed the street without realizing it, was standing before the six-footer. It was painted on a splintery piece of plywood. The "canvas'" bottom corner had been sanded smooth, but then it was as if the urge to paint had overcome the Artist's patience at prepping the surface. He'd had to stop with the menial tasks, to create, right then, at that instant. The board was covered with radiating starbursts, circles overlapping, roughly the size of the bottom of a gallon paint can, drips and runnels of paint, some so thick they threw shadowed lines across the board.

But there was something else.

When Darryl turned his head to the side he could see another picture within the pattern, about to burst out, and then it was gone. The jangling of change within the coffee can shattered his concentration.

"One penny for art, Ma'am," the Artist called out to a long-necked woman pushing a stroller who shook her head rather sadly as she passed them. "I know you got a penny to give, ma'am. Everybody's got a penny."

The Artist stepped between Darryl and the painting and spread his arms, the sweatshirt flapping from his frame. As the breeze kicked up from the Sound, an overpowering mixture of smells rolled over Darryl, pungent body odor, the sharp scent of turpentine and a stale-sweet current of marijuana. But beneath all that there was another smell, something decaying, thick and wet, the yeasty smell of sickness.

Darryl reached into his pocket, closed his fingers around half a dozen coins and dropped them into the can, not looking to see what they were. "Thanks, man—you're all right." The Artist smiled for just an instant, his teeth amazingly white and strong except for one yellowed stub on the left. He turned his back to Darryl and shook his can at a couple with Midwest Tourists stamped across their doughy features. "Just one penny, folks, everybody's got one penny to support the arts!"

TUESDAY 9:35

"Earth to Darryl! Come in, Darryl—Situation Urgent!" The wadded up ball of paper caught Darryl just above the right eyebrow. He jerked his head back, felt the casters on his chair slip and his hand brushed the lip of his Styrofoam coffee cup. The cup teetered from side to side, coffee slopping over the rim.

"Nice to have you back, Darryl," Lambert's flushed, heavy-cheeked face smiled at him from across the conference table. It was a schoolyard bully smile that played to his audience. Small coughs, snickers rose from Darryl's left and right. Blood rushed to the tips of his ears and he felt them heat up against his scalp. The others in the meeting room had to see it.

Darryl swallowed hard, reached out and steadied the coffee cup. He glanced down at the notepad lying in front of him. The spilled coffee had soaked the edges of the paper, curling them up. At the top he'd neatly written the date and time of the meeting. Below that was—what? He spread his short-fingered hand over the pad and looked around the table. No one but Lambert would meet his eyes. Darryl took a sip of coffee, keeping his hand over the notepad.

"Yeah, sorry, where were we?"

Lambert rolled his eyes and shifted his bulk forward in his chair, cuff-linked sleeves poking out just a little too far from his jacket. "Well, where we were, Darryl, is wondering why the hell you haven't locked up the *MacGregor's* account yet."

Darryl's eyes flicked down to the pad as if there was something useful there. "Yeah, *MacGregor's*—They said we'll need to come down five cents a unit on the three-and four-inch hasps before they'll sign."

Lambert's face reddened even darker. "Five cents per! You tell those Scots we'll drop two cents or they can haul their bog-trotting asses down to Home Depot if they want them any cheaper."

Darryl rubbed his forehead where the paper had hit him. "*MacGregor's* is the store name," he said slowly. "I don't think there's anybody from Scotland working there."

Lambert pointed across the table. "*You* don't crack wise with me, Darryl. *You* just get on the phone and do *your* damn job." With every other word Lambert punched the air toward Darryl with a hairy-knuckled finger.

Darryl closed his eyes—the urge welled up in him to lunge across the table, pin Lambert's wrist in his hands, and bite off his pointing finger. He could feel his teeth gnawing against tendon and bone. If he spit the severed finger out onto the tabletop would there only be small coughs from the others, nervous laughter? For a second, Darryl wondered if he'd actually bared his teeth at Lambert.

Lambert opened his mouth, closed it, opened it again, but said nothing for an instant. The heat from his eyes was almost palpable. Finally he looked away from Darryl, a small victory.

"Let's get back to work, people, hit those phones." Lambert levered himself out of his chair and left the room.

As the others filed out, none glancing back at him, Darryl moved his hand away from the paper. Under the date and time he'd covered the page with doodles, concentric circles, starbursts. A pair of interwoven lines that looked—well, he wasn't sure what they looked like. At the top and bottom of the scribbling he'd written ART in block letters, underlined it twice.

"Besides," Darryl continued to the empty room, "the peat bogs are in Ireland, not Scotland, right?"

WEDNESDAY 7:15 P.M.

Darryl privately thought of Wednesday as his "weekend briefing" night. Every Wednesday night Sara came home with a clear idea of where the weekend was headed. It apparently took two days to address the fall-out from the past weekend's dinner parties, rounds of golf, whatever else the partners and their minions did to take up their free time. Notes were compared, stories verified, and alliances fell firmly into place by Wednesday morning. As Sara liked to put it, by Wednesday afternoon everyone in the office had a pretty clear idea whose ass they needed to be kissing or in front of whose lips they needed to be wagging their own ass.

"So she just horned in on it, just like that," Sara swirled fettuccine on her fork and poked it toward Darryl. A thick white drop of alfredo sauce plopped onto the table past the edge of her plate. Her hair was still twisted into a French braid and her blazer hung on the back of her chair. The dining alcove was the short leg of an L in their condo, the living room running perpendicular to it. Over Sara's shoulder, Darryl could see most of downtown Seattle, Puget Sound beyond it an inky blackness. If he craned his head far enough to the right, he could just make out the space needle, it's saucer lit up for the night. The condo's interior was a ghost image on the plate glass. Darryl's own reflection looked out blankly at him.

"So Richard stops me in the hallway, saying this Debra and—Rick? Or is he Richard too? I need to find out, Anyway they're flying in Thursday night and not leaving 'til Sunday and since I—we—live downtown, can I take them around on Saturday, show them Seattle, what a great thing it would be, you know, all that crap, and then Lee just walks up and slips herself into the conversation."

Her voice took on a higher pitch, mimicking, mocking. "She goes, 'Justin and I were planning to come downtown Saturday too!' all excited like that. What a coincidence, Lee, I'm thinking. So she keeps going, 'Why don't all four of us meet them at the hotel, we can show them the Market, the Needle, Pioneer Square—maybe go on the Underground tour!' Like anyone wants to spend their Saturday walking through the goddamn basements of abandoned buildings. And

Richard just nodding and smiling like one of those bobble-headed dogs, and she actually says 'It'll be great 'cause you know, six is always more fun than four!' Have you ever heard that little saying before? Just try getting a table for six on Saturday on three days' notice." She stopped, took a swallow of wine. "What?" after a long pause.

Darryl blinked, "Um," he twisted in his chair, looking at the watercolor over his shoulder. "Do you really like that Farouz? I mean really *like* it?"

She pursed her lips, "Again with the painting, Darryl? Where is this coming from? Look how it catches the yellows and reds in the couch, doesn't dominate the wall. It's perfect."

"But what does it say to you?"

She rolled her eyes, "Say to me? It says 'Farouz stood in front of this meadow and painted some flowers.' It says 'Darryl and Sara have a nice piece of art that's worth maybe three times what they paid for it and it's going to keep going up in value.'"

She brought her hand to her mouth, "Oh God, Darryl, I just had a thought—What if Farouz dies, especially in some horrible, but well-publicized, accident? That thing would skyrocket!"

Darryl's alfredo sauce had congealed on the noodles. He poked the tines of his fork into it and said nothing.

"You know I'm just kidding, right?"

"I know."

Sara frowned, her high forehead creasing. A tiny smile played at the corners of her lips. "I'll tell you what. When we buy a big house on Mercer Island, I'll make sure you have a room all your own, where you can hang whatever pictures speak loudest to you."

He put his fork down and stared at the reflection of the watercolor in the window.

"I was just kidding again."

"I know."

FRIDAY 12:45 P.M.

"What am I doing?" Darryl muttered as he plodded down the steep sidewalk where Virginia met Western Avenue, his second latte of the day in his hand. Ahead of him the Pike Street market was filling up with the lunchtime crowd. A busker, anywhere between forty and sixty years old, leaned against the front of the original Starbucks store, his wiry, graying beard spreading out in a thick mat across his chest. He tapped one foot against the sidewalk as he squeezed an accordion and sang out "Like a Rolling Stone" mostly through his nose. At his side lay an enormous dog of indeterminate breed, a bandanna tied around its neck. In front of the dog, the man's accordion case held a few bills and a lot of change.

Darryl turned to his left past the accordion player and a balding black man in a worn Mariners jersey held his hand out, swaying from side to side and asked for a donation to the "United Negro Cannabis Fund," gold teeth glinting in the sunlight. Darryl shook his head and crossed Pike, stumbling a little on the cobblestones.

There he was.

The Artist had set up against the retaining wall again. His paintings spread out over seven or eight feet. He was far enough north of the actual market that he wouldn't bother the other vendors, those who'd paid the rent on their stalls. "One penny, folks." The can sent a hollow rattle over the seagulls' shrieks and traffic. "Everybody's got a penny."

Standing on the far side of a double-parked Honda, Darryl squinted at the large painting again. He'd jerked himself awake at three in the morning with a pattern of starburst and concentric circles fading before his eyes, his heart pounding, throat dry. A Lovecraftian story he'd read years ago had returned full-blown to his mind, a story about yammering *things* living in the subtle patterns of the everyday world. As he'd sat upright in bed, rubbing has hand across his sweating chest, Sara had rolled over just enough to see the clock, grunted something unintelligible and drifted back to sleep. Darryl had stayed awake, staring at the ceiling until the alarm blared at five-thirty.

As the Artist turned away shaking the can, Darryl moved around the front of the Honda. The painting seemed absurdly large compared to those around it. The starbursts and circles, thin spirals and runnels of paint, all placed haphazardly, crowding the center of the board, running past its edges.

But beneath the chaos, the screaming colors, Darryl suddenly saw another painting, the underlying structure that had drawn him across the street last Saturday, that had been in his mind this morning, this week. A bit of the starburst here, a curve of the plywood, the roughened texture giving rise to shape, and Darryl saw two figures in the starburst, arms wrapped around one another's body, the shoulders, the hip. They faced outward and he sensed a sort of grim determination in their features, an unbending will. The world could throw whatever it had at them, but they would face it together. Darryl's eyes unfocused as he took in the painting. Its outer edges blurred even as the couple's features swam up from the paint, the grain of the plywood. In the painting the man's brow was high and smooth, the woman's jaw thrust forward—their hair blew back away from their faces and their bodies were inclined as if leaning into a gale. The woman's fingers were interlaced with the man's, tendons and veins snapping out on her forearms.

Darryl's pulse pounded in his temples. He could taste that morning's latte burbling in the back of his throat.

"I call it *Into the Breech*, man. You like?"

At the Artist's voice Darryl blinked and stepped back, the latte slipped from his hand and imploded on the sidewalk, a miniature brown tsunami over his loafers. And then the painting was just the starburst again, the warped plywood. Darryl stretched his fingers out to where the hands had been so fiercely clenched. There was just a hint of knuckle, the thin bones of the woman's wrist, but if he looked too hard they, too, were gone.

"You saw them didn't you, man?" The Artist moved between Darryl and the painting. The familiar, overpowering mixture of smells rolled over Darryl, dried body odor, paint thinner, pot. And that other decaying smell, a body eating itself from within.

"Who are they?"

The Artist's dark face split into a grin. His teeth were white and even except for that yellowed stub on the left. "It's just art, my friend," he jangled the coffee can at the passing crowd. "One penny for art, folks! Can't you spare just a penny for art? I know you lovely ladies got to have a penny, just one between you," he spoke to a pair of coordinated sweat-suit wearing grandmothers who both affected a thousand yard stare as they swept past.

Darryl stuffed his hand in his pocket, pulled its contents out in the open and weeded out the receipts and business cards from the coins and bills. The chaff fluttered from his hand, but he clutched the money and dropped it into the can, not knowing how much he'd held. He thought he'd had a twenty, at least two fives, some ones, who knew how many quarters? How many pennies?

"Who are they?"

The Artist smiled, but he didn't look down into the coffee can. "I dunno, I call 'em Steve and Edie. I tell you, I was working on this, just feeling out the shapes, the whole, I dunno, *size* of the thing and then it was just like, *POW—*" he broke off into a long fit of coughing, wet, rattling coughing that hunched him over and buckled his knees. As the Artist wiped a hand across his mouth, Darryl could see a thin foam of blood at the corners of his lips. "Anyway," he continued, softer now, "it was just *pow* there they were right inside the painting. It's like that sometimes, when it's good, the painting, the creating, it bubbles up, bursts out, and you say 'where did that come from, man? Could that have come from me?' He tugged at the lobe of his ear and Darryl noticed how yellowish the whites of the man's eyes were, shot through with tiny broken veins. "Does it happen to you like that too, man? It's just there in the middle of your work? *Pow?*"

Darryl's fingers stretched out again toward the painting. "I—I'm not an artist. I sell things—fasteners, you know, nuts, bolts, hinges. I sell them to—" he stopped, feeling his teeth click together, the muscles on his jaw bunch. "I don't even really sell them, I sell companies the, how would you say it, the opportunity to buy them from someone else. I'm like a go-between. There's nothing to create." Darryl drifted off, feeling the same way he did every time he tried to explain his job to some new acquaintance. It was hard, it wasn't like he fought fires or transplanted hearts. How do you explain brokering retail contracts?

"I know it's a job," he murmured beneath his breath, "they pay me and I have to show up every day."

He traced what he thought were the lovers' intertwined fists. "How much is this?" Even as he asked, he pictured Sara's face as he drug the plywood into their apartment. Her eyes would narrow, her mouth pucker so small it would almost disappear.

The Artist chuckled low and shook his head. "Oh man, I don't sell these. These ain't for sale. I bring 'em to show people. So when I ask for that penny to buy more paint, canvas, whatever, they can see that this is what it's for. So they can see I'm not just begging, man. I'm not on the pipe, I'm no juice head." He narrowed his eyes just a little at Darryl. "Sure, I've smoked the weed, but I think it helps, you know, to see it all." He waved his hand at the plywood. "Mostly I buy paint with money. I don't eat much. But I got to make. To create." He covered his mouth and coughed again, long and wet, his yellowed eyes bugging out from his face.

Darryl's phone went off, a small klaxon at his hip. He jumped, looked around wildly, but by the time he'd taken it off his belt, its three rings were up and whoever was calling had been transferred to voice mail. In the top corner of the screen the time blinked. Christ, an hour and a half since he'd left the office. Lambert might not notice; but would the secretary mention when he'd left?

"I've got to go. I've got to go right now."

As he turned and crossed against the traffic, back toward Western Avenue, the Artist called out to him over the blaring horns. "Thanks for the donation man. Make something for yourself! Create something today!"

SATURDAY 2:35 P.M.

The weather held for the weekend, bright and sunny, seventy degrees, and the sloping floors of the three-storied Market were filled past capacity. Darryl walked a little behind the Sara and the others. Her voice carried over the crowd, playing tour guide to a city that she'd said more than once she loathed in the deepest part of her heart. ". . . And they say there's a ghost in one of the used bookshops here. She just appears between the stacks. I'm not sure which one."

Darryl shuffled his feet in the trying, stop-and-go movement that was the only way to walk through the crowd. Lee and Justin, Sara, and Debra and Rick . . . or Richard—Darryl hadn't paid that much attention during the introductions—managed to move through milling shoppers in a tight knot, glancing at the stalls with their bottles of organic honey, or Sleepless in Seattle T-shirts. Sometimes glancing west out the windows at the Cascades, a line of jagged teeth already capped with snow.

Ahead, Sara and the others reached the Market's northern terminus. The booths emptied out onto a sidewalk with the low retaining wall on the left. A few vendors had their goods stacked along the wall. "If we go up to the park, we'll have a good view of Mount Rainier," Sara said, as she slipped on a pair of Raybans the same red as her shoes, her purse, the bow holding her hair tightly against her skull. "You guys are so lucky with the weather today. It's usually pouring this time of year. I read somewhere that living in Seattle is like being married to a beautiful woman who's sick *all* the time." Lee and Justin laughed, heads nodding.

Darryl ran his tongue over his teeth, frowning but not surprised. He'd read that line to her from a G.M. Ford mystery, and she'd rolled her eyes and muttered that she was sick of the rain.

The concrete benches of Victor Steinbrueck Park were filled with people eating late lunches, some sprawled on the small mound of grass, shirts off, getting those last rays of sunshine. Others leaned against the peeling railing, watching the ferries disembarking, berthing, frothing wakes behind them.

Darryl's stomach clenched when he saw the Artist, set up at the edge of the grassy knoll. He still wore the same clothes, clutched the same coffee can. "One penny for art," sailed over the crowd's head. The Artist only had three or four paintings set up in a semi-circle. A plastic bag lay at his feet and a brown wrapped parcel leaned against the back of a bench, no more than two inches thick, as tall as the man's waist and about four feet long.

Darryl looked again—*Into the Breech*, where was it? Steve and Edie—Where were they? He'd said it wasn't for sale. Why wasn't it here?

He snuck a glance over his shoulder; Sara and her cronies had moved to the railing, both Lee and Sara pointing first to the condo-skirted bulge of West Seattle, and then farther out towards Bremerton. Nobody seemed to notice his absence.

When the Artist spotted Darryl walking toward him, his dark face split into a grin and he reached into his the thigh pocket of his ripped fatigue pants, "Hey, Man, Darryl, right?" The drawstring bag at the man's feet had SEATTLE ART SUPPLY stenciled along its misshapen side.

"I got something of yours, Darryl." He freed his hand and held out a slim leather business card case and a small bundle of papers. "You dropped 'em here yesterday." He tapped the case. "These had your name, where you work, I went by there, but I didn't think they'd let me see you. So I waited. Man, you move when you free from work, don't you? I tried to follow you but couldn't keep you in sight."

Darryl nodded absently, thinking of his hurried walk up to Capitol Hill last night. He took the cards and receipts from the outstretched hand, staring at the paint grimed into the knuckles, beneath the long nails. "Thanks," He looked around the park. Sara glanced over at him, frowned, then turned back to the view. "I, I actually gave you all the cash I had yesterday." Should he ask about the painting?

The Artist laughed, shaking his head just a fraction. "Wasn't looking for no re-ward, Darryl. Man, you already gave me plenty. More'n I'll sometimes get in a week. No, that just helped me find you. Figured you'd want them back, when you got to thinking about it. If I couldn't get you at your work, I knew you'd be back down here—been coming here all week." He set the coffee can down next to the bag. "I got something else for you. Help me with this," He bent to grab one end of the flat package.

As Darryl knelt beside him, he found the man's odor not overwhelming, but compelling, somehow. The smell of secrets, of living. They laid the parcel flat on the grass and the Artist pulled the tape away. Tourists and locals brushed past them. One man on the grassy hill raised himself on his elbows, watching. The Artist folded back the brown paper

"Is this one of yours?" Darryl kept his voice low. Maybe he could back out of here before Sara and the others came over to see what he was doing.

The Artist separated the last piece of tape and pulled the paper all the way off, letting it fall back on the grass. It was a blank canvas, stretched drum-tight over a wooden frame "Naw, man, no way. This is one of yours." He opened the bag up and dumped its contents around the perimeter of the canvas; tubes of paint, acrylics, oils, Darryl wasn't sure. There were a couple of rags and sponges, gray with wear and flecked with a rainbow of paint, a pair of rusted putty knives, but no brushes.

"No brushes," was the only thing Darryl could think to say.

"Brushes keep you too far away from it, Darryl," he unscrewed a tube and squeezed a thick worm of bright blue paint diagonally across the canvas. "It's like a barrier. Your fingers, that's what you use the most, just your fingers." Then it was red he pushed from another tube, rolling it as it emptied, spiraling it from the center of the canvas outward.

"Darryl, what the hell are you doing?" He glanced over his shoulder at Sara, standing there, Raybans clenched in one white knuckled fist. Lee and Justin were at her shoulders, Rick/Rich and Debra farther away, uncomfortably scanning the cityscape. The Artist hadn't looked up when she spoke. He' grabbed the rag and swirled the red and blue together into a muddy background. Darryl stepped closer to the canvas.

"Darryl, get away from him." In her eyes and from the rising pitch of her voice; he could see her picturing a thousand water-cooler conversations as Lee and Justin related his actions to the office. He almost felt sorry for her.

He edged closer to the canvas and the Artist handed him an open tube of yellow. *Daffodil* it read on the label across the tube's crimped end. The Artist's long, stained fingers wrapped around Darryl's wrist and guided his hand over the canvas, squeezing out bubbles of pigment. "I think if you look hard enough, you might find Steve and Edie in here, or maybe someone even better. I thought I'd help you look for them." He opened up two tubes at once and squeezed them out.

"Darryl, I swear to god, you are not going to do this to me—not here, not in front of them!"

Darryl dropped the empty paint tube and reached for another, then stopped, staring at the canvas. The paint was thick, covering the canvas from edge to edge, like frosting on a cake. Sara's voice receded, whistling down a long tunnel. He put his fingers into the paint, at first just the tips, but then splaying his hands flat on the canvas. The paint squished coldly between his fingers, up over the backs of his hands, layers of color, one on top the other.

He moved his fingers across the canvas, watching the designs appear, then pool in, then appear again. He smeared the paint out and it dripped over the edge of the canvas, falling with a thick plop. He plotted the curve of an ear, reached down for a sponge and dabbed it into a tracery of hair, hair swept back with the wind.

"I think they're in there," the Artist said. "I think you found them, Darryl."

Darryl no longer heard Sara's voice. If she had turned and left he didn't hear her heels clicking on the concrete. If she was still speaking, the words no longer mattered. The sun beat on his shoulders as his fingers moved across the canvas.

"Yes," Darryl said, "I think they're coming out together."

30

Corporate Art

TERRI GRIFFITH

Liz inserts her bus pass into the card reader. Expired, it says. "It can't be expired, I should have another week on this," she says to the driver. She fishes in her purse for dollar bills, some change, any money. Surely, she must have some loose coins in her purse. She feels the two people waiting on the steps behind her stare at her impatiently. This only makes her more nervous and clumsy.

"Don't worry about it," the driver says. "Just get on."

"Thanks," she mumbles.

Liz scans the seats for an orphaned newspaper, but finds none. She settles into an empty seat next to the window, takes off her gloves and wraps her bare hands around the stainless steel commuter mug to warm them. She's glad that no one is sitting next to her and that she can look out the window. Leaving early makes for an easy ride in. No chatty office gals. No moms escorting their kids to school. No heavily cologned management guy talking important businessman talk into his cell phone. Just early risers and corporate over-achievers. These are the only riders on the bus at six thirty-two in the morning, except of course, the minimum-wage workers who serve them.

Her career-girl camouflage is doing its job, and Liz is pleased by how well she blends in. She tries to identify who of her fellow commuters are actually ambitious and who are only pretending. The whole process is problematic. There are just too many factors to consider. A stranger just getting onto the bus might mistake Liz for one of these eager people. He would, of course, be wrong.

This comparatively quiet ride assures Liz that she is doing the right thing both morally and environmentally by taking public transportation. She saves a lot of money and it's terrifyingly expensive to park downtown, but it's the aspect of socialization Liz considers most important. She relies on these daily bus trips to keep her socialized, to prevent her from turning feral, like some dog tied to a tree in the back yard, never having human contact, never meeting other dogs.

Liz steps off the bus at her usual State Street stop right into the morning financial district bustle. Usually when she's early for work she goes to the corner coffee bar, chats up one of the coffee girls, and gets her second coffee of the day. Today though, her commute has gone swiftly, and she still has coffee left. It's extravagant and wasteful to just toss out perfectly good coffee, coffee she would be more than happy to have if her commute had lasted any longer.

Liz waits until the bus has pulled away and the passengers have scurried to their office buildings before opening her commuter mug and indulgently pouring its remains into the gutter. In the freezing cold of the morning, the hot coffee runs in a narrow, steaming rivulet into the storm drain. The whole scene makes Liz think of pee.

―――――――――

"Double short latte," she says to the guy at the cash register. She pays, then drops the few leftover coins into the jar marked "tips" and shuffles her way to the end of the counter to wait.

"Busy this morning," she says to the new barista, a cute girl with green eyes and a shaved head who is probably still in college although she looks much younger. Certainly if she were in high school, she'd be well on her way to class by now.

"People need their morning coffee," the barista says.

"Who makes yours?"

"I make my own."

"I bet you're good at it."

"Good enough." She smiles at Liz while she pulls the shots.

When the girl sets the drink on the counter, Liz reaches into her purse and takes out a five. Instead of putting the money into the tip jar, Liz pushes it across the counter. "Thank you," Liz mouths. The barista takes the money and slips it casually into the pocket on the front of her apron. Tomorrow when Liz comes in for her usual, the girl will remember her.

Liz pulls up the faux-fur-trimmed collar of her coat and fastens the top button at her neck before heading back into the chill. It will take considerably less than forty-five minutes to drink this latte, which is the amount of time remaining before she is expected to be sitting at her desk, ready for her first member of the morning. So, Liz walks up State, looking in shop windows, mentally trying on shoes and coats much nicer and more costly than the ones

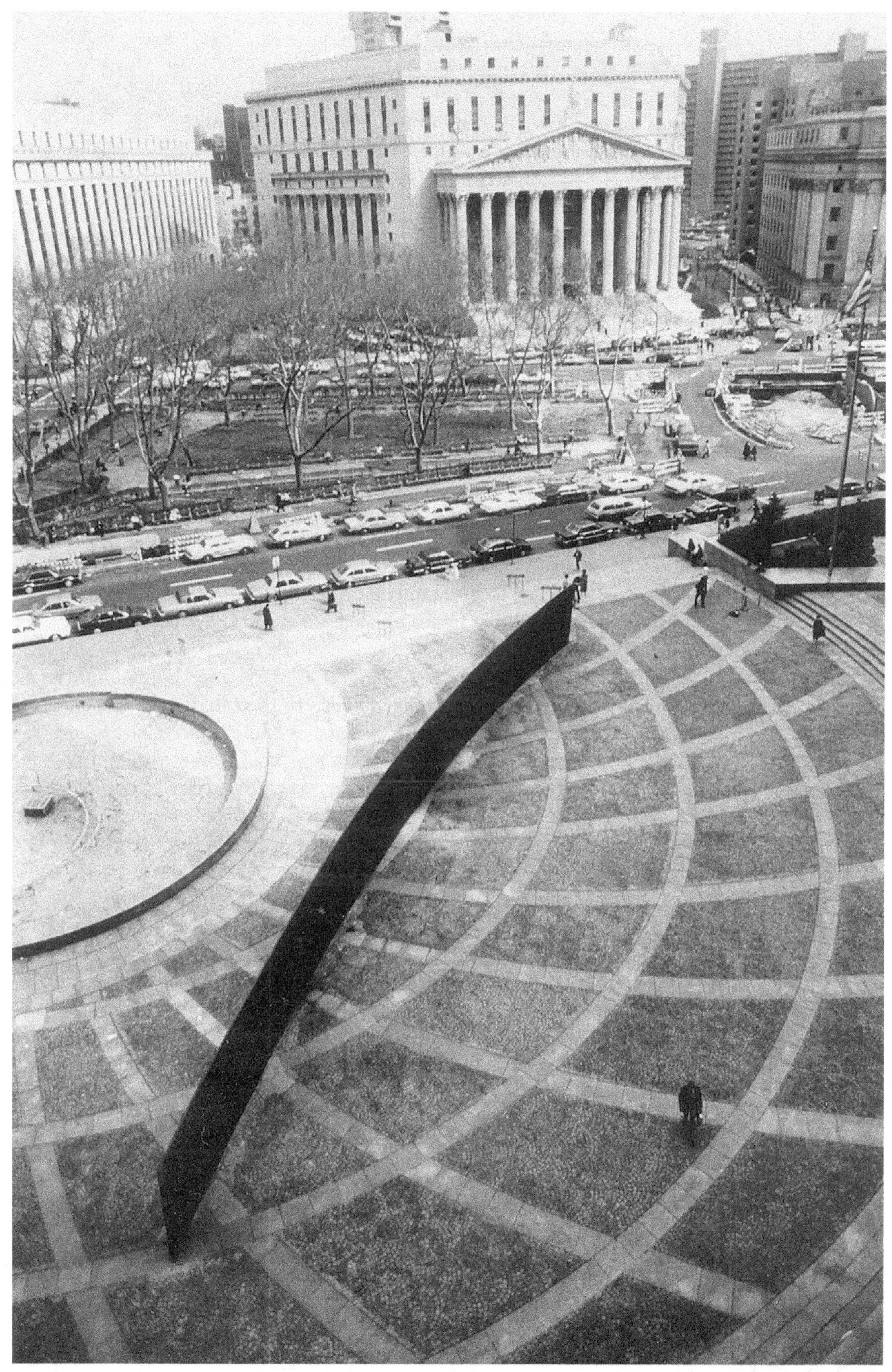

she's wearing. She watches a janitor in a dirty blue jumpsuit buff the floors that in less than two hours will be sullied, wet with melted, dingy snow, and stained a salty white.

Despite all the people rushing to their offices, downtown is muffled as it always is on a snow-filled morning. People hurry differently before work, more quietly than they do at the end of their day. No stopping to chat at the bus stop with co-workers, no yelling after occupied cabs, no frantic last minute dinner plans on cell phones. Just the comforting white noise of taxis and busses and feet sloshing across the sidewalk.

Liz is freezing and wishes she had not walked these extra few blocks away from The Credit Union. What has made her come to work so early when it would have been so simple to have just stayed in bed and called in sick?

Outside a tall, black glass building, an anonymous corporate headquarters, Liz sits and sips her coffee. The bench faces a large steel sculpture, placed there by the parent company as a "gift to its employees." When it was first installed the citizens of the financial district where practically giddy with delight. But really, this tilty slice of metal bisects the egress of the front door, forcing these same people to walk around it in order to enter the building. When leaving, they are faced with a wall of steel that stands between them and the street that will carry them home.

Liz doesn't know a thing about art, but of this she is sure: this sculpture is an act of violence against office workers and makes the building even more alienating. The company pretends this "gift" is there to add culture to the otherwise cultureless lives of the downtown employees. But Liz knows its true purpose is to mark this section of the downtown, to increase the perceived importance of the company and its headquarters. She watches the people pass and wonders if anyone really likes this sculpture, or only pretends to because it was made by someone famous.

The stream of workers flowing into the glass building is increasing, indicating that eight o'clock is approaching. She looks at her watch and wonders what she did with all that extra time. She should hurry off to her own cubicle, but she isn't quite ready. There's still latte left in her commuter mug.

For the third time this month, Liz finds herself sitting outside Theresa's office building, drinking coffee, contemplating the corporate art machine, and pretending she isn't waiting for Theresa to get off the southbound bus and walk inside.

31

The Bloomsbury Nudes

JAMESON CURRIER

I had overlooked the article until Keith pointed it out to me. "Didn't you know him? Was this the same guy?"

The article was buried at the bottom of one of those inside pages of the *Times* devoted to international news. It was about a sixty-two-year-old man whose body had washed ashore on the Amalfi coast. The dead man was a "former dancer" named Jared Tremaine.

Keith recognized the name because I had told him about Tremaine's relationship with the artist Clive Elliott and the strange events surrounding Elliott's death in London in 1981. Keith was something of a crime and mystery buff and a would-be novelist, always on the lookout for something or someone to write about. I had once thought that the details of Clive's life would interest him. Keith, never one to take any route I suggested, was more interested in the ex-dancer than the forgotten artist (which, in my estimation, didn't set him apart from anyone else). Jared Tremaine was a notoriously pretty man and widely admired as much for his looks as his talent. I remember the first time I saw him I felt as if God had sent an angel to torment me; I couldn't take my eyes off of him, but there was also the fear that if I looked too long I would become blind from his beauty. When I read the newspaper article Keith had discovered I realized that I had not heard anything of Jared in more than a decade. Since 1981, when I had last seen him, I had learned Jared was in Barcelona, choreographing parts of the Opening Ceremonies for the Olympics, and then, later, in Japan,

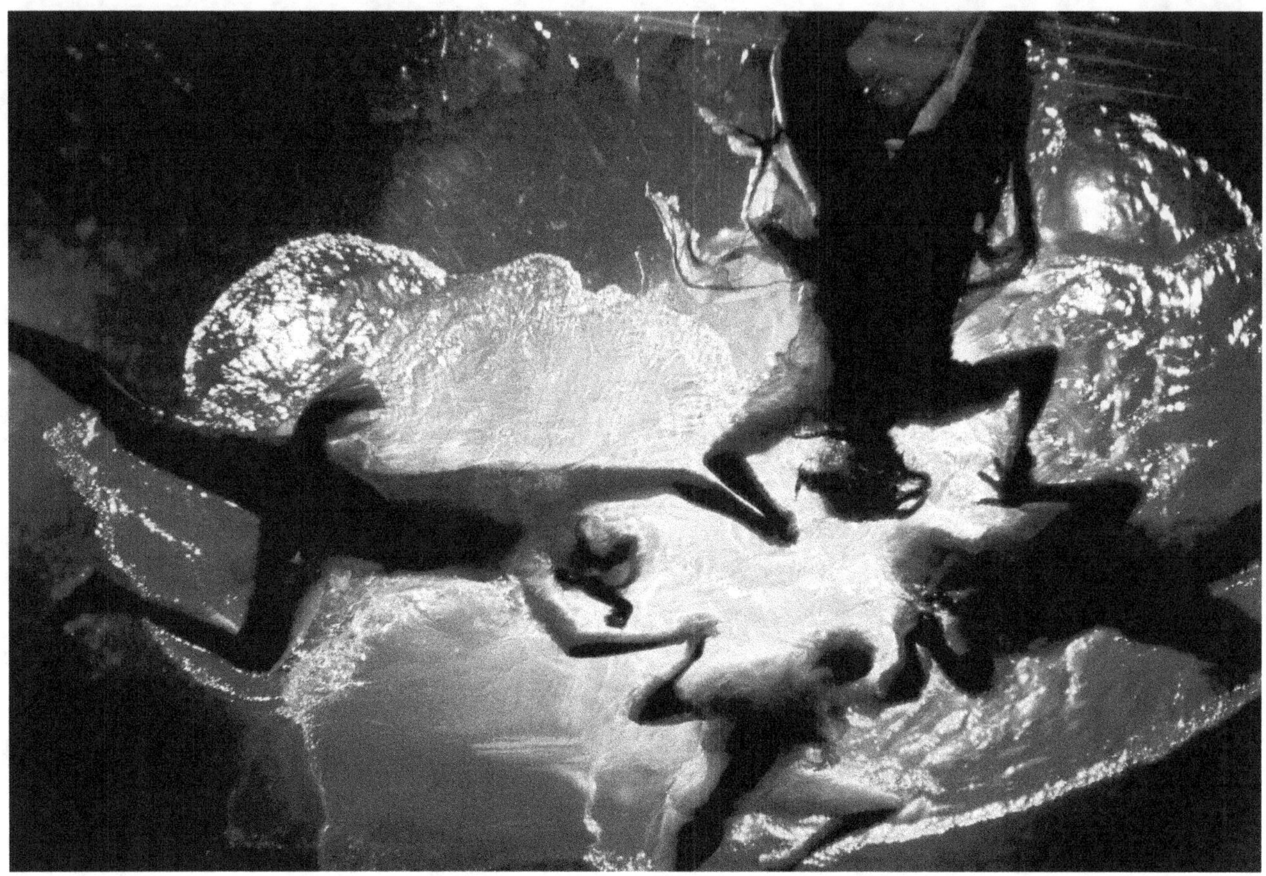

where he was said to be directing commercials and music videos starring American and British pop music stars. I had filed our friendship away as a memory, but something about Jared—and Elliott's death—had nonetheless clung to Keith's memory. Keith was something of a romantic; he could never think evil of anyone or of anyone as evil (perhaps another reason why his "true crime" stories lean more toward tragedy than horror).

Keith and I live in Somerset, not far from the Burnham seafront. I'm fifty-two now and run a gift shop, a favorite of the locals in search of a special present for one of their more peculiar (or flamboyantly queer) friends. There is an array of unusual souvenirs on the shelves—cheap, locally made snow globes, shot glasses, and ashtrays in case a tourist stumbles out of one of the arcades or pleasure parks and happens to find his way into our store. Keith, my business partner and lover (who is also in his early fifties), does most of the selling and dealing with customers; I tend to spend my time flipping through catalogs and brochures and visiting wholesale markets in search of the right items for our store or a special customer, sometimes bringing back an inexpensive antique that Keith will greet with a sigh and a roll of his eyes and an exasperated remark that the item will be unlikely to find a potential buyer. We're both collectors, and we've amassed quite an assortment of books, albums, movies, and *tchotchkes* that forever need dusting. We've done our best to keep abreast of the rapidly changing technology of camera cellphones, plasma screens, and iPods; we've even installed broadband at the store so we can swiftly cruise the 'Net when customers are scarce. We're the essence of the aging, queer British couple—suburban, bickering, and devoted to each other.

Twenty-seven years ago, however, I was single and in my twenties and determined to live and work in London as an openly gay artist. It was 1980 and I knew a few things about art history—I was appreciative of the Impressionists, frustrated by the Cubists, disliked most of the Modernists, and fell in love with the simplicity of the Pop artists. And I knew a few things about gay history—artists such as Michelangelo, da Vinci, Caravaggio, and Dürer were already part of the queer pantheon and scholars were hotly contesting the sexuality of John Singer Sargent and Thomas Eakins. And by 1980 Gilbert and George had successfully morphed from cheeky performance artists to being seriously considered *artistes* with *Dirty Word Pictures* and *The Penis*, Francis Bacon was drawing John Edwards, Andy Warhol was already an international legend, and David Hockney was experimenting with Polaroid pictures. But true art to me that year was the unmasking of the beauty of the male body via the Bruce Weber photographs in the American monthly magazine *GQ* and the hyperbutch illustrations of Tom of Finland that were reprinted in the London bar rags and imported porn slicks I could find in an underground specialty shop in Charring Cross. Clones ruled my imagination and libido and a male nude could suspend time for me, freeze me in place as I examined every nook and crack, yearning to understand both sex and love with another man. And even though I hadn't abandoned my desire to be a serious artist, I was sidelined by having to make a living as an assistant graphic designer at an advertising firm in Soho. This was long before Adobe and Quark and Photoshop made everything a lot easier and a little bit more fun, so most of my days were spent hunched over a mat with an X-Acto knife or a razor blade trying to make everything even and line up. I seldom got to draw anything at that miserable job. But every week I had a little more money in my pocket and on the weekends I went out dancing at whatever gay club was fashionable, be it drag or disco—Embassy, Regine's, Prince Albert's, Euston Tavern, The Bell, or Heaven.

I had known Clive Elliott as a teacher when I studied drawing with him in 1976 in Paris during a summer break from my college studies at Furness. At the time, my parents had wanted me to be anywhere but London, and I had ended up going to the university close to our home in Lancaster and working part-time at my father's lighting shop, mostly delivering lamps or helping install fixtures. My parents had acquiesced to my French sojourn, in part, because I had doodled a graphic of a winged foot for an ad contest sponsored by a local shoe company, which had been awarded first prize and printed in the newspaper, and I had expressed an interest in pursuing this artistic side of myself; and, in larger measure, to keep me from traveling to the raucous Liverpool clubs with my mates and their rock band and getting into all sorts of trouble. Drawing, as it were, was the lesser evil of the arts, and Paris, my parents believed, would be an educational experience for me.

Clive Elliott had made a splash at the beginning of the Pop Art phenomenon in Britain with a series of stark silhouettes of everyday items, such as familiar brand-name Coke bottles and Kleenex boxes, deceptively simple-looking paintings that were quickly snapped up by the Tate and the Modern in New York, though over the years they have been relegated to basement storerooms. The deep impression they made on the other artists of the movement has long been forgotten, particularly their impact on Americans such as Andy Warhol and Roy Lichtenstein, who seized on the notion of illustrating everyday items and took it to the next level. By the 1970s, Elliott had settled into being a respected and requested illustrator and designer—sometimes at work on a children's book, other times on the set design for an opera company—leaving behind the limelight and the large canvases unless something like a hefty commission determinedly yanked him back into it.

In Paris, in Clive's drawing class, we drew silhouettes of objects, learning how to form lines and shapes. I had had little artistic training other than a few school classes and a limited experimentation with my self-taught doodling. I felt that Clive knew I was one of the least talented pupils of the class. And the truth of the matter was I only wanted to be in Paris in order to explore its nightlife and get away from the prying eyes of my parents. Clive was fifty-six that year and had long before shed his own lithe silhouette. He was arrogant and conceited, like most great artists become when exposed to fame, but warm and insecure as a puppy once he felt comfortable with you and the bitter façade was dropped. In the classroom he could be condescending to his students. "I agree it is pretty, dear, but is it art?" was his favorite way of judging a drawing. As an art instructor he felt that a line should be seamless, even when it was shadowed, and there was always something about my work that was not straight enough for his liking—it was all too bent and disconnected to please him. "You seem to have lost control of your hand somewhere," he would say to me, leaning into my sketch. "Right about here. And here. And here. And here."

Clive would have disregarded my drawing talent entirely had I not caught Jared's attention.

Clive had met Jared in 1973 when Jared was twenty-nine and dancing with a Paris ballet troupe and already something of a legendary beauty, more breathtaking in person than he was onstage. Jared's parents had met in the Dutch Resistance and he had been born shortly after the end of World War II. He did not begin studying dance until he was sixteen, when he accompanied his younger sister Sabine to a dance class and was offered a small fee by the instructor to stay and help spot and lift the girls. Jared knew right away that he had no desire to "augment a ballerina" and he embarked on his own journey of pirouettes, jetés, and leaps into the history books. He trained with Roland Petit and the Paris Opera Ballet and made his debut at nineteen as the Nutcracker Prince. He might have gone overlooked were it not for the fact that the troupe had announced an "international exchange program" that would send Jared and three other dancers to Russia for a year in order to study with Pushkin and perform at the Kirov Ballet. That plan never materialized because of concerns over defections of the Russian dancers being sent to France, and Jared went to Vienna instead, where his Romeo in a production of the Berlioz ballet created a sensation and he caught the attention of film director Franco Zeffirelli. Zeffirelli flew Jared to Rome and screen tested him for a film version he was preparing of the Shakespeare play, but Jared's English was abysmal and the director found him "too distractingly beautiful." While in Italy Jared made a small film for Alberto Maresca, one of the lesser known Italian New Wave auteurs, and he returned to Paris where he danced Swan Lake to great acclaim and became a star attraction. Five years later, a motorbike accident in Cannes while he was the guest of a wealthy financier—Jared was riding down a slope in a chilly rain when the bike slid out from under him—caused a fracture in his ankle and sidelined him for months because the injury proved difficult to heal. Out of the limelight, he soon found his celebrity eclipsed by the Russian dancer Mikhail Baryshnikov, four years his junior.

That summer I spent in Paris, 1976, Jared was dancing less and less because of a reinjury to his ankle the season before. He was thirty-two and, in between physical therapy sessions, he was doing what most aging male ballet dancers do, looking for ways to expand his performance career with acting classes and modeling. Jared showed up in our drawing class one day to be drawn. He slipped out of his jeans and T-shirt and Clive, admiringly, told the seven of us to depict Jared as a silhouette. "Dear ones, take this magnificent specimen of *Homo sapiens* in front of you and attempt to have your line and shape contain all his beauty," Clive instructed the class. Like many male ballet stars Jared was tall and slender and athletic, with full, deeply muscled buttocks and a generous crotch. He was a good head taller than myself and Clive—slightly over six feet—and he had the smoothest skin imaginable, which would have made him feminine and ghostlike were it not for his extraordinary physique and the black coloration of his hair and eyes.

I didn't know anything of Jared except that he was extraordinary looking. I understood little about gay relationships then—I was twenty and had only had a handful of sexual encounters with men, and I could get an erection at the mere hint of another man's flesh. An "open relationship" between two gay men was simply a foreign and mystical concept to me—I had never even had a boyfriend. I remember I stood in front of my easel that day shifting from one leg to the other as I tried to see Jared's body as one continuous line, hoping to hide my sexual ache and avoid revealing too much about my own tortured interior. I wanted to know Jared, know what it was like to be with him and to be him, the envy of other men, to float easily through life and unabashedly shed my clothes for a roomful of strangers and be admired, and here I was instead, a frustrated young man with a charcoal pencil in my hand, nervously sweating, flustered and dizzy from the nearness of Jared's body.

Jared must have detected my squirming because I honestly don't believe my silhouette of him was striking enough to get his notice. But there was also something strange and restless about him—as if he were about to bolt at any moment and the only way he could remain in place was to find something curiously interesting about someone and detect the adoration reflected back at him. At the end of class we started a conversation while Clive was being monopolized by one of the more aggressive and less gifted female students, a petite Franco-Asian woman named Chloe who had made it clear she did not want to spend her class time drawing silhouettes.

"I will hear of that later," Jared said to me. His English was heavily accented and the tone of his voice, like many Europeans', emanated as much from his nose as his throat.

"He complains about us?" I asked, trying not to look at Jared dressing but unable to look elsewhere.

"To draw more attention to him," Jared answered and smiled. It was a gorgeous smile, the kind that deserved to be painted for all its mysterious complexity, not as a line but as a sharply detailed portrait like the *Mona Lisa,* "Involved with only him, you know?" he added. "What artist is not, yes? We are creatures of our design and not flattering, no?"

We began an awkward conversation in French—my vocabulary was minimal, even after years of classes. He asked me where I was staying in Paris and I launched into a flustered description of our neighborhood and the austere qualities of the dormitory where the students were housed. I was breathing heavily, trying to concentrate on my French and trying not to swoon like a girlish fool.

"There is a pleasant café near you," he said. "Café Florizelle. Meet me there. We have espresso and a long talk, yes?"

Outside the classroom Jared flirted and brazenly held my hand at the table, flattering me as "*la vraie beauté,*" and "*prachtige kunstenaar.*" He thought my sketch was the best in the class. He asked me about my family and "*Angleterre*" and he spoke fondly of his sister Sabine, who was teaching history at a school in Ghent. He followed me back to the dormitory and we began an affair that lasted until the end of the summer came and I returned to Lancaster. I call it affair because I also had no understanding then of what a sex buddy was—I could not emotionally disconnect myself from my partner during sex as Jared so easily did. And his body soon became more familiar to me than my own, capturing my desires and imagination more than any masterpiece on display at the Louvre. I ached to hear the sound of his voice, watch his lips move and his struggle for words as he criticized something he had recently seen—a soprano's aria or an actor's performance, watch the way he used his hands and wrists to express himself, smell the sweet-sour pulse of his breath as he leaned in closer to me to make his point clearer. My notebooks from those days are full of sketches of him. I had tried to capture the full beauty of his body as he lay stretched out or curled up on my bed, but I soon settled for smaller, more detailed portraits of his face and hands and legs. There is even a sequence of portraits of his face as I tried to render his expressions during the moments before, during, and after his orgasm—that rush of painful pleasure as it soared from his chest to his eyes. I can look at them today and still weep from the sheer beauty of his body and find myself amazed that I had been so close to it. I was ready to give up everything for him—to be with him in whatever way he wanted—a slave, an errand boy, the adoring fan, and yes, even his fuck buddy—anything as long as he did not leave me. "I am with Clive, you see," he would say gently when I protested every time he made an effort to leave my dorm room. "You break my heart when you depart me. You will leave me for another lover."

I leave *him*? I doubted that and sulked in his absence, trying to reconstruct his day away from me, obsessively wondering where he was and who else he was meeting and why. I often overlooked Jared's moodiness and depression because I was so overwhelmed by my own, and when it did surface in him and demand to be accounted for—that black despair of misunderstanding—I played the clown, or the fool, or the seducer, anything so he would not want to leave me. Jared's depression often had as much to do with Clive as it did with dancing—or not dancing—"He does not understand," Jared would moan and press his beautiful face into his hands while we were at a café and pretend to weep in a dramatic, theatrical fashion. "He does not get it," he would whisper as he pressed his lips against my chest if we were in my narrow little bed. "What it feels like to fly— *om te vliegen*—to have a control over the body—*ascenseur à un fantôme*—to be, how do you say it? Possessed by a spirit."

It was clear to me that Jared loved Clive and that Clive reciprocated that love, and it often left me feeling like an outsider. I ceased to exist when I was with both of them, because they were a couple and I was their friend, or student, or secret amour. My last weeks in Paris, Clive must have learned about my affair with Jared because I began to receive little invitations from him, sometimes during class—"Dennis, there's an exhibit I want to see in the Marais, can you walk with me after class to find the gallery?"—other times through a phone message scrawled on a piece of paper and shoved underneath my door—"Mr. Elliott called and asked if you can go to the opera tonight." Clive was always a gentleman, never trying to put a move on me or ask me of my feelings for Jared, and we became good friends. He'd grown up not far from Lancaster, in the Lake District, so we also had that in common. "My father used to deliver packages from the train station to Beatrix Potter," he told me. "She was quite old then and had given up publishing her stories and drawings because she was helping the farms and determined to save the land from developers. But if I accompanied my father in his van, she would always draw a little animal on a piece of paper for me to travel back home with—a small rabbit, perhaps, or a duck. She was my introduction into the world of art."

Two years later, in 1978, after spending agonizing time in classes in marketing and economics at Lancaster, I moved to London with a roommate, despite my parents' disappointment that I would not stay closer to them and eventually take over my father's shop. I was following a college mate I had become obsessively infatuated with after my summer fling with Jared, but after six weeks of our living together in the city in a tiny flat near Russell Square, Geoffrey announced that he was moving into a bigger place with his new boyfriend. I was both heartbroken and relieved and determined to make it on my own. My experience with Jared had left me wiser and stronger.

But I was thrilled when Jared's letter arrived at the beginning of 1980 to say that he and Clive were moving back to London. Clive was planning to design the sets for a West End play that was to star Jared. Whether Jared got the part in the play on his own talent or charisma, or through the aid of Clive's intervention or participation, I don't know, but Clive had promised the producer and director that he would create a bold, minimalist look for the play, designing the sets and costumes and any related merchandising materials.

It wasn't long, however, before the play's production budget had escalated out of control and a major investor had fallen through and the production was cancelled, but Clive and Jared still thought that living in London for a while would reinvigorate their careers, and Clive secured a teaching position at the University of London. Jared was also going to give choreography a try, working with a small avant-garde dance company and offering "master classes" for promising students.

Clive and Jared should have become as famous a gay couple as Benjamin and Peter or Gertrude and Alice, but too many personal setbacks and tragedies intervened and prevented this from happening and the public seldom got a chance to witness the full beauty of their relationship. I had no idea what part I was going to play for Jared when he arrived in London—resurrected lover or an ex-fling turned friend. I was still in love with him—I'm still in love with him today. Jared was my first love, which was why the painful news of his death in Italy unnerved me when Keith had presented the newspaper article to me. But by the time Jared and Clive arrived in London that fall I had progressed from wanting to make love to Jared's body to wanting to help him love himself and be happy. Jared did not exactly push me away, but he remained aloof and detached and there was no hint of wanting to resume our affair, and I began to have a closer friendship with Clive, introducing him to the better Indian restaurants in Bloomsbury and the art supply store on Tottenham Street. Occasionally, I would hear secondhand of Jared's depression through one of Clive's accounts, but I knew it was not from any regret over our affair or our diminishing friendship and more from the fact that Jared's career as a performer seemed to be drawing to an end whether he tried to pursue it or not.

———————

I'd love to blame the events of what happened that year on the townhouse Clive and Jared settled into on Gordon Square, not far from the British Museum. It was clearly too large and well beyond their means, one of the last buildings erected on the west side by Thomas Cubitt sometime in the mid-1850s. Their staff consisted of a housekeeper and a cook who showed up on sporadic days I could never figure out, their salaries paid for by the university, who had leased the house to Clive. At first glance the interior might have seemed like that of any grand, upper-crust quarters—not quite as extravagant as Apsley or Leighton or Spencer House, but certainly filled with antiques, curios, and relics of the Empire. But there was also something deeply troubling about its interior and furnishings. The entrance foyer was laid out with a swirl of black stones that swept up into a dark circular staircase and looked like the sprawling limbs of a giant tree. Above was a mock-domed ceiling flamboyantly painted in a Renaissance style with a battle scene between angels and demons. At one point the house had belonged to a colleague of Aliester Crowley and a member of the Hermetic Order of the Golden Dawn. Small touches of the dark arts popped out of nowhere—a sepia portrait of a frightened woman in a tarnished frame sealed with a ringlet of hair and pressed flowers, a large gilt mirror in the shape of a hexagram, an obelisk at the center of a paneled levitation box being used as a side table. The parlor was filled with gorgeously illustrated books on religion, mysticism, magic, and the occult, leather-bound volumes of *The Book of the Law*, *The Equinox*, *The Secrets of Conjuring*, *Deceptive Conceptions*, *Malleus Maleficarium*, *Clavis Salomonis*, *Pseudomonarchia Daemonum*, and early issues of *The Magic Circular*, *The Criterion*, and *The Tatler*. The lamps were shaded and fringed so that shadows of sickly colors filled most of the rooms. There was medieval armor and shields and swords and mounted antlers and tusks and animal-skin rugs. A bayonet that Clive had been told was used in the American Revolution hung on a wall. The previous renters had been a succession of scholars and professors and explorers, each leaving behind his own bizarre touches: exotic daggers and snuffboxes and tapestries and lanterns. One resident had been a noted collector of magicians' ephemera—there were small chests full of disappearing coins and scarves and gilded cages that had once been used on stages around the world and where now perched an assortment of stuffed doves and canaries. In every room there was a sense that someone was watching you and you were never alone—eyes stared out from grim photographs and gray marble sculptures and mounted animal heads, from behind wrought iron spokes or inside engravings and inlaid patterns on the sides and lids of wooden boxes, as if you were constantly in the presence of distressed and imprisoned spirits. The upper-floor rooms were equally ornate and disturbing, but Clive had cleared out a guest room and turned it into a study where his drawing desk, shipped from his Paris apartment, was placed, and Jared had achieved a similar effect in a large third-story room to create a space to exercise and dance.

"Everything in this place has a distinct history," Clive said to me the first time I came by for dinner. "This, for instance," he said, touching a chipped clay fragment of the face of the Buddha, whose chiseled-out eyes made it look soulless, "is from Afghanistan. Discovered by a French Catholic archeologist digging in a Muslim country."

"This belonged to Herr Wingard, the royal conjurer, almost a century ago," Jared added, reaching for an antique cane that rested inside an urn beside several black umbrellas. He tapped it on the ground and the cane changed colors—from a brown wood to a deep blue. He tapped it again and tossed it in the air and it changed into a bouquet of silk flowers, certainly one of the brighter, and less ominous artifacts within the house.

"And I particularly like this curio," Clive said, lifting a block of stone that was carved on the underside with a map to make a print. "The Seal of Solomon. Rumored to summon demons. It would be rare to find this as a woodcut—but carved in stone, it is priceless."

"We could retire if we found the right buyer for it," Jared explained.

"And face the wrath of God in the process," Clive added with a light laugh.

I'd love to lay blame for what happened on one of those relics, or even on one of those *objets d'art* Clive and Jared brought back to the house on their own. I had not known they were collectors of dark curiosities and when I asked Jared when it had started, he answered that it had only begun recently, since they had arrived in London. In that time, they had found a marble chess set with carved gargoyles as pawns in South Kensington and at the flea market in Notting Hill they had purchased a bronze figure of Osiris, holding the crook and flail and wearing a braided beard with a curled tip and the atef crown. But the truth of it is, I was partly to blame because I was the one who brought Bart Pearson to the house for dinner, and Bart was dark and curious and about as handsome a man as you could find anywhere.

I had met Bart at a pub in Islington and we'd had sex three or four times, but I was smart enough by then to know that I couldn't fall in love with him because he was the kind of man who wasn't interested in a commitment to a guy like me. But I loved showing Bart off to whomever I could and he loved being on display. Bart was tall, dark, broad-shouldered, and chiseled with muscles and furred with black hair—sideburned and goateed on his face and spread-eagled across his chest. A Tom of Finland clone breathed into life. I had tried to get him an interview as a model for a designer jean ad but the account executive on the team took one look at the Polaroid photo I had taken of Bart and proclaimed him "too bloody sexy" (and then asked for his phone number).

Bart wasn't conscious of the power of his looks, though he did like getting compliments; he also wasn't interested in going out with less appealing guys—no fats, femmes, or geezers need apply, no matter how much money was waved in his direction. He wasn't conceited or vain, just young and choosy like many gay men his age. I wouldn't say he was dim-witted, more easy going and unconcerned; much of the conversation you figured might be going over his head—stuff like politics and stock prices and theater trivia—was really being consciously tuned out and considered inconsequential. He was self-focused and a creature of habit, not roaming far from his flat, even when he was cruising—he liked spending time at the gym, playing football on Saturday mornings with his mates, helping his mum out during the week, and hanging out at the local pub at night. He liked to be around people who liked to be around him and in that regard he was no different than Clive or Jared.

Clive and Jared took an immediate liking to him, in large part because of his unspoiled simplicity. Jared more so, I knew. I soon learned from Bart, of course, what was happening between him and Jared. They would meet up at Bart's flat at night—Jared telling Clive he was going to the park, or for a walk to Russell Square where he might stop in to say hello to me, but actually hopping on his motorbike and cruising over to Islington to have sex with Bart in his tiny flat above a fish and chips takeaway. Other times, Bart would finish work—he did an early morning delivery route for convenience stores—and he'd park his van in front of the house on Gordon Square and pop in for a quick visit with Jared if Clive was away at the office. Since I knew what both he and Jared were like in bed—Jared passive and encasing, Bart eager and assertive, it wasn't difficult for me to summon up images of them together—Jared's long beautiful legs thrown up over Bart's wide shoulders, his buttocks swelling and rising off the bed as Bart's grip tightened and lifted to find a deeper or more pleasurable position. I could see the sheen of sweat gathering in the hollow of Jared's neck, smell the rank woodsy cologne Bart had a preference for when he thought he needed to make a special impression, and I knew how Jared would grasp for Bart's meaty arms just before he reached an orgasm.

Since Clive and Jared were so open about their "openness" I did not expect any problems would arise because of Jared's newfound infatuation with Bart, and I thought that, like his other affairs, this one would play itself out with time. I did suspect that something darker and more sinister was at work when I met Clive for dinner one night at a new Spanish restaurant that had opened on Charlotte Street and I asked him about the progress of his new drawings.

"I'm afraid this is all I've been able to do the last month," Clive said and reached for a briefcase he had carried from his office at the university. He slipped out a few sketches. He looked older and tired—worried semicircles had appeared beneath his eyes—and his hand trembled slightly as he handed me the drawings.

On top was a pencil sketch of a nude young man reclining on a bed. I was amazed that the body was so familiar to me—the dark hairy legs, the hirsute chest, the muttonchop sideburns, and goatee.

"I didn't know Bart posed for you," I said.

"He hasn't," Clive answered dryly.

The technique was different from the flat, stationary, and cartoonish style Clive normally used. The lines were broken and the effect gave the drawings more animation and passion. I flipped through the other sketches. They were of the same man, in a variety of sexual positions with another young man—long-legged and slenderly athletic, with the same balding pattern on his head as Jared. There was an inherent motion of desire that was seldom apparent in Clive's finished drawings. The final sketch was of Jared alone, seated on a bed with a look of despair. It was exactly as I had imagined Bart and Jared together in their tryst.

"Is this all imagined?" I asked. "Or were you a polite voyeur?"

"Hardly," Clive answered. "It's copied."

I gave him a quizzical look to show I didn't understand. He took one of the sketches out of my hand and pointed to the leggy young man. "That's me, not Jared. And this fellow is not Bart. His name was Theodore Rushton."

I wasn't following his logic. "What do you mean?"

"Did you know I once posed for Duncan Grant?"

"The Bloomsbury artist?"

Clive nodded. "I was eighteen. He picked me up on the train. He had a studio not far from here, at the back of Fitzroy Street, that had once been Whistler's studio. It was around 1938 and we had a friendly little romp and then he asked to draw me." He laughed and added, "It was all very illegal and pornographic and I was delighted that someone took a fancy to me. Duncan used to pass his nude sketches along to friends like party treats. I posed for him several times, alone and with a fellow named Theodore Rushton, who was an acquaintance of Edward le Bas. I think I've still got one or two of those drawings in the Paris flat."

"I don't understand."

"Neither do I exactly. It looks like Bart and Jared, but it's not."

"Are you sure you're not projecting something here?"

"Not at all. Teddy and I became involved with each other outside of Duncan's studio. I was living in a room above a store on Parker Street and spending my time shuttling between the Museum and the National Portrait Gallery, sketching. My father thought it was silly that I wanted to be a painter, but since I had told him I was coming to London to learn cartography he felt that I was entering an admirable field and would have a necessary talent if we went to war. Teddy was one of the most beautiful men in London. He was the son of one of Roger Sage's groomsmen at Marbleton Place."

"I don't know the name. Sage?"

Clive nodded. "Sage was from a wealthy Devonshire family. His great-grandfather had invented some kind of piston that everyone needed and the family was extremely well off. Roger Sage had been one of Duncan Grant's first lovers, caught up in that whole Strachey-Keynes melodrama. Sage and Strachey had a thing, too, if I'm not mistaken. Sage only dabbled in painting, which was why no one has ever really heard of him—he wasn't a part of the Bloomsbury set. In fact, they abhorred him—though not publicly. Only privately. But it was Sage, in fact, who had sketched Duncan nude first when he was eighteen and passed it on to his cousin Lytton, who wasn't amused by it at all. In fact, he was infuriated by it—as liberal as he was, Lytton was still something of a prude now and then—particularly when it came to one of his favorites, such as Duncan. And Lytton hated Sage because he was a great champion of anything having to do with the occult. Lytton was cynical of everything. Duncan escaped falling under Sage's spell—or being cursed by it—by remaining friends with him.

"Sage became more malevolent as he aged—he was notorious for instigating all sorts of sexual rituals under the influence of one drug or another. He taught Crowley a few things, too, if I'm not mistaken. Sage and Crowley passed around lovers the same way Duncan passed around his naughty little drawings. But Sage was very possessive of Teddy, more so than of any other man he was ever involved with. He was more than thirty years older than Teddy and had such a dark influence over him. He had created everything about Teddy, from paying for his education to fashioning his appearance. Teddy was like a beautiful wild beast, moody one moment, amiable the next. Sage refused to let Edward le Bas—another artist and collector—draw Teddy because he thought the fellow had no talent, so Edward suggested Duncan do a private drawing of Teddy for Sage. Sage thought it was the most delightful and wicked thing he had ever heard of—taunting an aging, old lover by sending him his newer, much younger one. But Duncan was a lot smarter than Sage. Sage hadn't expected that I would be thrown into the mix.

"When we met at Duncan's studio for that first portrait session, Teddy was desperate to leave Sage—and he would, for days at a time, holed up in my little room or at Edward's studio in Chelsea. He finally became so distraught that he confessed everything about our affair to Sage and said he was leaving him to live with me. He wanted us to go to Ireland together, or America—anywhere to get away from Sage—and the War—the Continent was going through such dramas because of Hitler and the Nazis. Then Parliament introduced the National Service Act and he registered for service. We were suddenly in the War and Teddy was gone. One day he just upped and left to fight. It devastated Sage. And it devastated him when Teddy was one of the casualties of Dunkirk. Sage blamed me for Teddy leaving. For Teddy's death. I think he would have blamed me for the War, if he could have. He had no idea how devastated I was. Sage had always been a heavy user of whatever was at hand. Opium. Heroin. Cocaine. He died during the last days of the blitz. May 10, 1941. It was never established if it was due to the shock of his house being bombed or from an overdose. His body was found unscathed in the rubble of his home."

"Why draw this now? After all these years?"

"Something's triggered it, I'm sure. Something about being back in London, walking through the same streets again. Maybe something in that house where we're staying. All those eyes looking at me all the time—you were so right about that—very unnerving once you realize it. And something familiar about Bart probably resurrected even more memories, because he does look so much like Teddy."

"You should try to work on something different," I suggested. "Inanimate. Without feeling. Go back to the silhouettes. It's what you do best."

"Perhaps," Clive answered. "Though there is some joy within this tug of memories."

I had another taste of suspicion that all was not well when about ten days later I arranged to meet Clive and Jared at Sotheby's. One of Clive's early silhouette paintings—The Wine Bottle with Glass—was up for sale and Clive was curious to see how it had held up. Clive had telephoned me at the office and thought the outing would be good for him; he had taken my suggestion to heart and thought a new round of silhouettes might make an admirable new project. "And if I'm going to be so damned melancholy," he said, "I might as well mope about how damn brilliant I used to be."

On Saturday afternoon at our appointed time, only Jared appeared. "Migraine," he explained about Clive's absence. "*Terrible*," he added in French. "He is becoming *impossible*."

We viewed the auction items and discussed the condition of Clive's painting so we could relay our impressions to him later, then shopped along Bond Street. Jared wanted a new wallet, something thin and sleek that didn't leave a "line" showing against his rear pants pocket. Bart's name only came up once during our outing, when we had strayed into a recessed alcove of a leather store where there were some vests and chaps and some more sexual attire and toys for sale. Jared picked up a small leather band—a cock ring—and said, "I bet Bart would like this."

I agreed—it was dark and simple, and something Bart would appreciate being given.

We had drinks at a pub, but Jared did not elaborate on his relationship with Bart (nor did I want to hear of it) and we avoided discussing Clive. Instead I listened to Jared describe the pupils in his master class, all talentless "jeune filles avec grandes chaussures," and sounding more like the critical Clive than the sensitive Jared I had fallen in love with. Then I followed Jared back to Gordon Square, thinking I would visit awhile with Clive, cheer him up with some recaps of a few movies I had seen. Almost at once when we were inside the house Jared made excuses about having to leave because he had forgotten to find a birthday item for one of his new pupils. I knew it was an excuse to meet up with Bart—Bart, at about that time, had finished his soccer game and his visit to his mum, and was probably coming out of the shower, clean and ready for a hook-up with Jared.

As soon as Jared left, I wandered upstairs to look for Clive. I found him in his second floor study, lying on a sofa. His shirt was unbuttoned and untucked, the sleeves rolled up to his elbows. He appeared to be ill and uncomfortable— his eyes were glassy and unfocused—I thought he must have been working and become exhausted because there were scattered pages of drawing paper around the room. I only had a few seconds to detect that they were more sketches of nude men coupling—Bart and Jared or Teddy and Clive—and a few other dif- ferent-looking men as well.

"Leave," he waved to me, annoyed that I had found and disturbed him. "I cannot see a bloody thing today. *Leave.*"

"Do you need a doctor?" I asked him. "Should I take you to a hospital?"

"Out," Clive ordered. "I can sleep—*or drink*—my way through it."

Unnerved by Clive's anger, I retreated to the hallway, where I had the impres- sion of something holding me in place and observing me. I don't know exactly what feeling it was that drew me to enter upon an exploration of the house; normally, I would have hurried away, particularly since Clive had left me so agitated.

I peered into a bedroom—it was tidy but cluttered with the kind of tchotchkes years later Keith and I would find so fascinating—crystal balls, black candlesticks, wicker baskets, dragon-shaped lamps, and a beautiful handmade quilt of five-pointed stars draped across the bed. There was another bedroom equally cluttered, with a large bronze gong suspended between a pair of demon- faced swordsmen. To the side of the room was a stark, large, black-tiled bathroom that felt to me like stepping into a vacuum. I confess that the house displeased me strangely. I was conscious of something powerful and controlling, and for a moment I was lightheaded, as if something had been pulled out of my body. I soon realized I was sweating, my forehead was burning as if I had a fever, and I was suddenly ready to leave but felt like I was pinned in place. In the hallway where I stood hung a series of grim and faded portraits of Edwardian and Victo- rian aristocrats looking locked up and trapped within their clothes, and I had an imagined flash of unhappy quarrels between the posers, conversations of spite- ful jealousies. As I tugged myself away from them and down the swirling black stone staircase, I spotted a small, carved wooden table on the ground floor near the entry to the parlor, guarding the door like a crouching beast. Sitting on the table beside a vase of dried flowers was a stack of cards, and as I moved closer to it, I noticed the artwork—an elaborate and stylized illustration, like those done by monks centuries before in a medieval monastery. It was only when I lifted the top card and turned it over that I realized it was a tarot deck. On the backside of the card in my hand were a winged, horned devil and an inverted pentagram. The Devil's card. I knew enough of mysticism and the occult to know that a tarot card is never interpreted at face value. But I also knew that I wanted to be out of the house—and that I should warn Clive and Jared that they should leave it, too.

————

I did my best to counsel them without alarming them. I left messages on their answering machines at the house on Gordon Square saying that I felt there was something seriously odd about it, and that they should move elsewhere because it felt like such an unhealthy and unhappy place. I went to Clive's office and Jared's dance studio to discuss it with them, but they were never there or would not see me—out on an errand, or with a pupil, or not feeling well and holed up "at home and not wanting to be disturbed." I went to the house, clapped that ominous-looking gargoyle knocker over and over against the door and banged with my fists, but no one ever answered it. I sat in the park so I could see the comings and goings in front of the house or at its windows, but no one ever arrived or departed while I waited, not the housekeeper, the cook, nor Bart. Sooner or later I would give up my surveillance, done in by the cold or the rain or my need to return to work. It was as if the house knew it could easily defeat me, and I would arrive back at my flat or my office and make another round of warning calls till one day I realized that I sounded like a madman and I should back off and not bother Clive and Jared any longer.

As it happened, I ran into Bart about a week later coming out of a pub as I was going inside. He looked thin and restless, his eyes darting back and forth as he stood in front of me. "You didn't warn me about the deep mess I would fall into," he said and added a laugh that sounded part observational and part nervous.

"What's been happening? I've been trying to reach Clive or Jared for weeks and I'm not getting anywhere. They seem to be avoiding me."

"Your mates are falling over to the dark side. Setting up little parties for all sorts of kinky fellas. Bondage. Candle wax. Body paint. You name it, they're trying it."

"I don't know what you mean."

"Yeah?" he asked and stubbed his cigarette out with the tip of his boot. I noticed that they were new ones. Black with engraved silver tips and oddly reminding me of the wicked curios on display at the house on Gordon Square.

"Your dancing fella likes to tie me up and taunt me with a few of his toys," he laughed. "Good thing is, I don't mind it—I know how to keep it all fun. But his old man is into some deep shit. I don't want to have to keep waving away the drugs, you get me? Come to think of it, I should tell 'em to add you to the guest list as referee, so nobody steps over the line."

"Are you sure?"

"We could have a lot of fun together again, if you like."

"I mean, are you sure about Clive? And Jared?"

"It's a dark world," he said. "Full of dirty secrets. Guess you just learned a few about your mates."

Even after he had left me, I was sure Bart was mistaken, and I put whatever worry I had about Clive and Jared out of my head because I was upset that I had been clearly dropped from their list of close friends (and I fell into bed with an Indian fellow named Rajan, who lived in a tiny flat behind Euston Station). But the next day, once I was back on my own home turf—my flat—Bart's conversation continued to bother me and I began obsessing again about Clive and Jared because I knew they were pushing me away. I tried reaching them at their various haunts, this time to confront them on their drug use, though rehearsing what I might say, not wanting to sound like a prude—after all, I had gladly shared a joint with both of them more than once.

Toward the end of the week, I took a long lunch and walked by the house and hit the knocker several times, but no one was home, so I walked over to the university and found Clive in a small office napping while pretending to read a book.

"Not sleeping well," he said, when I startled him with a light knock and he recognized me. "That house is like being in a dream factory. All sorts of things haunt me. I'm finding it more relaxing to be here."

"Perhaps you should move," I suggested.

"It's a terrific space," he answered. "And the university is subsidizing most of it. I doubt that I could get that elsewhere."

I offered to take him to lunch and we walked a few blocks to a pub he was fond of. Again, he brought along his briefcase and again he showed me his latest work. Even though I was somewhat prepared for what I would see this time, it was nonetheless startling. The two nude figures were now in a struggle for domination. The first sketch was a basic wrestling scenario, flat and uninspired, like something that could have been found on a Greek vase, but the following ones developed a stronger narrative, the dark-haired fellow submitting to the taller, fairer one, first on his knees, then bound to a chair and gagged. Any hint of romance and seduction was now replaced by the depiction of torture.

"Did this happen?" I asked him.

He gave me a vague look, as if he hadn't realized what he had drawn. "It started with a few wrestling poses for Duncan," he said. "But later on, it grew different. Teddy wanted me to tie him up so that he couldn't leave, but then he'd be begging me to let him go back to Sage. It was hard for me to separate what was real and what was fantasy with him. He wore me out. I finally told him that

I couldn't go on. That we had to end it. That was his breaking point. He threatened to kill me. Then kill Sage. Then kill himself. I never saw him after that."

"Does Jared know of these?"

"Jared?" he asked, as if he had forgotten him. "No."

"Has he said he was leaving you?"

"Jared?"

"Has he threatened you? Or Bart?"

"Bart? No. Not that I am aware."

"Has he hinted he's unhappy?"

A flicker of Clive's former personality resumed. "Dear boy, Jared's always been unhappy. I've never provided him the self-confidence that dancing—or his fans—have given him. He's taken this whole injury thing rather hard, I must say."

"You should tear these up," I said, handing him back the sketches. That moment I realized that I wanted to save him because I loved him. I loved his talent, his wit, his friendship, his inspiration. And I loved him because I still loved Jared. I couldn't bear to accept what was happening and I owed it to Clive and Jared—and myself—to help Clive get through it. "I can find you a program," I said next. "A clinic, if you need one."

He looked at me with his big brown eyes and said, "I'll pretend I didn't hear that."

"Roll up your sleeve. Show me your arm."

He narrowed his eyes and shifted away from me. "Young man," he said sternly. "I think it's time we part."

———

I tried to keep up with them, but I also had to work—I wasn't subsidized by a trust fund or a university grant or even by the credit cards of a sugar daddy. But I had no intention of letting Clive simply discard me because he was insulted by my offer of help. I waited a few days after my blowup with Clive and phoned Jared and made dinner plans with both of them for Saturday night, so they knew that I was thinking of them and that I wanted to stay in touch, no matter how they felt about me now. But on a cold, cloudy Friday afternoon, just as I was trying to get everything pending off my desk, I got a call at work. "Dennis?" the caller began in a faint voice. "Dennis? . . . Is that you?"

"What is it? . . . Clive?"

"Dennis? . . . Help?"

I rushed out of my office. A gray mist had settled over the city and I arrived at the house on Gordon Square damp, chilled, and panicked. The front door was locked, and I knocked and pounded but no one answered. I finally jimmied the lock on the servants' entrance below ground and made my way up the workday roots of the grand black staircase.

Clive was not in any of the first-floor rooms. There was a smell of stale cigarettes and booze, as if a party had recently ended, though all of the rooms were neat and tidy as I made a quick check of them. I bounded up the massive, swirling black-stone staircase two steps at a time. I found all three of them in Clive's bedroom. Clive and Jared were in bed, syringes and needles nearby. They were barely conscious. And in a corner of the room, facing the bed, was Bart. Nude, tied to a chair and gagged, his eyes fluttering to stay alive. Scattered on the floor were sketches, mirroring the events that had led up to the present scene.

I untied Bart and called for emergency assistance, waiting for the police and medics to arrive by stretching Bart out on the floor and stroking his hair. I tried not to notice that his body was in the exact position Clive had drawn in that first sketch he had shown me more than seven months before. "Baby, hold on," I said. "Help will be here soon."

There was more explaining needed than I could do on my own. I tried to be as clear as I could to all the authorities and officials who were canvassing the rooms for clues and details. Something in the house had possessed them, driven them all to this evil craziness. The interrogating officer looked at me as though I was the one who was loony.

Clive did not survive, but Bart recovered quickly, echoing my testimony to the officials that it had all been a bit too weird to believe. I stayed with Jared at the hospital until he was released, but Jared never attempted to explain or apologize for anything that had happened, and it was as if I were babysitting a corpse; neither of us had anything to say to the other and whatever emotional thread I felt was still attached to him he had purposely snipped. I couldn't blame him for what had happened so I loved him and hated him, hated what had become of all of us—Clive, Bart, him, and myself.

I was tugged through the next weeks by despair. The newspapers and television programs reported on Clive's death as though it were a scandal. Drugs were seized, more officers arrived with more questions. An inquest was held. Bart's and my account of the strange doings inside the house on Gordon Square were ridiculed by reporters. I skipped the funeral and memorials. Instead, I wandered around London crazed with grief and sorrow. I tried to remember what a decent man Clive had been with me, especially when he discovered how deeply I loved Jared, but there was a sense that my sadness was deserved because I was at fault. I was ashamed that I had been unable to save Clive. I had robbed the world of an immense talent. I had prevented masterpieces and great leaps of insight and the training of future talent. I missed days and days of work to the point of nearly losing my job. I drank too much. I overslept. I couldn't see Bart without breaking into sobs. I finally began to let go one afternoon when my boss told me to "straighten up, or else."

Clive Elliott is probably best remembered today as the promising artist of such iconic art as *The Soda Bottle* or *The Tissue Box*. Jared Tremaine became the executor of Elliott's estate, which is the primary reason why Clive's work has lapsed into obscurity. Jared never danced on stage again and, in part, I believe he blamed this on Clive, though I also believe that whatever artistic spirit had possessed him before—his ethereal yearning to dance—had been robbed from him by an unseen power while he lived in the house on Gordon Square. Bart Pearson did not live beyond the first decade of the AIDS epidemic and his illness and death six years later was the reason why I finally decided it was time to leave London behind. I went through every doctor's appointment and disappointment with him. We'd been best mates since Jared disappeared. I moved away in 1988, after having met Keith on a holiday in Brighton.

A decade later, sometime in 1998, as the power of the Internet was surfacing, I began to roam away from the chat rooms I had become so immediately fond of and into other areas of the Web. I stumbled onto a site that generated free tarot card readings, and learned that the fifteenth card—the Devil—can symbolize temptation and addiction. This triggered a memory and I began researching the Bloomsbury townhouse in Gordon Square that Clive and Jared had briefly rented that awful time in London and learned that the university had torn it down to make way for a new building, though no specific reasons were given for the destruction or what had happened to its contents. I searched for more details on Teddy Rushton and Roger Sage. I did not turn up much more than I already knew, though a few details surfaced, including a photograph of the two men, taken in "the foyer of a house of a friend." In the photograph, behind the two men, was the swirling, ominous black staircase of the house on Gordon Square. And yes, Theodore Rushton looked shockingly handsome and too similar to Bart Pearson for comfort.

After Clive's death and before Jared left town for wherever it was he was headed to—I can't remember the destination, nor did I want to hear about it at that moment—he came round to my flat with Clive's briefcase. "Some day, yes? *Bon art. Richesse,*" he said flatly, when he handed the sketches over to me. "*Peutêtre. Une nouvelle simple.*" Jared refused to ever see Bart again. When Bart died, I wrote Jared a letter that went unanswered.

My lover Keith still professes more interest in Jared's "true inner beauty" than in any of Clive's lurid sketches that I've buried at the bottom of one of our bedroom drawers. For years he has held on to this romantic vision of Bart and Jared roaming through London by motorbike, so much so, that I have also adopted it as one of my own and I have to remind myself that Clive was always there, too.

"Do you think it was an accident?" I asked Keith over breakfast as I folded up the newspaper to toss into the recycling bin. "Or did he jump to his death?" Jared's abandoned motorbike had been found the day before on the cliffs above Positano. The article had not elaborated on his fame or infamy. His dancing achievements were overlooked; his life with Clive invisible; the scandal in Gordon Square forgotten.

"Amalfi is such a gorgeous area," Keith answered. "One of the most beautiful places I've ever been to. The cliffs are very dramatic the way they hang over the Mediterranean. Like they are leaping out of the sea and into the sky. Rather inspiring and beautiful, I think, not at all depressing and suicidal. I can't imagine why anyone would be unhappy there, dear. Can you?"

32

Flatiron

ELIZABETH GRAVER

Her mother cleaned houses. The Point was private, a narrow spit of land. You had to get in through a gate, and the gate had a code, and each Spring and on the rare occasion of a burglary, the code was changed. 1918. 1022. 1492. Somebody's birthday. Somebody's wedding date or death date or—finally one Cass could make sense of—Columbus Sailed the Ocean Blue. Her mother wrote the numbers on a sticker inside the glove compartment. As they drove up, she'd ask Cass to open the box and read the code. You had to press the numbers on the silver keypad, and then the white metal gate would swing slowly open and they'd go through in the rusty Tercel, bumping along on the road that no one ever seemed to fix, past thickets of cat briar and blackberry and something that looked like bamboo, until there, the first house, shingled, sprawling and unheated and not exactly fancy, except that in front of it were several shiny, fancy cars, and some fancy bikes, and some grubby little kids with squinty blue eyes and stringy white-blond hair rich kids, though you'd never know to look.

In the summer, the Point was filled with these children, the lawns strewn with their bicycles and scooters, with their sandals, soccer balls and water guns. Inside the houses, the floors were grainy with sand. There were dirty socks and wet towels in the hallways, empty juice boxes and Popsicle sticks under the couches, Cheerios skittering across the kitchen floors. Sometimes the children were watched over by their mothers or nannies, but more often they ran about

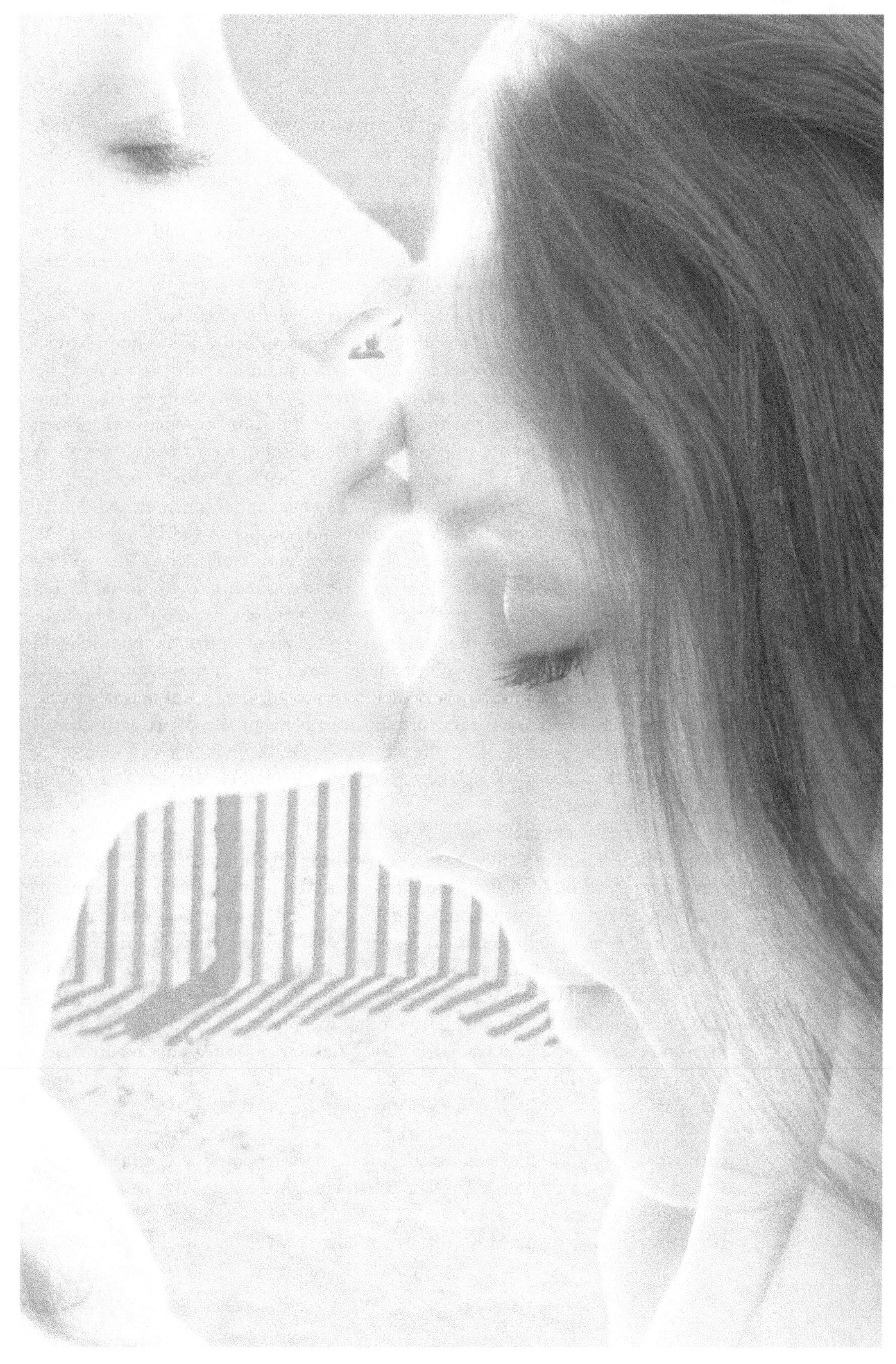

in gangs or rode their bikes down the road at breakneck speed, leaving their helmets in the grass. Off the Point, in the town where they lived, Cass's mother charged fifteen dollars an hour, but here she charged twenty—even more when Cass got old enough to really help—and no one seemed to mind. They'd leave the money on the mantle sometimes, the bills held down by a shell, or else a lady would hand it to them—hand it to Cass as if it were for her, as if she could take the whole wad and blow it on stuff for herself.

Everyone on the Point was related somehow, which was amazing to Cass, who had only her mother and grandmother, the rest of her relations never named or barely accounted for, her own father present only in her pale brown skin and in the way that by the time she turned fourteen, she was already several inches taller than her mother. Most of the mothers on the Point were older than hers, who was so tiny and pretty, still, so flat of belly and quick of voice, like Cass's sister, almost, except that no one ever thought they were sisters, no one even thought they were mother and daughter, their coloring too mismatched. Hurry up, Cassandra, grab the mop for me. Clorox and Soft Scrub and Pledge and Mr. Clean, except for the one house where they were only allowed to use natural cleaning supplies, mild, watery solutions with no smell; you could hardly tell they'd been there when they left. When Cass was younger, her mom had brought along a tub of toys for her—Barbies, markers, blocks—and sometimes kids on the Point would play with her. When she got older and her mom started paying her, she'd work for part of the time, then listen to her iPod, read magazines and daydream. Hey, she'd say if someone spoke to her, but she didn't get into real conversations. Sometimes, if no one was home, she'd convince her mother to let her put on the stereo, turn up the music. She'd swing her hips, grab her mom, and make her dance.

It was okay, spending summers like this. It was okay to hang out with her friends in the morning while her mother worked part-time at the insurance company (low pay, health benefits), and then, some afternoons, go with her mother to clean. Cass liked the summer houses, poking around, getting a cut of the money, even if half went straight to her college fund. A lot of girls didn't like their mothers; a lot of mothers made their girls stay in at night or nagged about grades or friends, but Cass's mom was okay, she was cool, she was nice, really—that's what Cass's friends noticed about her. Her mother was pretty, and mellow, and mostly nice, and even though Cass had been *unintentional*, her mom always made it seem like a good thing. I lucked out, she'd say, leaning over Cass's bed, lifting her hair so she could smooch her neck. Now get up, baby girl, or we'll be late.

The summer of the year Cass turned sixteen and got her driver's license, the code was 1416, a number neither she nor her mother could assign meaning to, though Cass enjoyed how it contained her age. On Labor Day weekend, most of the people packed up their things and returned to the city—New York, or Boston, or as far away as St. Louis. The following week and weekend, Cass and her mother came in to give the houses a good scrubbing, a semi-final cleaning—it was like this every year—but it wasn't until the day after Columbus Day that they closed down the houses for good. After school, Cass would take the school bus home and walk to Alliance Mutual, then drive with her mother past Stop & Shop and Big Value Outlet, into the village, over the drawbridge, past the ice cream stand until the road dead-ended at the Private sign and you took a sharp right, punched in the code, drove in.

As they had every year since Cass could remember, they covered couches with sheets, took pictures down from walls, vacuumed every room and rolled up rugs. As they had every year, they went through the cupboards, filling grocery bags with boxes of spaghetti and crackers, with unopened jars of sun-dried tomatoes and capers, with baking chocolate and honey labeled *Miel*. From the fridge, they rescued blocks of Parmesan cheese, jars of mayonnaise and ketchup. They threw out moldy lemons and garlic cloves dry in their husks, and when, finally, the fridge was empty, they unplugged it and scrubbed it down, leaving the door propped open with an ice tray.

Sometimes, if Cass's grandmother wasn't working at the health clinic where she answered phones, she came, too, and the three of them donned yellow rubber gloves and worked steadily, with pleasure reserved only for this final cleaning. Though they never talked about it, they all had a feeling of returning the house to nature, of stripping it down, delivering it to its proper place and time. The next week, they knew, Jerry Souza would come to turn the water off; once, years ago, Cass's mother had dated his cousin. Up to four hundred dollars for the closing of a big house. One house could take a day, or several afternoons, with two or three of them working non-stop, and they cleaned nine houses on the Point, more than their competitors, the Merry Maids, who did the rest.

Cass would do bedrooms but not toilets, Murphy's but not Lysol. Curtains were piled up to go to the dry cleaners, pillows squished into plastic bins. Towels were washed and stacked in the linen closet: face, hand, bath, beach. That year, in one house, Cass went even further, arranging the beach towels by color: shades of purples at the bottom of the pile, then pinks and magentas, yellows, oranges. She stacked the most mixed-up, splashiest towels in their own florescent section, ending with the blues and greens. What's taking you so long, her mother asked, poking her head into the closet, which was big enough to be a child's room. Look, Cass said, cracking herself up. A work of art, her mom said. Come on—we have mattresses to flip.

After several afternoons and a weekend of this, Cass had had enough. It was just the two of them that day. I have homework, Mom. Really, I've got stuff to do. And her mother stopping, then, to lean over herself as if she had a cramp. Was that when Cass first noticed her mother's index finger finding its way to her breast, pressing through the fabric of her T-shirt (which was Cass's)? Stop it, Mom, stop *touching* yourself.

Her mother looking up. "Huh? Oh, sorry, it's just—"

"What?"

"Nothing, there's just a little . . . I'm sure it's nothing."

Not nothing. Something. Treatable. Caught early. Not to worry not to worry. I'm a young woman, her mother told her brightly the night before she went into the hospital to have her left boob chopped off. You can be sure I'm not going anywhere.

Fourteen sixteen. It was written on the sticker in the glove compartment, but it was also written in Cass's brain, which she'd learned in school was the texture of toothpaste, floating in liquid, though now she pictured it filled with fatty, hidden lumps. She was not the sort of girl to spend much time alone. She liked her friends. She liked movies and dancing and talking on the phone late into the night while she doodled—horses and faces, swirls and shooting stars. She liked boys, sort of, well enough, and she was told she was pretty and believed it as she'd been told so many times, but she would not have sex with a boy, would not end up pregnant like her mother had or die of AIDS. Anyway, she preferred to look at how her friend Mara's earring sat nestled in her earlobe, how her collarbone jutted when she shrugged. She preferred to watch a girl's stomach show as she stretched, her belly button sitting there so round and dark, no hair. And now that her mother was getting her breast cut off, she noticed breasts everywhere: big, small and in between, and once, as she glanced up in the supermarket, an older woman in a purple tank top with nothing there at all, as flat-chested as a boy.

One-four-one-six. It meant something to somebody but nothing to her. Still, that fall, during the days when her mother lay in the hospital, during the days, even, when she lay at home, her breast draining blood and pus through a tube, bottles of Percoset and Tylenol with Codeine by her bed, Cass took the car and went to the Point, punched in the code, drove in. I have to look up something at the library, she'd tell her mom, or, I'm going to Mara's if you're okay alone, and sometimes she'd even head toward the library, head toward Mara's, but there was nothing inside her to let her actually arrive. She needed—what?—to pull out a quilt from a garment bag, to walk around a chilly kitchen with her coat still on, stepping over mice poison pellets, opening drawers. The loaded key ring from the key basket at home granted her access to this house, that house. She always locked up carefully when she left and returned the keys to the basket without making so much as a clink.

Dead, she might say aloud to the mirror in a chilly upstairs bathroom. Passed away last winter. No, it's just me now. I've taken over the business. She'd lift her sweatshirt, unstrap her bra and look, the left breast a little bigger than the right, both a little bigger than her mother's, the nipples dark. She'd cup them in her palms, feel them heavy, certain, water balloons inside her hands. Sometimes she'd close her eyes and pretend that they were someone else's—Mara's, or her friend Sandy's older sister's, or those of a girl she'd never met. Other times, she'd imagine they were gone—scars there, or the plain, happy flatness of a child. Oh no, I'm fine, she would say to the summer families after her mother's funeral. Thanks. Twenty-five an hour. Thirty an hour; I need to put myself through college. Forty; I need to pay the fucking rent. In the unheated air, her nipples puckered, bumps rose along her skin, and she'd re-hook her bra, pull down her sweatshirt, and go downstairs to a living room that felt suddenly familiar next to the place where she'd just been.

At first she just came a few times after school, but when her mother began chemo, when the vomiting started and the hair fell out, Cass started skipping school once or twice a week and coming to the Point instead. Afternoons, now, she was cleaning houses, taking her mother to the hospital, or sitting with her in their apartment, which seemed too crowded, suddenly, clogged with throw pillows, knickknacks, pictures of Cass in various life stages: a pimply twelve-year-old; a slit-eyed, ugly newborn, her face the violet color of a bruise. You're the best, Cass, her mom would say, and when her grandmother visited, she'd say it, too: You're a good girl. Her grandmother, who lived one town over with her husband, his daughter and his daughter's twin sons, brought them lasagna or meatloaf twice a week and got her mother's medicine, and the two other secretaries at the insurance agency brought a casserole and a roasted chicken, and her mom's boss sent a Stop & Shop gift basket of fruit. Cass did the wash for herself and her mother and shopped for frozen food and Ensure, and that was all okay, but sitting with her mom trying to chat about school was not, and cleaning houses alone or with her grandmother or her mom's friend Karen was not—no fun in it any more, no gossip and dancing, just dealing with other people's dirt.

On the Point, days when she should have been in school, she walked the maze of paths that wound through the thick brush behind the houses, crossing the occasional field or concrete foundation, ending, always, by a rocky beach. The colors were turning, the poison ivy red, the paths covered with dry leaves. Often, at the final closings, they found bittersweet branches in vases in the houses, orange berries to vacuum up, yellow shells to pry from between the floorboards. Cass would lift each vase carefully, try to get outside without making more of a mess, but always, the berries and husks came raining down. I need to take my mother to chemo, she kept telling her teachers, even her friends. There'd been a massive oil spill in Buzzard's Bay the year before, and though workers in plastic jumpsuits had scrubbed all summer, you could still see traces of it on the rocks, black splotches that looked like part of the stones until you touched them; then they were gummy and stained your hands. She saw a fox one day, staring at her from down the path. She saw rabbits hopping, birds wheeling. She was not a nature girl, but she liked running into animals, and she liked the way walking made her blood run fast, her thoughts grow dim.

At first, she went into this house, that house, but eventually, after she'd skipped school three or four times, she settled on a house to call her own. It was one of the smaller ones, which still meant it was big, with a new addition tacked onto one side. The furniture inside was faded, shabby: a scarred coffee table, a sun-bleached straw rug, a pinkish corduroy couch that had once (and still was, beneath the cushions) been red. Buoys hung from the slanted ceiling in the living room.

It was in this house that she found a space heater, plugged it in. It was here that she took the sheets off the couches, plugged in the radio and turned it to Magic 106.7. She was not afraid as she trespassed, perhaps because she'd been here before, and perhaps because she was quite sure that no one would come: the people were far away, living their other lives. She knew how to clean and would leave no traces. Anyway, it was her house, as she sat there. It was a house she lived in with roomfuls of girls her age, not the kids on the wall but other girls, ones she'd never met. Each night, they ordered out for pizza, built a fire and stayed up late dancing. They'd sleep wherever. By the time they woke in the morning, somebody would have cleaned up all the mess.

One foggy early November morning as Cass sat wrapped in a quilt, her feet tucked under her, a car drove up to the house. She had brought a Coke with her that day, and an apple, and now the nearly empty Coke can was perched on the arm of the couch and the apple core was browning on the floor. She had smoked a couple cigarettes (her mom called them cancer sticks but had smoked them too until recently, on the front stoop when she thought Cass was asleep) and had the window behind her open, the cold air passing, strange, over her head. She didn't hear the car's motor, or the car door closing. And then—my god—a person, inside the house. Cass stood up, knocking the Coke can to the floor.

"Shit," she said. "I—" She stooped to right the can.

A girl stood in the doorway, balancing a pile of books in her arms. As she looked up, her hair fell from beneath a baseball cap and something—anger? laughter? fear?—passed across her face. For a moment, watching her, Cass was actually unsure if she was real. Then the girl stepped inside, lowered the books to the coffee table and stared.

"Um, so . . . who are you?" she asked, wrinkling her nose as if she should have known.

"I—we clean for you, my mom does. I . . . Well, there was this bracelet, I got it for my birthday, and my mother said I could come look for it here. I think it fell off when I was cleaning after Columbus Day. I lost it—I mean, obviously, I guess. My mom is Marcie. You know?" The lie came out so nicely, astounding Cass, who rarely lied.

"Oh. Oh. Well—" The girl let out a little laugh and sank onto a couch. "I guess I don't need to tell you to make yourself at home."

She had big hoop earrings in her ears and wore a bulky knitted sweater in bright colors, and jeans with big holes in the knees, and black tights underneath. She didn't look quite like the summer people, a little wilder and brighter, but in her coloring—blonde, pale—and the straight, clean lines of her features, you could see how she was one of them, a girl flying by on her bicycle, a girl pulling her sneaker off to dump sand.

"I was just going," said Cass, then noticed the apple core, and a trickle of Coke making its way along the floor. "I'll just clean this up and—"

"Did you find it?"

"What?"

"Your bracelet?"

"No, but it doesn't matter." There were paper towels in the car; there was Fantastic, and 409. "I'll just clean this up." She knelt by the mess, suddenly desperate, on the brink of tears. She looked up to meet the girl's eyes, which she saw now were red-rimmed and watery, like a rabbit's, and tired.

"Are you okay?" The girl asked and took a step back.

Cass nodded. Are you, she almost asked but didn't dare.

"Listen, don't worry—I won't tell anyone you were here, if that's what you're worried about. As long as you didn't break or, you know, take anything. Not that there's anything to take."

Cass shook her head. "I told you, I was looking—" But she could never tell this stranger what she was looking for, even if she'd been able to explain it to herself.

"Do you need money?" the girl asked.

"No." Sometimes they found a quarter under the couch when they were vacuuming; sometimes they found a dime. They wiped the dust off the coins and set them on the mantle, though once or twice when she was younger, Cass had pocketed a coin behind her mother's back.

The girl nodded. "I didn't mean, I just thought—" She kicked off her shoes, folded her feet beneath her. "I'm supposed to be studying for my Generals."

"Your what?"

"The big exam we take to graduate. I'm finishing in January, if I make it. Then what?" She pointed to her books. "I have more in the car. You can hang out, if you want. It's weird to be here alone. The place is so packed in summer. My boyfriend was supposed to come with me, but at the last minute—"

She turned toward the window; was she about to cry? She was old, a senior in college, which made her, what—twenty, or twenty-one. Cass followed her gaze. A boxy blue station wagon was parked on the lawn. Cass had left the Tercel by the side of the road. For a moment she tried to picture the boyfriend behind the wheel, careless and at ease.

The girl turned back. "I decided to come anyway. I thought it might be good for me to be alone for once. Except you were here. I've got to say, you completely freaked me out when I walked in."

"Sorry," said Cass. "You freaked me out, too."

The girl's mouth twitched into a smile. "I'm Margery. What's your name?"

"Cass. Cassandra."

"Oh yeah. Now I remember you—I love your name. I think we even played together sometimes when we were little. You were younger. I liked little kids. Do you remember?"

"Yes," said Cass, though she didn't. There had been so many blonde girls, so many barefoot, sandy sisters, cousins and friends, and she'd never played with any of them for long. "Your name's nice, too," she said, a little lamely.

"It's my grandmother's. I'm still waiting for it to come back in fashion. I'm going to finish getting my stuff out of the car." Margery reached for her shoes.

Cass hesitated. "Do you want me to help you?"

"That'd be great." Margery smiled a wide, friendly smile, and for the first time in weeks, Cass felt a lightness in her chest.

"My parents would die," said Margery as they went out the door. "Marcie's kid breaking into the house, making herself at home. Like Goldilocks"—she sniffed the air—"except with a cigarette. Nobody smokes around here, you know. This is a Smoke Free Zone."

"I have a key," Cass said.

As she stood on the lawn with outstretched arms, Margery loaded her up with glossy, heavy books, and they brought it all inside—the books, a duffel bag, groceries and jugs of spring water, a laptop with an orange lid. When everything was in the house and Cass had cleaned up the Coke and apple core and butts, Margery took wood from the box next to the fireplace and built a fire. She made tea, boiling water in a pan on the stove, arranged her books in piles, plugged in her computer and cell phone, took a toaster from a cupboard and made toast. Finally, as the house filled up with the smells of toast and tea and fire, she took out a broom and starting sweeping mice poison pellets into a dustpan.

"These are disgusting." She dumped a batch of pellets into the trash and went for more. Cass watched as she swept and bent, her motions graceful; she looked like she played sports or maybe ran. "Not to mention cruel. I keep telling my mother. Did you know this stuff makes the mice dry up from the inside out? It dehydrates them until they die of thirst."

Cass shook her head. Her mother never let her near the poison. Go wait outside while I finish up, she said each October, and the week before Memorial Day, when they opened up the houses, her mom went in alone and vacuumed up the poison first. Sometimes, she'd miss a pellet, and later Cass would find it, turquoise blue, shaped like a little Pez candy, and have an urge to stick it in her mouth. Lately, alone in the houses, she had been sidestepping the poison, ignoring it, though it was everywhere, in half-filled boxes and scattered bits of blue. But now the floor was swept clean, the toast had popped up, Margery was pulling jam from a bag and digging in a drawer for napkins.

"Can I help?" Cass asked once more, but Margery waved her off.

"That's okay—I know where stuff is. Of course you do, too. How long have you been coming here? No, don't tell me. What I don't know can't be used against me—or you."

"I've cleaned this house a million times." Cass pointed at the utility closet. We store the napkins in a plastic bin."

Margery handed her a mug of tea. "I'm kidding, okay? *Mi casa es tu casa.* Do you speak Spanish?"

"*Poquito.*"

"Portuguese?"

"No."

"My boyfriend is from Mexico. He's been teaching me Spanish but I'm not any good. French just pops out of my mouth instead. We were supposed to go to Mexico after he graduates in May. Now"—she shook her head—"who knows. Do you like art?"

"Art? I guess," Cass said. In fact, art had been her favorite subject the year before, the way you got to look at people, the way the fruit looked like bodies, the bodies like fruit. One day they'd drawn a woman in a bathing suit, a real live woman who stood on a box, statue-still, until her muscles started to jump. The teacher had held up her drawing to show the class, and when she'd brought it home, her mom had found a frame for it and hung it above the couch, next to school photos of Cass from kindergarten through sixth grade. "I didn't have room to take art this year."

"That's too bad. Well, I have lots of books if you want to look at them. I need to switch the music, though. I can't concentrate with this, and I forgot my iPod in my dorm."

Margery spun the radio dial until she found classical music; then she settled on one couch and Cass sat on the other, their toast and tea near them on the floor. Margery picked up a notebook and pen, opened a book and lowered her eyes to it, and Cass also reached for a book, pulling it, heavy, into her lap. And then they were sitting, quietly, together, as if they both lived there, and the pictures in the book were of haystacks and oceans, sunflowers and men in hats in boats. It was France. You could tell that from the titles. A few of the pictures looked familiar but many did not, and it didn't seem like homework at all, to look at so many colors, to leaf through books whose paper smelled like glue and candy, while across from you a blond girl sat, girl of the house, king of the castle. But nice. She seemed, for a time, to forget that Cass was there.

Then she glanced up, looked over. "How old are you?" she asked.

"Me? Sixteen."

"God, you're a baby. You seem older. You're very self-possessed."

Cass shrugged. A teacher had called her the same thing the year before—self-possessed—and while she'd known it was meant as a compliment, it had made her feel hidden, too serious, not fun enough: they hadn't seen her dancing, heard her jokes. "How old are you?" she asked Margery.

"Ancient. Twenty-one. I can't believe I'm graduating. I really, truly don't mind that you come here, by the way. This house just sits here, all winter long. It's always bugged me. When I was little I thought it must be sad without us in it. Now it just seems like a waste."

"It's not heated."

"Still." She reached for her mug but didn't drink from it, just pressed its warmth to her cheek and set it down. "I remember your mom. She's pretty. Like you."

Cass might have looked down, then, flushed. She might have mumbled thanks and turned away. Instead, she raised her eyes to meet Margery's, and as she did, she felt the brownness of her own irises, the gold flecks, the greenish rims. She could see herself from outside, as if she were in a painting—a whole girl, smooth, strong and pretty; a half-girl, for what did she know about her insides, about anyone's, a garden inside you, full of flowers, or was it mildew, aphids, pellets, mold? She looked at Margery and Margery looked back. A ledge, another ledge, a little further, yes. Something will happen, Cass thought with strange certainty, and just as she thought it, her mouth opened, the round words formed. "Thanks," she said. "You're pretty, too."

She stayed for a few hours that day, went home and made dinner for her mother, returned the next morning to find a fire roaring, the books in new piles, Margery in jogging clothes, her color high.

"It was creepy here at night," Margery said. "I don't know what I was thinking, coming here alone. I called Tomas and had a horrible conversation. Then I called my mom and had an even worse one. Today, for some reason, my cell thinks this is a dead zone." She laughed. "Maybe my ancestors' spirits are helping me. This morning I went running and skinny-dipped off Nani's—that's my great-grandmother's—rock." She undid her ponytail and shook out her hair, which was, Cass saw now, wet at the ends, its blond turned dark.

"You swam?" Cass hunched into her sweatshirt. Her own hair was down, too, as long as Margery's but darker, and much curlier. Mara called it seaweed hair and liked to braid it. When Cass was younger, dodging the hairbrush, her mother used to threaten to cut it all off but never did.

"I can't come here without swimming," Margery said. "I feel much better now. How about you? I'm glad you came back. Are you okay?"

Cass nodded. She didn't want to trade stories with Margery—jerky boyfriend, cancer mother—not here, where you couldn't even hear the sound of cars. The day before, she had stopped at the store on her way home and bought pork chops, egg noodles and applesauce. She made a home-cooked meal, and her mother nearly finished it. Later, she crawled into bed with her mom and spent the night there, the way she used to as a little girl. As she lay there, a car drove by blasting music—louder, louder, softer, gone—and one neighbor's son shouted for another neighbor's son, and the people downstairs, new renters, spoke in Portuguese, their voices fast until eventually, they, too, were quiet. When, finally, Cass's sleep came, it was careful, even vigilant, as if her mother were a baby in the bed.

She brought a book that day, *One Flew Over the Cuckoo's Nest;* she was supposed to be reading it for school. Instead, though, she read Margery's books, or rather looked at them, for they had few words. She looked at sculptures of faces rising, half-formed, out of rocks; at paintings of ladies on swings with fat angels with little penises flying over them; at one of brown women with no shirts on, bent at the waist, their long breasts hanging down, obscene, or maybe beautiful.

"They expect us to know the whole fucking history of Western Art," Margery said, but she didn't sound unhappy, exactly. At one point, she pulled out a stack of postcards and asked Cass to quiz her. Cass would pick a card from the pile and Margery would have to tell her who the painter was and the year he was born and the year he died and something about his Movement, and Cass would look at the writing—some printed, some handwritten—on the back of the card, and say yes or no or there's more. Because the postcards were small, Margery came to sit on the same couch as Cass, and because the day was cold, the space heater chuffing, the fire dying, they both put their feet under the red quilt. Was that when Cass closed her hand around the arch of Margery's foot in its thick, wool sock? Was that when she felt the foot flex into her and heard a sigh—part surprise, part pleasure—escape from Margery's lips? Margery might have moved her foot away, then. Instead, she glanced at Cass, who looked down and held up another card. Manet, said Margery. Dejeuner sur L'Herbe. It's a total cliché by now; it'll never be on the test. What about this one? A woman holding a child, the child sleepy, her mouth parted. Mary Cassatt. My grandparents have one. A real one? Yeah, it's in a vault; it's too valuable to hang. Like how valuable? I don't know—close to a million, maybe. Cass's hand flew from Margery's foot to her own mouth. You've got to be kidding me, she said.

When Margery said some of the names, her lips pursed, and she spoke from the back of her throat. DuChamps. Mat-teese. That painting looked like wrapping paper, blue figures dancing; Cass had seen it before. There was one postcard she didn't want to flip toward Margery the first time she saw it: three men on a floor, their shirts off, scraping the wood, planing it down, and the sawdust spirals were curly, and the floor was light and shiny except for where it wasn't, the men casting shadows as they worked. Cass's eyes slid from the painting to Margery, whose eyes were shiny, too, whose wrist came pale and blue-veined from inside her sweater, whose hair was like the hair of girls in fairy tales, let down your golden hair.

Cass turned the card around. 1875, she read on the back. "I like this one," she said, and by now their legs were intertwined, she could feel Margery's breath rise and fall, they were curled together, two girls on a couch, two women.

"Me too," said Margery. "I saw it in Paris."

"You went there?"

"I did junior year abroad, and then I stayed until I ran out of money."

"What was it like?"

"It was . . . hard to describe. It's full of people from all over, and there's museums practically on every block. The best part for me, though, was that when I'm speaking French, it's like I'm a whole new person, you know? As if I"—she sighed, and for a moment, Cass could see what she'd look like when she was very old—"could be anyone." She took the postcard and squinted at the writing on the back. "Gustave Caillebotte. 1848 through 1894. He did another famous one. Hold on, let me see."

Rifling through the cards, she came up with another. A man and a woman were walking down a sidewalk, both in black, with an umbrella over their heads. Behind them, on the long street, were rows of slick, square stones, each in its place, though, briefly, Cass pictured a stone missing, a foot catching, a body falling down. There was no grass in the picture to break your fall; there was not one single tree. What would she do in a place like that? She would walk and walk, speak French, be anyone. She would go inside a sand-colored building to a sand-colored room, far from the push and pull of sea. She would like it there for a while, the place clean and pretty and full of straight lines, like nothing she'd ever seen. Then she would miss her mother and come home.

"Look," Margery said. "How you can only see part of this guy, and how the building zooms away from you? He was really into perspective. That's a flatiron building." She handed the card to Cass and shut her eyes. "Paris Street; Rainy Day. 1848 through 1894. 1848—"

"A what building?" Cass interrupted. They had a flatiron at home, stuffed somewhere deep in the cabinet beneath the bathroom sink. For a month or so, when she was fourteen, she had experimented with straightening her hair.

Margery opened her eyes. "Flatiron, shaped like a clothes iron. I think it is, anyway, but don't quote me—I'm not exactly sure. It's by the Gare St.-Lazare. It's amazing—nothing much has changed. The buildings are so solid over there. Over a hundred years later, and it still looks just like that."

They kissed, then. Later—an hour later and years later—Cass would try to figure out who started it, whose lips moved through the air, who leaned in first, but she never could decide. They kissed once, then twice, the postcards heaped across their laps, and Margery's mouth tasted of tea and humanness, and her smell was somehow terribly familiar, though exactly what it reminded her of, Cass could not say. She shut her eyes to it, closed her eyes to the postcards, the room, the house and, outside, the slope of bushes, the beach with its oil-stained rocks, the sea. Nobody came to this house in the fall. Nobody looked in the windows or ate in the kitchen or touched each other on this old, faded couch smelling of damp and salt.

It was three o'clock. School was just letting out. Her friends were going to their lockers, jostling each other, making plans. At home, her mother was napping, pink bucket by her bed. They kissed for five minutes, maybe more, mouths searching, eyes shut, hands in each other's hair. She thought she could taste Margery's sadness, taste her sweetness, and something else—a bitterness, almost, metallic and coated, like when you've drunk too much and slept too long, or was the taste coming from herself? After a while their hands moved from under the quilt to each other's waists, bare beneath their clothes, and then Cass dared her fingers to travel to the bottom edge of Margery's bra. But Margery stopped her, gently, hand on top of hand.

"I don't think—" she said. "I'm not—"

Cass sat up. Abruptly she was furious, though she couldn't say why. It wasn't just because Margery had stopped her; it wasn't just because her belly was coiled with a desire so tight it felt like pain. For a moment, she wanted to tell Margery about her mother: sick, dying, sick. But she couldn't do that; her mother wasn't going anywhere, not now, not anytime soon, and Margery's pity would only make things worse. She stood up and as she did, the quilt fell to the floor, the postcards, too. She leaned to steady herself on the couch, then crossed her arms over her chest. Margery looked up at her, her hair mussed, her eyes unreadable.

"You're really young," she said.

"Yeah, well, I need to get home."

"Come back tomorrow. I have two more days before I've got to be back at school, if I can make it that long out here."

"I have school, too." Not once had Margery asked her why she wasn't there.

"I know. I just thought—"

"Whatever you thought," Cass said, "was wrong."

Week by week, her mother got better. She was up and about. No spread, a successful surgery. She made Cass read the letter from her doctor. She was better; she was fine, except for no nipple on her left breast, as if someone had forgotten to finish the drawing. She's fine, Cass told her friends when they asked, which was rarely at first, then not at all. I might be an artist, she told her mother one day as they made dinner, and then she laughed—a throaty, knowing laugh that would follow her into adulthood—because she knew she had no interest, not in that, not really.

But the way the building stretched. But the arch of the umbrellas and the couple leaning on each other, or not leaning, exactly, more just walking together, looking at the world, while behind them the cobblestones—was that what you called them?—the stones on the road sat square and shiny, each in its place, and other people walked in pairs, or alone. Flatiron. It was a word she would always remember. Over a hundred years later and nothing has changed, Margery said. It still looks just like that.

"Flatiron" was commissioned by Chicago Public Radio, and first presented as a live dramatic reading by Stories on Stage in January, 2004."

33

Skating

STEPHEN SOUCY

The phone rang.

No one else could hear it.

I looked to my family: no one moves. Like in the film by Alain Resnais, *Last Year at Marienbad,* People were stopped. Stopped in time.

Are they even there?

The phone rings.

I'm home for Christmas from Los Angeles. On holiday break from the well-known television show I write for—a situation comedy featuring a psychiatrist with a radio gig, giving advice to listeners who call in.

Surrounded by family, by all those married relatives, coupled and sipping champagne from delicate hand-blown flutes from a set that came from Venice, Italy.

My two nieces and two nephews run from room to room: living, dining, kitchen, then slide across the floor, fingers outstretched, like baseball players grasping for home, reaching for my ankles and yell, PICK ME UP! PICK *ME* UP! UNCLE ALEX!

The phone rings.

I stand in the living room.

The phone glowed, alive and bright. Vibrating. Lit on the dresser of my childhood bedroom, reflected in the mirror that was, at one point, attached horizontally—and later—vertically, as I grew taller.

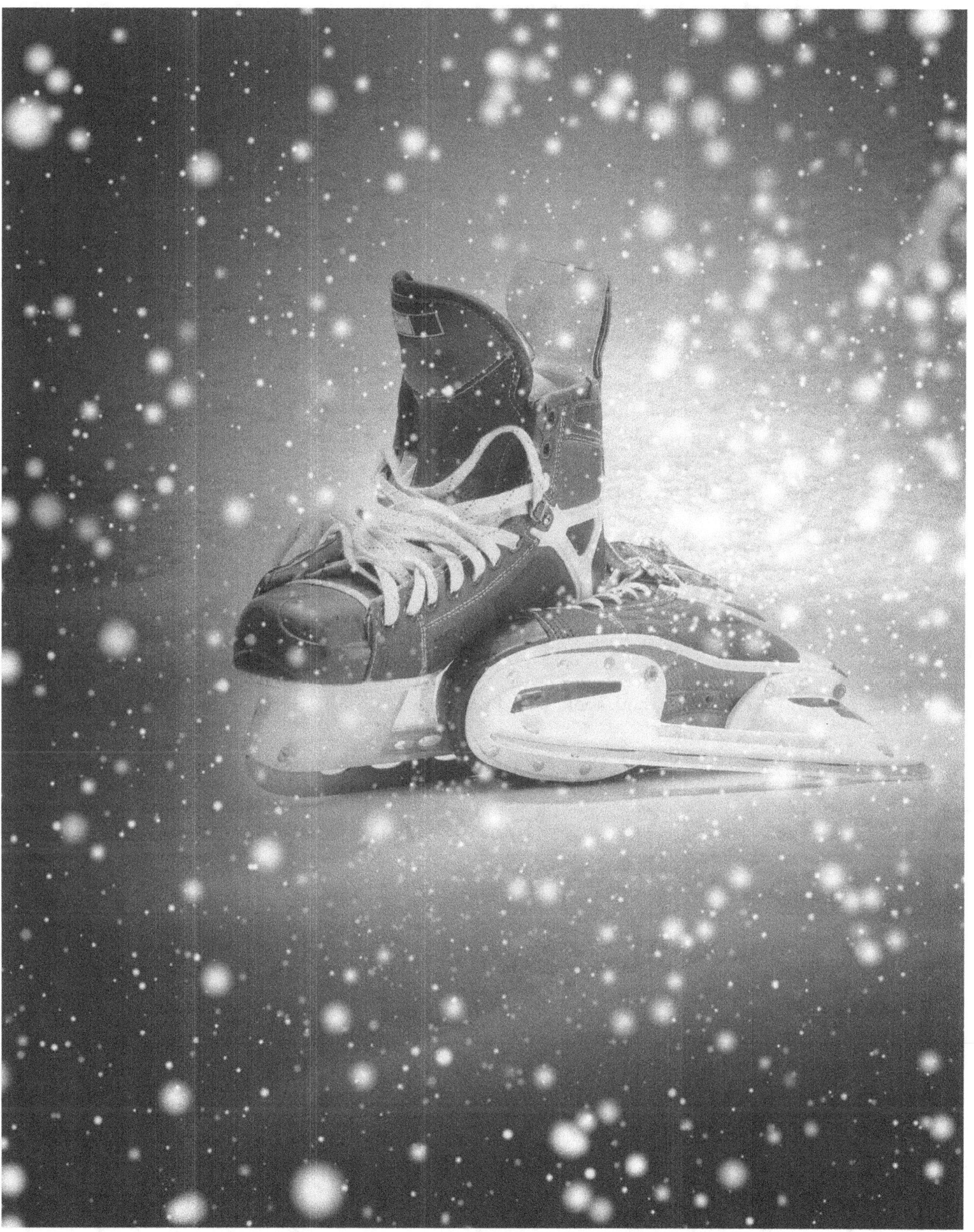

He's on my mind of course, on this particular day. It's been nearly seven years.

Had Wayne ever been in my childhood bedroom? For some reason I can't recall.

I leave the children to my brother and climb the steps, enter the room, take my cell phone in hand, it reads: *BLOCKED CALLER.*

I answer, and hear: "Merry Christmas, Alex."

The sound of rushing air intertwined with the sound of his voice. A feeling of vertigo, for me.

Merry Christmas, Alex.

An impossibility.

I look at the disbelief written upon my face in the mirror's reflection and imagine the ghostly outline of Wayne as he was seven years ago, at my side.

"Who is this?"

"It's me Alex. I'm here."

"I'm serious: who is this?"

I can tell of course. How could I ever forget the sound of his voice, and his laughter—the shy way he would look down and eyes slightly averted—when all I wanted to do was hold his gaze?

"Wayne."

"Yes."

"How?"

"Don't think about how. Just get here."

"Where?"

"Saratoga. I'll be waiting."

"What do you mean? Waiting where?"

"To see you. I don't have long."

Nervous laughter. "You're not alive. This . . ."

"It is. I'm here. For you."

The signal on my phone fades. There's an unexpected burst of static. I move instinctually toward the only window in the room, for clearer reception and drop to my knees before the iced-over window in the room. The electric candle with its red bulb melts the frost into an ellipsoidal-shaped hole that I can see through, down to the blanket of snow on the lawn below.

"This is crazy. This is a joke. I'm hanging up."

"Don't." Panic.

I push the phone hard against my ear until it hurts, straining to decipher the gentle hum in the connection that sounds like waves crashing on a faraway beach and a faint tinkling of bells.

"Ten o'clock. Do you remember the ice rink?"

"Of course."

"The Gideon Putnam Hotel. Room 305?"

"I know those places, haven't been back since. It's . . ."

I feel a sensation: like the tips of fingers on my face.

I close my eyes in that moment and imagine myself behind the wheel of my mother's car. I drive the road that weaves through Saratoga State Park, between the majestically tall pine trees that reach to the stars in the clear and cold night sky; dense branches covered like flocked Christmas trees. I see this image as I have in years past, as I know I will again later this night.

I move in past, present, and future.

"Meet me at ten o'clock. The Adirondack Trust Bank on Broadway." He says.

"I'll be there." I commit.

The call ends.

Wayne Bowman is somewhere. His spirit with voice, blood coursing through his veins. Or is he gone?

He's *somewhere.*

In life, he stood slightly taller than six feet; he held muscle well and his skin had a tinge of bronze—the American Indian in his mixed blood. His eyes were an unremarkable brown until the light hit them just right and they gleamed brilliant, like the inside of a kaleidoscope pointed at the sun. His hair was thin, and a worry, for he dreaded more than anything losing it before he turned thirty.

But Wayne never turned thirty.

This has to be a prank. No such thing as resurrection of the dead. How could it not be? Someone privy to my past was playing a terrible joke.

The phone is dead, but I still speak: "I stood next to your casket, Wayne."

I turn the bedroom light on. My eyes are drawn to the black plastic clock with the silver hands that are now immobile. It belonged to Wayne. His mother had invited me back to her small apartment that was constructed and arranged for her disability, her permanently damaged leg. She asked me to choose a few things to remember her son by. I chose the clock because it stood steadfast on the bedside table next to us, while we slept.

I'll be there.

———

My mother yells that the family is leaving soon for Mass and will I be coming along?

I feign illness and the house quickly becomes quiet. I watch the cars back slowly out of the driveway and climb the hill in a dull procession.

I remember the day of the burial. Twenty-four at the time, I stood with my head bowed somberly, under a green canvas tent that sheltered the few mourners from freezing drizzle that descended unremittingly from a slate-gray sky. The reserved plot was situated at a corner of a large, unremarkable cemetery with an undesirable view of a shopping mall. I stood shivering beside the dark mahogany casket where Wayne's body, completely drained of its essential fluids, would decay.

———

I rifle through my father's coat pockets for car keys, and find a hidden pack of cigarettes instead. Then into the kitchen, where the keys sit waiting on the table. I grab my coat and move swiftly out the door.

Much of the street is lit brilliantly, strands of single-colored lights wrapped around trees covered in snow, and luminariums; small white candles lit and placed inside white paper bags that glow like phosphorescence.

The thirty-minute drive to Saratoga is treacherous. Snow falls fast, which makes visibility poor and maneuvering slow. Route 9 is all but deserted except for a few state-operated snowplows, their bright revolving yellow lights on the roofs of their cabs and headlights illuminating a good stretch of road.

I keep driving, heading toward downtown and before long I'm on Broadway, the main thoroughfare of this peaceful city that's known best for summer horse racing. As I approach the intersection, ten minutes late, I'm somewhat relieved to see no one standing there, awaiting my arrival.

I park the car and step out: nothing but the delicate and gentle sound of a snowfall. There is absolutely no one on the street, which isn't surprising considering the hour and the night.

Wayne's former second-floor apartment is directly across from where I stand. The lights are on and I can see a Christmas tree standing tall in front of the arch-shaped window through gauze-like curtains.

I walk the wide pedestrian-friendly sidewalk, as I had several years before, past the darkened shops: tuxedos on half-mannequins in one window, a Bagel Bakery, and Compton's Diner, open only for breakfast every day of the year. After so many months of walking past the place with Wayne at my side, we never ate there.

I reach the steps, covered with snow. They lead to the front door of the three-story red brick building. On the landing, just outside the broken front door that never locked, there are three mailboxes. Wayne's name is still discernible, but has been crossed out crudely with a ballpoint pen and a new one is written clumsily above it.

No explanation, no detail, just crossed out.

I push the large wooden door; it opens easily. The entrance foyer is pitch-dark. I wish for an instant to ascend the stairs and find Wayne awaiting my arrival like he had on our last Christmas Eve together.

I pull the door closed and return to the street corner. Still: no one there. Looking at my watch, I decide to give it fifteen minutes.

At the thirteen-minute mark, I'm back in the car with the engine running. The windows are freezing over, so I turn the defroster on full. As the driver side window slowly clears, the Adirondack Trust clock comes into view and there's someone standing beside it: a man in a long black dress coat. He rubs his palms together and blows into them for warmth. Then he thrusts his hands deep into his pockets, which was something Wayne used to do.

My heart races and for a moment I grip the steering wheel to brace myself. I take the keys from the ignition and open the door. The man who stands on the corner hears this and slowly turns in my direction. The snow begins to fall fast, it's like a cloud has opened up and let out a deluge. I'm snow blind, yet I still cross the street, and find the illuminated clock with no one standing beside it.

I'm dreaming, I think, as I move tentatively toward the apparition that now stands just outside the front glass doors of the bank. I see Wayne's face clearly in the light of the streetlamp; he has not aged. The strong, jutting chin, his face, lightly peppered with tiny scars—proof of an adolescent struggle with acne. His eyes shine brightly with life. Wayne says my name clearly, and then reaches out and pulls me into a strong hug.

He is real. This I cannot doubt, after seeing him, feeling his heart beat. The feelings that I had pushed aside, the love I still felt for Wayne overwhelms in that unprepared-for moment. I realize that everything I'd come to believe throughout the course of my life and education was now being called into question. How could this be real? I didn't have the answer, but was more than willing to suspend disbelief.

Another thing I think of while standing there, holding the ghost of a dead man in my arms, is that I had convinced myself that seven years was enough time to feel immune to the loss of someone. But as I hold Wayne I realize what a lie it is to pretend that I had moved on.

"Where have you been?" I ask.

"That doesn't matter, Alex."

I step away and look carefully into Wayne's face.

"You don't believe in me."

"I just—don't understand." I say.

"You have to believe, or I can't stay."

"Tell me I'm not crazy, Wayne. I don't see how this is real."

"Do you believe in me or not?"

I think for a moment longer, then reach out for Wayne's hand and take it into my own. "I do."

Wayne, with the shy and sheepish look that I now remember so clearly and forcefully, pulls me toward the steps that lead to his former apartment.

"Come on."

"Where are we going?"

"Upstairs."

"We can't, someone lives up there now." I look up. The apartment is now dark. "The lights were on before."

"Trust me."

Wayne climbs the steps and waits for me to follow. I do, then watch as Wayne enters the dark foyer. The staircase curves right on the way up to the second floor landing. I walk carefully, one hand holding the banister while the other holds tightly to the back of Wayne's coat. It's so dark that I'm unable to see the door to the apartment. I recall the rolled bathroom towel Wayne used to keep at the bottom of the door that prevented light from escaping and cold air from coming in. All of these details come flooding back, and I cringe to think of what will happen when Wayne tries to open the door of the apartment he hasn't lived in for years.

Wayne opens the door without a key, and warm light immediately fills the hallway.

He looks back at me proudly and smiles.

"Here we are."

It's like time has traveled back upon itself and carried both of us with it. The room is exactly as I remember: the same rust-colored carpeting, drawn shades that cover each window, a black leather couch, the two sliding doors that lead to the bedroom where Wayne's waterbed is. This is the place where we spent our first night together after meeting in a bar, the room where we fell in love.

By some twist in logic, I see a younger version of myself sitting on the couch next to Wayne in front of an oversized and lit Christmas tree, covered with strings of popcorn and reams of tinsel. I wear a red, long-sleeved Polo shirt, the one I'd worn that year—proof being images captured in photographs that are now in a dusty album back in Los Angeles.

I watch as we exchange gifts, a child-like twinkle in our eyes. I marvel at how the scene is plays out exactly as it had years ago. Wayne has bought me a brown leather aviator's jacket, I give him two turntables and a stack of 12" dance records that I bought at a tiny store in Greenwich Village, so that Wayne could spin once he's hired for his first gig as a club DJ—his talent and his dream.

We sit together, Vince Guaraldi Christmas music playing on the stereo, until it's time to unplug the tree and move into the bedroom. I turn away and open the door to leave because I know what comes next: a miserable Christmas morning where I find Wayne dead from a Grand mal seizure.

When I step out onto the threshold, I find myself back outside, stepping onto the sidewalk.

"Shall we go?" Wayne asks.

"Where?"

"To right now, to Christmas Present." Wayne places his hand on my shoulder and when he takes it away, I'm standing at the spot in the State Park where we had gone skating years before. The rink has been closed for several seasons. When I was a child, my family would take me here during the day, an excellent place for a winter outing. Wayne had lived in Saratoga his entire life, and had never been, because he'd never learned to skate. I had pledged to teach him and within no time Wayne was gliding on the ice like an expert, doing figure 8's and skating backwards.

But now, in the present, the place is completely deserted. The snow is untouched, pristine under the light of the moon.

"It's been closed for years."

"I know. It's easy to forget that the world goes on without you, that things are always in a state of flux here."

In the blink of an eye, I watch as the area transforms itself into the vision in my mind. Suddenly the snow melts away and the ice appears, shimmering. Several pine trees are lit with strands of white lights—the place is radiant. I turn back and find Wayne lacing up a pair of black skates. There's another pair, blades stuck in the snow, beside him.

"Let's go skating." Wayne says and is up and on the ice.

I am not far behind. Together we move smoothly and with grace over the ice, under the moon, as the earth turns on its axis.

We collapse against a snow bank. Winded, it takes a minute for me to catch my breath.

"I'm in worse shape than I thought."

"You look great," Wayne says.

"Thanks." I look away, slightly embarrassed by the compliment.

We sit in silence for a while, revel in the beauty of the moment.

"So why here? Out of all the places in the world, why bring me back here?"

"Because this is where your present meets your future."

"I don't understand."

"You will." There's a brief silence and then Wayne says, "Our last night together, just before everything went black, the image of this place came to me; an image of us skating together out here like we had so many times before. And then, the rink suddenly never ended. It went on and on forever and I just skated away."

I reach for Wayne's hand and hold it.

"Where've you been, can you tell me? Why are you here now?"

Wayne doesn't have an answer so I turn away, then look back again quickly, afraid he might disappear if I keep my eyes averted for too long.

"You were so important to me. I had no idea how much. I wondered for a long time after you died, if I'd ever be able to go on with someone else, and I think I've tried, even if only half-heartedly. Your love has never been replaced."

"I know, but now it's time. Time for you to go on."

Wayne's eyes gleam in the light. He smiles.

"Thank you." I say, and look at Wayne one last time. I let go of his hand.

When I look up again, I'm sitting alone. The ice skating rink is gone. The trees stand tall and are engulfed in darkness.

Only one set of footprints lead to where I sit.

I take the skates off, find my boots a few feet away, and start the half-mile walk back to downtown, back to my car.

In ten minutes, I reach the park entrance and see a Jeep Cherokee pulled over to the side of road on Route 9. I watch as a man gets out of the car and lifts the hood above the engine.

I approach.

"Hello there. Need some help?"

"Hi." The man steps away from the vehicle and enters the light of a street lamp.

"Did you breakdown?"

"Yeah, I guess. The car's a rental. I'm not sure why but it just stopped running. I've plenty of gas."

"That's odd. Mind if I try?"

"By all means."

I climb into the car, the key hangs from the ignition. I try it and the car turns-over immediately.

"I'm feeling a little silly right about now. I swear it wasn't working."

The man laughs; I smile.

"I believe you. Rentals can be temperamental sometimes." I say.

"I was on my way back to the Gideon Putnam Hotel. Can I give you a lift somewhere?"

I hesitate and turn to look back in the direction I'd just walked from.

"It's the least I can do."

"Sure. My car's a few blocks up on Broadway."

"Cool. Jump in." The man offers his hand. "I'm David, by the way. Nice to meet you."

"I'm Alex. Pleasure."

"So, is it some kind of a tradition?"

"What's that?"

"Do you always go skating first thing Christmas morning?" David points to the skates that hang down from my shoulder.

I laugh, "Not usually. Truth is, I was visiting with a friend."

"And I was coming back from my folk's house. A late dinner."

"Where are you from?" I ask.

"Originally? From here, but now I live in Los Angeles."

I glance at my watch; it's just after midnight.

34

The Man Who
Walks Beside the Sea

SEAN PADRAIC MCCARTHY

The painting hung in the front room of the gallery. Every season since she lost Eve, Nora would pray that it wouldn't be purchased, and to date it had not. Nora would only travel to the gallery after the crowds had thinned and the sun had shifted its angle crossing the sky. The trees bare and the chill of winter beginning to creep. Most of the shops, the restaurants, closed down as the season came to a close, but the gallery stayed open. A converted old home, a Greek Revival, the far end of Commercial Street, crumbling brick steps, and an effigy of Poseidon carved in wood above the door. Poseidon had one hand raised, open palm, in the manner of Moses, and in the other his trident hung low. Eyes empty, lost and without pupils, and that only seemed right. The Greeks had always left the eyes empty, and Nora sometimes wondered if it signified looking further, having seen too much, or perhaps seeing nothing at all. A reflection of life. The empty hunger of the sea. A reflection Nora saw regularly when she stared into the mirror.

The painting itself was of the sea, but Poseidon wasn't in it. The artist had been fairly talented, but the technique was nothing innovative, nothing spectacular. It was merely a painting of the waves, the curve of the town and the tower rising from the hill in the background, and a man walking alone along the beach. Head down and hands in the pockets of his long, heavy coat. He was walking away and you couldn't see his face. A seagull perched in the sand behind him. Blank, black eyes. The gallery owner had told Nora on her second

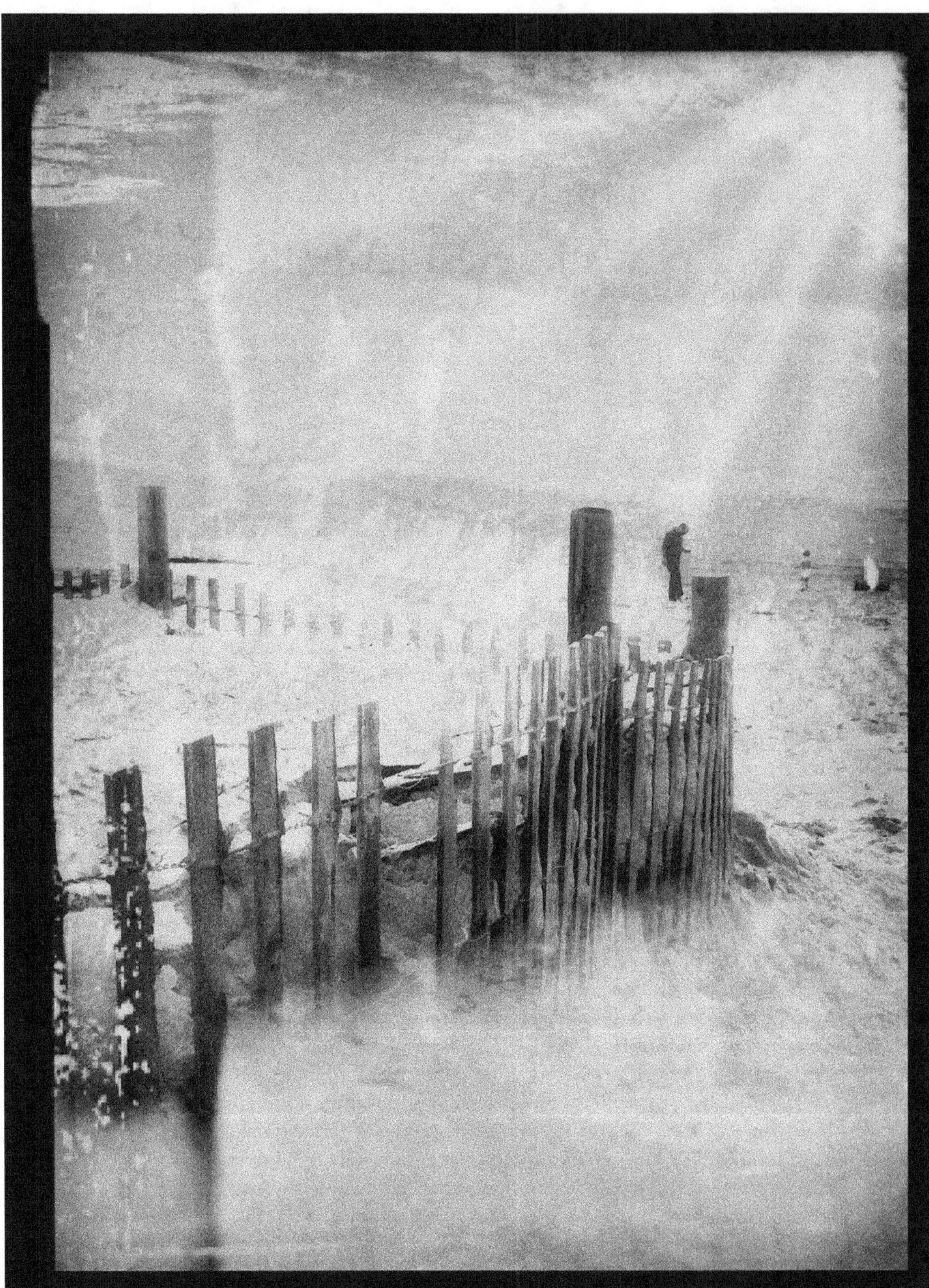

visit to the gallery that he only kept the piece on continuous display because he had promised the artist that he would, until it was sold. It was the artist's dying wish and he had been something of a friend, the gallery owner had told Nora. Nora had never met him, but the owner said he was a small, quiet man with a flat top and glasses, large brown eyes, who had moved to the town because he couldn't face himself being queer anywhere else. It was too much for him, too much for his parents—he had lived in his childhood bedroom for thirteen years after graduating college—and then he moved, and then he was sick within three or four years. And then he was dead. He had sold a few paintings, mostly land-scapes. The owner had liked the artist, he said, because he didn't come to the town to showboat, or even to look for love necessarily. He had merely come to be left alone. He could do that here, he said. He was kind of pathetic in a way. But we're all pathetic, I guess, aren't we? he asked, smiling quick. Isn't that why we're out here, at the end of the world?

But Nora's life hadn't been pathetic. At least not until she moved to the Lower Cape. Truro. Even in summer Truro never seemed as congested as the other towns. P-town in particular. Truro was too spread out. Sand dunes and hills and small, scraggly trees. It had drawn her here. The quiet. Nora had grown up in Manhattan in a family with money that went so far back no one was exactly sure how it was acquired, and she had started modeling—at her own insistence—at thirteen, done reasonably well, and followed the circuit until she was thirty. And then she was pregnant, the father an unwitting accomplice; Nora had told him she was still on birth control, and she was not. She knew him only casually. He wrote for *GQ*, and had beautiful blue eyes, and after a night of drinks she had brought him back to her apartment and slammed shut the door. Easy prey. As soon as her dress was up, he was on his knees, kissing the inside of her thighs. Promising her anything. He would do anything.

She had never told him about the pregnancy, the baby. She feared that if she did, he may have tried to insist she have an abortion, or he may have insisted he be allowed to be involved. And that was not what Nora was looking for. She didn't want him involved. She wanted a child, and she wanted quiet, and she had moved to Truro.

Eve was born in June.

Nora's parents had come to be with her when she delivered, and then her mother had stayed throughout the summer, deep into October. But with the seasons changing, the people vanishing, her mother grew disquiet, needed to return to the city. She liked being surrounded by people, streams of bodies and noise and volatility. It was what she was used to. She broke the news to Nora as gently as she could, and Nora feigned disappointment, but if truth be told, she was happy to see her go. There was a girl in town who was able to help her watch the baby when she needed to go out, and she didn't need to go out very often. There were few places to go.

Nora had a modest house on a hill, with a clear view of the sea, and she had enough people coming and going. She was finding she liked the company of people with simpler lives. Small talk with the man who delivered her milk in the morning, the women she met when she had enlisted Eve in a play group in town, and an occasional dinner with a fisherman who lived in Wellfleet. The fisherman was older. His name was Peter. Gray hair styled like Caesar's, and hard, red skin. Weathered blue eyes, sad and amused, and crow's feet abundant. He had massive forearms and sculptured lips, and he proposed to her after the third time she had slept with him, but Nora had said no. She wasn't looking for marriage. Not now.

She continued to sleep with him after that. She liked the physical contact. His rough fingers, and his heavy body lying beside her. He was wonderful in bed, and could bring her to climax quicker than any man she had known before, but he was looking for something different. He would bring her little girl, now three years old, small presents. Beads and colored stones from the shops downtown, and animals he had carved during his time on the water. Whales and mermaids and goats and dogs and birds. And the little girl was thrilled whenever he did. And then when she was gone, he had tried to be there even more for Nora, but Nora couldn't have that. She didn't want him. She didn't want anybody.

She had lost Eve in late September. A warm day and an empty beach. Both in their bikinis. They were on the ocean side of the town, and there was a pull—more of one than usual following a weekend storm—but there was always a pull, always heavy surf, and it was never a major concern because the little girl never waded far out into the water. If Nora wasn't holding her hand, never past her knees. Sometimes she would lay in the surf, propped on her elbows, one eye shut and facing the dunes, as the waves rolled over her, content and still for what seemed an impossible length of time for such a small child, or she would bring down her pail and shovel to build a castle, but that was all. She loved the water, but she wasn't a swimmer, not yet, and there didn't seem to be an urgent need to be concerned.

Nora couldn't have dozed off for more than five minutes. At most ten. Eve hadn't even been near the water's edge when she did, she was sitting beside Nora, sifting sand through her fingers and talking about seals. Nora had taken her on a whale watch the week before and they had seen three seals swimming danger-ously close to the boat. Nora had told her of the legend of selkies, the seals shed-ding their skins and running to the shore to sunbathe on the beach, and that's all she had been talking about ever since she wanted to know if they still had their feet when they were inside their seal skin.

"But where do they come from Mummy?" she had asked on the beach.

Nora, head back and eyes shut, had become proficient at tuning her out. Murmured yeses and nos ready on her lips. She loved the beach this time of year.

"Souls," she whispered.

"Like ghosts?'

"Mmm . . . humm."

"Of who?"

"People who have drowned," Nora murmured, "or have been lost at sea."

"Mummy," the girl had said after a period of quiet. "I don't want to get bigger."

"You don't? Why not?"

"Because I'm afraid I'll never see my Mummy again."

"But why do you think that, honey?" Nora had asked. The sun was hot on her forehead. She opened her eyes just for a moment. A seagull was circling above them, and the sun had moved to the center of the sky. The last days before the equinox, the last days of warm sun.

"Well, I'll have to move to my own house," said Eve.

Nora smiled, reached with her fingertips, patted the girl's shoulder. "Not for a long time."

The waves broke on the shore, and Nora felt a spray of mist.

"Mummy, can you come here for a minute?" Eve asked.

"Why?" said Nora, her thoughts fading. "Is something wrong?"

"No."

"Then why?"

"Because I miss you."

When she woke she reached out again to her before she opened her eyes. The girl would still be sitting there, of course she would be sitting there. But she was not. Air. Sand. Nothing. And then Nora bolted up, immediately beginning to panic. Her first thought, what she wanted to believe, was that Eve must have headed up towards the dunes. She scanned the water as soon as her eyes shot open, and there was nothing. Just a small boat far on the horizon, and heavy clumps of brown seaweed being pushed forward, pulled back. Nothing. If Eve had gone into the water, there would be a sign of something. It was too big, too open. Nora would see her. She would have to be able to see her. She couldn't see her.

Nora had run to the water's edge, and then up the dunes. Losing time. No matter which way she went she was losing time. And then she saw the man further down the beach. A tall, slope-shouldered man, heavily dressed in gray or black, staring at the sand as he moved along. He seemed to be walking slowly, but no matter how fast Nora ran she couldn't catch up to him; he just grew smaller in the distance. She finally stopped, out of breath, and stared at him a moment longer. He was alone. That much she was sure of. Even from here she could at least discern that. He was alone. But what if he had seen Eve? He must have passed by while Nora was sleeping. He could be able to tell her something. Anything. But she was losing time. If she kept chasing after him, away from where Eve had been, she would lose more time, and this close to the water, time meant everything. Nora turned and began sprinting back.

There were three days of vigils. Candles and songs, poems from neighbors, questions from police, and people camped along the beach. And then she washed ashore down in Orleans.

Eve was lifeless and blue, but despite three days in the water, she looked very peaceful. Merely asleep. As precious as she had been when Nora had last seen her. There were little to no signs of decomposition. The coroner couldn't explain it, but Nora wasn't committed to debating how long the girl had been dead, not yet, not then. All that mattered was she was gone now. He said there were no signs of struggle, foul play. Eve had drowned, her body full of sea water. Nora had sat with her in the room for hours on end, waiting, and praying against hope, that something would change, that she would somehow awaken, but of course she did not, and it took the coroner and a local priest more than an hour to convince Nora she had to go home. She requested a private burial. The fisherman, her parents, and a brother and sister. Two friends from the town. And then she had gone back to her home and shut the doors for winter.

———

She first saw the painting in the gallery the following March. The pain of grief still gnawed at her like hunger, but there was nothing she could do to fill it. Nothing she wanted to do. Nothing had meaning, had purpose. She had gone into town to pick up a few groceries, and ducked into the gallery when it started to rain. Sleet. Snow. And the wind howling in from the sea. The gallery owner was bundled in scarf and hat, pulled down tight over his ears, behind his desk. Two sweaters.

"The heat's not working," he said. "The furnace. I planned on getting it fixed last fall, then put it off, and then it was February, and I figured if it made it this far, I could get through the season, wait until next fall. You know how that goes."

Nora had nodded, but she wasn't really listening. Her heart was pounding in her chest. She was staring at the painting, hanging on the wall facing the window, and her mouth was dry and her thoughts racing. The drops of rain still dribbling down her cheeks, the tip of her nose. She had dropped twenty-five pounds that winter, twenty-five pounds she could not afford to lose, and her body was shaking. A rattling cage.

"I have a space heater—I bought it in case of an emergency like this—but I'm terrified of those things. Simply terrified. Every year you hear about the fires those things cause." He noticed Nora staring and got up from his stool. "I can move that if you want, hang it up by itself so you can get a better feel for it," he said, coming around the counter, but Nora had merely shaken her head, mouthed a thank you, and was then back out the door and into rain.

Back at home, she couldn't get the picture out of her head. It almost seemed a cruel joke, the same man, walking away. But perhaps it was coincidence. Or perhaps it was just a local man who liked to walk the beach. The beaches. And the artist had captured him that way. The artist was local, that much seemed sure—Nora had noticed the Pilgrim Tower in the background—and if she found him, she could ask him. Who the man was, where she could find him. If nothing else, maybe he had been the last to see her little girl alive, could offer her an explanation. Or maybe just a memory. Eve by the water's edge, running through the sand. Perhaps shaking Nora's arm, trying to wake her. Something, anything, to add to her picture. At least another moment, a snapshot in time.

She had gone to the girl's room to straighten the bed. The bed didn't need straightening—no one but Nora had been in the room since Eve had gone, and she kept the room exactly as it had been—but it had become part of her daily routine, and the routine helped. Structure. Structure helped you cope, that's what people said. Eve had only been out of her crib three months when she drowned. Nora had had a hard time taking her out of her crib, her only baby, but Eve had been thrilled. A Little Mermaid comforter and pillowcase, and jumping on the bed so her head nearly hit the ceiling. Nora still kept her stuffed animals lined against the wall. Baby Simba from The Lion King, a panda bear she named Boo-boo, dogs and turtles and a small, long beaked Seagull. And then there was the doll she dragged with her every day since she had learned to crawl. Ratty, gnatty hair fanning over her bald spot in back, and one lazy eye. Louie. Louie looked as if she had been through a war, and every time Nora looked at her now, she found herself caught between laughing and crying. Only something that had been loved could ever possibly get worn so quickly.

Potty training had been more difficult than leaving the crib, and Nora had tried to develop a reward system with her. "What do you want?" she had asked. "Do you want a sticker? Or do you want a piece of candy?"

But Eve had just looked at her, her lips pursed sadly. "A hug?" she had said, and Nora pulled her close. "Mummy?"

"Yes?"

"Am I growing up?"

Now Nora took a seat on the bed, and looked out the window, toward the sea, the breakers in the distance. The house was creaking around her. The house wasn't old, but it was hard—nearly impossible—to keep a house new so close to the sea. The sea was constantly out there, especially this time of year, carried on the wind, whistling through the cracks around the windows, loosening shingles on the roof above. The sea was relentless. It wanted everything, everyone, for its own.

It was the next day that she returned to the gallery and the owner told her about the artist, the painting. He had others, too, that he showed to her quickly but none that caught her eye. A hollow man with sunken cheeks sitting on a wooden chair in a blue room, a painting of a woman in the parking booth below the Pilgrim Tower—the style reminiscent of Edward Hopper—and the Windmill in Orleans. Orleans, Nora wondered. Why did Eve choose to travel to Orleans? She almost told the gallery owner that her father owned a Picasso, and at any other point in her life she might have done just that, but not now. She doubted he cared. She didn't care. She had needed to stop in the street, her feet cold in the slush and snow, and take three deep breaths before even coming inside. He recognized her immediately, made reference to the painting, and then alluded to coming down in price if she were interested. He could let it go for six hundred dollars.

Nora told the man she wasn't sure. But six hundred dollars wasn't the problem. Six hundred dollars was nothing. She didn't want the painting, didn't want it in her home. She just wanted to know that it was there, that it was real. That she could see it when need be.

The owner's skin looked dry today, flaky at the scalp, and he smelled faintly of garlic. The heat was working now, the hat and scarf gone. "I think he considered it his most accomplished piece," he said. "He never said that directly, but I could tell by his demeanor when we first looked at it together, when he first brought it in."

Nora held out her hand, fingers inches before the canvas, and the gallery owner looked at her sideways, more than likely wondering if she were crazy, she imagined.

"What did he call it?" she asked.

"He didn't." The man paused. "At least not that he ever mentioned. I just call it November. It looks like November."

"He must have painted it down on one of the beaches along 6A," she said.

The owner shrugged. "Maybe. Or he could have just taken a picture, used a postcard. Lord knows there are enough of them around."

"Did he ever mention the man?" she asked.

The owner stepped closer. He opened his mouth, paused for a bit. "I never asked," he said at last. "He really wasn't one to volunteer information. Like I said, he was quiet. Really very sweet. The picture made him nervous though. I meant it when I said I believe he looked at it as his most accomplished work, but as excited as he was with it, there was something else. His hands were shaking when we looked at it, when I promised him I would show it until it sold. He wasn't looking very good, and I figured it was the least I could do. He obviously didn't have much more time."

"And did he ever say anything else about it?" she asked. "After that, I mean."

"No. He really couldn't. I think he was dead about a week later. Two at most."

————

The fisherman still came by to visit, but if Nora ever let him in, she did her best to keep it brief. Sometimes she would just meet him at the door, open it a few inches, explain she wasn't feeling well. He usually took no for an answer, but not always. He never looked angry, but his eyes always looked concerned, even when he was doing his best to smile. He would cook for her sometimes. He was a very good cook, and if she wouldn't let him in, he would just hand off whatever he had made, right there at the door. She wouldn't let him touch her. She wouldn't let anybody touch her—it didn't seem right. Nothing that brought pleasure—that could bring pleasure—seemed right any longer, and that was another thing she liked about the painting. It intrigued her and frightened her, and maybe even comforted, but it brought no pleasure.

———————

During the second winter, she visited a psychic downtown, but the woman's answers were generic, empty, and then grasping for straws, grasping for any-thing, Nora began to attempt to contact Eve through the mirror. She wanted to know, needed to know, if she were out there—if her soul resided somewhere other than the sea—and she had read about a technique for communing with loved ones, communing with the dead, in a book written by a doctor of some sort. It was a hypnotic exercise requiring you to refrain from caffeine and dairy for a day, and then you needed to listen to relaxing music, possibly view some works of art, and then, at twilight, with a dim candle lit behind you, you needed to gaze into a mirror.

At her feet she lay pictures of Eve. Drawings she had done. Coloring books, her blanket, toys. Louie. The child's belongings were supposed to help the seer focus, help evoke memories. Nora had little trouble evoking memories but she wanted to follow the directions exactly as instructed, and she hoped that having Eve's cherished possessions close by would aid in drawing her baby back to her, draw her near. A step closer to communion. The secret, the book had said, was to gaze past the mirror more than gaze directly into it. It should feel as though you were looking into the distance, and then after a time, the surface might become cloudy, might become black, and then if all was quiet, if you were relaxed enough, something, someone may start to appear. Or possibly you might hear something. Feel something.

She tried six times in a two-week period, and each time, the results were the same. Nothing. After the sixth, she scrambled herself some egg whites—she had refrained from eating entirely before this attempt, hoping that the fast could help induce visions—and then she slipped into her coat and walked to the beach.

Nora's home was not directly on the beach, but less than a quarter mile away. A lumpy, curvy road wound through the woods and led you to the path that broke through the dunes. In season the road and the path would be spotted with bikers, hikers, and joggers. Small children trailing their parents and dragging boogie boards. But today she saw no one.

The temperature had dipped below freezing, but the sky above was deep blue. The closer she drew to the water, the bluer it seemed. It was the same beach where she had lost Eve. Each time Nora came down here, she retraced that day in her head. What they had said, what they had done. What she had done. What she hadn't. It all came back clearly as she trudged through the sand, the familiar pain stabbing at her soul, the day somehow locked in time, and the sounds about her seeming to change. The roar of the ocean was still there, but it was lighter, quieter, and warmer. She was more in touch with the sounds of that day than even the visuals, and if she shut her eyes as she sat in the sand, she could still hear her little girl's voice. She remembered looking up at one point, telling Eve she was too pretty to have sand all over her face. "The sand loves me, Mummy," Eve had said.

Her hope was always the same each time she visited—the man she had seen in the distance would come walking back. If he were local, someone who walked the beach routinely, chances were she would run into him again. But even as she held out hope for this, she wondered how she would know if it were him. She had only seen him from the back, never seen his face. Did not know if he were old or young. But the walk, she told herself. She would recognize the walk, the slouch of the shoulders.

Nora kept her eyes shut for ten minutes or more, shivering in the cold and listening to the wind and when she opened them there were heads bobbing in the surf. Two of them. Snouts raised and whiskers. At first she thought they were dogs—someone had let their dogs in the water in February—but then they dipped and she saw their tails. Seals. They couldn't have been more than ten yards offshore.

"It's a different place this time of year, isn't it?"

Nora looked up and tried to force a smile. An older woman, probably mid-seventies. Blue plastic sunglasses, a rolled, brimmed hat. "Truro?" Nora asked.

"The sea." The woman stepped closer, poking the sand with her walking stick. "It's older in the winter," she said, her mouth agape as she stared out upon the water. Lines running from the corners of her mouth down to her neck. "In season, with the crowds, it seems a lot younger—the sand warm and skies clear. A lot safer, too, I suppose. It's more difficult to imagine it claiming you on a beautiful day."

Nora was silent. She looked back upon the water.

She heard the woman take a breath. "But it really doesn't discriminate, season to season, I mean. That famous pirate ship they're always talking about— the Whydah or whatever it was called—that sank in mid-spring, I believe. Or maybe it was late spring, I'm not sure. I saw something about it on the National Geographic Channel, and they're still excavating it offshore here, from what I understand."

Nora stood, folded her arms. The woman was shorter than she originally seemed. Maybe less than five feet tall. "Was it right off this beach?" Nora asked.

"Wellfleet, I think," the woman said, "but the wreckage scattered three or four miles. They opened a museum to it a little while back. I guess it must have been something. For days after it broke apart the corpses were washing ashore." The woman smiled. Straight white teeth. More than likely not her own. "Most of them were pirates, but a lot of them were the captives, too. One was just a little boy." She breathed in again. "You're not from around here, are you?"

The wind picked up, and Nora brushed the hair from eyes. "New York, originally."

"You must be the woman who lost the child a couple years back, the little girl?"

Nora didn't answer. She never did, when people commented, people asked. She couldn't. She wasn't sure why. She just couldn't. Admitting it, talking about it, finalized it somehow, and she wasn't ready for that. Not yet.

The woman sighed again. "It doesn't make any sense, does it? Any loss of life, but particularly when they're young. I lost my boy thirty-four years ago, now. Hard to believe it's been thirty-four years, but it has. Seems like yesterday. I can still seem him so clearly. Blue eyes and curly hair, an infectious smile. It was probably the smile that got me, the reason he always got his way. He never came back though. He was out with his friends, probably drinking though I'm not sure now that it matters—he was in high school, and that's what they do. They all went into the water, but he never came back. So, of course, we had nothing to bury. It's a strange thing when you find yourself praying that they'll find your child's body. Something. Anything. I prayed for months."

Nora looked at the woman a moment, and then back upon the water. She wondered if the woman was looking to share her grief. Thirty-four years and still looking to share her grief. But Nora wasn't interested in sharing. Friends, the fisherman, had tried to get her to join support groups, to be with people going through the same thing. But nobody was going through the same thing, that much she was sure of. Each case, each child, was unique, so how could they be going through the same thing? And pain was different for everyone. She had no doubt this woman still experienced pain when thinking of her son, but was it anything even remotely close to Nora's? A pain so fresh, so new? She couldn't believe that it was, ever could be, but here this woman was looking for an ear, perhaps a word of kindness, shared sympathy, and Nora felt momentarily ashamed for downplaying any of it at all. Where would she herself be in thirty-two years?

"Do you ever feel his presence more when you're down here?" she asked at last. "Does it help?"

"I do," said the woman, "but I'm not sure it helps. In some ways it's more frustrating. You feel that they are still out there, somehow, but there's nothing you can do. The sea is cluttered with souls, so at the very least, you know they have company."

———

She dreamed of Eve that night. It wasn't unusual for her to dream of Eve, but usually the dreams were heartbreaking but mundane. Eve was back, wasn't dead, had never been dead, and maybe Nora was fixing her lunch or following closely behind her as she rode her small bike with training wheels, with bells. Talking about jellyfish and turtles. And each of these dreams ended the same way. Nora would wake to reality, the illusion shattered, her little girl dead. There was always a hint towards the end of these dreams of what was coming, reality looming, Nora's thoughts beginning to race as she realized, remembered, that she had lost her, and then the little girl would look at her and smile, sometimes whispering words Nora could not hear, and then Nora would struggle not to wake, to stay with her, but of course she never could, and then she would again pull the blankets up tight around her, listen to the wind. But this dream was different.

In this dream, Eve was floating, spinning through the depths of the sea, her eyes closed and hair streaming as sharks and fish passed her by. There were others about, too, but Nora could not clearly make out their faces. Different attire, clothes that spanned the ages. Long gowns and ragged breeches, and some in bathing suits, and some not in clothes at all. Completely naked and completely blue. They were all blue and they all had their eyes closed, the only things they all had in common, but then Eve's eyes slowly opened, staring out as if looking into the lens of a camera, and a small bubble of air passed from her lips. Breathing. She was breathing.

Nora bolted up in bed. The room was dark, empty, the moonlight spreading across the floor. She had a radio playing softly in the corner. The quiet voice of a late night D.J., a talk show of some sort, something about the windmills they wanted to build along the shore. A long steady line of them. Nora went to her window, and she could see the lighthouse beacon spinning in the distance. She wondered how much sailors used them anymore, and if they used them at all.

She looked into the mirror again just before dawn. Her belly empty and her mind tired, still looking for sleep. But she couldn't sleep, hadn't been able to fall back to sleep after the dream. She lit the candle behind her and watched the shadows of the light dancing in the glass. Half her own face illuminated and warm, and the other half black. Swallowed by shadows. She wondered if people really saw the things they attested to in an exercise such as this or if it was just the mind playing tricks on them. If you stared at anything long enough, your mind would play tricks on you.

She tried to focus, to keep her thoughts from wandering, but you had to walk a thin line. If you focused too hard, concentrated too much, you couldn't relax, and the book had stressed the importance of feeling relaxed. If you didn't feel relaxed, opening your mind, chances were you would not succeed. Nora narrowed her eyes a bit, thought of the child's voice, the doll—Louie—and a song Eve used to sing from a children's show—*"Has anyone seen my good friend, Drew? He's a big brown cow, he goes 'Moo, moo, moo!'"*

She concentrated on her breathing, slow and measured, and she felt something then. A tingling on the back of her hands, running up her arms—the hairs standing on end—and reaching her shoulders. The tingling was somehow both warm and electric, and in the reflection of the candle flame, flickering in the mirror, she thought she saw a tiny figure dart across the expanse. Long legs and running gait, looking too lanky to be a small child. It was there and then gone, and then there again, moving closer, passing in and out of sight as if moving down a long corridor with many rooms. In and out, room to room. Flickering on and off in her field of vision. Nora's heart began to race, and her mouth felt dry, metallic with fear. The figure was closer now, and the features were beginning to become clearer. A face. Nora tried to sit still. It was now coming too quickly. A face. Did she want to see a face? She wasn't sure. It wasn't Eve, couldn't be Eve, and now it was moving faster. And then it suddenly came to stop. Staring. Standing in the middle of the hall. Nora gasped for her breath and bolted upright in the chair. The candle flickered behind her, and then the room was lost to darkness, the blue gray of dawn rising just outside the window.

She went to the gallery, but the painting was no longer on the wall across from the window. In its place was a contemporary lithograph. A farmhouse in the snow. Dark shadows and a dark blue night. One warm square of yellow light in the center of the house. A window. And the stark shadow of the smoke from the chimney trailing across the snow. Nora's heart began to flutter, panic. She looked to the desk, but the owner wasn't there. She moved her eyes quickly around the room, looking for her painting, but it was nowhere to be seen, and then she heard noise coming from out back. She called out hello, and the owner popped through the curtain. Sawdust lacing his hair, a thin coat covering his glasses.

He took off the glasses, cleaned them with the edge of his shirt, and looked at her again. It was raining again outside, but just a bit warmer. Hints of spring. The gallery owner didn't look well today. Thinner, paler, his eyes slightly gaunt. A bit of watery snot dripping from his nose. He pulled a Kleenex from his pocket, wiped it away.

"I have a miserable cold," he said, "so you might not want to get too close." He was wheezing, his breath raspy and short. "I was just out back doing a little framing. A local boy has talked me into letting him have a show, and I figured what the hell—he has a little talent, comes from a little money, and is willing to put it all up front for the framing. And business has been slow, so I figure it can't hurt."

"You moved the painting," she said.

He hesitated, his mouth open for a pause, almost as if he were debating going forward. "Sold it," he said at last. "I sold it just yesterday. To be honest I was beginning to think I would never sell the thing, especially not this time of year." He wiped his nose again, and then he blew it. "People aren't usually interested in looking at that sort of thing right about now—walking in off a gray cold street to look at a gray cold picture. In season, sure. There's something romantic about it in season—they want to look at it, but don't want to experience it. I'm tired of looking at it, tired of winter. If I make it through this one it will be a Godsend. Anyway, it was starting to depress me—so I put it in the window. Like I said, he just bought it yesterday. A big guy, gray hair, blue eyes."

"Do you know his name?" she asked, her heart picking up again.

The man wheezed again. "I do," he said, "I think. He paid with credit, so it must be on the slip." He went behind the counter, popped open the drawer. "I don't bother processing these things until the end of the week." He pulled out a small pile, squinted through his glasses as he began sifting through. "Here it is," he said. "Peter. Peter Reingold. He lives over in Wellfleet. He said he was a fisherman."

He was outside splitting wood when she pulled into the driveway. Down to a blue T-shirt despite the temperature. His face was red, his head steaming in the cold, and his eyes lit up immediately as soon as he saw her step out of the car. She hadn't been over to see him since before she lost Eve.

He put down his axe, and quickly, nervously pulled out a red bandana to wipe his brow before opening the door to usher her into the house. It was a small house with wide hardwood planks and a potbellied coal stove in the corner of the living room. Peter worked out of the bay side but lived on the side of the open sea. His means were modest and he could have sold the house, the land, for an enormous sum of money, but the house had been in his family a long time and he had never seen the need. Never been married, never had any children. When he had proposed to Nora he had made it clear he would adopt Eve immediately, but that hadn't swayed her.

He offered her a drink. Coffee. Water. Tea. A beer. He had a fridge full of beer, he said. And then he pulled out a chair so she could have seat at the table in the kitchen. He pulled on a sweater.

"I'll get cold as soon as I stop working," he said, the sweat still streaming down his cheeks. "As long as I'm moving, I'm fine. Are you cold? I can light the stove. I usually don't light it when I'm in and out, no point. Waste of coal. The way things are going, I don't want to waste."

Nora shook her head. She wasn't cold. She forced a small smile. It was good to see him, she said. She wanted him to know that. It wasn't why she had come, and she didn't know if she would tell him why she came, but he had always been kind to her, and he had always made her feel good. At least back then. She took a beer. A Belgian-style beer of some sort. *La Fin Du Monde.* It was brewed in Canada, he said. He liked Canadians, the way they looked at things, and he only drank good beer, he had told her in the past. He liked different ones, different tastes. He liked to keep it interesting. And if you couldn't drink to enjoy the taste, there wasn't much point in drinking. Not for him. He rarely drank to get drunk. Whenever he said this, there was usually a light in his eyes, and he would follow it up with "But that's not to say it never happens."

And it had happened a few times between them. Whenever it did, they had always ended up in bed. Inhibitions lost. She remembered she had sometimes spoken dirty to him during those times—Eve sound asleep in her room down the hall—and that had always sent him over the edge. A few words from heaven, he said. And a few words from heaven were always enough to catch him then and there, bring him to the edge. Finish the night. And thinking about that now made her smile again. He had often seemed to be so much a boy. Despite his age, his gray hair and wide chest. How he had gotten into fishing, she had never figured out. His mother had been a teacher. His father a surgeon. That at least, he said, had paid for the boat.

He told her he missed her, and she smiled again. She told him she missed a lot of things. He talked about the upcoming season. He wasn't going to waste much time before heading out. The earlier the better, and he had already signed on four men for a crew. All shifty characters, he said, but they were all reliable— good hands—and they made the days out at sea that much more interesting. It could be hard, stuck out there for days. That was the worst part of it, he said. The loneliness. By the second beer they had moved into the living room. There were several pictures in there. A black and white photograph of an enormous hotel on the cliffs of the sea in San Francisco—the picture was very old, the people in the foreground in Victorian garb: dresses and petticoats, black suits and bowlers and their faces unclear. Another, a reproduction of Millet's The Angelus—the farmer and his wife standing in the freshly plowed field, heads bent in prayer—an original oil painting of a windswept tree, and there on the far wall, the painting she had come looking for. Her painting.

He saw her staring at it, her eyes fixed. She sat on the couch, sitting forward, her knees pressed close together. The familiar anxiety and comfort swirling inside her. She had yet to figure out how the picture could bring forth both feelings at once. It made little sense. Like waking in a dark room and knowing there is someone there with you. Having to look, but not wanting to. But you have to because you know once you do, it will all be better. And so you pull the sheet down from over your head . . .

"You like it?" He was smiling again now. He had seen the reaction in her eyes, had known the picture had done something. A chance for another connection, perhaps.

"I do," she said. "But I think there's more to it than that." She sipped her beer.

"I bought it over in P-Town," he said. "I went over there for a beer the other day, and I saw it—passed it in the window. I don't usually buy anything that expensive, that impulsively, but I really like it. The artist died a couple years back the guy behind the desk told me. I thought that was kind of funny because of the subject matter, the guy there on the beach."

She glanced at him quickly. He was sitting across from her on the edge of his seat. "Why is that?" she asked.

"Well, because of the lore. The dealer said the artist came from Ohio or something, so I thought it was kind of a funny coincidence that he chose to paint the man on the beach. I mean, maybe he picked it up somewhere, I don't know, but it's not really a story you hear people passing around anymore. I heard it once from an old fisherman about thirty years ago as he was on his way out the door, and I suppose you might find it in some old books about the Cape. The myths and legends and all that."

"Who do they say he is?" she asked.

Peter smiled. "The Man Who Walks Beside the Sea. Death, I suppose. Or at least a harbinger of Death. It used to be said that sailors would sometimes see him standing on the beach, and then turning and walking away, as they tried to make it back to shore in the midst of a storm. The thing was, whenever they did, it usually meant they weren't going to make it back in. The ship usually grounded and was then torn apart in the waves and the wind. And if not it was just pulled back out and never seen again. The souls becoming his. Or at least the sea's. The old guy who told me about him seemed to believe it, but then again, he seemed to believe a lot of things. You spend that much time at sea, your mind starts to wander, thinking, creating, and fearing, and stories sometimes seem to take on a bit more truth than they normally would. Besides, out there it helps to be superstitious. Keeps you alert."

Nora looked back at the picture. Here in his home, if you looked away and looked back again quickly, the waves in the painting almost seemed to be moving. A strange but wonderful effect. "As dark as it is," she said, "you don't get exactly what I'd call a bad feeling looking at it though."

"No, you don't," said Peter. "That's one thing I liked about it."

She looked into his eyes then. "And what would you do if you saw him?"

"Well, I certainly wouldn't head into shore." He laughed a little, sipped at his beer. "I think I'd probably turn back."

He was sitting beside her then, his beer on the floor, and after a moment, she felt a hand on her knee, and then moving further along, up her thigh. He turned to kiss her, his lips first on her cheek, and then her throat, and Nora arched her neck as he did, her eyes still on the picture, her thoughts racing back to the beach, that day in the sun. The bubbling surf and gobs of brown seaweed. The lone seagull circling, wings crooked and webbed-feet extended, as if about to land. But the bird never landed; it was taken on the wind until it broke back into flight, and then it was gone. And Nora knew what she had seen. The man had been real. Solid and moving. And thinking back now, she had known even then who he was. What he was. She felt it, the feeling so strong. And she couldn't catch him because she wasn't supposed to catch him. And if she had? She wondered what would have happened if she had.

Peter put his hands upon her shoulders, easing her back on the couch, and as he did, she didn't resist. Nor did she stop him as he unbuttoned her jeans, faded and soft, and pulled them over her hips, the heels of her feet. The fire in the stove was crackling, the door open, and small sparks of red ash were floating about the room, and Peter moved his lips over her shoulder, her breasts, her belly. Nora was quiet, her eyes closed. It had been so long since she had felt anything like this, the feeling both sublime and removed. Something that shouldn't be hers but felt too good to let go. She listened to the wind, higher now, picking up and pulling at the windows, pushing to get in. And carried on the wind was the sound of the sea. It was the one thing you could never escape down here, not this time of year.

■ *35*

Black Silk

DEB TABER

hree black shapes move on Emma's dining room wall, serpentine bodies with spines that swing like lethargic silverfish. They arrange themselves into filigree designs against the cranberry paint. They are the Aal.

Cilia pulsate in waves down the sides of the Aal. Emma watches, motionless. Even as her mind tells her to smash them and run, her muscles relax and her body wilts into the nearest red velvet chair. The undulating hair gives the design a haloed effect and Emma thinks of snake angels, terrible and beautiful. Unknowable.

A need fills her. She must make note of the creatures' design, to feel it flow out from her own fingers so she will understand. Her sketchpad is in the other room. Her charcoals are in her hand.

The pulsing of the cilia slows as Emma draws, allowing her to see the translucent hairs that run down either side of each sinuous body. Two creatures branch from a single stem. The third is by itself, a black silk rope that has begun to fray. The pattern reminds her of Turkish writing, or a piece of ancient lacework pulled out of context.

As she finishes her drawing, the cilia move faster again and Emma feels a deep sense of pleasure, as if the room is filled with praise for her. She draws another and the pleasure grows. She fills her sketchpad and sets up her easel. She

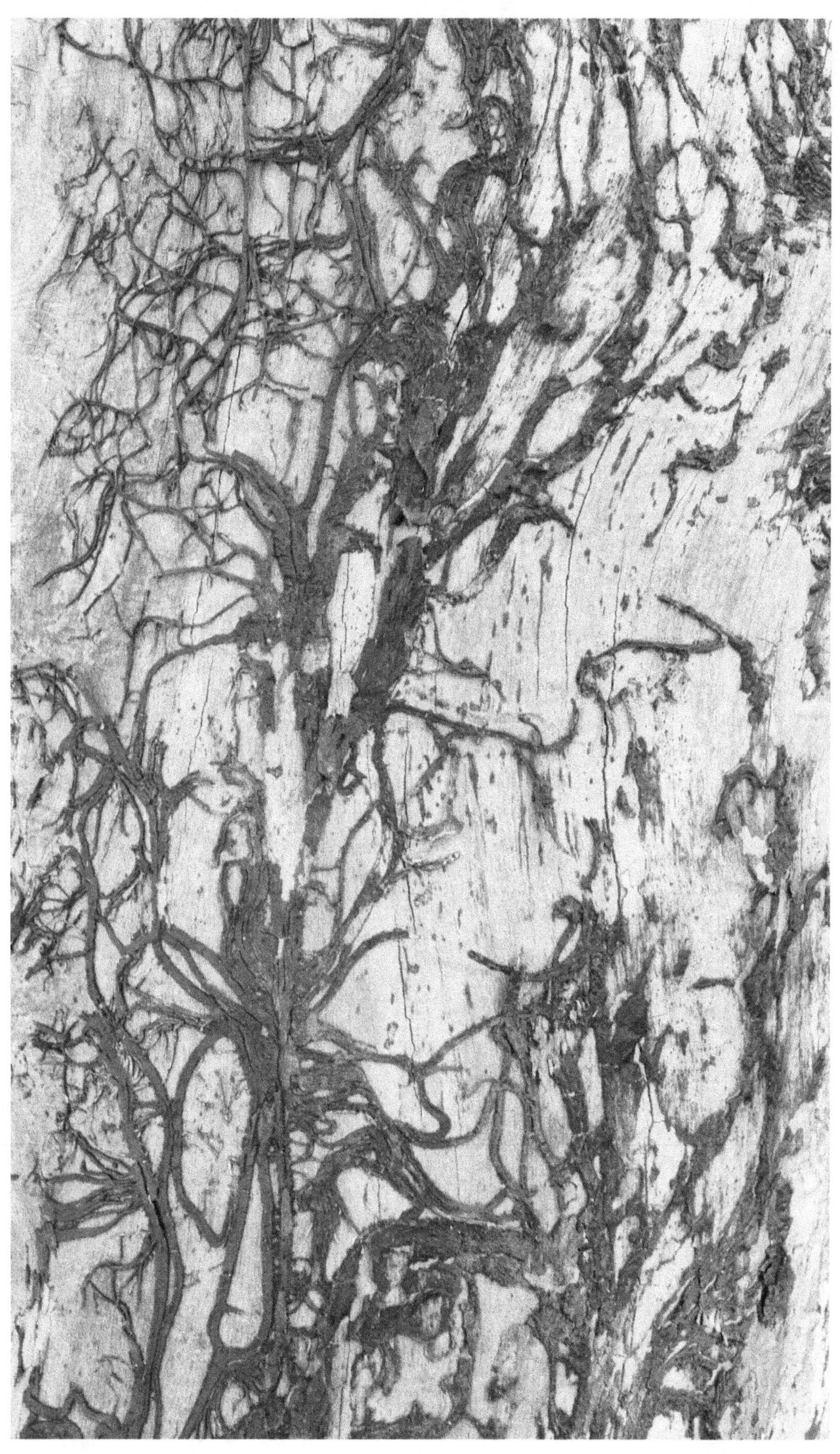

paints until her arms will move no more, then drifts into a sated sleep. She is barely ten feet from the silent motion of the Aal.

———————

Emma's paintings describe the creatures with photographic realism, then with blurred impressions. She experiments, drawing the Aal in greens and blues, purples and golds.

Her works fill the galleries, the shapes of the Aal on display for crowds that are fascinated and repulsed. Some of the patrons come back again, looking longer each time, studying the curving forms. They want to touch but are afraid to cross the velvet ropes. They leave unsatisfied.

Emma, also, needs something more. More shape, more life, something she can feel under her skin, not just beneath her brush. Her hands mold form. In clay, in wax, in plaster, in metal.

———————

The first sculptures of the Aal are unveiled. A wall of plaster bas-reliefs dominates the gallery, the curving lines of the Aal static and surreal under frosted lights. Beneath this display are three bronzes, so vivid that patrons can taste the metal on their tongues.

In front of one sculpture stands Simon. He has known Emma since their art school days, and has come to see her work. His eyes trace every curve a thousand times, trying to grasp the tail of a feeling that slips around the edges of his mind. The sculptures, the paintings, are incomplete.

He leaves when the gallery closes, returning when it opens the next day to look again. The gallery owners do not bother him. They are drawn to the artwork the same way, but they are afraid of it and can't stay in the room for long. They hide in their offices and trace their own black designs on white paper, but their symbols are hard and sharp. There is no life in them.

———————

Emma lies on the heavy oak table, oblivious to the house around her. Dust has settled on the furniture. Hair and lint gather into tiny monsters in the corners of the floors. Her body vibrates, straining to match the pulse of the Aal. She smiles. Blackness writhes on the wall before her and Emma burrows into the waves of pleasure. For the first time, a single Aal lifts itself up, a narrow head or tail testing the air. It judges the distance from wall to table, measures the path from red to brown. The gap is too great. Instead of leaping, it flows over its companions and down to the floor. Carpet and wood pass quickly beneath it and then it is on Emma, cilia tickling her skin.

Fear surges in Emma and she fights herself. Trying to make her body get up, trying to make it stay lying down. Tiny hairs pulse quickly, sending out waves of contentment so Emma can't think why she would ever want the creature gone. The Aal continues to touch her, to explore.

When it is stopped by the belt at her waist, Emma sits up and removes all her clothing. She will let it feel her shape unhindered, as she has felt it take shape beneath the skin of her hands so many times before. She lies back down and closes her eyes as it caresses every inch of her skin and hair, silken underbelly raising goosebumps in its wake. The other two Aal, now fully separate, join them on the table. Emma can feel the patterns they form.

The first casts a small loop at the front of her throat and arranges itself in curves around her shoulder blade and belly. The second meanders across her belly and hips, one end trailing around her thigh. They take their time creating the pattern, testing the uses of the third dimension Emma's body provides after so long on the flat red wall.

The cilia on all three Aal move slowly, brushing gently against the fine hair of her body. A sensation like ice on raw, unhealed skin pierces Emma's belly where the two Aal overlap. She whimpers and the creatures pulse faster, covering her discomfort with satisfaction. The cold deepens as her skin separates beneath her ribcage, creating an opening wide enough for the third Aal to slip through. Emma gasps at the shock of the creature entering her, pain and pleasure signals convoluted in her mind. The hole closes, sealing the Aal inside.

Simon has grown anxious in his days at the gallery. He knows there is more than Emma's paintings are telling him, but she doesn't answer her phone and the gallery owners haven't heard from her in weeks. He stands outside Emma's window and peers in. A form, vaguely human, lies motionless on a table. Something else moves in the background.

A black snake.

Simon pounds on the door, knowing Emma will not respond. When he checks the window again only the small, dark form stirs.

Forms.

It's hard to see through the dirt on the window, but it looks like one wall is covered with snakes. He breaks the window with a rock and lets himself in. Rocks and broken glass will save Emma from the snakes, and then she can tell him what the paintings mean.

Emma lies unmoving on the table. Simon comes closer. He forgets to be afraid of snakes. There is Emma, nude and covered in dust, and then again there is Emma, or half-Emma, protruding from herself like double vision sculpted in flesh. The second self grows out of her side and a little behind, as if she were trying to catch up to herself but hadn't quite. The head or tail of a lifeless black creature pokes out from between the whole Emma's legs. Birth becomes death.

Simon has forgotten why there is a rock in his hand. The Aal soothe him with the essence they exude by the waving of their silken hair. One slips down off the wall and curls around his chest and shoulders. The thing at the edge of his mind is satisfied.

He takes Emma into the yard and buries her like a beloved pet. When she is gone, he turns the dining room table on its side and sits behind it, shielded from view of the front window.

There are six Aal on the wall now, on their way to becoming eighteen. Some divide in half, others into multiple smaller sections, adding tiny accents to their designs. The last Aal is with Simon, and he knows what it needs.

———

The Aal are more careful with Simon than they were with Emma. They learn quickly. They want him whole and alive or they have no hands, no feet, no eyes. No way to be a part of this world or shape it in their own image.

Simon lies on the floor and his Aal ensures that his muscles relax, that he is enjoying himself. The silken ebony underbelly of the creature traces every cell of his skin, the only lover he will ever have. Pleasure, pride, relaxation. He knows nothing else, but his hands trace filigree designs into the plush grey carpet.

———

Simon is Simon-and-a-half. Almost a half. This makes it harder to walk when he must go to the toilet or feed himself. The right side of his doubling body is heavy and drags, but so far he still just needs to feed the one. The second absorbs from the first. Emma's stores of food are running low, but the Aal are content and he trusts that there is enough. There are blackberries out in the garden, near where he buried Emma.

Emma.

The Aal give him pleasure when he says her name out loud. It is a feeling like being cradled in his mother's arms, only he can't picture his human mother now. There is only Emma, and the Aal, and his growing twin. He continues the painting and sculpting, filling the garden with statues and shipping them to the galleries under Emma's name. The owners believe she has become a recluse, refusing to talk to anyone, even on the phone. Simon has, too, but not for long. When his brother is finished, they will move to a new city where they can show their creations under Simon's name. The two of them, along with the Aal, will create together.

———

The Aal inside Simon-and-three-quarters moves constantly, twinning itself as it twins him, using the three dimensions of his body to cast intricate patterns through tissue and blood. It ensures that the cells that move stay moving and the cells at rest stay at rest. They learned this from Emma, too late.

The second Simon is eating now, and between them the Simons are using too much food. They won't starve, but they are growing weak. The Aal will remember, and before the next twinning they will make sure that there is more. The human body is inefficient but complexly ornamental. Enjoyable.

Both Simons' hair grows long as they separate, sometimes waving when a breeze comes through the broken window, creating interesting patterns of shadow on the walls when the afternoon sun is low.

––––––––

The twinning is complete.

––––––––

The gallery owners begin to tire of hiding from Emma's work and talking to her unseen assistant on the phone. They insist on a meeting. Simon agrees.

When the owners tell the slender, long-haired man not to bring any more artwork, he smiles with only a hint of sadness. His hair stirs slightly in a barely perceptible breeze, and he hesitates like a man who thinks he might have forgotten something.

"All right," he says, looking pleased to hear his own voice.

"From Emma," he says, and hands them each a small silver charm on a black silk cord, slightly frayed.

The charms are beautifully rendered miniatures of Emma's sculptures. Each is unique, a pattern of lines and curves. A command. The gallery owners thank Simon and hide the charms away in their pockets, hide themselves away in their offices where little black symbols mean even less than they did before. Soon, one by one, they will take the charms out of their pockets and put them on.

36

Graffiti

ROBERT GUFFEY

1. Halation

Halation. Dove. Faded Jeans. Downing. Ice Blue. Domicile. Snow. Chalk Board. Inferno Red. Royal Twilight. Robin's Egg.

These were the first. I will always associate them with the early years, the years when I first figured out what I wanted to be. For so many decades I've been documenting my life with colors. Now I'll try to use words. I hope they're capable of being anywhere near as accurate.

I started my apprenticeship when I was eleven. My two older brothers first tagged an office building when they were fifteen, sixteen. Something like that. My brothers are four, five years older than me. I looked up to them, wanted to be exactly like them. So I picked up a spray can and went with them at night, scaling the sides of freeway overpasses and hopping chain link fences and creeping through alleyways and along the roofs of office buildings and staking out the houses of our enemies. By the time I was eight I knew the secret byways of the city as if I'd built it myself—better than if I'd built it myself. No architect, no matter how masterful, could ever have been as intimate with that city as me and my brothers were in those years.

By the time I was fourteen both of my brothers had been thrown in jail. That's when I saw the truth: this is what happens to young men in this city when they want to express themselves.

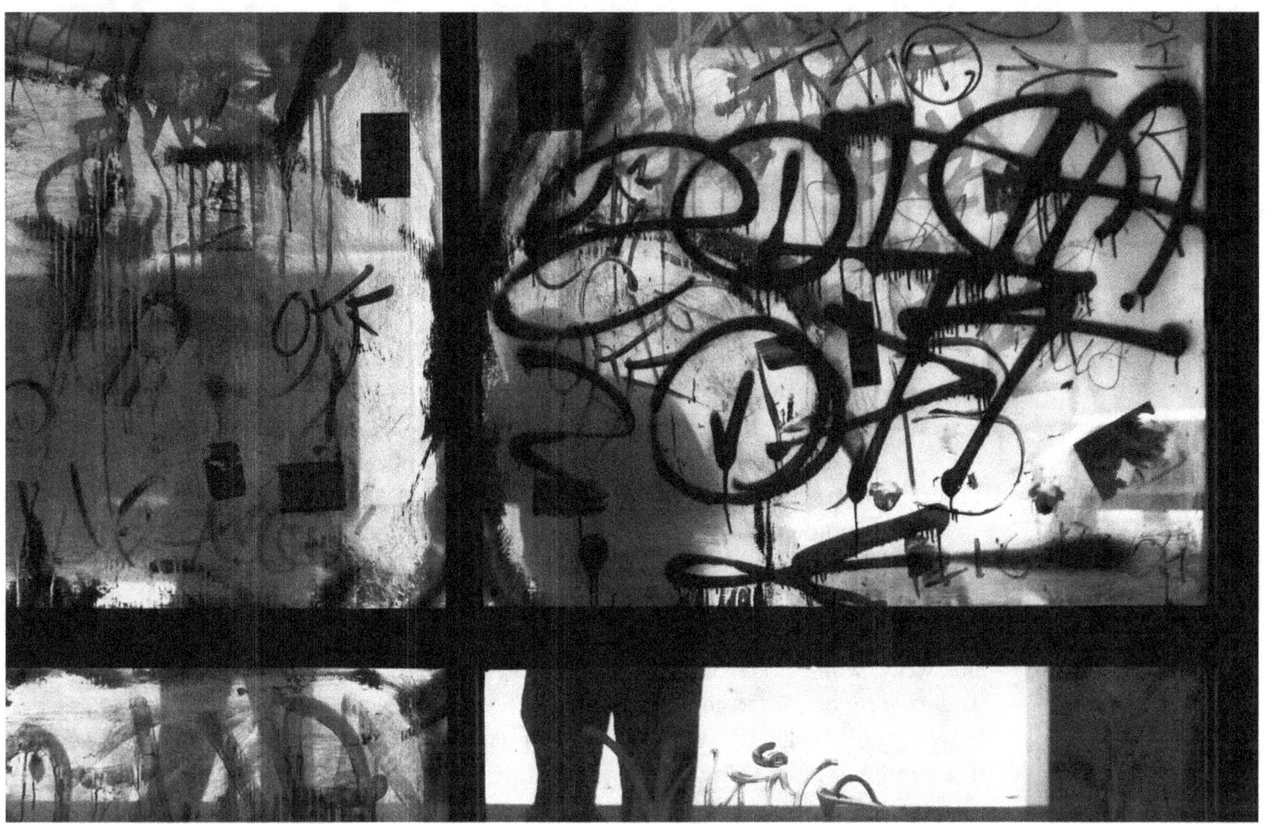

Back then I never thought I'd go to college or have a profession. I figured, this is my neighborhood. This is my life. There's nothing else for me.

I just wanted to leave my mark on something before it was all over.

I didn't think of tagging as a way to destroy other people's property. I genuinely enjoyed the smell of the paint and the look of the design once the image was complete. My brothers? They just liked to fuck shit up. Not me. Sure, it all started as a way to mark my territory, like a dog pissing on a fire hydrant. But after a few years, after feeling the persistent ache in my heart when seeing my favorite designs wiped out over and over again by government hacks, I realized how meaningful tagging was to me. I didn't want to just "fuck shit up." I wanted to improve shit . . . improve it until it wasn't shit anymore.

My counselor seemed to understand me, at least a little bit. I had always thought of Mr. Malevich as just some skinny white dude who worked in a closet-sized office at Wilson High. But when I was caught spray painting over the logo of the school's football team, Malevich was the one who volunteered to help me direct my artistic impulses into more constructive channels. My mom (Dad didn't care, he'd been AWOL for years) pleaded with Malevich to help her turn me around so I didn't end up like my brothers.

Mr. Malevich insisted that "the soul of an artist" was trapped inside me. "With the proper encouragement, it shouldn't be difficult to release his inner artist into the world." He talked that way. He was a bit of a hippie.

Of course, I hated him.

2. Dove

After school every day Mr. Malevich dedicated an hour of his own time to instructing me in the history of the arts. Using the image search function in Google, Malevich took me on a guided, virtual tour through all the great works of centuries past. I wasn't very cooperative, I have to admit. Though I was impressed by the techniques, I couldn't quite connect with the subject matter. That is, until I reached the twentieth century. And one particular painting.

But that happened almost by accident. Malevich didn't show me the piece. I found it on my own.

One afternoon Malevich was called out of his office by the Dean, so he told me to wait in my straight-back wooden chair until he came back.

"Don't get into trouble while I'm gone," he said. I think he was just joking.

The second the door closed, I decided to satisfy my curiosity. What's with this weird white dude? I thought. Why is he goin' out of his way to help me? There's gotta be somethin' more to it.

I thought Malevich was some kind of narc who was setting me up for a fall. The previous summer my brother, Sergio, tried to buy pot off some white dude he didn't know, and it turned out the guy was a cop. Shit like that happened all the time where I lived. So I always had to be on guard. Sergio had warned me: Don't trust no white dude who wants to give you shit for free.

So I punched in Malevich's name into Google to see if the guy was for real. If he existed, there had to be some kind of record of him having a job before Wilson High, right?

Well, I didn't find Malevich's employment record, but what I did find stunned me. I discovered the work of Kazimir Malevich, a Russian painter. I couldn't believe what I was seeing. It was a painting called Black Square completed way back in 1915. The title said it all. A black square bordered by white. I stared into the center of that impenetrable blackness for several minutes. It was nothing more than oil on canvas, and yet for me it was a tunnel that had been dug deep into that flat nondescript surface, a secret passageway leading into the heart of another world, one far different and more magical than ours. The blackness wasn't depressing, not at all. Its mystery intrigued me. Links on Malevich's Wikipedia page led me to similar paintings: Composition No. 10, for example, by Piet Mondrian. What were these abstract blocks of intense color? There was something about its total lack of meaning that enthralled me. This was nothing like the sanctimonious, tepid religious murals I saw in church, with their in-your-face moral teachings that were so impossible to avoid. This was something less . . . and something more. It was nothing except what I wanted it to be.

I was so hypnotized, I didn't even hear Malevich come back into the room.

"Hey," Malevich said, seeing me behind his desk, "I thought I said to stay out of—"

I didn't allow him to finish. "Are you related?" I said.

"To who?"

I hit the back arrow, then pointed at the few Kazimir Malevich paintings displayed on Wikipedia.

Malevich glanced at the abstract images. He smiled. "Ah . . . well, who knows? Perhaps, distantly. I wouldn't know. My great-grandfather was Russian, but I never knew him. Kazimir Malevich was part of the Russian constructivism movement of the early twentieth century. But we haven't gotten that far yet. I'm afraid we're still stuck in the Enlightenment."

"I say we skip ahead."

3. Faded Jeans

So we did.

I couldn't get enough of abstract expressionism, minimalism, Conceptual Art, Pop Art, and, yes, Russian constructivism. I was particularly drawn toward Mark Rothko and Robert Rauschenberg. I didn't even know why. There was something about their work that simply connected to me at a level I couldn't even understand.

Mr. Malevich didn't understand it either, but then again he didn't care to understand. He was just glad he'd succeeded in getting through to this dense, reluctant hooligan using only his knowledge of art. He encouraged me to sign up for a summer art class. I suppose he figured it'd keep me off the street and out of trouble.

He was only half-right.

4. Downing

The art class did keep me off the street. My mom used up her meager savings to invest in paint supplies. She did everything she could to encourage me to pursue this new obsession. I quickly pumped out imitation after imitation of Rothko and Rauschenberg and Mondrian. My art teacher was pleased . . . more than pleased. I received straight A's on assignment after assignment. But after awhile, even this meager recognition wasn't enough to satisfy my new hunger. I desired a far larger canvas.

One night, beginning at twilight, I snuck onto campus with several spray cans and a ladder. I worked very hard, harder than I'd ever worked before, all the way until sunup.

By the next morning, an immense Rothko painting had replaced the fresh new logo for the Wilson High football team.

5. Ice Blue

Everybody was furious with me, of course. My art teacher, the Dean, Mr. Malevich, my mom, the police.

Why did you do it? they all asked over and over again.

I didn't understand. After all, I did exactly what they told me to do. I successfully expressed my inner turmoil. I was making real art this time, not just ugly black squiggles. Hadn't that been the point of "reeducating" me after school for so many months? To improve my technique? To teach me to turn ugliness into beauty?

Nobody agreed with me, particularly not the social workers.

I ended up having to pay for my "crime."

My mom took away my art supplies, and I was forced to work—for free—for the Graffiti Prevention Taskforce in Long Beach. The Mayor of Long Beach had recently declared a two square mile area of the city to be a "Graffiti Free Zone." Kids caught tagging in Long Beach were forced to clean up graffiti within that zone for several months to make up for their "bad" behavior.

I was angry. Indignant. I felt like a puppy whose face was being shoved into his own puddle of urine. I couldn't wait to get back on the street and do something even more spectacular. What would it be next time? City Hall? The police station? The roof of the Mayor's house?

One state representative had been making noises about punishing taggers with public spankings. Jesus. I wanted to find out where this dick lived and spray paint the words "SPANK ME" on his front door. No hi-brow Mondrian icon this time, just straight up FUCK YOU disobedience.

There was one problem: I would be eighteen soon. I'd be forced to serve real jail time for practicing my art. Well, fuck them then, I thought. If that's the way they reward an artistic spirit, then bring it on, motherfuckers.

When I ended up in jail, at least I wouldn't be in there for the same reason my brothers were. That was the only thought that gave me hope. In my mind I couldn't avoid being imprisoned, but at least I could do it with a bit more dignity than my brothers. I knew where I was headed. It was all just a matter of time.

But one day everything . . . everything . . . changed. I was in the back room of the Graffiti Prevention Taskforce Headquarters trying to decide which can of paint to choose for that morning's job. Some kid had sprayed his gang name (THUMPER) in bold black letters on the wall of the Long Beach Main Post Office on Long Beach Blvd. Okay, here we go again, I thought, another sellout job.

Now, instead of throwing paint on a wall with skillful, artistic intent I would be forced to toss paint in haphazard streaks on the wall of the Post

Office. Why was one style of vandalism more acceptable than the other? I didn't understand.

My supervisor, Mark Hernandez, some two-faced Mexican dude in a suit and tie—a fair weather Chicano "revolutionary" whose high ideals had somehow landed him behind a desk filling out forms in triplicate—was constantly riding me to make the paint "blend in" with the background, which is fuckin' impossible. Instead of blending in, the best the Taskforce could do was create incongruous blocks of color.

I had many choices of colors on my state-sanctioned palette: Ice Blue. Halation. Dove. Faded Jeans. Downing. Snow. Chalk Board. Domicile. Inferno Red.

That day I chose the first one I saw: Ice Blue.

This afternoon's team (me and two other pimply-faced kids, Pedro and Armondo) chose not to use the "ghosting" technique Hernandez had requested. "Ghosting" is where you carefully follow the outline of the tagged scrawls rather than block it out entirely. No, sir . . . no ghosting today . . . today we decided it would be simpler to overlay a simple rectangle over the tag.

Armed with brushes and rollers, we did just that.

Sorry, Thumper, I thought, I know how it feels, man. I have to do it. I've got no damn choice.

I felt like a traitor. I felt like Hernandez. While I worked, Hernandez's fat face laughed at me in my mind, spat on what little was left of my self-respect.

After a few hours, the three of us stepped back from the wall, sweat pouring down our backs in the 3:00 P.M. summer heat, and checked out what we had done.

"Looks okay," Pedro said. "Let's knock off for the day."

"Shit, sounds good to me," Armondo said.

I couldn't say anything. I couldn't believe what I was seeing. I was too busy being stunned again.

Rothko. Rauschenberg. Malevich.

While working on the wall, I hadn't really *seen* it.

They were all there, compressed into an Icy Blue rectangle of pure, vivid emotion. *Tranquility.* A block of coolness forever protected from the summer heat. Right there on the front of the main Post Office. Subsidized by the U.S. government. Painted by members of the Graffiti Prevention Taskforce.

Abstract Art, with a capital A, casting its shadow over Thumper's spidery scrawl.

I glanced from building to building, reassessing the handiwork of past Taskforce teams, seeing suddenly the beauty hidden within these haphazard blocks of garish colors. Accidental art. Rothko, as reinterpreted by a child.

What canvases . . . so damn large . . . so many possibilities . . . .

"So what do *you* think?" Pedro said.

"I think it's fantastic," I whispered, "perfect."

Pedro shrugged and said to Armondo, "Okay, well . . . let's go get a beer."

"You got the I.D.?" Armondo said.

"On a hot day like this? Shit, man, I wouldn't leave the house without it. You comin' with us?"

"What?" I said.

"Whose *ass* is your head in today, man? You wanna go get a beer?"

"No . . . no, uh . . . I've got things to do . . . you think you can put my roller and brush away for me when you go back to Headquarters?"

"Okay, yeah, whatever." Pedro shrugged, circled his right temple with his index finger, then led Armondo toward Jack's Liquor Store across the street.

Not many people on the Taskforce liked me. They disapproved of my open hostility toward them. Toward everything associated with the Team.

But now . . .now I saw the whole operation in a vastly different light.

I took off running down Long Beach Boulevard, hopped on the 92 bus, and headed for home.

6. Domicile

I greeted my mom with a smile on my face. I planted a kiss on her chubby cheeks and thanked her for setting me on the right path. She looked startled. So pleased.

I locked myself in my room and began planning. I needed spray paint . . . a lot of it . . . .

7. Snow

The next morning, when I got the phone call, I was half-asleep. The Taskforce was now calling me in for a special job. Some idiot had painted a bunch of squiggly black lines on the side of Acres of Books, the oldest bookstore in the city. Hernandez was confused. Usually tags signify something. These squiggles didn't seem to signify anything in particular. They were just a whole lot of nothing that needed to be removed as soon as possible.

"I can't wait to clean up the mess," I said.

Hernandez said, "Cut the sarcasm, okay? Just get your butt down here now."

"But I'm not being sarcastic, sir," I said. "I really can't wait to get on the job. I understand the situation better now. Really. I understand why the Taskforce is important. We're painting over the trash. We're bringing beauty back to the city. Real beauty."

There was a moment of silence, as if Hernandez didn't know what to say. "Okay," he said, "well . . . get movin'."

"Yes, sir," I said, hanging up the phone and slipping on my tattered work jeans. The same jeans I'd worn the night before.

I grabbed a candy bar out of the refrigerator on the way out the door.

"What about breakfast?" my mom said as she got dressed for work. "There's cereal in the cupboard."

"Not for me," I said, smiling, "no time. I've got work to do. Real work."

8. Chalk Board

The second I stepped through the front door of HQ I demanded to be the supervisor on this job. Every day the boys had the opportunity to volunteer to take on more responsibilities . . . it was part of the GPT's democratic process . . . but for some strange reason, none of the boys ever volunteered to be the supervisor. The supervisor always had to be appointed by Hernandez.

Except today. Except for *me.*

Mr. Hernandez was pleasantly surprised. "I like seeing initiative from a young man like you," he said. "This turnabout . . . it's a wise move on your part."

9. Inferno Red

I chose the color, the instruments, the technique. I was careful about which boy would help paint these three overlapping rectangles, even more careful about how these precious geometric shapes would be laid down on the wall. I had a clear vision in my mind how they should appear. The other boys were confused as to why I was being so pushy.

"Man, you're really tryin' to get in good with Hernandez, ain't you?" said Pedro.

"What a kiss ass," said Armondo.

I didn't listen to them. My brain was obsessed with Inferno Red.

Yes, I chose Inferno Red for this one . . . the perfect shade of discovery.

10. Royal Twilight

The other two boys were ready to quit five minutes before 3:00 P.M. That's when we were allowed to go back home and return to our meaningless lives with our meaningless friends and girlfriends.

I stayed behind. I worked till 4:35. The job had to be done right.

When I was finished, a perfect block of urban-born frustration—the forbidden thought of arson given actual form and substance—had been imprinted on the faded red brick. Forever. Or as long as the building remained standing.

If somebody else tagged it, I could replace it with a brand new color from my palette. And the city would foot the bill.

I stood there in front of my mural, my fists balled at my sides, staring up at that fiery image as pedestrians wandered past, all of them unaware of the conflagration stirring in my skull.

11. Robin's Egg

I returned to HQ, my clothes covered in sweat. I dragged my feet into the back room and returned my partners' tools to their cubbyholes.

"You're late," said Hernandez, appearing in the doorway. "Where've you been?"

"I had to get the job done right."

Hernandez studied my face for a moment, as if trying to gauge my honesty. He nodded and said, "I can't wait to assess it." He turned to leave, then paused in the doorway and added, "Keep this up, Emmanuel, and you might be able to leave the Taskforce early."

"Yes, sir. Thank you, sir." I smiled, but not on the inside. On the inside I was panicking.

Oh no, I didn't want to leave. Not now. Not when I had finally stumbled upon my true calling.

I would just have to do something to get myself assigned back to the GPT. I knew that wouldn't be too difficult.

Possibilities . . .

Halation. Dove. Faded Jeans. Downing. Ice Blue. Domicile. Snow. Chalk Board. Inferno Red. Royal Twilight. Robin's Egg. Concrete. Electric Light. Stucco Pink. Rust Orange. Bulldozer. Neon Blue. Midnight Ocean. Asphalt. Steel Sheen. Urban Camouflage . . .

. . . too many for my brain to contain . . . so many colors I'd never even heard of.

Who could exhaust them all in a lifetime?

Not me.

Not *yet*.

37

_______, John

SYLVIA MARTINEZ BANKS

"So this is what a runaway bride looks like," Jess says as he closes the heavy door to the Jeep behind me. It's one of those Jeeps with canvas attached over the top and sides, opaque plastic windows in the back.

I slip off my fur-lined boot, cross my right leg over my left knee and wave my pedicured foot at him once he's in the driver's seat. "Yeah, that's it. Touch my cold foot, cuz."

He reveals a dimple underneath his stubble and shakes his head.

My cousin Jess is the epitome of a Texan stereotype: cowboy boots, Wrangler jeans, a t-shirt underneath a denim jacket, and a black cowboy hat, of course. Back home in San Francisco, this outfit might be seen during Halloween or in the Castro year-round with some leather chaps, maybe. But here, it's as common as a cold.

"Admitting cold feet is the first step," he says and winks.

I say nothing.

"Nice ring," he says as he shifts gears.

I don't thank him the way you're supposed to thank people when they compliment your stuff. Instead, I size him up with the squinting of my eyes, looking for hidden meaning in his comment.

"Really. No judgment here, Clari. I like the guy."

Jess is like a brother to me, although I've never really had a brother to know if my simile is accurate. He's ten years older than I am, but we've gotten close

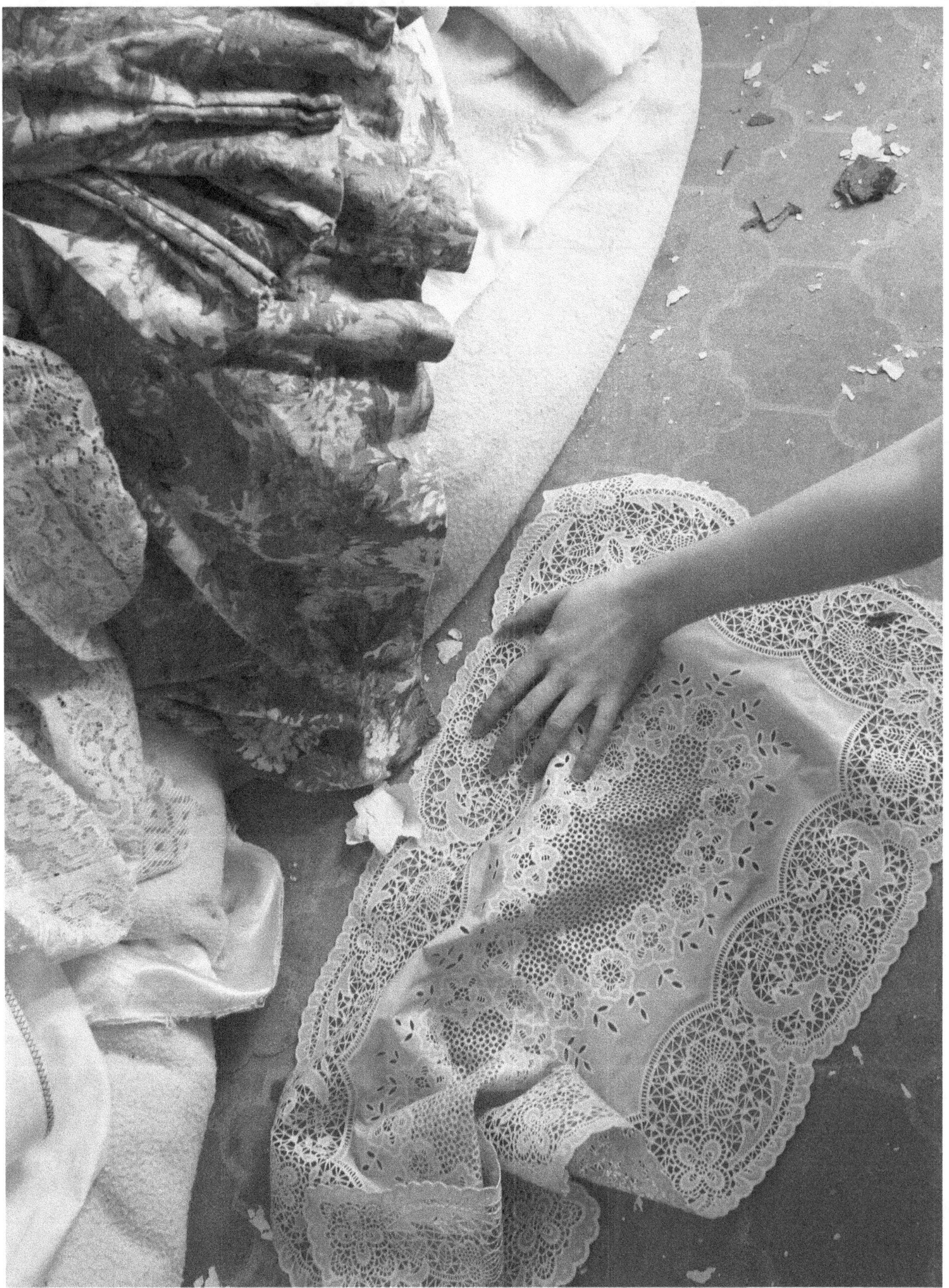

because he's the only cousin of mine from Texas who's traveled to California often. He's one of the few of my Texas family members who isn't afraid to fly.

Maybe that's why he and I get along so well.

"So really, though, Clari. Your wedding's next month, and you decide to come to Texas now . . . just to get away?" His southern drawl is subtle. I wonder how I sound to him.

"Something wrong with that?"

"Not at all, cuz." His inquisitive expression doesn't match his words.

Truth is, though, I think better away from home, and I do want to take it all in, the marriage thing, that is. I'm twenty-five. Young, they say, to get married these days, but I know who I am. I always have. As the wedding gets closer, though, I've had these little feelings of uneasiness, and I can't quite pinpoint what they are.

It all started when my mom asked me what my married name would be. We were shopping for her dress for the wedding, and she was choosing between an off-white dress with a pearly jacket, and a simple but elegant beige one. I liked the way the beige one looked on her, but it wasn't my decision to make, so I said nothing. She ended up picking the off-white one. The way she asked the question was as simple as if she were asking me where I wanted to go for lunch. I had never even thought about what would become of my name, to be truthful. Then I did that night. I took a mental inventory of the surnames of my sisters and aunts and noted that women in my family either replaced their last names with their husband's, or they slid their last name to the middle and input their husband's at the end like on one of those slider tile toys I used to love as a kid. A Razo for a García. A García moving over for a Sánchez.

But they matched their new surnames. I don't look like a Jones.

I asked Marcus that night at our apartment what he thought I should do. His response: Whatever makes you happy. That's when I suddenly got scared.

"So what are your plans while you're here?" Jess asks.

"I don't know. See family. Maybe head out to San Antonio to see the Alamo. Take a ride on the Riverwalk."

"The tourist thing."

"I guess so. Just have a good time."

"Yeah. You city girls get bored of Beeville real fast."

It's true. Beeville is a snoozer, where my dad grew up. He's the only one of his 8 brothers and sisters that left Texas. He joined the Navy and never went back. Thank you, Dad. One thing I'll give Beeville, though, is that it has everything you need for a life: A hospital, a Wal-Mart, one high school, a bowling alley, a movie theater, a morgue.

"I'll take you up to the Lake on Sunday if you want to see the new lake house."

"That's right. You and Gracie actually did it." Gracie is Jess' twin sister who lives in Austin. They kept talking about building a house out by Lake Medina and they actually did it. It's supposed to be a mirror image house where his side matches hers. "I can't wait to see it."

The ride from the airport to Beeville is two hours, but we stop mid-way to get some dinner. It's a restaurant that looks like a house in the middle of nowhere. It's called Shorty's Place.

"Is this a real Texas roadhouse?" I ask Jess.

He gives me a look that makes me believe there really is such a thing as a stupid question. He opens the door to the restaurant, and a few men tip their hat to me as I walk in. It's funny to me the way men are courteous to women around here. It's not flirtatious. At least I don't think so. It's more like that's just how things are done here. I actually like it.

My salad shows up with brown squiggly, crunchy things on top, and my ranch dressing on the side of my chicken strips looks odd. The waitress seems to notice my confusion, and I see Jess notice the waitress' long legs. Men. "Everything okay, ma'am?" Ma'am is a name I become accustomed to while I'm here. It makes me think of a good way to explain the *usted* pronoun to my students.

"Everything is fine, thank you." As soon as she is out of hearing range, I ask Jess, "Dude, what's up with my ranch dressing?"

He laughs. "You're kidding me, right? It's gravy, not ranch dressing."

I am disgusted. I tell Jess how I've been on this South Beach Diet for a few weeks now to get ready for wearing my swimsuit in Maui. I don't have my list of okay foods with me, but something tells me gravy is not on that list. I eat the chicken dry.

"You don't need to lose any weight. If anything, you need to eat the gravy."

I shrug off the vague compliment and take the gravy cup off my plate. "So, what's new with you, Jess?"

"Nothin' at all with me. My body shop is doing fine. The economy's down the tubes, but people still get in accidents."

"That's good for you, I guess."

"Yeah."

"How's Junior doing? I haven't seen him in a while."

"You know he's pitching for Texas A & M International now, right." He eats his ribs with his fingers. "Partial scholarship."

I squeeze the lemon wedge into my water. "That's great! Where's that?"

"Laredo."

"Do you get to see any of his games?"

"The season doesn't start until spring."

"Oh yeah, that's right."

He reminds me that it's November, but that pretty much means nothing to me since I've never kept up with the seasons of sports. I wipe the corners of my mouth with a napkin and then put the napkin on my plate.

"I can drive you out to the Alamo tomorrow if you want."

"Perfect," I say. "So Jess, can I ask you a question?" Segue has never been my thing. Not with the people I'm closest to, anyway.

"Shoot."

"When you were married to Carmen, I can't remember. Did she take your last name?"

"Yeah, but I got it back in the divorce." He grins.

I smile and let out a small laugh. Since it's been a few years since their split, it seemed okay to bring it up. Jess and Carmen were married for a little over a year. She got pregnant soon after they got married, but she lost the baby the day before the Fourth of July. I remember that detail because I was watching fireworks at the Berkeley Marina with Marcus when Jess called to tell me.

He was silent at first, so I thought that maybe the call had dropped. But then he kept clearing his throat, and he seemed to struggle to speak.

"Jess?"

"The baby . . ."

"Jess." The fireworks went from decorating the sky to sounding like gunshots.

"Our baby died." Then he told me how they went to have the ultrasound done the day before to find out the sex of the baby, and instead found out the baby wasn't alive anymore.

It would have been a girl.

Jess and Carmen were never the same because Carmen was never the same after that. In fact, she seemed to change into a different person. She changed her hair color, lost a lot of weight, and never had any fire in her smile anymore. She seemed like a puppet without a hand. She ended up moving to New York with one of her aunts. I think Junior was the only thing that kept Jess from losing it. Junior is Jess' son from a high school relationship.

"Why are you asking, Clari? What's Marcus' last name?"

"Jones."

"You'll be Mrs. Jones, then?"

"I have no idea. It sounds funny on me, doesn't' it?"

"It sounds fine to me. You'll get used to it."

The fear makes another appearance, but I dismiss it fast. "I guess."

We walk into our grandmother's house, the same house where my dad and Jess' mom grew up. I feel tall, even though I'm only 5'2". Everyone who comes to Beeville always pays her a visit first, as if her house is a tollbooth into the city. The ceilings are low, and the ground feels like it's up on planks, if that makes any sense. The house is like one big rectangle; you can see the end of it as soon as you walk in. First you're in the living room, then you're in the bedroom, and then you're in the kitchen. And that's it for the big stuff. The kitchen has a tiny room with a washer and dryer on one side, and there's a door leading to a bathroom on the other side. The back door leads to a block of unkempt land. Her house is the only one on this block. That would be unheard of in the Bay Area. I always find it hard to believe she and my grandfather raised eight kids here in this tiny house.

She divorced him after 34 years. Why bother at that point, I asked my mom when I found out about their divorce. She then told me about a baby born out of an affair he had with a woman much younger than him. Supposedly, he looks just like my dad.

"Hi," I say to my grandmother in Spanish. She is sitting on her bed watching a variety show on a Spanish station hosted by a man with a staticky voice that sounds falsely excited. Aside from my father being her son and my being named after her mother, I feel no connection to her.

"Gracie?" she asks. There are three Gracies in our family, but I attribute her error to being 91.

"No, Abuela. Yo soy Clarissa."

"¿Una de las hijas de Joseph?"

"Sí." I give her a hug. She is so small, 4'10 and 90 lbs., maybe. Her short, fine hair is a blend of muted browns, and her spirited brown eyes have a bluish hint to them. Her skin is wrinkly and dark. She doesn't say anything more to me, but she continues to look at me. Her hair has to be dyed, I wonder to myself.

I walk around the rectangle and look at the pictures that are all over the house. Some are on the walls; some are on shelves and tables. I stop at one of my parents on their wedding day, which strikes me as odd because they've been divorced since I was two. My mom is breathtakingly beautiful, happiness in human form, wearing a white pillbox hat over her bobbed, dark hair. I've always been told I look like her when she was my age, and I now feel how much of a compliment that is. She's wearing bright red lipstick that outlines a large, genuine smile. Her skin looks so fair and so smooth, and her brown eyes glimmer. My dad looks cologne-model-handsome, in his sailor uniform with his dark hair parted to one side and slicked back like young Elvis. He's smiling just as real as my mom. I notice his head leaning slightly on hers, and her hand on his, gripping it gently. I remember seeing this photo before, but it doesn't have an effect on me until now. I wish I could take it with me.

I see my wedding invitation on my grandmother's refrigerator, secured by a magnet that is two red dice, a six and a one. It says Las Vegas in tiny letters between the parallel dots on the six. I know she won't be there because she doesn't fly, but I like seeing something I sent out a month ago in a new setting.

"Clari's the one that's getting married next month," Jess says in a loud voice that catches me off guard. He speaks to her in English. I forgot. Most of my generation of cousins in Texas don't speak Spanish even though all their parents do. I do because it's one of my loves - what I studied in college. I started teaching high school Spanish two years ago.

"Oh," she says.

I stand next to her kitchen table and see her signature snack: a jar of instant Folger's coffee next to half a bag of Cheetos folded over. My dad commented to me when I came with him once that that's been her afternoon snack for as long as he can remember. Maybe there's something in the combination that keeps her ticking.

I'll stick to South Beach, though. I've lost 6 lbs. already, although I miss bagels.

"We're going to go now, Grandma," Jess yells. I feel rescued by these words. I feel bad that I don't feel comfortable in my own grandmother's house, but sometimes things are just what they are. I've had a close relationship with my mom's mother, so I guess that's why I never feel like I've been missing much.

"What now?" Jess asks.

"I don't know. Maybe head back to your parents' house. I'm kind of tired." They have two extra rooms, so I always stay with them while I'm here. Jess usually stays there instead of at his house when I visit, too.

"Works for me."

I can't sleep. I look around my cousin Gracie's room and think it must be in the same shape as when she moved away to college. Her furniture is an antique white, and the walls and bedding are different shades of pink. There are cheerleading trophies and photos of her at different stages of her life. My favorite is the one of her smiling as she crouches down next to a golden retriever. Her giant smile shows her missing front teeth.

I open my laptop and instantly have Internet access through a network named Wally.

I am in the middle of searching for information on the Alamo when Marcus calls. I texted him when I landed that I got in okay, but I haven't called him since.

"Hey Love." His voice sounds foreign from where I sit.

"Hey."

"You having a good time?"

"So far. Just tired. I want to get some rest because Jess and I plan to head out to San Antonio in the morning."

"Seeing the Alamo, right?"

"Yeah."

"Okay. I won't keep you long. Just wanted to say good night."

"Okay."

"I love you, Clari."

"I love you, too. I'll talk to you later."

"Okay. Good night."

I press the end button once, and then press it again in a long hold to turn off the phone.

I decide to read instead of perusing the information on the Alamo site. I open a book to a story I started last week about a guy considering joining an exclusive club in which he has to assume the identity of a famous artist. He finds his actual life boring and is searching for something to make life more exciting. I finish the story and learn that he becomes paranoid when he thinks he also has to assume the same death that artist did in his own life. In the end he's running away from this club, by leaving his job and leaving town.

I'm still not sleepy, so I put my headphones on and listen to the new Jason Mraz I downloaded before I left California.

Calm down, deep breaths
And get yourself dressed instead
Of running around and pulling on your threads
And breaking yourself up.

I imagine in great detail about which famous artist I'd choose if I were to join a club like the guy in the story. Frida Kahlo, of course. I imagine I am her, joined eyebrows and braids and all, in her blue house that I visited when I studied abroad in Mexico City. I imagine intense physical pain that echoes the pain I feel inside about my marriage, about my life. I can smell the oily paints in the stained pallet in my hand as I sit in front of my easel, blank canvas before me.

I re-open my laptop to find out when and how she died because I realize I know many things about her, but I don't know that.

Hold your own,
Know your name
And go your own way.
And everything will be fine.

I awake and turn my phone back on. There's a text message that says <good morning> from Marcus. I don't respond. I head out to the living room in my pajamas instead.

"Jess, do your parents have a treadmill here?"

"We have a road outside."

"Never mind."

"Good morning, *Tía Lucía*," I say. My aunt comes out of her room fully dressed, made-up and all.

"Good morning, *Clarissa. ¿Dormiste okay?* I made some desayuno. Está on la estufa for you." She always speaks in a fast Spanglish that sounds conflicted, like each language is fighting against each other.

I answer in English only. *"I slept fine. Thank you. And thank you for making breakfast."*

I look on the stove. Thick white tortillas, eggs, bacon, and some cinnamon rolls. I take a mental inventory of the protein and then shrug. Being respectful requires that I eat South Texas instead of South Beach this morning.

"Jesse *dijo* that y'all *van a ir a* the Alamo *hoy.*"

"Yeah. I've actually never been."

"*Tienes que ir a* Goliad, pues, too."

"*What's Goliad?*"

"It's *donde* the Presidio La Bahía *está.*"

"*Hm. Never heard of it.*"

"More lives were lost there than at the Alamo and San Jacinto combined," Jess says not even lifting his eyes away from the local paper he's reading. I realize at this moment that even though he doesn't speak Spanish, he has to understand a lot having grown up around his mom's hybrid language.

In the morning light I notice Jess' hairline is receding. When does that happen for men? Does it happen to women? There are so many things I don't know.

"I'm off to *la iglesia ahora*, y'all." My constantly thinking mind pauses at her last word, y'all, and I'm excited that I have discovered an English translation for vosotros for my students back at home.

"*Okay, Tia. See you later. Have a great day.*"

While eating breakfast, I look up Presidio La Bahía on my computer. I am intrigued that Goliad is an anagram created out of Father Miguel Hidalgo's name, the priest said to be the father of Mexico's Independence. They just dropped the H and switched the letters around. But why not just name it Hidalgo instead of making it all complicated by scrambling the letters? I'll have to look it up more tonight.

I tell Jess I'll check it out on my next visit, but that I'd still like to go to the Alamo today. "Sure thing," he says, folding his newspaper closed. He then looks at my plate. "Want some gravy with your breakfast burrito?"

"Shut up."

On the ride to San Antonio, I finally text Marcus back. <on my way to alamo>

< i remember>

<haha>

"So what's really going on with you, Clari?"

I inhale a deep breath. The skyline in Texas looks like a blend of translucent grays, like a watercolor painting that's still wet. I don't think I've ever seen a blue Texas sky. "What do you mean?"

"Why are you here?" He doesn't look at me when he asks me this.

"I just needed to get away for a bit."

"Why?" He looks at me now.

I exhale. "I just needed a break from it. The planning. It's like the wedding's all anyone talks about."

"Come on. Give me a break. You women live for this stuff."

Frida Kahlo enters my mind and I wonder what she felt before she married Diego Rivera. Did she have doubts before such a rocky marriage? Why did she marry him again after they got divorced? I know he was twenty years older than her, but how old was she when she got married the first time?

"Jess, I had a bridal shower two weeks ago, and my mom cried over a porcelain teapot from Macy's."

"Aw. Coffee pots are what really get me."

I smile and shake my head. "Really, Jess. It's just so out of hand. And then did I tell you about the bachelorette party last weekend? One of my bridesmaids threw up in my shoe and there was a cake shaped like a penis."

He's smiling now, teeth showing. "You didn't like the penis cake?"

I aim a heavy sigh towards my cousin. I definitely appreciated the parties, but I would have enjoyed them more if they didn't feel so much like a Bon Voyage party. In Spanish, they're even called *Despedida de Soltera*: Farewell to being single. Like I'm supposed to morph into one entity with my husband once I say, *I do*. "Can we just drop it and go to the Alamo, cuz?"

"As you wish, Clari." He looks at me with sincere eyes. "Just let me know if something else is bothering you. You know you can talk to me."

I do know that, but there are just some things that seem so taboo to talk about a month before your wedding, after the invitations have been sent out and put on refrigerators with dice magnets.

To my surprise, there is no entrance fee to get into the Alamo. I pick up a brochure and the first sentence is that the Alamo was originally named *Misón San Antonio de Valero*. Does everything have a former name? The line is long, so I read as I wait. Jess is reading, too. By the end of the brochure, I learn that the Alamo symbolizes a heroic struggle against overwhelming odds—where men made the ultimate sacrifice for freedom.

I think of my friend Rich back home who's brother was recently killed in Iraq. Men are still dying for our freedom. Rich's brother, Army Sgt. Jonathan Martínez, was just 29.

As we make our way around the side, the first part of our self-guided tour is a look at a low horizontal marble wall, etched with the names of the heroes who died here. From where we walk, the last name on the list is the first thing I see.

______, *John*
a Black Freedman

Everyone else on the list has a last name except for him, so his name stands out more to me. I wonder how this John didn't get a last name. If he had been a slave at one time, wouldn't he have assumed the name of his master? Maybe he dropped it when he became free? There are quite a few other Johns on the list, but they all have last names like Thomson, Wilson, Flanders, Jones.

Jess shows me the six flags and tells me that that's how many flags have flown over Texas, and that that's where the theme parks got their name.

I am taking it all in, so I just nod and raise my eyebrows. My mind is in academic mode, and I am loving it all. And even though we have already passed surname-less John, he is still with me.

I take my hand off the wall after reading a sign to keep off the walls. Oops. But all the carved graffiti tells me my tactile crime was nothing. I read the carvings as we weave into different parts of the Alamo. Jimmy loves Maria and Bobby was here. Someone else just carved a star.

As we get further into the mission, there are display cases with guns, artillery, clothing worn by Davy Crockett, who I learn didn't even like the name Davy. What's up with that? People knew that but just kept calling him something he didn't want to be called? In one of the cases, there are bits and pieces of plates, burnt buttons, coins, keys. Nothing seems whole around here, yet all the pieces are so powerful despite being fragments.

My phone vibrates three times against my thigh. <call me>

I tell Jess I plan to make a call outside, and he is so busy reading the Alamo information next to the display cases that he hardly notices. Isn't he from Texas? Shouldn't he know all this stuff already? Then again, I'm from San Francisco and have never been to Alcatraz. Visiting a jail has no appeal to me.

"You okay, Clarissa?" Marcus rarely calls me by my full name, so I know he's concerned.

"I'm good," I say as I walk next to a stream with carp in its murky waters. They move their thick, puckered lips to the surface. Are they searching for air or for food? I notice a very old couple looking at me as I talk. They smile with super-perfect teeth that I realize they must be dentures. I aim a slight upcurve of my lips towards them. "The Alamo is pretty cool."

"Are you sure you're good?" I see the couple still smiling at me. I exhale.

I want to tell Marcus that no, I'm not. Good. That I'm scared. That I don't know why I'm so scared when our relationship is everything I've ever dreamed of. How I even had a tangible list for what kind of man I wanted to marry and he fit every characteristic on that list. But how I'm so, so scared, because all the marriages around me fail. And the ones that survive, don't seem happy.

I want to say into my cell phone how when I get scared, I run. Put on my running shoes. Get on a plane. Fly. But how can I tell him all this without him thinking it's about him? It's not him I'm running from.

Calm down, deep breaths
And get yourself dressed instead
Of running around and pulling on your threads

And breaking yourself up.

I imagine I am Frida again, and I wish I could show Marcus the painted self-portrait in front of me. I would show him the fear in my head with images above my joined eyebrows, but below my braided hair. I would paint twelve tiny orange pills from my youth, my first love Joey Marquez holding his beautiful baby boy, red dice with the dots too blurry to see what the roll was, the photo of my young and smiling parents, torn apart. And a girl, running on the inside of a wheel, going nowhere but wanting to. So wanting to. Or at least thinking she wants to. Beneath me would be a Lone Star for Texas, a Mona Lisa smiling sun for California, and a green Alameda Park for Mexico City, with the 4 P.M. rain coming down in a torrent, of course. Each place would float independently of each other, but all holding my face up. Above me would be the faces of my mothers, and the mothers of my mother and father and their mothers, too. The sky would be blue and gray, more gray than blue.

I would put the Alamo's hero wall in there, too, and I would put "__________, John" in there, but he'd be the first on the list instead of the last.

"I'm good, Marcus. No need to worry. Kay?"

I can feel the air of his sigh through my cell phone. "Okay."

Then he says something sweet, I know from his tone, but I am too lost in all my thoughts to really hear. Instead, I think of Frida again and ponder her death at age 47. I have yet to decide if it was because of complications resulting from a pulmonary embolism, or a cleverly disguised suicide like some people believe.

"I'll be home in a couple days, Marcus," I say. "Don't worry about me." I look at the carp, still searching for something but never finding it. Then I notice the bench is empty where the old couple was. I look all around the courtyard, and they are nowhere to be seen.

38

Gesso

LOIS BARR

We held the egg yolks in our upturned hands as the whites slithered through our fingers down the drain. Then we placed the yolks on paper towels. Gently, we slid the plump yellows around to absorb any remaining globules of white. Judith, our tempera instructor, had taught us to puncture them with our palette knives and funnel them through a fold at the edge of the towels into plastic flasks. How quickly the sac emptied, leaving just a yellow stain on the paper: a simple pleasure at a point in my life when not too much surprised or pleased me. Then we filled jars with water and chose our subjects from the flowers Judith had cut in the gardens.

A new student slipped in while we stood at the sink. She wore a long white suede coat with the lapels turned up so that only the tips of her spiky platinum hair and her big gray glasses were visible. When she removed the coat, she lost all of her volume. Several layers of beige Italian-knit sweat clothes hung on her skeletal frame. I examined her as she took off the sunglasses. Her narrow face made her brown eyes look enormous. She was on the young side. Thirty or so. At my age everyone looks young. I got closer to examine her case of supplies. Her pigment jars contained colors so intense that I wanted to grab them, but I could tell my scrutiny made her uncomfortable.

Judith welcomed her, and asked us to introduce ourselves. We complied eagerly, but the new student didn't say her name and avoided looking at us.

"Have you ever studied tempera before?" Judith asked.

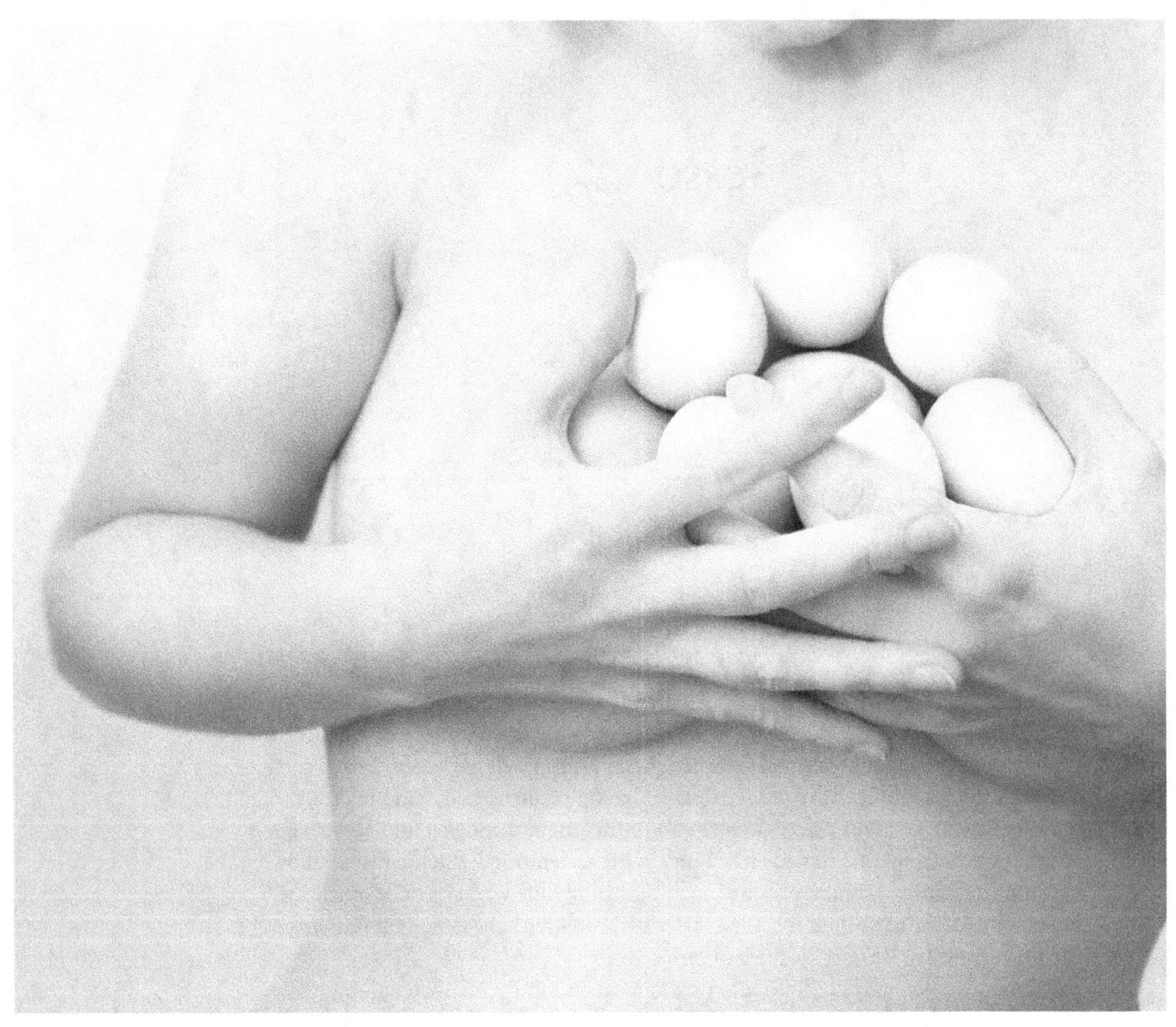

"Yes, well, sort of . . . I . . . worked with *Hay viyer* . . ."

I was so distressed by her mispronunciation of Javier, that I didn't catch the fellow's last name. She said she had studied with him as a private student for seven years. Judith was keen to hear the details, and she seemed to know not only who Javier was but that he had moved to New York City. Judith joked about Javier's bad manners and his ill-reputed gesso. She called it a toxic goop. The woman shrugged her shoulders and said, "He never taught me how to mix it. He always prepared my boards before I got there. But I've been trying to make my own gesso for a while."

"Where on earth did you get a recipe?" Judith was eager to know.

"I didn't, I mean I just tried to figure it out."

While I listened in on their conversation, the others set about painting. Then Judith went to coach them with their work. I wanted to hear more of this woman's story. I asked her again about the recipe for gesso, but all she would say was that she thought Javier had withheld an ingredient. Evidently, her paint never again glided onto to the surface the way it did with the concoction he mixed in his studio. She had followed the vague indications in Renaissance master Cennino D'Andrea Cennini's treatise: she boiled rabbit skins and mixed in gypsum in varying amounts in search of the perfect background for her boards. I asked specific questions about proportions to no avail. I decided to offer her one of my clayboards that I'd picked up on sale, but she declined it, taking out instead a two-by-three-inch piece of wood with a milky finish, a set of Kolinsky sable brushes, and a small gold mirror.

The hum of fluorescent lights accompanied our work at tables arranged in rows. The long narrow room always seemed intimate and safe when we were busy painting. In front Millie and Priscilla sat head to head, both immaculately coiffed, in starched robin's egg blue dental smocks provided by Millie's brother. They worked hurriedly from photographs. They had a tennis game right after class. Across from them Suzanne painted sensuous October roses strewn randomly on dark green velvet and forgot her fretful newborn baby for a few hours. Behind Suzanne, a retired music teacher, Jocelyn, cautiously mixed a Windsor violet and a cadmium lemon. She compared her muddy gray with dismay to the rich hue Judith had produced in the demonstration. Jane, also a retired teacher, prepared a detailed pencil sketch of holly leaves and berries. I, a professor of Spanish on sabbatical, was pressing pesky little air bubbles out of my paint with the palette knife. Hesitant as to how to approach my subject, I finally began, inspired by the amber reflections of the vase I'd brought from home, the arching lines of the thistle leaves, and the plump lavender blossoms.

Some time later I tired of the thistles. The lavender seemed dull and the composition was awkward; moreover, I had made a hole in the clayboard from lifting my mistakes. So, I got up to stretch and saw that the new student was executing a replica of her hand in the act of painting. You could see the purple veins that stood out on her pale flesh, even the hairs on her minute paintbrush. She had painted the mirror and the painting itself. Proportion, shading, glints of light, all executed in miniature. Although it wasn't finished, it promised to be a little masterpiece. As I bent over to take a closer look, she flinched, so I backed away and returned to my work.

At noon I joined our new classmate at the sink to wash my brushes and palette. I wanted to ask her more about her work, but she quickly pulled her sleeves down—not before I saw the scars—dried her hands and backed away. She packed up her supplies and left silently. Hastily, I crammed my brushes and pigments into my bags and followed her out the door. She got into in a silver Karmann Ghia and sped away. Without thinking, I followed her. The work on Alfonsina Storni's poem, "Voy a dormir/I Am Going to Sleep," could wait. My research on the poet who'd walked into the sea at Mar del Plata in 1938 to end it all was less compelling than this mysterious painter.

The woman sped down the winding wooded roads to a walled Normandy mansion, a massive new construction in a ravine close to the lake. Lacking the courage to follow her in, I sat in the car out front and sketched the stone wall and the turret. The drawing was dreadful, so I ripped it out. I felt strange and lonely sitting there, so I called my colleague Natalie who lives nearby. Natalie didn't know the woman's name, but she knew from neighborhood gossip that the woman's husband had custody of their four kids. He'd taken them away from her, and the only thing she'd gotten was the newly built mansion. According to Natalie, the woman didn't talk to anyone and rarely left home. Rumor had it that the entire house was empty; she had sold the furniture to pay the mortgage and the utility bills. When Natalie inquired about my research project, I made an excuse to get off the phone.

That night, I pulled out my prized possession, a recent acquisition. On yellowing onionskin, I held a handwritten version of Alfonsina Storni's last poem that predated the one that was found alongside a good-bye letter to her son. I had outlined all the changes she had made in the second version and had begun to analyze how her choice of imperative verbs reflected her resolve to control her destiny in the face of advanced cancer. In my last poetry seminar I had unwittingly mentioned some of the variants and my brightest student Julián Sangredo picked right up on it. He interrupted my lecture to ask where I had seen those changes. I tried to get him off the trail by mentioning that I recollected seeing comments about them in Gómez Paz or Forgione's work, but he said, *"¡Bah, es imposible!* No one says anything about any earlier version; I'm absolutely sure." I changed the topic by announcing the rubrics for their final paper, but he stayed after class to grill me with questions. I told him I'd be more than willing to set up a time to talk if he would e-mail me. But why should I meet with that arrogant little Argentine boy when he's chosen to write his dissertation with Otto? Won't they be surprised when I pull this breakthrough out of my hat? Now that Sangredo was on my trail, I needed to finish my work very soon.

I calmed myself down remembering that he was just a graduate student, and I had plenty of time to craft my monograph; furthermore, I was rather tired of the intrigue in the department and intrigued by tempera painting. Ten more glorious months to indulge myself. I deserved it. My first sabbatical in twenty-one years of teaching. I put Alfonsina Storni back into her file and went to the computer to investigate my new fascination.

Something about this isolated and frightened painter captivated me. Using her address, I found her name, Bianca Jennings; furthermore, I ran an online credit check and learned that she had amassed an enormous amount of debt. There were no websites with her artwork. For the next several days I neglected my research to observe her house. I sketched the stone edifice and the weeds growing through crevices in the walkways. Nothing pleased me. Once I stayed until after dark watching for signs of life but observed only a rectangle of light coming from the turret. Then yesterday at dusk, as I drove up, I noticed that the wrought iron gate was slightly ajar.

I bounded out of my car and followed the winding flagstone driveway up to the house. One door of the carriage house was ajar, so I walked in. Her old silver roadster seemed even smaller in the enormous space. In the dim light I could see two walls of cages. As I approached a cage, I was greeted by eager whiskered noses and pink eyes. The floor was littered with bits of lettuce, pellets of food and pellet-sized droppings. Near the doorway to the house were a laundry sink and a rough-hewn table with bloodstains that had soaked into the wood—burnt umber and bright crimson. Above the table on the wall a hunting knife hung from a hook. The smell from the animals indicated that their cages needed cleaning, but the odor as I slipped quietly into the house made me gag.

I followed a humming sound to the kitchen that had oversized stainless steel appliances, but no table or chairs. There was one large pot on the cook-top, a sieve, and a funnel. In the pot several rabbit carcasses had turned a grayish-green. Their bloody fur was in the trash compactor. I opened the refrigerator. It was empty except for a carton of yogurt. On the marble counter sat a small jar of white tablets, a mortar and pestle, and a spoon smeared with yogurt and, stuck to the yogurt, white granules. I ran my finger on the counter and found traces of the white chalky powder. Suddenly the silence of the house became oppressive, and I called Bianca's name as loudly as I could. My cries had the odd reverberation of nightmares or those silly teenage horror movies. And I continued to call out to her as I raced up the marble stairs and ran from empty room to empty room. Finally, I came to an oak doorway that I thought would lead to the stone tower. I entered a narrow winding stairway dimly lit by small oblong leaded glass windows. At the landing at the top of the stairs—darkness. I groped the unfinished plywood walls and found a door. It was locked, so I banged with both fists. I could tell from the hollow sound of the wood that it was flimsy, so I heaved my body weight against it over and over until the door gave way.

The soft light of sunset came in from a skylight. I found the switch and turned on an overhead light. The round walls were covered with minute tempera paintings and in the middle of the room there was a tall metal bookcase filled with jars marked *gesso*. Behind the bookcase, Bianca lay on a canvas colored cot. She was pallid, barely distinguishable from the bed's surface. I held her slender wrist to check for a pulse. It was weak. I wiped a bit of whitish foam from the side of her mouth and shook her arms, but there was no response. I pushed vigorously on her chest and felt a rib give way. For what seemed an eternity, my breath ballooned into her body. When she resumed breathing, she opened her eyes, stared at me in terror and closed them again.

"Bianca, can you hear me?" I shook her gently.

"I want to sleep. Please, turn down the lights." She responded so softly I wasn't sure she had spoken. My effort to save her seemed futile and cruel. But I couldn't leave her alone to die. There was no phone in the room, so I ran downstairs to the kitchen and called 911. As soon as I caught my breath, I returned to her studio but avoided staring at her inert body. Pacing back and forth in the small room, I examined miniature portraits of her bony feet, of her scarred wrists, of her unsmiling mouth. I opened a casement window to listen for the ambulance. When I heard it in the distance, I slipped a dozen bottles labeled *gesso* and several jars of pigment into my bag and hurried downstairs. I pulled bolts and latches and opened wide the arched double doors at the entryway. Then I ran back to the kitchen and slipped out through the garage. My heart pounding louder than the engine of my car, I rounded the corner of her street as the ambulance raced by me.

Today I returned to tempera class. My classmates were assembled at the sink cracking eggs. Jocelyn said they had missed me, and I mumbled something about being tied up with my beloved poet. Priscilla observed that I had lost weight. Suzanne offered to show me the technique Judith had taught the week before, and Jane related that the woman who painted the miniature of her hand hadn't come back. "She was too good for us," said Millie with a knowing smile.

Judith brought in a basket full of fall flowers and set them out for us to choose. I selected the thistles. I made a rapid sketch. The proportions were perfect. Then I set out the water, egg yolk, and brushes and chose my pigments: violet, alizarin crimson, terra vert, white, cobalt blue and ultramarine. As I began to mix the colors, Judith bent over to check how I was doing. I flinched. She picked up one of my new jars of pigment and ran her finger across the smooth surface of my little wooden panel. Her raised eyebrow formulated a question. I averted her eyes. Focusing my attention on the palette, I added a drop of yolk to the grains of color, and began to grind them with my knife. With quick elegant strokes I formed the thistle's head. The paint glided ever so smoothly onto the board. The lavender was intense and luminous.

"Gesso" first appeared in *Ekakshara*, June 2009.

Contributor's Notes

1 STEVE HIMMER. *I See What You Mean*

Steve Himmer is author of the novel *The Bee-Loud Glade*, and his stories have appeared in a number of journals and anthologies. He edits the webjournal Necessary Fiction, teaches at Emerson College in Boston, and has a website: *http://www.stevehimmer.com.*

*Bears are a subject I come back to again and again, almost helplessly. I've written an academic thesis about polar bears, an (unpublished) novel about black bears, and short stories about both of those and grizzly bears, too. But when I saw a photograph of Lawrence Argent's sculpture "I See What You Mean" standing outside and peering into Denver's convention center, it was like seeing something fundamental about bears, something I'd struggled to realize about them, made tangible, giant, and blue. I wish I could say the story came quickly after that, but they rarely do. I tried writing from the bear's point of view, and I tried other approaches, but the image of that big blue bear stewed in my head for months before I finally asked myself what kind of person, with what kind of life, might the sight of that bear really impact. And once that protagonist became clear to me, the story came together. Or at least the first draft of it did.

2 MICHAEL MENDOLIA. *Transparent Tigers and Towers of Blood*

Michael Mendolia's fiction can be found in the journals *Ganymede* and *Diverse Voices Quarterly*. He holds a Ph.D. from the University of Pennsylvania, and currently lives in Paris.

*I find Jorge Luis Borges' short story "Tlon, Uqbar, Orbis Tertius" intoxicating. Its remarkable premise involves a massive conspiracy of intellectuals who document an entire imaginary world and even sneak forged entries about it into encyclopedias. In my story, "Transparent Tigers and Towers of Blood," whose title is a phrase taken from the English translation of the Borges story, I tried to recreate the tension between a formal, academically rigorous narrator and a mysterious situation into which deeper investigation only sparks further befuddlement. As in the Borges story, the truth remains tantalizingly obscure, and it is unclear which of numerous potential realities will prevail.

3 FRED SKOLNIK. *Creativity*

Fred Skolnik is the editor in chief of the 22-volume second edition of the *Encyclopaedia Judaica*, winner of the 2007 Dartmouth Medal. He was born in New York and has lived in Israel since 1963. Now writing full time he has published over 30 stories in the past 2 years (in *TriQuarterly, Gargoyle, The MacGuffin, Minnetonka Review* (Pushcart nomination), *Los Angeles Review, Prism Review, Underground Voices, Lunch Hour Stories, 34th Parallel, River Poets Journal, Third Wednesday, Sonar4, Skive, Neon, Johnny America,* etc.). His novel *The Other Shore* will be published by Aqueous Books in 2011 and his novella *Like Soldiers Everywhere* has appeared as an ebook (Cantarabooks).

*The first paragraph of the story-within-the-story ("She was wearing a dark, expensive-looking coat . . .") came to me just as I describe it, out of nowhere, and I then began to write it and got stuck, also just as I describe it. The first paragraph of the actual story ("Point A . . .") came to me a few days later, also out of nowhere, and quickly enough I made the connection between the two, so that the work of art in question became the unfinished story and the story itself a kind of journey leading me to an understanding of why I did not wish to write it.

4 V. GEBBIE. *The Return of the Baker, Edwin Tregear*

Vanessa Gebbie is Welsh and lives in the UK. Author of two short story collections, she is also contributing editor of 'Short Circuit, a Guide to the Art of the Short Story' (Salt Publishing). Her first novel will be published in 2011. She can be reached online at *www.vanessagebbie.com.*

**The Return of the Baker,* Edwin Tregear was inspired by a visit to the Geevor and Levant tin-mining museum in Cornwall, UK. I became fascinated by the device that transported miners into the shaft—the man-engine. One of the last examples of this technology to be used in the UK, this device failed in October 1919 causing the deaths of over thirty miners. The story is fiction, as are the characters, but the description of the man-engine is correct, the central incident is historically accurate, and Levant tin mine and the town of St. Just both exist. This story won a prize at the Fish Publishing international short story competition in 2009.

5   RICHARD C. ZIMLER. *Stealing Memories*

Richard Zimler has published eight novels over the past 14 years. His most popular work is "The Last Kabbalist of Lisbon," which has been translated into 22 languages. His new novel, "The Warsaw Anagrams" was named 2010 Book of the Year in Portugal, where he has lived for the last 20 years. It will be released in America by The Overlook Press in July of 2011. His website is www.zimler.com

*I wrote *Stealing Memories* after reading an essay about Fernand Léger's painting by a close friend of mine who is an excellent art critic, Timothy Hyman. At the time, I was thinking a lot about my family because one of my two older brothers had recently died (despite the desperate effort that I'd made, along with my parents and friends, to save his life). While I was grieving, my surviving brother—a troubled and unhappy person who refused to see our dying brother for the last five years of his life—wrote me a series of sadistic letters in which he accused me of being a disgusting and cowardly person, and our parents of being negligent monsters. This was a terrible betrayal of me at my lowest moment. In *Stealing Memories*, my anger over his letters mixed together with the trauma caused by my other brother's death—and my interest in Léger—to create an intricate and emotionally charged story of love, death, betrayal and grief.

6   BENJAMIN ROBINSON. *The Bridge House*

Benjamin Robinson is a writer and artist. He was born in Northern Ireland in 1964. His essays and short stories have appeared in *Quantum Genre In The Planet Of Arts* (e-book/anthology edited by V. Ulea), *A cappella Zoo, Existere, Crannóg, Dandelion, The Benefactor, Yuan Yang, Sein und Werden*; online at *3:AM Magazine, Recirca, 10,000 Tons of Black Ink, TQRstories* and *Dogmatika*. His art has been exhibited in Ireland, Germany and the UK. He lives in Dublin with his wife and young son.

*The flared double curves that make up the two connected enclosures of Richard Serra›s interactive sculpture, "Torqued Torus Inversion"—transposed to the mid nineteen eighties—provided me with a narrative framework for the fate of an aspiring artist, whose father—like Serra's—had worked in a shipyard (in the protagonist's case, Harland and Wolff in Belfast). I saw in Serra›s rusted curves of buckled steel the forces that built the modern world, and the trajectory of a life torqued out of shape. Prefiguring the story's dénouement, Jeff Koons' *Balloon Flower (Magenta)*—seductively slick and effortlessly hollow—is the antithesis of Serra's aesthetic.

7   ROBERT MCGOWAN. *An Ephemeral Exertion*

Robert McGowan's fiction and essays are published as book contributions and in several dozen prominent literary journals in America and abroad, including *Chautauqua Literary Journal, Connecticut Review, Crucible, The Dos Passos Review, Etchings* (Australia), *LIT, The Louisiana Review, The Savage Kick* (UK), *South Dakota Review*, and have been anthologized. McGowan's work as an artist is in numerous collections internationally, including Bank of America, Bank of Korea, and the Smithsonian American Art Museum (SAAM), Smithsonian Institution. He lives in Memphis.

*Because of my long history as a visual artist, the art world and the artist's experience find a place in many of my fictions, as do various bodies of my own visual work, invariably as the work of my fictional artist characters. The stories always follow long after, sometimes years after, completion of the drawings, photographs, or sculptures that show up in them. The color drawings executed late in his life by my character Aubry Allen, in "An Ephemeral Exertion," are based on a set of digital photographs I'd some time earlier taken of splashes of direct and indirect sunlight washing over the walls of my home. These images seemed naturally to pair with my character Aubry Allen as he withdrew somewhat into himself and his smaller world near the end of his life. I am unendingly fascinated by the merging of the real world of my own visual work with the imagined world of a fiction that incorporates them.

8   LISA ANNELOUISE RENTZ. *Glove*

Lisa Annelouise Rentz's work is archived at *eatgoodbread.com*. Her writing and drawings have been published in the past fifteen years by Etchings, You Are Here, Paysans Sans Peur press, *Salon.com, Alternet.org*, and They Draw and Cook.

*"Glove" is a patchwork of real art and artists whose details I've forgotten over the years: my mother did take me to an art show, in the 1980s, where the artist actually was killed on his way to the reception; for a long time I had a page pinned to a wall—in some apartment or two, and torn from a National Geographic, I bet—of a woman who had decoupaged the interior of her camper; and at one point, I did have an unfulfilled crush on a painter, whose work inspired the 'Revolution' painting I made up. "Glove" is a slow story, built on twenty-five-year-old memories, first drafted in 2000, and now published in 2011. My crush once told me (and I remember this impressionistically as well) that people often joked to him *Must be easy being an artist, sleeping in, just painting . . .* and he always replied, *No, each painting has taken me a lifetime.*

9   MARSHALL MOORE. *Flesh, Blood, and Some of the Parts (Le sang du monde)*

Marshall Moore is the author of two novels (*An Ideal for Living* and *The Concrete Sky*) and two short story collections (*Black Shapes in a Darkened Room* and the forthcoming *The Infernal Republic*). He also runs a publishing company in Hong

Kong, Typhoon Media Ltd. For more information, please visit marshallmoore. com and/or typhoon-media.com.

*I'd started on this story just before a trip to Europe back in 2005. As sometimes happens, I'd reached the end of the formative idea and the work had ground to a halt. In Vienna, a friend and I had gone to the Kunstforum to see a Magritte retrospective. When I saw the discomfiting, corpuscular *Le sang du monde* for the first time, the rest of the story (plus the title) came to me all at once. I'd known all along how the story would end, more or less, but this image (roughly, a landscape-heap of body parts and blood vessels) compelled me to reconsider the route I was taking. I took a seat on the bench in the middle of the gallery, pulled my notebook out of my backpack, and started writing. I finished the story in a creative white heat in a flat I subsequently rented in Budapest.

10   RICHARD K. WEEMS. *Artistic Endeavor*

Richard K. Weems (*www.weemsnet.net*) is the author of *The Need for Character* (Revelever Publications, 2004) and *Anything He Wants* (Spire Press, 2006), finalist for the Eric Hoffer Book Award. His short story publications include *North American Review*, *The Gettysburg Review*, *The Mississippi Review*, *Other Voices*, *Crescent Review*, *The Florida Review* and *The Beloit Fiction Journal*. "Artistic Endeavor" appeared in Richard's full-length collection, *Anything He Wants*.

*Professional wrestling is my unguilty pleasure. Not so much for its soap-operatic drama, but for its displays of self-destruction: men and women subjecting themselves to years of surgery, scar tissue and chronic pain for the sake of entertainment. The driving force behind "Artistic Endeavor" became a challenge to meet self-destruction (emotional and physical), abuse (see previous) and artistic expression. If art is an expression beyond the self, then the individual artist can become a squirrel in the road, and I wanted to see if my narrator could make that leap.

11   MARTIN ROSE. *Scanner Days, Starry Nights*

Martin Rose lives in New Jersey, where he writes a range of fiction from the fantastic to the macabre, holds a degree in graphic design, and enjoys blurring the line between art and life. More details are available at *www.MartinRoseHorror. com*.

*My mother was obsessed with Vincent Van Gogh, and *Starry Night* used to hang up in her room. I know that image so well I could draw it from memory—the town, the swirling night sky. Now, you can obtain the same image printed on your credit card, an incredible social statement of the corruption of artistic authenticity. In our virtual world, we have lost our connection to fearless, artistic sensibility, and seek to destroy it. Frustrated by the failure of people to realize everything beginning to unravel all around us in the days before the bank failures, to realize the choke-hold corporations have on art in the copyright wars, and to acknowledge that our paper world is dissolving in the face of the digital, the story took shape.

12   GRACE TALUSAN. *The Book of Life and Death*

Grace Talusan has been awarded an Artist Grant in Fiction Writing from the Massachusetts Cultural Council, a residency at Hedgebrook, and other fellow-ships and awards. She has published prose in *Best American Medical Writing 2009, Creative Nonfiction, Brevity,* and many other publications. She earned an MFA in fiction from the University of California, Irvine. Currently, she teaches writing at Grub Street and Tufts University.

*"The Book of Life and Death" was inspired from many art sources. Although not on public display in galleries or museums, I've come across photos in Filipino family albums of people posing in front of coffins. This isn't a death ritual that I've seen Americans participate in, and since I grew up in the United States, I always wondered what role it played in the grieving process for Filipinos. I was also inspired by a New York Times Sunday magazine article, "A Good Provider is One Who Leaves." Filipinos are so invisible in media that when there is coverage on Filipinos or Filipino Americans, I get multiple emails from my Filipino writers' listserv as well as from relatives and friends. The article was about overseas workers who may spend most of their lives earning money away from their families. Lastly, I was inspired by the story of Anne of Green Gables. I remember watching the mini-series with my Filipino nanny when I was a girl. We both cried watching it and I'm embarrassed to say, that was the first time that I realized my nanny had a whole life—longings, desires, grief—that I had never even considered before. All of these outside sources came together and suggested this story.

13   FRED MCGAVRAN. *A Photograph From the Permanent Collection*

A graduate of Kenyon College and Harvard Law School, Fred McGavran recently retired from Frost Brown Todd LLC in Cincinnati, Ohio, where he defended psychiatric malpractice cases and litigated business cases. In June he was ordained a deacon in The Episcopal Diocese of Southern Ohio, where he serves as Assistant Chaplain for Episcopal Retirement Homes. In 2009 the Ohio Arts Council awarded him a $10,000 Individual Achievement Award for The Reincarnation of Horlach Spenser, a story that appeared in Issue 37 of Harvard Review. Black Lawrence Press published The Butterfly Collector, an award win-ning collection of his short stories in December 2009. The collection is going into a second printing.

*I have always been fascinated by Nineteenth-Century photographs, where the subjects had to hold a pose for a minute or more for the photographer to expose the film. The rigid poses are mirrored by the rigid personality of the narrator in the story, who is shocked out of his frozen view of the world when he encounters an unexpected photograph at the exhibition. I wanted to link an artistic medium with a personality disorder.

14 JOHN MORGAN WILSON. *The Pull of the Current*

John Morgan Wilson is a journalist, documentary writer, and fiction writer. Among his awards are the Edgar Allan Poe Award ("the Edgar") from Mystery Writers of America for Best First Novel and three Lambda Literary Awards for Best Gay Men's Mystery. John's early Benjamin Justice mysteries, including *Simple Justice*, his 1997 Edgar winner, have been reissued by Bold Strokes Books. His short stories have appeared in *Ellery Queen's Mystery Magazine*, *Blithe House Quarterly*, *Best Gay Stories 2009*, and other anthologies. He lives in West Hollywood, California.

*I came across a reproduction of John Singer Sargent's "Tommies Bathing" years ago in *Smithsonian* magazine, illustrating an article about the iconic artist. I was intrigued not only with the watercolor itself, but with the artist's personal story as a closeted gay man living in a darkly repressive time. *Smithsonian* touched rather lightly on that aspect of Sargent's life, but also mentioned his physical isolation from others in his later years, which suggested a good deal about the subtext of the painting. For me, it became not only an expression of male sensuality and intimacy, but also disconnection, loneliness, and missed possibilities. When asked to contribute to this collection, I decided to explore my feelings about "Tommies Bathing" more deeply, and began writing my story without knowing where it was going or how it would end.

15 KEYAN BOWES. *The Intra-Galactic Shakespeare Festival*

Keyan Bowes is a peripatetic writer who lives in a stream of stories and occasionally grabs one long enough to type it in. A graduate of the 2007 Clarion Workshop for science fiction and fantasy writers, Keyan has had work accepted by Strange Horizons, Cabinet des Fees, Expanded Horizons, Big Pulp, and several anthologies. The Rumpelstiltskin Retellings, a story in poetry-blog format, was made into an award-winning short film. She is currently working on two Young Adult adventure novels. *www.keyanbowes.org*

*Shakespeare's plays have fascinated me since my parents took me to plays in the park as a small child: The mix of high purpose and comedy, the fantastic cast of characters. They are performed all over the world, in multiple languages, so why not one-step further, out to the galaxy? The Merchant of Venice, which I studied in school, was one of my favorites. Only when I looked back at it later did I see that Shakespeare had used with quite prosaic elements: a merchant, a moneylender—

and a heroine who rises to the occasion. This story was fun to write, but took a long time to edit into its current shape. Special thanks to Ellen Kushner and Delia Sherman, who helped me do it at Clarion 2007.

16   RENI KIEFFER. *Right Where it Belongs*

Reni Kieffer was born and raised as the child of an author and chose the path of becoming one herself after ditching the idea to become a veterinarian because she couldn't bear the sight of blood. She got a home full of animals instead and published her first book at the age of 16, a tour-diary that she had written together with her mother about the British band Take That. The diary was a huge success and the author-team continued working together and have published thirteen books in Germany, Austria and Switzerland. *Right Where It Belongs* is Reni's first short story published in the US.

*Music is my fuel, my inspiration, my constant companion while writing. "Right Where it Belongs" evolved as I was listening to two Nine Inch Nails songs on loop, Right Where it Belongs and All the Love in the World. The melancholy of the first and the hidden contempt of the second merged and created the main character of my story within a couple of minutes. Writing it was like transforming the lyrics into a scene that reflected the pain, anger and hopelessness of both songs. If you get the chance, listen to the songs while reading, they're the ultimate soundtrack.

17   ANDREW HOOK. *Ennui*

Andrew Hook's short fiction has appeared in over 90 magazines and anthologies since 1994. Some of these stories have been collected in three books: "The Virtual Menagerie" (Elastic Press, 2002), "Beyond Each Blue Horizon" (Crowswing Books, 2005), and "Residue" (Half-Cut Publications, 2006). Longer works include "Moon Beaver" (ENC Press, 2004), "And God Created Zombies (NewCon Press, 2009), and "Ponthe Oldenguine" (Atomic Fez, 2010). Andrew's website: *www.andrew-hook.com*

*"Ennui" was conceived after watching the 1967 movie *Deux ou Trois Choses Que Je Sais d'Elle* (Two Or Three Things I Know About Her), directed by Jean-Luc Godard. Godard's movies have often been an influence—whether directly through dialogue or indirectly as collages of imagery. In the film, the 'her' referred to in the title is the city of Paris, and—in brief—the movie's partial concern is that in order for someone to live in society they are forced, on whatever level or scale, to prostitute themselves. I've taken that concept and expanded it to include prostitution of humankind by external forces, in this case, a UFO; with the backdrop of Paris, the 'replication' of the coffee cup scene, and the general inability of the characters to affect their situation being drawn from the film. Godard acts as a

springboard for me, often obliquely, with two of my previously published stories ("Cinemad" and "Unchained Melody") being directly inspired by *Le Mépris* and *Bande à Part*, respectively. Written directly after watching the movie, the first draft took just a couple of hours. About thirty minutes later, I discovered the Art From Art guidelines and realized I had found the perfect market.

18   ALEX MACLENNAN. *Four Minutes Time*

Alex MacLennan's debut novel, *The Zookeeper*, was a finalist for the 2007 Lambda Literary, Violet Quill, and Edmund White Debut Fiction awards. A short story, "Touching the Pole," was featured in *Stress City: A Big Book of Fiction by 51 D.C. Guys* in 2008. Alex holds an MFA in Creative Writing from American University, was named a Writer to Watch by *Washingtonian* Magazine in 2006, and currently writes for an international environmental group.

*Sam Taylor-Wood's "Still Life" stopped me cold midway through an inspiring— if challenging—summer in England in 2004. I was in London doing research on another project, and when I stumbled upon the work amidst the Tate Modern's bullishly provocative collection, the lush and classical still life seemed as unmoored as I often felt during those long, isolated days. When the image fell in upon itself, revealing itself as a video exploration of decay, it was a revelation. After watching the four-minute sequence multiple times, I took my temporary loneliness home, and began to write.

19   LAUREN ALWAN. *Self Portrait: Untitled*

Lauren Alwan's fiction has appeared in the *Alaska Quarterly Review*, *StoryQuarterly*, and most recently in the *Sycamore Review*, as a finalist for the Wabash Prize in Fiction. She is the recipient of a Pushcart Prize nomination and a graduate of the Warren Wilson Program for Writers. Lauren lives in Northern California where she is at work on a first collection of fiction. "Self-Portrait: Untitled" originally appeared in Fish Stories: A Literary Anthology of Fiction and Poetry and is reprinted here by permission of the author.

*Like the narrator in "Self Portrait: Untitled," I too had a drawing book, and in fact the story began with writings prompted by images from a sketchbook I had in school. From those passages, the narrator emerged, a girl who understands her world only by drawing it. As it turned out, the portrayal also became one of time and place—Los Angeles in the late sixties was itself in a kind of adolescence and, like the narrator, moving toward an unpredictable future. I am grateful for the immeasurable help this story received in Pam Houston's Creede workshop and from the editorial guidance of the staff at FishStories.

20   FELICE PICANO. *Absolute Ebony*

Felice Picano recently guest edited Volume 7 of the prestigious, Paris-based, literary annual Van Gogh's Ear. Along with Professor Lazaro Lima, he co-edited, Ambientes: GLBT Latino/a Writing Today, published by The University of Wisconsin Press. His collection of personal essays, True Stories, will be put out by Chelsea Station Press in 2011.

*"Absolute Ebony" came to me in a dream and one image especially—in the bedroom—was so strong it haunted me all day. Just before I woke up a voice said to me: *This is a story by Nathaniel Hawthorne.* I knew he'd written about artists— "The Artist of the Beautiful," "The Marble Faun." etc. So I got out my *Collected Stories of Hawthorne* and scanned the tales. I never found this story. Then I understood it was a story to be told as though Hawthorne or one of his contemporaries were writing it. Once that was understood, writing it only took a few days.

21   BILLY O'CALLAGHAN. *The Things We Lose, The Things We Leave Behind*

Billy O'Callaghan is the author of two short story collections, 'In Exile' (2008) and 'In Too Deep' (2009), both published by Mercier Press. Winner of the George A. Birmingham Award, the Lunch Hour Stories Prize and the Molly Keane Creative Writing Award, he is a three-time finalist for the RTE Radio 1 P.J. O'Connor Award for Drama. Recent work has appeared or is forthcoming in Alfred Hitchcock Mystery Magazine, Bellevue Literary Review, Confrontation, Hayden's Ferry Review, the Los Angeles Review, Narrative Magazine, Pearl, the Southeast Review, Versal and Waccamaw.

*The story, "The Things We Lose, The Things We Leave Behind" was at least partially inspired by the 1945 Jack Butler Yeats oil-on-canvas, entitled: "End of the Season." The painting depicts two men standing back to back on a broken shoreline. One, the taller of the two, is gazing out to sea where a boat looks to be battling a storm. Island life has long held a fascination for me, and it is something that I have tried to explore in several of my stories. Minute details that hold little importance in a city tend to matter a great deal on islands. There is such a sense of life on islands, and also a kind of timelessness. Yeats has a violent, expressionistic style that always feels ideally suited to depicting the wild and rugged terrain of Ireland's western and southwestern coastlines, and in particular its many scattershot islands. He defines limits in his work, distilling everything down to a kind of breathless simplicity, some moment of absolute truth. Within the frame there is land and there is sea, and usually there is weather. A lot of weather. But also, invariably, there are people, hunch-shouldered and beaten down but still battling the elements for their surviving share, still fighting to live. And these people have stories just waiting to be told.

22　DAVID GULLEN. *Installation 72*

David Gullen has had over twenty short stories published. Recent work has been featured by PS Publishing for their Catastrophia anthology, and in the winter 2010 edition of GUD magazine.

*With Installation 72, I wanted to combine social comment with very disturbing imagery. Horror all too often fails because it relies on predictable shock, startlement—and so it becomes simply a pleasurable thrill. My idea was to create a situation where dreadful things could be "normalized" into society, where they become desirable, popular even fashionable. With Installation 72, the reaction of the audience is more important than whether the events depicted are actually real.

23　RON SAVAGE. *Retrospective*

Ron Savage has published more than ninety stories worldwide. He is the recipient of the Editor's Circle Award in Best New Writing (Hopewell) and has recently been nominated for the Pushcart Prize. He has been a guest fiction editor for Crazyhorse, and his new novel Scar Keeper (Hilliard & Harris) will be out in the summer. Publications include the North American Review, Shenandoah, The Baltimore Review and the Magazine of Fantasy and Science Fiction. *http://www. ronsavage.net*

*The inspiration for my story came from my aunt who has been an artist for most of her life. She is now in her eighties and still going strong. A couple of falls ago, my wife and I finally had a chance to go to Paris. One of our first stops was the impressionist collection at the Musée d'Orsay—and that had an impact. Most of my story, though, was simply my imagination.

24　KEVIN W. REARDON. *Three Shades*

Kevin W. Reardon's stories have appeared in journals and anthologies including *The James White Review, Fresh Men, ParaSpheres,* and *Unspeakable Horror.* He holds the M.F.A. in Writing from Sarah Lawrence College and a B.A. from Brandeis University. His short story "Teamwork" was the 2003 winner of the Richard Hall Memorial Short Story Contest, sponsored by Lambda Literary Foundation.

*"Three Shades" was inspired by many afternoons at the Metropolitan Museum of Art. The Gian Lorenzo Bernini Bacchanal, a Baroque sculpture depicting several imps teasing a faun, is pivotal in the story. Bryan and Russell are kindred spirits who both interpret their world vis-à-vis art. However, an essential difference in their personalities comes out through their reactions to this sculpture. Russell was raised Roman Catholic and carries the general burden of Original Sin along with specific guilt resulting from his own actions. He sees this joyous scene, experiences

shame and looks away. In contrast, Bryan was raised as a Jehovah's Witness, but was rejected by his parents' faith early enough that he was able to embrace the sensual world. Perhaps Bryan is too familiar with the pleasures of the flesh. When Bryan sees Bacchus, his visceral appreciation resonates with the thrill that the 18-year-old sculptor must have felt as he created this masterwork. Unfortunately, these young men never discuss the art. Bryan, Russell and Laurent are lost souls, three shades adrift in their corporeal forms through this Museum where, beneath every arch and in every corner, there is evidence of some greater meaning.

25 ANNE WHITEHOUSE. *A Visit to the Stock Exchange*

Anne Whitehouse was born and grew up in Birmingham, Alabama, and has a BA from Harvard College and an MFA from Columbia University's School of the Arts. She is the author of the poetry collections Blessings and Curses (Poetic Matrix Press, 2009), Bear in Mind (Finishing Line Press, 2010) and The Surveyor's Hand (Compton Press, 1981). Her novel Fall Love (2001) is now available as an e-book from Feedbooks, Smashwords, Amazon, and as its own application on iTunes. Her poetry and short stories have been published widely in literary magazines, journals, and anthologies; and her essays, feature articles, and book reviews have appeared in major newspapers throughout the US. She lives in New York City. *www.annewhitehouse.com*

*"A Visit to the Stock Exchange" is about the age-old conflict between art and commerce as expressed through the mixed emotions of a painter who creates art to sell but is unhappy about the buyers. Elizabeth comes to feel that her paintings exact such a high cost from her in terms of effort that money seems an inadequate compensation. The triumph of having her work acquired by the rich and prominent is countered by her overwhelming sense of loss when her painting "disappears" into a private collection, where her art may be welcome but she is not. Elizabeth struggles against economic hardship and sexism, as well as the difficulties of raising a family and pursuing her art, yet her flower paintings, as perfect and complete as a Northern Renaissance still life, give no clue to the chaotic and difficult existence in which they were conceived and created. The character of Elizabeth was suggested to me by an artist I once knew—who is no longer alive. Her art awakened my admiration at the same time that the circumstances of her life aroused my sympathy and distress and inspired me to write this story.

26 STEVE RASNIC TEM. *La Mariée*

Steve Rasnic Tem's latest book is *In Concert* from Centipede Press, collecting all his short story collaborations with wife Melanie Tem. His audio short story collection, Invisible, is available from Speaking Volumes LLC. His first two novels

Excavation and *The Book of Days* have been re-released as ebooks from *crossroad-press.com*. You can visit the Tem home on the web at *www.m-s-tem.com*.

*La Mariée came to me because of the Chagall painting of the same name. I'm an enormous fan of Chagall (my publisher has recently gotten permission to reproduce several of his paintings in my collaborative collection with my wife, IN CONCERT) and for me, no painter better embodies that feeling of romantic, nostalgic longing. And I felt this painting in particular makes the promise of a rare and beautiful moment available to the ordinary viewer.

27   TRACY DEBRINCAT. *Call It a Hat*

Grateful acknowledgment to the editors of *The Pinch*, who initially published Tracy DeBrincat's *Call It A Hat*, and to Subito Press, which released her debut fiction collection *Moon Is Cotton & She Laugh All Night*, in which the story also appears. Tracy DeBrincat's award-winning short stories and poetry have been published widely in literary journals from *Another Chicago Magazine* to *Zyzzyva*. Her debut fiction collection, *Moon Is Cotton & She Laugh All Night*, was published in 2010 by Subito Press/University of Colorado, Boulder. She is a freelance creative advertising consultant in the entertainment industry and loves living in Los Angeles.

*With its juxtaposition of sweetness and brutality, Stravinsky's "The Rite of Spring" is the clamorous backdrop for my protagonist Lydia's flights of paranoia, ecstasy, longing and fear. "Call It A Hat" sprang from various events that occurred to me while attending the Los Angeles Philharmonic over the years: mind-movies inspired by music, Technicolor daydreams in half-sleep, sneaking into better seats and one very memorable hairpiece. Lydia's emotional currents reflect the movements of the music, and are subject to the sensory whirl around her as she considers what appears to be a very secure, stable proposal.

28   PEDRO PONCE. *The Piazza De Chirico*

*Pedro Ponce is the author of Alien Autopsy, a collection of short fictions, and Superstitions of Apartment Life, a compendium of urban folklore taken from fictional and nonfictional sources. His latest work is the novella Homeland: A Panorama in 50 States, a dystopian narrative based on etchings by Francisco Goya.

"The Piazza de Chirico" is my attempt to use Giorgio de Chirico's haunting imagery to structure a written narrative. In a 1982 essay, Sanford Schwartz observed that De Chirico "builds his pictures with the same spooky dominion that children have when they rearrange the contents of doll houses or when they position their toys for the night." It's this same sense of the uncanny embodied in the everyday that I wanted to evoke on the page. I pursued this project first as historical fiction, but had more success when I abandoned realism and, instead, just "wrote" the paintings.

29   DAVID C. PINNT. *One Penny for Art*

David C. Pinnt lives and works near Denver Colorado. His fiction has appeared in a variety of anthologies and periodicals, including Permuted Press' *The World is Dead*, *Andromeda Spaceways Inflight Magazine*, and Pill Hill Press' *Wretched Moments*.

*In the mid-90's I moved from a small town in Western Colorado to Seattle and was absolutely enthralled with the Pike Place Market, its ongoing whirlwind of vendors, buskers, fish-hawkers and artists. I may or may not have seen the artist character from my story in real life, but a few years later, in my first "grown-up" job, I experienced a great deal of difficulty with the transition from earlier artistic aspirations into my new-found responsibilities. More and more I was drawn to thoughts of these street artists and their conviction to put art of any sort as their highest priority regardless of the consequences. "1 Penny for Art" grew from my own discomfort at putting aside artistic inspiration for real-world concerns.

30   TERRI GRIFFITH. *Corporate Art*

Terri Griffith's writing has appeared in *Bloom, Suspect Thoughts, Bust* and in the anthologies *Without a Net: The Female Experience of Growing Up Working Class* and *Are We Feeling Better Yet?* Along with Nicholas Alexander Hayes, she is co-authoring a transgressive retelling of the Greek Myths. Terri is the co-editor of the forthcoming anthology *The Legacy of The New Art Examiner: Thirty Years of Independent Arts Journalism*. Her debut novel *So Much Better* is available from Green Lantern Press.

*"Corporate Art" is inspired by Richard Serra's sculpture "Tilted Arc," which was a site-specific work originally installed on Manhattan's Federal Plaza. After much litigation, the work was removed. Many of the complaints came from Federal Building workers. Although I am a fan of Serra and oppose the removal of "Tilted Arc," I was still intrigued by the story that seemed a perfect example of the way the public can come to think of contemporary artists as arrogant, and contemporary artists can interpret the public as ignorant—the sad way that those who should be natural allies can become adversaries.

31   JAMESON CURRIER. *The Bloomsbury Nudes*

Jameson Currier is the author of two novels, *Where the Rainbow Ends* and *The Wolf at the Door*, and four collections of fiction, *Dancing on the Moon; Desire,*

Lust, Passion, Sex; Still Dancing; and *The Haunted Heart and Other Tales.* His newest novel, *The Third Buddha,* will be published this year.

*In 1988, on the death of a close friend, I came into possession of several Bloomsbury artifacts—correspondence of Lytton Strachey, a sketch by Dora Carrington, and a drawing by Duncan Grant. I knew more of Virginia Woolf than I did of these other Bloomsbury folks, but over the course of many years more knowledge seeped in and my appreciation for these artists deepened. I had always been intrigued by Duncan Grant, an openly gay artist, and was particularly impressed by his nude sketches that I had seen in a catalog published by the Anthony d'Offay Gallery in London. I learned more about these nude drawings through the writings of Douglas Blair Turnbaugh, particularly *Duncan Grant and the Bloomsbury Group*, published in 1987, as well as from the advent of the Internet and the exhibits and information on the artist available through the Leslie/Lohman Gallery in New York and Adonis Art of London. For years I had toyed with the idea of creating a fictional back-story of the men who had posed for these sketches, and I researched quite a bit on who they might have been. When I sat down in 2007 to write this story, I was influenced by a lot of the horror anthologies I was reading at the time, and I decided it was apropos to have a young artist be one of Duncan Grant's nude models, and that's how I came to the character of Clive Elliot. It was during this writing process that I decided to overlap the influences of Aleister Crowley, another legendary British fellow whose life and career and writings had always intrigued me. In the story, Clive Elliott, Jared Tremaine, Bart Pearson, Roger Sage, and Teddy Rushton are all fictional characters and Crowley's link and association with the men of the Bloomsbury group is purely from my own speculation.

32   ELIZABETH GRAVER. *Flatiron*

Elizabeth Graver is the author of a story collection *Have You Seen Me?* and three novels: *Unravelling, The Honey Thief,* and *Awake.* Her work has appeared in *Best American Short Stories; Prize Stories: The O. Henry Awards* and *The Pushcart Prize Anthology.* She teaches at Boston College.

*"Flatiron" began as part of an "assignment"—I, along with two other writers—was asked to write a story that somehow contained or used as a springboard Gustave Caillebotte's 1877 painting "Paris Street, Rainy Day," which hangs in the Art Institute of Chicago. The stories were then read by actors as part of Chicago's "Stories on Stage" series and aired on Illinois NPR. Years before, in the Musee D'Orsay in Paris, I'd been transfixed by a different Caillebotte painting, "The Floor Scrapers," so I managed to work it into the story as well. Though I'm only now making the connection, I think perhaps the two paintings—one so upright and geometric, the other of bare-chested men laboring together on a floor—sug-

gested to me some of the issues of social class, order, disorder, and sexuality in the story. "Flatiron" eventually ended up leading me to the subject of my current novel-in-progress, though none of the characters in the story figure the novel, except on the outskirts, in my mind.

33   STEPHEN SOUCY. *Skating*

Stephen Soucy is a writer, publisher, and filmmaker based in Los Angeles. He started Modernist Press in 2008, and his first edited collection of short fiction featuring fourteen writers, *Nine Hundred and Sixty-Nine: West Hollywood Stories* sold over 3,000 copies as a Print-On-Demand book. Stephen's at work on his first novel and his short film, *Slant,* is scheduled for release mid-2011. He can be reached via www.modernistpress.com.

*I thought of compiling this collection, *Art From Art,* after writing "Skating." I had always wanted to compose my own inspired-by version of *A Christmas Carol* by Charles Dickens, and part of the resulting story is based in fact—I did lose a good friend, and someone I was very much in love with, when he had a grand mal seizure at age twenty-six. The loss I felt and the difficulty of moving on is hopefully captured in "Skating." I never had the chance to properly say good-bye to Wayne Cross, and this story was an attempt at true closure.

34   SEAN PADRAIC MCCARTHY. *The Man Who Walks Beside the Sea*

Sean Padraic McCarthy's short stories have been recently published, or are forthcoming in, *Glimmer Train, Confrontation, The Sewanee Review, Bayou Magazine, Hayden's Ferry Review, Another Chicago Magazine, Cadillac Cicatrix, Red Cedar Review, South Dakota Review, Sou'wester, The Evansville Review,* and *Blue Mesa Review* among others. His short fiction has been nominated twice in recent years for the Pushcart Prize, and he lives in Mansfield, Massachusetts with his wife and children.

*I started working on "The Man Who Walks Beside the Sea" after attending a conference on "Spirituality, Faith, and Mental Health" for my job with the Department of Mental Health in Massachusetts. One of the speakers, a psychiatrist who works with survivors of severe trauma and violence, discussed how a former client of his, a woman who had lost all her children in the Khmer Rouge labor camps, told him of her visions of an American dressed in black walking along the sea. After dreaming of this man several times, she implored upon the American people to help her build a Buddhist temple near the seashore in Boston. The psychiatrist believed her dreams were a sign of a healing journey, and that even victims of horribly traumatic events can go on to lead beautiful and meaningful lives. The image in the painting came to me after the idea for the story. Nora is drawn to it immediately because she sees someone else has seen what she has seen, and as she searches for her own healing she finds the image to be both haunting and comforting, the man both a harbinger of death and something of a Christ. I chose Truro and Provincetown as the setting because of the artistic community there, the many galleries, and because of the extremes the area experiences, the continuing cycle of life and death, crowds in the summer and the quiet desolation in the winter. For many of the natives, I imagine, the latter can often be more comforting.

35   DEB TABER. *Black Silk*

Deb Taber is Senior Book Editor at Apex Publishing, a critically acclaimed small press specializing in dark science fiction and horror. Her fiction has been published in Shadowed Realms and Fantasy Magazine, with a forthcoming story in the Dark Futures anthology; her nonfiction has appeared in a variety of print and online venues. By day, she edits nonfiction for print and electronic media, and she can also be found designing lighting for theatre and dance performances throughout the Pacific Northwest.

*"Black Silk" isn't based in the works of any master; it crept up on me much in the way of the Aal. I sat in a writers' workshop, thinking I was fully absorbed in listening to those around me talk about improving their craft. At the end of three hours, my pages were covered in doodles, dark and branching and looped in mysterious designs. Embedded in those loops and coils were the memories of the session, bits and pieces of the techniques that allow artists and writers craft the stories they want to tell. The next time I reached for something to write, those shapes were there, compelling in some ways, repulsive in others. They had a story to tell.

36   ROBERT GUFFEY. *Graffiti*

Robert Guffey's first book, a collection of novellas entitled *Spies & Saucers*, is forthcoming from PS Publishing. His short stories, articles and interviews have appeared in such magazines and anthologies as *After Shocks* edited by Jeremy Lassen, *Catastrophia* edited by Allen Ashley, *Chimeraworld* edited by Mike Philbin, *Dark Jesters* edited by Nick Cato and L.L. Soares, *Escape Clause* edited by Clélie Rich, *Flurb* edited by Rudy Rucker, *Modern Magic* edited by W.H. Horner, *The New York Review of Science Fiction* edited by David Hartwell, *The Pedestal* edited by John Amen, and *The Third Alternative* edited by Andy Cox. Further stories are scheduled to appear in *Aoife's Kiss* edited by Tyree Campbell and *Postscripts* edited by Peter Crowther and Nick Gevers. He teaches English at CSU Long Beach and can be contacted at rguffey@hotmail.com.

*Graffiti has always fascinated me. Growing up in Old Torrance, only a few blocks from the city limits of Carson (the birthplace of several different Crip and Blood gangs with illustrious names like Don't Give a Fuck and Too Many Hoes), I saw a hell of a lot of graffiti growing up. I remember those illegible black scrawls appearing magically on the front of my deteriorating apartment complex just off Carson Street, some of the letters taller than an average human being. City workers would arrive to paint over the words, but you could still see where the letters had once been. A few days later the graffiti would reappear as if by sorcery. As a child, I imagined these characters to be rune-like sigils imbued with esoteric wisdom. In the Spring of 2006, my girlfriend (now my wife) showed me a satirical short documentary called "The Subconscious Art of Graffiti Removal." In a tongue-in-cheek manner, it attempted to prove that government-sponsored graffiti removers were secretly driven by artistic motives. I decided to take this premise at face value and imagined a frustrated young artist who discovers how to create subversive art, and manages to slip it under the radar of cultural norms, by shifting his perceptions just slightly. Like graffiti, perceptual psychology has always fascinated me as well. "Graffiti" combines both of these interests into a single tale.

37   SYLVIA MARTÍNEZ BANKS. _____ , *John*

Sylvia Martínez Banks earned a BA in English from UC Davis, is a graduate student in English at Cal State East Bay, and is an alum of VONA. She has also been published by the *San Francisco Examiner*, *Tattoo Highway*, *The November 3rd Club*, *Occam's Razor*, and *Word Riot*. She lives in the San Francisco Bay Area with her husband and two children. She is currently working on her first collection of short stories.

*" _____ , John" was inspired by several works of art. A few weeks before writing this story, I had gone to Texas from California with my father to visit family and to work on a detailed family tree. I ended up feeling guided toward a story about a young woman contemplating her identity before getting married. On that trip, I had read the story, "The Identity Club," by Richard Burgin and had also listened to Jason Mraz's song, "Details in the Fabric," both of which make their way into the story and affect the protagonist, even leading to Frida Kahlo's influence on her. I had also visited the Alamo and Goliad on this trip and kept feeling drawn towards the idea of identity in a name. The title " _____ , John" came to me when I saw it at the Alamo. The main character struggles with the symbolic meaning of taking her fiancé's last name, but at the Alamo sees freedom in no last name at all.

38   LOIS BARR. *Gesso*

A Spanish professor at Lake Forest College, Lois Barr has published books, articles and reviews on Latin American and Spanish literature. Her poems and stories have appeared or will appear in *East on Central*, *94 Creations*, *Love After 70*, *Food Memories*, and two zines, *The New Vilna Review* and the University of Iowa's *Daily Palette*.

*Like the narrator of "Gesso," I was a Spanish professor on sabbatical taking a course in Renaissance painting at the Chicago Botanic Gardens. Judith was our tempera teacher. The students were very much like the women in the story. One day a painfully thin but very talented painter came to class. She had a recipe for gesso, but did not share it. Like the narrator, I saw the scars on her wrists as she washed her hands. When she left class, I resisted the urge to follow her. The genesis of the story came when I thought about the act of breaking eggs into our hands to make the base for the paints. Every writer has to break some eggs, and there is an act of theft in every artwork. As I began to ask questions about jealousy and thievery among artists and academics, the obsessions of the narrator and Blanca came to life. As far as Alfonsina Storni's poem, "Voy a dormir/I Am Going to Sleep," I haven't seen studies of an earlier version. Perhaps a researcher somewhere is hoarding it.